The History of the University of East Anglia Norwich

The History of the University of East Anglia Norwich

MICHAEL SANDERSON

HAMBLEDON AND LONDON
London and New York

Hambledon and London

102 Gloucester Avenue
London, NW1 8HX

838 Broadway
New York
NY 10003-4812

First Published 2002

ISBN 1 85285 336 0

A description of this book is available from the
British Library and from the Library of Congress.

Typeset by John Saunders Design & Production, Reading

Printed on acid-free paper and bound in
Great Britain by Cambridge University Press

Contents

Illustrations

Between Pages 170 and 171

1 The Vice-Chancellor's Office, Council House and Registry
2 Earlham Golf Course, 1961
3 The University Village in late 1963
4 Denys Lasdun with his plan for UEA, 25 April 1963
5 University site, 14 March 1965
6 Lasdun's skyline
7 Ziggurats
8 Rick Mather's Constable Terrace
9 Sports Day at the Ziggurats
10 The Sainsbury Centre: the presentation announcement, 26 November 1973
11 The Sainsbury Centre in snow
12 The Sainsbury Centre, interior
13 The spinal walkway

Between Pages 234 and 235

14 Frank Thistlethwaite, the first Vice-Chancellor
15 Appeal Garden Party, 1962: Viscount Cranbrook, Frank Thistlethwaite, Lord Macintosh and Timothy Colman
16 Gordon Tilsley, Timothy Colman and Sir Edmund Bacon, 1974, at the retirement of Sir Edmund as Chairman of the Appeals Committee
17 Sir Lincoln Ralphs
18 Sir Solly Zuckerman
19 Lord Mackintosh
20 Sir Charles Wilson
21 The first executive, 1963

Between Pages 298 and 299

Tables

Acknowledgements

This history has had a long gestation. In June 1978 Frank Thistlethwaite, the first Vice-Chancellor, proposed to initiate a project on the History of the University. A small committee was set up under Professor J.R. Jones to gather archival material and take oral and written evidence. The Vice-Chancellor said that "I hope in due course this exercise will result in the publication of a History of the University of East Anglia".[1]

Professor Jones' committee laid some useful foundations. Gordon Tilsley, the former Town Clerk of Norwich and a leading figure among the founders of UEA, wrote a memoir and presented his invaluable papers to the archives. Several early participants wrote letters of reminiscence to Frank Thistlethwaite and an exhibition on the history of UEA was planned.[2] Although the Committee drafted a twenty chapter outline covering the first thirteen years of the University (not followed in this volume), there was no intention that any of them would actually write the history at that stage. The academics were busy with their own projects and it was probably still too close to the University's founding to get a historical perspective. Professor Jones, in a candid moment also suggested that anybody who took on the writing of the "real" history would do so "perhaps naively".[3]

The matter rested for many years until 1994 when the then Vice-Chancellor, Professor Derek Burke, revived the project and invited me to undertake it. I in turn was delayed by the need to write other matters for a forthcoming Research Assessment Exercise but this had the fortuitous effect that it became realistic and appropriate to regard the year 2000 as the terminal point of the history. By happy coincidence I also reach this point with the longest service – and longest memory – of any member of the University.

Many people have helped me in this task and it is a pleasure to be able to acknowledge them. Chief of all has been the founding Vice-Chancellor, Frank Thistlethwaite, who left his papers to the University archives to which he gave me unique access. It was a privilege and a pleasure to be able to discuss with him aspects of those years when the University was being created. He read Chapters 1-8 and his suggestions and corrections greatly improved the text. This was also so for the second Vice-Chancellor, Sir Michael Thompson, who added valuable insights to Chapters 9 and 10 which

I could not have gleaned from documentation. Derek Burke, Dame Elizabeth Estève-Coll and Vincent Watts have likewise read all the chapters relating to their periods of office and I am grateful for their advice, corrections and comments.

Closely associated with the Vice-Chancellors have been two people who have been at UEA for many years. Patricia Whitt MBE, the Personal Assistant to three Vice-Chancellors, and Michael Paulson Ellis OBE, the Registrar and Secretary to five of them. Both have been unfailing sources of encouragement and funds of knowledge. Miss Whitt read Chapters 1-11 and her meticulous corrections have been essential to the final text. Mr Paulson Ellis has acted as the general manager of the project, helping to keep it on track and facilitating its progress to publication.

In the course of research I have tried to recover for the archives any papers, especially of the founders of UEA. In this I have had some good fortune. Gwynneth, Viscountess Mackintosh of Halifax, found the annotated typescripts of the speeches of the first Viscount Mackintosh (her father-in-law) when promoting the University in the region in 1960-64. I am particularly grateful to Lady Mackintosh for making these available. Lady Enid Ralphs showed me many letters and other papers of her late husband, Sir Lincoln Ralphs, discussed them with me and was able to resolve the authorship of an important document in UEA's origins.

Sir Arthur South provided a packet of materials relating to the vital period when he gained City support for the emerging University. Mr W.E. Etherington, the former Principal of Keswick Hall College, made available several files of papers about the merger of the College and the University. All these materials have either been deposited in or photographed for the UEA archives. Professor Brian Thorne lent me his typescript reports on the Counselling Service. In addition, I have had access to two sets of private papers still retained by the owners. One is the papers of Professor R.H. Campbell, the Pro Vice-Chancellor 1969-71, which threw much light on student unrest and the building of the Plain. The other is those of Mr Michael Everitt of the architects Feilden and Mawson, which relate to the Library Building.

Some people have written memoirs of their days at UEA. Those of Gordon Tilsley and Frank Thistlethwaite are major sources. In addition those of Professor Norman Sheppard throw light on the early days of Chemistry. Rosemary Bohr (née Spencer) and Mary Vallanjon have written useful short accounts of student life. In many ways the most remarkable is the 102 page manuscript student memoirs of Christopher Wrigley, later Professor of History at Nottingham University, President of the Historical Association and an Hon Litt.D. of the University.

I have also tried to retrieve memory by interviewing participants in UEA's story and a complete list is in the Bibliography. I would just indicate a few now outside the University. Professor Roy Campbell, a key figure of the 1960s, met me in Stranraer for a long talk about those days as well as providing unique papers. Sir Timothy Colman KG has a record of public service to the University of unrivalled length and it was a privilege to be able to talk with him about this. It was also good fortune to be able to interview some of the early founders and supporters of the University; Gordon Tilsley; Sir Arthur South; Lady Ralphs who told me of Sir Lincoln's activities; Sir Charles Wilson; Lord Annan, Chairman and member of the original Academic Planning Board and Raymond Frostick, who played a crucial role at various points of the University's history from the early involvement of the Junior Chamber of Commerce in the 1960s to the appointment of the latest Vice-Chancellors of the 1990s. Finally Professor John Tarrant, now Vice-Chancellor of the University of Huddersfield, made time in a busy schedule to throw much light on the time when he was Deputy Vice-Chancellor to Derek Burke.

Architects and other outside experts have been patient in explaining their activities to a layman. It was a privilege to talk with Sir Denys Lasdun CH about his great work in the design of the Plain. I am also grateful to Peter McKinley of Denys Lasdun and Partners who participated in my talk with Sir Denys. Both read Chapter 8 and I am especially grateful to Mr McKinley for his careful annotation of this chapter, which saved me from many errors, especially on technical matters, and I have retained his wording. From Feilden and Mawson, David Luckhurst, Marshall Hopkins and Michael Everitt told me much about their contribution to the building of the Village and the Plain. Also outside the University Miss Rosamund Strode threw much light on the connection of Benjamin Britten with UEA and generously made available her transcripts of Britten correspondence. The files of interviews with the above and all others in the 'Personal Interviews' section of the bibliography will be deposited in the University Archives and I am very appreciative of all those who were kind enough to talk to me.

Within the University I am indebted to several people who have helped me with access to documentation. To Deirdre Sharp, the University Archivist; Sue Koria of the Committee Office (housing all University Committee minutes) for her considerable knowledge of UEA documentation and Lorraine Bozza of the Files Office (in effect the contemporary archives). Pat Piner was very helpful in making available the early press cuttings and Anne Ogden the Press and Publicity Officer the later ones. Derek Lummis provided materials from cupboards to which he alone seemed to have access. Hayley Garrard made available Alumni data from computer records. Paddy Anstey and Janet Anderson provided me with valuable reports they have compiled on computer use and employment. Dr Steven Hooper, the Director of the Sainsbury Research Unit, gave much helpful advice about the Sainsbury Collection. The University is rich in audio-visual material and I am grateful to Wally Tyacke of the Audio-Visual Centre and David Cleveland of the East Anglian Film Archive for enabling me to see or hear this, while Evelyn Mould and Anna Marie Triggs were very helpful with photographic illustrations. I am also indebted to Dr Stefan Muthesius for making available the typescript of his book on the architecture of UEA.

Outside the University I am grateful to the following for making records available. Dr Jenny Doctor, the Director of the Britten-Pears Library gave permission to cite the correspondence of Benjamin Britten. The quotations from the letters of Benjamin Britten, which may not be further reproduced without the written permission of the Trustees are © copyright the Trustees of the Britten-Pears Foundation. The Master and Fellows of Churchill College Cambridge and Mr Christopher Cockcroft gave permission to use and cite from the papers of Sir John Cockcroft OM. Norwich City College archives provided their prospectuses and newscuttings books. The Norfolk Record Office holds the Minutes of the Norwich Higher Education Committee. I have also benefited from the Cambridge University Library Official Publications Room for their matchless collection of official publications and the expertise of their staff in locating them. Eastern Counties Newspapers made available microfilm of the Eastern Daily Press pre-1963. I am also grateful to the BBC Sound Archives for making available material for me to hear in the national Sound Archive in the British Library.

This project could not have been brought to completion without the very generous help of the University. I was granted two periods of research leave and a sufficient budget for research and travel. The later stages of the project have been assisted by Alan Preece. Much of the typing was done by Mrs Patricia Dalley, whose careful work has been invaluable. The full text has been read and refereed by Michael Paulson Ellis and Professor Roy Church. I am especially grateful for their memories, suggestions and corrections, which have both saved me from serious errors and directed my attention to significant themes. All have greatly improved the text. I am indebted to Audrey Judkins for compiling the index so efficiently. The production of publication has been handled by Martin Sheppard of Hambledon and London. I am very grateful for the care with which this has been done.

Finally I thank my wife Anne Sanderson, herself a long-serving member of UEA, for her helpful checking of the bibliography and her constant and encouraging support through the task. Although the work has been a labour I have always been conscious that it has been a privilege to attempt to shape the first historical view of the early decades of the University. People tell me that it will be "definitive". Of course it is not, any more than any other history. The story will be told and retold many times in the future from different viewpoints and with different emphases. But this is a version that derives a particular authenticity from being close enough to the origins for memory to be recaptured but sufficiently distant to gain some initial perspective. At the 1985 Congregation the Chancellor, Professor Owen Chadwick, himself a highly distinguished historian, said "I want the graduates to think that they are part of a very long tradition". I hope that this book goes some way to meet this intention.

Abbreviations

AAC	Academic Advisory Committee
ACNP	Advisory Committee on Novel Foods and Processes
AERE	Atomic Energy Research Establishment (Harwell)
AFRC	Agriculture and Food Research Council
APB	Academic Planning Board
APU	Anglia Polytechnic University
APWP	Academic Planning Working Party
ARC	Agricultural Research Council
ASP	Papers of Sir Arthur South
ASTMS	Association of Scientific Technical and Managerial Staff
AUT	Association of University Teachers
AVC	Audio Visual Centre
BBP	Benjamin Britten Papers
BIO	School of Biological Sciences
BSCL	British Sugar Corporation Laboratories
CARE	Centre for Applied Research in Education
CC	County Council
CCS	Common Course Structure
CEAS	Centre of East Anglian Studies
CEB	Centre for English Language and British Studies
CHE	School of Chemistry
CRU	Climatic Research Unit
CSERGE	Centre for Social and Economic Research on the Global Environment
CVCP	Committee of Vice Chancellors and Principals
DES	Department of Education and Science
DEV	School of Development Studies
DLP	Denys Lasdun and Partners
DOS	Dean of Students
DTI	Department of Trade and Industry
EAS	School of English and American Studies
EADT	*East Anglian Daily Times*
EDP	*Eastern Daily Press*
EDU	School of Education

EEN	*Eastern Evening News*
ENV	School of Environmental Sciences
ESRC	Economic and Social Research Council
EUR	School of European Studies
FAM	School of Fine Arts and Music
FOG	Frame of Government Committee
FRI	Food Research Institute (see also IFRN)
FT	Frank Thistlethwaite
FTP	Frank Thistlethwaite Papers
GCP	Gerald Crompton Papers
GTP	Gordon Tilsley Papers
HEFCE	Higher Education Funding Council for England
HUDG	History in Universities Defence Group
ICER	Institute for Connective Environmental Research
IFRN	Institute of Food Research, Norwich
ILTHE	Institute for Learning and Teaching in Higher Education
IS	International Socialists
IT	Information Technology
JCR	Junior Common Room
JEI	Jackson Environment Institute
JII	John Innes Institute
JIC	John Innes Centre
LAW	School of Law
LFA	Loan financed accommodation
LLT	School of Language, Linguistics and Translation Studies
LTR	Low Temperature Research
MAP	School of Mathematics and Physics
NFU	National Farmers Union
NNAA	Norfolk and Norwich Association of Architects
NORCAT	Norfolk College of Arts and Technology (King's Lynn)
NRO	Norfolk Records Office
NRP	Norwich Research Park
NUS	National Union of Students
ODG	Overseas Development Group
ORS	Overseas Research Student Scheme
PCFC	Polytechnics and Colleges Funding Council
PR	Personal Reminiscences of Gordon Tilsley (typescript)
PRC	Planning and Resources Committee
PRCS	Premature Retirement Compensation Scheme
PRO	Public Records Office (Kew)
PVC	Pro Vice-Chancellor

QAA	Quality Assurance Agency
RAE	Research Assessment Exercise
RC	Royal Commission
RDC	Rural District Council
RHCP	Roy Campbell Papers
RIBA	Royal Institute of British Architects
SAGA	Sand and Gravel Association
SAPC	Student Amenities Policy Committee
SCR	Senior Common Room
SCUE	Standing Conference on University Entrance
SCVA	Sainsbury Centre for Visual Arts
SISJAC	Sainsbury Institute for the Study of Japanese Art and Culture
SL	Spartacist League
SLC	Student Loans Company
SOC	School of Economic and Social Studies
SOC SOC	Socialist Society
SZP	Solly Zuckerman Papers
TEFL	Teaching English as a Foreign Language
THES	*Times Higher Education Supplement*
TQA	Teaching Quality Assessment
UAU	Universities Athletics Union
UCCA	Universities Central Council on Admissions
UEA	University of East Anglia
UEASU	University of East Anglia Students Union
UFC	Universities Funding Council
UGC	University Grants Commission
USAAF	United States of America Air Force
VC	Vice-Chancellor
VCO	Vice Chancellor's Office
VSO	Voluntary Service Overseas
VSU	Voluntary Service Unit
WEA	Workers' Educational Association

1

A University for Norwich

Norwich is the natural and traditional focus of a large area in East
Anglia with a rich heritage from the past . . . the City and the area
around it has an unobscured and solid thread of cultural progress
of a kind which would be extremely suitable as a background for an
institution of University rank.

Memorandum, 1947[1]

Norwich is a "fine city". The phrase was first used by George Borrow in the
mid nineteenth century and still appears proudly on the boundary signs that
welcome the incoming motorist. The city had developed from a series of
hamlets into a market centre in the Danish period, 870-920, coming to
replace the nearby great Roman town of Caistor as the chief centre of the area.
In this pre-conquest period Norfolk was emerging as one of the most popu-
lous and wealthy regions of England. The Normans gave it its distinctive
landmarks and status – the castle (originally in wood and then in stone from
1120), the cathedral from 1096 and the market by St Peter Mancroft, still the
largest open market in England. It also received its first charter in 1194. It is
notable that three of the cities where new universities were founded in the
1960s, Colchester, Lancaster and Norwich, received their civic charters in the
five years to 1194.

Norwich's medieval wealth was based on wool; by the fourteenth century it
was the chief centre of worsted manufacture in the land and the sixth richest
town in England. No other medieval town had as many as five bridges across
its river. With wealth went culture and civic concern. Norwich retains from
the middle ages the Great Hospital (1256), one of the pioneering institutions
for the care of the sick and aged. St Andrews Hall remains the only friars'
church in England surviving in its entirety, while Mother Julian of Norwich
(1373-1416) has acquired a new reputation as a woman spiritual writer of
national repute: "all shall be well and all manner of things shall be well".

From the 1550s Dutch and Walloon 'strangers' further stimulated the textile
trade with their finer cloths and the city became a major centre of ecclesiastical
silversmithing with an assay office from the sixteenth to the eighteenth
century. In 1612 John Harrington declared, "I should judge this city to be

another utopia". By the early eighteenth century Norwich was pre-eminent among early Georgian provincial cities, the largest outside London until over-taken by Bristol in the 1730s.[2] The Georgian Norwich gentleman would perambulate Gentleman's Walk, take his refreshment in Thomas Ivory's Assembly House with its Music Room (1754), be entertained there or in the adjacent Theatre Royal (1768) and stroll in Chapel Field Gardens. Indeed the Assembly House, Theatre Royal and Chapel Field Gardens were all laid out as contiguous amenities in the mid eighteenth century as the first integrated leisure complex in England. Should our gentleman fall sick then the Norfolk and Norwich Hospital (1772) would minister to his needs. All these institutions survive and reflect into the twentieth century something of the quality of culture already evident in early modern Norwich. The nineteenth and early twentieth centuries added the Triennial Music Festival (1824), Nugent Monck's Norwich Players (1911) and the Maddermarket Theatre (1921), one of the most important pioneers of amateur drama in England.

The strong distinctive character of Norwich in the late nineteenth and early twentieth centuries impressed observers. Percy Lubbock remembered it in the 1880s and 1890s: "The heart of Norwich, in the region about the market-place, has a very distinguished air. It impressed me with the dignity and the grand style of a capital city . . . Norwich had a personal, self-conscious look, aware of its own being; it was from Norwich, not from London that one could learn to think of a city as a body of life and character."[3] A few years later R.H. Mottram, one of the University's first group of honorary graduates, claimed that "there is no other town that has had for eight hundred years, cathedral and castle and a large share of industrial prosperity and agricultural markets of national importance".[4]

Nor has Norwich and the region been without its notable personalities: Sir Edward Coke, the Chief Justice under James I; Sir Thomas Browne, the eminent doctor and philosopher; Elizabeth Fry, the prison reformer; and Horatio Nelson. East Anglia's great skies, dry light and landscapes inspired two notable schools of painting, the Norwich School of John and J. B. Crome and J. S. Cotman, and the Suffolk School of Constable and Gainsborough. The University has rightly paid tribute to the memories of Fry, Nelson and Constable by naming buildings after them. It had the privilege of holding Coke's library for a time in the sixties and still occupies Elizabeth Fry's resi-dence at Earlham Hall.

Norwich is moreover the centre of the great region of East Anglia, which Mottram characterised as "a province, a non-metropolitan district of strong local flavour".[5] The huge bulge of East Anglia thrusts out into the North Sea towards Holland with which in prehistoric times it formed a land bridge. In the eighteenth century it was easier to send Norfolk grain to the Low

Countries by sea than to the midlands and it is still easier to get from Norwich to Amsterdam than to London. Dutch gables and Flemish bricks are still to be seen, though the characteristic building material is flint, a Norfolk industry from stone age times. The characteristic landscape is not "very flat" as in Noël Coward's famous *Private Lives* canard. The Norfolk landscape rolls gently though no higher than 300 feet, with wheat and barley fields, clumps of pine on sandy soil, Saxon round towers and later medieval churches faced with flint. What is distinctive is its low level of population density, the predominance of arable agriculture and relatively dry climate. Indeed in the eighteenth century Norfolk was a centre of the agricultural revolution associated with Thomas Coke and his friends – enclosure, crop rotation, selective animal breeding. The fine country houses of the great landowners, Holkham, Houghton, and Raynham, are witnesses to the wealth and taste of their time. The region's tradition of agricultural innovation raised expectations that a University might contribute to it and this was an important issue in the University's early days.

In cast of mind East Anglia prides itself on its independence; 'do different' is a saying adopted by the University as its motto. It was a centre of Lollardy in the Reformation and Independency in the Civil War, when it supported Cromwell, an East Anglian squire. The strength of its Nonconformity in Victorian times continued this tradition. The region has a remoteness, since the bulge creates distances greater than expected and its transport links, until recently, have not been good. This enhances its sense of being a distinct region and Norwich's feeling of being a major regional metropolitan centre. These matters have proved significant. The very long and strong cultural and civic traditions, the separate distinctiveness of the region, and the centrality of Norwich's metropolitan role within it, were the most powerful and convincing arguments used by the city in its claims for a University in the 1960s.

In spite of these characteristics, Norwich still lacked a university in the mid twentieth century. Had universities been created outside Oxford and Cambridge at any time from the late middle ages to the eighteenth century then Norwich would have merited one. But the civic and provincial universities movement in England was a late Victorian one and Norwich was unable to take part in it. The civic universities arose in the great industrial cities of the north and midlands in response to rising population, its concentrations in large urban centres and the need for scientific and technical manpower for the industries of those areas. They were also conspicuous expressions of civic pride in arriviste towns whose rise to national prominence was much later than that of Norwich. Yet Norwich could not join them in the 1870s and 1880s and thereafter.

There were various reasons for this. First, Norwich's population by 1911 was too small. The populations of cities with civic universities chartered between 1899 and 1909 ranged from 704,000 (Liverpool) to 339,000 (Bristol). Norwich's population in 1911 was only 121,000. It was also much less than the populations of Newcastle (247,000) and Nottingham (240,000), which had minor colleges taking the degrees of Durham and London.

Secondly, Norwich's decline from the largest provincial city in England in the early eighteenth century to twenty-third by 1901 reflected its declining industrial strength. The woollen textile spinning and weaving which had been an important source of Norwich's wealth since the fourteenth century had passed from the city to the West Riding of Yorkshire. There the proximity of coal, which Norwich lacked, gave an advantage to the steam-powered factories of Leeds and its region. Norwich, where half the population in the eighteenth century depended on handweaving cloth, was desperately vulnerable. The handweavers of Norwich moved to fancier work or other jobs. A steam-powered mill was built in Norwich in 1839 but this was hardly an Industrial Revolution to match that of the north. Victorian Norwich came to depend on other industries: brewing (there were twenty four breweries in 1836 thriving on the local barley fields); leatherworking and shoes; Boulton and Paul's wire netting from 1850; and Colman's mustard. Its most dynamic areas were in finance, the Norwich Union being founded in 1797, and particularly banking. There were six banks in Norwich by 1800, and Barclays emerged from them as the leader. But Norwich, lacking coal and minerals, missed the Industrial Revolution of the nineteenth century. It could not become a Manchester, Liverpool or Birmingham. Norwich sank back into being a pleasant, rather remote provincial town, a gentry social centre and market with fine period architecture relatively free of the dirt, smoke stack industries, teeming slums and social problems of larger and more successful cities. But it was not in that first league of Victorian cities for whom a civic university was an urgent need and credible adornment.

Thirdly, the East Anglian rural hinterland went into a sharp decline just as the civic universities movement was getting underway. The influx of cheap grain from the USA, Australia and elsewhere brought about an agricultural depression in England, especially in the 1880s and 1890s. The East Anglian wheat and barley growers were particularly hard hit and, denied the protection of a tariff, had to endure a halving of wheat and barley prices between the early 1870s and mid 1890s. Low farm rents, incomes and profits, diminishing fortunes, unrenewed tenancies, labour laid off and emigration was the result. Norwich was left as an old city with a relatively low population, falling back, overtaken in industry and wealth and set in a surrounding region seriously depressed for other reasons. This was not a realistic time or venue for a serious University movement.

In the 1900s there were however, whiffs of expectation in the air. In the 1890s Cambridge University used to run University Extension lectures in Norwich. These were courses of about ten lectures given by Cambridge dons on subjects of general interest. The audiences were usually the cultured middle classes, notably women, who were there for interest and pleasure rather than to pass examinations or for university entrance. By coincidence the founder of the nationwide University Extension Movement, James Stuart, came to live in Norwich in 1898. He was a former Professor of Engineering at Cambridge and had married a Norwich woman, Laura Elizabeth Colman, the daughter of J. J. Colman.[6] Stuart accordingly became a director of Colmans, living in Carrow Abbey. So there was a direct connection through this Norwich worthy between the City and the University Extension Movement generally, though Stuart does not seem to have involved himself in the movement in Norwich. In 1901 this extension work came under the auspices of the new Technical College, opened in 1891.[7] From 1901 members of this group began to call themselves the "Norwich University Extension Society". Of course this did not imply that Norwich had a University nor that Extension Society activity was intended to be the roots of a university proper – though in Reading it proved to be. But the conjunction of the two words "Norwich University" inspired dreams and expectations for the next sixty years. A plaque in the box office of Cinema City in the Stuart and Suckling Halls commemorates this. Moreover in 1901 the Technical College began to prepare students for London University matriculation and B.Sc. examinations. This too suggested that there was an institution in Norwich which was in some sense an outpost of London University and that through London University, it might become a university college in its own right. This was to prompt action nearly forty years later.

There was also a more nebulous and subtle point. In the 1900s, when the great Victorian cities were securing charters for their civic universities, there was much talk of these cities as reviving the ideals of the Italian city states and free German cities of the late middle ages and Renaissance.[8] It was particularly so in Birmingham and Liverpool. Having an independent university had been a mark of these older continental cities as it was now to be in Victorian England as a symbol of civic pride. Accordingly it was no coincidence that the 1902 series of lectures of the new Norwich University Extension Society was on "Famous Cities" by F. A. Kirkpatrick, with the first one on "The City as Sovereign State". Norwich was scenting some of the wafts of this neo-medievalist civic thinking in the 1900s and having a university was one of the strains in this heady aroma. It has been suggested that early proposals for a university in Norwich came in 1910,[9] but there is no evidence for this. *The Times*, which reported Norwich affairs closely, made no reference to any such development in Norwich 1909-13, although it noted the beginnings of the Sussex University Movement in 1913.[10]

The first initiative in Norwich came immediately after the First World War. The war had resulted in an optimistic attitude towards education. Children attending secondary schools increased from 187,000 in 1914 to 337,000 by 1920, while H. A. L. Fisher's Education Act raised the school-leaving age to fourteen. The new civic universities had also played a vital role in the creation and development of new war technology. This changed the public perception of universities from being that they were institutions relevant only to a tiny elite to an awareness that they were a national resource from which the increasing number of secondary school pupils could benefit. A short-lived economic boom following the end of the war added to the sense of optimism. In this atmosphere of heightened appreciation of education some towns hoped that the pre-war period of granting charters to universities could be resumed. Brighton and Norwich sought to jump on this bandwagon.

In 1918 a proposal to found and endow a college in the city was put forward by a committee under Sir George Chamberlin.[11] Chamberlin (1846-1928) was the proprietor of one of the finest fashion department stores in Norwich, on the Guildhall Hill site of the present Tesco's. He was Lord Mayor of Norwich in 1916 and 1918 and knighted in 1919.[12] He envisaged it as a War Memorial College and it was hoped that Cambridge would help the college come into being, just as Oxford had recently fostered Reading. They quickly acquired subscriptions and promises amounting to £60,000. Then in July 1919 a request was made to the Board of Education that they should contribute £100,000 conditional upon a similar sum being raised locally. The Board of Education, however, refused the scheme which Norwich abandoned in October 1920.

There were various understandable reasons for this. Although £60,000 had been promised in Norwich, only £20,000 was raised. This was tiny when the UGC explained that the necessary annual income of a small university in 1920 was about £100,000. In any case the turning of the post-war boom into the first of the inter-war slumps prompted education cuts in December 1920. If Norwich had not abandoned the scheme in October it would certainly have been quashed two months later. Secondly, Norwich had, perhaps unwisely, stressed that the proposed college would serve the city and region. The Board would not have been impressed with the modesty of a university with such localised ambitions. The 1960s movement was careful to avoid this error. It was also unclear where a university with no money could be housed. The Registrar of Reading University imaginatively suggested St. Andrews Hall,[13] but this got nowhere as did an attempt to persuade the Board of Education to upgrade the recently created Technical College to university status. The City accepted the setback, but Norwich, like Brighton, had usefully made a serious claim that it wanted a university some forty years before its eventually successful outcome.[14]

The movement surprisingly revived in 1939 with striking new developments at the Technical College. In January the City Council recommended that the new college should be built on the Ipswich Road at a cost of £199,000. In the course of the debate G. F. Johnson said that the new Norwich College would be "the university of the city's working class people".[15] This was a grand claim in the face of a failed attempt by Sir Robert Bignold (Leader of the Conservatives and Chairman of Norwich Union) to minimise the college by halving its building programme. Johnson's phrase and idea caught on. In March the Principal of the College, Dr H. W. Howes, speaking at the annual dinner of the Norwich and District Master Bakers Association, delivered some visionary words: "I am looking ahead to the day when the building which will go up on the Ipswich Road . . . will not be a technical school, but will be designated a university college. I do not think that day is so far off as some people imagine."[16]

In the same month Alderman F. C. Jex, the leader of Labour on the City Council and Chairman of the Education Committee, supported these claims. He wrote "I see no reason at all why Norwich should not be recognised and receive University College status".[17] He called for "benevolent educationalists with financial resources" to endow the college. "This would afford an opportunity for our boys and girls to reach university standard without having to meet the terrific cost of university training in other parts of the country." He repeated Johnson's claim, "I look upon this college as providing the university for the working classes". This was not merely rhetoric, for on 21 April 1939 the Director of Education and the College Principal were recorded as about to visit London University to investigate the possibility of establishing a university college in Norwich.[18] The coming of the war, however, made any further advance out of the question although the Norwich College was then larger than twenty-two other major technical colleges, six of which later became universities.

As the First World War had created an atmosphere favourable to education so even more so did the Second. The 1944 Butler Education Act raised the school leaving age to fifteen. The Act was expected to increase access to the grammar school and hence to university and aroused considerable enthusiasm for education generally. Two major reports at the end of the war signalled the need for an expansion of technological manpower and of the universities to produce them. Lord Eustace Percy in 1945 called for the maintenance of the post-1943 annual output of engineers at at least three thousand a year and an increase of university graduates supplied to industry.[19] Sir Alan

Barlow was even more demanding. He wanted a doubling of the output of university scientists from two and a half thousand to five thousand a year. This was to be brought about not only by expanding existing universities but by the creation of a new one. The student population had risen from 50,002 in 1938/9 to 65,452 in 1946/7 but clearly further expansion was being assumed.[20] Various cities now saw an opportunity to revive or start a university movement. Norwich was one of them.

Even outsiders saw the justice of the claim. Dr J. A. Bowie of Dundee, a well-known figure in management education, suggested Norwich as the location of a new university in March 1946 and this attracted local attention.[21] The Norwich Movement revived in 1946 as did those in Bradford, Brighton, Stoke and York.[22] A meeting was convened by the Mayor of Norwich, Alderman S. A. Bailey, on 14 June, and the *Eastern Daily Press* gave its cautious support.[23] Education Officers J. W. Beeson, W. O. Bell and Dr Lincoln Ralphs prepared an important memorandum rehearsing the arguments for a university in Norwich.[24] They noted Sir Alan Barlow's report published in April, its call for a doubling of university students and Barlow's assumption that this would need more new institutions. In this Barlow differed from Percy, who preferred merely to expand existing universities.[25] Norwich had a case in that, as there was no other civic university within a hundred miles, "there is no other town in England of similar size which is situated so far from a university or university college". Nor was there so sizeable an aggregate population of 500,000 (Norwich and Norfolk) so distant from a university. They estimated, still thinking locally, that the region would produce a potential 400-480 university students. This seemed appropriate. Reading had been told that it needed a nucleus of 300-500 students and Reading was succeeding with a lower population (97,000) than Norwich (126,000). Of course not all students would be local but East Anglians who went elsewhere would be balanced by incomers, as at Reading.

Norwich could be made attractive by developing distinctive studies. The obvious one was agriculture: "the city has a rich agricultural hinterland and there certainly would appear to be need for some extension of agricultural education facilities in the region". The counter-argument to that was the Loveday Report on Higher Agricultural Education, which had suggested that there was ample provision for graduates in agriculture. Norwich saw a niche in intermediate sub-graduate agricultural studies. They were on safe ground in seeing the need for degrees in horticulture and agricultural engineering. Lincoln Ralphs noted that several "responsible individuals" had stressed the importance of agricultural engineering which "is in my view, a subject in which the Committee have the strongest claim for a separate institution".[26] Overall they thought that the annual costs of a university college would be £120,000 to £150,000 but had no idea what Norwich could contribute to this.

A subsequent memorandum reasserted Norwich's chief claims – its fine cultural heritage, the vast area it had to serve, its ability to serve local industry and enrich educational life.[27] They reassessed the local supply of entrants at 300 rather than 400-480. They emphasised industry more and agriculture less, possibly aware that the UGC was bound to be influenced by Loveday. Their strongest arguments were the region's remoteness, its long cultural tradition and prior university claims.

Armed with these arguments a deputation from Norwich went to see the UGC on 14 May 1947.[28] They were not to know that the UGC had already taken a cool view of Barlow's proposals for new universities. With the exception of R.H. Tawney, the notable champion of expanding educational opportunities, their view was that Barlow's "proposal for the establishment of a new university is not one which they could support".[29] It was better to build up existing institutions, as a new university would divert staff and scarce materials from elsewhere and would in any case be too small to be economical. But intriguingly they conceded that East Anglia was a region of "unsatisfied local need for a centre of university education".[30] The deputation met the Chairman, Sir Walter Moberley, and his Vice-Chairman, Arthur Trueman. They emphasised the informal exploratory nature of the approach and repeated the arguments of the 1946 and 1947 memoranda. Moberley was courteous if not encouraging. The UGC was increasing its financial support for universities and he conceded that East Anglia "has extremely strong claims founded on its geographical position". But he emphasised the four limiting factors working against expansion at this time. First, there was a seven year gap in training teachers for universities. Secondly, there was a grave shortage of labour and materials for the building industry and existing universities had building programmes which had to take priority in the allocations which the Ministry of Works made to the Ministry of Education. The lack of building resources was crucial and the Norwich deputation had no existing buildings to suggest on which a nascent university could be based. Thirdly, Moberley stressed that the deputation should decide on a range of subjects for the proposed university since this would affect their demand for buildings.[31] This was the nub of Norwich's problem. The 1947 memorandum had deliberately not specified subjects. They knew that only those to do with agriculture gave Norwich distinctive credibility. Yet they also knew that official policy following Loveday was that agriculture was amply supplied with university education already. To base a university movement on sub-graduate work was hardly credible either. Fourthly, Moberley argued, there was no demographic need for university expansion in the 1940s. Due to the declining birthrate in the 1930s and war years, the numbers of eighteen-year-olds would not rise until after 1960. Moberley's view was that the Norwich project was a long-term but not an immediate prospect. He clearly held the same view of Brighton, York and Bradford, whose 1947 claims were likewise denied. Yet a later UGC document suggested that the Norwich claim had been considered "with some seriousness" and that "Sir Walter Moberly was rather more encouraging to the Norwich deputation than he had been to the Sussex authorities or to York".[32]

Some string pulling behind the scenes was to no avail. The Norwich MP John Paton asked the government whether they would look with favour on the university project in Norwich. The Treasury and UGC agreed that their approach should be "rather cautious".[33] The Norwich people contacted Sir Will Spens, the former wartime Regional Director of East Anglia, who had a discreet Athenaeum lunch with Moberly and tried to broker some arrangement whereby Cambridge University would "sponsor" the Norwich application, but it came to nothing.[34] It was at Spens's suggestion that, later in October, a Norwich delegation went to Hull which gave them some advice. Hull stressed its substantial land holdings (150 acres), residences, endowments, the financial backing of the local authorities, their high catchment (80 per cent) of students from a ten mile radius, and their research for local industry.[35] It was a useful meeting but indicated to Norwich just how far behind its own movement was and what it lacked to make the project successful. On the return to Norwich the Town Clerk, Bernard Storey, called a meeting for 22 October which decided that it was not worth proceeding further.[36]

This realistically recognised not only the position of the UGC but the general mood in Norwich. For example Gordon Tilsley, Storey's successor as Town Clerk, was amazed that there was no reference to the 1946/7 movement in the Education Committee minutes and no reference to the UGC and Hull visits in the local press.[37] There was no broad support for the movement in Norwich in 1946. Even Beeson, in whose name the main document was written, was not personally enthusiastic, and discouragingly poured cold water on the initiative which he thought would be too difficult.[38] He was right. The 1946 movement accordingly lapsed, but it had been valuable in keeping the idea of a Norwich University alive both in the mind of the UGC and the people of Norwich itself.

There was a twenty-six year interval between the 1919 and 1946 movements but there was to be no such delay between the post Second World War initiative and the ultimately successful one beginning at the end of the 1950s. This was because strong social changes began to transform the need for university expansion.

In the first place there was a 'trend' to staying on in the sixth form. The number of pupils in sixth forms rose between 1947 and 1958 from 32,000 to 53,000. What was remarkable was the fact that this increase had been brought about with age cohorts whose birth rate had been declining in the 1920s and 1930s. It did not merely reflect the fact that there were more children to enter sixth forms; on the contrary, there were fewer. It was a real trend to staying on at school with 40 per cent of fourteen-year-olds in 1954 going into the sixth form as seventeen-year-olds in 1957.[39]

Why should this have come about contrary to the demographic expectation? After the 1944 Education Act grammar schools could only be entered by intelligent children selected by examination. Fee paying was no longer the back door entry for the academically less able. Accordingly the academic quality of grammar schools in the 1950s would have been considerably better than that in the 1930s and more would look forward to the sixth form to develop their abilities. Secondly, sixth forms in the 1950s were taught by a high calibre of teachers. Many had entered grammar school teaching in the 1930s when recruitment was very selective and the profession attractive. A good war record enhanced the quality of the best. Although real wages for schoolmasters fell in the early 1950s and diminished the attractiveness of school teaching, that older generation was too established to leave and the 1950s sixth formers were among the last to benefit from teachers who brought qualities from an earlier age. Thirdly, pupils could now afford to stay on. The full employment and generally prosperous times of the 1950s enabled parents to let children stay beyond the minimum school-leaving age. Also the 1944 Act had removed the costs not only of fees but of significant burdens such as stationery and books. Fourthly, the 1950s saw important occupational shifts which benefited the more highly educated. Occupational groups 1-4 (managerial and professional) rose by 27.1 per cent over the decade and groups 5-7 (manual, unskilled) fell by 0.4 per cent.[40] These precise figures were not known until the 1961 census but the perception of the rise of increasing opportunities for white collar 'executives' were evident to contemporaries. All these factors moved more children into sixth forms and raised their aspirations to higher education beyond.

This trend was given a much greater urgency by the 'bulge' of the increasing birth rate since the war. Births had fallen steadily from 1920 to 1933 and had removed any demographic pressure on the universities from 1938 to 1951. The birth rate, however, rose in the later stages of the war. Accordingly the populations of eighteen-year-olds in the UK was to rise from 649,000 in 1959 to a peak of 959,000 in 1965, with 1964-67 being the most difficult years of the bulge.[41] By the 1970s numbers of eighteen-year-olds would be also in the 700-800,000 rather than the 600,000 range of the

1950s. The sharp peak of 1964-67 was unusual but even when it subsided it did so at a higher level in the 1970s than it had left in the 1950s. Moreover, from the standpoint of 1958, a second sharp rise was already evident in the period 1973-75. When the effects of the "trend" and the "bulge" combined in the 1960s the pressure on universities would be insupportable with existing facilities. Lord Robbins' committee estimated that, unless there was a considerable expansion, by 1967 there would be a shortfall of 25,000 young people a year qualified to go to university but for whom there would be no places. These were the kind of considerations which in the 1950s began to move the idea of a university in Norwich from the remote sidelines into the centre stage of practical possibility.[42]

Given the increasing awareness in the 1950s of the general need for university expansion in the 1960s, it is worth considering the documentation which specifically began to shape Norwich thinking in the late 1950s. This was read and often annotated by a leading figure in the movement, Gordon Tilsley, the Town Clerk of Norwich. Many of these items began to pinpoint Norwich as a likely new site for a university and this powerfully reinforced the confidence of the reviving movement.

An able Association of University Teachers Report of 1958 presented the familiar figures on eighteen-year-olds. But it added a new dimension by pointing out that, if the IQ appropriate for university education was 122.5, 6.7 per cent of the population merited it. Yet since in 1954 only 3.2 per cent were so educated there was a case on psychometric grounds for doubling the university population. In their view this was best done by creating new universities, since merely expanding existing ones beyond 4500 would destroy the personal contact of staff and students. "This implies that new universities ought to be created . . . and sites such as Norwich, York and Leamington have been suggested because the existing town or city provides a nucleus of cultured life."[43]

A few months later the UGC published its 1958 report on the 1952-57 period.[44] This too was avidly read by Norwich promoters. Here there were two ideas which they did well to disregard since they ran counter to Norwich intentions and in any case were soon reversed by the UGC itself. The first was the UGCs belief that the expansion could be accommodated by the expansion of existing institutions, plus Brighton. The second was that more biology was not to be encouraged, But some positive ideas encouraged Norwich's thinking. The UGC hoped that along with expansion there "is a need for constant experiment in the organisation of university teaching and design of university curricula". This was enthusiastically underlined in the Norwich copy. So was the UGC's calling for more management education and the importance of halls of residence.

Another influential study feeding into the thinking of the early movement was a report by the WEA Norfolk Federation. In 1958 they had written to J. W. Beeson, the Director of Education for Norwich, giving their support for "the claims of Norwich as an ideal centre for a new university". In 1959 they followed up with a formal report.[45] It rehearsed the usual demographic arguments for national expansion. It based its claims for Norwich on the distinctive regional character of East Anglia. This could not be served by Cambridge, a national university, nor by the nearest civic universities, Leicester and Nottingham, which were of the east midlands and not at all distinctively East Anglian. Only a university in the great "provincial capital" of Norwich would suffice. A university would in turn bring more culture to the region and, not to be overlooked, at least £160,000 a year in government money apart from millions in capital grants. The most valuable contribution of the WEA's report was some excellent thinking about the curriculum. In particular they floated the idea of interdisciplinarity. They noted "A high proportion of new developments are either outside the normal boundaries or where the boundaries overlap", and they specified biochemistry and communications. These were remarkably prescient in foreshadowing the views of the first Vice-Chancellor, Frank Thistlethwaite. The WEA also foresaw the Centre of East Anglian Studies with suggestions for East Anglian studies in geography, history and economics. For languages they suggested Dutch and Scandinavian as well as the common ones. In science they saw Norwich as having a special role in marine biology, nutrition and, of course, in agriculture and agricultural engineering, in which "we look forward to the greatest development". The WEA report was one of the best discussions of curriculum to influence the embryo University. Their predictions of subjects and combinations – interdisciplinary biochemistry, East Anglian studies, Scandinavian, marine and food science – all came to fruition. Even the miscues – agricultural engineering and Dutch – were sensible and appropriate. The WEA provided a further service to the movement by running a series of lectures through the Autumn of 1959 on the proposed "University for Norwich".

At the same time in 1959 Professor Balchin of Swansea surveyed the position of the universities. He was clear that the expansion, on which all agreed, could best be catered for by creating more universities rather than expanding existing ones. The optimum size of universities, in the opinion of those days, was 3000-4500 and the older ones were at the limit of expansion. He analysed likely centres from the point of view of population, hinterland and distance from existing universities. Norwich was identified as a leading contender with a population of 121,000 and a hinterland of 250,000. Ipswich had 108,000 plus 250,000 respectively – Gordon Tilsley underlined the comparative

Norwich and Ipswich figures. Norwich with York also had the strongest claims as a cultural centre. Balchin rightly foresaw Norwich, Brighton, York, Canterbury as justifiable sites, with Norwich second only to Brighton on population grounds.[46]

Finally in 1959 the Federation of British Industry added its voice to the call for expansion.[47] They accepted the UGC's estimate of the need to increase the student population from 100,000 to 130-140,000. But they did not want universities to be larger than 3000. They then embarked on some faulty arithmetic which inadvertently made a forceful point. They assumed that most of the expansion could be brought about by an expansion of existing universities. Yet this course of action would still have left a shortfall of 17,000. They unwittingly showed, contrary to their policies, that six *new* universities were required, not merely two or three. But they specified Norwich and York, along with Brighton as "particularly suitable" to provide the extra places.

The positive messages that Norwich received from these reports, often specifically annotated by the Town Clerk, were these. There was an IQ argument, hitherto overlooked, for expanding university entrants to 6.7 per cent of eighteen-year-olds, there was a need for experiments in curricular design and notably interdisciplinary combinations, industry needed more graduates, new halls of residence were desirable, a city with a population of 121,000 and a hinterland of 250,000 and a strong cultural background had especial claims to a university. All these points reinforced Norwich's aspirations. But even more important, four of the reports – those of the Association of University Teachers, the Federation of British Industry, the Workers' Educational Association and Balchin – called for expansion by creating more new universities and not merely relying on expanding existing ones. The mood was sharply changing against creating civic mega-universities and in favour of spreading the benefits around and encouraging curricular diversification. But most important of all, all the reports that called for new universities specifically identified Norwich as a city with a priority claim. By the late 1950s the arguments in favour of a "University for Norwich" were unanswerable and the tide of opinion seemed unstoppable.

Events in Brighton reactivated the Norwich movement in the Spring of 1958. Yet again proposals for a University in Brighton were rejected in 1956 but at last were accepted in February 1958. This prompted further thoughts in Norwich, which had shared disappointment with Brighton after both world wars. Might it not now share its success? The credit for starting the 1958 movement lies with two men, Dr Lincoln Ralphs the Chief Education Officer for Norfolk and Andrew Ryrie, a director of Colman's.

Lincoln Ralphs, a heavily built man of immense energy and real ability, was Chief Education Officer for Norfolk from 1950-74. A graduate of Sheffield both in science and law he became President of the National Union of Students and of the International Confederation of Students in 1937-38. He came to Norfolk after the war as deputy to W. O. Bell, whom he succeeded.[48] Most crucially it was Ralphs who actually wrote the document (ascribed to Beeson and Bell) advocating a university in 1946. Ralphs thus provided the direct continuity between the 1946 and 1958 movements. Ralphs was the first Methodist layman to preach in Norwich Cathedral and was a President of the National Sunday School Union. This was to prove significant as three major figures in the formation of UEA, Ralphs, Viscount Mackintosh of Halifax and Gordon Tilsley were Methodists of Park Lane Chapel and the first two were leading figures in the Sunday School Movement. On 16 April 1958, while addressing the Norwich Rotary Club, Ralphs reflected that it was a pity that Norwich was being developed by the second Elizabethans and not the first, "I doubt if they would have left the third city in their land without a university".[49] The fact that the first Elizabethans did precisely that did not diminish the rhetorical point.

By coincidence the theme was quite independently taken up by Andrew Ryrie, Secretary and later Vice-Chairman of Colmans. He was a different personality from Ralphs. Arthur South remembered Ryrie as "a small chap, full of energy, a little terrier, a tough little Scots lawyer".[50] Valerie Guttsman, who served with him in Labour politics recalled his quick spoken, bubbling, lively, jumpy manner, "a monkey on a stick".[51] He was a future Lord Mayor and then unusually, became a Labour Councillor after his mayoralty and after leaving Colmans. He was an "ideas man", very caring on welfare measures, but possibly lacked the weight of Ralphs and some future participants in the university movement. In 1958 he was President of the Norwich Chamber of Commerce and in that capacity was distributing prizes to Lowestoft Technical College at the South Pier Pavilion, Lowestoft. This was on 17 April, the day after Ralphs' address to the Rotary Club. Ryrie told his Lowestoft audience that there were going to be more universities, recalled the earlier Norwich movements, and said that it was time to take it up again.[52] Interestingly, Ryrie's motives were to provide more industrial manpower: he envisaged a University growing out of the upgraded Norwich Technical College.

Ralphs, seeing the report of Ryrie's speech, then determined to get the bandwagon rolling. This also began a friendship between Ralphs and Ryrie who had otherwise barely known each other. Ralphs wrote to the local press that it may be "now or never" for a Norwich university movement. A university would enrich Norwich's cultural life and convey East Anglia's own heritage to others coming from or destined to live in industrial areas. It was interesting that Ryrie's emphasis had been on producing industrial manpower; Ralphs' was on enriching and diffusing culture. Both arguments ran together in the founding of the university.[53]

Ryrie made the university the theme of his presidential address to the Chamber of Commerce on 31 May and in June the movement suddenly took off. Ralphs opened up a salvo of communications to the *Eastern Daily Press*[54] and this began to draw in other major figures. Sam Peel, the chairman of Norfolk CC Education Committee, in effect Ralphs' boss, gave his support, suggesting that they start the university by using temporary huts quickly and that they emphasise Finance as a specialism, since it coincided with the 150th anniversary of the Norwich Union.[55] Equally important, Peel got in touch with Arthur South, the Chairman of Norwich Education Committee, urging cooperation in the university endeavour.[56] Sam Peel jollied South along. Referring to an Alderman North who had played a part in establishing University College Leicester, he bantered that "what North could do in the West, South might do in the East".[57] South (later Sir Arthur) was a Norwich businessman and furrier who was then deputy leader of the Labour Party on the Norwich Council. He was a precocious public figure and was the youngest councillor in England when elected to Norwich Council in 1935 at the age of twenty. He had also been one of the youngest Sheriffs and the youngest Labour Lord Mayor in 1956.[58] A stocky, pugnacious, energetic man he was to become a new driving force in the university movement.

Tom Eaton, an ex Lord Mayor, local solicitor and city councillor since 1949, was also drawn in.[59] He called for the Lord Mayor to convene a meeting to advance the university. He feared that Ryrie's idea might "dissolve once more into thin air". He was clearly unaware of the networking behind the scenes and the close interlacing of Ryrie, Ralphs, Peel and South that had so quickly come about. Moreover now that Ralphs had the bit between his teeth, it was unlikely that things would now lapse. But Eaton's show of interest was valuable in spreading concern beyond officials and politicians specifically concerned with education in the city and county. From the second week of June interest spread into Norfolk. J. E. Webster, the Chairman of Cromer Urban District Council, saw the university as giving people "of this area" the education to compete for "important jobs".[60] In North Walsham, K. N. Marshall, Lieutenant Colonel, the headmaster of Paston School, praised the idea of the university for its potential contribution to agriculture and veterinary science.[61] The redoubtable Miss Mary Duff, Principal of Norwich Training College, also used their Commemoration Day to express her hopes for the university.[62] There were further threads in the web in that Lincoln Ralphs' wife Enid taught with Miss Duff at the Training College and Miss Duff's brother – Sir James Duff, Vice-Chancellor of Durham – was Chairman of Sussex University's Planning Board and gave much informal advice in the formation of the UEA.

By June talks were going on between Ryrie, Ralphs, Herbert Frazer the leader of the Council, Fred Jex, Bernard Storey the Town Clerk, J. W. Beeson the Director of Education for Norwich and Arthur South. So quickly had opinion come together in Norwich in June 1958 that it caught the national attention. *The Times* noted "the enthusiasm of a large section of opinion in the city" for a university and that "an influential part of local opinion believes that if Norwich is ever going to get its own university, this is the time".[63]

Arthur South took up the running. He hosted a lunch party on 8 July in a private room at Purdy's Restaurant in Tombland. Purdy's was then the best restaurant in Norwich and the venue of several early meetings to do with the origins of the university. At this meeting with South were familiar figures, Ryrie, Ralphs, Beeson, Frazer, Jex, Storey the Town Clerk and R. P. Braund the Vice-Chairman of the Education Committee. Jex, Beeson and Storey had been participants in the abortive 1946 movement and South recalled that Ryrie found Jex and Beeson rather discouraged by their earlier experiences and even thought the 1958 initiative "was unlikely to be achieved".[64] South had taken no part in the 1946 attempt to create a university and, like Ryrie, brought an enthusiasm untainted by disappointment. Ralphs was young and tough enough to drive through both 1946 and 1958 movements.

The Purdy lunch agreed that Beeson and Ralphs should survey the area for potential sites for a university.[65] They had data from Brighton about their site and finances.[66] The party agreed to approach Sir Robert Bignold of Norwich Union to get his support, financial and otherwise. They also thought of getting advice from Sir John Wolfenden, the Vice-Chancellor of Reading, and decided on the crucial step of approaching the UGC to discuss the establishment of a University College in Norwich. Andrew Ryrie immediately telephoned the UGC after the lunch to arrange a meeting with its Chairman, Sir Keith Murray, to tell him of Norwich's ideas: "it gives us the opportunity of getting some up to date information about the attitude of the University Grants Committee without comitting the city or the county in any way".[67] South and Ralphs thought this an excellent idea. Accordingly Ryrie went to see Murray at the UGC offices in Belgrave Square on 16 July 1958.

This was a crucial meeting. Ryrie and Murray had been at Edinburgh University together and found that they had "a lot of mutual acquaintances", which eased their relationship. Ryrie stressed to Murray the "strong growing opinion in Norwich in favour of the establishment of a University" and Murray indicated what factors would be necessary for success. He would be looking for the support of the locality, a site of at least 100 acres plus playing fields, an endowment fund of around £250,000, plenty of available lodgings accommodation and "some academic support, which obviously in our case would come through Cambridge". But he added several words of caution.

Murray thought that up to 1962 there was only enough money for the existing universities plus Brighton. But he could not speculate what extra leeway there might be after 1963. He also suggested that "certain cities nearer the industrial life of the country and with larger populations would have some priority, particularly if the slant was to be towards the sciences and the technical".[68] This seemed rather a dampener on Norwich as the centre of an agricultural district, especially since Murray (an agricultural economist) also indicated that in the UGC's view there was not much point in offering agriculture as a specialism since university places for agriculture "were sufficient". Nonetheless Sir Keith urged Norwich to put in an application and Ryrie came away optimistic. Meanwhile Lincoln Ralphs kept Norwich opinion simmering with two influential articles on "A University for Norwich" in which he equally optimistically claimed that it "would be hard to believe" that the UGC would be unsympathetic when it saw the strength of local support.[69]

In his meeting with Ryrie Murray had scotched an issue still ambiguous within the movement. He made it clear that the proposed new university should *not* be based on the Technical College. This had been a suggestion in Ryrie's Lowestoft speech. Most movements hitherto in the 1900s, 1919, and 1939, had grown out of the 'Tech' or somehow involved it. The Principal of King's Lynn Technical College had proposed a university college in Norwich but also incorporating county technical colleges and the training college.[70] Oddly, convoluted as it sounded, it presaged the situation in the late 1990s. It found no favour, though it would have given the university a strong vocational element. Ralphs was aware, however, that many in the city were apprehensive about the potential adverse impact of a University on the "Tech". He also recalled, and revealed much later, that he had been "called over the coals" by the Chairman of Governors of the City College in the fear that the University "might detract" from the College.[71]

In September the movement acquired a valuable new supporter, R. Q. (Dick) Gurney. Won over by a speech by Ralphs, he told the latter, "I am dead keen on this University for Norwich . . . I back you to the hilt". This was valuable since he was the next President of the Chamber of Commerce and High Sheriff of Norfolk. He was aware that "this might bring additional weight to bear so that this scheme may be brought to fruition".[72] Gurney was also a local director of Barclays Bank and in the future was one of the largest personal donors to the university appeal while his family gave the first private land for the university. Lincoln Ralphs regarded Gurney's support as "the best piece of news I have had in years".[73] Ryrie, who was more circumspect, agreed on the importance of Gurney's support, but was suspicious, "I am at a loss to know who is inviting whom at this stage", and did not want to "extend the body of conspirators" – the inner circle of pioneers of the movement.

Perhaps Ryrie had a sense that Dick Gurney, for all his public position, good will and generosity, might be a cause of difficulty.[74]

The summer over, the movement resumed strongly. On 8 October 1958 Arthur South presided over a meeting in Norwich City Hall to consider Ryrie's meeting with Sir Keith Murray and the way forward. This set up a small group – South, Ryrie, Ralphs, Gurney (now quickly taking a prominent part), Jex and Sir Ronald Keefe, a local solicitor and the leader of the Conservatives on Norwich City Council. These were "to issue invitations to serve on a committee whose object would be the promotion of a university in Norwich". This committee would include local people of note and was to become the Promotion Committee, a term proposed by Gordon Tilsley. Then from this large body a sub-committee was to be formed specifically to make a submission to the UGC. The movement was now acquiring a formal structure to bring about substantive action.[75]

It was significant that this meeting had taken place in the City Hall and that it was South, a Norwich City Councillor, who had presided over the Purdy lunch on 8 July and the City Hall meeting of 8 October. In the view of Gordon Tilsley, who took over from Bernard Storey as Town Clerk from 1 February 1959, Norwich City Council was "the most dynamic political force in East Anglia" and the City Hall the seat of operations. By contrast the County Council, under its Chairman Sir Bartle Edwards, was lethargic. It aimed to keep the rates low and do as little as possible. Sir Bartle did not even trouble to attend the first meeting of the Promotion Committee. His own views expressed at a local school was that curbing inflation had to take priority, even if it slowed down the building of schools.[76] This when inflation was virtually nil, 1958 was a recession and the birth bulge was rolling through the schools. This attitude meant that he was likely to be unenthusiastic about such a huge project as the University promised to be. Gordon Tilsley pitied Lincoln Ralphs' position as the County Chief Education Officer, "it was sad that a man of such imagination and energy should have been working for a body which gave him so little support".[77] This accounts for the shift in leadership in the movement from the initiatives of Ryrie and Ralphs in the Spring to those of South, a city politician, in the summer and autumn of 1958. It also accounts for the lack of county grandees. For example Sir Edmund Bacon Bt, later so important for UEA, was not yet involved.

Gordon Tilsley proposed that Viscount Mackintosh of Halifax be invited to become Chairman of the new Promotion Committee. They knew each other through Park Lane Methodist Chapel. So a small party, South, Ryrie, Ralphs, Tilsley and Beeson went to see him in his Chapelfield office, the Norwich headquarters of his toffee firm. Gordon Tilsley provided Arthur South with a brief with which to persuade their quarry. This stressed the usual arguments – the demography, the advantages to the city, the recent go-ahead for Brighton.[78] Tilsley recalls in his own words:[79]

> "I think it was Arthur [South] who put the proposal and we chatted gently round it. Then Lord Mackintosh said "I suppose you'll be wanting some brass?" I replied, "About £500,000 I imagine". This as it turned out two or three years later was much too modest [£1,500,000 million was the target of the eventual appeal], but the figure clearly quickened his interest and he said, "I'll go and get Eric" – his younger brother.
>
> When he was out of the room Lincoln remarked, "This is a good sign – he never does anything important without consulting Eric". Eric then came and partici- pated in the discussion and before we left we had the promise we were seeking about our future Chairman.
>
> It might have left the delicate question of who was to be Chairman of the Executive Committee which had the crucial task of preparing the application to the UGC. It might have been expected to fall to Ryrie or Ralphs, but there was unease about this. Harold solved the problem himself: "Oh I shall be the Chairman of the Executive. I'm not willing to be a figurehead. I'm coming into this to work . . . Now who is coming to help me on the Executive?"

Mackintosh's assumption of the chairmanship not only of the Promotion Committee but, by pre-emptive self-appointment, of the executive also caused some surprise since he was not expected to do both. Mackintosh's act was not one of brash assertiveness but, in spite of the breezy language, one of great social finesse. He appreciated that by taking this position himself he would remove any bad feeling among individuals already in the field who might have hoped for this post yet not been elected to it. If he could get them all to work under him he would avoid dividing the movement however slightly. Secondly, he knew with total realism that he was the only figure of both East Anglian and national stature for both tasks. Even Sir Edmund Bacon, the Lord Lieutenant and leading figure in landowning circles in Norfolk, was not yet much involved in the university.[80] No one in city or county could match his record of lifetime achievement, reputation and authority and they all knew it.

Who was Harold Mackintosh? His parents had started the famous toffee firm in Halifax, where he was born in 1891. He never went to university but spent those years in Germany learning the language and running a toffee factory in Krefeld, and even playing international hockey for the German national team before the First World War. He became involved in Norwich when, as a result of a casual lunchtime encounter at the Savoy Hotel, he bought A. J. Caley's Norwich confectionery and Christmas crackers firm from Unilever in 1932. He himself moved to live just outside Norwich in Thickthorn Hall in 1947. His main achievement was to build up the confectionery firm but, as a public figure, his influence extended wider. He was a major figure in the British Empire Cancer Campaign and the Halifax Building Society and most importantly was the driving force behind the National Savings movement in war and peace. He was a devout Methodist with immense enthusiasm for the Sunday School Movement, becoming President of the World Sunday School Association.[81] Honours came to him early and late. He was knighted in 1922 at the age of thirty-one, the youngest person (except Sir John Alcock, the Atlantic aviator) ever to receive a knighthood. A baronetcy followed in 1935, a barony in 1948 and a viscountcy in 1958. The last honour, granted just before the university promoters approached him, may have reinforced his own insistence that what he had to offer was his executive energy and not merely his new figurehead title. It was also thought that, now sixty-seven, he was actually grateful to be given this fresh interest to stimulate his last years.

Although he had not been to university, he had a strong scholarly inclination. He had been a fluent Germanist. He had an unrivalled collection and knowledge of early Toby jugs and was a published expert on Ralph Wood and Staffordshire pottery. He also had strong views on universities. He sent his son John to university in the USA since he did not regard any British universities adequate for training in business administration. This was something he would have liked a new university in Norwich to address, just as he would have been delighted by UEA's later forte in art history. Such was the man who took over as Chairman of the Promotion and Executive Committees and who was to guide the creation of the University until his death in 1964.

An "invitations" Committee began to approach notable county figures to enlist their support. Lincoln Ralphs approached the Countess of Albemarle, Ruth Lady Fermoy and Sir Bartle Edwards.[82] Andrew Ryrie tackled Lord Mancroft of Norwich Union, who was delighted to join, as was the Marquess of Townshend.[83] Getting the support of Sir Bartle Edwards, however, raised City-County sensibilities. R. B. Boyce, Clerk of the County Council, in noting the activity of Tilsley, his City counterpart, asked Ralphs "are you content to let them take the initiative at this stage?" Ralphs, ever politically sensitive, stressed that it was not a question of surrendering initiative to the City but of cooperation.[84] But would the County cooperate with the City? Bartle Edwards's position in November was that the University project was as yet "wishful thinking on the part of those devoted to education": he could not yet associate himself with it until the County Council had discussed it. In contrast, Sam Peel and E. G. Gooch, Chairman and Vice-Chairman of the County Education Committee, were keen on the University. Gooch was also Labour MP for North Norfolk and accordingly committed to Labour's policy of creating new universities.[85] Peel used to joke that he was keeping Sir Bartle's chair warm for him since Peel and Gooch would represent the county and Sir Bartle would join when he could.[86] Ralphs accepted this but thought that Edwards was being disingenuous, and had certainly no reason to believe that the university project was "merely one of wishful thinking". But Ralphs and Boyce accepted that Sir Bartle's position was delicate. He could not, as Chairman of the County Council lend his weight to the movement without Council support and certainly not give the impression he was implicitly committing the Council. This added to the sensitivity of Ralphs' position. He was a driving force of the movement but with only ambivalent support from his County Council Chairman whose "point of view is perhaps a restricted one" – as his Clerk put it. Yet Ralphs did have the support of his Education Committee led by Peel and Gooch, who attended the Promotions Committee in Edward's absence. Ralphs saw that the county could not be left behind and the movement needed its support. Also the county's natural disposition not to spend money should not be excused by the argument that the university was chiefly a city project. He told Tilsley, "I am particularly anxious that we should not precipitate a county versus city dispute . . . I hope you will agree that we don't want to have too much of Norwich at this stage".[87]

Ralphs continued to be sensitive about these matters. He suggested to Tilsley that they should not always meet in the City Hall, "the City Council is so strongly represented that patterns of procedure appropriate to the City Council are already being advocated as appropriate to the university and I am sure this is wrong".[88] Ralphs was concerned that they must make it clear "that the university rises above authority boundaries". There would be dangers if the university movement were too closely associated with the city and City Hall or if tensions were precipitated between city and county. But the level-headed good sense of Tilsley and Ralphs working together prevented this.

The Promotion Committee first met at the City Hall on 2 February 1959. To indicate the nature of their task and the context of the problem Gordon Tilsley prepared a notable paper.[89] Gordon Tilsley was the Deputy Town Clerk, taking over as Town Clerk in February 1959, by pleasing coincidence with the start of the Promotion Committee. But he had already been a leading figure in the movement from 1958, notably in the approach to Mackintosh. In effect he was acting as the chief administrator of the embryo University and only ceased this task on the appointment of the full-time Registrar and Secretary George Chadwick in 1962. His careful preparation of lucid documents and keeping the committees on track and moving forward is one of the most impressive features of these early years. He was one of a handful of genuine founding fathers of the University, which recognised this with the awarding of his richly deserved Hon DCL in 1981.

His preparatory document rehearsed the arguments for expansion and the claims of Norwich. He laid out the lines of submission to the UGC and in effect set the agenda for the coming year. He summed up, "it seems clear, therefore, that the University Promotion Committee must plan an institution which will be independent from the outset, which will teach and foster research in a wide range of subjects and which will have a potential student population of say, 1500 to 2000. Such a university could play a substantial part in solving the national problem as well as serving East Anglia."[90]

At its first meeting the Promotion Committee consisted of representatives of Norwich City and Norfolk County Councils, and their Education Committees and officers. Also the meeting had drawn in officials from Ipswich, Great Yarmouth, Lowestoft, East and West Suffolk County Councils. It was a recognition, although Tilsley's terminology was still "University of Norwich" that they needed East Anglian support. Tilsley stressed the need for Suffolk local government to support the project. If Suffolk had tried to found a university at the same time both would have failed.[91] The Chief Education Officer of East Suffolk presciently referred throughout the meeting to "a university for East Anglia". This was an issue which would have to be resolved eventually. Thirdly, some landowners had declared their allegiance – Sir Edmund Bacon, Marquess Townshend of Raynham, Mr J. D. Alston and the Earl of Stradbroke. With business, professional and religious figures it was already well balanced and well grounded in the region. Later in 1959 when it made its submission to the UGC the Promotion Committee consisted of seventy-six people:

Local government Norwich and Norfolk	14
Local government Suffolk	10
Industry and business	16
Academics	13
Landed gentry	9
Churchmen	4
Women's organisations	3
Legal and medical	3
MPs	3
Trade unionist	1

The Promotion Committee on 2 February received Tilsley's memorandum and established an Executive Committee to prepare an approach to the UGC. This in effect was the first proto-council of the University. This in turn was rather large and created a smaller steering committee to arrange the UGC meeting. This consisted of Ralphs, Tilsley, Miss Mary Duff, J.W. Beeson, the Director of Education of Norwich, and Don Farrow, the Chief Education Officer for Great Yarmouth, who met on 10 February to do this.[92] Sir Keith Murray had written to Mackintosh offering his assistance and they were determined to take it up, so Tilsley, Ralphs and Beeson went to the 1 Belgrave Square offices of the UGC on 20 February. They had good private reason for confidence. Denis Buxton of Caister Hall near Great Yarmouth, a friend of Tom Eaton's, not only expressed his support for the university but revealed a connection with Murray and the UGC. He said that a university in Norwich "was a possibility and not just a dream. I know Sir Keith Murray of the University Grants Committee and he confirmed this in a brief conversation the other day".[93] This was an encouraging thought as Ralphs and Tilsley went to see Murray a few weeks later.

Sir Keith explained that at that time the government proposals to expand student numbers to 124,000 by the mid 1960s could be satisfied by existing institutions plus Sussex. Six English universities had populations under two thousand and still had considerable room for expansion. The UGC's capital up to 1963 was already allocated. But after 1963 a new proposal like that of Norwich could be considered, especially since further expansion to 138,000 was envisaged by the latter part of the 1960s. "In short, therefore, Norwich should formulate their proposals during the next twelve months and make an application in the early part of 1960." This was much the same position that Murray had made clear to Ryrie in 1958.[94]

As regards size, in response to Ralphs, Sir Keith said that he envisaged universities of a size 3000-6000 students but attained through slow growth. He did not think there was any possibility of expanding to a full student population within ten years; Keele had taken ten years to reach 1000. (UEA's later policy, almost a slogan, was 3000 in ten years). Murray also gave advice about curriculum. Arts and pure science were "clearly essential", some applied science in relation to local industrial interests "might be attractive". But there was no need for more medical schools and – disappointingly for East Anglia – "no weight should be attached to agriculture". Social Studies "might be a possible subject". He also advised that a large single campus site was essential not necessarily close to a city centre.

Murray insisted that Norwich should not form links with any existing university. The old notion of new universities serving an apprenticeship under the tutelage of established institutions did not appeal to him. In his view they should be independent from the start. Also Murray did not favour recruiting distinguished academics onto the Promotion Committee, since such academics might have undue influence "and it might result in proposals either unnecessarily conservative or 'cranky'". There were no academics on the original Promotion Committee. Murray's view rather cut across some recent actions of the Promotion Committee. For example, the first item considered by the steering committee was making approaches to Cambridge and London to "establish an informal link" and get the support of notable academics. Also Murray was not happy to learn that prior to coming to see him the deputation had had lunch at the House of Lords with Lord Chorley, Professor of Law at London University, and various AUT officials. Murray would have been positively angry if he had known that one of these officials suggested that Lord Chorley could provide a useful access to Murray for the Norwich group.[95] Murray always wanted direct relations between the UGC and Norwich. He did not want their views influenced by other academics, still less by academic interest groups. Tilsley was to bear Murray's warning in mind when he was faced with a curious offer later in the summer.

Finally, Murray said that he would like to see local bodies providing 2 to 5 per cent of the capital outlay as an earnest of local support, the UGC meeting the rest. There should also be recurrent annual support from local authorities in the area. Tilsley told Murray that he was confident that local authorities would probably contribute 1d. rate to this purpose.[96] This was the balance of caution and encouragement, and the guidelines of sensible advice, within which Norwich was to shape its application in the coming year. The meeting finished with an agreement that Norwich would make a formal application by the beginning of 1960.

This seemed satisfactory, but Andrew Ryrie, who was not present at the 20 February meeting, was becoming anxious.[97] He thought that Murray was just as non-committal about Norwich as he had been when he had first seen him last July. He feared that "we may be moving in too leisurely fashion". He had hoped that the February deputation would have got some firmer "agreement in principle" with Murray and would itself have had the "framework of an application". This was rather unreasonable. But Ryrie was right in urging that the application to the UGC be made late in 1959 rather than early 1960 and that Norwich should not lose its place as "next in the queue after Brighton".

Back in Norwich the steering committee began to address the question of local authority finance. They thought in terms of 1000 students at £3000 a place plus £1000 per residential place which would demand £4,000,000 in initial costs. £200,000 raised from local authorities would provide 5 per cent of this, the desirable proportion suggested by Murray. Norwich and Norfolk could not raise this alone. A "University for Norwich" was going to have to be presented as one for East Anglia.[98]

Encouraging developments were taking place even as they met. Early in February the North Walsham Urban District Council expressed its whole-hearted support for the proposals for a University at Norwich and "consider any contributions from public funds would be money well spent".[99] The other local authorities in Norfolk were informed of the resolution. By April, apart from Norwich and Norfolk, twelve boroughs, urban or district councils supported North Walsham's proposition; three agreed with the University but withheld agreement about finance; three others were non-committal; and eight had not replied. It suggested a good balance of Norfolk opinion in favour of a university, all the more remarkable since many of these areas were very rural and remote and did not obviously stand to gain much from such an institution in Norwich.

In May Norwich Education Committee met and Tilsley explained to them that for the financial year 1d. rate for Norfolk and for East and West Suffolk (then separate and only merged in 1974), Yarmouth, Ipswich and Norwich yielded £45,930, with Norfolk County at £13,594 quite the largest contributor. Enquiries of other universities revealed that scarcely any had received capital cost help from local authorities, except Keele which had been given £40,500 by Stoke and Staffordshire. Sussex had been given a site at a nominal rent. But all eleven universities surveyed received annual contributions from local authorities ranging from Manchester's 0.33d. to Exeter's 1.79d. rate;[100] or, put another way, from Manchester's £60,000 plus to Leicester's £12,000.[101] A few days later Tilsley was able to tell the UGC that Norwich Education Committee would recommend to the City Council that grants of £15,000 a year (a remarkable 2d. rate) would be paid towards the current expenses of the University and that the city should bear the costs of the site. In addition Norfolk Education Committee would recommend to the County Council that it contribute £13,600 a year (1d. rate).[102] LEAs could do this under Section 84 of the 1944 Education Act and it was accordingly done.[103] By the end of 1959 the undertakings were

	£
Norwich	15,000
Norfolk	13,600
East Suffolk	9400
Ipswich	7500
West Suffolk	5000
Gt. Yarmouth	3500
	54,000

This £54,000 promised by local authorities exceeded the £40,000 received by Brighton. Only Leeds, Nottingham, Manchester and Birmingham received more at that time. After the University began, the Isle of Ely gave £2000 in 1962/63 and Huntingdon County Council £2000 a year for three years 1962/63 to 1964/65.[104] We shall see the history of these local annual contributions in a later chapter. But at the same time they were certainly sufficiently sizeable to impress the UGC as evidence of local support.[105]

Local support of a different kind also materialised at this time. Sir Roy Harrod, the distinguished Oxford economist, had joined the Promotion

Committee. Sometime in the Spring of 1959 he approached Tilsley offering the services of himself and his friends. His "friends" turned out to be Lord Adrian OM, Master of Trinity College and Vice-Chancellor of Cambridge, one of the most distinguished academics in the land; Sir John Cockcroft OM of the Atomic Energy Authority and Master-Elect of Churchill College, Cambridge; Professor (later Sir) Neville Mott, Cavendish Professor of Physics and Master of Gonville and Caius College, Cambridge; Miss Mary Lascelles, Vice Mistress of Somerville College, Oxford; Professor W. J. H. Sprott, Professor of Philosophy at Nottingham; and Sir Solly Zuckerman, Chief Government Scientific Adviser. To these were added Dr David Thomson, Master of Sidney Sussex College, Cambridge, who seems to have been recruited by Ralphs.[106] Tilsley found this galaxy of eminence "staggering" and even embarrassing.[107] It prompted the question of what all these people had in common and why they should be at all interested in a putative university in Norwich. There was obviously a Cambridge connection binding Adrian, Cockcroft, Mott and Thomson. But the real link was less obvious. It was that almost all had country houses and holiday homes in North Norfolk: Zuckerman at Burnham Thorpe, Harrod at Bayfield Brecks near Holt, Sprott at Blakeney, Lascelles, Adrian and Cockcroft in Cley. Cockcroft's son was also at Gresham's School, Holt. Of these Harrod was the leader and "unquestionably the keenest of our academic sub-committee".[108] Harrod further helped the movement by broadcasting about it on the programme "Sign Post" on the Midland Home Service 27 August 1959. Tilsley, however, remembered Murray's warnings against the dangers of being too influenced by eminent academics. The UGC was suspicious of fledgling universities receiving guidance from bodies other than itself and its own UGC appointed Academic Planning Boards. Murray shrewdly suggested that they be made into a separate Academic Advisory Committee to provide them with a purpose.[109] This was done and they embarked on unofficial and stimulating discussions of curricula in their pleasant north Norfolk retreats.

Norwich also got some good advice from further afield by tapping the experience of Brighton, which was well ahead of them in progress. W. G. Stone, the Director of Education for Brighton, came to talk to the promoters on 6 July 1959. He indicated the main features of the Brighton movement, many of which were similar to those in Norwich. They too had failed before, in 1911 and 1947, when they proposed upgrading the Technical College. They had secured £40,000 from their LEAs and a site from Brighton Corporation. They were now thinking of a public appeal and forming the university into a limited company to receive and administer funds. They were sufficiently advanced to have set up a Council of mixed membership, a third each, from LEAs, local prominent persons and the university. An Academic Planning

Board was already guiding their planning and they were preparing to apply for a Royal Charter.[110] All this reassured the Norwich promoters that they were taking the right course of action and showed the steps ahead. A key point of difference was in the choice of the pre-charter corporate form. Brighton had formed a limited company, but Norwich, with the shrewd legal advice of Gordon Tilsley, formed a trust.[111] Tilsley liked the trust form and used it in conjunction with his work for the Norwich Triennial Festival. Tilsley's view was that this would ease the transition of Executive Committee into Council and Promotion Committee into Court when the university was created by Charter. So it proved.

Increasing enthusiasm in Norwich began to mesh with a major change in policy at the UGC in 1959. In the summer of 1958 Murray was taking a rather discouraging line. He told Edward Hale (whom Ryrie was trying to "cultivate" as a distant acquaintance) not to raise unjustifiable optimism in Norwich,[112] and he himself told Ryrie that he could not "conscientiously encourage Norwich".[113] But by 1959 after a close discussion of "trend" and "bulge" statistics in July, they became convinced by the end of the year that "the Committee have little doubt that some provision for new institutions will be needed" and by March 1960 that the claims of Norwich were very strong and it "should be encouraged to go ahead, the sooner the better".[114] The summer of 1959 and the July meeting seems to mark a shift in the attitude of the UGC from restraint to the acceptance of the need for expansion. This was to be crucial for UEA.

A vital matter decided in the summer of 1959 was the name of the university. In the first half of 1959 the terms "proposed University of Norwich" or "for Norwich" were commonly used by the Promotion and Executive Committees. Gordon Tilsley who wrote the minutes personally preferred "University of Norwich". The *Eastern Daily Press*, however, often called it "East Anglia University" or "University of East Anglia" at the same time. Suffolk folk at the first Promotion Committee in February 1959 used the term "University for East Anglia". The need for LEA and other money from outside Norwich and Norfolk forced the choice towards "East Anglia".[115] On 4 August 1959 the Executive Committee discussed the matter and on the proposal of Wallace Morfey of Ipswich they decided on "The University of East Anglia, Norwich". Tilsley admits that this had led to "a certain blurring of identity which has always dogged the University".[116] We are familiar with outsiders whose idea of the location of the university ranges from somewhere in the Fens to anywhere north of Ilford. This became dangerous when East Anglia and Essex became confused in the public mind during the times of spectacular student unrest at Colchester, for which UEA was sometimes blamed.[117] Moreover "Norwich" and "Norfolk" have a ring to them which

"East Anglia" somehow does not. The UGC thought of the new universities as the "Shakespeareans". Their names, Canterbury, York, Lancaster, Warwick (Norfolk yes, but not really East Anglia), "might easily be a couple of lines from *King Henry IV Part II*" thought Sir John Wolfenden, the Chairman of the UGC.[118] Paradoxically the Earl of Cranbrook, Lord Lieutenant of Suffolk and the leading non-Norfolk figure in the movement, had no particular wish for "East Anglia"'. He told Lord Mackintosh "incidentally I regret that it is not going to be called University of Norwich".[119]

As part of their preparations the Promotion Committee not only received advice from Brighton but also visited Nottingham in November 1959. Nottingham University had grown from less than a thousand to 2500 over eleven years and was projected to grow to 4000, which made its experience relevant to Norwich.[120] The Vice-Chancellor, B. J. Hallward, made some useful suggestions. He recommended that a new Vice-Chancellor should be given six months leave to look at other universities to get ideas and see the consequences of error. This advice was followed profitably at Norwich on the appointment of Frank Thistlethwaite as Vice-Chancellor and before UEA opened. Hallward advocated a "loose" centre to a site to allow the expansion of administrative and library buildings without conflicting with faculties. To this end he urged the appointment of an landscape architect to work with individual architects. UEA went one better by having one architect for the whole site plus a landscape architect. This obviated Nottingham's problems of having separate architects for separate buildings. Hallward also thought desirable a range of restaurants to keep students on the site for evening meals, and he liked an art gallery and a chapel on campus. Norwich followed all these practices. In response to a query from Tilsley, Hallward was strongly in favour of a Court of local well-wishers who received an annual report after a "magnificent lunch". This too became a Norwich feature.

By November 1959 the Promotion Committee was ready to make a submission to the UGC.[121] They had a strong case to make. They reminded the UGC of the long-standing nature of Norwich's claims to a University going back to the early years of the century, and assured them of the unanimous enthusiasm in the region for a University, "it has truly been said that East Anglia has seldom been so united or so enthusiastic". A university would provide an increase in educational opportunities in the region and an apex for the general system of education there. It would enrich the cultural life of the area and stimulate local industry. The isolation of the region also meant that a University in Norwich would be over a hundred miles from the nearest university except Cambridge. The proposed University already had impressive assets of £54,000 promised annually by the local authorities of Norfolk and Suffolk. An extensive 165 acre site at Earlham had recently been given by the City Council. The submission was able to lay stress on the prosperity of the region's agriculture, fisheries, food and light industry. Equally convincing was the immense cultural heritage of the city and region, its fine buildings, artistic traditions, musical festival, museums, theatres and learned societies. Four pages of the submission stressed cultural matters. Norwich was probably more impressive on this broad cultural front than any of the new universities, with the possible exception of York. Norwich stood ready to contribute to meeting the national problem of the shortage of university places and thereby to "add vastly to the educational and cultural life of the region".

On 16 December 1959 a deputation led by Lord Mackintosh went to be interviewed by the UGC on their submission.[122] The East Anglian deputation consisted of Lord Mackintosh, Michael Bulman (the Lord Mayor of Norwich and a surgeon at the Norfolk and Norwich Hospital), Lord Adrian, R.Q. Gurney, Sir Roy Harrod, W.M. Morfey, Lincoln Ralphs and Gordon Tilsley. A deputation from York was visiting on the same day. When they saw Michael Ramsay, the Archbishop of York, leading out the York delegation, the Norwich delegation was comforted to be able to field such academic big guns as Adrian and Harrod. The interview began with an introductory presentation by Lord Mackintosh.[123] He stressed the immense enthusiasm of East Anglia for the projected university, the financial support of £54,000 from local authorities, the 165 acre site given by Norwich Corporation, and Norwich's regional capital status with its history and economic activity. He concluded that they were "ready and eager to go forward".

The subsequent interview was unremarkable, which suggests that the submission had been sufficiently full, clear and convincing. Lord Adrian referred to the cleavage between Oxford and Cambridge on the one hand and the provincial universities on the other. He argued that the new universities like Norwich could fit into this gap and "approximate more closely to the older universities". Various minor matters were touched on. Dr Kitty Anderson was impressed with the new City Library in Norwich and the city and county's vast collection of historical records. Professor Asa Briggs was told that UEA might take a slightly higher percentage of local students than the national average. Sir Keith Murray asked searchingly whether Norwich would have difficulty if they were asked to build for three to four thousand students and "the deputation were emphatic that it would make no difference". Sir Roy Harrod, in response to a question about the curriculum, defensively replied that discussions had been "somewhat conservative" and they were looking to the UGC for some views. Murray sharply volleyed by saying that on the contrary the UGC were looking to UEA for experimental ideas. Mackintosh, the ex-international hockey player, neatly stepped in and whacked the ball back to Murray with a suggestion about business administration which saved the rally.

The only potentially awkward area of questioning was over residences and lodgings, shrewdly pursued by Professor Ronald Edwards. He pointed out that if UEA claimed to provide residences for two thirds to three quarters of students then it would be most unusual, but that in any case a university of three thousand students would require lodgings for one thousand students. Were these really available in a city the size of Norwich? Tilsley realised that this was one area where their submission was not watertight and with characteristic thoroughness analysed the problem on his return to Norwich.[124] He showed that there were 29,174 houses in Norwich and the immediate fringe area with potential space to offer bedsits and that when the Royal Agricultural Show had visited Norwich in 1957 eight hundred such rooms had been found. Tilsley did not reveal all his calculations to the UGC but was able to reassure them that Norwich could cope. As the meeting ended one over-eager member of the deputation suggested that if Murray could decide quickly local authorities could incorporate the financial commitments into their forthcoming budgets. The urbane Murray was not to be hurried by such a ploy, "twisting his tail" as he put it, and smilingly assured them that there would be no unnecessary delay. Mackintosh had pleasing memories of the UGC meeting: "They treated us in a friendly fashion and promised us a quick and careful consideration of our request. Then we waited."[125]

They did not have to wait very long. On 19 April 1960 the UGC sent one of the most important documents in the history of the University. Their letter said that they "have been authorised by the Government to enter into discussions with your University Promotion Board with a view to the establishment of the proposed University College of East Anglia at Norwich".[126] They noted with pleasure the available site and assurances of financial support from local authorities. An Academic Planning Board would have to be appointed to prepare a draft Royal Charter and advise on the organisation of the "College". Then the UGC would recommend grants for capital development to meet the essential building needs and in due course recurrent grants at the beginning of the next quinquennium. There was some stage management in the dating and sending of the letter. Tilsley recalled, "it had been their intention to send it in the previous week, but feeling that it would be difficult to handle the intense publicity on Maundy Thursday, I asked Sir Cecil Syers, their Secretary, always an obliging chap, to hold the letter back until after the holiday, and this he did."[127]

The letter was greeted with almost unalloyed joy. The unease was created by the curious use of the words "University College". This was an old fashioned Victorian term for a college on its way to becoming a university but under the supervision of an older one – usually London University – until its academic standards were regarded as satisfactory for independence. Yet the new universities were supposed to be independent from the start and Murray had warned Norwich not to get involved with any other university which might suggest subservience. Tilsley immediately queried and objected to the term. He telephoned the UGC the same day and had been assured by Sir Cecil Syers that the term had "no significance". It had been used for Keele and Brighton but was not intended to bear its Victorian connotations. Sir Cecil told Tilsley that he would raise the matter of dropping the term "College" from the beginning.[128] Lord Mancroft put it most strikingly, "University College might do very well for Wagga Wagga or Walthamstow but . . . I don't see why we should not be a "University"."[129] This was Murray's view also. Sir Cecil sounded out Murray, who sounded out the CVPC, who agreed that East Anglia could be a "university" from the start. Tilsley was gratified: "So what Keele and Sussex had accepted and York were willing to submit to, Lord Mackintosh successfully resisted."[130]

Lord Mackintosh proudly issued a press release notifying the contents of the UGC letter.[131] He expressed gratitude for "the overwhelming support given by all sections of the community throughout the whole of East Anglia and the substantial financial assistance of the local education authorities. These were the two factors which had led to the "splendid result". Now they would have to "bend all their energies to ensuring that the University College of East Anglia shall be of the highest quality possible". The dream was not yet realised but the letter of 19 April 1960 was one of the first great milestones. Now some solid foundations would have to be laid in 1960-62.

2

Laying the Foundations

East Anglia has seldom been so united or so enthusiastic as it is over this project . . . the time has now come for a University to be formed in East Anglia in accordance with the present national policy of founding and expanding universities.[1]

Petition of the Promotion Committee of
the University of East Anglia

Getting the approval of the UGC for a university in Norwich had been hard enough. But now major tasks – raising the money, securing a site, drafting the charter and discussing the curriculum – lay ahead. Scarcely any of them was more important and troublesome than the appointment of a founding Vice-Chancellor.

Hardly had the promotion of the university been announced than well-wishers began recommending likely colleagues. Quite the most realistic was Sir Roy Harrod's backing of Robert Blake, the distinguished historian of the Queen's College, Oxford, who also had the support of Sir John Cockcroft.[2] More systematically the Academic Advisory Committee was individually asked to think of possible names. A plethora was put forward: headmasters, dons, chief education officers, civil servants, most of them quite unaware that they were under consideration. Some selection criteria were proposed. Professor W. H. Sprott held "very firmly that the person who is appointed should not be a headmaster" since he would be too schoolmasterly with students.[3] This was to prove no problem since Dr Eric James, High Master of Manchester Grammar School, who was on the early Norwich lists (though oddly confused with Dr R. L. James of Harrow School), was appointed Vice-Chancellor of York. The Bishop of Norwich wanted a Vice-Chancellor sensitive to religion, which became an issue later on.[4]

In September 1960 the task was formally taken over by the new Academic Planning Board appointed by the UGC. This was a very high-level body under the chairmanship of Dr (later Sir) Charles Wilson, then Vice-Chancellor of Leicester. It consisted of Noel (later Lord) Annan, the Provost of King's College, Cambridge; Professor Sir Christopher Ingold FRS, a chemist from University College, London; Professor (later Sir) Denys Page

FBA, a classics scholar and Master of Jesus College Cambridge; Dr (later Sir) Lincoln Ralphs, the Chief Education Officer of Norfolk; E.T. (later Sir Edgar) Williams DSO, Warden of Rhodes House, Oxford; and Professor Sir Solly Zuckerman FRS (later Lord Zuckerman of Burnham Thorpe), Professor of Anatomy at Birmingham University and Chief Scientific Adviser to the government. They could be expected to have a wide knowledge of university affairs and personnel. By November 1960 the APB had refined the names down to six with C.H. Waddington, the distinguished Professor of Genetics at Edinburgh University, and Robert Blake as front runners. At this point the contenders were still probably unaware of their participation in a contest. Zuckerman strongly backed Waddington and Charles Wilson told Zuckerman, "I am perfectly happy about Waddington too . . . we'll find out whether he is willing to be considered".[5]

Norwich too began to express a view, unaware of the contenders. Canon R.A. Edwards, the Vice-Dean of Norwich, urged that the new Vice-Chancellor should be "a man of wide sympathies and [with] an appreciation of the spiritual and cultural values that had contributed to our civilization."[6] Did he really mean *religious* values? The *EDP* agreed that this was "a good reflection of informed public opinion". This flash of concern about religion was to cause problems as the selection process unfolded. It caused concern because Professor C. H. Waddington was a biologist of wide cultural and philosophical interests but of doubtful Christianity. His book *The Ethical Animal* treated Christianity as one set of views among others. He was a Darwinian evolutionist. Tilsley, who had actually read the book, told Lord Mackintosh, his fellow worshipper at Park Lane Methodist Chapel, that "I would judge his [Waddington's] views would be surprising to anybody brought up in accordance with conventional Christian morality".[7] Lord Mackintosh, a devout Methodist and very well informed on theological matters, determined to read the book for himself. This was more difficult than it sounded, not due to the subtlety of Waddington's argument but because the pages in the Norwich Public Library copy were bound in the wrong order. This unfortunate book finally vanished in the fire that destroyed the library in 1994.

Since nobody except Solly Zuckerman knew Waddington he was invited to lunch with the APB at the Union Club, in St. James Street in London, so that his views could be sounded out.[8] Beyond banalities on the desirability of a balance of arts and sciences, some of Waddington's strange views were revealed. He thought it would be possible to have a lower standard pass degree but the Chairman ruled it out as unfeasible. He envisaged some staff concentrating on research and others on teaching. Very oddly, he said he would want to be an autocrat for fifteen years (he was then aged fifty-five) before admitting democracy in university government! Most strangely he claimed to want a faculty of theology with initial instruction in divinity. For someone whose own religious views were very much in question this was an extraordinary flight of fancy. These were bizarre policies which UEA narrowly escaped.

As if from nowhere another candidate appeared on the scene, Dr J.F. Lockwood the Master of Birkbeck College and Vice-Chancellor of London University 1955-1958. He too was taken to lunch but whereas Waddington's views were provocative, Lockwood's were so evenly balanced as to be negligible.[9] He admitted that he had not given much thought to the problems of the new universities but he would break down the barriers between subjects. Thereafter his comments became opaquely ambivalent. The development of vocational subjects was "valuable" but "should not go too far", prefabricated buildings were "essential" but also a "menace". Asked by Zuckerman about business administration courses he said that their absence had not weakened British industry but that universities had not considered the needs of the business community. Zuckerman never found out whether Lockwood intended to rectify this at UEA. Lockwood gave the impression of someone long used to seeing the merits of every side of every question but now too elderly (at fifty-seven) to entertain clear forceful views of what he wanted to carry out in a new university.

The APB sized up the two candidates realistically. Waddington was the keener and more vital and had ideas. Lockwood had had the administrative experience of being a Vice-Chancellor before. But there were doubts whether Waddington could create a good community among senior colleagues. Lockwood would be more acceptable to Norwich society. Most of the APB preferred Waddington, only Lincoln Ralphs opting for Lockwood. Yet in truth neither was suitable, both were too old at fifty-five and fifty-seven to start a new university.[10] Waddington had too many odd views; Lockwood scarcely any at all. This was precisely Sir Roy Harrod's opinion. He was "deeply disappointed" that the APB was even considering these names; they were both too old and unreceptive to new ideas, and he had "resolute opposition" to both. Harrod again pressed Blake's claims and his "deep roots in and deep affection for the county".[11] Otherwise the APB must find men of "calibre in the middle life" in Cambridge or elsewhere. Harrod was right and this presaged trouble that was to brew when the APB with their recommendation of Waddington met the Executive Committee of the Norwich promoters a few days later.

The Executive Committee held its own meeting which revealed a unanimity of viewpoint.[12] Lord Adrian was scathing. He regarded Waddington as "unorthodox, a socialist, a modernist and keen on abstract art". Adrian "doubted his [Waddington's] ability to handle opposition and he was mildly paranoid about other genetic groups. He did not think he would handle opposition with skill and there was a criticism that his humanism was empty and sterile." Moreover, there were his "two wives"; for he was a divorcee, then socially unacceptable for one in so public a position. Bishop Fleming also was "dubious about Professor Waddington", Richard Gurney feared a "Norfolk reaction" against him, and Lord Mackintosh came to the view that he was "too big a risk". This was a parlous situation. The APB wanted to appoint Waddington but leading members of the Academic Advisory Committee and the Executive Committee did not want him at any price.

On 27 January 1961 the APB and Executive Committee met with some acrimony.[13] Richard Gurney raised the question of churchgoing and on some consternation being caused (on whose part is not clear), the Chairman agreed that Gurney had raised a crucial point of local feeling but, "Test Act – could not agree to taking such factors into account." The Bishop sensing a dangerous drift in the discussion intervened "No Test Act on VC", but queried whether Waddington would appoint professors whose attitudes were as non-religious as his own. This would arouse wide resentment. Charles Wilson was "somewhat taken aback" at this talk of wide resentment. Zuckerman then interposed that "this talk is anti university – would shut down universities".

In fact the row had at its heart a white heat of fury and pain not evident in Tilsley's verbatim note account. Gurney had not just been concerned that Waddington did not go to church or was a divorcee or even an atheist. He made the wounding remark that he was "not even a Christian".[14] Sir Solly Zuckerman, who took this as an anti-semitic slight, exploded. Gurney recalled his own astonishment:[15]

> After a moment's stunned silence, Lord Zuckerman, Sir Zolly Zuckerman, as he then was, launched forth and gave me [the Lord Mayor of Norwich] the biggest dressing-down I have ever had in my life e.g. the private life of the individual concerned was no concern of mine or of the Committee, and that even a Primary School Headmaster could not have his religious views questioned by the Governors when applying for a post.
>   When he eventually ran out of breath I rather timidly replied that I had not in my busy life, come all the way from Norwich to London, just to act as a rubber stamp and I could see no point in such a meeting, which was, after all, completely private, unless we each said what we really thought.

But Gurney was not off the hook. He recalled, "Lord Annan entered the fray. Sir Zolly had been blistering enough. Lord Annan pulverised me and I could think of no reply . . . I do not remember ever having felt so small and

stupid and insignificant." Gurney clearly did not know that Annan was a
prominent agnostic in Cambridge and that his chief academic work had been
a biography of Leslie Stephen, a leading Victorian agnostic rationalist.
Accordingly, any suggestions that a Norwich Vice-Chancellor or a professor
had to be a Christian were deeply offensive to Zuckerman and Annan for
different reasons.

The meeting rambled on with some participants trying to calm the situa-
tion. Lincoln Ralphs suggested that they were not concerned with
Waddington's lack of Christian views but the impact on the locality of such a
Vice-Chancellor and his staff. Lord Cranbrook agreed with Zuckerman that
the University would be doomed if the personal religious views of the Vice-
Chancellor were taken into account. The Bishop, now rather alarmed and
frankly unclear what he should say, concluded emolliently and surprisingly,
"Christian views irrelevant".[16]

Passions lasted well after the meeting. Zuckerman told "Bill" Williams, "I
was shocked to the core by what happened".[17] But beyond his own personal
feelings Zuckerman saw the deeper issue. A University of East Anglia is not
"some kind of private charity". Taxpayers' money was going to be infinitely
more important than that of local ratepayers and philanthropists. He was
"appalled by Mr Gurney's intervention", and the shamefaced and equivocal
support of the Bishop, but "I do not accept that their view is representative of
opinion in East Anglia". He hoped it was "a piece of ill considered eccen-
tricity". If not, the UGC should get tough, remove the site to Suffolk or "the
whole idea of a University of East Anglia should be scrapped."[18] This was a
very dangerous situation. Andrew Ryrie's unease that Gurney might be
trouble was coming to pass.

If Zuckerman's anger persisted so did the Bishop's embarrassment. He
was a fair-minded man and wrote to Tilsley of his concern, "I have been
going over that meeting in my mind self critically and wondering what I
might have said and not said . . . I was taken a great deal unawares by the
form the meeting subsequently took. I'm awfully sorry that we have got
landed in these difficulties."[19] The whole matter of religion had been raised
by Richard Gurney not by the Bishop, who had become embarrassed and
perhaps equally so by having to pretend that Christian belief did not matter.
It was as if all the objections to Waddington – his divorce, Darwinism, autocratic attitudes, socialism all focused on this unmentionable issue of his
atheism.

The Executive Committee and the APB then held separate meetings. There
was a total difference of opinion between them. Gurney admitted that his
views had exacerbated the APB and Lord Cranbrook thought that the criticisms of Waddington "had consolidated the Planning Board in their support

of him". But Lord Mackintosh thought they were right, since he had heard disquieting reports from Edinburgh that Waddington did not get on well with people of opposing views.[20] The APB held its own meeting.[21] They received a letter from the Bishop assuring them that he was not committed to the view that the Vice-Chancellor must be a practising Christian. Lincoln Ralphs likewise told them that "religion was no issue among local people" and that the Executive Committee was not totally associated with the views of Gurney. Accordingly the APB determined to press on with Waddington, whom they regarded as "head and shoulders above all other candidates". Late in the day they decided to get some proper evidence on his personality "from an impartial source", not just unsubstantiated rumours passed from Edinburgh to Lord Mackintosh.

Charles Wilson was now getting very concerned about the delay because the later Norwich appointed a Vice-Chancellor the more behind they would be in choosing an architect from a limited field. Wilson was not the only one concerned about the delay. Sir Keith Murray wrote in some reproof to Lord Mackintosh. "This is all very disturbing since as you know, the Government made its decision to go ahead in York and Norwich on the grounds of urgency. This is the first time that this difficulty has occurred and it does seem a serious setback."[22] But there was a further delay as Lord Mackintosh departed for a holiday in South Africa where, as a sideline, he hoped to entice the High Commissioner, Sir John Maud, to Norwich as Vice-Chancellor.[23] Wilson went to the West Indies where incidentally he picked up some adverse views on Waddington (who had recently been there) which added to his anxieties.

The APB was still searching for a Vice-Chancellor.[24] More names were raised: headmasters, newspaper editors, more and more dons. The months drifted by and Wilson became increasingly worried, "we are already the object of a good deal of eyebrow raising over this election".[25] The local MP John Paton was even asking questions in Parliament about it,[26] and it may have been at this time that Sir Keith Murray wrote to Lord Mackintosh virtually threatening that if Norwich would not accept the recommendations of the APB then there would be no university in Norwich at all. The veiled Zuckerman threat of 30 January looked as if it might become a reality. Tilsley thought this "unfortunate and possibly disgraceful", but clearly Murray felt he must resolve the situation.[27]

Behind this tension lay a misunderstanding about the division of power and responsibility between the Academic Planning Board and the Executive Committee in Norwich. Lincoln Ralphs took the view that the appointment of the Vice-Chancellor was made by the Executive or Promotion Committee after the APB had "nominated".[28] Charles Wilson was quite clear that the responsibility of appointment lay with the APB and he was undoubtedly right. The APB terms of reference were that it should "select and nominate, in consultation with the Executive Committee". The APB had consulted and had selected and Murray was right to back them. "Bill" Williams wrote privately to Murray at the UGC about his unease about divisions in Norwich, suggesting that the UGC should make it "absolutely clear" that the final decision lay with the APB. He also objected to the presence of Lincoln Ralphs as a local man on the APB, especially since he took a contrary view.[29] Ralphs was more reasonably suspicious about this shadowy academic world of appointments without advertisement. He was also "astonished at the way in which academics can abuse colleagues whose appointments they do not desire and eulogise over others whom they would care to see appointed".[30] The Executive Committee and the APB met on 25 May and, in spite of misgivings, appointed Waddington. Waddington accepted subject to further conversations with Lord Mackintosh, Wilson and Murray. He seemed enthusiastic: "I feel somewhat overwhelmed at the magnitude and opportunity of the task which you have invited me to undertake. It is one of the most challenging and exciting assignments which can fall to the lot of a scholar and I look forward very much to being able to tackle it."[31] Charles Wilson told Lord Mackintosh that "I am enormously relieved and I hope that we shall have his unconditional acceptance soon".[32]

They never got it. Waddington, only *after* he had been appointed, "got down to the brass tacks of what the job really is"[33] and claimed to be "extremely disappointed". The terms were not good enough, the salary of £4000 a year to the age of sixty-five did not match his present £3500 to age seventy, plus his consultancy fees of £1300, plus his wife's salary of £1850. In fact the offered salary of £4000 was quite standard for a Vice-Chancellor, and was the same as Sussex. It was also then the salary of a Lieutenant-General or a Vice-Admiral. The idea that a new Vice-Chancellor of a small new university should be paid more than very high-ranking military officers seems an extravagant pretension on Waddington's part. He also thought that the UGC support of £1,500,000 was insufficient and did not provide for residences, and most of all he was not willing to sacrifice his research. Waddington did not mention the key factor. Charles Wilson invited Waddington to visit him in Leicester to see just what a heavy burden being a Vice-Chancellor entailed. It was only then that Waddington appreciated what he was taking on and sacrificing. Frank Thistlethwaite thought that this was a brilliant Macchiavellian move on Wilson's part to break the impasse between the UGC and Norwich by depicting the work of a new Vice-Chancellor as horrific. Sir Charles insists that he was just giving Waddington a realistic view of his task.[34] Waddington certainly received some kind of message, changed his mind and withdrew his candidature. Lord Mackintosh closed the matter with a cool letter to Waddington suggesting that he had wasted their time

It was a fortunate escape. Waddington would probably not have made a good Vice-Chancellor. He was too old and had too many odd views. His religious, possibly political attitudes and marital life style would also have been at odds with some important sections of Norfolk society. He was too self-centredly concerned about his money and his research, at which he was genuinely distinguished. He clearly had no idea that it was up to him to raise the funds for residences and quite underestimated the public role he would have to play in East Anglia. To an extent he was also a victim of the way Vice-Chancellors were appointed in those days. Since posts were not advertised, people were discussed without even being aware of it, or wanting to be candidates. No proper references were taken, and the raising of the religious issue was improper and would have been forbidden by Clause 22 of the University's charter, not yet then drawn up. It is also remarkable that the post was offered and accepted before any discussion of terms or salary took place. There was nothing peculiar to Norwich in this since 1961 was still the world of "soundings" rather than of modern management selection. Waddington returned to Edinburgh to continue his scientific career which left the way clear for the final satisfactory stage of the proceedings.

In July 1961 the APB started again. More names were suggested and sounded out. At one point the list contained seventy names, but these were whittled down to four excellent candidates. They were C.W.L. Bevan, Professor of Chemistry at Ibadan, C.K. Dunham, Professor of Geology at Durham, E.M. Wright, Professor of Mathematics at Aberdeen, and Frank Thistlethwaite, a historian and Fellow of St. John's College, Cambridge. Thistlethwaite was the only one who had been neither a professor nor a Pro-Vice-Chancellor, but it was he who carried the day.

The interviews took place in the Senate House, London University on 27 July 1961. We possess notes rapidly taken by both Gordon Tilsley and E. T. Williams while Thistlethwaite was actually speaking on that day.[35] He was strongly in favour of university expansion and looked for a university of minimum size of three thousand. He was interested in the regrouping of subjects outside the usual faculties, for example combining literature and history. The students could be given a broader context of studies followed by specialism later in the degree. He did not see much feasibility in arts students studying science or vice-versa though he would like to try giving arts students a course on the history of scientific thought. He envisaged a residential but not a collegiate university. Teaching should be in small-scale groups with compulsory essay writing and he wanted an extended twelve week term to include a non-teaching reading period. To facilitate the emphasis on reading, the library should be open until midnight. Finally he thought that agriculture would be an appropriate subject – not knowing that it was ruled out. These are the kind of ideas with which he impressed the interviewing APB.

Here was a succession of ideas, totally sensible but not banal, many of which were to carry straight through into UEA practice. Charles Wilson, who had been on the Sussex Planning Board, murmured to Tilsley who was acting as Secretary, "This chap's thought things through further than they have in Brighton".[36] It suggested a potential Vice-Chancellor who had already given much thought to the task and who would be innovatory and the Board was rightly impressed. Denys Page and Noel Annan, who already knew Thistlethwaite at Cambridge, were respectively "surprised" and "staggered" at the confidence of his performance. Zuckerman preferred Thistlethwaite, since his ideas were in accord with those of the APB and he would attract good staff. Sir Walter Worboys of ICI, who had joined the APB after its initiation, was taken with Thistlethwaite's imagination and originality while the Chairman, Charles Wilson, found Thistlethwaite "charmingly diffident, very captivating" with "bite and drive". Of the interviewing panel five clearly put Thistlethwaite first, one was for his nearest contender and one divided his favour. This was a decisive selection.

Gordon Tilsley wrote to Lord Mackintosh with evident enthusiasm and relief, describing the new appointee:[37]

> Mr Thistlethwaite is about forty-five with experience of Cambridge and of American universities. Although he hadn't the experience of universities of the United Kingdom such as that possessed by Professor Wright, he fairly "sizzled" with ideas about new universities and seemed to have absorbed all the best of what he had seen in America without swallowing anything uncritically. The Board came to the conclusion that he was the man to advance their ideas – in fact in the discussion he showed that he had already thought out some of their ideas more deeply than they had and they felt that if Norwich was to be distinctive and exciting, he was the man . . . they unanimously favoured Mr Thistlethwaite.

Who was Frank Thistlethwaite? He was born in Burnley in 1915 into a Victorian cotton manufacturing family. After attending Burnley Grammar School, he went to the Quaker Bootham School in York where he enjoyed a successful academic, sporting and musical career. Both his upbringing and schooling provided that background in liberalism and nonconformist spirituality that was to shape some of his later attitudes at UEA. From Bootham he went as an exhibitioner to St John's College, Cambridge, reading both the Historical and English triposes, gaining a double first. He then went as a Commonwealth Fund Fellow in American History to the University of Minnesota in 1938 and was there at the outbreak of war. The war drew him into the British Press Service in New York and he became head of the

Information Department, servicing the American press and radio about the British war effort. In 1941 he returned to Britain to join the Royal Air Force and trained as a radar plotter at Rudlow Manor. It was appreciated that his American experience could be put to better use, so he was seconded to the newly formed Joint American Secretariat in the office of the War Cabinet. By 1944, at the age of twenty-nine, he had risen to be Joint Head of the Secretariat and Temporary Principal.[38]

At the end of the war he returned to St John's as Fellow and Lecturer in History and taught at the Faculty of Economics and Politics. From time to time he visited the United States: the University of Rochester in 1950, Princeton in 1954 and Pennsylvania in 1956, nurturing his increasing expertise as a leading British scholar of American history. It culminated in a best-selling book, *The Great Experiment: an Introduction to the History of the American People* in 1955. He further helped to establish American studies in Britain as Secretary of the first Fulbright Conference on American Studies and as the co-founder and first Chairman of the British Association for American Studies.

Frank Thistlethwaite had been thinking about the new universities for longer than the APB might have supposed. As early as Spring 1959 he had chatted informally with Asa Briggs (soon to leave Leeds for Sussex) about constructing curricula for a new university while cruising on Lake Maggiore. He himself was restless to leave Cambridge. He had failed to succeed Briggs at Leeds and had declined a post as Dean of Arts at George Washington University, St Louis. He was preoccupied with other tasks when the Norwich movement was in its early stages and, though aware of rumours that East Anglia was having difficulty in finding a Vice-Chancellor, did not relate this to his own ambitions. In Spring 1961 when, unknown to him, the Norwich search was stalling, Thistlethwaite approached Noel Annan, who encouraged him to think of UEA. Then by chance Thistlethwaite, as Steward of St John's, organised a lunch for a group of visiting Vice-Chancellors. He recalled,

> After the luncheon at which I was a host, Charles Wilson sought me out and we walked through the John's Backs together on a pleasant July afternoon talking in a general way about me and my plans and my views about new universities . . . it is clear that he was assessing me as a possible candidate for the Norwich Vice-Chancellorship.[39]

So it was that within a few days he was called to meet the APB on 27 July. It is intriguing that on that very day Eric James, the new Vice-Chancellor of York (who had been on a Norwich list), offered Thistlethwaite the chair of history at York.[40] Thistlethwaite replied, not without irony, that he was interested in "working in the newly developing universities" but he had commitments "actual and pending". He did not add that it was as a rival Vice-Chancellor.

Thistlethwaite's record and qualities impressed the APB selectors: his nonconformist liberalism, his own interdisciplinary undergraduate studies, his very considerable administrative experience at a high level at an early age, his ability to bring an American viewpoint. But there was something else they would not have known about. At the age of seventeen he had played the first movement of Beethoven's Third Piano Concerto at a public concert in York. The *Yorkshire Post* praised his "firm touch, decisive attack . . . admirable verve". Here already was an artistic sensibility and sense of theatre which was to be brought to UEA. Above all there was the courage and control of nerve to perform under pressure in an exposed public situation. These last were the qualities that were to be called upon again when the university faced troubled times at the end of the decade.

The Board not only acquired Frank Thistlethwaite as Vice-Chancellor but Mrs Jane Thistlethwaite as "full-time unpaid professional Vice-Chancellor's lady". She was an American lady of energy, charm and talent in her own right. She had been raised in St Paul Minnesota, and had attended Minnesota University and Yale University Drama School, where she studied stage design. Her father, by profession a commercial lobbyist to the Minnesota State Legislature, was also a noted etcher. Jane Thistlethwaite brought her own artistic talent and expertise to Norwich as a Governor of Norwich Art School, to the Norwich Museum Mellon Foundation project on the Norwich School of Painters and as Chairman of the Friends of Norwich Museums. But her chief work was in helping her husband to shape the new University.[41]

The new Vice-Chancellor took office from 1 October 1961 at a salary of £4000 (the same as Sussex). He was also to be provided with an official residence "in or around Norwich".[42] This was Wood Hall in Hethersett, a fine period house in nearly twelve acres of grounds. It had been a sixteenth-century farm house converted to a Victorian parsonage, "a delightful small country house of character and historical patina". It had belonged to the Holmes family, Norwich shoe manufacturers, but had fallen into some disrepair.[43] The Thistlethwaites actually found the house for themselves on the advice of Mary Watt, Lord Mackintosh's daughter, who lived in the village. The house was bought for £13,000, the UGC providing £12,000 of this. The initial idea was that it should be a temporary home until a new house could be built near the University, and at one time there were plans for a residence to be built off Colney Lane. However it cost over £38,000 to get Wood Hall into good order – it then depended on a well for water and cesspit for sewage. Having spent that money on refurbishment, it made more sense to retain the fine house as a residence rather than build a new one. A substantial property was needed not only as an attractive perquisite of the office but as a centre for entertainment. What it has saved the University in hotel bills will long since have recouped the initial cost. Moreover a Hethersett address in the county was more appropriate for a UEA Vice-Chancellor than a house in Norwich, which would have identified the university too closely with the city. For the first year of his appointment the new Vice-Chancellor commuted from Cambridge to Norwich – once acquiring a speeding fine in his eagerness. But in December 1962 he moved into Wood Hall to face one of the severest winters of the century.

Finally, the new Vice-Chancellor acquired a place from which to operate. He began at a table in the Town Clerk's department at the City Hall. Then, from 21 December 1961, at Number 4 The Cathedral Close, rented at £150 a year, which became the administrative base. In 1970 a plaque was put up at 4 The Close to indicate that this was where the University began. On 11 October 1962 the University moved to Earlham Hall leased initially for seven years. In fact the Vice-Chancellor remained there until 1975. The University is still there (2002).

Shortly after his appointment Thistlethwaite fittingly wrote to Lincoln Ralphs, perhaps the most important and earliest of the Founding Fathers and the East Anglian representative on the APB. He spoke of his "sense both of the great responsibility involved and of high excitement at its possibilities".[44] Norwich was fortunate, after many troubles, to have made such an appointment.

The next task was to raise the initial funds to get the University started. The local financing of the University was to come from local authorities and then from private local business, industry, agriculture and individual well-wishers. The outlook was promising. Bernard Waley Cohen, the Lord Mayor of London, told the new Vice-Chancellor that "Norfolk is a rich county and I hope they anti [sic] up well".[45] The sequencing of this had to be carefully done. The local authority finance had to be assured *before* the approach to the UGC in December 1959, since it was a basis of the submission. Yet the appeal for private funds was only appropriate *after* the UGC had given its approval in April 1960. In this way they would avoid the embarrassments of 1919 and 1947 when money raised for the University had to be directed to other purposes or returned to the donors.

In the very early days, when the University was merely a suggestion, money was already being pledged. W.G. Munnings of Diss, the brother of the painter Sir Alfred Munnings, offered £500 in July 1958 and said he would try to persuade his famous brother to do the same.[46] Rev. C. G. Deeks, the Methodist Minister of Acle, gave £5 in December 1958 saying "it seems to me a good thing if we could get everybody to have a share in this University so that it could be 'ours'",[47] and Costessey Secondary Modern School promised to raise £100.[48] Lincoln Ralphs was so touched by this early support that he publicised it in the *EDP* to indicate that there was potential financial backing for the project.[49]

As well as receiving the generosity of individuals, the promoters decided to make some early tentative approaches to business even before the visit to the UGC. The Steering Committee appealed to Colmans, Fisons, Mackintosh, Norvic (Shoes), Norwich Union, Ransomes (agricultural machinery) and the CWS.[50] They also started visiting leading businessmen personally. [51] The Lord Mayor and Town Clerk called on Mr Tresfon of Boulton and Paul. Tresfon was plain spoken. He told them that there was a shortage of graduates in engineering and business management, "He said that as industry would be subscribing its shareholders' money, industry would wish to see that the shareholders would ultimately benefit by obtaining trained staff in return." Fortunately this crude cost-benefit approach was not typical, but it indicated that it might be difficult to raise enthusiasm if business's horizons were limited to getting "trained staff". Nonetheless the Finance Committee decided to carry on making "a private approach to a number of the prominent industrial undertakings of the area".[52] Twenty-six firms were targeted, fourteen in Norwich and Norfolk and twelve in Ipswich and Suffolk.[53]

Another strategy was to employ a professional fund-raising organisation. Sir James Duff, the Vice-Chancellor of Durham and Chairman of the Sussex APB, often gave judicious advice through his sister Mary, the Principal of Norwich Training College.[54] He advised against it on two grounds. Firstly big money only came from big firms and they paid no attention to agencies. Secondly, the UGC was most influenced by LEA support. Lincoln Ralphs was of the same mind; the early offers of money he had received convinced him that there was enough local goodwill and cash to match it.[55] Nonetheless, the Finance Committee decided to explore the possibility.[56]

Dr M. A. Hooker of the John F. Rich Company of USA had approached the promoters in the summer of 1959. Hooker (ex Marlborough and Oxford) had experience of fund-raising for Coventry Cathedral and was well recommended. His company would handle individual approaches, mail, press relations and take a fee rather than a percentage. Tilsley was impressed with Hooker's "air of competence and his approach to his job". Hooker explained his work further to the Finance Committee on 2 May 1960 and it became clear that it was chiefly with public schools. The Finance Committee thought that if they used an agency at all it would be Hooker, but there was unease that the Promotion Committee would lose control, and that industrial firms might be offended and prefer a direct approach from the prominent East Anglian individuals behind the University. The Rich Company had also never raised more than £300,000 in Britain and had no experience of a sum as large as UEA would need.[57]

The decision not to use agents was linked with another policy which was clarifying at this time. There was an idea that Brighton, Norwich and York should mount a joint appeal to avoid the success of any one draining support from the others. The three universities cooperated to coordinate the timing of the appeals but decided against one combined effort. Lord Mackintosh "had in the first place wondered whether a joint appeal would be suitable but on reflection he was satisfied that this would be impracticable".[58] Sir Keith Murray also advised against a triple joint appeal. Brighton, making their appeal first, generously agreed that it should be accompanied by a nationally publicised statement that the Norwich and York appeals would follow later. Accordingly, on Lord Mackintosh's suggestion, a joint letter was published in *The Times* giving advance notice of forthcoming appeals by Norwich and York and hoping that current appeals would not weaken future claims.[59] Brighton had decided to go it alone and also to run their appeal without using Hooker and the Rich organisation.[60] Norwich followed suit.

1961 was chiefly occupied with appointing the new Vice-Chancellor. But on 9 October 1961 Lord Mackintosh proposed the setting up of an Appeal Committee separate from the Finance Committee. This began to meet on 6 November 1961 with a view to launching an appeal in Spring 1962. The chairman, invited by Sir Edmund Bacon, was Timothy Colman, then a young man of thirty-two and undertaking one of his first major acts of public service.[61] The Colman family had been associated with the region around Norwich since the seventeenth century and Timothy Colman himself was the great-grandson of Jeremiah James Colman, the founder of the famous mustard firm. At the age of thirteen he had embarked on a career in the Royal Navy, where he served for ten years. Due to family bereavements he returned to Norwich in 1953 to work in the family business of Reckitt and Colman. He became the manager of the factory at Carrow but then had to take over the extensive family estates as a farmer. His family also had a holding in Eastern Counties Newspapers and he joined the board of the company in 1957, which became his chief business interest. He thus brought to his position as Chairman of the Appeal a wide knowledge of East Anglian agriculture, industry and business and the local personalities in those worlds.

He was ably supported in the Appeal Committee by, among others, Harold and Eric Mackintosh, Andrew Ryrie, Arthur South, R. Q. Gurney of Barclays Bank, the builder R. G. Carter, and large farmers and landowners Sir Edmund Bacon, J. D. Alston and Viscount Althorp (the father of the future Princess of Wales). They envisaged launching an appeal in April 1962. Although they postponed deciding on the exact target figure, they regarded £750,00 as a minimum,[62] raised to £1,000,000.[63] They learnt from the Sussex experience where a too low target of £1,500,000 had been met too quickly, leading to difficulties in reviving enthusiasm for a revised target.

Two potential types of donor interested the committee at the outset, Americans and East Anglian farmers. Arthur South raised the issue of potential interest in the USA. They thought that they could appeal to Quakers due to the connection of Earlham Hall with the University. Also the New England counties of USA were settled by East Anglians. There was a Norfolk, Virginia, a Norwich in Connecticut, and a Norwich University in Vermont. There was even an Earlham College in Richmond, Indiana. This was a Quaker school founded in 1847 shortly after Joseph John Gurney (of Earlham Hall, Norwich) had developed Quakerism in the area in the 1830s. Lincoln Ralphs wrote to the College and the President replied with good wishes but no offer of money.[64] Less tenuously sentimental, many American airmen who had served in East Anglian airfields in the war had memories of Norwich. The links were maintained through visits to cemeteries and the donation of a USAAF memorial library in Norwich Central Library. Lord Althorp contacted Colonel Kneen of Sculthorpe to get in touch with ex-servicemen's organisations. Otherwise they thought an American appeal should only be mounted on the prior success of a home appeal.[65] Lord Mancroft was actually touring the USA in January 1962 and tried to publicise the future University and its need for support.

By then, however, opinion had blown very cool on American possibilities. Michael Bulman, the distinguished surgeon and Lord Mayor of Norwich, had just been to Norwich, Connecticut, where he had friends. Bulman was uneasy about raising the matter of the University: "there was a danger of putting ourselves in the position of poor relations towards our friends in America without securing any financial benefit from the humiliation".[66] A friend of Bulman's, Herbert Dickerson, an Englishman who had been a Norwich Congregationalist Minister, was very discouraging. He thought Americans "much colder, much less trustworthy"; they would only be interested in contributing to something specific like a room with a plaque to "see something for their money" or a scholarship confined to a Norwich Connecticut boy visiting UEA.[67] Colman was shown Dickerson's comments and sensibly agreed to set American initiatives aside until they had raised £1,250,000 in England.[68] This was surely right. To base an appeal on the identity of certain place names in East Anglia and the USA was mere sentimentality. There was also something distasteful in appealing for money to former members of the USAAF who had already risked lives and lost comrades in East Anglia during the war.

An appeal to East Anglian farmers would be more firmly based. Farmers were doing very well indeed in these years. The early 1960s was a peak period for price subsidies for farming, productivity was growing at 6 per cent a year, there was a boom in investment and agricultural machinery after 1958, and the output of wheat, barley and sugar beet (all typical East Anglian crops) rose sharply over the late 1950s and early 1960s.[69] This was a good time to appeal to farmers as Colman, a large farmer himself, knew. Timothy Colman, J. D. Alston and Viscount Althorp therefore arranged to discuss the appeal to farmers. The Norfolk and Suffolk NFU Chairmen were contacted at a lunch arranged for farmers on 5 February 1962.[70] The Norfolk NFU contacted five thousand members and another lunch was arranged for March 1962. This was "reasonably well attended" with a favourable reaction.[71] The chief benefit of this farmers' drive was the remarkable £11,000 covenanted by seventeen members of the Alston family. The family were as remarkable as their gift. They had come from Scotland in 1903, like other Scots farmers, to pioneer a new East Anglian farming of dairying and sugar beet. They were leading dairy farmers in East Anglia, using Ayrshire cattle.[72] Confusingly there were ten James Alstons in East Anglia at this time, many of whom were among the seventeen supporters of UEA.

The Appeal Committee also approached industry. Almost at once they drew up a list of the top hundred company directors who could be approached personally. Unilever responded immediately with a promise of £25,000.[73] By February 1962 they had raised £500,000 in donations from Norwich firms, which was "a most satisfactory situation". In March 1962 a small deputation visited King's Lynn to meet heads of local industry and similar visits were planned for Great Yarmouth, Lowestoft and Ipswich.[74] The Norwich brewers had "tentatively" decided to support UEA. Why "tentatively"? Given the gargantuan levels of student beer drinking one wonders that they should have thought twice about ensuring that Norwich had a university as soon as possible.[75]

In these early months before the appeal proper was launched in May 1962, a strategic problem was emerging. It was evident that the area around Ipswich and South Suffolk might prefer to support a new university in Colchester. The new Vice-Chancellor had consulted his friend Noel Annan who was the Chairman of the Colchester APB, who assured him that there was no reason why UEA should not appeal as far as the southern boundary of Suffolk.[76] This was not quite the point, however; it was a matter of where locals' perceptions of their loyalties lay. The populations of East and West Suffolk south of a line roughly from Aldeburgh to Lakenheath are closer to Colchester than to Norwich. Moreover Ipswich is about fifteen miles from Colchester but about forty miles from Norwich. This raised acutely the whole issue of "East Anglia", where it was and Norwich's relation to it. Osborne Peacock, the advertising agency which prepared the appeal brochure faced this problem.

They agreed that a map of East Anglia should be included in the brochure but "the inland boundaries should be faded off in some way to avoid a too clear definition of the area to be covered".[77] They could try to fudge it but it did not affect sentiment in Suffolk. The real problem of the Appeal Committee was concerned about "the indifference to the university of which there was evidence in Ipswich. It was felt that in Ipswich there was a general lack of information about the university and there was a divided loyalty caused by the establishment of a university at Colchester."[78] The Appeal Committee hoped that Great Yarmouth and Lowestoft would get more involved, which might act as an incentive to Ipswich "to play a full part in the creation of the University of East Anglia". Andrew Ryrie, ever fertile in ideas, proposed naming halls of residence Norfolk and Suffolk Terraces to encourage a sense of involvement. This was eventually done. To tackle this problem more immediate visits were made to the main towns of Norfolk and Suffolk, culminating in a successful presentation by the Vice-Chancellor at the Ipswich Chamber of Commerce,[79] which was "a great success and the subject of much popular comment",[80] followed by a big reception held by Lord Mackintosh in the same city on 1 May 1962.[81]

Local professional people were also appealed to.[82] Sir Ronald Keefe drew up a list of solicitors to approach and Dr Anthony Batty Shaw, the well-known consultant physician at the Norfolk and Norwich Hospital and Secretary of the Norwich Medico-Chirurgical Society, was in touch with doctors who would contribute.[83] It was assumed that schoolteachers being less affluent would prefer to contribute by school rather than individually.[84]

Early in 1962 the Appeal Committee was firming up its arrangements before the formal launch on 17 May 1962. The original intention to appeal for £1,000,000 was raised to £1,500,000. This was realistic. Essex had appealed for £400,000 and raised it to £1,000,000, Sussex had asked for £500,000, raised it in a year, and had had to keep the fund open. The Warwick appeal was for £1,000,000, while York had raised £1,500,000 before its appeal, which it then decided should aim for £2,000,000.[85] It looked as though others had aimed too low and UEA was right to raise its expectations. Norwich was rather concerned that York was to launch its own appeal for £2,000,000 on 14 May – three days before the Norwich launch. Timothy Colman, however, took the sensible view that far from undermining the Norwich effort it would make a bigger *national* impact to have two appeals in the same week. It would also indicate to national firms that they should look on all the new university appeals in the same light.[86] York's £2,000,000 target would also show that Norwich's £1,500,000 was reasonable and realistic.

Even before the time of the launch they had already raised over £700,000. For the historical record it is worth printing this list of honour in full.[87]

Companies	£
John Mackintosh & Sons	100,000
Norwich Union	100,000
J. & J. Colman	75,000
Anglia Television	50,000
Laurence Scott	40,000
British Sugar Corporation	25,000
Boulton & Paul	25,000
Eastern Counties Newspapers	25,000
Unilever	25,000
Jarrold & Sons	23,000
Steward & Patteson	15,000
Guinness, Son & Co.	10,000
Norvic Shoe Co.	10,000
Mann Egerton & Co.	10,000
Richard Clay & Co.	10,000
Bullard & Sons	10,000
Watney Mann (Norwich)	7500
East Anglian Daily Times	6000
Bonds (Norwich)	5700
E. Lacon & Co.	5000
Esso Petroleum Co.	5000
Bally's	5000
John Copeman & Sons	5000

Individuals	
Mr H. C. Drayton	16,400
Mr Timothy Colman	15,000
Alston family (seventeen members)	11,200
Lord Mackintosh	10,000
Lord Elveden (A.F.B. Guinness)	10,000
Mrs Geoffrey Colman	5000
Sir Edmund Bacon	5000
Mr Eric D. Mackintosh	5000
Mr E. W. Trafford	5000
Hon. John Mackintosh	3000
Lord and Lady Althorp	3000
Mr R. Q.Gurney	2500

The firms, as one would expect, reflected the commercial and industrial structure of the city and region – confectionery, insurance, mustard and food, light engineering, brewing, printing and publishing, shoes. Of the individuals, by contrast, most derived a substantial part of their income from land and agriculture – Drayton, the Colmans, the Alstons, Bacon and Althorp, while Viscount Elveden, as a member of the Guinness family also received an income from brewing. To have raised nearly half the target before the formal start of the appeal augured well for the campaign proper.

The appeal was formally launched by Lord Mackintosh in the City Hall on 17 May 1962. He had originally thought of a press launch at the Savoy Hotel in London in the morning and then – quick dash by train – at Norwich in the afternoon. But this arduous if glamorous programme was sensibly replaced with a launch at the City Hall at noon and a reception in the Castle in the evening. At the midday meeting Lord Mackintosh stressed the generosity of Norwich business and at the evening reception the cultural life of East Anglia and the future role of the University in it.[88] Two brochures were prepared.[89] These explained who the Vice-Chancellor was and what was to be taught. In this they emphasised marine and food science and management studies as relevant to needs of East Anglia. It was explained that private money was needed for University residences, raising the standard of buildings, the library, a concert hall, common rooms and an endowment for research. The second brochure emphasised also the beauty of the site and the distinction of the recently appointed architect Denys Lasdun. The tone of the brochures was actually shaped by private advice from Sir Keith Murray to Frank Thistlethwaite. Murray explained the UGC view that private funds should be used as capital funds for building residential halls. Murray also advised that 60 per cent of appeal money be used for building and 40 per cent for an endowment, not 50/50. Residences were to be the priority. Hence the second brochure has rather idealistic drawings of young men (not women) in residence, wearing ties, jackets and gowns, with firm clean shaven jaws, earnestly reading broadsheet newspapers or discussing thoughtfully. This was the vision of a university that Norwich wanted to see. Emphasis was also laid on the need for universities not to be entirely reliant on the state, as an independent element in their finance was appropriate to institutions in a free society. This appeal to private enterprise was also attractive to conservative rural Norfolk and Suffolk.[90]

So the appeal got under way. A permanent Secretary had been appointed in Group Captain G. R. Montgomery CBE, a former Air Attaché in Tokyo and commandant of Bircham Newton near Hunstanton. He had actually retired to the Broads and become Secretary of the Friends of Norwich Cathedral. Through this connection Colman and Bacon urged him to take on the University appeal.[91] Montgomery agreed and went on a training course run by no less than Dr M. A. Hooker, whose services had been declined earlier but who felt no grudge and was very helpful. Montgomery had a valuable assistant in Mrs Pamela Stenson, who had worked for Guinness and who was the widow of a Guinness area director. They toured about East Anglia meeting local farmers and businessmen, explaining the purpose of the university and leaving covenant forms for them to consider. The technique with firms was for a senior member of the Appeals Committee to approach the senior director of a company. For example, Arthur South tackled Sir Robert Bignold, head of the Norwich Union. Sir Robert disliked the idea of a local university and had no use for academics but it says much for Sir Arthur's powers of persuasion that Norwich Union matched Mackintosh's at the head of the company donors' list of contributions.[92] A lesser figure would tackle someone lower down so that the idea of supporting the University was implanted at two levels and a special team went to see directors of smaller Norwich firms.

This was the hard grind of the appeal but it needed a touch of showmanship to excite the imagination and who better to provide it than Lord Mackintosh. First, Lord Mackintosh, often accompanied by the Vice-Chancellor and Timothy Colman, kept up an energetic schedule of lively public speaking in support of the University – to farmers, the press, Suffolk people in Ipswich, the Promotion Committee, business firms and receptions all over the place. His style varied subtlety from broad encouragement and uplift to closely argued facts and figures depending on his audience. Always energetic and punchy, often interspersed with calculatedly impromptu jokes and stories (not written out), these speeches were a vital contribution of Lord Mackintosh to the cause.[93] Secondly, he offered a gamble. He had originally thought of wagering that Norwich would meet its £1,500,000 target before York reached £2,000,000. This was not a very eye-catching proposition so with a characteristic flair he raised the stakes and introduced his famous heifer. He recalled,

> It was now that I made what I suppose I must now call my celebrated wager: I bet Lord Harewood, whom I had known, you will recall, since his boyhood, that our appeal for East Anglia would have raised more than his appeal for York. I went further. If York have achieved a higher figure in their appeal than we have by the end of the year, I stated, "I will give them one of my herd of pedigree Hereford cattle, or its equivalent in Premium Bonds". The *Yorkshire Post* described my offer as a wager that "smacked of the eighteenth century and Regency bucks risking their estates ..." But in my heart of hearts I did not think I was risking much, because our appeal machinery was so sound and our enthusiasm was so great.[94]

By 12 June they had raised their donations to £796,611, but they were initially disappointed by the results of their appeals to some large national companies.[95] Mackintosh, Norwich Union and Colman's were there with the largest sums as both Norwich and national firms. Lower down were Unilever, Guinness, British Oxygen, Boots, Rank Hovis McDougall and Esso. But not many of the other major companies one might have expected. Some said that they were restricting support to the new universities in their immediate area. Norwich realised that it had to appeal even more strongly to the region.[96]

A scheme was drawn up dividing the region into seventeen areas as far afield as Huntingdon in the west and a line Huntingdon-Newmarket-Bury-Ipswich in the south. Representatives were appointed to contact local gentry and businessmen – Lord Althorp and Lady Fermoy for King's Lynn, Lady Albemarle for Felixstowe and so forth. The Royal Family as residents of Sandringham and major East Anglian landowners gave generously. It is a piquant thought that mutual concern about the UEA appeal was another factor drawing closer the Windsor, Spencer (Althorp) and Fermoy families and their recently born daughter-in-law to be, Diana.[97]

In October 1962 there was a sustained appeal to the locality and a good deal of speaking to local groups – the NFU, Lowestoft Rotary, Norwich Business and Professional Women's Club. A special press conference was held to appeal to farmers, stressing the role of biology and food research studies which the University intended to pursue.[98] There were nine thousand farmers in East Anglia and they were specially targeted in late 1962. Also by October the Appeals Committee was very relieved to find that major national firms, whose absence had been noted earlier in the year, were now substantial contributors. These included clearing banks, Shell, W. H. Smith, Marks and Spencer, Lloyd's of London.[99] The banks seem to have coordinated their gifts to the new universities, £2500 being the standard amount. Barclays gave £7000 to UEA, however, though this compared modestly with the £52,500 they donated to Warwick. Lord Mackintosh was adept at dealing with large companies. He was quite blatant in suggesting to firms that supplied Mackintosh's with raw materials that they should support UEA. He could also wave aside modest offers without embarrassment and keep talking until he had secured a sum *he* thought worthy of the firm he was soliciting. This all helped to raise the funds from £1,135,000 on 30 October to £1,210,000 by the end of the year.[100]

This was creditable but Lord Mackintosh had lost his bet since Norwich had "just been pipped" by York's £1,215,000. He recalled,

> I did not welsh on my wager with Lord Harewood. I chose and sent off Witchingham Topaz, a lovely creature worth, I suppose, about 200 guineas, on her journey to York. I gave her a final grooming before she was led into the float. I was sorry to part with her but the wager, even though I lost it, had done both universities an enormous amount of good. *The Times* had even written a very amusing 'fourth leader' about it and, though I had lost it, it was cheering to know that if the

contest had lasted a day longer, we should have won it, because on New Year's day another £10,000 came in for our appeal. As the cattle float started off north on its way I slapped on to its side one of our yellow and blue posters which read:

UNIVERSITY OF EAST ANGLIA APPEAL–PLEASE GIVE

I thought we might as well pick up whatever support was going on its journey.[101]

After the departure of Witchingham Topaz the appeal still continued. In 1963 Mackintosh wanted to draw in smaller firms in the region and modest sums from individuals. He said, "My strong feeling was that we had to create an atmosphere in which nobody would want to be left out".[102] He put it vividly that he wanted four shillings a head from every man, woman and child in East Anglia.[103] Montgomery doubted the wisdom of this since it might cause some resentment in what was a lowly paid region. It is difficult to see why, say, Suffolk agricultural labourers or East Coast fishermen should feel any obligation to the cause. More realistically many small Norwich businessmen began to support the appeal since they could expect to profit handsomely from the extra trade brought by the University's members. These included, for example, Butcher's drapers, the Royal Hotel, Wilkinson's leather shop, Dipple's opticians, Loose's glass shop, Pilch's sports store and Coe the photographers. Norwich firms like these were among the most direct beneficiaries of a university population of consumers.[104] Unlike many of the larger Norwich firms, most of these smaller retailers continue to thrive.

By July 1963 the appeal had raised £1,327,890 and by now growth was falling off as Mackintosh expected. There were still some large local sums coming in: £7000 from May and Baker on Sweetbriar Road (subsequently Rhône Poulenc and now Aventis Cropscience), and £10,000 from Erie Resistor in Great Yarmouth.[105] The Appeals Committee would have been touched by small sums from modest groups – Ailwyn Bingo Club, the children of Horning Primary School, Dereham Methodist Youth Club and others. These were the four shillings a head people Mackintosh had hoped to appeal to at the end. The disinterested generosity of these not very affluent local people, especially outside Norwich, is worth remembering. One hopes that many of them benefited from UEA social events or sports facilities even if they did not become students.

Thereafter there was little more money to be raised. By 1966, four years after the launch, the appeal had raised £1,404,000 still not quite meeting the £1,500,000 target. Its growth at various points was as follows

1962	17 May	700,000
	24 July	919,000
	22 August	1,000,000
	30 October	1,135,000
	11 December	1,186,000
1963	1 January	1,210,000
	10 May	1,268,000
	13 June	1,300,563
	18 July	1,327,890
	18 November	1,355,000
1964	17 February	1,370,000
	31 July	1,383,000
1965	31 July	1,397,000
1966	8 July	1,404,000

This compared creditably if not splendidly with the other new universities by January 1967.[106]

Warwick	£2,750,000
Lancaster	£2,200,000
York	£1,850,000
East Anglia	£1,400,000
Essex	£1,300,000
Sussex	£1,000,000
Kent	£600,000

£1,400,000 had been raised mostly from the city and region.[107] This was an act of great generosity but it was also a splendid long-term investment, even viewed in narrowly financial terms. The Norwich Junior Chamber of Commerce thought that only modest business benefits would be derived from the University on the grounds that teachers were poorly paid and had no significant spending power.[108] They probably underestimated this. By 1970 UEA was spending £1,800,000 a year in the region,[109] by 1973 £3,000,000,[110] and by 1988 £18,000,000 a year.[111] By 1980 the *Eastern Evening News* regarded UEA as the largest employer in Norwich,[112] but even if it was only one of these (along with Norwich Union and the Health Service) by 1988 it was providing 1700 jobs in the city.

The sad counterpart of that is that many of the leading firms which supported UEA in the appeal have since lost their identity or importance in the Norwich economy. Mackintoshes was taken over by Nestlé and closed down in Norwich in 1996. Boulton and Paul has closed; Reckitt and Colman sold off the Colman food division in Norwich. Norwich Union and CGU have merged and a reduced involvement with Norwich is anticipated. Norvic shoe firm is no more, May and Baker were taken over by Rhône Poulenc and are now Aventis Cropscience. The brewers (Steward and Patteson, Bullard, Lacon) who were so "tentative" are no longer independent Norwich names. In the ebb and flow of economic life the University has proved more long lasting, stable and ultimately more important as a generator of Norwich incomes and jobs than many of its commercial progenitors.

As well as money the University received many gifts of fine silver at this time, notably from several Suffolk landowners. The University acquired a very fine collection of silver, candlesticks, rose bowls, soup ladles, salvers, épergnes and the like, too valuable to be on regular display but a delight at formal dinners.[113] The Appeal of course remains open indefinitely but in some formal senses ceased in October 1966.[114] The Appeal Office at 4 The Close was closed down, Group Captain Montgomery became the Honorary Secretary and Mrs Stenson retired. It had been a fine effort run by Timothy Colman and Lord Mackintosh, administered with great energy by Group Captain Montgomery.

The next foundation block that needed to be put in place was the curriculum. What was this proposed university to teach that would make it distinctive? The first body to consider this was the Academic Sub-Committee. This was the group of eminent academics with residences in Norfolk whose services Sir Roy Harrod had offered to the rather surprised Gordon Tilsley and the Promotion Committee. They met at Harrod's house at Bayfield Brecks, Holt, in August 1959 to lay down some sensible sugges-tions.[115] In science they uncontroversially agreed that degrees in mathe-matics, physics and chemistry should be a minimum. Engineering however, posed problems. It was an expensive subject and more appropriate in large industrial centres. On the other hand, it was thought that there was likely to be a rapid increase in the demand for engineers and Norwich could play its part, probably in electronics and light engineering. A consensus agreed that a degree in mechanical sciences would be desirable.

Some people in Norwich thought that this was the way the new university should go. An intriguing letter written by Russell Taylor was sent to Arthur South and the Massachusetts Institute of Technology asking for advice, since "many of us feel that we should like to have a university more like MIT than the usual imitation of an Arts College".[116] Taylor was the son of the owner of the Castle Hotel and a member of Norwich Education Committee. There is no record of a reply but it was an early example of concern about how involved the new university should be with technology. The Academic Sub-Committee's attitude to mechanical engineering took the same view.

In the life sciences Harrod's group realistically saw that there could be no

School of Medicine but envisaged Biology related to Genetics and Agriculture. The whole question of Agriculture was to be a central problem for UEA. The committee faced it head on. They admitted that there was no seeming need for more graduates in the subject and even the existing output could not be placed. Yet they felt that UEA could not avoid having a degree in agriculture. The region was a major centre of British agriculture, its chief industry. Several adjacent industries and careers in fertilisers and food processing, both important in the region, would welcome graduates with qualifications in agriculture and biology.

Arts provided fewer problems. History, law and modern languages were regarded as desirable in spite of the expected high costs of a law library. Economics too should be included but, they thought, as part of a group of social studies subjects including philosophy – on the lines of Modern Greats at Oxford with which Harrod was familiar. Although UEA was to be a new university, they saw some role for Latin as part of modern languages in support of law, history or English literature. But they saw no need for theology. These were sensible deliberations and many elements carried over into UEA practice, notably economics as part of Modern Greats (the Harrod influence) and non-zoological biology (the Zuckerman influence). They were also right to consider Engineering and Agriculture though neither came to fruition.

Following the Bayfield Brecks meeting Gordon Tilsley (the Secretary) was asked to make further investigations in three areas, law, agriculture and architecture. A discussion with J. F. Warren of the Law Society was discouraging.[117] Although an increasing intake into the profession would come from the universities, most existing provincial university law departments had ample room for expansion and some were too small to be economical. There was no need for yet another in Norwich. Tilsley concluded that it was a "dubious venture".

His conversation with F. Rayns of Norfolk Agricultural Station was more promising. Rayns agreed with Sir Keith Murray (who had been an agricultural economist) that there was only a limited demand for agriculture graduates. Norfolk boys needing a degree in agriculture had to go to Cambridge (difficult to enter) and Reading (where most went). It seemed odd that East Anglian agriculture was serviced by a university 130 miles away. Rayns thought that "for a university at Norwich an agricultural department was inescapable". He agreed on the importance of food technology as a study but noted that agricultural engineering had had difficulties at Cambridge due to staffing. The real problem would be cost: it would need a 300 acre farm and equipment costing hardly less than £100,000. This would give the promoters pause.[118]

Tilsley had a similar ambivalent discussion about architecture with Mr Ricketts of the RIBA.[119] Entry into the profession, 900 a year, was already excessive and likely to fall to 500. Existing universities could easily meet this need. This was a pity, as Norwich's own variety and age of buildings made it "an excellent place for a School of Architecture". A serious paradox was emerging from the committee's deliberations and Tilsley's conversations. The national and Norwich rhetoric emphasised the need to expand higher education for the vocational manpower needs of the economy and professions. Yet there was no feeling in major areas like law, medicine, agriculture or architecture that there was any need for expansion and certainly not at a new university. One of the most influential of Harrod's group was Sir John Cockcroft. His personal views were on these lines. He told the Robbins Committee that there was no need for more classics, medicine, agriculture, theology, botany, zoology or physics. The real need was for more engineers (which Norwich was unlikely to be allowed to do) and mathematicians (which schools could not produce).[120] Already Norwich's attempts to devise vocational degrees was meeting discouragement and it was being forced to think more in terms of liberal education which, hopefully, could be adapted to a range of careers.

Between November 1959 and April 1960 working parties on various subjects were set up while the result of the application to the UGC was awaited. Tilsley also took the advice of Sir James Duff, the Chairman of the Sussex Academic Planning Board.[121] Duff kept a keen interest in Norwich through his sister Mary, who was on the Promotion and Appeal Committees. He was firmly of the view that "one could not envisage a University College of East Anglia without agriculture"; and he thought it worth battling with the UGC over the point, since he knew them to be discouraging about agriculture. If full-scale engineering was not possible then he thought that electronics should be offered; he knew this was Cockcroft's view also. But he was scathing about some arts subjects: "he said there were far too many people about the country who had studied French or English or German and nothing else and the only thing they could do was to teach the subject". He advised a grouping of arts subjects into a "broader field of knowledge". He was, however, much in favour of social studies, which he hoped would "loom large". Both these views on arts groupings and social studies carried through into UEA practice.[122]

The working parties on agriculture and architecture made some recommendations. That on agriculture enthusiastically suggested that East Anglia would welcome a department of agriculture and horticulture and that there was a "definite shortage" of highly trained specialists in agriculture. They took the wind from their sails, however, by noting that the UGC held a contrary view and would make no funds available for Norwich. Much more promising was the proposal of Dr John Corran, Chief Chemist of J. & J. Colman, for a department of agricultural chemistry and food science. This was given sharper focus by the fact that the Agricultural Research Council's Low Temperature Research Station at Cambridge would have to move after 1966. It seemed highly probable that Norwich might get the non-meat food research, if meat went to Bristol. Dr Corran and Dr Bate Smith, the Director of the Cambridge LTR station, were in close touch and this was a further factor moving Norwich's thoughts away from unrealistic expectations about agriculture to biology-based food technology, "unquestionably a Department of Food Technology would be very attractive to local opinion".[123]

Local architects were very keen on the establishment of a faculty of architecture but recognised that it was best to defer the matter since existing provision was sufficient. So it was with law. More positively, leading figures on the Promotion Committee, including Sir Edmund Bacon and Lord Mackintosh, were strongly in favour of business management as a postgraduate study. Finally the local clergy of Norfolk and Suffolk, sensing the coolness of the Academic Sub-Committee to Theology, held a meeting of all denominations on 18 November 1960 in the Assembly House in Norwich. This unanimously called for a professor and department of Christian Theology on the grounds that there was a shortage of Religious Instruction teachers, and it could train schoolteachers, candidates for the Ministry and be part of general culture.[124]

By this time the Academic Advisory Committee had been superseded by the Academic Planning Board appointed by the UGC. But they had been a distinguished and useful body making several useful pointers to the future – economics in the context of social studies, biology related to food technology, electronics rather than full scale engineering. Even subjects which had only a delayed introduction, like law, or others which never arrived, like agriculture, architecture and theology, merited and received a fair airing.

The Academic Planning Board was appointed by the UGC in July 1960 and one of their tasks was "to consider the range of subjects to be studied". Sir Solly Zuckerman was the only member of the old voluntary self-appointed Academic Advisory Committee who was on the new APB. The APB first met on 27 July 1960 when the Chairman, Dr Charles Wilson, set the course that there were advantages in keeping to traditional lines but they must "introduce something of a distinctive character". Accordingly there was no need to discuss whether to teach English or mathematics; rather they should focus on what would be distinctive. Wilson himself had been an Oxford politics don before becoming Vice-Chancellor of Leicester. More significantly he had been on the Sussex APB and helped to shape the combinations of arts and social studies which were a distinctive feature of Brighton and which in turn influenced Norwich.[125]

Noel Annan, the Provost of King's College, Cambridge, opened the case for the Arts.[126] He liked the Brighton system by which single subject specialisms were replaced with groupings in social studies and English studies – shades of Sir James Duff, the Chairman of Sussex APB. These covered combinations of literature, language, philosophy and history, each nurturing the other. Charles Wilson, who had contributed to these groupings at Sussex, would have smoked his pipe and listened approvingly. Annan wanted to go further, "to make the Norwich curriculum as idiosyncratic as possible" and hence "memorable". He did not want ancient and medieval history and most controversially rejected European studies. He wanted the core to be English studies then related to America, Russia, China, the Middle East, Africa or the Commonwealth. He said, "I therefore envisage a compulsory core of English studies that would include courses ranging from literature to sociology; and a choice of two, three and possibly four, areas outside Britain which the student would study either in literary, historical or sociological terms". His very questionable rejection of European studies was based on his stupendously mistaken belief that Europe had ceased to count and was no longer a "part of the world which will particularly affect Britain in the future". Annan also had quite a modest view of UEA. He thought it should aim at being a "liberal arts college", that Norwich would be "low in the University peck order", and that very few of its students would be capable of abstract reasoning in philosophy or economic theory. This was a remarkably pessimistic view of the potential student body and seems inconsistent with the broad international sweep of studies he was expecting students to embrace.

Annan made his proposals more specific in November and it was then clear just how generalised his view of UEA degrees was to be.[127] For instance, the proposed degree in economics would consist of five courses in economics mixed with three in history and six others, chiefly sociology and politics. It gave substance to a private cutting remark (unknown to Annan) by Sir Maurice Bowra, the classicist Warden of Wadham, "I expect Noel will insist on your centering everything on Sociology". Annan clearly did not believe that UEA students would be capable of anything like the rigours of economics at Cambridge or the solidity of the civic universities. A degree in "Economics" barely a third of which contained economics would have been professionally valueless.[128]

Annan had been bold and imaginative in laying out his views but his companions did not follow him all the way. Edgar Williams liked the spirit of Annan's approach but was uneasy that there was "a danger of studying no one subject in depth" in all this rich mix;[129] certainly the economics pattern suggested this. Sir Christopher Ingold thought that these claims to do Russian and Chinese would be useless, since all students would take American Studies as a "soft option". Charles Wilson certainly did not want UEA to be a "Liberal Arts College" as Annan had suggested, with its implications of a wide scatter of not very rigorous specialised arts subjects.[130] Denys Page also thought Annan was sacrificing depth to breadth and all this talk of Russian and Chinese was making Norwich look not only different but "odd". Page (unlike Wilson, Annan and Williams) did not like Sussex's breadth of curriculum either. He frankly preferred single subject degrees in history and English on the Cambridge Tripos model.

Another arts area specifically advanced was a proposal for a B.Ed. degree in education.[131] The proponent of this was Lincoln Ralphs, one of the earliest advocates of the university. As Chief Education Officer of Norfolk he represented local interests on the APB and naturally had a particular concern for education. He wanted UEA to do teacher training, arranging full- and part-time courses for serving teachers, engaging in educational research and running extramural adult education. Ralphs assumed that "a considerable number" of students going to UEA would become schoolteachers and that they would be "a more second rate type of student",[132] who could use the B.Ed. to prepare for teaching in secondary modern schools.[133] The other members of the APB did not like the sound of this at all. They thought that a B.Ed. was both too general in content but too narrowly specific in purpose. Wilson was especially doubtful about degrees which had a declared career intention at the outset.[134] Ralphs rightly retorted that there seemed to be no such difficulty over degrees in law, medicine or engineering but, with an uncharacteristic loss of tactical sense, he dangerously back-tracked by suggesting that there would be "very little professional training in it", which made the rest ponder what the point was at all. He also antagonised the scientists by suggesting geography as a suitable subject for schoolteachers, whereas Zuckerman had a view of environmental sciences as much more "high grade operation" than this "casual application for teachers". Charles Wilson made it clear that he did not see the B.Ed. as fitting into the UEA pattern. It was an undesirable vocational first degree and not as academically acceptable as the others. Ralphs took it in good part but had the long-term satisfaction of seeing most of his ideas accepted by the University over the years.[135]

The third major debate on arts subjects was over languages.[136] This was inevitably influenced by Annan's view that Europe had ceased to be the centre of the world and that studies should be oriented to the Great Powers, Third World and Commonwealth. When the APB met in September Annan expounded his view of Russian, American and Chinese studies. Sir Christopher Ingold, a no-nonsense chemist, pointed out that students would not study Russian and Chinese since these languages were so difficult and took so long to learn that everybody would do American instead. To avoid this Annan suggested that a foreign language be made compulsory. But here again the same problem would arise: Russian would be neglected for French, since in Annan's view, "French would be the soft option". There was parallel debate among the scientists. Ingold took the view that German and Russian were useful for scientists but French "had no place" in scientific studies. Sir Solly Zuckerman had no particular view about French, his own world being very much an Anglo-American one. A dangerous situation for French had emerged. The most vociferous scientist (Ingold) was hostile to French and the most influential (Zuckerman) indifferent. The most forceful arts man regarded the heartland of Europe, including France, as finished as a world centre and the study of French as a "soft option". Only the Chairman, Charles Wilson, sustained the view that French was of first importance for the arts man and listened to this anti-French debate with considerable scepticism.

By November 1960 Annan crystallised his views even more firmly, stressing that the key arts study should be Britain in conjunction with USA, Russia, China and other non-European countries. He was frank: "it is an essential part of the scheme that European studies [the study of French, German] are *NOT* included". Moreover the Russian and Chinese languages would have to be learnt in a "propaedeutic" year before coming to university. Learning Russian and Chinese in one year while at school studying A levels at the same time seemed absurd, as did any expectation that students would take a year off without financial support. Nobody would come to Norwich on those terms. Annan's radical views split his fellows. Denys Page and Edgar Williams thought that there was too much sacrificing of depth to breadth and that all this emphasis on Russia and China was eccentric. Ingold thought that there was an unrealistically short time for new difficult language learning. This forced Annan into an untenable position. He thought there would be time for language learning if it were kept clear of reading literature, which ran counter to the whole object of using languages to integrate them into literary and historical studies, which he had been advocating in the previous year.[137] By mid-1961 it must be admitted that the discussion of languages, while very imaginative, was at an unsatisfactory stage. Expectations were quite unrealistic about difficult foreign languages, about which none of the APB seemed to have any first-hand knowledge, and Annan's forcefulness had obviated the necessary debate about European studies. In July 1961 Thistlethwaite arrived as Vice-Chancellor with his own views, but this was an area where the APB discussions were of only limited use to him.

The APB discussion of the Arts subjects had been imaginative and stimulating. Even when it became unrealistic, it raised the right controversies.

Annan's Sussex- influenced view of an integrated curriculum was rather too wide and unspecialised for the rest of the committee. He took an unnecessarily pessimistic view of the possibility of economics, for example, and had his scheme been adopted it would have resulted in degrees too unfocused to be credible outside. Secondly, Lincoln Ralphs was very unlucky to have been given such short shrift over his B.Ed. In fact his sensible ideas were put into practice at UEA some years later – the B.Ed. degree, a School of Education, educational research, and extramural development. Finally Annan's view of languages was quite misleading; his rejection of European studies and specifically French and his exaggerated view of the importance for Britain of some backward Communist countries was idiosyncratic and in retrospect mistaken. Lord Annan, interviewed on 26 September 1996, was astonished at the negative attitudes to Europe he had expressed at that time. "It was clearly very bad advice", he said with disarming charm. We have the benefit of hindsight, whereas Annan was trying to make imaginative predictions looking forward. One understands the group dynamic. There was an imperative concern to make UEA appear different and innovative. Annan, who had considerable gusty charm, clearly took on this role. By contrast Denys Page's conservative preference for single-subject degrees appears inappropriately unexciting. But some good things did emerge from the debate. UEA's interdisciplinarity in arts and social studies was influenced by the APB. Most of Lincoln Ralph's proposals were incorporated. Annan was most valuable in prompting Norwich to look more widely to the USA, Russia and development studies, while his views about Europe had no lasting influence and did no lasting damage.

The debate on the sciences was focused on the environmental sciences and biology. Sir Christopher Ingold opened the discussion by considering the basic sciences of mathematics, physics and chemistry.[138] He envisaged departments of each of these, each with a professor and grouped in a Faculty of Science with students being able to take combinations of courses across these departments. It was as simple as that. Ingold, then aged sixty-seven, was the eldest member of the APB and had been Professor of Chemistry at University College London since 1930. Sensibly conservative, he was not inclined to broad flights of fancy. His proposal seemed a mix of interdisciplinarity and single-subject organisation and occasioned no contentious debate within the APB. He could not have foreseen that no other APB recommendation was to lead to such furious acrimony in the future when the first Professor of Chemistry demanded not just a department in a faculty but an entirely separate single subject School.

Thinking about the life sciences depended largely on Sir Solly Zuckerman, whose proposals were both more imaginative and less contentious. He was the most distinguished and worldly member of the APB. He was also the only one who had served on the preceding Academic Advisory Committee. Around the time of his involvement with these bodies he was very much interested in environmental matters.[139] These included the integration of forestry and agriculture in marginal areas, the effect of toxic chemicals on agricultural products and foodstuffs, and the environmental effects of population growth. He saw clearly that this whole mixed life science area was one which a new university could develop as a specialism. He wrote to Ingold,

> If one had it in mind to do something absolutely new and fresh in science, I am wondering whether Norwich could not embark in its Faculty of Science on a Division of Environmental Sciences – meteorology, oceanography, geology, conservation, etc. If it were, I am quite certain that nobody could ever be able to say that scientists were trained in a narrow way. Conservation would lead to the social sciences, population studies, etc . . . Such a department would of course be based upon basic training in physics, chemistry and mathematics but for that matter so is every other part of science.[140]

He drew up a detailed scheme for a degree in environmental sciences. The first year was to be the same as for biology students. The second year was to include ecology, soil science, meteorology, geography, economic geography, statistics plus chemistry and physics. Then the third year was divided into optional areas – meteorology and oceanography, conservation including forestry, land use, population, transport studies – where there would be links with economics and social studies.[141] Zuckerman had clearly given a good deal of thought to this, which was well worked out, interdisciplinary but solid. There was no discussion of this proposal. It was so authoritative and obviously right that the APB were happy to leave it so. Zuckerman was in any case always careful to "square" his fellow scientist Ingold before the meeting. The Royal Society added some further detail on marine sciences and areas they would like to see developed – biology of fish, geology of the sea floor, wave and current motions – and these too were noted by the APB.[142] It all fed into the creation of UEA's distinctive School of Environmental Sciences which Zuckerman was proud to recognise as his "specific contribution". He himself retained a genuine interest in the School. He subsequently became a Professor at Large and arranged annual international seminars for the School, financed by the Ford Foundation at Zuckerman's persuasion.[143]

Lincoln Ralphs alone was uneasy about Zuckerman's view of environmental sciences, since he preferred a more traditional form of geography for schoolteachers. He wrote to Professor S. W. Wooldridge, "I am of the opinion that the University is not giving sufficient attention to the place of geography".[144] He felt he was a lone voice and urged the Royal Geographical Society and the

Geographical Association to put pressure on the University. Dr Alice Garnett of Sheffield University and the Geographical Association held a similar view that the new universities were neglecting old-fashioned geography (she had likewise been trying to influence Warwick).[145] Dr E.M. Yates of King's College London, to whom Ralphs had sent the ENV curriculum, thought that it was too wide to fit a graduate to teach geography in a school.[146] This was music to Ralph's ears but Zuckerman could not have cared less.

The other distinctive area of UEA science was to be biology. Ingold left this largely to Zuckerman, though Ingold was certain in his own mind that biology "will become a huge subject in itself" and one of the chief developments of science as a whole would be "the constant expansion of the biological sciences".[147] Zuckerman held very high expectations of biology at UEA. He astonished Annan by asserting that "the first professor of biology will be a Fellow of the Royal Society and the School of Biology at East Anglia will shortly be far superior to that of Cambridge".[148] Zuckerman drew up a detailed plan.[149] There was a very broad first year, considering such matters as the cell, enzymes, proteins, carbohydrates and fats, reproduction, genetics and diversity of form. In the second year studies were divided into ecology, including flora and fauna, plant breeding and general academic biology for teachers. Then in the third year the student would carry on with deepening the area of this second year choice and focus on one specialised part of it. In Zuckerman's view "the biology course should not be full of facts and emphasis should be laid on the commonness of mechanisms throughout the living world".[150] Noel Annan thought that all science students should take biology in the first year.[151] Zuckerman agreed with this as did Ingold, so there was nothing more to discuss. What was to be distinctive about Norwich, however, was the lack of separate Departments of Zoology and Botany; it would be about what was "unitary in living systems", as Annan put it. Zuckerman liked that and underlined the words in his copy. He later wrote to Ingold, "the really important thing is that young biologists should approach the subject in terms of the general principles which affect all living matter".[152] This approach to biology was to find perfect sympathy in T.A. Bennet Clark CBE, FRS, the distinguished Professor of Botany at King's College London. Bennet Clark, at the end of his career, was profoundly dissatisfied with the narrow compartmentalisation of forms of biology at the University of London, and was seeking some way of developing a more integrated form of biology and biochemistry.[153] The Zuckerman-APB thinking for Norwich provided this perfect opportunity and Bennet Clark came to UEA to found the new School of Biological Sciences in this spirit.

Two scientific matters the APB did not discuss were agriculture and engineering. Charles Wilson told them frankly that the UGC did not want these subjects at Norwich; it would provide no money for them and so there was no point in discussing them. The rejection of agriculture at the outset was just as well since, during Sir John Wolfenden's chairmanship of the UGC 1963-68, he had to require three universities to run down their existing departments of agriculture.[154] His policy was to concentrate in fewer and bigger schools and deprive the others of finance. Had UEA started agriculture in 1963 against UGC advice it would have been totally vulnerable to this squeeze and could not have survived.

Another matter which the scientists were not interested in discussing was interdisciplinary courses in science for arts students. Noel Annan and Edgar Williams were keen on this idea in the wake of C. P. Snow's influential *Two Cultures* (1959). Ingold put a stop to it. He thought that humanists and scientists were fundamentally different in outlook and "he was not hopeful of any ultimate intellectual link between them".[155] History for scientists had met "little sympathy" at UCL, while science for humanists was an "intolerable burden" for teachers and taught and had likewise been abandoned at UCL. The strong implication was that science students should be far too busy to spend time on arts courses while science teachers had better things to do than teach unreceptive arts students not good enough to do science properly.[156]

In the summer of 1961 Frank Thistlethwaite was appointed Vice-Chancellor. He had his own views on the curriculum, which he discussed with the APB. He outlined schemes for Schools of European Studies, English Studies and Overseas Studies. They all had in common three first year courses, in the History of Western Europe since 1492, Introduction to Philosophical and Scientific Method, and Modern Government, to give a multidisciplinary grounding. Then the Schools went their own way. Thistlethwaite clearly differed from Annan in reinstating European Studies. The Europeanists could specialise in literature or history with several interdisciplinary options, including philosophy and inevitably language. In his preliminary thinking Thistlethwaite, again differing from Annan, included French. Likewise in English Studies, students would divide into historians and lettrists. Social Studies would comprise economics, politics, sociology, philosophy, economic history and eventually psychology. It was rather generously broad but allowed for more specialism than the Annan model, for example nine out of fourteen courses could have been in economics. Finally, he proposed an imaginative School of Development Studies which very much followed the spirit of the best aspects of Noel Annan's advice and, from the basis of economics and politics, branched out to study the Commonwealth, USSR, Africa and India.

Charles Wilson noted the organisation by multi-subject schools rather than by traditional departments and wondered if there was sufficient specialisation and depth. The Vice-Chancellor replied that "he accepted the fact that the Schools arrangements would not provide the same depth of specialisation as that of a conventional Honours course; but he felt that the advantage of providing the student with a broad contextual framework outweighed this and that the arrangement was more appropriate to the needs of the under-graduates to be catered for". This was a fair and concise expression of the philosophy behind the curricular thinking of the early years of UEA. Thistlethwaite defended Development Studies as a coherent mix providing a course of interest for foreign students and those working in underdeveloped countries. Annan made a valuable suggestion that there could be "luxury dons" in the living arts. The new Vice-Chancellor agreed and envisaged a lecturer in art history while Charles Wilson referred to his director of music at Leicester. It was a germ of the future School of Fine Arts and Music.

All were aware that UEA was light on the vocational side. Noel Annan had stressed the need to cater for technology since "it would be unwise in the present climate of opinion for the University not to be seen to be doing its duty in this respect". Fine words, but empty given the constraints of the time. They knew they could do nothing about agriculture or engineering but hoped to approach them via food technology and electronics. There was no demand for doctors, lawyers or architects. The Vice-Chancellor was aware of the interest of Lord Mackintosh and Sir Edmund Bacon in business administration but saw this only as a postgraduate development for a later stage. The Bishop's hope for clergy training fell on deaf ears and the nearby Keswick Hall Church of England Teacher Training College blocked the need for contributions in that area. There seemed to be very little scope for the development of vocationalism at the middle class professional level.

There would have been a more radical alternative: to move into the area of vocational technical education by providing degrees in, say, hotel management, building construction, fashion design including shoes, automotive engineering including farm machinery. All would have been relevant to Norwich and East Anglia and all subjects worth studying on three year degree courses, as happens now. Lincoln Ralphs had perhaps too easily set aside that letter from the Principal of King's Lynn Technical College and the whole tradition of claims for a University of Norwich coming from the Norwich "Tech". Certainly the members of the APB were too eminently academic to consider a university moving into these technical areas. They saw their task as devising an essentially *academic* university curriculum. The one secular figure on the APB, Sir Walter Worboys of ICI, was supposed to be looking after the needs of industry, but he was nothing like as forceful as Ralphs, Annan, Ingold and Zuckerman in the deliberations. Annan more than most was aware of these issues.[157] A few years later he reflected that Lord Taylor's committee on higher education in 1962 had suggested bringing all higher education under comprehensive universities, thus enabling universities to deal at a high level with subjects hitherto restricted to technical and training colleges.[158] Annan thought this was "impossible given the state of opinion in the universities at the time". Partly because it affronted the traditional notion of the BA or BSc degree and partly because it seemed to introduce subjects less amenable to research. It would certainly have been impossible given the new Vice-Chancellor's approach. He stated firmly that a university pursued "the truth in fundamental matters for its own sake . . . [it] is not a training or technical college."[159] This High Victorian view of liberal education in the tradition of Newman and Mill would probably have been shared by most arts men on the APB, all Fellows of Oxford and Cambridge colleges. But it left UEA weak in vocational subjects in the 1960s and its students vulnerable in the job market. Sadly it also prevented closer links with Norwich City College, so that that institution was eventually married not with UEA, its natural partner, but with the Anglia Polytechnic University in Chelmsford and Cambridge.

The APB, its deliberations completed, then reported to the UGC digesting the foregoing discussions. In science there would be mathematics, physics, chemistry and biology with a distinctive overlapping of botany and zoology. They indicated an intention to start environmental sciences in the near future. In the arts they explained the Schools of European, English, Social and Overseas Studies and their interdisciplinary approach. They suggested that they would look at ways of serving agriculture and food technology and expressed future intentions for business administration and education.[160] The UGC responded very favourably.[161] They were "very interested" in the Humanities Schools and had no comment to make. On the science side they thought that it was not desirable for all students to do biology in the first year, nor should they study three sciences in an honours degree. They liked the School of Biology and agreed that environmental studies and business administration should be left until the University was established. Once again they firmly ruled out agriculture. The UGC response had been overwhelmingly approving. There was now enough consensus between the APB, the UGC and the Vice-Chancellor to give UEA a clear and distinctive curriculum.

Devising a form of government for the new University was not so arduous a problem for the APB as their other tasks. There were ample precedents. Lincoln Ralphs told the Executive Committee that "The Charter would be on the normal pattern of a civic university".[162] Specifically the APB was using the draft charter of the University of Sussex as a pattern and they had a working copy of the Sussex draft (20 May 1959). Charles Wilson had been on the Sussex APB and so was perfectly familiar with it. This was largely unremarkable. It stated that the university was to be "both a teaching and an examining body", no religious tests should be imposed on students or staff, and women were to be eligible for any office. The structure was likewise predictable with the Queen as Visitor, a Chancellor, Court, Council, Senate, Students Union and Schools of Studies. It was unlikely that Norwich would adopt anything very controversial or deviant.

The pivot of the system was the power relationship of the Senate and the Council and here some interesting views emerged. Sir Roy Harrod visited Keele and found unsatisfactory circumstances that Norwich would do well to avoid.[163] At one level professors had far too much departmental power, leading to the frustration of non-professorial staff. They were revising their regulations for Senate to give non-professors a louder voice. This situation was made even worse by the fact that the Principal, Sir George Barnes, did not think much of his Senate. Too few of his professors had had any experience of university administration before coming to Keele. He found that "a body of men, however able, if without previous experience of administration or of the world beyond the cloister is unfitted to do this work wisely", and more bluntly, "a combination of youth and inexperience can wreck a Senate". Accordingly, Barnes relied on a Council of laymen and academics from *other* universities to control his Senate and give proper guidance to the University. The parlous situation at Keele gave some salutory warnings to Norwich.[164]

Harrod's visit to Keele had been a piece of private enterprise for the early Academic Advisory Committee. But it was the official duty of the APB to decide these matters following a draft provided by the Privy Council. When the APB began to discuss the constitutional organisation, they and the chairman assumed that there would be a Court, Council and Senate. Charles Wilson thought that a third of the Council should come from the Senate. Denys Page pointed out that at Brighton twenty-four out of a council of thirty-eight were laymen and this was too many, so he thought Wilson's assumption of one third academics was too few. Annan and Ingold deviously favoured a large Senate of fifty to seventy on the grounds that its unwieldy size would lead to the diffusion of power among small groups and give greater authority to the Vice-Chancellor. When the APB discussed Faculty structure with the Vice-Chancellor in 1961 they envisaged Boards of Schools comprising all staff of disciplines involved.[165] They also thought that there should be Boards of Studies for individual disciplines but were less sure – horrendous thought – of a third tier of Faculties for Arts and Sciences combining Schools in contiguous areas.[166] There clearly had to be a happy medium between autocratic Deans for life operating with no democratic Board (which is what Ingold wanted!) and three tiers of "local government" – (Boards of Schools, Boards of Studies and Boards of Faculties) – with the interminable bureaucracy they implied. They came to the view that Deans should be appointed for no more than ten years.[167] To avoid the Keele problem a third of Senate should be non-professorial staff, large as that might make the Senate.

The APB reported to UGC in rather bland terms. The Court would meet annually to receive the Vice-Chancellor's annual report and comment on the progress of the University. The Council would be the body "with final responsibility for the administration and finance of the University". It would be thirty to forty in size and have a "strong academic representation" but, as required by the Privy Council, there would be a majority of lay members. The Senate would be the "main academic governing body" and have one third non-professorial membership. They coyly made no reference to government below the Senate about which they were still unsure in spite of their recent discussions in September 1961. This did not escape the notice of Sir Keith Murray, who welcomed the main features but asked for a fuller clarification in due course.[168] This seems to have prompted the Vice-Chancellor to decide on his own intentions.[169] The focus was to be the School Board of all members of a School. He saw no need for umbrella Faculties of Arts or Sciences combining Boards. Nor did individual subjects need full Boards though no doubt they could meet in committees. This was both democratic and economical and was what came into being in the next year.

On the basis of these discussions the Promotion Committee petitioned for a Charter in May 1963. This was approved on 16 December 1963 and sealed on 5 March 1964. It now hangs in the Council Chamber.[170] This created the University as a corporate body "to advance learning and knowledge by teaching and research". It was also to be both a teaching and an examining body. This sounds self-evident but was innovatory. For much of the nineteenth and twentieth centuries many university colleges had been teaching bodies with their examining done by the University of London. Conversely the University of London between 1858 and 1900 had been an examining, not a teaching body. The new universities were not only to teach but were given the right to examine their own teaching from the outset. Otherwise the Charter set out the officers and institutions of the University, Court, Council, Senate, Assembly, Schools of Study with their Deans and Boards. The Court was a very large body of notable figures in East Anglia who wished the University well and which meets annually to receive the Vice-Chancellor's report and, as rare occasion demands, to elect the Chancellor. Frank Thistlethwaite originally regarded it as an anachronism but was persuaded by Gordon Tilsley of its necessity as a regional sounding-board.[171] In particular it gave a formal role to members of the original Promotion Committee who made a happy elision into the Court as the Executive Committee did into the

Council. The Assembly was to be a meeting of all members of teaching and related staff to discuss and declare opinions on any University matter. It was the UEA equivalent of Oxford's Congregation and Cambridge's Regent House but without their legislative power. It could make life uncomfortable for the Vice-Chancellor and his Administration but was a necessary part of checks and balances. The Charter also set up an Academic Advisory Committee required by the Privy Council to carry on from the APB which ceased on the granting of the Charter. Lincoln Ralphs and Solly Zuckerman, as Norfolk residents, were members of the APB who continued on the new AAC. Zuckerman had the unusual distinction of serving on the original Academic Advisory Sub-Committee (Harrod's group), the APB and then the Privy Council appointed AAC. The last was finally dissolved in February 1969, ending a long chain of advice and guidance by distinguished academics to the fledgling University.

Three clauses of the Charter are worth comment. By Clause 21 the University may not pay a dividend to its members. This was supposed to distinguish modern universities from Victorian and Georgian Oxford and Cambridge. In those days fellows were paid from the profits of their colleges struck at the annual audit. They were in effect shareholders in their houses. Nowadays there is an argument that universities would benefit from private capital from investors, including their own employees. It is odd that a university should seem to deprive itself of this opportunity by Clause 21. In practice members of the university have invested in the capitalisation of new UEA buildings through a Business Expansion Scheme run by Hodgson Martin. Sensibly nobody invoked Clause 21 against this. The next, Clause 22, requires that no religious racial or political test could be imposed on any member of the University. It was in effect a modern version of the Universities' Tests Act of 1871 and sounded obviously liberal in its day. Yet it leaves the University vulnerable to students and staff with neo-Nazi or Stalinist views or influenced by brainwashing cults not envisaged in 1960. There is nothing much the University can do about this under Clause 22 save to hope that such cases are sufficiently few as to be overwhelmed by the prevailing plurality and diversity of opinion that is the characteristic of a liberal university. Clause 23 states the equality of men and women in the eligibility for offices and degrees. Today it seems odd that it was felt necessary to express this. In practice it is disregarded since, for example, there are Women's Advisers who are specifically women. These three clauses, 21, 22 and 23, must have seemed self-evident, liberal even highminded in 1963. With the short passage of time they have been overtaken by shifts of attitude – the recognition of the need for private capital in public institutions and the concept of the stakeholder, the acceptance of affirmative action feminism, and the increased dangers of political and religious bigotry.

This is no reason to change the Charter, which has served the University well over the years.[172]

An essential concomitant of the Charter Clause 3 (21) was the grant of arms by the Royal College of Arms. These were to be symbols of the new corporate status of the University. Frank Thistlethwaite consulted his friend Michael Maclagan, a medieval historian, Fellow of Trinity College, Oxford, and Pursuivant of the College of Arms. Maclagan suggested three gold crowns on an azure ground – the symbols of the ancient kingdom of East Anglia. He pointed out that this was also the logo of Scandinavian Airlines, "but that's a problem for Swedish heraldry not ours".[173] So the coat of arms was devised by A. Colin Cole, Portcullis Pursuivant of Arms.[174] There were the three crowns, an angel bearing a sword as a word play on Anglia, Norwich Castle with three St George's banners flying from turrets, and lions with money bags around their necks to symbolise Lord Mackintosh's leadership of the National Savings Movement. The coat of arms also incorporated a motto. Frank Thistlethwaite describes how he arrived at his choice:

> Ever since coming to Norwich I had enjoyed the Norfolk dialect saying "In Norfolk we du different". I had in fact used the phrase as a theme of an early speech; this was picked up by the *Eastern Evening News* which titled its leader that evening "Du Different a Virtue" (21 October 1961). And later when at a meeting of Deans in my room, Thomas Bennet Clark suggested it as a possible motto I jumped at it.[175]

The College of Arms changed it to "Do Different" and so it remained. Opinion was mixed. Frank Thistlethwaite recalled that some people were uneasy that it may seem to be making fun of the Norfolk dialect. Jill Aitken, the daughter of the Archdeacon of Norwich and an early student, disliked it since "people expect us to be different in the wrong sort of way".[176] In contrast, R. H. Mottram, a leading Norfolk author and UEA's first Hon. Litt.D, was delighted since he often used the expression himself.[177] Overall the *Eastern Daily Press* found most people pleased with the motto.[178]

The students also wanted their own symbols. Taking the colours of the arms – blue, gold and black – the Students' Union devised a scarf: this was already being sold by London Street outfitters by the start of the first Spring Term after the students arrived.[179] Curiously this was *before* the University had decided on its official colours. It was not until the beginning of the second year that the official colours of the University were announced as blue and black (but not yellow).[180] In practice scarves retain the three colours; sporting shirts the blue and black only. Small matters, but all part of the corporate identity and all linked since the Charter obliged the University to have a coat of arms while the colours that were adopted for everyday wear in ties and scarves helped to bind the community.

The University also acquired a ceremonial mace. This was made by Christopher Lawrence, the head silversmith with Gerald Benney. It was the generous gift of the Norwich Junior Chamber of Commerce.[181] The Junior Chamber had started in 1960 and almost from the start took an interest in the University as the other fledgling Norwich institution of the sixties. They formed a University Committee which held twenty-two meetings in 1962/63 and organised a May Ball (14 June) in 1963. The University was not yet open but this was to raise money to present the University with a silver mace. It was a great success and 400 people attended at Earlham Hall. The mace was duly presented to Lord Mackintosh by Norman Gomm, President of the Junior Chamber, on 18 April 1964. The Chamber then organised the University's first May Ball in July 1964. It is noteworthy that a leading figure in the University Committee was Raymond Frostick a young Norwich solicitor and later a lifetime friend of the University, and Chairman of Council and Pro-Chancellor. The mace remains a centre of attention in the Council House foyer and when carried proudly at Congregations. It is a symbol of the early warm and generous support of the Norwich business and professional classes in the early sixties.

The final major matter that had to be settled in the University's foundation was its precise location. There was no shortage of possible sites, but a fundamental issue was raised at the outset: was it to be in the City of Norwich itself or out in the surrounding countryside?

There was a body of opinion, chiefly voiced by a local architect Bruce Henderson-Gray, which wanted the university to be an integral part of Norwich. They favoured a site forming a wedge right into the city centre starting from the cattle market behind the Castle then through Ber Street and King Street to Bracondale Woods and Carrow Abbey with their houses and grounds, thence to the open country on the southern outskirts of the city.[182] The arguments in its favour were that "it offers most of the advantages of a compact medieval town". It would redevelop the redundant cattle market where the University's administrative buildings could be built and it would remove the slums from Ber Street and King Street while using the street infrastructure. Most importantly, in Henderson-Gray's view, it would ensure that the City and the University would be thoroughly integrated with each other – students thronging the Norwich streets and citizens enjoying the facilities of the University. Norwich was urged not to be like Sussex with its Falmer site some miles away from Brighton.[183] This had a certain medieval attractiveness; castle, cathedral, market, university, medieval walls (in Ber Street and Carrow) all snugly together like some fifteenth-century Italian city. Moreover it fitted in with the not yet published Robbins Report (1963) which was "in favour of fostering further development within large cities" and hoped that of the new universities "a large number will be in great centres of population or their vicinity".[184] Too late. The locations and sites of the new universities had already been decided and the UGC's policies were not those of Robbins.

The Henderson-Gray proposals were quite impracticable. Their proposed site was only sixty-five acres and the UGC made it plain that it required a minimal site of two hundred acres with adjacent land for further expansion to accommodate a university of three thousand students. The surrounding land was needed for hard surface sports areas, more and more residences, and beyond that for playing fields. Unforeseeable subsequent developments were also inevitable. In UEA's case major scientific research establishments (John Innes Institute, Food Research Institute, British Sugar Corporation) gathered round the University in a way that would have been quite impossible in the Ber Street site. Moreover, students like to be rowdy from time to time. High-volume discotheques and drunken parties best take place in private and would not have been welcomed in close proximity to other residents of the city. Also Henderson-Gray totally underestimated the amount of traffic the University would generate. UEA soon had the largest car park in Norfolk; this alone would have swallowed up a large portion of the Ber Street site. All the cars flowing into Norwich every morning rather than away from it to the west would have created impossible problems of congestion. The city site would have entailed a vast amount of compulsory purchase and demolition of existing property, entailing high costs and delay even before building could start. In any case the whole site was riddled with marl workings in unstable and steeply sloping ground which would have exacerbated the problems of the architects and builders.

Horace Rowley, the City Engineer and Planning Officer, rejected the site. The Academic Advisory Committee walked over it and likewise rejected it for the reasons explained above.[185] Yet still Henderson-Gray and the Norwich Society persisted. This led to a Planning Enquiry in December 1960.[186] Lord Mackintosh, Horace Rowley and Professor W. H. Sprott for the Academic Advisory Sub-Committee all expressed their rejection of the Ber Street site. Tilsley feared that the message was still not getting through and decided on a *coup de grâce*. He telephoned Sir Cecil Syers, the Secretary of the UGC. Syers jumped on the next train and duly appeared in the Council Chamber the same afternoon. His message was blunt. "If all Norwich has to offer is the Ber Street site, there will be no University in Norwich." Eric Blain, the barrister for the promoters, now had an unanswerable case. The Promotion Committee did not want Ber Street, the City would not let them have it and, even if they had, the UGC would not accept it. That was the end of this imaginative but impracticable proposal.

The University was going to be built on the outskirts of Norwich, but where? Arthur South as early as the summer of 1958 was thinking of Colney Hall in conjunction with the golf course at Earlham.[188] Lincoln Ralphs went over there and peered through the windows, being unable to get in or contact the owner. Colney Hall was too far away, however, was certainly no adequate site in itself and they received no offer of it as a gift as they hoped, so it dropped out of consideration. There were various other proposals too unrealistic to be in the running. Andrew Ryrie suggested demolishing the Prison and the Barracks and using Mousehold Heath.[188] J. and J. Colman Ltd generously offered a small site at the junction of Bracondale and Martineau Lane. The Promotion Committee considered it but, at twenty-seven acres, it was far too small. The County Hall was built there instead. Mr Edward Bush offered 120 acres at Markshall on the Ipswich Road. But this was also too small, would have been expensive and difficult to drain, and the owner wanted to sell rather than donate.

This left four sites seriously considered by the Promotion Committee. First there was the airfield at Horsham St Faith, an RAF fighter station during the war and post war years. It had the advantage of huge, if bleak, space and some existing administrative and residential buildings. Andrew Ryrie saw it as an opportunity to get a quick start for the University,[189] but others were less keen. Lord Mackintosh went to see the Secretary of State for Air on 29 April 1959 who in effect ruled it out, as it would be required by the RAF for the foreseeable future. Horsham later became useful residences for the University in 1965 but there was no question of waiting until then before starting the University itself.

Secondly, there was the possibility of land on the Crown Point Estate to the south east of Norwich on the road to Bungay. This was owned by Mr Timothy Colman, who lived nearby in Bixley Manor. The idea for this came from the County Planning Committee and Tilsley approached Colman on the matter. Colman's position was that he would be "extremely reluctant" to give up any of this land until other possibilities had been explored. It was left as a last resort. This was actually an act of great generosity by Timothy Colman, who did not reject the proposal out of hand as he might reasonably have done but put himself at the risk of making a considerable sacrifice. Few could have known this at the time but fortunately it was not necessary.

This focused attention on the two most likely sites, Eaton and Earlham. Both were about two miles to the south of Norwich, Eaton to the south east and Earlham to the north west of the Newmarket Road, the main southern exit from Norwich to London. The Eaton site was proposed by Horace Rowley, the City Engineer.[190] He thought that the land between Newmarket Road and Marston Lane and adjoining Eaton Golf Course would be suitable for the University. He knew that Major Gurney was willing to sell and had been discussing it with Bassett Hornor, his agent. Various other owners were also interviewed by Tilsley and expressed their interest in selling to the University. The adjacent golf course was owned by R. Q. Gurney and leased to Eaton Golf Club until 1971, after which the University could purchase it. The whole area would have been 349 acres at a cost of £125,000 to £175,000. But possession of the golf course was not necessary to get the University started. This was not the site chosen but extensive residential building took place there instead. This indirectly played its part in the development of the University since many university people came to live there. I did so myself and there were five other UEA staff members close by.

The ultimately preferred site was the Earlham Golf Course. The wry joke in Norwich was that they were going to lose one golf course or another although the Eaton course was not essential to that site.[191] The Earlham land had originally been the home farm to Earlham Hall. It had been acquired by Norwich City Council in 1925 and laid out as a golf course as an unemployment relief measure in the early 1930s. It was certainly the most attractive site of all, well-wooded with a south facing slope down to the River Yare, with room to expand across the river and to Colney, with untouchable but delightful Earlham Park to the rear.[192] At 165 acres with the possibility of expansion it was acceptable to the UGC with their 200 acre criterion. The Academic Advisory Sub-Committee liked the Earlham site. A group including Adrian, Cockcroft, Harrod, Zuckerman and Tilsley gathered at Thickthorn Hall and then toured the site in Sir John Cockcroft's large Bentley. They thought it ideal and that it "accords fully with the trend followed in other modern civic universities of obtaining a site to allow for all possible expansion".[193] The Promotion Committee also preferred the Earlham site. Tilsley and Horace Rowley personally favoured Eaton on the grounds that it would preserve the scenic beauties of the Yare Valley and building development was going to take place in Eaton anyway. The Norwich Society and the City Planning Committee also favoured Eaton.

When, however, the City Council came to debate this in October 1959 they declined the advice of the Planning Committee and plumped for Earlham instead. This was on the motion of Alderman H. Frazer, the Labour Leader of the City Council. He had been a strong protagonist for the Earlham site on the University Promotion Committee and carried this through on to the City Council where he had more influence.[194] The arguments for Earlham were persuasive. The City Council already owned Earlham Golf Course (and Earlham Park and the surrounding housing estates) from the 1925 purchase. Thus it would cost it no money to give it to the University. On the other hand, it would have had to spend up to £175,000 buying land at Eaton from several owners to make that gift. It was also aware that the University Promotion Committee preferred Earlham. Finally, by giving up Eaton, the City would deprive itself of 120 acres allocated for housing in the Development Plan when land for housing within the City boundary was desperately short. The arguments for Eaton and Earlham were so evenly balanced that there was no acrimonious party division over the matter and supporters of Eaton had not much difficulty in backing Earlham. The *Eastern Daily Press* shifted its advocacy in this way.

On 23 November 1959 the Executive Committee was formally notified that the City Council would make the Earlham site available. When the UGC architect came to Norwich and spent an hour walking over the terrain, he said "he could not think of anything better".[195] The availability of the Earlham site free of charge was to be an essential factor in the UGC's willingness to sanction a University of East Anglia. It was not only a splendid location but a token of the earnest support of the city for the project. Before an area of great landscape value like the Yare Valley could be developed, the Council had to ask the Minister of Housing and Local Government for authority to grant permission to the developers – the University. On receiving objections the Minister decided that there should be a public local enquiry first, which was fixed for 13 December 1960.

This gave opportunities for the objectors. The golfers had an understandable grievance since they would lose a very fine course. But the Earlham Golf Club comprised only four hundred members. They were not self-supporting and cost the Council £2000 a year in subsidies. It was judged that their loss of amenity was outweighed by the importance to the city of a University for several thousand. Moreover the whole course site would now be open to all comers to walk through and enjoy the valley. The Parks Department, which had lavished loving care on the golf course, gave it up with "grave reluctance" but could hardly object. The chief objectors were Henderson-Gray, the Norwich Society and those who wanted the University physically integrated with the centre of Norwich. Their arguments and their dismissal at the enquiry by Sir Cecil Syers of the UGC we have seen. The Inquiry Inspector, Mr R. G. M. Chase, decided accordingly, in favour of Earlham and advised his Minister accordingly. The Minister "agreed with his Inspector that the land at Earlham would serve well as a site for the University and he is not satisfied on the evidence before him that any of the alternative sites suggested would be as suitable".[196]

With this decision another foundation block was laid. Critics were not entirely silenced. The occasional golfer would thwack a ball along the old fairways as a gesture of defiance even as the buildings were being erected. Sociologists expressed reservations. The key one was that too many universities were being built on green field sites away from cities and this risked creating closed communities of students, isolated from urban and by implication "real" life. A critic who had taught at UEA observed, "one cannot help thinking that for many of the students who live within the campus the world will start at Earlham Road and stop at the River Yare". It was an exaggerated fear and underestimated the enterprise of students in the search of social life – and the enterprise of Norwich taxi drivers in running cheap taxi services between the University and the City.[197]

As well as acquiring Earlham Golf Course the University also acquired the use of the adjoining Earlham Hall. This was the property of the Bacon family but was historically famous as the residence of the Gurney family, who had leased it since 1786. Joseph John Gurney, the banker, had lived in Earlham Hall, as had his sister Elizabeth Fry the prison reformer. It was a fine mansion. The critic Percy Lubbock, whose home it was in the late nineteenth century, remembered it:

> Earlham was the wonder of the world. And indeed it was a beautiful old house, red and mellow, spacious, sun-bathed. There were gables of flint and brick with a date on them, 1642, which I suppose marked the earliest core of the building. But later on, perhaps in the reign of Queen Anne, the older building had been all but swallowed up in a house with a big garden-front, to the south, and rows of high sash-windows, and two projecting wings to the north that reached out and enclosed you as you arrived, as you drove up in the family carriage, palpitating with excitement, to the semi-circle of steps before the front-door.[198]

So it still is. The Hall, rented by the Gurney family until 1912, passed into the hands of the City of Norwich in 1925. The Hall itself had been a nursing home, and a wartime maternity home; subsequently a school, it was still being used as an extension of the nearby Bluebell School. But the Education Committee agreed to vacate the Hall and the City Council to lease it to the University for seven years, later increased to twenty-one. Renovation and decoration enabled the Vice-Chancellor and his staff to move in on 11 October 1962. Frank Thistlethwaite remembered that "on that day I saw an owl perched at noon in a niche on the north front, surely a good omen for a new learned life for the Hall".[199] At Earlham the University had acquired a beautiful site to stimulate the imagination of its architect Denys Lasdun and a gracious historic headquarters now given a new lease of life. It was a perfectly judged set of decisions.

In many ways the culmination of these founding developments was the appointment of the first Chancellor. Viscount Mackintosh of Halifax was the inevitable choice, not only as the leader of the UEA foundation movement but as the major national figure in Norwich. He served as Chancellor from 7

January to 27 December 1964 but died before he could be installed. He was delighted, his only disappointment being having to relinquish his Chairmanship of the Council to Sir Edmund Bacon. I met him once during his year as Chancellor. He held large parties at Thickthorn Hall for members of the University. The last two were just before Christmas, 9 November and 11 December 1964, and I attended the latter.[200] I admired the Hall, his collection of Norwich School paintings and the general generosity of the occasion. Towards the end of the evening I was standing by the glass cabinets displaying his collection of Toby jugs on which he was a proud expert. He came up quietly behind me and in avuncular tones commented "Well it will soon be Christmas". He asked if I were interested in the jugs and told me a little about them. Then to my surprise he said, "Here, have a toffee", which I took gratefully. In later life I came to wonder if I had imagined the episode but Sir Solly Zuckerman likewise recalled that after a meeting of the original Academic Advisory Committee at Thickthorn Hall the committee were surprised on leaving to be presented with boxes of toffees.[201] Lord Adrian, OM and Nobel Laureate, received his gravely as if it were the greatest honour ever bestowed upon him. The party and the personal incident illustrated several aspects of Lord Mackintosh's personality and attitude to the University. There was a generosity, a genuine interest in individuals, the flair for unexpected and vivid behaviour especially if promoting something – National Savings, his toffees or UEA. He must have taken pleasure in seeing the scores of youngish people milling about the Hall since they were the life blood and energy that would bring life to his University. This is what he now lacked himself. His face that evening was heavy and grey, for he was approaching death and he died of a seizure about a fortnight later, just after Christmas, on 27 December 1964.

He had had the satisfaction of seeing the University come into being and he is commemorated by a portrait in the Council Chamber, a copy by Cowan Dobson of his own portrait for the National Savings Movement.[202] Lord Mackintosh's death rounds off the story of the origins and founding of the University. Now a community of scholars was getting to work.

3

What and How to Teach

I have taken on the job of building up the new University of East Anglia as its first Vice-Chancellor . . . the real excitement of the project is that we have a completely free hand to think out afresh what we should teach and how we should teach it.[1]

Frank Thistlewaite, 26 October 1961

The University began in the specially built prefabricated Village on the other side of Earlham Road, opposite Earlham Park and Hall. Sir Keith Murray opened it on 29 September 1963 in his last public engagement as Chairman of the UGC and praised the ingenuity and enterprise of UEA in creating the Village as a means of receiving students as soon as possible. In his view it proved that "elegance need not be sacrificed to speed". His delight was genuine. He thanked Frank Thistlethwaite for "such a wonderful day and one of the most satisfying in what is now quite a long life. You have achieved so much in so short a time".[2] In the invited party celebrating the opening was John Gurney of Walsingham, the still anonymous donor of the twelve acre site on which it was built. Sir Keith Murray retired the day after opening the UEA Village and was succeeded by Sir John Wolfenden. On 23 October the Robbins Report was published with its calls for further expansion of higher education. It was accepted by the government the next day and supported by the Committee of Vice-Chancellor and Principles the day after that. This was the heady atmosphere in which UEA started life in the Village as the first students arrived on 7 October 1963.

The village was to be the crucible for a new curriculum and research agenda and new approaches to teaching. In the latter UEA had two distinctive characteristics, the seminar and the coursework system. The seminar was a small group of students discussing a topic chiefly among themselves but under the guidance of the tutor. Frank Thistlethwaite was very keen on the system as essential for personal teaching. He appreciated that the Oxbridge tutorial system would not be possible with UGC staff/student ratios of 1 : 10. But the small group would be feasible under these conditions. He had experienced seminars as a student at Minnesota and a teacher at Pennsylvania. He recalls, it is not an easy medium for the teacher, one has to learn special techniques of setting topics, conducting discussion at a proper intellectual level, bringing out the shy in argument and rationing the voluble . . . but at its best the seminar is more satisfying than the tutorial. I determined to make it the basic teaching unit supplemented by more formal lectures of the traditional kind.[3]

The Vice-Chancellor's close friend Ian Watt, who had come from California, was also deeply committed to the seminar.[4] He said that he found the undergraduate "proseminar" "the most satisfactory method of teaching that I have ever encountered".[5] In Ian Watt's view the seminar had to strike a balance "between autocracy and anarchy". It was best suited to philosophical, literary and historical studies, but less so where the factual basis of a subject was "exceptionally definite". The Hale Committee, to which UEA gave evidence, was supportive of this view, and stressed the importance of active participation by students to exercise the mind, "teaching by discussion rightly used, is a way of making the student do for himself what is too often done for him."[6]

The seminar system did not meet with universal acceptance and it was subject to debate and criticism throughout the sixties. In 1965 a seminar on seminars was held which revealed some important divergences in approach.[7] In literature the view of the seminar was that it should be "self-propelled" after a "launching charge" by the tutor. The students should run it themselves with the tutor becoming unobtrusive and not concerned about the transmission of information. Professor James McFarlane admitted that this was his technique, sitting at the back of the group, not measuring the success of the seminar by how much information was disseminated and accepting that there would be a long period when discussion might be arid.[8] The sciences by contrast had less use for seminar discussion at the undergraduate level. Professor Bennet Clark interposed tellingly that biologists "do not discuss how many petals a buttercup has, they have to learn how to find this fact out. When the fact is then scientifically known it does not lend itself to discussion and opinion."[9] It was evident that there was already a wide variety of attitudes to the seminar, and to its purpose and value.

Malcolm Bradbury wittily caught this confusion of purpose and the vulnerability of the seminar form to the idiosyncrasies of tutors and pupils.[10]

> Classes at Watermouth are not simply occasions for the one-directional transmission of knowledge; no, they are events, moments of communal interaction, or, like Howard's party, happenings ...
>
> There are others where you have to sit and listen to tutors in self-therapy, talking about their problems or their wives or their need to relate; there are other classes where almost the reverse happens, and the students become objects of therapy...

There are classes where the teacher, not wanting to direct the movement of mind unduly, will remain silent throughout the class, awaiting spontaneous explosions of intelligence from his students; there are classes, indeed, where the silence never gets broken. There are other classes where the teacher never appears in person at all, but materializes suddenly into existence on a screen in the corner of the room, beamed there from the audio-visual centre.

This is amusing but the seminar came to be regarded as an element in three problems in the sixties. First, students were sceptical of their value. When opinion was tested in 1968, opinion was cool.[11]

Student attitudes to teaching forms (percentages)

	Lecture	Seminar
Favourable	41	38
Unfavourable	7	23
Non-commital	53	40

Students preferred lectures to seminars, which were too often seen as aimless and insufficiently structured discussion. The danger was that when the "troubles" struck in 1968 the seminar was seen as one source of discontent: they were too large, dominated by too few, insufficiently concerned with learning, and the lecturer had a confused role as both participant but also the judge awarding marks for assessment.[12] The sciences disregarded the system knowing that the seminar arose in nineteenth-century Germany and USA for *postgraduates* but was less appropriate for undergraduates who could not yet be expected to have the background of knowledge to sustain a useful exchange of ideas. Such were the kinds of criticisms levelled at the seminar system in the late sixties.

Second, the seminar system did entail very high costs in faculty time.[13]

Percentage of faculty time spent on

	Undergraduate teaching	Research
1966	56	32
1967	48	25
1972	41	22

It was also evident by 1972 at the professorial level. UEA professors spent much more time on teaching (38 per cent) than the national average (26.1 per cent) but less on research (16.0 per cent) compared with the national average (18 per cent). That UEA professors were spending half the time on research that they spent on teaching, and that that research time was lower than the national average, was dangerous. Teaching at UEA in the 1960s was arduous in getting many courses started and teaching large numbers of small groups.

But it was a high-risk strategy when university reputations were increasingly to be based on research.

The reliance on seminars with a deteriorating staff student ratio posed problems by the end of the Sixties.[14] UEA's staff student ratio was 1 to 12.8 compared with the national average of 1 to 11.08. The distinctive use of seminars and continuous assessment was extremely time-consuming. A working party considered that the only response would be an increase in seminar size, more use of graduate students, fewer seminars, cutting back research time further. A worsening staff student ratio "would certainly involve a jettisoning of some of the most important and basic principles of the University". They were right of course. The ratio did deteriorate and most of their proposals or fears came to pass.

A third possibly adverse effect of seminars was evident in the first EAS degree results in 1966. Of the fifty-five EAS graduates over two thirds (67.2 per cent) gained 2/2 degrees. It suggested that the seminar system applied to literature and history had produced a body of students who simply did not know enough. This, however, may be to take too academic a view. In this 2/2 category were actors, journalists, organisers of all kinds of bodies and events. It is arguable that the seminar system had nurtured these articulate personalities while not raising them to academic excellence or overburdening them with examinable information.

The seminar system was run in conjunction with continuous assessment based on coursework. Students were to gain coursework grades for their essay work and seminar performance and these grades made up a proportion of the final assessment of degree classification along with the final examinations. Coursework could count from 40 per cent to 50 per cent of the whole. This was another idea with which the Vice-Chancellor was familiar in the USA:

> I had long thought that to judge a candidate for a degree entirely on his or her performance in a series of written three hour examinations did not necessarily test the full range of that candidate's capacities. While such an examination was critically important in assessing memory and ability to write lucidly and quickly under stress, it could not assess other qualities equally important, notably the ability to undertake a sustained piece of work over time. Hence I introduced the practice of including coursework marks, especially for term papers, as well as written examination marks as an element in the "Final Assessment" for the final degree.[15]

Thistlethwaite also saw that to gain a grade at the end of a course could be attractive to American visiting students, who could gain credits at UEA they could transfer to their degrees back home. It foresaw the system of the Common Course Structure and portable grades now virtually universal in British universities. But he did not like the idea of continuous assessment when it was interpreted as the testing of students week by week, so that virtually everything they did or said was assessed and credited in some way. Its great virtue has been that it has led to a steady consistent work by students given the reassurance that when they entered the final examinations they already had credit "in the bank" towards the final degree result. A strong critic of the new universities thought that UEA's coursework system, not basing the degree result entirely on final examinations, was "the most important advance in educational practice made by any of the new universities". The stress on coursework further emphasised the importance of the seminar.[16]

UEA presented its views on coursework to the Hale Committee. Hale raised some obvious objections.[17] The coursework component in the final assessment reduced the independent role of the external examiner. The teacher's relationship to the student was also compromised if he was the examiner at the same time as tutor. Hale also shrewdly pointed out the unfairness of counting earlier inferior work alongside mature work in deciding the degree classification. Notwithstanding, students liked the coursework system, 65 per cent claimed to have been attracted to UEA by it. But they came to see its problems. By 1968 a quarter of students thought that coursework took stress out of examinations but 35 per cent thought that it created ongoing stress over a long period. By an extraordinary reversal, nearly two thirds of third years had changed their minds about whether coursework was a good thing or not, probably reflecting the anxieties of the third year.[18]

The distinctive use of the seminar and coursework called for the need for some form of training. Indeed, it was surprising that there was none in the early sixties. But in 1968 a Working Party on the Training of University Teachers was established and they brought in consultants from the Tavistock Institute who ran short courses on group behaviour and small group teaching. Some of this seemed rather weird to the participants - sitting in a group waiting for the tension of silence to force someone to speak - and smacked more of psychiatry than getting on with teaching. But by 1971 forty-eight faculty Training of University Teachers had attended courses at UEA and sixteen had been on away courses, almost all lecturers. Scarcely any senior faculty participated, presumably carrying on what they had been doing in whatever other university they had come from.

Frank Thistlethwaite's basic philosophy of curriculum planning was multi-disciplinary. As a scholar who had moved between and combined history, English and economics he wanted the same intellectual excitement for students that he had found.[19] He was also influenced by the precedents of Keele and Sussex in combining subjects and the belief that "many of the great breakthroughs or growing points have recently been at the interstices between established disciplines".[20] He also hoped to attract faculty who wanted to move away from the departmentalism of Oxford, Cambridge and the civic universities; this was most notable in the attraction of Thomas Bennet Clark from King's College, London. Thistlethwaite also wanted to use the preliminary course to break down the single-subject assumptions of sixth formers.[21] It would also provide a pause to enable them to sample and choose before taking their honours courses without getting too tracked into a specialism in their first year. The idea of a first year in which students mixed the subjects of their Schools up to a preliminary examination was agreed by Arts Deans in 1962.[22]

Thistlethwaite regretted that some faculty wanted to get started on professional training in the first year to prepare for Honours, so moving away from the original intention. This was especially so with the sciences and economics, subjects which were sequential and block-building in their learning process and where specific foundations had to be laid to make future work possible. Stuart Maclure seized on UEA's distinctive "liberality", the keeping of options open which "forces students to be free from the narrower forms of specialisation".[23] He wondered paradoxically whether students given such choice would feel as free as those allowed to "bury themselves from choice in some all-consuming yet lop-sided study". This view was echoed in the University by those who held that "free choice confuses rather than gratifies" and that too many students picked up courses which never constituted "anything as secure and significant as a programme".[24] Thistlethwaite was not then so concerned about unspecialised first degrees, as his assumption was that a third of students would do fourth year postgraduate degrees where appropriate specialism would be possible.[25] It was also a clearly stated assumption of Albert Sloman, the Vice-Chancellor of Essex University.[26]

This attempt to spread the curriculum in the sixties universities was matched by a similar, less successful concern at the sixth form level. The Standing Conference on University Entrance (SCUE), wanted to reduce specialisation and broaden the scope of study in the sixth form. In 1967 they proposed two A's and four elective subjects. In 1968 they proposed five major subjects studied through two years. In 1969 they suggested the replacing of A levels with a first year examination in five subjects a mixture of arts and sciences followed by a second year examination in two or three subjects.[27] Universities became rather punch drunk with these annual proposals, which they regularly rejected. It would have meant students coming up to university less well prepared in the sciences, languages and mathematics. For the arts it might have been of less consequence, even beneficial. The working party came to the view that "there is no pressing need for reform". Though such was the craze for change in the sixties, and the anxiety not to appear resistant to it that the working party made the extraordinarily silly comment that "it would be churlish to oppose reform simply because there is no particular need for it". Good sense, however, prevailed and the University politely told SCUE that change was unnecessary.[28] The "gold standard" of the English A levels was thus preserved. The proposed A level reforms tacitly assumed a "catching up" first year at university and a four year degree. But by the end of the decade it was clear that neither was to materialise.

The Schools at UEA were to be multi-disciplinary, except Chemistry, and students were expected to keep within the School subjects in those days. Students could not initially combine subjects across Schools, though it was expected that there would be pressure for this to carry UEA's interdisciplinarity to its logical conclusion. The vital turning point came in 1967 when a student was allowed to combine courses in philosophy and art history although technically being in the School of Economic and Social Studies.[29] It was an important precedent opening up a healthy trade across Schools in curricular diversification. With these broader considerations in mind let us turn to consider the activities and interests of the Schools themselves.

The founding arts School was that of English Studies. The historians already offered a wide sweep of English history.[30] Dr Jane Martindale and Dr Roger Virgoe covered the early and late middle ages. Dr Hassell Smith's Tudor interests closely linked the School with the region of East Anglia, having worked on the social structure of sixteenth-century Norfolk. A strength of history in the School then lay in seventeenth-century studies. Professor Robert Ashton had started as an economic historian interested in the Crown and the money market. His work at UEA was on the origins of the Civil War, integrating economic with religious, political and social history. The later seventeenth century was covered by Professor J. R. Jones, who was then especially concerned to relate English post-Restoration history to its European setting, notably French and Dutch. The eighteenth century was covered by Dr Brian Hill, then working on Robert Harley, and the early nineteenth by Dr Patricia Hollis. Dr Robert Shannon was the School's specialist on Victorian history with notable interests in Gladstone culminating in his major biography. Shannon also edited a series of books for Routledge aiming to combine the approaches of history and literature then typical of UEA. Indeed from UEA Patricia Hollis, Michael Sanderson and A. E. Dyson contributed volumes to it - an indication of genuine interdisciplinary interests of the time. Dr Geoffrey Searle's sphere was late Victorian and early twentieth-century history; he was then preparing his work on National Efficiency. Finally in 1970 they were joined by Dr Paul Kennedy, a leading authority on twentieth-century British and world history and perhaps the most distinguished historian to pass through UEA.

This was a very able body of scholars. Apart from Ashton and Jones, Shannon, Hassell Smith, Searle and Kennedy all became professors. Kennedy became the prestigious Dilworth Professor at Yale University, a best-selling author and an Hon. Litt D. of UEA. Patricia Hollis, combining an academic career with an outstanding one in public and political service, became the Baroness Hollis of Heigham. Of more importance to the students, they all seemed to be good to excellent teachers. Christopher Wrigley, then a student and himself a future professor, gives a vivid picture of Professor Robert Ashton. "He clearly enjoyed giving them [his lectures], prowling the front of the lecture theatre, varying the volume and tone of his voice in a most theatrical manner. He was a good figure of a man, smartly yet comfortably dressed, moustached." Wrigley was also appreciative of all his teachers, "I think I was very well taught in history . . . all were good."[31]

An important interdisciplinary venture was the Centre of East Anglian Studies to forge further links with the region. This was proposed by Hassell Smith in 1966, who saw it as a coordination of the arts, history, sociology and archaeology.[32] The Vice-Chancellor endorsed this in a speech at Bury St Edmunds in 1967 and he wished to include contemporary economic and social studies in its scope.[33] This was appropriate since Professor C. R. Ross was Deputy Chairman of the East Anglia Economic Development Council. In 1967 the CEAS was established in Earlham Hall under Hassell Smith as Director since it was decided not to have it in Stowmarket as part of a Museum of East Anglian Rural Life but to keep it at UEA.[34] The Vice-Chancellor tried to raise money for it from the Leverhulme Trust, now run by Sir Keith Murray, the former Chairman of the UGC under whose benign influence UEA had been established. Murray made it clear that Leverhulme was not interested in East Anglian Studies as such but that they would support social sciences. This was in accord with the Vice-Chancellor's view, so a project on the location of East Anglian industry was devised and the Leverhulme Trust provided £40,000 in 1968.[35]

The Centre quickly became engaged in other projects by the end of the decade. They compiled an index of materials on East Anglia held in public and private libraries.[36] Particularly important was the Norwich Survey under Alan Carter. This was a study of the archaeology of Norwich and its buildings of the fifteenth to the seventeenth century, financed by Norwich Corporation and the government's Inspectorate of Ancient Monuments. The British Academy supported an edition of the papers of Nathaniel Bacon of Stiffkey, 1547-1622, and a Norfolk volume of the International Corpus of Pre-Reformation Stained Glass. Paul Ashbee, the Centre's archaeologist, continued his work at Sutton Hoo as co-director of the British Museum's excavation there. They also made a major study of the location of industry of

East Anglia. The links with the local community were emphasised by twelve members of the CEAS committee being local laymen, the Chairman, Michael Riviere, being a local businessman and editor of *Norfolk Archaeology*.[37]

With history in EAS was English literature. Its founding Dean was Ian Watt, a former close associate of Frank Thistlethwaite's and one who could bring a historical and sociological dimension to the study of English literature. He was firmly in favour of the association of English literature and history. He told Martin Bell, the television interviewer, that this would provide graduates with "wider interests and training" which would "equip them for a greater variety of things".[38] Notwithstanding Watt's return to the USA, these beliefs remained. His successor was Nicholas Brooke, a specialist in seventeenth-century drama. His colleagues Colin Clarke, Bob Woodings, Roger Fowler, Jocelyn Houseman, Peter Mercer and Lorna Sage were involved in an appropriately wide range of interests - D. H. Lawrence, George Gissing, linguistics, the eighteenth-century novel and critical theory. A. E. Dyson acquired a wider reputation outside literature as the editor of the notorious *Black Papers*, casting doubt on some of the expansionist assumptions of the sixties.

However, what was distinctive about English Literature at UEA was its nurturing of creative writing. The School had two first-rate novelists on the staff: Angus Wilson and Malcolm Bradbury, both later knighted. In the sixties Wilson published fiction,[39] as well as critical work on Jane Austen and Dickens, though he disliked writing criticism at the same time as his novels, the former constraining his imagination. He felt that teaching at UEA had improved his depiction of young people, since he now had more contact with them. He was also keen on the link with history since his early training was as an Oxford historian; it was this aspect of the School that had induced him to accept Ian Watt's invitation to join.[40] Malcolm Bradbury was already a notable humorous novelist as well as a critic of American literature. Unlike Angus Wilson, Bradbury could write criticism (fluently) at the same time as fiction (very slowly). He was soon devastatingly to dissect the follies of a new university (not UEA surely) in *The History Man*. The collaboration of Wilson and Bradbury was to lead to the course on creative writing for which UEA became famous.

Its origins are legendary. Bradbury was attracted to UEA partly by Angus Wilson. Because of the presence of both by the late 1960s a number of undergraduates were encouraged to write, including Rose Tremain, Snoo Wilson and Jonathan Powell. A mysterious course called "Tutorials in American Literature" was set up to enable Snoo Wilson and Powell to write plays under its guise. Angus Wilson and Bradbury then thought of formalising this as an undergraduate course, which was not entirely satisfactory; they then realised that a postgraduate, professionally oriented MA was required. This started in 1970 with a single student, Ian McEwan, a Sussex graduate. His extraordinary success in that year and subsequently helped to kick-start the new course, accepted in the University and of ever increasing reputation at large.[41]

The historians and "lettrists" as they came to be called worked fairly well together, as Thistlethwaite hoped. But there were always fissiparous tendencies under the surface. Michael Beloff on his visit found historians who rejected literary evidence as too impressionistic and who frankly wanted a separate School of History.[42] On the other hand were literary scholars interested in the literary merit of works, irrespective of their historical context, which they regarded as irrelevant. It was a difference of intellectual approach that ultimately led to the split of history and literature in 1994. A more serious problem in the running of the School was the perpetual imbalance of more students studying literature than history, with the best students being those of literature. There were various reasons for this. The name of the School did not readily advertise its historical content to UCCA applicants, and shrewd applicants claimed to be historians to gain easier entry and transferred to literature later, perhaps with the perception that literature was more pleasant than the grind of history. Whatever the reason, literature was always flooded with applicants and transferees.[43] It was an unforeseen problem in running a dual subject School of subjects more diverse than they had been conceived to be.

In 1967 the School became the School of English and American Studies, with a full programme of American history and literature courses being offered. Malcolm Bradbury had joined in 1965 and he was joined by Howard Temperley, an American historian, in 1967. In 1969 they were joined by Christopher Bigsby, the future Professor of American literature, broadcaster and novelist, and Roger Thompson the historian. In contrast with English studies, the Americanists were much firmer in their belief in the unity of literature and history to the extent that the American historians declined to join the School of History in 1994 rather than break their literary links.

In spite of Noel Annan's view that Europe should not be a focus of attention, the Vice-Chancellor decided on a School of European Studies. It was hoped that Geoffrey Barraclough, a distinguished German historian, would start the School as founding Dean but he left for Texas instead. By good fortune this left the way clear for James McFarlane, a former colleague and friend at Newcastle of the Registrar and Secretary George Chadwick. He was a Germanist who had developed an expertise in Scandinavian languages, becoming an authority on Ibsen. He had edited the Oxford edition of Ibsen's work and was recognised with a Norwegian royal decoration. Frank Thistlethwaite describes him as "tall, large and saturnine, Mack had a powerful somewhat Scandinavian presence, great charm and charisma".[44] He had been an Oxford soccer blue and had even played professionally for Sunderland. He and the Vice-Chancellor wanted to develop a strong Russian and Slavic languages sector. The whole thrust of EUR was to be North European German-Scandinavian-Russian. For Frank Thistlethwaite this was a conscious policy: "I was anxious on general grounds to provide a counterpoise to the dominance of French in our literary culture." This was a crucial issue, possibly even a policy mistake, which is worth addressing at the outset.

The APB had been indifferent to French. Frank Thistlethwaite's arrival in July 1961 restored not only European Studies but also the possibility of French.[45] But by the Vice-Chancellor's Report for 1962-63 it was clear that the emphasis would be Slavonic and Northern European. There was seemingly good reason for this. In 1959, when the UEA campaign was beginning, British universities produced 669 graduates in single honours French compared with 265 in German, eighty-one in Spanish, forty in Russian and the rest in small numbers. It made sense for UEA to be different in trying to build up minor languages rather than add to the over-predominance of French graduates.

Yet scarcely had the new School been running for a year than the Vice-Chancellor signalled another change of policy. He admitted that,

> to have excluded France from the initial areas of study of the School when the resources available to the University were necessarily limited . . . was a decision which one realised in advance would bring with it certain embarrassments; nobody pretends that European Studies of any real coherence are possible for long without acknowledging the existence of France and the contribution to Europe of French culture.[46]

Accordingly it was proposed to introduce French Studies at the earliest opportunity, with French language in the language laboratory from September 1964 and full coverage of French literature and language from 1966.

Dr (later Professor) John Fletcher was the first appointment in October 1966 and thereafter French was built up rapidly. French was clearly responding to student demand and in its first year French "rapidly established itself as a large and important sector in the School". Well-qualified applicants for places were much more numerous than for any other sectors of the School. More history majors also preferred to study the French language than any other. Accordingly early policy errors were rectified.

The School started in October 1964. It already had a twenty-booth Tandberg language laboratory providing tuition in nine European languages. The Language Centre emerged as a semi-autonomous unit in 1967 with Veronica du Feu as Director from 1968.[47] The appointment of Dr John

Coates in 1968 enabled UEA to offer the unusual specialisms of Finno-Ugrian studies. Scholarly endeavour flourished. There was McFarlane's work on Ibsen, Anthony Cross's writings on eighteenth-century Russia and the Russo-British link. Also on the literary side, John Fletcher developed studies on Samuel Beckett, Haydn Mason on Voltaire, Brian Rowley on German literature and John Flower on French drama. It was indicative of the quality and quantity of this output that Drs Cross, Mason, Kochan, Berghahn, Flower, Price, Elsworth and Burrow all achieved professorships at other prestigious universities as a result of their UEA work in the sixties. Out of this wide range in literature and various European languages developed the undergraduate programme in Comparative Literature in 1968, with John Fletcher becoming the Professor of Comparative Literature in 1969.

Students of French and German enjoyed the challenge of a year's work and study abroad in those countries. Students of Russian could not then do this but instead were taken on an extended study tour.[48] It was accordingly much more difficult to achieve high language performance in Russian than in other main languages of the School. It was another argument for reinstating French to a central role.

The third arts School was that of Social Studies (later Economic and Social Studies). The Vice-Chancellor looked to Oxford PPE as a model and he took the advice of Sir Roy Harrod, one of the Academic Advisory Committee, about attracting an Oxford economist. Frank Thistlethwaite felt that Roy Harrod was not happy with his appointment, since he would have preferred Robert Blake.[49] So contacting Harrod was politic and it also proved beneficial. Harrod put Thistlethwaite in touch with C.R. "Dick" Ross, Fellow and Bursar of Hertford College, an economic adviser to the Treasury and a member of Lord Franks' World Bank mission to Pakistan.[50] The friendship of Dick Ross and Marcus Dick, the former Senior Tutor of Balliol College and UEA's Professor of Philosophy had the surprising effect of wrong-footing Thistlethwaite. He had intended to include politics in SOC on the Oxford PPE model and had actually interviewed someone for the Chair. He then found that Ross and Dick, both Oxford tutors of PPE, were so hostile to politics as taught at Oxford that they refused to countenance its introduction at UEA. Taken aback by the "revolt", Thistlethwaite agreed. It accounts for the odd feature that puzzled many in SOC at the time, that politics was not there from the start and had to be introduced later when it had no chance to grow to an effective size. However, as in PPE, philosophy was a part of SOC taught by Marcus Dick and colleagues. Although located in SOC philosophy was taught to all the Arts Schools. We shall see more of Marcus Dick later.

Dick Ross was Professor of Economics, Dean of the School of Social Studies and Pro Vice-Chancellor. During his time at UEA, he kept up his

Whitehall contacts and led economic missions to Malta and Tanzania. He left in 1969 to join the OECD, then to become deputy head of the Central Policy Review Staff (the original "Think Tank") in the Cabinet Office and then subsequently as Vice-President of the European Investment Bank in Luxembourg. He was an outstandingly able man ultimately honoured with a CB, and it was UEA's good fortune to have his services in the 1960s.

SOC in the sixties taught economics, sociology, economic history and philosophy, with students majoring in one of the subjects and minoring in one or more of the others. The Vice-Chancellor was keen on sociology. He established it at UEA as a result of his own professional concerns in Cambridge as an economic historian interested in migration. Indeed Frank Thistlethwaite had helped to lay some of the groundwork for its establishment as a Tripos subject.[51] Roy Emerson was the Professor of Sociology and developed a range of valuable research projects at this time. The first of these was the Suffolk Village project, whose aim was to study fifty villages and the effect of urbanisation on rural society.[52] The £12,000 cost was met by East and West Suffolk County Councils and the Social Science Research Council, with Richard Scase (later Professor of Sociology at the University of Kent in Canterbury) doing much of the fieldwork. The report, *Suffolk Some Social Trends*, showed that drift from the land had ceased and that further dramatic decline was unlikely.[53] More importantly it showed Suffolk that UEA was not solely concerned with Norwich and Norfolk. It was an early use of computers in sociological research at UEA and it established sociology as an external grant earner. The next project secured £40,000 from the Leverhulme Trust for a five year study of the location of industry in East Anglia, largely run by Emerson, but as a joint Social Studies and Environmental Studies project under the auspices of the Centre of East Anglian Studies. Thirdly, Emerson began a study of nurse recruitment in Yarmouth and Lowestoft. It drew Emerson into medical sociology and medical administration, ultimately as Chairman of Norfolk Family Practitioner Committee, and much else for which he was awarded the OBE.[54]

The School of Social Studies spawned the Overseas Development Group which came into being in 1967. In the APB Noel Annan had been enthusiastic about developing studies beyond Europe and this was a thread in the thinking behind this. Frank Thistlethwaite also wanted to include Third or Underdeveloped World Studies to balance the emphasis on Europe in EUR. He was equally clear that these should be contemporary rather than historical studies and be actually "concerned with assisting the well-being of the peoples of the developing world".[55] Accordingly Athole Mackintosh was brought in to set up the Group within SOC.[56] Mackintosh had worked in the Treasury, been Deputy Director of the Overseas Development Institute, and had worked on assignments to the Caribbean, Malaysia and Ceylon.[57] The Dean of SOC, Dick Ross, shared such interests himself, having been on economic missions to several developing countries, including Peru, Pakistan and Tanzania. The Group was to be unusual in two ways. The members of the Group would be expected to spend up to a third of their time overseas on research and consultancy assignments or secondment to overseas governments. The Group was also not intended to be fully financed by the University. It was expected partly to finance itself by payments for professional services from governments and aid financing agencies. It became involved in a number of projects worldwide. The most important was in Malaysia, their first team project, evaluating natural resources in Johore. Other members had interests in Caribbean tourism, land reform in Chile and Peru, nutrition in Uganda and much else. In 1973 it was established as the separate School of Development Studies.

Frank Thistlethwaite had a professional interest in several of the subject areas of the Arts Schools considered so far - history, English, economics and sociology. The School of Fine Arts and Music combined two of his private passions. He had long been enthusiastic about architecture and was an accomplished pianist. Frank Thistlethwaite said that he "wanted to bridge the gulf peculiar to this country, between universities and music academies whereby a bright and musically gifted eighteen year old has to choose between a performing career and sacrificing the university experience or vice versa".[58]

Frank Thistlethwaite decided to get advice from Benjamin Britten. He wrote to him in November 1963: "I hesitate to write to you because I know how many demands must be made on your time; but I am most anxious to do what I can to encourage music-making and musical studies in this University . . . and I should greatly value your interest and advice."[59] The Vice-Chancellor had had no connection with Britten up to this point but wrote to him as England's foremost composer. Equally important, Britten was an East Anglian through and through. He was born in Lowestoft, educated at Gresham's School Holt, his first publically performed work was at the Norfolk and Norwich Triennial Festival in 1936, his most famous opera *Peter Grimes* was set in Aldeburgh and *Gloriana* partly in Norwich. He had long been resident in the area, at Snape from 1938 and at Crag House and then the Red House Aldeburgh from 1947, and he had founded the Aldeburgh Festival in 1948. When Frank Thistlethwaite approached him Britten's own career was moving into a period of high prestige. The *War Requiem* had been performed (1962), the Aldeburgh Festival was expanding, he was befriended by royalty and becoming an "establishment figure" from 1963.[60] He was on the eve of receiving the Order of Merit in 1965. In due course, after Britten's return from

Venice where he was writing *Curlew River*, he and Peter Pears and Frank Thistlethwaite met in March 1964.

Britten and Pears gave general encouragement but a subsequent meeting in May attended by Imogen Holst yielded practical advice. Miss Holst, the daughter of Gustav Holst, had been Britten's musical assistant. She was a first-rate teacher and compiled a long memorandum for Frank Thistlethwaite based on her experience at Dartington Hall in the 1940s and 1950s.[61] There was some careful thinking about the client students - performers, teachers, those with a hobby interest - interestingly reflected in Philip Ledger's own later thinking.[62] Holst envisaged a very practical course with orchestras, choirs, composition, sight reading and instrument maintenance. Thistlethwaite was appreciative but then thought that it was more appropriate for a training college and lacked the academic element for a university. He later changed his mind. Ledger's view of the curriculum embodied the inevitable practical training for instrumentalists with more academic matters - history, musical criticism, acoustics, writing on style. The Vice-Chancellor told Britten that to establish music "as an academic discipline, on all fours with the other humanities, the emphasis will inevitably be on music history and criticism". But they would combine this with the practical work for teachers that Imogen Holst envisaged.[63] Britten expressed himself uneasy about "the return to a more academic view of the position",[64] being adamant that the School should combine practical composition and performance with academic studies.[65]

Philip Ledger was appointed as Director of Music in March 1965. The term Director rather than Professor was intended to convey the practical and not exclusively academic nature of the post. A graduate of King's College Cambridge, he had been Master of Music at Chelmsford Cathedral for three years and had been working with Britten at Aldeburgh from 1963. Britten acted as his referee for the UEA post, praising Ledger as "a first-rate musician of quite uncommon gifts . . . a splendid musical scholar".[66] He congratulated the Vice-Chancellor on his "excellent choice for your Director of Music, I am sure all will be well. He is a close friend of both Imogen Holst and myself".[67] It forged further UEA links with Britten and Aldeburgh. In 1965 Britten also became President of the University Music Society and Honorary Music Adviser to the University. Links were also forged with Norwich Cathedral, the Organist Brian Runnett being also a part-time lecturer at the University while the Dean and Chapter established an organ scholarship tenable by a music student at UEA.[68]

The School of Fine Arts and Music began in the Village in October 1965. Although they had only two music students, the musicians made an impact with a splendid production of Handel's *Saul* in May 1966. This followed a fine

Dido and Aeneas in 1965, performed by the Music Society before the creation of FAM. The Council made a grant to Ledger to enable him to mount a series of choral and orchestral concerts at St Andrews Hall. The Aeolian String Quartet also accepted an invitation to make UEA its base, playing chamber concerts and helping the student string players.[69] Peter Pears held master classes at UEA in April 1967,[70] and when the Queen opened the new Aldeburgh Festival Concert Hall in the Maltings in Snape in June 1967 Ledger was the organist and the UEA choir sang.[71] Ledger became Artistic Director of the Aldeburgh Festival and directed the Festival Singers from 1968 to 1973. It had been intended to award the degree of Hon. Mus. D. to Britten with the first group of honorary graduands in 1966 but his serious ill health prevented this. The degree was eventually conferred in 1967 in a joint ceremony with Sir Frederick Ashton. Curiously, although Britten appreciated the honour, such ceremonies left him feeling depressed (he declined an invitation to the pre-Congregation dinner). To cheer himself up after the event he drove from UEA to Lowestoft, to visit his family home and buy some bloaters before returning to Aldeburgh.[72] His real appreciation was shown in his conducting two performances of the *War Requiem* in Norwich Cathedral on 1 and 2 December 1967.[73] Ledger was co-conductor and Mary Wells (Mrs Ledger) and Peter Pears were soloists. It was a most impressive event with choirs and orchestra in the nave and the audience in the clerestory, some of whom were visibly moved by the performance. This was a high point of the University's musical impact on Norwich in the sixties.

Music needed its own purpose-built premises and this was made possible by a grant from the Nuffield Foundation. The Foundation decided to make a "birthday gift" to all the new universities and the Vice-Chancellor wished to use this for a Music Centre with a concert room, electronic music studio, practice rooms and offices.[74] There was also an Aldeburgh link here. The Music Centre was designed and built by Philip Dowson of Ove Arup. Arup's who had built the main buildings of the Maltings at Snape in 1967, also built the Pears-Britten Music School at Snape shortly after that at UEA. Britten took a direct interest in the new music building at UEA. Ledger recalled "I did talk to Ben about the new UEA Music Centre and he was deeply concerned to achieve proper soundproofing. Derek Sugden helped John Braithwaite with this".[75] Derek Sugden was Arup's authority on musical acoustics and both the Maltings and UEA benefited from his expertise. Philip Ledger and Julian Webb of UEA provided the music for the acoustic tests of the Maltings in 1967 and the rebuilt Maltings in 1970. UEA's Music School opened in 1973.

Music was also helped by the foundation of the Arthur Batchelor Lectures, endowed by his daughter Diana in 1963. Batchelor was an artist who lived in Norwich from 1912 and was active in both artistic and musical circles. He helped run the Norwich String Quartet Concerts which Britten had attended as a young man. His daughter Diana used to play in an amateur orchestra run by Imogen Holst. Fittingly Miss Holst gave the first Arthur Batchelor lectures on some East Anglian Composers.[76] Another benefit to the UEA music students was the Hesse student scheme for attending the Aldeburgh Festival. Princess Margaret of Hesse had the idea of bringing young students to Aldeburgh by providing the cost of tickets and bed and breakfast accommodation.[77] In return, the students would help with the running of the Festival. The scheme was already operating from 1959 before UEA started and so provided another opportunity for UEA students to widen their education. UEA students became Hesse students in the 1960s and learnt much about festival and concert management. The UEA choir also had the chance of singing at Aldeburgh with the Festival Singers and the Festival Chorus. They were rigorously auditioned and the Norwich section (including the best of other local choirs as well as UEA) was rehearsed by Philip Ledger in Norwich before going to Snape.

Music was especially noteworthy at UEA in the sixties and provided that mix of the academic and the practical that Frank Thistlethwaite had wanted. Much was owed to the Aldeburgh connection and to Britten himself, who "really minded" about UEA.[78] Britten, unlike Peter Pears, was always uneasy about academics but he cared about the musical education of the young and about East Anglia. This underlay his genuine support for UEA. So did the mutual regard of Britten and Ledger and the energy of the latter. Ledger left UEA to return to King's College, Cambridge, as Director of Music and thence to be Principal of the Royal Scottish Academy of Music and Drama, for which he was knighted.

Fine visual art was the other part of FAM. Frank Thistlethwaite's original intention was to unite the fine arts in a way that would bring together like-minded people. He also wanted to get away from a too theoretical academic approach to art which dominated British universities, largely through the influence of the Courtauld Institute. He wanted to break down the distinction between the university department and the art school and "broaden the conventional syllabus to include such subjects as aesthetics and the actual creation of art objects". Thistlethwaite pursued the tiny handful of people who were both skilled practising artists and also historians and critics, but to no avail. The Vice-Chancellor then consulted Sir Anthony Blunt, the Director of the Courtauld Institute, whom he had known at Cambridge in the 1930s even though Blunt "presided over the institution which was the embodiment of the Germanic tradition of art history which I was trying to break away from." With Blunt's help Peter Lasko was appointed as the first professor; he was Courtauld educated, an Assistant Keeper at the British

Museum and an expert in early medieval art. A Berliner, he had attended the same school there as the Librarian Willi Guttsman. UEA thus came within the orbit of the Courtauld's influence, contrary to Frank Thistlethwaite's intentions.[79] Indeed Lasko eventually left UEA to succeed Blunt as the Director of the Courtauld. It was another pleasing irony that when rankings were given to university departments for research, UEA and the Courtauld were two out of only three departments sharing the very highest grade.

What was lost was a vision that the UEA School of Fine Arts would be a practical school engaging not only in academic work but in practical painting, pottery, scenery design, and having close links with the Norwich School of Art. One evening the Vice-Chancellor had a flash of this vision in Philip Ledger's production of *Saul* combining music, stage and costume design, theatre production and remarkable choreography (by Jenny Abramsky then a student and later BBC Executive and Controller of BBC Radio). Otherwise the artists turned their attention to becoming a first-rate department of academic art history. They rapidly built up collections of 100,000 prints and 30,000 slides necessary for teaching and started vacation courses to enable students to undertake projects abroad or elsewhere in Britain during the summer. The most important development of this was the scheme to study in Venice at the Venezia Isola degli Studi which already catered for Warwick students.[80] This began in 1972. The art historians in the sixties did not have that high profile the musicians had gained from the Britten-Aldeburgh-Ledger link or the same opportunity for public performance and display. But they got on with their work and published eight books between 1967 and 1972 on a range of subjects from Gothic Art to Pier Francesco Mola, from the kingdom of the Franks to Victorian architecture. It laid the foundations for a reputation which was to attract the gift of the Sainsbury Collection and Building in the 1970s and UEA's emergence as one of the major British centres of art history.

Biology was a particularly appropriate study for East Anglia. It is the richest agricultural region in the country and also important for forestry, particularly in the Brecklands around Thetford. There were important fisheries in the coastal towns and a fishery research station at Lowestoft. Most of the manufacturing industries of the region were biologically based - starch, mustard, confectionery, leather, fertiliser and pharmaceuticals. The Natural History societies of Norfolk and Suffolk were among the most active in Britain and the Norfolk Naturalists' Trust which owns and manages many nature reserves was the first county Naturalists' Trust to be formed in 1926. The strong natural history tradition, its varied ecology and terrain and bio-based economy all called for the study of biological sciences at the new university.[81]

The shape of the School of Biological Sciences (BIO) was formed by discussion between Thomas Bennet Clark and Sir Solly Zuckerman. Both were agreed on the integration of Botany and Zoology. Indeed it was the narrowness of the study of biology at the University of London that had driven Bennet Clark from King's College London to start the new venture in Norwich. A root of the thinking of both Bennet Clark and Zuckerman was the Royal Society Report on Biology in 1961.[82] This was concerned that there were still too many departments teaching classical descriptive biology rather than developing newer analytic forms such as the borderlands of biophysics, biochemistry and genetics. They recommended a new School of Biology not divided into formal departments but with more application of physics and chemistry to the subject. The report finished presciently, "the creation of new universities offers an admirable opportunity for experimenting in this way". This was in line with Bennet Clark's thinking; indeed he was a member of the Advisory Council on Scientific Policy which requested the Royal Society to write the report in the first place. As an FRS and senior Professor of Botany he was of course consulted by the committee writing the report. So there was a consonance between Zuckerman's scheme for UEA in 1960, the Royal Society report of 1961 and Bennet Clark's well-known views.

In 1962 Bennet Clark began to form his School. He wanted Jack Dainty as Professor of Biophysics. Dainty was a rare example of a physicist genuinely interested not only in biology but in the natural history and nature reserves of the Norfolk coast.[83] Bennet Clark envisaged himself as the Professor of Botany and Dainty as Professor of Biophysics, both supported by Readers in Zoology and Biochemistry. Zuckerman was concerned at this, fearing that emphasising biophysics so early would make BIO "more off-centre than I believe would be acceptable to many".[84] Zuckerman wanted a chair of biophysics in the "near future" but not at the expense of a chair in zoology. Zuckerman felt the need for more animal physiology than Bennet Clark was proposing. After conversations with Thistlethwaite, Bennet Clark hastened to reassure Zuckerman.[85] In the study of morphology "animals must bulk larger than plants" and there would be a Professor of Zoology so animals would not be neglected. Bennet Clark was well aware that in the Royal Society Council botanists were "a very small and powerless minority", compared with animal interests. At UEA, "I want to hold an even balance". Accordingly zoologist J.A. Kitching FRS was appointed to the third chair. BIO gave UEA two Fellows of the Royal Society at its outset, placing it nineteenth in rank order of British universities with Fellows of the Royal Society, and the best of the new universities.[86]

BIO embarked on a wide range of research initially in a prefab built in the back yard of Earlham Hall.[87] Dainty worked on the salt and water relations in

plants and their uptake of food through the roots. Kitching studied the physiology of a single-celled organism living in ponds. He was noted for his
annual expeditions with students to his own marine laboratory at Lough Ine
in Ireland to study anemones, sea urchins and crabs. Dr Croghan was likewise
concerned with sea creatures, the crustacea of the Baltic, and Dr G. C. Kearn
with fish parasites. This interest in marine matters gave a useful point of association for East Anglian sea and river interests. Three members of the School,
Dr Hewitt, Dr Gibson and Dr Balls, were involved with animal genetics,
Hewitt with locusts and Balls with large South African toads. Gibson's work
was the most relevant to medical research being concerned with the biology
of schizophrenia. The biochemists, led by Dr David Davies, formed a distinct
body. They examined the "pathway" of chemical events controlling growth in
plants. Dr Maurice Wilkins studied "biological clocks" influencing the
growth and flowering of plants. Dr Shelton was concerned with the respira-
tion of the lower vertebrates, finding that diving ducks reduced their heart-
beats tenfold when under water. Dr Noble Nesbitt studied insects able to
absorb water from the atmosphere, while Dr Brian Lewis sought to eradicate
the fungus infection of crops and stored vegetables.[88]

BIO had some interesting facilities. Pride of place was the £156,000 Philips
EM 200 electron microscope which could create images of x 2 million magni-
fication from 20-70 millionths of a millimetre sections. This was the equivalent of a pinhead three and a half miles wide. The School also had the use of a
considerable botanical garden made available through the generosity of
Maurice Mason. Mr Mason was a farmer at Fincham near Swaffham who
journeyed every winter to the tropics and sub tropics in search of new plants.
He had been doing this for twenty years and on his fifteen acre site at Talbot
Manor had accumulated a collection of considerable importance. He allowed
it to be used as a university botanical garden and after his retirement
proposed to give it to the University along with his valuable botanical
library.[89] UEA, however, never took possession, due to its distance from
Norwich.

At the end of the sixties Bennet Clark looked back on the problems of
carrying out his scheme. In particular he found the level of mathematics of
school leavers insufficient for what he wanted them to do at UEA.
Accordingly he had had to undertake too much remedial mathematical
teaching at the expense of the botany and zoology they had come to study.
This led to further problems, since BIO claimed to cover so much in its quest
for the integration of so many aspects of biology. He feared he was producing
jacks of all trades and found the cutting back of branches of biology exacerbated the "inadequacy" of the scheme.[90] He tried to increase the specialisation in the later part of the course but recognised that it really needed an

added fourth year. When the Village opened Bennet Clark was interviewed by Martin Bell for BBC TV.[91] Bell was rather sceptical when assured that UEA would not only cover a wider range of biology than elsewhere but would be specialised as well. The realities of the sixties forced Bennet Clark privately to recognise that Bell's polite scepticism was justified.

The firm establishment of Biology led to further developments at UEA. The Agricultural Research Council felt that many of their research institutes were too isolated and that there was a danger that they would run out of steam for lack of stimulating contact with other scholars. Accordingly it was ARC policy under Sir Gordon Cox to site research institutes near to universities.[92] Cox saw UEA as such a linkage and several factors must have weighed with him. Bennet Clark was a prominent member of the ARC and under him biological research was a forte at UEA. East Anglia was a premier region for agriculture and Sir Solly Zuckerman, a keen supporter of UEA, was a powerful influence on all science policy. Zuckerman chaired the committee urging the resiting of research institutes near to universities and this influenced the ARC and its specific view of UEA as such a university.[93] Cox came to the view that UEA was a suitable University to act as a unifying nucleus for a constellation of Research Institutes.[94] Accordingly the Food Research Institute in Bristol was divided into two, with Bristol left to concentrate on red meat and all other food research transferred to a Food Research Institute in Norwich adjacent to UEA. It was set up in 1964 and moved to its present Colney Lane site in 1968. It was joined by what had been the Low Temperature Research Station in Cambridge, originally dating from the early 1920s. This closed in 1966 and part of it continued as part of the new FRI at UEA. The FRI developed a special interest in potatoes, poultry and eggs, soft fruit and food chemistry and microbiology generally.[95]

This was also the case with the John Innes Institute. John Innes had made his money in the wine trade and property development. On his death in 1904 he left money for the founding of a Horticultural Institute at Merton Park and Manor. Under its first two directors, William Bateson and Sir Daniel Hall, it developed as a world centre for plant genetics - indeed it was Bateson who first used the term "genetics" in 1905. With the outbreak of the Second World War the Institute moved from Merton to Bayfordbury on the outskirts of Hertford. In 1945 it came under the Ministry of Agriculture and from 1956 under the ARC. In the 1950s it was a very strong centre for genetics, plant breeding and cell biology applied to a whole range of plants from tomatoes and roses to potatoes (with the Commonwealth Potato Collection) and soft fruits. To associate this powerful research tradition and expertise with that of BIO under Bennet Clark - who was already on the Board of the Institute before he came to UEA - would create a major mutually stimulating nexus of biological research.[96] This is what Cox and Zuckerman envisaged. As early as 1963 a scheme was drawn up indicating the strengths the John Innes Institute could bring to UEA.[97] Senate determined "that every effort be made to foster a close association between the University and the John Innes Institute".[98] Accordingly the Institute hoped to move to Colney, just across the river from the Plain early in 1967. They would also have a field station of 165 acres at Stanfield near East Dereham. The wealth of the John Innes charity also enabled them to establish three chairs in the School of Biology, in applied genetics, cell biology and pure genetics. So the staff of the Institute would enrich the teaching of biology.[99] Productivity of British farmers nearly doubled between the 1950s and 1990s: improved crop varieties were a major element in this with the John Innes Institute as a "main centre".[100]

Gordon Cox wanted the John Innes Institute to fuse with Professor Roy Markham's department of microbiology at Cambridge on its move to Norwich. This was done and Markham became the new Director of the Institute. He made a shrewd initial decision. He was clear that he wanted the new permanent buildings of the Institute to be built across the river on the other side of Colney Lane and not on the Plain as part of the Lasdun buildings, "adjacent" to BIO as Frank Thistlethwaite had assumed in 1966 in his letter to Zuckerman. The point was of some significance, since there was some anxiety that the John Innes Institute would be swallowed up and lose its identity in UEA. A slight distancing, a pleasant walk through a wood, over the river Yare and across the lane was a gentle assertion of this independence. Far from becoming an absorbed sub-section of BIO, the John Innes Institute remains wealthy and prestigious, recognised by the award of a knighthood in 1995 to Professor Sir David Hopwood FRS, the John Innes Professor of Genetics.

At the same time as the John Innes Institute came to Colney Lane, the FRI and the British Sugar Corporation laboratories were being built on the Plain side of Colney Lane. The research staff of the British Sugar Corporation also moved in August 1967 from Bramcote near Nottingham to their new laboratories at Colney Lane.[101] These were opened by Fred Peart in 1968 and Sir Edmund Bacon, the Chairman of the BSC for eleven years then retired, content at this fusion of his BSC and UEA interests.

The other major centre associated with UEA was the Lowestoft Fisheries Laboratory.[102] This remained, of course, in Lowestoft where it provided space and supervision for marine biologists; conversely, staff of the laboratory could study for doctorates in BIO and their senior specialists taught at UEA as honorary lecturers while the director was given professorial status. Since a number of BIO faculty already had marine interests it was a good marriage. In its links with the FRI, JII, BSC and the Fisheries Laboratory BIO contributed to a powerful network of biological research all of whose components were particularly appropriate for the East Anglian region.

There had been the assumption in the early days of the UEA movement that the region wanted a School of Agriculture at the new university. [103] Yet East Anglia was quite well supplied with agricultural education and research. These included the Norfolk Experimental Farm at Sprowston, the Ministry of Agriculture Experimental Husbandry Farms at Terrington and Boxworth, the Norfolk School of Agriculture at Easton taking fifteen to eighteen year olds, the Burlingham Horticultural Station, King's Lynn Technical College for agricultural education; and there was a good day release agricultural and horticultural apprenticeship scheme. Necessary graduates could come locally from Cambridge.

The promoters had the problem of suggesting that the University would be useful to local agriculture without raising expectations unrealistically. In July 1961 the Appeal Committee "strongly advocated setting up a faculty of agriculture and allied food technology" because of "the concentration in East Anglia of large companies concerned in the agricultural and food industries". However by the end of the year the policy was clear that "the undergraduate study of agriculture is at present adequately covered by other universities".[104] So they would concentrate on developing biology and consider agricultural education at the postgraduate level later. In any case agricultural colleges were increasing in scope and most training of farmers was likely to be done there.[105] The Vice-Chancellor explained this view in tours around the region in early 1962, though some local farmers still regretted that there was no chair of agriculture.[106] By the time the University opened it had a firm and credible position. Bennet Clark explained to the Norfolk Agricultural Club that UEA was not going to have a School of Agriculture because the UGC had decided to have no more. But UEA would offer a School of Biology with its feet "firmly in the mud".[107] BIO's range of research, and its close links with its associated Research Institutes often supported by the ARC, was a fair response to the expectations of the farming community. It soon became clear that UEA was right not to have an agriculture faculty (not that it had any choice) when in 1966 the UGC reviewing the demand for agriculture graduates suggested that some university agriculture departments should close down.

Another of the new science Schools was that of Environmental Sciences. It will be remembered that Solly Zuckerman had persuasively argued for this in the APB and that it was to be of a more scientific character than the geography advocated by Lincoln Ralphs.[108] Thistlethwaite was keen on Zuckerman's ideas, though there was no obvious English precedent. Thistlethwaite visited various schools of earth sciences in the USA for ideas. It was difficult to start, because each of the external assessors wanted to appoint a Dean in their own specialism.[109] "Environmental" could mean almost anything. A School of Environmental Studies had opened at Lancaster University in 1963 with a botanical and geographical emphasis which then shifted abruptly to the study of the physics of the upper atmosphere. UEA had actually been sent some proposals for a Faculty of Field Sciences - biology, geography, geology, climatology, oceanography, geophysics in the context of agriculture and forestry.[110] It was evident that almost anything could be included here. Thistlethwaite wanted to stick to Zuckerman's ideas as a firm rock in a potential quagmire. He told Zuckerman in 1965 "it is important that you should like it because the original idea was yours".[111] To resolve the focus of the new School Thistlethwaite asked two of the most impressive interviewees for the post of Dean to discuss the problem with him and a few colleagues. These were Keith Clayton, a geographer from LSE, and Brian Funnell, a geologist from Cambridge. After a round table discussion on 25 February 1967, Thistlethwaite amazed the pair by offering the job of creating the School to both of them. They accepted. Thistlethwaite was delighted that this combination of earth sciences and geography reaching into social sciences was in the Zuckerman spirit. He wrote to Zuckerman many years later, "you will be glad to know that the structure of studies is still very largely faithful to your original idea".[112]

The School opened in October 1967, with Keith Clayton as Dean. They started with the physics, chemistry and biology of the earth and locational analysis. Most notably, considerable time was to be spent in the field using the coastal and inland terrain of Norfolk as a field laboratory - "pebble collection outings to Cromer on a cold foggy day" as a student affectionately remembered.[113] To this end they acquired various pieces of equipment both delicately scientific (the stereoscan electron microscope) and the rugged (a three ton lorry, a drilling rig and the bottom thirty feet of a bore hole in the Antarctic ice sheet). It well illustrated the mixed scientific and practical character of the School. It clearly proved attractive since they received six hundred applications and a quarter making ENV their first choice, the highest proportion in the University. After the first year students studied economic geography, geophysics, hydrology, oceanography, rock chemistry and soil science, urban and regional planning, then meteorology and climatology, tropical resources and ecology. It was a rich and attractive mix.

They began with a wide range of research interests. Most notably the Natural Environment Research Council provided support for a major study of Broadland's pollution and the seeping of nitrates into the water and its consequent clogging with weeds. The NERC also financed a study by Dr John Tarrant on the vexed question of Norfolk hedgerows, their destruction and contribution to the ecology. One unusual investigation bringing home the practical value of environmental studies was an estimation of the position of a crashed plane, calculated from the position of recovered debris and bodies. This was done by Dr J. G. Harvey for the Navy. Professor Clayton began his long-term work on coastal erosion on the East Anglian coast and studies in the North Sea and the Wash with the research boat *Envoy*. In 1969-70 the School enticed Fred Vine from Princeton, who was notable for his work on the geology of the Pacific Ocean floor. He was soon, as one of the pioneers of the study of ocean floor spreading, a fundamental part of the theory of plate tectonics, to become the youngest Fellow of the Royal Society in 1974. Then in 1970-71 ENV marked a new growth by securing finance for a Unit of Climatic Research to be led by Professor Hubert Lamb of the Meteorological Office, a pioneer of historical climate change. The development of ENV under Keith Clayton was one of the successes of UEA in the 1960s. In 1971 Clayton was appointed to the Natural Environment Research Council and the Nature Conservancy. His subsequent appointment to the UGC and service as its Vice-Chairman earned him a CBE. Frank Thistlethwaite regarded him as "one of UEA's most distinguished founding fathers".

Chemical Sciences at UEA were forged out of a significant controversy at a high level which throws light on the working of the scientific establishment of the 1960s and its curricular attitudes. The APB, and especially Sir Christopher Ingold, the physical chemist, envisaged an interdisciplinary group of physical sciences. Thistlethwaite recalled "as a Board we remained determined not to succumb to conventional departmental rigidities. We were feeling our way towards some sort of interdisciplinary grouping of physical sciences led by the central discipline of chemistry".[114] However, when they came to appoint the first professor early in 1962 they had to choose between two contrasting views. One was a physical chemist in the Ingold mould interested in the interdisciplinary linkages UEA espoused. The other was Alan Katritzky, the ultimate appointee. He was thirty-one, "breathtakingly young, abrasively dynamic and with the firmest ideas". He was an organic chemist, a Fellow of Churchill College, Cambridge, and a lecturer in Sir Alexander Todd's department. One of his "firm ideas" was that he should be the head of a single-subject chemistry department, not one accommodating other disciplines as Ingold and the APB wanted. Thistlethwaite needed Katritzky's dynamism and leadership and was prepared to sacrifice the interdisciplinary ideal for it in this instance, chemistry being a universe of sciences in itself.

The matter did not end there, for even after he was appointed Katritzky felt that he had to fight a long-running battle through 1962. He was suspicious that Thomas Bennet Clark (whom he regarded as a "socialist" and a "burst professor") wanted chemistry merely as a "minor appendage" to biology. He was also resentful of the lingering influence of Ingold. He challenged Frank Thistlethwaite: "Who did he think should determine the syllabus for chemistry; the new professor in whom he should have every confidence, or Sir Christopher Ingold?"[115]

In May Katritzky sent a long memorandum to the Vice-Chancellor urging a separate School of Chemistry,[116] outlining its curriculum and proposing a rapid build up of students to 310 undergraduates and 101 research students by 1969. Katritzky was accordingly dismayed when talks with the Registrar on 6 June revealed that the science build up was to be much slower than he had assumed and that his claims for a separate Department of Chemistry were being undermined. Katritzky felt he had a battle on his hands, especially since he had just declined the chair at Munich and arranged to sell his Cambridge house.[117] He was adamant that he was not leaving Cambridge to come to "an American liberal Arts College or a glorified technical college" in Norwich. Katritzky began to elicit support. He went to see the Master at Churchill College, Sir John Cockcroft, to tell him his problems on 12 June.[118] Although Katritzky did not know it, Cockcroft acted speedily. The next day he drove to Norwich to see Thistlethwaite and the day after that to see Lord Mackintosh at Cley. He was going to visit Solly Zuckerman, nearby at Burnham Thorpe, after that but the meeting was cancelled; instead he wrote to Zuckerman about it rather later, by which time Zuckerman was well informed of the issue.[119] Sir Christopher Ingold, unaware of Cockcroft's soundings, reiterated his strong opposition to what he saw as Katritzky's undermining of the APB plans. Ingold told Thistlethwaite, "I think that chemistry would commit scientific suicide if it should cut itself even partly off from its stem. Ideally physics and chemistry are one subject and should be run by a single scientific team." He pointed out from his own syllabus at University College, London, the common need of chemistry and physics for thermodynamics, kinetic theory and atomic structure; "my main purpose is to illustrate the magnitude of the needs of chemistry for cooperation from the more basic science of physics".[120]

The difference between Katritzky and Ingold and the whole role of chemistry at UEA was thrashed out at a meeting between Katritzky, Ingold, Thistlethwaite and Zuckerman in the University of London Senate House on 24 August 1962. Thistlethwaite explained the situation to Zuckerman, that Katritzky "is very chemistry orientated and although he is quite prepared to include a fair proportion of physics, mathematics and biology in his first year course, he is anxious that these ancillary subjects should be tailored to chemistry". Ingold "is unhappy about this and rather suspects Katritzky, who in any case is not his kind of chemist, of trying to take the bit between his teeth".

But Thistlethwaite was concerned "we should be careful not to dampen Katritzky's quite remarkable energy and enthusiasm for we cannot do without it".[121] Zuckerman duly replied that he was on Ingold's side, "what Katritzky proposes doing is not in line with the general conception which we agreed for the science Schools".[122] For Zuckerman chemistry was more closely linked with physics than with biology and Katritzky was wrong to divide it.

Katritzky could not know that Zuckerman had already taken up a hostile position before the 24 August meeting, since he looked to Zuckerman to counteract Ingold. Katritzky shrewdly continued building up support elsewhere. He contacted Sir Robert Robinson, his former Oxford tutor and mentor. As a Nobel prizewinner and member of the Order of Merit Robinson's views carried considerable weight. Katritzky sent Robinson a copy of his proposals for the School of Chemistry and duly received his approval.[123] He was thus able to tell the Vice-Chancellor on the eve of the 24 August meeting that Sir Robert Robinson approved his plans and "Lord Todd [the Professor of Chemistry at Cambridge]) was in full agreement with my approach".[124]

When the Senate House meeting took place Zuckerman was not present - his absence, given his preconceived support of Ingold, helping Katritzky. Also Cockcroft had still not made representations to Zuckerman on Katritzky's part. But in "a long and heated meeting" on the 24 August Katritzky found that he was supported by Bennet Clark, "who agrees completely with my view", against Ingold's stubborn difficulty.[125] At this meeting a curriculum was agreed heavily weighted to chemistry as Katritzky wanted - 50 per cent in the first year, 80 per cent in the second and 100 per cent in the third. Katritzky was content with this but was concerned that Ingold still wanted a combined School of Physics and Chemistry under a Physicist Dean. Katritzky kept Robinson informed and asked for any further support he could give. Sir Robert replied forcefully, "I should like to contest strongly the extraordinary idea that chemistry is a branch of physics . . . this ridiculous contention must be squashed at an early stage or it will do a great deal of damage".[126] To this Katritzky was able to add evidence from Sussex, where the subsuming of chemistry in a School of Physical Sciences had led to a lack of representation for scientists as a whole and the treatment of the Professor of Chemistry as a surrogate Dean. "Eaborn [the Professor of Chemistry] advises me strongly to ensure that mistakes made at Sussex were not repeated at East Anglia, and he felt that an independent School of Chemistry was of primary importance."[127]

Katritzky's point carried the day. The APB agreed to establish three independent Schools, Biology, Chemistry, and Mathematics and Physics, each under its own Dean with Katritzky as Dean of the School of Chemical

Sciences.[128] Behind these struggles of 1962 lay issues much wider than those of UEA. In chemical education at that time there was a fundamental difference between two traditions - that of Oxford, which was very focused on single-subject chemistry and that of Cambridge, with a broader more interdisciplinary degree. Katritzky was a graduate of Oxford though a teacher at Cambridge and, aware of both traditions, much preferred the former. This conflict of traditions was further overlaid by the long-standing rivalry and even personal antagonism of Sir Christopher Ingold and Sir Robert Robinson. This directly affected UEA because of Ingold's membership of the APB and of Katritzky being a pupil and protégé of Robinson. This fed into Ingold's suspicion of Katritzky with his Robinson connection and his espousal of an Oxford-type single-subject chemistry curriculum. The clash had already been evident at Katritzky's selection interview in March 1962, when Ingold opposed Katritzky and Dr J. W. Linnet from Oxford supported him. Katritzky regarded the personal antagonism of Robinson and Ingold (sometimes regarded as the finest British chemist not to win a Nobel Prize) as a great pity for British chemistry. He later tried to build bridges with Ingold and felt that Sir Christopher was won over to UEA by the professorial appointments of Norman Sheppard and especially Stephen Mason, whom Ingold particularly liked.

This controversy and Katritzky's part in it had several implications for UEA. First, it meant that an Oxford approach to chemistry came to UEA rather than a Cambridge or UCL one. Secondly, Katritzky asserted the principle of the single-subject school against the prevailing ethos of multidisciplinarity which shaped the other Schools and which was central to Thistlethwaite's thinking and that of the APB. In retrospect Thistlethwaite takes the view that Katritzky was undoubtedly right.[129] Sir Charles Wilson, with long experience of many universities, reflects that chemists usually prefer to be in single-subject departments, just as biologists often like to be interdisciplinary. UEA was true to form.[130] Thirdly, Katritzky, by insisting on being his own Dean, and for more than the normal three years, won Thistlethwaite over to the need for strong management especially in expensive science schools.[131] Katritzky and the School of Chemical Sciences were thus elements challenging the UEA aversion to single-subject disciplines and professorial hierarchy, though for Katritzky chemistry was a multidisciplinary subject in itself.

Katritzky quickly built his staff, six from Cambridge and two from Oxford (Katritzky had doctorates from both), including Norman Sheppard, the distinguished physical chemist who was lured from a fellowship at Trinity College Cambridge.[132] As the course evolved, many of Ingold's objections would have been allayed. The five week introductory course covered atomic and molecular structure and kinetics - the kind of subjects referred to in Ingold's letter to the Vice-Chancellor in June. The research of the School "covers the range of synthetic, structural and kinetic problems in all of the main branches of chemistry . . . a principal general interest which serves to unify the research effort of the School is the development and the application of various branches of chemical spectroscopy". Katritzky's own speciality was heterocyclic chemistry in which he became a leading world authority. Norman Sheppard's was in infrared and Stephen Mason's in ultraviolet spectroscopy.

Katritzky was proud of the fact that in the five years 1964-70 he had rapidly expanded the School to 206 undergraduates. But this was only achieved by admitting applicants with the lowest A level admissions requirements in the University (CCD, or even three Es for those who put UEA first choice).[133] Following this, numbers were drastically cut back and the 1970 level was not attained again until twenty-three years later in 1993. The policy with postgraduates was also unusual. Again Katritzky's determination to build a large graduate School (ninety-two by 1970) led to their accepting postgraduates of low first degree level. In 1966 it was quite the largest graduate School (eighty-one) but with only a quarter of their postgraduates having first class or upper second degrees. Biology by contrast had only thirty-four postgraduates but with two thirds having firsts or 2/1s.[134] Yet this was not so ill judged as it might appear, since about half the chemistry postgraduates took up industrial employment, whereas most other Schools' postgraduates went overwhelmingly into academic careers.[135] There was clearly a demand in the chemical industry for competent but not academically first-rate entrants which the School could supply in good number. Katritzky took the view that A levels were not a good predictor of degree success; he wanted to give more potential students a chance and believed that more young people should have been going to university in the sixties. As regards his postgraduates, he took many Cambridge 2/2s, of good quality. Above all, he saw the need to develop the School rapidly and sizeably and especially the need to create a large graduate School active in research.

Forged in controversy, Katritzky's creation and running of CHE in the sixties, while out of tune with some UEA attitudes of that decade, presaged certain features of the future. The move to single-subject degrees, scepticism against combining too many subjects superficially (contrary to Bennet Clark's optimism about biology), the insistence on strong management, and the willingness to go for rapid growth at the expense of formal qualifications, the driving emphasis on research, all made CHE unusual in the sixties but foresaw attitudes of the late 1980s and 1990s. He created a notable School and brought a forcefulness that Thistlethwaite knew he could not do without.

The School of Mathematics and Physics opened in 1964 without the birth pangs surrounding Chemistry. The obvious connection of physics and mathematics was uncontentious and students of both followed a common first year. Donald Osborne from Cambridge became the first Professor of Physics and Dean. He described the mutual interests of the School neatly:

> the concern of the mathematicians for fluid mechanics is matched by that of the physicists for liquid helium and liquid metals, and the mathematicians interested in solid mechanics have ideas to exchange with solid state physicists. Some physicists and some mathematicians take an interest in those materials which have both liquid and solid properties and in doing so find common ground with biologists in the University and with such industries as paper making and printing.[136]

In 1966 Peter Stocker was appointed as Reader in Computing and Director Designate of the Computing Centre, the start of a major development for the University. Liquid metals became a specialism of the physicists under Professor Norman Cusack. In 1966 he acquired a very high pressure container in a steel reinforced room "in which potentially dangerous experiments may be conducted by an operator located safely outside".[137] In the following year this was joined by a helium refrigerator which could reach temperatures down to 0.05°K for low temperature physics. It certainly made physics sound rather more fun than the Humanities. The most eye-catching "invention" that emerged from physics in the sixties was a device by Dr C. C. Matheson and Dr J. G. Wright for detecting rust on railway lines by light, developed in collaboration with Messrs Bellingham and Stanley Ltd. The prototype was presented to the School in 1972 after five years' work. Unfortunately, this did not develop. The School was not then as interested in links with industry as Matheson was. Indeed the University signed disclaimers of interest in the patent. The inventors moved away to other careers and Frank Thistlethwaite now regrets they did not then forge more links with industry. But attitudes were different then and the bias of the department very "pure". Physics started well but had to wait until 1973 before moving into its purpose-built accommodation in the new Science Building with its wider opportunities.

As the Schools developed their research so they increasingly drew in research grants from outside bodies (see Table 1).

That the University had started well was suggested by the reports of the first external examiners.[138] In biology Professor J. A. Ramsay thought that "a bold experiment seems to have got off to a promising start" and for history Professor Charles Wilson of Cambridge judged "the general standard seemed to me to be entirely satisfactory".[139] In economics the level was "much the same as it would be elsewhere", and in sociology A. H. Halsey of Oxford found it "a good university standard" and economic history "very satisfactory." In

Table 1 Research Grants to UEA, 1964/5-1970/1
(£ *unless otherwise specified*)

	BIO	CHE	EAS	ENV	MAP	SOC	FAM	EUR
1964–65	163,344	33975			13,726	11,004		
1965–6	169,478	87,157			26,333			
1966–67	229,680	86,011			46,887	9510		5000 DM
								$1500
1967–68	271,725	121,474 +$3320			63,968	12,940		
1968–69	299,081	99,361		67,309	71,900	26,970		
1969–70	215,858	85,689		20,720	42,486	840	300	1000
1970–71	50,731	43,126	500	88,689	60,105	1117		1900
		+13,600 DM						

chemistry reactions were cooler, "below average but not unreasonable . . . overall favourable". Only in mathematics, perhaps predictably, was the verdict "disappointing".[140]

As well as the balanced curriculum offered in the 1960s, there were also interesting hopes for the future which did not materialise. On the science side the University had wanted a Medical School almost since the beginning. The Vice-Chancellor had expressed this interest to the UGC in May 1964 and reiterated it in March 1966 on the grounds of the large catchment area of a population of 1,600,000, the strengths of biology and the possibility of rebuilding a hospital near to the University Plain.[141] The Royal Commission consequently recommended that if Cambridge University decided against undergraduate clinical teaching on a substantial scale then the development of a medical school in Norwich would be an alternative. Since there was no likelihood of Cambridge foregoing medical education, UEA reasonably had to wait until further maturity.[142]

It did not, however, remain idle. In 1967 it returned to its claims. It pointed out the national shortage of doctors and the shortage in East Anglia, and the fact that East Anglia was the only hospital region in Britain without an undergraduate medical school. There were only four professors in the medical school in Cambridge, the last two as recently as 1962 and 1965. On the positive side there were nearly 9000 beds in the region, and the Norfolk and Norwich Hospital had a long history and already taught medical students. The case was unanswerable but it was equally unthinkable that a new and unproved University scarcely three or four years old and as yet unbuilt, was going to be given a medical school, a prestigious privilege for which the newer civics had had to wait for many decades.[143]

UEA had to lay the foundations of credibility. This was partly done by developing its biological sciences. Also there were positive initiatives to develop areas of joint interest and cooperative research between the University and the Norfolk and Norwich Hospital.[144] Twenty-seven members of local hospitals expressed an interest in co-operating with the University and various areas were identified. These included research on human cytogenetics and the use of ultra sound. As well as these links with biology and physics, there was also potential with sociology. Professor Roy Emerson was moving in the direction of medical sociology and proposed studies on the interaction of medical and social services in the region and problems of nurse recruitment in Yarmouth and Lowestoft. The University and Hospital groups were pleasantly surprised to find several areas of overlapping research in both institutions - blood flow in arteries, physiology of the eye, enzyme biochemistry and the hormonal regulation of metabolism. It all added to the strength of UEA's claims, which was to bear fruit in its departments of nursing and physiotherapy in the 1990s, bringing closer the future founding of a Medical School.[145]

The chemists wanted a separate School of Molecular Technology combining polymer science, colour chemistry, ceramics and metallurgy. With the backing of Ingold, Cockcroft and Todd, it would have been a good match with chemistry, and have enhanced its relevance to industry and possible career opportunities. The high cost prevented its coming into being, however, especially when cuts began to bite. A School of Psychology went the same way, though there was a shortage of university places in psychology and potential applicants still enquire after it.[146] In any case the UGC told UEA in 1967 to shift its focus towards arts rather than science-based subjects.[147]

On the arts side there were high hopes for a School of Management and Technology. Lord Mackintosh had wanted a School of Business from the beginning, since he had sent his own son to the USA for lack of anything suitable in England. He told the UGC, and was fond of telling groups in East Anglia, that UEA would provide for this field. Lord Franks, shortly before becoming Chancellor, had written an influential report on management education, though he saw it only as a graduate study.[148] The subject was in the air. The difficulties of devising such a course were, however, evident from what was going to be packed into it - economics, sociology, technology (not that UEA did much technology), mathematics, computing, even philosophy and industrial design. It had a lot of the worst features of management education thinking of the sixties - a complete rag-bag of too many subjects too superficially covered. This too fell by the way.[149] The School of Social Studies had thoughts about human or behavioural sciences and also about a graduate Centre of Advanced Study in Social Science.[150] This was clearly premature, since SOC had only just produced its first output of undergraduates and it was still too small and undeveloped in its own research. Indeed the six professors and senior lecturers in economics and sociology had published only one book between them at that stage. Nonetheless these plans are indicative of lively forward-thinking. Some were premature, a School of Management has since come about and a School of Medicine was approved in 2000. The chief loss was probably Molecular Technology.

In many ways the Library is the most important part of the University. Accordingly the Librarian was the second appointment made by the Vice-Chancellor, following the Registrar. Thistlethwaite admired the library at the London School of Economics and was delighted when the Librarian there recommended his own deputy, Willi Guttsman, for UEA. Guttsman was a Jewish émigré from Berlin who had come to England, and had worked as an agricultural labourer before becoming a student at LSE, where he rose to become deputy librarian. He was a political sociologist of distinction with his work on the British political elite. His linguistic range, social science expertise and scholarly reputation made him an ideal appointment. His wife Valerie, after a career in local politics, became Lord Mayor of Norwich. Guttsman also brought from LSE Elizabeth Fudakowska as his deputy. She was a scholar of French literature who came from Poland after the War. Thistlethwaite recalled that Norfolk gentry with a taste for rare books were looking forward to "a cosy bibliophilic crony" as University Librarian. This rigorous Germanic sociologist, supported by his graciously calm Polish deputy, was not what they expected, but Guttsman and Fudakowska were absolutely right for UEA.[151]

The Library began in the Jacobean Hall and then in the Georgian dining room of Earlham Hall before it moved to the Village in August 1964. Teams of helpers, including local sixth formers, moved 30,000 books in three days to a former common room block in the Village. Then after Christmas 1964 a former assembly room in the Village was taken over for another 20,000 books.[152] The layout of the Library then was six rooms, quiet rooms leading off from a noisy concourse area with catalogues and social space. It was immediately to the left on the main entrance to the Village.

Some Cambridge well-wishers of the new University - Lord Adrian, Noel Annan and Sir Eric Ashby - generously proposed that books from the Cambridge University Library should be lent to UEA to help the Library get started. There was, however, a strong movement in the Cambridge Senate to stop this on various grounds.[153] It would not only inconvenience Cambridge University Library users, and increase wear and tear on their books, but it would also jeopardise their copyright library status if they sent books elsewhere. It could also have stultified UEA if its library grant were cut on the grounds that it would always be subsidised by Cambridge. The motion was lost by a surprisingly close vote of 212 to 188 after an acrimonious debate. Cambridge was right to keep its books to itself.

The Library got down to work in the Village, starting with an initial grant from the UGC of £175,000. In spite of its temporary accommodation, the Library had much to be proud of. It kept open seventy-eight hours a week including weekends, longer than any other university library. One of its strengths was Frank Thistlethwaite's policy of appointing staff who were academic subject specialists, one strongly affirmed by the UGC.[154] A record library of 500 records was started in 1965. The Library also began to receive some notable donations. In 1964 the Earl of Leicester decided to deposit 130 law books of his ancestor Sir Edward Coke (1552-1634), the famous Lord Chief Justice.[155] They included three early printed copies of Magna Carta, two annotated in Coke's hand. They were all repaired in Cambridge to be made available to the world of learning. The gesture proved short-lived since Lord Leicester required the return of the books in 1971. The Hon. J. V. Saumarez gave the Journals of the House of Commons and the House of Lords and E.M. Forster the novelist donated a set of the *Biographie Universelle, 1811-28*. Of particular importance was the agreement, 1966-67 with the Norfolk and Norwich Library to purchase books from this splendid nineteenth century subscription library. When their lease finished in 1973, UEA would take over most of their stock.

The chief problem for the University Library was rising costs. Book prices had trebled between 1963 and 1967, then the 1967 devaluation of the pound led to a further 12.4 per cent increase 1966/7 to 1967/8. Nonetheless the expansion of activities continued.

Table 2 Library Holdings

	Bookstock	Issues	Cumulative Expenditure on books and journals	Students
1963	16,000			
1964	31,640	5502		
1965	50,109	16,005	£100,000	
1966	69,014	34,026	£160,000	1220
1967	88,875	49,808	£200,000	1724
1968	108,909	75,553	£221,609	2123
1969	126,039	96,205	£261,467	2358
1970	147,500	117,618	£319,853	2722
1971	170,172	133,868	£387,477	2802

This was impressive, though Guttsman pointed out that the newest university in Germany, Bochum, would open with a stock of 200,000 books collected in two years, and with a foundation grant ten times that of UEA.[156]

In 1966 the building of the new library on the Plain began and on 19 August 1968 they began to move into their new home. The first day was a disaster. The lift broke down and most of the 10,000 books shifted that day had to be hoisted by hand up and down six floors of staircases. The new Library, which cost £392,000, was formally opened by the Chancellor, Lord Franks, on 25 October 1968 with capacity for 200,000 volumes and seating capacity for 700 readers.[157] The new building enabled the Library to advance in technology. By 1968-69 the Librarian decided that some kind of punched card or computerised system of issuing would be needed as the bookstock rose over 100,000. A punched card system was started for science books in Autumn 1969 and a fully computerised system in January 1971. As the Librarian put it dramatically, "while those who had assisted in the nine months gestation held their breath . . . the infant burst forth with no more disturbance than the gentle whirr of the collectadata which also accompanies the operation". Much of the credit for this was due to Dr Christopher Aslin, the Science Librarian. A Telex was acquired for inter library loans and in 1969/70 it received its first batch of video tapes and a Sony Video Recorder for playing them. At the scholarly level a thousand books of R. W. Ketton Cremer of Felbrigg Hall were incorporated into the Library. He was a distinguished local historian and an Honorary Litt.D. of the University. Blickling Hall, by arrangement with the National Trust, also made available seventeenth- and eighteenth-century books for historical research. The Library had started excellently on its first decade.[158]

From the beginning there were plans to support teaching not only with books but with television. Anglia Television already ran a Dawn University of early morning lectures in 1962/63.[159] As soon as the Village opened, there was a closed circuit TV link from Cambridge set up by Anglia TV.[160] George Kitson Clark lectured on Victorian history and Fred Hoyle on mathematics. This was an imaginative idea but carried uneasy implications. Students had not come to UEA to attend lectures at Cambridge and it suggested that Norwich was a poor relation needing the assistance of its neighbour. This burgeoned into a broader idea whereby Cambridge, London, Essex, Hull and UEA should set up a TV link to send teaching reciprocally to each other. The Vice-Chancellor attended a meeting to this effect on 21 February 1964. Peter Laslett, the Cambridge historian, was the chairman of a working party financed by the Gulbenkian Foundation. He had been a BBC producer of Third Programme talks 1946-49 and was Chairman of the Viewers' and Listeners' Association founded in 1960. In Cambridge the Advisory Centre for Education ran a TV week in June 1965 which attracted much publicity.[161] But later in the year the UGC flatly declined to finance even a TV pilot at UEA.[162] So Laslett's hopes for inter-university TV teaching and the UEA's role in the five universities scheme never materialised,[163] but it did lead on nationally to the University of the Air and the Open University.[164]

The Working Party on TV at UEA, set up in 1964, nevertheless,continued to deliberate.[165] It concluded in 1966 that closed-circuit TV should be installed in the University starting in 1966 with a Director of TV to be appointed for 1967. It was seen as of especial relevance to Science Schools for the demonstration of closely filmed experiments, all the members of the working party being scientists except the chairman, Professor James Mcfarlane. The valuable outcome was the Audio Visual Centre (AVC), where Malcolm Freegard was appointed Director in 1967. He was a man of many parts, a Cambridge soccer blue, President of the Marlowe Society at Cambridge, bomber pilot, school master at Gresham's School and BBC TV producer.[166] His engineer was Mr W. C. Tyacke, former head of Outside Broadcasts for Harlech TV and subsequently Director of the AVC. They set up shop in 1968. The UGC had now given UEA £32,000 for equipment and some was lent and given by Anglia TV and the BBC.[167] In January 1970 they moved into the AVC studios on the Plain. These were linked with the teaching buildings and the Library for transmission from the Centre.[168] Biology was the chief user and they even had a small TV studio of their own.[169] Overall about a quarter of the teaching faculty had made use of the AVC by 1971, which produced about six hours of television programmes a week.[170] As well as making TV video recordings, the AVC also ran the Central Photographic Unit and supported Nexus, the student TV Society, enabling students to produce their own programmes, a worthwhile extra-curricular activity and providing some with media experience for later life. This academic activity was the heart of the new University's purpose. But there were other, sometimes lighter, aspects to the life of the community and to these we now turn.

4

A Community of Scholars

"The world of learning is essentially a Community . . . of teachers
and of pupils . . . living together as a Community."[1]

Launcelot Fleming, Bishop of Norwich, January 1964[2]

The initial attitude of Norwich to the University was almost uniformly
favourable. Gordon Tilsley speaks of the "warmth of feeling" locally towards
the new University; it was like being in the "middle of a glowing fire".[3] This
was also evident in the attitude of ordinary people interviewed in the streets
of Norwich by the BBC.[4] A young woman said, "I think it will liven the old
place up a bit". "Good luck to it", added a young man. A thoughtful middle-
aged woman thought it would bring "quite a lot of trade to the place as well
as, shall we say, dignity". Another young woman thought, "it's about time we
did something for the youth of Norwich", and a clergyman took the view that
East Anglia had a distinctive character and Norwich was the sort of place
where there ought to be a university. The play *Roots* by Arnold Wesker (a
future honorary graduate of the University) was produced in 1959, depicting
cultural stultification in south Norfolk and, through the character of
"Beattie", a yearning for intellectual stimulus. These attitudes represented a
predictable mix of assumptions: Norwich had a cultural tradition but it
needed livening up and a university would help youth and bring in trade. So
when the first term ended it was felt that UEA had "fitted comfortably into
Norwich", apart from some jealous rowdiness from the "Earlham teds".[5]

There were some rare occasions where the value of the University was
brought into question. One came significantly from Leonard Howes, the
Lord Mayor. He generously entertained the students at the City Hall.[6] But he
had his reservations, "I think we are overdoing the university lark", he told a
City Club dinner three weeks later. He thought university students were
"very good fellows" but added, "I wish the schools would stress the values of
craftsmanship more than at the moment". This was expressed in jocular
faux naif terms but Howes was absolutely right in his perceptiveness. It is
arguable that what the economy needed at that time was not graduates, especially arts graduates. The real lack was secondary technical schools

producing engineers, craftsmen and technologists for industry. As millions were being spent on new universities in the 1960s the Secondary Technical Schools were being allowed to wither away.[7] Alderman Howes to his credit had put his finger on a sensitive and unfashionable point. There was also an extraordinary episode when the Academic Planning Board was being entertained at a reception at the City Hall. Somebody, it is now not known who, made the observation that universities were not necessary for modern youth, that all they were fit for was the army. At this Edgar Williams of the APB – who in a former life was Brigadier "Bill" Williams DSO, a Montgomery staff officer and "a hard boiled customer not afraid of making highly wounding remarks"[8] – went over to the speaker and gave him a public dressing down that was absolutely electrifying.[9] Howes' comments had some justification; those of the unfortunate last speaker were simply foolish. But expressions of slight regard for the University were unusual in Norwich in the early sixties.

Yet outside Norwich, even in the honeymoon period, localities could be cool about the new University. Ipswich found it difficult to get enthusiastic about UEA. Their view was that Norwich would enjoy the glory, "much of it at the expense of places like Ipswich".[10] It was absurd in their opinion for every household in the region to contribute to UEA, as Mackintosh wanted, "as a university to them is about as remote and useful as the man in the moon". At Yarmouth, L. F. Bunnewell of the Education Committee queried the point of Yarmouth supporting UEA.[11] Only one Yarmouth student had gone to UEA; they were better supporting Hull, which at least had three. When student troubles arose in 1968 Yarmouth was the first to withdraw its £4000 grant to the University. Most seriously, a tough-minded old lady in Depwade raised a more fundamental issue. Dr Edith Mellor objected to Depwade Rural District Council contributing £100 to UEA on the grounds that under the 1933 Local Government Act a Rural District Council could not levy an education rate. She was no philistine but a Doctor of Science who had studied at universities in England and France. But she thought "there was too much nonsense and sentimentality talked about UEA".[12] It required the Local Government Act of 1963 to enable Depwade to make its contribution, which it did in time for the opening. It was a remarkable instance where the UEA movement brought about a change in national legislation. One can understand the cool attitudes outside Norwich. Norwich stood to gain a great deal of money and some culture from the University. But it was not self-evident what the gain would be to a ratepaying King's Lynn shopkeeper, Thetford hotelier or Castle Acre agricultural labourer. *The Eastern Daily Press* tried to answer the Ipswich objections by appealing to the role of a university in Norwich as "a heritage of thousands of East Anglians as yet unborn". This all sounded rather metaphysical and suggested that East Anglian students would go to their local university, which was very unlikely and quite misleading in the early sixties.

So what kind of students wanted to come to the new University of East Anglia? When the early students arrived in the Village in October 1963 they looked more like students of the 1950s than those of the late 1960s. Still and TV photographic evidence shows girls wearing skirts (many in the tartan and check then in fashion) and jumpers and high heeled shoes. The young men were short-haired and wearing suits and ties. They have the appearance of schoolteachers, secretaries and bank clerks, which must have been reassuring to Norwich.[13] They even impressed the *Daily Telegraph*, one of whose reporters gushingly found in them "a wonderful freshness of outlook and a splendid combination of curiosity and kindness, of self-possession without aggression".[14]

But where did they come from? The school background of the early intakes in 1964-66 were analysed at the time and show an interesting shift.

	1964[15]	1965[16]	1966[17]
LEA Schools	78.6	68	49
Independent	10.7	19	29
Direct Grant	8.7	13	22

What is remarkable is that initially UEA seemed to be fulfilling Robbins hopes that university expansion would widen the opportunities for higher education. That over three quarters of students came from LEA schools in 1964 suggested this. But, as UEA's facilities improved, its reputation (or very existence) became better known and the new universities acquired a certain chic, partly derived from Sussex, so the picture changed. It became more a "public school" university with barely a half coming from LEA schools and just over a half from the Independent and direct grant sectors.

The school background was itself a reflection of the social origins of the students.

	Non Manual		Manual	
	Professional, Administrative Managerial	Clerical	Manual Skilled	Manual Semi- and Unskilled
1965[18]	65	16	10	9
1966[19]	69	20	11	0

Harold Perkin puts this another way and comparatively:[20]

Table 3   Percentages in Social Classes

	Intakes	I and II	III	IV and V
Sussex	1966	70	10	20
Essex	1965–67	68	14	18
UEA	1966	62	14	24
Kent	1966	62	14	24
Warwick	1966	60	20	20
Lancaster	1966	54	19	27
All British Universities	1958–59	62	11	27

UEA's "comfortable" social origins were evident. It was in the middle of the range of new universities in taking upper middle-class students – though none was quite as "posh" as Sussex in those days.[21] Academically too they were rather good. In 1965 the percentage of students with three Cs and above at A level was consistently above the national average.

	Humanities	Social Studies	Pure Science
UEA	69	69	59
National	60	56	57

(excluding Oxford and Cambridge)

In terms of geographical origin, eight of the first (1963) intake of 112 came from East Anglia (7.1 per cent), including two from Norwich itself, Jill Aitken the daughter of the Archdeacon of Norwich and another young woman from Norwich High School for Girls. Frank Mattison found for 1965 that more than half of applications and admissions came from an area east of a line from the Wash to the Isle of Wight. 6.8 per cent of freshmen came from Norfolk, Suffolk, Cambridgeshire, Ely and Huntingdonshire.[22] By 1967 4.8 per cent of the student body came from East Anglia,[23] and it seemed to have settled round about 4 per cent by the early 1970s.[24] This may seem rather low and certainly belie the expectations of some that the University would especially serve the region. Yet East Anglia only supplied 2.5- 3.0 per cent of the national student population. So East Anglian young people made a greater impact on the intakes of UEA than they did on other universities at large. It was an argument that could be used to justify local authority support for the University. Finally, there was a predominance of women in the student body in the initial stages. It is evident in the early photographs and fifty-one of the first seventy-nine graduates were women.

The admissions situation in the 1960s remained quite healthy. In the admissions season 1965/6 for 1966 entry 913 applicants put UEA as first choice and 513 actually came. The quality too remained good by national standards. The following percentage of students attained the top three UCCA classifications for A levels: 64 per cent in 1965, 53 per cent in 1966 and 47 per cent in 1967; compared with national figures of 53 per cent for 1965, 55 per cent for 1966 and 50 per cent for 1967.[25] A sharp fall in admissions between 1969 from 12,587 in 1969 down to 7968 by 1972 ended the optimism of the sixties.[26] This was attributed to the diminished reputation of the University consequent on well-publicised student unrest, a general waning in fashion for the "new" universities and a possible confusion with Essex, whose troubles had been notorious.[27]

If the students were good, so were the faculty. When Frank Thistlethwaite was first interviewed following his appointment he said, "I hope because of the attractions of a new university and the attractions of Norwich we shall be able to get the pick of some of the best and youngest talent in British universities from all over the place".[28] The first faculty were scholars of high calibre. Of the sixty-one appointed in 1962-65, two thirds (67.2 per cent) had first class degrees and of the 140 appointed up to 1967 55.7 per cent had firsts.[29] A visiting professor from Yale, Elting Morison, found "I was amazed at the high standard of the faculty".[30] From another viewpoint, a Cambridge don found that 56 per cent of professors at UEA had Cambridge degrees compared with Cambridge's own 62 per cent and an English average of 30 per cent. In fact UEA was the only British university except Cambridge with a majority of Cambridge graduates among its professors.[31] The assiduity with which this data was compiled and discreetly publicised at the time now looks fussy and even distasteful, not least to some distinguished Scottish professors to whom Cambridge was no more marvellous than Glasgow and Edinburgh. But in the early sixties it was vital for the "new" universities that they showed that they were not academically second-rate newcomers but could compare favourably with established institutions.

Some of the early faculty were distinguished in other ways. Seven professors had already been professors elsewhere or Fellows of Oxford or Cambridge colleges. This was significant since Sir George Barnes of Keele urged Norwich to appoint some men of previous administrative experience, the lack of which he felt at Keele.[32] UEA accordingly had a good leavening of experienced men in early appointments – Marcus Dick, Dick Ross, Ian Watt, Thomas Bennet Clark – who were crucial helpmates to the Vice-Chancellor. The early men also contained several of current or future recognised distinction – three knighthoods (two British, one Norwegian), one CB, 3 CBEs, 3 OBEs and four FRSs.

The quality of the first generation of faculty requires some explanation. I questioned a number who were still at UEA in 1995 about what attracted them to UEA.[33] Many were attracted by the city and area, its countryside and sailing, often familiar from holiday experiences before the founding of the University. Many were also attracted by the possibility of a new university, of starting something new with potential new thinking and being part of a founding group. Two were attracted by professors already at UEA and inevitably some saw it as a promotion, with greater further promotion prospects arising from starting in a new institution.

Most regarded becoming a university lecturer as a "step up" from their parental origins, which were heavily lower middle class with some manual, craftsman, clerical element (cabinet maker, schoolteacher, poultry farmer, baker, clerk, local government clerk, gardener). Two who came from professional or business families were unable to say whether they had moved up or down socially. Salaries were also quite attractive in the early sixties. Thistlethwaite referred to his faculty as "academics content with meagre salaries",[34] but in truth an assistant lecturer was then in the salary range of an army captain, a lecturer in that of a major and lieutenant colonel and a senior lecturer in that of a colonel – which now seems rather extravagant. University teachers were also given an 11 per cent increase from 1 April 1963 to encourage recruitment for the expansion.[35] So for most new faculty at UEA their choice of career was then a rational social and financial advance, though it did not remain so. Those early appointments who stayed at UEA did so because they liked their colleagues, the science facilities, stable family relationships and especially the desire to provide continuity of education for their children in the excellent Norwich schools. More tellingly all had been "broadly satisfied with their experience at UEA" and none regretted not having taken careers in business and industry. It is a pleasant picture of men positively attracted to UEA, behaving with economic and social rationality for the time, happy to stay for good reason and all rising to senior positions through administration or research according to inclination.

Students are rightly less impressed by the background of faculty than their effectiveness as teachers. The student newspaper *Mandate*, tested this in 1969 and found the following student reactions to forty-three profiled faculty.[36]

	Favourable	Neutral	Critical
EAS	17	6	4
EUR	9	6	1
	26	2	5
	(60.4 per cent)	(27.9 per cent)	(11.6 per cent)

It suggested a broadly good faculty in the 1960s. Unfortunately, *Mandate* did no more of these profiles.

The compactness of the Village helped to create a genuine community spirit among the early faculty. The new Vice-Chancellor, as a former Steward of his Cambridge college, and Marcus Dick, as former Senior Tutor of Balliol, wanted to bring a certain Oxbridge style to the University.[37] Thistlethwaite was unsuccessful in encouraging punting on the Yare – he paid for two punts himself but they sank or were lost. Croquet on Earlham Hall lawn also proved abortive. But a Senior Common Room in Earlham Lodge met a real need and was a striking success. Earlham Lodge was a Georgian house in the Village at the foot of the slope down to the river and close to Earlham Church. Frank Thistlethwaite saw the need for an SCR straight away. He suggested a Faculty dinner once a week to "talk over common problems and clear our minds about the way ahead ... I hope we may take the opportunity on this occasion to form ourselves into a Senior Common Room".[8] The weekly dinners must have much contracted by 1964 since I never recall going to such events. But the SCR in Earlham Lodge did thrive. Anne Franks and Jane Thistlethwaite were given carte blanche to furnish it with good old furniture, chintzy armchairs, mahogany side tables and restful side lights. The Lodge served coffee and tea through the day and was a place to relax and socialise in a series of fine rooms, each with a different character and atmosphere: a rich brown sitting room overlooking a magnificent beech tree at the front; a small green panelled writing room at the rear; rather feminine drawing rooms on the first floor. The beech tree, believed to be four hundred years old, died and was felled in 1996. In summer a terrace overlooking the river at the back was a popular venue. The SCR even had a genuine butler, Benham, "Tall and of great bearing and dignity", as Thistlethwaite describes him, he had been in service in great houses in Norfolk and butler to an ADC of George VI.[39] He was virtually retired when he came to UEA but by a unique dispensation was allowed to continue after the age of sixty-five for as long as he wished, so valued and unique were his services. The style he could bring to the University's formal hospitality when dealing with the City and County were inestimable. The SCR also had its own wine store, £10,000 worth laid down in the cellars of Earlham Hall with a loan from the University Council and managed by Professor Robert Ashton and his wine committee of *bons viveurs*. Wine tastings and buffets were held on the lawn of Earlham Hall and pleasant symposia discussing academic papers over claret in the Lodge. One of the quaintest traditions of the Lodge was a wager book in which members wagered bottles of claret on various propositions. In one the Vice-Chancellor bet someone that Barry Goldwater would (or not) gain the Republican nomination, in another a literary lecturer wagered that a certain quotation was from Matthew Arnold. The book has since been lost as surely as the age of which it was a part. Faculty wives were not forgotten for a UEA Women's Club was presided over by Jane Thistlethwaite and sometimes met in Wood

Hall. Its wide range of social activities helped to integrate wives and especially newcomers into the life of UEA.[40] All these activities, ranging from the slightly pretentious to the practical, forged a sense of community. Bob Ashton called it "the golden days of UEA – the Garden of Eden before the Fall". For Nicholas Brooke it was like "a country house party that went on just a bit too long".

The students lived their own lives apart from their studies. Where they were to live was an initial problem, since before the building of residences the University needed plenty of lodgings. The UGC had required assurances about accommodation which were broadly met. Norwich needed a hundred lodgings providing bed and breakfast for 1963 and an estimated 1500 by 1968 with 500 students in residences. Norwich posed various problems. The City College and Keswick Hall Teachers Training College students already occupied "digs". Moreover, 40 per cent of Norwich housing was corporation housing mostly built in the 1930s and many not big enough for a third guest bedroom. [41] Of the 41,000 houses within the city boundary only about 10,000 had a rateable value of over £25 – a size suitable for lodgings, whereas outside the city boundary there were 11,000 houses mostly smaller. The industrial structure of Norwich also created difficulties. Many potential landladies preferred to work in the light industry of Mackintosh's and Colman's rather than take lodgers. This led to unnecessary fears that students would have to live in seaside boarding houses in Great Yarmouth. These proved groundless, but the fact that they were aired at all (by the British Council) might have been dangerous for university recruitment.[42]

It was Daphne Powlett as Accommodation Officer who grappled with these problems.[43] Miss Powlett was an ex WAAF officer and house director for the YWCA, a fluent French-speaking Francophile, canal and culture lover. With great energy she searched for and inspected lodgings. They were on weekly terms so that a landlady had the security of knowing that she could remove a troublesome student within a few days. Students were not supposed to be away for a night without permission of their adviser.[44] The University gave "considerable thought" to whether there should be a curfew time to be back in lodgings and whether men should be banned from calling on women in lodgings. Both were sensibly regarded as unenforceable, but they illustrate the paternalist care with which the University regarded its role *in loco parentis* in those days. The genuine appreciation of the vital role of the landladies was expressed in an annual tea party for them hosted by the Vice-Chancellor.[45]

Overseeing all student matters, their discipline and welfare, was the Dean of Students. This rather American role was filled by Marcus Dick, the Professor of Philosophy. He was a former senior tutor of Balliol College Oxford and regarded as one of the star catches of UEA. He relished the new life. As he told Anthony Sampson, "I feel ten years younger than I did when I left Balliol and twenty years younger than I did when I was a scholar at Winchester".[46] He also found that the excitement of the early years at UEA "reminded him of Monty's headquarters in the desert".[47] Among his many talents he had been a TV quiz master on the BBC's *Down You Go* in the early 1950s. His first wife was a Norfolk lady, the daughter of D.A.J. Buxton of Caister Hall, Yarmouth, who had taken a keen interest in the origins of UEA. Marcus ran and oversaw all student matters, discipline, lodgings, relations with the Students' Union. He was also senior resident tutor at Horsham. The first time I met him he was arranging the raising of a punt sunk in the river – no problem was too small or large for him. There was an attractive, worldly, raffish side to his personality – his baggy clothes, 1930s Balliol shuffle and knowing leery smile. He smoked too much but was unflappable. Sir Maurice Bowra described Marcus as one of "the new kind of don; they gave tutorials with a bottle of whisky by the armchair".[48] Thistlethwaite less scurrilously captured his personality, "of great charm and lively social graces . . . he had the panache and authority to command respect."[49]

Marcus was an atheist but, as a philosopher, well appreciated the role of religion in student life. Many of the founding fathers were Christians and Lincoln Ralphs was one of the first to assume that religion would be an "essential element in university life".[50] One of the ceremonies at the opening of the University had been Thanksgiving Services at the Anglican and Catholic cathedrals. There was a good deal of religious faith among the students. A survey made in 1966 found the following extent of belief.

	Belief in God	Belief in life after death (*percentages*)	Belief in the divinity of Christ
Men	47	27.9	29.7
Women	60	50.9	50
Scientists	49.4	22.9	30.1
Arts	50	47.2	40.7

There was more belief among women than men and more among arts students than scientists. There was enough for the churches to work on.[51] The spread of student affiliation was then about 90 Anglicans, 80 Roman Catholics, 30-50 Methodists, 15 Presbyterians, 12-15 Quakers, 9-10 Congregationalists.[52]

The Bishop of Norwich, Launcelot Fleming, was admired by the Vice-Chancellor as a helpful force for good.[53] Fleming set up a local churches committee, including other denominations, and they suggested that the University should recognise chaplains or delegates from the main churches.

The Anglican chaplain was appointed by the Bishop and paid by the Diocese. The first was Rev. John Giles, a Wykehamist and Cambridge rowing blue. A chaplain's committee was formed in the Village and from it evolved the idea of a chaplaincy building on the Plain.[54] It was envisaged that there would be a large room to be used for worship interdenominationally or by individual denominations. The building would also contain chaplains' offices and a social space. It was to be financed by outside sources. There was some unease about the last proposition on the grounds that worship would divide even Christian denominations and that students were better off mixing with the wider community in existing churches.[55] Senate decided, however, that "the large room proposed for devotional purposes would have no permanent ecclesiastical furniture or decoration associating it with any one religion or denomination but would be capable of being freely converted for secular use and would be freely available to all religions and denominations".[56]

An appeal committee was therefore set up to launch an appeal for funds to meet the cost of £20-30,000, with the University agreeing to match pound for pound up to £15,000 out of its own appeal money.[57] Charles Jewson, a Norwich businessman in timber and a prominent Baptist, was chairman of the appeal and under him £27,000 was raised. This enabled the Chaplaincy to open in the Autumn Term of 1971.[58] The Chaplaincy did not meet with universal approval. Atheists and agnostics in the Assembly deplored the allocation of a central site to the building and of Appeal funds to its building and thought that the University should not give facilities to specifically Christian denominations. In fact, the siting was the decision of the architect Bernard Feilden on spatial grounds rather than any considerations of the centrality of religion. At the other pole, it was thought that Fleming's successor as Bishop of Norwich, the low church Maurice Wood, had reservations about an ecumenical and multi-faith chaplaincy. Wood arrived late at the opening ceremony and rather distanced himself from it. Bishop Wood accordingly missed the Vice-Chancellor's opening address and was later pointedly sent a copy. In this Thistlethwaite stressed that UEA was a modern secular university, yet the Chaplaincy Centre was "informed by the aspirations of contemporary religious thought and belief in the context of a modern university community".[59] Most drawn to the Chaplaincy would be Christians, but since UEA received students from all over the world "others of the world's great religions have the full right to use the Chaplaincy for their own occasions of meeting and worship". The opening ceremony in January 1972 indeed contained Jewish and Islamic participants and prayers. One good effect of the Centre was the possibility of relocating the Annual University Service. In the sixties this was held in the Anglican cathedral and became too exclusively Anglican, associated with the cathedral and civic dignitaries. Accordingly very few, even Christian, students attended. Holding it in the Chaplaincy returned it to the University and its community.[60]

The Chaplaincy was a University matter but much student social life was facilitated by the Students' Union.[61] It arose oddly informally. The Lord Mayor gave a party for students and it was suddenly realised that someone had to give a vote of thanks. The Registrar, George Chadwick, lighted on Dick Snelling, who duly performed and was then subsequently elected President of the new Union. They pressed for action on student issues, successfully getting the bus route extended to the Village. They also had funds, with cheques countersigned by Dr Ken Joy on behalf of the University, to distribute to a range of social and sporting societies.

There was always a strong moral element in student leisure life.[62] They started a Voluntary Service Unit which visited the Cheshire Home in East Carleton to do repairs and painting and to chat with the elderly and severely disabled people resident there. They also visited old people living alone. In the late sixties VSU's range of activities under its president Jan Sheppard was very extensive.[63] She was a mature student who had taught with Voluntary Service Overseas in Uganda. Several ex-VSO students helped to create a voluntary service ethos at UEA at this time, and by 1969 there were six of them who had had prior experience with VSO.[64] The VSU worked through City institutions, including Friends of the Old People of Norwich and the City Welfare Department, so that activity was coordinated where it was needed. They did visiting, shopping, gardening, painting and decorating. But as one remarked, "it's usually just a matter of keeping someone company for a little while, but it is greatly appreciated. The old people seem to enjoy talking to someone young."[65] They regularly visited Little Plumstead Hospital for mentally handicapped children, the Wednesday Club for the mentally handi-capped at Princes Street Congregational Church, the physically handicapped at Bishop Herbert House, went swimming with the disabled on Sunday mornings and took patients at Thorpe St Andrew's Hospital for outings. By the early 1970s VSU had 150-200 student members (nearly 10 per cent of the student body).[66] Apart from the good they did in the city, they brought incal-culable benefit to the reputation of the University. When the image of the "student" deteriorated at the end of the sixties, the VSU's good-hearted and caring voluntary work stood out as one of the few areas of university life the Norwich citizen could understand and respect.

Another moral dimension of student activities was the raising of funds to enable a black South African student to study at UEA. Sir Robert Birley, the former headmaster of Eton and then a professor at Witwatersrand University, came to UEA to speak on educational apartheid in South Africa on 10 February 1966. [67] It was decided to raise £1500 to bring a student to

UEA, the initiative being that of the Students' Union backed by Marcus Dick as Dean of Students, who became chairman of a body of trustees. There were some arguments against the scheme – that the money would be better spent in South Africa itself, that any putative student would have to leave South Africa illegally and would never be allowed back, nor could he avoid being patronised by his philanthropic patrons.[68] However, Senate agreed to waive fees and half the cost of residences and in 1968 a South African student, Reg Africa from Johannesburg, arrived in the School of Social Studies. The whole matter raised student consciousness of the South African apartheid situation and so incidentally helped to shape attitudes to the Barclays Bank issue in the years of student disturbance, as we shall see. In 1966 the Student Support and Aid Fund was raising £10,000 a year, supporting schools in South Africa, Zimbabwe, Namibia and Tanzania, and helping black students at universities in Africa rather than at UEA. It raised over £100,000 in its thirty years to 1996.[69]

Students enjoyed the usual range of sports with playing fields at Horsham from October 1965. Some idea of their relative importance is given by the Students' Union expenditure on them in the mid sixties: sailing £527, hockey £388, cricket £370, soccer £368, rugby football £346, squash £101, water skiing £96, basketball £95.[70] The pre-eminence of sailing was specifically East Anglian due to the nearby Broads. Sailing got off to a strong start with forty of the 130 students of 1964 having joined the sailing club. E.C. Landamore & Co of Wroxham presented one of their National Twelve sailing dinghies as a gift to the University.[71] The expansion of sporting activity led to the appointment of a Director of Physical Education in 1968. This was Haydn Morris, a Welsh and British Lions Rugby International and rugby selector for the British Universities Sport Federation. He unanswerably defended the keeping free of Wednesday afternoons for sports. It enabled UEA students to participate in inter university UAU competitions, matches against local opposition and Cambridge colleges, and to enjoy horse riding and golf facilities set aside for them. In the sixties UEA sporting teams achieved success remarkably rapidly especially after Morris's appointment. UEA became regional champions in both rugger and hockey in 1967-68. In 1968-69 the rugby team lost only one game and were regional champions again in 1969-70, reflecting Haydn Morris's expertise. Women's tennis and fencing were also strong.

The University was also enthusiastic about theatre, both dramatic and musical in the sixties, the big assembly room in the Village proving an excellent venue. The first President of the Drama Society was John Rhys Davies, the future successful film actor, whom Halliwell describes as a "heavyweight British character actor, a good roisterer". [72] His ebullient personality energised drama at UEA, and he starred in UEA's first play *The Crucible* by Arthur

Miller (a future honorary graduate), which was produced by Professor Nicholas Brooke. The York Mystery Cycle was presented at St Peter Mancroft and in 1966-67 UEA reached the finals of the NUS drama competition. Notable productions of *The Devils, The Workhouse Donkey* and *The Birthday Party* brought the new drama to UEA. UEA drama also fostered the talents of Rose Tremain the novelist, Snoo Wilson the playwright and Jenny Abramsky the BBC executive, who were all active in acting, writing and producing in these years.

Finally, the debating society was a thriving activity in the mid 1960s under Christopher Wrigley. They attracted notable visiting speakers to participate in debates – John Biffen, Michael Meacher, the future Bishop Bill Westwood. They extended into inter-university debates with Essex and Cambridge and a high point was the winning of the Observer Mace Competition in 1968. They also reached out into the City by organising the sixth-form debate competition for local schools. The Vice-Chancellor gave them a gavel as a trophy. They relaxed with style too, with an annual dinner at a local restaurant attended by Frank and Jane Thistlethwaite.[73] By 1964-65 there were already some forty student societies. All this acting, debating, sporting activity and philanthropy were important elements in creating a university of well-rounded culture and immensely enriching for the students who participated. Indeed most of these activities were generated by student initiative and enterprise.[74]

The Students' Union, in keeping with older universities, decided to have a "rag" to raise money for local charities. This kind of licensed tomfoolery, anachronistically reminiscent of the Oxbridge of the 1920s and 1930s, can sometimes do more harm than good. The early rags began well, however, in terms of image. There were suitably "daring" incidents, a pram race with girls in substantial nightgowns, and stealing a traffic policeman's dais. There was also some elegance with the Rag Queen arriving in a Rolls Royce at the Norwood Rooms in full evening dress for the Rag Ball, attended by the Lord Mayor and Chief Constable. It was noted, however, at the outset that the Norwich population did not understand the purpose of rag. The 1965 rag was rather similar. Only a few people watched the procession in poor weather and, raised a "disappointing" £1700 compared with £1200 in the previous year.[75] That of 1967 raised £2000. The rags, always hostages to fortune, had started modestly well, raised a little money for disproportionate effort, and had not aroused too much antagonism. But they were never so effective in their generation of good will or dispensing of philanthropy as a good concert or drama production or the unobtrusive work of VSU. With the troubles from 1968 the rags became a disastrous liability.

Students also played their part in the twinning of Norwich and Rouen. In

1966 a group of three faculty and seventeen students made a four day visit to the Law Faculty at Rouen University for a round of receptions and visits to notable sites.[76] In the next year twenty students from Rouen made a return visit to a programme designed "to compete with the lavish display of hospitality they received in Rouen". [77] The high costs, limited number of students involved and doubt about what these visits achieved beyond ceremonial symbolism meant that they could not continue on this scale and frequency. Students were still visiting Rouen in the early 1970s, however, as part of a Norwich group of athletes, itself part of a larger twinning visit.[78] The visits of the mid sixties were of an age when the University was more affluent and could play a social role on behalf of the city. Thereafter they became less justifiable.

Outside the University, students enjoyed the normal range of cinema, the theatres at the Maddermarket and the Theatre Royal, drinking in the many pubs, dancing at the Samson and Hercules, hearing jazz in the Orford Jazz Cellar, folk music at the Jacquard, going for a meal at Purdy's Restaurant in Tombland. A notable venue was the Jolly Butcher's pub in Ber Street run by the singer Anna. She was an Italian woman of an immigrant family from Pontallani which had settled in Norwich before the First World War in what was then a cosmopolitan Latin quarter of Norwich. Anna established herself as a blues singer, especially with American soldiers who came into Norwich from surrounding air bases in the Second World War. Early UEA students caught the later stages of this interesting culture mix. Some enterprising girl students spent their leisure in an even racier institution. They took jobs as hostesses (not strippers) in the gambling and strip club at the Washington Hotel. It was "seedy and revolting and pretty boring" but it supplemented the student grant.[79] Some night-clubbing students also frequented the Washington.[80] Within the Village the bar and the sailing club boat house were venues for social life and lively parties.

Part of the purpose of this socialising in all manner of venues was to establish or cement romantic relationships. These were remarkably frequent. One survey found that of a hundred students thirty had a boy or girl friend in the University and this within just over a year of the Village starting.[81] It was to be expected from so socially minded a body of students that they should form a UEA society for former graduates. The Vice-Chancellor supported them and in May 1971 150 former students met in London to put this into effect. A steering committee was set up, with Alastair Gordon as Chairman. He was later tragically killed in the Moorgate tube crash in 1975. They organised reunions in Norwich and enabled graduates to communicate with each other. The society thrives, its reunions acquiring an increasingly nostalgic fascination with the passing years.

What happened to our graduates in the sixties? It was not evident that this was going to be an easy area for the University. Its curricular balance was very much towards liberal education in the arts and lacking in technical professional training which would have led graduates direct into related employment. Some rather ambivalent attitudes were also expressed by some of the University's creators. Lincoln Ralphs addressing Beccles Rotary Club in 1963 claimed that UEA would have a "liberalising effect" and they did not want to produce students who would "cash their certificates on the highest market".[82] The Vice-Chancellor similarly told graduates at the Congregation in 1972 that "to make the assumption that you will get a better job when you leave the university with your degree would be a great mistake".[83] This did not auger well for guiding students into employment.

The trend of employment was as follows, down to the nadir of 1971.

Table 4   Employment Trends

	Research and further academic study	Postgraduate and Teacher Training	Other full-time training	Direct employment	Industry	Unemployed or unknown
			Arts			
			(percentages)			
1966	14.3	26.8	17.8	7.1	(1.8)	5.3
1967	12.9	16.7	6.1	39.4	(10.6)	18.9
1968	8.7	19.1	8.7	25.7	(7.1)	33.3
1969*						
1970	9 2	12.7	6.6	29.9	(7.1)	39.1
1971	4.2	14.6	5.5	19.3	(4.4)	51.2
1972	7.6	16.5	5.7	17.7	(2.8)	45.9
			Sciences			
1966	43.5	13	4.3	26	(8.7)	13
1967	21.8	21.8	4.6	31	(20.7)	20.6
1968	8.7	19.1	8.7	25.7	(7.1)	20.9
1969*						
1970	15.9	13	25	30.7	(16.3)	34.4
1971	16.1	14.3	1.1	18.4	(5.6)	42.8
1972	14	22.3	5.2	20	(5.6)	34

* Due to changes in the classification of years covered there are none for 1969 alone.

The first output of seventy-nine students went overwhelmingly into research, further study and teacher training. Few went into direct employment and very few into industry. Indeed the Appointments Officer noted that the emphasis on English and biology, and with 64 per cent of the graduates being women contributed "a combination of circumstances not calculated to breed expectation in the industrialist's heart."[84] By the next year teaching still remained the most popular occupation even for scientists, "the predeliction of our scientists to teaching careers is noteworthy".[85] Indeed providing science teachers for schools may have been an especially valuable role of UEA in its early years. The Appointments Officer (David Ward) wanted to "stimulate students interest in the intellectual challenge of industry". Accordingly, he solicited the opinions of various businessmen about UEA graduates. These are so illuminating as showing industrial attitudes to UEA and the wide disparity of views within industry itself that they are worth indicating here.[86]

Favourable

1. UEA has made a good start. Do not turn to vocational training.
2. Impressed with the calibre of UEA students. Do not teach techniques.
3. No need to "gear more closely" to industry; business sense cannot be taught.
4. The combination of chemistry and economics is liked.
5. The University has no need to train. Employers look for potential and liked UEA students.

Adverse

1. UEA graduates have no idea whether their studies can be of any use to industry.
2. They need to develop leadership.
3. They need to understand statistics more.
4. Students do not know enough about industry and need to redress their poor image of it.
5. They need to understand that profit is worthwhile and that following an industrial career is not selling one's soul.
6. "Social Science" is a soft option.
7. Computing courses and vacation work should be related to local firms.
8. Industry needs more specialists and technicians "the dilettante will choose UEA precisely because he does not have to commit himself."

These views of the mid to late 1960s show the difficulty of UEA in responding to "industry". There were too many conflicting attitudes. Also, as well as UEA's lack of specific vocational technical training, its graduates on their greenfield campus in a cathedral city were too generally ignorant of or hostile to industry.

In the late 1960s and early 1970s certain trends became plain. After the unusual first graduation year, 12-16 per cent of arts graduates and 10-14 per cent of scientists opted for teacher training. Fewer arts students took up research but scientists sustained healthy proportions of 14-17 per cent. There were, however, two disturbing trends. Proportions of both arts and science graduates entering industry sharply and consistently reduced while the proportions of unemployed or untraceable graduates rose equally sharply to unacceptably high levels. That over half of arts and 40 per cent of science graduates were in this category by 1971 was worrying and damaging. In part it may have been due to a hostility to looking for jobs on the part of the radical generation of students of 1968-71.[87] Employers too may have become very wary of employing potentially disruptive graduates at a time when university students and universities experienced a sharp fall in public estimation. Industry had its own problems, since the years 1970-72 experienced the highest levels of unemployment since the war. This prompted comment that from 1971 only graduates of the "highest calibre" would be successful in seeking employment.[88] The Senate noted that graduates had become a "bulk commodity" and cited Lord Todd's view in his Presidential Address to the British Association that the expansion of prolonged education had presented society with "acute problems".[89] The Admissions Officer noted gloomily that the expansion was likely to continue with a doubling of graduates in the 1970s, though "there is little sign that the implications have been considered by the parties most likely to be affected". The layman taxpayer could be forgiven for wondering what the point was of expanding higher education for those lower than of the "highest calibre" if there was no need for them. It also seemed odd that the university expansion had been intended to solve problems of the early sixties only to find Lord Todd suggesting a decade, and several million pounds, later that the very expansion itself had created yet more "acute problems".

In practice the only way forward was for graduates to accept formerly non-graduate jobs. Graduate technicians in industry almost doubled 1965-8 to 12,791, which was very close to the total recruitment of graduates into industry (12,736).[90] The concept of a "graduate job" was changing: for example, UEA social studies graduates were working as a milk roundsman, bus conductor and goods vehicle driver.[91] The Times also highlighted the fact that UEA PhDs in science were applying for jobs usually requiring only A levels.[92] The rapid university expansion of the sixties in an industrial economy not buoyant enough to sustain it or its output had led many students into unrealistic expectations. It contributed to the unrest and poor morale of those years. It is human nature that the general public were more outraged by student rebelliousness than by the wastage of their taxes that graduate unemployment and the expensive use of graduates in inferior jobs implied.

If we turn to postgraduates the picture was a bit healthier.[93]

Table 5   Subsequent Careers of UEA Postgraduates, 1964-69

	No Inform- ation	Continuing Postgraduate Education at another University	In Academic Employment	In Government Employment	In Industrial and Commerical Employment	Other	Total
BIO	1	5	16	5	1	0	28
CHEM	1	9	18	4	28	0	57
EAS	6	1	11	3	2	0	23
EUR	1	0	7	0	0	0	8
FAM	0	0	1	0	0	1	2
MAP	1	0	5	3	3	0	12
SOC	5	7	7	6	3	3	30
			65 (40.6 per cent)		37 (23.1 per cent)		

The strong output of biologists into academic life and especially of chemists into industry is creditable. The forays of some arts Schools into this field caused unease, however, the EAS and SOC figures suggesting that 30-40 per cent of their postgraduates were in danger of being drop outs or "perpetual students", always a risk at this level. On the positive side, around 80-90 per cent of postgraduates in biology, chemistry, mathematics and physics and European studies got some kind of employment. For less employable arts subjects, like English and social studies, the outcome at 60-70 per cent was more modest. But doing postgraduate work clearly paid off in employment in the sixties.

A high point of the sixties was the installation of Lord Franks of Headington OM as Chancellor, Lord Mackintosh having died before his formal installation. Lord Franks was proposed by Sir Edmund Bacon, who served on the board of Lloyds Bank of which Lord Franks was Chairman. They had been friends for many years. In his letter of invitation to Lord Franks, Sir Edmund Bacon said that UEA needed as Chancellor a man "of great national status with if possible a strong academic background" and that his friend was the man.[94]

Oliver Franks had had a remarkable career of great distinction. He was born in 1905, the son of a Congregationalist minister and college principal in Bristol. Success at Oxford had led to a Fellowship at the Queen's College and the Professorship of Moral Philosophy at Glasgow University at the early age of thirty-two. The war brought him to the Ministry of Supply, where he rose to be Permanent Secretary – the only temporary civil servant to reach this rank. In 1946 he returned to Queen's as Provost but continued his life of public service, effectively setting up the European programmes of the

Marshall Plan to receive American Marshall Aid for post-war European reconstruction.[95] The OEEC was largely his operation. Following this he became HM Ambassador to the United States in Washington between 1948 and 1952, covering the creation of NATO and the Korean War. On his return he became a banker as Chairman of Lloyds Bank, Chairman of the Committee of London Clearing Banks and leader of the World Bank mission to India and Pakistan. It was on this task that Professor C.R. Ross, UEA's first Pro Vice-Chancellor worked with Franks, forging another link with the future Chancellor. In 1962 he was ennobled and returned to Oxford as Provost of Worcester College.

It was unkindly said of Franks that when you broke the ice there was a lot of tepid water underneath. The words were actually those of Isaiah Berlin who was seeking to deny them. I had the privilege of spending a day in Oxford talking to Lord Franks in 1966 and I found him not only impressive, as I expected, but also warm and pleasant, forthcoming and even humorous. In 1960 his rigour and puritanism are thought to have lost him the Oxford Chancellorship to the worldly Harold Macmillan. UEA had better judgement and Lord Franks became its Chancellor in 1966, lending the prestige of his name and the dignity of his presence to the University for the nineteen years of his Chancellorship.

The Installation on 23 April 1966 was a splendid occasion.[96] It was preceded by a civic reception in Norwich Castle hosted by the Lord Mayor and Lady Mayoress, Mr and Mrs C.B. Jewson. The Installation itself took place on the following day in St Andrews Hall. Lord Franks in his address gave some insight into his own thinking that universities had to be places of useful knowledge but also places concerned with values and activities worth pursuing for their own sake. The Vice-Chancellor conferred the honorary degree of DCL on the new Chancellor. Following this a group of distinguished men and women were also made honorary doctors of the University: Asa Briggs, the historian; R.H. Mottram, the Norwich novelist; A.L. Hodgkin, the Nobel laureate physiologist; Dorothy Hodgkin, the crystallographer and also Nobel laureate; Paul Samuelson, the economist; Sir Eric Ashby, a leader in higher education and Robert Gardiner the Executive Secretary of the United Nations Economic Commission for Africa. Finally, and especially fittingly, came Sir Charles Wilson, the Chairman of UEA's Academic Planning Board. After the Installation the participants processed to the Cathedral for a service of thanksgiving and the morning ended with an excellent buffet lunch in marquees on the lawn behind Earlham Hall.

The Installation was also notable for the first public display of the new academic gowns designed by Cecil Beaton. Hitherto the Vice-Chancellor had worn a conventional gown from Ede and Ravenscroft. Something more striking was required, since the Vice-Chancellor saw degree days as "an attractive form of theatre" and that a theatrical costume was appropriate for "the principal characters in the drama". So why not call in a top theatrical designer? He recalls,

> I wrote to Cecil Beaton. At that time he was at the height of his success as the scenic and costume designer of *My Fair Lady* and it occurred to me that he just might be intrigued by the idea of designing the costumes for the theatre of a new university, for we were fashionable at the time. He accepted and I called on him for the first of a number of enjoyable sessions at his house during 1965. He was, I suppose, mannered and the highest of elegant camp . . . but I enjoyed his company and admired his professionalism. There was nothing of the show off or dilettante.[97]

Beaton devised a Vice-Chancellor's gown of tan with fire-coloured velvet facings, the Pro Vice-Chancellor's blue with orange trimmings and for the Public Orator two shades of purple with orange lining at the sleeves. All were eclipsed by that of the Chancellor. His gown is of scarlet with striking gold and orange facings and bishop sleeves.[98] There is a famous theatrical reference here which may have been unconscious on Beaton's part. It echoed the gorgeous design by Roger Furse for the first act costume of Henry V in Laurence Olivier's film. The scarlet body and especially striking back is offset by the half chevron facings of red and gold. Beaton of course knew Olivier well, had designed for him and would certainly have known professionally of the Furse costume. The Chancellor's hat is an even more direct artistic reference. It is modelled on the Arnolfini hat in Van Eyck's 1434 painting of the Arnolfini marriage and is hence strikingly taller than the Tudor velvet cap.[99] The whole outfit, made by Joshua Taylor of Cambridge, cost an amazingly modest £100.

The undergraduate gowns are short smokey blue capes with originally a tricorne cap since abandoned for the more traditional square mortar board. The new costumes met a generally favourable reception. It was said of the Chancellor's and Vice-Chancellor's gowns that "their flamboyance might have better suited the stage of Covent Garden than the Senate".[100] This was both to seize and miss the point; they were never worn in Senate but were designed for the theatre of Congregation. The *Sunday Times* thought that "Beaton's undergraduate is second cousin to the Carnaby Street Mod". Oddly the gowns received most publicity not in 1966 but in the next year when they were modelled by hostesses from Pye Radio at a radio trade show. The models, older and more glamorous than students, made them look like costumes from *The Avengers*. The ogling photographers publicised them as far as Australia and Istanbul. This was UEA as sixties fashion statement.

Beaton was paid a £500 honorarium fee. UEA did not know it but Beaton received £750 for the Fonteyn and Nureyev costumes for *Marguérite and Armand* at Covent Garden. He had just earned about $21,000 for the designs for the film of *My Fair Lady*.[101] So his work for UEA was a small act of generosity on Beaton's part. He was in the USA when the first Congregation was held and so did not see his handiwork in motion. But it continued to give pleasure and the success of the unusual venture prompted Essex to commission Hardy Amies to design for them.

If the Installation of 1966 was a high point of UEA's sixties, the decade ended with the University bathed in a prestigious glow as Lord Clark chose to finish his television series on Civilisation at UEA. He stood before Denys Lasdun's terrace residences and praised the students:

> When I have the good fortune to visit one of our new universities, it seems to me that the inheritors of all our catastrophes look cheerful enough . . . I doubt if so many people have ever been as well-fed, as well-read, as bright-minded, as curious and as critical as the young are today.[102]

This was immensely gratifying publicity. Frank Thistlethwaite visited Lord Clark at Saltwood Castle and wrote to him how "very proud" he was and of his "sheer gratitude" that UEA had been featured in *Civilization*.[103] By now UEA was entering a dark period and needed all the favourable publicity it could get, as we shall see. But let us now turn to those UEA buildings which acted as the background to Kenneth Clark's encomium as symbols of sixties high culture.

5

Building the Environment

We have got a magnificent site on the edge of Norwich . . . with I
believe the best architect going.[1]

Frank Thistlethwaite, 26 October 1961

Until now I had thought of Lasdun as a man of somewhat inflated
reputation due to his temperament etc. but after seeing the
University I realised that he is a master of the first order . . .
powerful and too tremendous – but wonderful for an entire
University and worth any amount of friction.[2]

Sir Isaiah Berlin, 3 March 1967

The new universities were not only places of higher education. Most of them
accepted that they had a duty to the environment and that their architecture
itself should educate the aesthetic sensibilities of the inhabitants. Following
the insistence of Sir Keith Murray and the UGC, they all had spacious greenfield sites which invited some kind of architectural statement. A fine site had
not always led to fine architecture. There was the example of Keele, where the
opportunities of the site had been lost by being covered by a campus of piece-
meal development. Keele's historian regards the concern to avoid this in the
future as the chief lesson which Keele taught to the new universities of the
sixties.[3] It was a lesson not likely to be lost on Frank Thistlethwaite, who was
deeply interested in architecture. Indeed as a schoolboy he had had an ambi-
tion to become an architect himself and precociously subscribed to the
Architectural Review and took a National Institute of Industrial Psychology
test in 1931 which confirmed his architectural aptitudes.[4] At the end of his
career he was admitted as an honorary Fellow of the Royal Institute of British
Architects in recognition of his commissioning and support of the major
architects who created the Plain as the most architecturally interesting of all
the new universities. Thistlethwaite was determined that the University of
East Anglia should not merely be a collection of serviceable buildings but be a
stimulating environment in which all could take pride and pleasure.

This was more ambitious than local opinion originally supposed. The
Norfolk and Norwich Association of Architects was quick to suggest at the

beginning of 1960 that local architects should design the university and that local builders should build it. If a "more prominent architect" was appointed then, in their view, he should farm out individual buildings to local architects. Moreover, they claimed, that any approach to the RIBA should be supported by the Norwich Association and there should be no local competition, since this would be far too costly for a local firm. These rather self-seeking claims were met with the cool response that they "would be carefully considered".[5] The suggestion was in fact exactly contrary to what UEA was to become – a bold unified statement by a major international architect, not a series of discrete buildings by able and competent local men.

The search for a major figure initially settled on Sir Leslie Martin, the Professor of Architecture at Cambridge. The APB said that it would support him and the Executive Committee resolved to invite him to become the University's architect.[6] Martin had made his reputation as architect to the LCC between 1953 and 1956. At this time he was heavily involved in university building – College Hall at Leicester University (1958-61), Caius College Cambridge (1960-62) and Oxford libraries (1961-64). Martin, while grateful for the honour of the invitation and complimenting the University on its "magnificent site", saw his contribution as a limited one. He could draw up a master plan for the layout of the site but other architects would have to be brought in for individual buildings.[7] This was not really what Norwich wanted – but Martin, as his projects cited above show, was exceptionally busy with university work elsewhere in 1961. Frank Thistlethwaite had further discussion with Martin in October 1961 but the latter was growing cool and deferred firm acceptance of his appointment until the University could provide more detail on the buildings needed.[8] These discussions of 1961 proved abortive and further delay could not be tolerated.

Charles Wilson, the chairman of the APB and former Vice-Chancellor of Leicester University, then suggested Denys Lasdun who had built a hall of residence for him at Leicester. Thistlethwaite also knew him as the runner-up in a competition for the design of student rooms at St John's, Cambridge. Thistlethwaite had been on the building committee and had been taken with Lasdun's stepped back design for residences. He saw that, while perhaps too bold for the Cambridge Backs, they would be appropriate for the free space of Earlham. So Thistlethwaite went to talk to Lasdun. "We met on 10 October 1961 at his small office then in Albany Terrace. We liked each other and he was attracted by what would of course be a major commission".[9] It is notable that this first meeting was on the very day after the report to the Executive Committee that Leslie Martin was losing interest.

Within a few months Denys Lasdun was invited to become the Architect in January 1962 and formally accepted in March. He was chosen "not only because of his outstanding reputation but also because it was thought that he would be able to plan the University's development as a single unified concept, so that the University would become a consistent whole".[10] This was what the NNAA and Sir Leslie Martin would not have been able to deliver. The local press welcomed the appointment as "long-awaited" and Lasdun personally as a "brilliant architect of wide ranging vision"[11]

In 1962 Denys Lasdun was forty-eight. Born in London, the son of a businessman engineer, he went to Rugby School and thence to study at the Architectural Association, where he immersed himself in the writings and work of Le Corbusier and was especially influenced by his Pavillon Suisse (1930) in Paris. Before the war he worked with Wells Coates, the founder of the Modern Architectural Research Group (MARS) and moved from them to join Berthold Lubetkin and the Tecton Group (1937-38), whose use of concrete, notably at London Zoo, presaged Lasdun's later use of the material – not least at UEA. (Tecton used in situ concrete whereas that at UEA was largely pre-cast). During the war he built airfields as a major in the Royal Engineers, then after it he returned to Tecton. He established an individual reputation in the 1950s with the Hallfield Primary Schools in Paddington in 1955, the Cluster Block flats in Bethnal Green (1956-59), Peter Robinson's store in the Strand (1958) and luxury flats in St James (1957-61), setting up Denys Lasdun and Partners in 1960. He was also engaged in university building at Liverpool, Leicester and Fitzwilliam House in Cambridge.[12]

Certain stylistic features soon to be evident at UEA were already evident in this earlier work, including the separation of services and activities with bridges and walkways at Hallfield and Bethnal Green and the teaching wall in Peter Robinson's store. The famous ziggurats of the UEA residences had already been a feature of Lasdun's proposals for residences at St John's College, Cambridge. But most important was the Royal College of Physicians in Regent's Park (1960-64). Sir Denys stressed that the Royal College was the "seminal" building, it contains the "quintessential formal language of UEA . . . all the vocabulary was there".[13] The bunker-like extension staircases, terrace and pillars all have visual resonances familiar to inhabitants of the UEA Plain.

Also, several aesthetic characteristics were already established before his coming to UEA. First, he believed firmly in the use of concrete. It was the material used by Le Corbusier in the buildings Lasdun had visited and admired in Paris in the early 1930s, and also the medium in which the Tecton Group had expertise. Lasdun saw the possibilities of "a substance; a muddy mixture of marl, clay, lime, sand, gravel, water heavily laced with steel – reinforced concrete I began to get very excited . . . Believe me, the sweetest music you will ever hear is 'concrete' on your own site".[14] Secondly, he was influenced by Le Corbusier's perception that most activities take place on platforms; indeed platforms, connections and interlocking spaces came to be themes of the Lasdun programme on the Plain.[15] Thirdly, he greatly admired the Greek theatre at Epidauros, of architecture layered into the slope of the landscape. This integration of building and landscape was also to be evident at UEA, "the [UEA] buildings are conceived as architectural hills and valleys, from the air they are like an outcrop of stone". Fourthly, he liked the idea of water flowing over concrete or concrete spanning falling or flowing water, famously evident at Frank Lloyd Wright's influential house Fallingwater (1936), which combined reinforced concrete and terrace platforms over a waterfall. Some of these features were intended and some realised in the UEA residences. Finally, Lasdun saw his task as architect "to give the client, not what he wants but what he never dreamed he wanted and, when he gets it, he recognises it as something he wanted all the time".[16] Such was the man of decisive vision who undertook to build UEA in the 1960s.

The conditions of his employment were laid down.[17] He was to deal with the Site Development Committee acting for the University as employer and specifically with the Estates Office, which was to cause initial problems. The Development Plan was estimated to cost £6,000,000 and the architect's fees were a half per cent of this. The fees for individual buildings undertaken by his firm were 5.75 per cent of the cost. Where the UGC would not meet the full costs, the University would make up the difference out of its own funds. UEA expected to spend £500,000 in addition to the £6,000,000 to be contributed by the UGC. This being satisfactory Lasdun began to devise his master plan, emphasising that "there will be no question of trying to create a University for Norwich at long distance".[18] Sir Denys likened running such a project to directing a jazz band. There was a team with the partners in charge, Denys Lasdun and Alexander Redhouse and the Associate Peter McKinley, under whom worked nine of their architects for specific jobs. Each architect, like an instrumentalist, comes in for his specific task but the overall design and concept lies firmly with the leader of the band, Lasdun himself. The drawings and models were made in London, but architects, especially Peter McKinley, would visit UEA about twice a week as necessary.[19] There they would deal with the Estates Office staff, J. Cory Dixon, Gordon Marshall, Malcolm Crowder, Peter Yorke and Ron Skipper.

His brief was for a university of three thousand students on a site of 272 acres (165 acres at Earlham given by the City Council plus further land over the river purchased by the University). The University was intended to reach three thousand in ten years but Lasdun was asked to take account of the possibility of an expansion to double that thereafter. The individual disciplines were to relate to each other and be physically close and to "foster a striving towards the unity of knowledge". The University was to be highly residential with two thirds of students in residence, but there were to be no colleges or halls of residence. Students were to identify socially with their Schools and on the small scale with their "staircase" in residence, a unit of about twelve students.[20] Frank Thistlethwaite recalled that the "concept was urban, buildings linked by walkways, square and street, free of traffic, rather like an Italian Renaissance hill town".[21] This was in accord with Lasdun's view that "architecture is in a sense a microcosm of the city".[22] On revisiting the University in 1989 Sir Denys remarked, "It's like a little city – it's probably the most urban modern university in the country".[23] The Library was to be near the arts schools, which had to be given a sense of identity. Thistlethwaite recalled, "that was about as much of a briefing that I gave Denys; but he seemed to think it sufficient".[24] With these broad considerations Denys Lasdun and Partners got to work, being expected to report back in about a year.

In the meantime the University needed some other temporary accommodation if it was to receive students in 1963. This was long before any Lasdun buildings would or could be ready for use. As early as October 1961 Frank Thistlethwaite had expressed his intention of starting teaching in temporary accommodation.[25] It was a bold stroke and totally justified by events. It also gave rise to some of the most satisfying buildings (now vanished) the University ever enjoyed.

The Gurney family had anonymously given a twelve acre, steeply sloping site of rough scrub and woodland by the river on the other side of Earlham Road opposite the park. The idea of building a temporary Village there to start off the University came from Denys Lasdun, although he was not to build that part of the site. Frank Thistlethwaite persuaded the UGC to approve the "temporary village" on the grounds that he intended a fast build-up of students to 733 by 1965/66 (in practice it was even faster to 804), and that there would be postgraduate scientists needing laboratories from the start. The cost was estimated at £250,000-£260,000, with which the UGC concurred.[26] So in December 1962 the Norwich firm of Feilden and Mawson, with David Mawson as partner in charge, was appointed as architects to create a Village to consist of 88,000 square feet of accommodation. David Luckhurst, then aged twenty-eight and having only been with the firm for three weeks, was asked to design this new Village. On Christmas Eve 1962 the Medway Building and Supplies company were granted the contract for the buildings themselves and immediately began the designing and subsequent production in their factory in Rochester. Several firms had to cooperate with Feilden and Mawson as architect. These included Medway, the producers of the pre-fabricated buildings; Jack Stockings, the quantity surveyors; Harry

Pointer, for clearing and levelling the site and laying the underground services; R.G. Carter, the builders of the concrete platforms for the buildings; and Bush Builders, subcontractors for the construction. It was said that Norwich had never seen a job of this nature with seven major contractors running concurrently. They were co-ordinated by Mr C. Davies, the Clerk of Works, a tower of strength and one of the unsung heroes of UEA's initial days.[27]

Because of the steeply sloping site it had to be terraced, so that buildings would sit on flat ground. This level surface was achieved by scooping off the earth and refilling with gravel. The work would have been difficult in normal times but 1962/63 was one of the worst winters of the century, with severe frost and snow for eleven weeks following Christmas 1962. The soil was frozen solid three feet down which even broke bulldozer blades. Anti-freeze had to be mixed with the concrete and mortar and the laid concrete had immediately to be covered with hay and polythene. The grass was so unyieldingly frozen that it had to be ripped up with pneumatic drills in order to allow Pointer's digging machines to start the service laying. In the process they cut an uncharted 33,000 volt oil-filled cable crossing the site and not on the plans provided by Eastern Electricity, plunging part of Norwich into darkness. The digger driver was lucky to escape with his life. Following the freeze the thaw came in March, turning the site to mud which had to be covered with metal tracking to enable the lorries to move the pre-fabricated materials to the building positions.

In the meantime Medway started constructing the components of the buildings in Rochester from February 1963. The Medway system consisted of Douglas fir four-inch posts and beams with wall panels which took part of the roof load.[28] Pre-cast concrete and brickwork formed the foundations and provided level platforms, important on so sloping a site. The panels used in Norwich were variously waterproof plywood, Colourglaze asbestos and Western Red Cedar boarding. These were stippled with Arpax, a paint-like solution developed during the war for camouflage. The roofs were flat, built up with several layers of Arpax and finished with stone chippings. But for the large assembly hall a pitched roof was chosen. Amazingly, after the freeze and the mud, the erection of the buildings began on schedule on 1 April, with the Medway teams putting up the superstructure with roofing and glazing at rate of 8000 square feet a week.

David Luckhurst for Feilden and Mawson designed the layout of the Village and an early sketch suggests that some rethinking was necessary.[29] For example the Students' Common Room was originally to be right alongside Earlham Road. This would have entailed severe problems of very noisy social events being heard by passing traffic and nearby houses creating an image of rowdy irresponsibility. It was then moved to the lower end of the site, as far as possible from resident neighbours. The library, which was not accounted for on the original plan, then took over the Student Common Room space. This also had the further advantage that the public attending concerts and plays in the Village were drawn past the Library, offices and laboratories and given the impression of university life as one of sober and purposeful activity. This imagery always mattered but especially in the early days.

Since the original buildings in the Village no longer exist it is worth recalling them. At the top of the slope by Wilberforce Road was the Library and Dining Room. A path then led down towards lecture theatres and arts offices with Earlham Lodge (housing the Senior Common Room) and a superb beech tree at the foot of the slope. By a gravel car turnaround were a bookshop and a banking hall where a workman was tragically killed falling from its low roof during construction. Over to the right were H blocks for the sciences, chemistry, biology, mathematics and physics. Beside the Students Union, now at the lower end of the slope, was the Assembly Hall used for social events, drama, examinations, congregations and the like. Behind both was a large barn splendidly restored in 1968 by Feilden and Mawson as an even more secluded venue for parties and discos, which became all the noisier in the sixties.

The Village was intended, very successfully, to compose a university in miniature and to foster an academic community. As the Plain was built the Village would take on the role of a nursery for new subjects developing and waiting to be transplanted to the main site. It was a feature of the design that the buildings should be at least thirty feet apart not only to give a sense of spaciousness but to prevent the spread of fire. Indeed, in Easter 1963 a fire was started in a biology laboratory, probably by vandals, but it did not affect adjacent buildings. There were originally intended to be fourteen buildings in the Village but by a curious typing error this was changed to fifteen which Feilden and Mawson duly provided; by double irony one fell down but was quickly replaced.[30] By mid June 1963 all the buildings were erected and by the end of July the internal finishings by Bush and R.G. Carter were completed – all in four months. The final painting was completed at the end of August and furnishings installed ready for the official opening by Sir Keith Murray in September 1963 to receive students on 7 October 1963. The whole Village cost £266,400 and was supposed to last ten years, but so good was its building that it lasted nearer thirty.[31] Its construction against adversity and urgency was an impressive achievement by David Luckhurst who was later to play an even greater role in the shaping of UEA. David Mawson, the responsible partner, was recognised with an honorary MA in 1995. It was a delightful environment in which to work with offices spacious enough to hold a seminar, good quality woodwork and flooring, warmly heated in winter but cool and airy in summer. It provided some of the best working conditions I have experienced at UEA.

The other temporary buildings which the University needed were residences. Norwich could not provide enough lodgings while residences on the Plain could not be expected to be ready until the late 1960s. Even then they could not meet all needs. On the northern boundary of Norwich at Horsham St Faith was an airfield with ample former RAF accommodation. As early as 1960 Sir Roy Harrod was thinking in these terms. He regretted that there would be no residence for three years and raised the point with Gordon Tilsley , "Keele started in its first year with Nissen huts, I was wondering whether there were any for sale at St Faith's aerodrome that we could take over ?"[32] Horsham had been empty since July 1963 and the Ministry of Defence could not decide if it needed it. The City wanted the airfield as a civic airport and the University wanted it for residences. Both eventually came about. Sir Edmund Bacon used some behind-the-scenes influence. His brother-in-law James Ramsden was Under Secretary of State for War, "I told him what a jam the War Office would put us in if they took over St Faith's Airfield. I did this off the record and I don't think it will do any harm".[33] The Ministry of Defence decided that it had no further use for Horsham and so UEA acquired the RAF accommodation and ten acres of playing fields on a twenty-one year lease.[34] The University spent £221,000 on refurbishing and £120,000 on furniture and equipment for rooms for eighty-eight men in the sergeants' quarters and 151 women in the officers' quarters. Together with the airmens' quarters it in all provided more than 400 residential places. These were all ready for the new academic year starting in 1965. It struck some outsiders as quaint. A visitor recalled, "I arrived [at Horsham] late at night . I thought the place looked rather like a barracks. I was surprised next morning to find it really was one".[35]

So successful did Horsham prove that a new three-storey 212 room block – "Z block"- was built and opened in 1969. It was financed by a loan to be repaid from student rents over thirty years. The new Z block was built in less than ten months by John Laing using their Easiform system building.[36] It initially seemed unattractive to students to live four miles away from the University in ex-RAF barracks linked by a shuttle bus. Yet Horsham rapidly developed its own powerful ethos with its bar, discos and distinctive forms of rowdiness. "Horschwitz", as it was tastelessly called by some, presided over by the excellent Oliver Wilson, himself a former inmate of a German prisoner of war camp, was an environment which worked.

As the temporary buildings were being erected and occupied, Denys Lasdun busied himself with his brief and his plans for the Plain. He began by paying close attention to the site. Indeed most of Lasdun's work had been in cities; for him UEA was unusual in being on a large rural virgin site. He flew over it in a helicopter and walked over it for the first time with the Vice-Chancellor and Gordon Tilsley in January 1962 and then many times more "in all seasons, in mist, snow, wind and sun",[37] deeply impressed with its possibilities. They noted that the area had a slight rainfall of twenty-six inches a year and high average figures for sunshine. They were concerned to find, however, that Norwich had a higher than average record of lightning strikes which was going to need a radio active discharge system with fifteen foot masts as lightning-conductors on the buildings and a Franklin rod on the boiler house chimneys. As regards the building ground, its southern facing slope, rising seventy feet from the River Yare was inevitably to shape the whole concept. The subtle contours of the site, doubly sloping both to the south and the west, were carefully modelled back in Denys Lasdun and Partners' London offices, since the new UEA would become part of this land-scape.

Certain principles began to emerge. The University must be concentrated and compact to create a sense of identity. The spread should be limited to preserve the natural landscape as distinct from the urban environment of the university itself. Because the ground sloped so markedly the "linkage" should be routes on horizontal levels against the natural slope of the ground. So part of the design would incorporate decks and platforms with walkways elevated above the sloping ground beneath. These were to be a distinctive feature of UEA, carrying not only circulating walkers above but service ducts under the walkway, all separated from the flow of vehicle traffic below at ground level. Lasdun also saw a further value in walkways for academics since "every moment of walking is a moment of thinking".[38] Horizontally working against the slope was one principle. But another was that the buildings should appear to "cascade" down the slope, "the buildings are dispersed around a sequence of central spaces cascading down the slope and leading to a large re-entrant rough grass area, a "land-locked harbour". The latter was an assertion of the natural green of the landscape, interpenetrating and contrasting with the urban grey of the building. Indeed Lasdun likened it to creating "what is virtually an outcrop of stone on the side of a hill leading down to a river".[39]

With these broad considerations Denys Lasdun and his twelve colleagues began to form their Development Plan, moving between Norwich and his London offices in Queen Anne Street. He presented the Plan to the Executive Committee on 7 December 1962 and it was then published in April 1963, a year after his appointment.[40] The Plan was for a University which would contain three thousand students in ten years with the possibility of expansion to six thousand thereafter. Academic assumptions were also to shape the architectural design, although inevitably when Lasdun was devising the Plan in 1962 there were very few academics around with whom he could discuss their needs. Nonetheless Thistlethwaite had his own very clear strategic ideas which shaped Lasdun's thinking. "Individual disciplines will so far as possible be related to one another", so they would not be housed in separate departments but in broadly based Schools of Study. The site was conceived as a semicircle with a radius of not more than five minutes slow walking time. Since it sloped north to south and also down to the river, the entrance was to be at its highest point. The pedestrian route would not follow the slopes but be on walkways running behind the residences and alongside the Schools, providing entrance to the buildings two or more floors above ground level. Vehicle traffic would be kept separate from the walkways and below them on roads at ground level. Focuses of the site would be University House, Senate House and Library, all on the northern part. The teaching block, not yet called the Teaching Wall, would snake down the slope from north east to south west with arts and science buildings intermixed in a long sequence, a "long sausage", to encourage intellectual contact between different disciplines. It was also an important principle that grassed areas should penetrate and intermingle with built up areas. The most prominent of these was to be a rough grassed area reaching up from the river between the residences to the teaching wall, later to be called by Lasdun "the Harbour" though the term did not catch on and has not lasted. The whole site was to be open to the public; there was to be no "Cordon Sanitaire".

As regards individual buildings the Library was originally to be at the north end of the University with two thousand reading places and housing a small picture gallery. University House was originally intended to contain all the dining facilities for the University as well as common rooms, an assembly hall and theatre. The Senate House would serve as the administrative centre of the university and be placed at the north east of the site close to the entrance. The residential blocks were already thought out. Lasdun envisaged crescents of residence blocks which came to be called ziggurats, rather like claws stretching down to the river. After fifteen years it was intended that there should be five crescents comprising an amazing forty-six ziggurat blocks; wide swards of grass would separate the crescents interpenetrating the natural green and concrete built areas. Each group of a dozen students would have their individual study bedrooms of 120 square feet, each group having its own front door, kitchen and breakfast room. In fact only two crescents were ever built – Norfolk and Suffolk Terraces – and it takes some imagination to envisage the original bold plan of five such ranges stretching down to the river. The residences were to be in the design of a series of stepped ziggurats with the height of the teaching wall behind them. The whole was to create an effect of "urban spaces cascading down into other urban spaces", as Lasdun put it. This cascading effect is best seen from some way down the River Yare, looking back.

There would be other buildings, the Sports Centre and the Chaplaincy and it is interesting to note that Lasdun envisaged that the old quarry on the north side of the site could be made into an open air theatre. The University decided to restrict the use of cars to a quarter of the total university population. Parking would be dispersed through the site without the need for a large separate car park. The quarry theatre never materialised but a large car park did, yet it is remarkable how much of the original concept was carried through into the final version – the walkways separated from roads, the teaching wall, the crescents of ziggurat residences, the harbour of grass between Norfolk and Suffolk Terraces. The chief differences are the assumption that there would be more than twice as much ziggurat residence accommodation. Nor has University House emerged as quite the multi-function building originally intended. Most strikingly the original intention of having the river brought right up to the residences and flowing actually beneath one of them was not possible because Norfolk Terrace was not completed. It was overall a grand design, most of the spirit of which has been retained. What has also been retained is the acronym "UEA" which Lasdun used on his plans for brevity and which became the identifying title of the University.

Denys Lasdun accompanied by the Vice-Chancellor presented his plans to an appreciative press at Earlham Hall on 25 April 1963.[41] His presentational style was notably impressive as objects and models of buildings, initially covered by sheets, were successively unveiled with the sheets removed one by one as if by some master magician.[42] It was praised as "a very competent and imaginative plan . . . a commendable achievement". Sir Denys recalls that the atmosphere was one of considerable excitement and approval. But the audience spotted the inevitable dilemma. Lasdun claimed that the University would not be "a little separate oasis" but part of the fabric of Norwich.[43] It was geographically within the City as bounded by the River Yare and satellite sites merging with the City fabric were proposed for long-term expansion.[44]

Yet so carefully planned was the campus as an integrated town plan in itself that the *Builder* thought "one cannot help thinking that for many of the students who live within the campus their world would start at Earlham Road and stop at the River Yare. This kind of university life is a far cry from town and gown college life and perhaps even further from the dispersed life of the red brick universities". People from Norwich could come to the campus to walk by the river and attend social functions. But the students, it was feared, would not so naturally integrate with Norwich as the Oxbridge man walking out of his college gates straight into his university town or the civic university student with his university buildings set amid the streets of a Victorian city. The integrated campus would undoubtedly facilitate the creation of a community but its danger might be to encourage one too inward-looking, even too self-obsessed as in the years of unrest. This was hardly Lasdun's fault, however, it was a consequence of the greenfield, 250 acre site policy of Sir Keith Murray and the UGC of the time. The City gave outline planning approval to the plan which was exhibited in the Castle along with the architectural models to help with the Appeal Fund.

Denys Lasdun's presentation in April 1963 was a great success in Norwich, but back in London the UGC was displeased. They were annoyed with the University, rather than with the architect, for disclosing details of the plan to the press in circumstances of high publicity before presenting them for approval to the UGC. The Vice-Chancellor expressed his regret to Sir Keith Murray, explaining that they had needed to publish the plans to get Outline Planning Permission from the City Planning Committee. Denys Lasdun reasonably explained that the plan was only a first draft without cost exercises but that he had always met cost limits before on university buildings. The UGC had visited his offices on 7 March to see the Development Plans. Murray made it clear that the UGC would not be "hustled", building had to be kept to cost limits with plans and schedules properly approved by the UGC.[45]

Cory Dixon, who was highly regarded by the UGC, had contacted the UGC in "great distress" to complain that the architect was ignoring him, was insisting on dealing with the UGC direct and was not discussing his plans with the local authorities.[46] It had also been made clear by the UGC and the University that individual buildings should not be designed before the general plan was approved.[47] The arrangement was that Lasdun should provide the overall development plan and then, if this were satisfactory, he would be invited to design the first buildings. This was made clear at a meeting with Sir Keith Murray at the UGC. Lasdun claimed, however, that he had not understood at the outset that work on the Development Plan was to be separate from work on the buildings: "if you had put this proposition to us at the very beginning we would not have undertaken work at all on this University."[48] His position was understandable since the UGC limited consultant architects fees to a quarter per cent of project costs, which was not very attractive unless the architect could also design the individual buildings. This may have been a factor in Sir Leslie Martin's reluctance to be merely an overall planner, since he had not the time to design buildings. Certainly Lasdun would have been aware that UEA's intention was to have a fully integrated scheme with the overall planner also designing the buildings, this being a major reason for turning to him and not staying with Martin.

The UGC was becoming uneasy about Norwich. They began to fear that Denys Lasdun was intending to "do a Spence" as they put it, devise a splendid plan (as Sir Basil Spence had done in Sussex) which was bound to be "far out with our cost limits", and lead to the kind of trouble they had had with Sussex. They were even suspicious of the influence of Lord Mackintosh and his flair for publicity. They felt that it was as if the Vice-Chancellor and the architect were so swept up in their enthusiasm for the architectural plans that they were engaging insufficiently with UEA officials, the local authority or the UGC itself.[49] The instincts of the UGC had to be for control and restraint whereas those of the University and its architect were properly for an ambitious creative vision and the drive to carry it through.

Lasdun had taken somewhat longer than expected on the Development Plan since he had been unwell with mumps around May 1963. At the same time he had been doing necessary outline work on designing individual buildings.[50] It was decided to go ahead with the Development Plan but a Site Development Committee was set up to work with the architect. There were also some difficulties about fees. The UGC was trying to control the situation whereby architects employed consultants who in turn required fees without reducing their own fees for work taken off them. Lasdun had specifically arranged in his own contract that his fees would not be reduced.[51] Accordingly not all members of this new Site Development Committee who had to work with Denys Lasdun were his unqualified admirers. Sir Lincoln Ralphs who was invited to sit on the committee reflected that "our architect is likely to continue to prove difficult".[52] This was a harsh view, and Sir Lincoln Ralphs could be a demanding man, but it represented the tensions perhaps inseparable from such a vast creative project and with the many diverse personalities.

On 30 September 1963 Denys Lasdun presented his Development Plan II with important modifications in the light of discussions since April. By now there were ample faculty at UEA to make their desires known. Lasdun had originally seen the teaching area as a long building containing sections for arts and sciences. The Arts Schools, however, "wanted some sort of building in which they could feel their own identity, some sort of court, some sort of planning device which was not just a long sausage of a building". Hence the idea that the present buildings should eventually form one side of a series of courtyards. The spur buildings now stretching from the Teaching Wall towards the boiler house were to form second and third sides. Ultimately it was intended to build a parallel Teaching Wall alongside the existing one on the Earlham Park side to complete the fourth side of what would have been courts. This of course was never done. Lasdun regarded this new thinking as "the real discovery" of the Second Plan. He described with enthusiasm the building which goes from one side of the site to the other, which combines small rooms, big rooms, specialist rooms which can be prefabricated . . . which can cope both with the known factors of teaching and the imponderable additions and changes that might be wanted in the future . . . it is a sort of way of planning which allows departments to move around freely with vertical circulations at frequent intervals . . . it was an immensely important discovery.

However the full plan was not to be. The long Teaching Wall, with its spurs providing the big rooms, stands as a building in its own right, although without the parallel building, which never materialised, the courts and the intended catenation could not be formed.

The second major change of the second plan was that Thistlethwaite and the Librarian, Willi Guttsman, convinced Lasdun that the Library should be a free-standing centrally-placed building with room around for expansion. In the original version it would have been in an increasingly built up area of contiguous buildings at the top of the site. The Librarian was absolutely right and this was one of the most far-sighted changes for the better. Thirdly, Denys Lasdun aired a proper grievance which had a profound consequence. There was a lot of chopping and changing about the location of the Food Research Institute, whether it should be on the Plain or outside it. He was dismayed to find out from a third party that it was to be built by another architect, David Luckhurst, the designer of the Village, and it was to be at the southern end of the site. Understandably annoyed as he was, Lasdun saw that this resolved a jigsaw and changed a fundamental policy. Since the Food Research Institute needed to be near Biology, then the School of Biology had to be located at the southern end of the Teaching Wall.[53] The location of Biology was also influenced by its need for a large biology garden to the rear and this location in the Wall provided it adjacent space. Biology in turn had to be next to Chemistry and thence to Physics and to Environmental Sciences in sequence. This overturned Lasdun's (architectural) and probably Thistlethwaite's (curricular) assumptions "that there should be a mixture of Arts and Sciences. We mixed Arts and Sciences in this basket". Now the Arts Schools were grouped sequentially at the top of the north-east end of the line and the sciences together at the south west end. Lasdun described the chief conceptual difference between the first and second plans as a change from "a centroid moving outwards" to "a ring of buildings which will move outwards".[54] An American critic thought that this "continuous teaching environment", the Wall, "may well be Britain's most significant design concept for higher education".[55]

On 1 November 1963 Denys Lasdun presented his detailed building programme for the sequence of work.[56]

	Contracts placed	Works completed	Cost
Early 1964	Entrance Road, part playing fields	1964	£50,000
Mid 1964	Boiler House	1965	£200,000
October 1964	Residences	1966 July/December	£700,000
November 1964	Chemistry	September 1966	
April 1965	Biology	July/September 1967	
October 1965	Arts	July/September 1967	£1,750,000
July 1965	Library	April 1967	£300,000
July 1965	University House	July/September 1967	£500,000

He made it clear that he would design and build all of these buildings or none of them. The University wanted him not only to devise the overall structure but to set the aesthetic style of the initial building. Whatever confusions there had been about this were resolved and Lasdun got to work.

A crucial initial decision that was to stamp the whole aesthetic of the project was to build in concrete. Sir Basil Spence had used brick beautifully at Sussex University and it was said that Lasdun had originally intended to use bricks at UEA but had gone over to concrete. "This caused uneasiness among members of the Norwich Town Planning Committee", but they were satisfied that "it will be good to look at".[57] In fact, Lasdun had never contemplated using brick except briefly in areas where concrete blocks were eventually used. It was already evident that he was determined on concrete at the time of his first Development Plan in December 1962. He justified it on the interesting aesthetic grounds that,

> the infinite variety of colour in the valley landscape makes the choice of external materials and colour of particular importance. Of all the suitable materials available today concrete in its natural grey state appears to enhance the colours of the landscape to greatest advantage. It is important therefore that there should be a predominance of this material with its range of neutral colours depending on whether it is pre-cast, in situ or in the form of concrete blocks.

By his Development Plan of 1963 the aesthetic argument was clinched by the economic one. The building industry was heavily committed nationally and regionally. So the buildings had to be erected "quickly and cheaply". To achieve this object prefabrication was necessary. As a local producer of precast concrete explained, "concrete is now proven to be the most economical form of construction in a multitude of cases, particularly when one takes into account that it is long lasting, fire resistant, needs no painting or other forms of protection and maintenance ... economy is achieved over site methods by mechanisation and therefore less labour, less waste of national materials and particularly important in this modern age – speed of construction".

Moreover, pre-stressed concrete with high tensile wires cast into the concrete "gives the structure enormous strength – much greater than could be given to it by a similar amount of reinforcing steel".[58] This technique had been used in England since 1947. Lasdun's early experience with Tecton, notable users of concrete in various forms, spanned the periods 1938-48 before and after the introduction of pre-stressed concrete. His airfield building had also given him a familiarity with reinforced concrete, which preceded the pre-stressed form. All these factors, aesthetic, cost, and his early experience, shaped Lasdun's view about the desirability of concrete as the medium for UEA.

The decision about concrete obviated a quaint bit of whimsy. The Lord Lieutenant of Suffolk as a former Christ Church, Oxford man asked his old college if it would give him one of the stones of their building to be incorporated into the new buildings at UEA. The curious grounds for this were that Cardinal Wolsey, the founder of Christ Church was from Ipswich and hence an East Anglian. Surprisingly Christ Church agreed to provide a stone (where did they take it from?) and UEA agreed to accept it.[59] Although generously meant this had inappropriate overtones – that "proper" universities were built of stone, that an apostolic succession from, even a tiny gesture of connection with, Oxford was somehow desirable to validate a new institution. Lasdun's bold plan in concrete was a "doing different" assertion of independence from that kind of traditionalism which the Christ Church masonry would have symbolised. The stone never arrived and Lasdun knew nothing of it. The only natural stone in the UEA buildings of the Lasdun, Feilden and Mawson period is in the foyer of the Council Chamber – a facing of finely knapped Norfolk flint. Perhaps the only natural stone in the exterior are the sets at the end of Norfolk Terrace. They came from the forecourt of the demolished Norwich Station, which used to stand at the foot of Grapes Hill.[60]

The builders got to work. The building method for the residences was to make pre-cast concrete slabs and panels on the site using vertical steel and horizontal timber moulds. Ten vertical casting batteries, based on those developed by the Building Research Station, manufactured wall and floor elements each up to four tons in weight. The largest units would take three days to produce and the small a day and a half. This pre-cast concrete made on site was produced by Formcrete. It was erected by rail-mounted tower cranes operating in conjunction with a remote controller trolley.[61] For the teaching buildings pre-cast concrete components were made locally in their own works by Anglian Building Products. This was for parts needing "technical and exact control of the quality and dimensional accuracy of concrete . . . the controlled conditions of a factory with modern apparatus and skilled craftsmen are necessary to produce quality concrete products". They claimed that economy was achieved over in situ methods by mechanisation with less labour and less waste of materials. Also Anglian Building Products had devised a system whereby the set concrete could be released from the moulding shutters not by oil but a releasing agent which gave a more attractive surface and which they had previously used at St Catherine's College, Oxford. Four large repetitive basic components were assembled on site with a rigid in situ spine.[62] They, and the in situ materials, were erected by tower cranes within the building, extending upwards as the building rose and with the voids being filled as the cranes were dismantled.

Lasdun explained his dual strategy of a mix of in situ and factory made materials, for the Teaching Wall,

> a system of prefabricated parts was proposed. The elements would be made under strictly controlled conditions and then transported to the site and assembled by a small semi-skilled gang. The floors are made of structural concrete in the form of a flat slab of constant depth. This slab supported by three parallel rows of concrete columns is composed of pre-cast ribbed slab units and edge beams with the central section cast in situ to stabilise the building.[63]

The standardised dimensions of slabs and panels relate to a series of modules themselves of uniform dimensions of 2 feet 7½ inches (800 mm) with a clearance height of 9 feet 6 inches or 11 feet from floor to floor. Most users of the teaching buildings on the Plain are not aware that rooms big and small, long or square are all multiples of these modular dimensions. It is also intriguing that this idea of devising modules differently combinable derived from the work of Le Corbusier and his Domino skeleton of reinforced concrete columns and slabs as early as 1914 – an early influence on Lasdun.[64] The spoil earth dug out to enable the foundations to be laid was tipped by the river to stabilise part of the marshland for possible playing fields. Bernard Feilden later planned a steep mound formed from excavated spoil earth at the north end of the site by the old quarry where Lasdun had proposed to form an amphitheatre. The grading for the mound was carried out by "a very skilled and sensitive digger driver Cyril Loynes"[65] who deserves credit for the sharply eye catching, now tree covered, feature of the otherwise gently sloping landscape of the Plain. Mr Loynes subsequently worked on the careful grading of the land around Norman Foster's Sainsbury Centre.

The first building on the Plain and perhaps the most immediately striking for the visitor is the Boiler House.[66] It was decided to bring all the central services together in a long low building on sloping ground against the background of the belt of trees dividing Earlham Park from the Plain. The roof could be used as a car park and it was originally envisaged that a bridge or walkway would link this with the teaching buildings. A 33 KV Eastern Electricity Board substation is at the east end of the building and next to it an

11 KV substation serving the boiler house itself. The boiler house was planned to contain eight oil-fired boilers fuelled with 250,000 gallons of fuel in six storage tanks. Only three were installed. The boilers then operated at 150 pounds per square inch, a pressure producing an impressive 25 million British thermal units per hour. They have since been replaced by tower pressure equipment. The equally remarkable exterior is dominated by two elegant 140 foot chimneys, although a group of four was first intended. Their optimum height and cross section design was shaped as a result of a smoke model test at the National Physical Laboratory. The whole complex cost just over £750,000.

Despite the Lasdun central section never having been built, the building is very impressive. The Vice-Chancellor showing some Scandinavian visitors around the site found to his surprise that this was the building that most enthused them.[67] But it could also confuse the locals. In an overheard conversation on a bus passing along Earlham Road one elderly lady asked another, "What's that? A biscuit factory?", to receive the reply "No, you can see the chimneys, it's the crematorium".[68] Lasdun made the bold and correct decision to make a striking feature of the chimneys and in this UEA contrasts with the rather feebly apologetic and half-hidden chimneys at the University of Kent in Canterbury.[69] They are also an example of a recurrent powerful image in Lasdun's aesthetic. He first used the theme of paired verticals in the portal of his first house design, Silver Greys at Oxshott in Surrey in 1934 "Lasdun would resort time and time again to the theme of paired verticals in his buildings".[70] UEA is fortunate to have one of the most powerful examples of them in the Boiler House chimneys.

After such essential services the next important building was the Library. Willi Guttsman, the Librarian, had written an excellent brief for his building.[71] He wanted a single building with no departmental libraries. It was to be a borrowing library with books and readers in close proximity and with no barriers between them, "there should therefore be as much access to the stack as is technically and economically possible. Indeed stack and reading space should be interpenetrating". Just before coming to UEA Guttsman had visited various libraries in the USA and this confirmed his views about the desirability of open-plan libraries and even the conjunction of picture gallery space within them. Before the new universities of the sixties university libraries tended to have a division of function between restricted stacks and reading rooms. He wanted to break this down. He envisaged a thousand reading places and a bookstock of 500,000 volumes. The stacks would be the core of the building with reading areas radiating from them, with each floor to be open plan. Distinctive features he wanted were to be rooms for rare books and manuscripts, and a music room and picture gallery as part of the concourse. He also insisted on separate offices for library staff.[72] This was partly a reaction against his experience at LSE where assistant librarians had no private studies and partly recognition of German practice where university librarians were expected to have subject specialisms and personal rooms.

Denys Lasdun's original intention was for the Library to be part of a closely-integrated central core of buildings along with the Senate House and University House. Guttsman was uneasy about this on various grounds. It would have been too close to a road with its attendant noise and he also doubted whether there was enough room for further expansion. Accordingly the Library was moved down the slope away from the administrative building, as a free-standing building with land around it for expansion.[73] Guttsman got on well with Lasdun, possibly because of his thoughtful briefing papers. For example, Lasdun proposed a staircase going the whole length of the building which would have been very open and a source of noise at the heart of the building. He also suggested reading floors and stack floors divided at half levels. Willi Guttsman disagreed with both of these features and they were dropped.[74]

Denys Lasdun presented his specific designs for the Library in September 1964, locating the Library near to the "main central space of the University" on the network of pedestrian circulation.[75] He proposed building it in two stages, 1966/7 and 1971/2, with the original block being doubled in size to form a near square. He took great care over two particular problems. Sun glare on the windows was to be deflected by a wall and transom arrangement with the window-glass set well back and shaded. This works well. He was also conscious of the very heavy weight of the books borne by the Library floors. The floors accordingly were one foot thick reinforced concrete slabs on a grid of 20 inch by 20 inch columns with column heads mushroomed for load-bearing and the foundations were to be driven concrete piles. Sir John Cockcroft, who took a special interest in the Library, regarded the construction schedules and cost as "not at all unreasonable".[76] And so it proved. The Library, when opened for use in 1968, was praised as one of the most spacious and relaxed in atmosphere of any of the new university libraries.[77]

Accordingly Denys Lasdun's subsequent disengagement from the University buildings caused Willi Guttsman considerable anxiety. The Library still needed the completion of its second stage – "a mirror image of the present one and the building is a stump without it".[78] Guttsman wanted Lasdun to be retained for the Library Phase II. After negotiations it was arranged that Feilden and Mawson would be the architects for the Library II but that Denys Lasdun would be retained as the designer and paid a fee by Feilden and Mawson.[79] This overcame the problem that the copyright on the design was held by Denys Lasdun and Partners, DLP. But the legal responsibility and detailed design and working drawings would be the work of Feilden and Mawson. Michael Everitt of Feilden and Mawson took great care to obtain the exact pre-cast concrete colour and quality of Phase I, consulting Shockcrete in Cambridge about this. Max Fordham was the new service engineer. He was then at an early stage in his career but subsequently a leading figure in the profession. He played an important part in making both parts of the Library look the same, although Phase II was cheaper. There are differences in window design and the air conditioning by Fordham is also simple but effective. It actually looks like one seamless building and most people do not realise it is actually two by two different architects but with the continuity of Denys Lasdun's design. It is one of the most successful buildings on the Plain, a tribute to Willi Guttsman's briefing and ideas, Denys Lasdun's concept, and Feilden and Mawson's sensitive completion of it. It is a castle keep of a building, a central citadel of learning and an assertion of what the University is really about. There is room for expansion and Sir Denys was rightly concerned that that surrounding area is not encroached upon by other buildings.

The lecture theatres were largely thought out by Ian Watt, the Professor of English and a close friend of the Vice-Chancellor.[80] He argued that, since it was unlikely that a theatre and a concert hall would be built on the Plain, it was better to design large lecture theatres which could also serve this purpose. He envisaged a 400 seater lecture theatre with a dais running the width of the interior at one end to serve as a stage, with lighting, access doors to the side and cine-projection facilities. A second lecture theatre for 200 could be used for concerts with a dais strong enough to bear a grand piano. The final plan incorporates this but on a larger scale. Two main lecture theatres of 500 and 250 seats were to be complemented by two 150 seaters beneath at a total cost of £205,886. The original intention was that all the lecture theatres should have ceilings of suspended painted plaster, but this feature was abandoned leaving the ducts and roof stanchions exposed. Indeed the false ceiling was specifically omitted from the large lecture theatre in order to make it suitable for music. Both are comfortable to speak in without microphones, probably because of the high rake of the seating.

Most working activity would take place in the Teaching Wall. The Chemistry Building was the first teaching building on the Plain, taking priority with the residences. The original demands by Alan Katritzky were understandably ambitious and the UGC told the University to cut them. They required the research space per person to be cut from 90 to 80 square feet and demurred at so many special rooms. With cuts they thought the cost could be kept to £756,000.[81] In the light of this Lasdun drew up his plans.[82] He was being asked to design and erect the Chemistry Building in a third of the time recommended by the UGC, "the time factor has therefore been one of our main considerations in developing the design and structure of this building". It was to be in five storeys, eventually in two continuous parallel blocks each 50 feet wide and 100 feet apart, though as we have seen the parallel blocks never materialised. For speed and cheapness it would be in prefabricated parts, with floors of reinforced concrete in the form of structural slabs or pre-cast ribbed slab units and edge beams. There was to be a maximum repetition of pre-cast units in what was to become the familiar module of 2 feet 7½ inches. Uniquely the draining system from the Chemistry Building was to be of borosilicate glass discharging into the main sewer with a sampling chamber before discharge. Otherwise it set the pattern for the whole Teaching Wall, both for arts and sciences.

Since the pattern for the Chemistry, Biology and Arts Buildings had to be identical and were to be part of an integral Wall, it was suggested by the quantity surveyor that the same contractor should build all three.[83] Accordingly various contractors tendered for the buildings and R.G. Carter won the contract with a tender of £675,797 for the Chemistry Building.[84] The Arts Building was to be contiguous with Chemistry in the Wall. But, whereas the original intention was for Arts and Sciences to intermingle, Chemistry prevented this by placing firmly locked doors between themselves and Arts I. This made good sense, as it was quite unacceptable to have arts students wandering into chemistry laboratories and there had to be security doors to prevent the spread of fire following some chemical accident in other parts of the Wall. Interconnection and intermingling between the Schools would be along the walkway.

The ideas for the Arts Building came from Ian Watt.[85] He suggested a single building for all the Arts Schools, close to the Library and with office rooms for small tutorials and larger seminar rooms for groups of twelve to twenty-five students. He also wanted good circulating and meeting space with foyers and (fancifully) bay windows and verandas for intimate encounters. This was largely carried out.[86] It is notable how much of the Chemistry Building design was the same as the Arts – the five storeys, the fifty foot width, the prefabricated concrete construction, the foundations of bored cast in situ concrete piles and the inevitable 2 foot 7 inches module with the 21 foot column spacings. The Arts Building has proved very flexible, its internal walls are of non-load-bearing concrete blocks and have been quite easy to move about, changing the size of rooms according to need. When Arts I was being built I entered the shell of the building. It looked like a multi storey car park dripping with wet. All the structural modules were there but it required imagination to envisage how it would be filled with rooms and corridors. This was the point, the structure is immensely strong; the interior walls, on the other hand, are flexible and easily dispensable. In the sixties they were plastered and painted, a luxury dropped in the seventies.

Biology was to start just before Arts in July 1965 and be completed about the same time in July 1967. As with Chemistry, Biology chanced its arm with its demands to the UGC. Likewise the UGC's reaction was that there was too much space devoted to research (26,770 square feet), but unusually suggested that the University had underestimated the cost which they put at £ 1,700,000 rather than £1,300,000 .[87] Biology was to be located at the lower end of the Wall to be near to the biology-based research institutes (the Food Research Institute, the John Innes Institute and the British Sugar Corporation laboratories).[88] It was to be a seven storey building with an aquarium in the basement and an animal house on the fifth floor. In between was to be zoology, biophysics, botany, genetics and biochemistry.

The Mathematics and Physics Building posed particularly interesting problems. The original intention was to locate it between Chemistry and the Arts Building so that mathematics using arts subjects, notably economics, would have access to it. But in September 1966 it was decided to place it between Chemistry and Biology as requiring mathematics even more. So in Autumn 1966 there was a rethinking of the sequence of the Teaching Wall from west to east: Biology, gap (which Lasdun assumed would be filled by the John Innes Institute), Mathematics and Physics, gap, Chemistry, Arts.[89] So the Wall was not one straight line but originally consisted of blocks not all were yet connected to each other, which changed the angle of direction in the middle where there was a gap. The gap between Biology and Chemistry was completed by Feilden and Mawson architects to Denys Lasdun's plan after DLP had ceased responsibility for the building of the Wall. There was an interesting problem in that the length of the gap between the existing buildings necessitated a narrowed-down version of the Lasdun plan in some places and a widening in others. This is barely visible to the eye so skilfully was it dealt with, nor is the change in concrete colour which has weathered down to uniformity. When Denys Lasdun inspected Feilden and Mawson's completion of his design on the Wall he appreciated the problem and, to David Luckhurst's pleasure, approved the solution.

The demands of the physicists were quite the most testing in the design of any building. They included rooms reinforced with two inch steel plate to withstand explosions; rooms for compressors creating vibrations which must not affect other rooms, especially the balance room; a room with a floor capable of accepting a five ton electromagnet at 1000 lbs per square foot; another for fluid dynamics with heavy loading and subject to flooding; and rooms that were variously dark, radioactive, non-magnetic and freezing.[90] Every conceivable condition and contrary condition had to be catered for in rooms in the same building. This was built by Feilden and Mawson with Marshall "Hoppy" Hopkins having special responsibility for the Maths and Physics Building. Distinctive features were the need for a preponderance of small rooms which in turn necessitated a double corridor with stairs and lift shafts in the centre – unlike the central single corridors in the Arts Buildings. Particularly striking is the lecture theatre on the roof adding to the sculptural features of lift shafts and water tanks which break up the straight horizontals of the roof line.[91] This was seen by Hopkins as a particular tribute to the Lasdun concept, offsetting horizontal lines with strong vertical blocks. The building requirements of physics, however, already raised issues about this problematic subject. It was plain that it was to be quite disproportionately expensive and demanding on the resources of other parts of the University. This was in spite of certain lower cost features such as anodised aluminium rather than bronze window frames for example. The question whether it was all worth it was not publically raised. Frank Thistlethwaite privately had doubts and consulted Sir John Cockcroft, only to be told that not to have physics as a subject in the new university was unthinkable. But the extravagant building demands suggested that either the University or the UGC should have pondered whether proliferating physics departments were really appropriate for the nation at large or Norwich in particular.

The Computing Centre was located on the north-eastern boundary of the Harbour between the Chemistry "bridge" and the Lecture Theatres.[92] This was a small but demanding building needing airlocks, air-conditioning and pad foundations to diminish vibration. It was built to an "extremely tight" schedule to receive the computer in June 1968. Nobody could have predicted at the time how all-embracing and important computing would become in the University and how worthwhile its costs (*pari passu* with the equally unpredictably diminishing importance of physics).

The Wall was where teaching went on. But the residences were more central to students lives and attracted particular attention from the public at large. The nature of the residences to be built depended on some fundamental thinking about the social organisation of student life. Were they to be colleges like Oxford and Cambridge or residences as in many civic universities, or some smaller kind of unit? Sir Roy Harrod, for example, as early as 1960 was arguing that there should be Halls of Residence, each with separate refectories and that all students should belong to and eat at their Hall, whether they lived there on not.[93] This was an extravagant Christ Church, Oxford, view of unreality. More influentially, and realistically, Charles Wilson of the Academic Planning Board had come firmly to the view that a collegiate system was out of the question.[94] He thought that even the Durham collegiate system was merely a pale imitation of Oxbridge and, unless a college both admitted and taught, there was no point in bothering with it merely as a place of residence. For a small university, colleges teaching, admitting and providing residence and catering made no sense. Yet if a full-blown college system seemed impracticable, the APB and Wilson were equally clear that a high degree of residential accommodation was necessary, combined with centralised catering. [95] It was going to be up to the new Vice-Chancellor to decide the detail.

Frank Thistlethwaite was equally clear that UEA must be "highly residential". This was on broadly educational grounds and also took account of the fact that Norwich could not provide enough lodgings. So 60 per cent of students would have to be in residences provided by the University, "residential accommodation must therefore be an integral part of the building programme".[96] He reviewed the alternatives. A unitary system of centralised facilities in a "union" had certain advantages – it was cheap to build and in a small university there was no need to disperse facilities. The "federal" approach devolving facilities to colleges and other residential units also had advantages – it created small manageable communities in which students of different academic disciplines would mix. But colleges would be costly and the UGC had made it clear that the initial capital costs of residential accommodation must be borne by the University. Without UGC finance "to embark upon the collegiate plan might be hazardous". He then focused on his solution.[97] If colleges were impracticable yet, in his experience as a Cambridge college tutor, the heart of the college was the staircase, "the true unit of common living". He thought modern students were impatient with the imposed formality of colleges – formal dining, gowns, fixed hours, but that there was a preference for "on campus residence without collegiate trappings". The staircase with twelve study bedrooms and a communal kitchen/breakfast room/ common room was his solution. "Therefore it is proposed that the modulus of student residence should be the staircase of about a dozen study bedrooms together with kitchen and common room." The cost per student would be about £1000 and thus £600,000 taken from the Appeal Fund would house 600 students. This together with 800 in lodgings would provide for 1400 students all fed centrally. In context, York, Kent, Lancaster had opted for some form of collegiate structure whereas East Anglia was at one with Sussex, Essex and Warwick in deciding against it.

Lasdun went ahead accordingly, designing a series of "ziggurats" or "Aztec pyramids" in crescent terraces. There were intended to be five of them, as we have seen, but only two were built. Each pyramid had a central staircase off which corridors branched to left and right. On the south side of the corridors were bed-sitting rooms so that each corridor had about a dozen rooms forming each unit. The layers of rooms were stacked, as in a pyramid, with more rooms at the base then fewer stage by stage to the top of the stepped design. At the top was a flat for a resident tutor or visiting guest, and water tanks. The layout of the rooms converged to a point like the prow of a ship and the room at this apex point was the communal kitchen and breakfast room for the corridor at that level, also acting as a social common room. The stepping of the ziggurats was subtly contoured to the slope of the ground in ways which the eye appreciates without initially understanding why. For example in Suffolk Terrace, higher up the slope, there are three pyramids of seven storeys and one of six storeys. In Norfolk Terrace, slightly lower down the slope, there are three of eight storeys, two of seven and one of six. The overall effect is one of an even roof level on changing levels of ground which creates a sense of unity and homogeneity which is extremely satisfying to the eye. Since the levels were stepped the roof of the room below acted as a terrace for the room above. It was one of the pleasures of the residences that an occupant could step out of his large window onto a personal terrace looking towards the greenery of the harbour, trees and the river and broad beyond. All the rooms looked to the south. The back of the building was "blind" concrete with a walkway running the length linking the entrance doors to each ziggurat at the back. The whole effect Lasdun likened to "vineyards in France". He was fond of this imagery of a vineyard or a rocky outcrop on a slope in his concept of the UEA site.[98]

There was another image too. This was evident in the drainage, where "rainwater is collected in gutters in the roof of each floor, discharged from one to the next at the prow of each breakfast room and drained to the River Yare".[99] As the buildings cascaded down the slope figuratively, so water cascaded literally and spectacularly down the ziggurats in time of rainfall. This characteristic of water falling over or underneath concrete was another powerful Lasdun image. It may derive from Frank Lloyd Wright's famous house Fallingwater in 1936, where concrete platforms extended over a waterfall. Curtis thinks that this "may have touched a special chord in Lasdun's imagination". There are certainly echoes of it in his original intention of bringing water of the river right up to the residence and having it flow under some concrete spans. The water cascading down the ziggurats is the remnant of the idea. Such was the bold design and a superb work of imagination.

But there were doubters. The estates bursar, J.F. Cory Dixon, began to have profound unease about the Lasdun designs. He saw that Lasdun regarded building the residences as pyramid crescents as vital to his design. Yet Dixon did not believe that the buildings could be achieved within the UGC cost limits. He argued that the weight of more than a few storeys must increase the construction costs and the use of stepped design was an expensive way of providing volume, while having bedrooms on only one side of a corridor increased the circulation space in proportion to the accommodation.[100] He wanted an assurance from Denys Lasdun that there was no necessity for the residences to be in the form of stepped crescents. He wrote to Lasdun saying that he appreciated that Lasdun felt "passionately" about his stepped crescents but that he – Dixon – would be happier with "more traditional slabs, courts or quadrangles".[101] Thistlethwaite also went to see Denys Lasdun to receive assurances that they could be built to UGC costs.[102] Cory Dixon's deep objections to the stepped crescents made his position incompatible with Lasdun's. The Vice-Chancellor recalled that Cory Dixon himself "had his own strong views about buildings, their design and architects"[103]. The impasse was broken when Cory Dixon resigned to become the successful estates officer for the University of Surrey. He was succeeded by his deputy, Gordon Marshall, who had come with him to UEA from the University of Liverpool.

The grounds of Cory Dixon's unease did not depart with him but fell to his successor. Marshall appealed to the UGC that UEA could not bring the costs of the residences below the UGC limits unless they could guarantee a thousand residences. The UGC replied coolly that they were not interested in any particular form of building or architectural design and "they could not give any university any increase over the s.b.u. [study bedroom unit] formula for any purpose".[104] The UGC had set cost limits of £885,000 though the University now estimated the cost at £935,555.[105] The UGC would not budge.

This problem was linked with another, about how much of the Appeal funds should be properly used on these exceptional buildings. The Vice-Chancellor early became aware that local East Anglians who had supported the Appeal were resistant to the greater part of their contributions being devoted to residences.[106] They took the view that the government should pay for them. The Vice-Chancellor saw that he had to stress how important residences were; indeed it was always made clear in the running of the Appeal that residences were to be an object of the raised funds. Timothy Colman as chairman of the Appeal was very concerned that too much Appeal money should not be diverted to building of residences and away from the creation of a substantial endowment fund. He took the view that many local contributors were motivated by a concern to help the University "to achieve independence and freedom from Government control" by having an endowment fund.[107] Residences were secondary. Indeed if residences had been the prime objective he thought that only about half a million pounds would have been raised not the expected £1,250,000. He was also concerned that the original proposals for 500 bedrooms had risen to 680. Here was the squeeze. Gordon Marshall was telling the UGC that they needed a thousand bedrooms to get within the UGC cost limits. Yet Colman was concerned that rising bedroom numbers even well below that level would swallow up the Appeal money, leave the University under endowed and arouse feelings of bad faith among those Appeal supporters whose priority concern was endowment for independence not building. In practice, so committed was the University and Lasdun to the ziggurat residences that Appeal money was used to make up the shortfall. In the end they cost £1,000,000 at a cost per student room of £1300[108] and the UGC congratulated Lasdun on their being "extraordinarily good value for money".[109]

Reaction to the residences was generally favourable. Jonathan Mardle, the popular local journalist, was poetic on entering the residences on their first day of occupancy:

> Light floods in from a wide window, opening out on to a little terrace, and commanding a view of the green valley of the Yare, with a curving line of willows marking the course of the stream. Indeed the buildings might be compared to a ship with companion ways leading down to the cabins between decks . . . each set of study bedrooms has a combined kitchen and common room placed in the angle of the building as if it were in the bows of the ship . . . the studies are carpeted. They have sofa bedsteads, wardrobes, washbasins, desks, bookshelves and armchairs . . . these rooms have already begun to look homely, with bright coverlets spread on the beds, books and bits of pottery on the shelves and pictures pinned on the walls.[110]

This was a good and fair description of the building in the mid sixties. There were some inevitable difficulties.[111] The students were concerned about the pinoleum window blinds. They were woven in France from Czechoslovakian reeds and certainly looked smart. But they proved to be virtually transparent so that students in a lit bedroom at night were visible to an observer in the dark outside.[112] The students complained that "having transparent blinds is a matter of great concern particularly to women residents".[113] The students took the matter into their own hands covering the windows with papers, which diminished the aesthetic effect of the attractive blinds. More drastically they organised vigilante patrols to warn off peeping toms.[114] The matter that bothered most students, however, was that the room at the apex was intended as a social room with occasional light cooking. Increasingly they wanted to use it as a serious kitchen with more elaborate cooking facilities.[115] But overall, in spite of criticisms of detail, it was agreed that "the students are on the whole satisfied [since] the rooms have been particularly well designed".[116] The result was that by the 1970s UEA housed a higher proportion of its students, 70 per cent, than Oxford or Cambridge.[117]

No building caused more problems than University House, largely because it proved very difficult to decide what it should comprise. The first assumption, as early as August 1962, was that it should be 80,000 square feet and contain the Senate House, theatres and a large hall. By March 1963 a medical centre and Senior Common Room was added to make a building of 102,000 square feet, but by July the SCR itself was expanded making the total building 110,000 square feet. The Estates Officer, Cory Dixon, envisaged common rooms so capacious that space could be set aside for table tennis, billiards and card rooms. The Vice-Chancellor sternly disapproved, "I do not think that these rather trivial amusements ought to be specifically encouraged in a University"; in his view the space should be used for music and art.[118] The UGC was also alarmed at the ambitious scale and told Cory Dixon that five (!) committee rooms as well as the Council Room was excessive and the plan should be cut by 1000 square feet.[119]

At this point the architects were appointed for the building and it was hoped that some order would be brought into these shifting demands. But the drive for increasing scale remained unabated. In February 1964 the common room space was doubled and the building itself increased to 133,000 square feet. A drama studio was added above the theatre. Yet by June the theatre had vanished altogether. By November 1964 the University faced up to the fact that it had no clear idea what was to be in this University House and still less on what scale. The Vice-Chancellor told Lasdun that he would have to delay on University House and have an "agonising reappraisal". He admitted that it was entirely the University's fault since they had not fully thought through the role of catering and student amenities, "we have not fully thought out, as we should have done, the implications of the original strategic decision".[120] Alexander Redhouse of DLP and Gordon Marshall made a visit to French universities in December 1964 to see how they handled central services

In April 1965 it was decided to divide the functions between a University House, with no medical centre, hall, theatre or SCR, and a Senate House, with a hall and SCR. This, however, did not restrain over extravagant planning. The President of the SCR, Marcus Dick, made some proposals for a SCR more reminiscent of a wealthy Oxford college whence he had come: a large dining room with waitress service, five guest bedrooms with en suite bathrooms, silver store, steward's office, pantry and cellarage.[121] 1965 thinking was now for two separate buildings, a University House of 40,560 square feet and a Senate House of 35,437 square feet. But in June 1966 the matter was rethought yet again with the idea of having University House and the Senate House all in one building at a cost of over £600,000. The result was Lasdun's scheme of March 1967 which represented the highest level of expectations.[122] There would have been a Senate House on the top floor with Vice-Chancellor's offices, then an Appointments Office and below that the whole of the SCR with a 268 seater dining room and Council Chamber suite. There would have been guest bedrooms, dining and committee room suite, a secretary and technicians' club. Then below that the whole of the Students' Union with two 400 seater dining rooms, quiet and games rooms and then silver and wine stores in the basement. The whole would have cost £643,130 and have been staffed by 118 staff. It would have combined in one multi-storied palace virtually every conceivable administrative, social and catering function of the University. By September 1967 the costs had escalated to £678,000 and completion been deferred to 1971.[123] But by now Senate was getting "seriously alarmed" at the delays, rising costs and constantly changing concepts of the provision of central services. It was now seven years since the first ideas had been put forward, and three of the ablest chairmen from outside the University (Lord Cranbrook, Lincoln Ralphs and Gordon Tilsley), charged with the Committee to plan central services, had followed each other without bringing a building to conclusion. The catering advisers J. Lyons, had come and gone in exasperation.

The consequences of all this were adverse for the University. Timothy Colman told the Vice-Chancellor, "one becomes conscious talking to both students and visitors from Norwich of the very real need for some form of social nucleus on the Plain".[124] An outside architectural critic was more condemnatory, "for a university to have to exist for five years without a restaurant, without a bank and without shops is absurd".[125] This stricture was rather exaggerated. Many remarkably good planning decisions were taken in those early days – the Village and Horsham, the location of the Library, the landscaping and so forth. But the whole matter of the Senate and University House(s) and central services was the most intractable. It reminds us that the environment we experience and take for granted was not inevitable but merely one of a whole spectrum of alternatives and combinations, only one of which came into being. It also reminds us of the highly optimistic assumptions in the 1960s about possibilities and the availability of resources to fulfil them – Marcus Dick's extravagant expectations for the SCR in 1965 and Lasdun's hugely ambitious scheme of March 1967 belong to a vanished age. In the end the administrative, student amenity, restaurant, shop, medical and theatre buildings were all to become quite discrete blocks, close but totally separate. These matters were only solved by Lasdun's successors after he had left and the University had made up its mind what it wanted. It was the great achievement of Sir Bernard Feilden and his architects. This project dragged on because the urgency to resolve it was lessened by the fact that many of the facilities already existed elsewhere. The administration was in Earlham Hall, and rather good student amenities and catering and banks in the Village. Many people liked, and certainly all benefited from, the regular short pleasant walk through Earlham Park from the Plain to meals in the Village. But it could be argued that the long-term spatial separation of Plain, Earlham Hall and Village was an element in the lack of integrated unity which fed into the Troubles, as we shall see.

In addition to what was created it was hoped that the Plain would also be the site of some very large projects financed jointly with the City. There was a proposal for a Concert Hall and Civic Theatre for 2000 people financed partly by the UGC and with £250,000 from Norwich.[126] The City Council actually voted in favour of this and 20 per cent was to be contributed by the Arts Council.[127] All this would have comprised Mackintosh Hall, a worthy tribute to UEA'S first Chancellor and Norwich's foremost businessman. The University could not decide, however, whether it wanted a raked theatre or a flat-floor examination hall.[128] The UGC made it clear that it was not interested in assembly halls.[129] The City for its part had second thoughts, since they faced costs of refurbishing St Andrew's Hall in the centre of the City, which removed much need for another public hall in the University some[130] miles away. By 1968 the Vice-Chancellor reflected, "Mackintosh Hall was so far in the future as not to be worth worrying about".[131] A similar idea was a swimming pool. The City varied in its view whether it wanted a large pool on the site or whether it should invest instead in smaller learning pools. The University would provide the site and staff, the City a substantial part of the capital. The University would have predominant use of it in term time and the City in vacations. The project revived again in 1972, but neither Mackintosh Hall nor the swimming pool materialised, victims of cuts and more urgent priorities.[132]

The physical form of the University was not only its buildings but also its total landscaped environment. The term "Plain" was adopted for the campus on the Yare valley slope. The analogy was supposed to be not the common English-American use of a wide open flat grassy landscape but the East Anglian-Dutch (*plein*) meaning of a space surrounded by nearby buildings. Bank Plain and St Andrews Plain in Norwich were examples of the usage. Lasdun was conscious that the Plain was "an exceptionally fine landscape of which the University is custodian".[133] He wrote an initial report in 1965 advocating the keeping of Earlham Hall, Earlham Lodge and the church as remnants of the old Earlham Village, though there was hardly any prospect of demolishing them.[134] He discussed the retention of the trees of the golf course and valley, and calculated the sports and playing fields needs for the University. He appreciated, however, that the whole matter needed a specialist landscape architect and called in Brenda Colvin in 1966.

Brenda Colvin's friend, Lady Evershed, for whom she had worked, told the Vice-Chancellor that "she is a perfectionist and is sad at being brought in at such a late date".[135] She set to work in great detail surveying trees, vegetation and the whole ecology, and made several interesting proposals.[136] Willows grew in the wet of the river valley but they needed proper cropping and replanting. Brenda Colvin arranged with the firm of Edgar Watts to manage the willow spinney, cropping and planting for cricket bats. The willows would contrast with the Cringleford pines and she proposed planting scarlet willows for further contrast. She suggested keeping the marsh then by the river (now the Broad) for biological interest, with occasional winter cutting of reeds to preserve its character. She also envisaged a Broad fed from the river which she advised should be dredged. The grass parkland should be mown to fine turf near the buildings but then scythed to about six inches further away. The pit or quarry to the east should be retained with tree planting on the ridge above. She also wanted extensive tree planting on the eastern boundary to screen off the site from Bluebell Road housing development and urged the retention of sweet chestnuts on the approach to Earlham Road. Her meticulous, almost tree by tree survey about pruning, removing, replacing and new planting lay behind the fine treescape the University enjoys, partly inherited from the old golf course and valley parkland but selected and shaped by Brenda Colvin.

Brenda Colvin was under no illusion about the role of man in creating landscape. She told Roy Campbell, who acted as her host at UEA, that "most people think the landscape is normally green: it isn't, it is black".[137] Frank Thistlethwaite asked her to write him a letter expressing her views with which he could impress Council. Her words are worth recording:

> The English landscape is very largely a man made work of art, but I doubt if the general public realise that its quality depends on constant care . . . our generation benefits from their [earlier landowners] forethought and generosity. We accept the privileges, too often with little thought of the related responsibilities to the future . . . I feel that any landowner, more especially a University has the responsibilities of ensuring for the future, the benefits, inherited from the past.[138]

Well said. The University within its financial constraints has tried to fulfil this duty to its landscaped environment.

Also as regards the surrounding environment, much care was taken over the access road to the Plain alongside Earlham Park.[139] Norwich Corporation granted a perpetual easement to the University to build a twenty-five foot carriageway with a ten foot footpath from the cottages by the park gates on Earlham Road to the University site. The University would construct the road and also another leading to it from Earlham Hall. The traditional "cow drive" from Bluebell Road to Earlham Park was to be retained and kept safe from traffic. It was not to form the basis of another road but to remain a traditional footpath. The City Planning Office was especially concerned that the University and its access roads should not become a short cut to Colney hence the deliberate non-development of the "cow drive". So it is still there between Blackdale School and the University car park. The relation of the new access road to Earlham Park itself caused concern. There was always a wish that local people could have easy access from Earlham Park into the University site. Hence the broad gate in the park hedge near the University end of the access road. Otherwise the Earlham Park nursery had to be fenced from the road for security. But Denys Lasdun insisted that, apart from that stretch, there should be no fencing or hedging which would interfere with the concept of a road running through parkland. Hence the low fence and beech hedge was set low in a ha-ha, allowing uninterrupted views and echoing the ha-ha that already divided Earlham Hall from its parkland to the rear of the house. Lasdun also wanted a footbridge over Earlham Road for pedestrians walking between the Village and the Plain, fearing serious accidents.[140] The bridge was never built but mercifully accidents have not occurred. The access road having the end of Arts II and the Registry tower as its terminal line of sight and with the park on the right is especially satisfying for the incoming visitor.

UEA was in effect a small town and this posed problems of sewage and water supply. It was hoped that a new sewage works would be built nearby at Colney capable of dealing with 2,800,000 gallons per day, and this would take the sewage from the Plain. However a difficulty posed by the University was that it produced not only human waste but toxic materials from laboratories which were to pass into the sewage system.[141] In the event the Ministry of Housing rejected the proposal for the sewage works at Colney. It would have entailed effluent flowing along the River Yare through Earlham Park and the University grounds to Cringleford. It was decided instead to expand the sewage works at Whitlingham which discharged into the Yare, inoffensively, downstream from Norwich.[142] The sewage from the Plain goes into the main sewer running along the Yare valley. A walker along the valley down to Cringleford will find the manhole covers unobtrusively at various intervals. Conversely it was originally thought that the City would not be able to supply water to the University and that it would need its own bore hole. In 1963, however, it was decided that this was not necessary.[143] Accordingly both sewage and water supply were not quite such problems as had been initially feared.

Reaction to Lasdun's new buildings on the Plain was divided. Informed opinion was deeply appreciative. Terence Bendixson, in a considered appraisal, regarded UEA as "at one extreme among the universities now being built in Britain. It is a spectacular personal statement" which he

1. The Vice-Chancellor's Office, Council House and Registry.

2. Earlham Golf Course, 1961, from approximately the present entrance to the Registry.

3. The University Village in late 1963.

4. Denys Lasdun with his plan for UEA, 25 April 1963.

5. University site, 14 March 1965. Building the Ziggurats.

6. Lasdun's skyline.

7. Ziggurats.

8. Rick Mather's Constable Terrace.

9. Sports Day at the Ziggurats.

10. The Sainsbury Centre. The presentation announcement 26 November 1973. Timothy Colman, Sir Robert Sainsbury, Frank Thistlethwaite, Lady Sainsbury.

11. The Sainsbury Centre in snow.

12. The Sainsbury Centre, interior.

77

13. The spinal walkway, the Ziggurats to the left, the Teaching Wall is to the right.

compared to Barry's Houses of Parliament and Lutyens's Viceroy's Lodge in Delhi.[144] He praised the "spectacular views" from the walkways and suggested that the green of the pines "against the soft, delicate, grey of ubiquitous concrete" conjured up a feeling of Scandinavia. Bendixson admired the "tremendous impact and cohesiveness of East Anglia" and appreciated that it was a university city in its own right.

Some local opinion was less appreciative. Following the open day in November 1967 a spate of letters attacked the buildings. One deplored the valley "desecrated by concrete blocks hideous to behold". Another called it "a monstrosity and a blot on the landscape", while another found it aesthetically distasteful . . . it would take a sea of virginia creeper to soften their insensitivity". Indeed in the 1990s extensive use is being made of creepers to that purpose. It would be easy to dismiss such comment as ignorant philistinism and it will be remembered that the Plain was only partially built amid scarred earth and rubble. Yet there always has been a stream of sincere opinion disliking the texture and angularity of the concrete as an intrusion into the landscape rather than a complement to it.

After ten years, however, when the Plain was completed, Sir James Richards, long time editor of the *Architectural Review* found it "a great citadel of buildings". Lasdun's nucleus had "endowed the university with a positive character . . . it remains a powerful complex . . . one walks in the air with as much of the building falling away beneath as towering over one". Moreover after ten years the concrete was still wearing well.[145] Also the *Spectator*, reviewing a Lasdun retrospective at the RIBA, saw his UEA buildings as a "positive contribution" to the landscape of the Yare valley.[146]

Other critics, while accepting the overall design, saw faults in the materials and execution. Harold Perkin in 1969 observed that "the execution in grey shuttered concrete already showing characteristic weather drip stains is less than impressive . . . it is a pity that so imaginative a scheme should be marred in the execution".[147] Tony Birks, the architectural historian, similarly deplored that with East Anglia's 200 days of rainfall, "surfaces look miserable when they are wet".[148] It was unfortunate that some of the filming of UEA for the widely seen Lasdun Exhibition at the Royal Academy in 1998 was done in wet weather with the concrete rain-soaked, streaked and damp. Malcolm Bradbury suggested that it really needed South of France sunlight whereas pollution drifting across the North Sea left it stained and dark in winter.[149] Denys Lasdun accepted that the disadvantage of the concrete was the weathering and for his next building, the National Theatre, used silver sand and white cement in the concrete to lighten the staining. Staining results, however, from the porosity of the concrete rather than its colour.

In May 1964 the programme ran into financial difficulties. The UGC was allowing the University to spend more than intended on residences and the Village, but insisted that it must all come from a capital allocation of £3,120,000, which was going to leave the University £378,700 overspent.[150] This meant that at least one major building would have to be postponed, either Biology or Arts I.[151] The latter was chosen. Lasdun's approach would have been to extend the financial programme over three years but the UGC would not allow this.[152] Another alternative was to build the residences entirely from Appeal money, but there was unease about that on grounds we have seen. Lasdun thought that expecting the same facilities at a lower cost was unrealistic, and reducing the facilities was also undesirable, so the best way out was to delay the programme of starts. Lasdun was dismayed that the University was transferring UGC money to the residences, since this would reduce the overall capital for the rest of the site. He had understood that the residences would be paid for out of the University's own funds.[153] Pro Vice-Chancellor Ross made it clear to Lasdun that the Appeal would only finance 500 residence places and that the University would have to postpone Arts I and leave out the lifts.[154] Lasdun rightly thought that the last suggestion was out of all proportion to the savings. He also pointed out that postponing Arts I would entail a financial loss due to the reduction in the size of the contract for prefabricated units on the main site.[155]

A meeting of Deans on 29 May 1964, after being briefed by Dick Ross and Gordon Marshall, came to the stark conclusion that the University could not continue the development programme within the capital grant and it was doubtful whether the projects, especially University House, could be financed within the UGC limits.[156] Lasdun was clear that the root of the problem was the transfer of capital from the rest of the site to the residences to save the Appeal funds. When the University went to see the UGC they emphasised another problem: namely, that to keep costs low and make the best use of industrialised building they needed to contract for Chemistry, Biology and Arts simultaneously. The UGC insisted, however, on the delay of starts on University House, Arts and Biology. In return they would sanction an overspend of £300,000, the limit of what they would regard as acceptable.[157] But there was an uneasy feeling that cost control was becoming increasingly difficult amid the excitement of the magnificent concepts.

Through 1967 and 1968 problems compounded. There were delays. The restaurant was supposed to be ready by October 1969 but still was not sited by October 1968. Thistlethwaite personally told Lasdun that he was very concerned that the time-scale for Arts II, the Lecture Theatre and University House "was going absolutely for six", putting the whole University development into jeopardy.[158] But of more concern was the problem of high costs.

The UGC made it clear "how expensive the site works were ... our percentage cost of site works was exceptionally high". The UGC was insistent that external site works must not exceed 2½ per cent of the value of the buildings. Professor Roy Campbell, who was charged by the Vice-Chancellor with responsibility of dealing with the architect, had been told this on his visit to the UGC on the morning of 19 January 1968.[159] When he moved on to visit Denys Lasdun and Partners (DLP) the same afternoon it became clear that the site works for the Centre (the Restaurant, SCR, JCR, shops, Sports Hall, Senate House) would certainly amount to 2½ per cent in Lasdun's plans.[160] Yet, although the architects appreciated the problem, they over-optimistically thought that the UGC would be flexible and persuadable.

Overall there was increasing anxiety about financial control. Matters came to a head in a clash over the appointment of a quantity surveyor. DLP wanted Davis, Belfield and Everest, who had already done much work on the Plain, whereas the University wanted Jack Stockings who had been less involved. Attitudes began to crystallise – whether "a refusal to work with Stockings might well lead to a termination of the appointment of DLP".[161] Lasdun accepted Stockings but, as Timothy Colman shrewdly observed on being told, "I'm afraid this signifies a postponement rather than a solution to our problems".[162] By then matters were moving swiftly to a conclusion.

In October 1968 the University decided to "disengage" from DLP as architects of the University.[163] At a meeting on 29 October 1968 Sir Edmund Bacon formally told Denys Lasdun that they were not proposing to continue his appointment as Development Plan architect beyond the end of the year.[164] He was invited to continue as architect for the Arts II and Mathematics and Physics buildings but no longer for the Centre, and he agreed to this. He was concerned that the University would not spoil what he had already achieved, "letting expediency and squalor follow" the Development Plan's departure, with "a creeping devaluation of the environment" which he cared for.[165] His fears were needless. The University was far too appreciative of what Denys Lasdun had achieved for it to impugn his reputation or sully his legacy.

In particular Peter Lasko, the Professor of Art History, dissenting from the decision to disengage from DLP, reminded the University that whatever problems with costs here or materials there yet, "we are dealing with over three million pounds worth of building put up in less than three years and not a seaside bungalow". It would have been miraculous if nothing had gone wrong, yet it was too easy to focus on these and leave the virtues underappreciated. He deplored that the University had never made any expression of thanks or appreciation to Denys Lasdun "one of the outstanding architects of our day with an international reputation second to none".[166] The Vice-Chancellor regarded Lasko's paper as "an expression of the grand aesthetic, it could not be answered".

Nor did it have any effect. Council formally disengaged from DLP but confirmed that he should continue with Arts II, but the MAP building was to be abandoned and DLP was to play no part in the design of the Centre.[167] Thus the dividing line between the old and the new was clearly drawn. The press presentation was amicable. Lasdun said that "the moment has come when we have completed the nucleus and established the vernacular and we can allow another architect to carry on their work while safeguarding our concept".[168] But when Kenneth Clark stood in front of the Lasdun ziggurats as a symbol of 1960s civilisation their architect had departed.

In any case there were more fundamental reasons why the disengagement from DLP was likely by the end of the decade. It was always intended that Denys Lasdun, having devised the main plan and designed the initial buildings, should hand over to a successor. When he left he had been working for UEA for seven years. Timothy Colman noted that he "had carried on much further than many members of the Council envisaged when he was appointed".[169] Secondly, the whole financial situation had changed. Financial cuts meant that the UGC no longer had funds to dispense as generously as in the early 1960s. The Conservative government cut the universities building programme before leaving office in 1964. The new Labour government delayed building programmes in all universities for six months and then allocated £54,500,000 for the period January 1965 to March 1966; £33,000,000 for 1966-67 and £25,000,000 for 1967-68.[170] In 1967-68 the UGC made fifteen per cent cuts in sums for new buildings and in 1968 there was a UGC moratorium on all new building. Moreover, there was a fear that the UGC was switching its priorities away from the expansion of the new universities to building up the older civics.[171] A much cheaper form of architecture was now needed, especially since it was made clear that the UGC would no longer finance residences. Any possibility of completing the five intended residential terraces vanished. So did the idea of parallel teaching walls and the Mackintosh Hall. Thirdly, the financial constraints changed the mood of the clients. In the early sixties Council wanted a distinctive architectural statement from a major architect – which it got. Yet when Denys Lasdun left the room on 29 October, after being told of the termination, Sir Edmund Bacon observed gloomily, "we did not want to build for posterity".[172] Yet Lasdun did and was doing so. It was a sign that the parting of the ways was inevitable. In any case the Vice-Chancellor and others felt that "Mr Lasdun was beginning to have enough of the University".[173] He was engaged on the Institute of Education and the School of Oriental and African Studies for London University from 1965, residences at Christ's College, Cambridge, from 1966.

He was also turning his mind away from the academics and gentry of Norfolk to the arguably more exciting and high profile project of working with Sir Laurence Olivier on the National Theatre.

The Lasdun buildings at UEA received proper recognition. They were given a Civic Trust award in 1969 and praised as the boldest of all the twenty-two new universities established in the 1960s and as "one of the most outstanding new university designs in Britain". A RIBA publication called Lasdun's creation of UEA "an architectural event of the first importance".[174] Lasdun himself went on to receive the RIBA Gold Medal, a CBE (1965) and knighthood (1976), and was made a Companion of Honour in 1995. The University awarded him the honorary degree of Litt.D. in 1974 as a fitting expression of gratitude to the man who more than any other gave the University its physical form. It is also pleasing to record that Sir Denys's son graduated at UEA in 1983. When Dame Elizabeth Estève-Coll became Vice-Chancellor in 1995 she invited Frank Thistlethwaite and Sir Denys Lasdun together to a private lunch at UEA to discuss with her their original thinking about the University and its academic and material formation.

When Lasdun severed his connection he left behind instructions or hopes for the future and many of his suggestions have been observed.[175] He wanted the Harbour to be retained, a green wedge leading up the Wall between the residence terraces. He wanted the wet area by the river to be preserved, he assumed as a marsh, but the subsequent Broad was consistent with his 1963 plan. He hoped that the river would be spanned by a footbridge, which came about as part of the Broad development. He also assumed that the Library would be completed, which was done seamlessly with Lasdun's original block. Finally, the Teaching Wall was to be continued and the gap filled.

Many of his expectations could not be realised. He anticipated the further development of upper-level pedestrian walkways with a footbridge over Earlham Road and an overhead link from the Boiler House to the walkway system. He hoped that more residence terraces would be built in his ziggurat style to complete his intended five ranges, but this became unthinkable. Tony Birks makes a vivid analogy, Lasdun's plan "will never be judged in full, for like a dinosaur . . . it is becoming fossilised through lack of adequate finance, and only a few central vertebrae and ribs lie on the ground giving little idea of its full extent and shape".[176] Most fundamentally Lasdun wanted the site to retain its predominance of concrete. But the walkways and extra ziggurats did not materialise due to cost, and the new buildings by Norman Foster and Rick Mather broke away from the concrete aesthetic while retaining the overall grey and white tone colour. There was also a major remaining unsolved problem which was that of the main entrance to the University. Lasdun admitted that "the missing element in this University is any sense of a front door . . . still we're stopping at the top end, we never seem to get the neck connected to the head".[177] So there were many guidelines, problems and new opportunities for Denys Lasdun's successor.

The Council reviewed the situation in November 1968 and noted the changes in the whole situation since Lasdun's first plans: the UCG no longer financing residences, their reduction of the real value of cost limits by 15 per cent, the pressure of local authorities to integrate the University with its development plans for the area.[178] To succeed Denys Lasdun they wanted "an architect of sufficient stature . . . who lives and works locally", and chose Bernard Fielden, with the knowledge that he would be strongly supported by the UGC.

Bernard Feilden was already well known to the University. He was a partner in Feilden and Mawson, the architects of the University Village and of the adjacent Food Research Institute, both by David Luckhurst. In the wider world he was a consultant architect to Norwich Cathedral, York Minster and St Paul's Cathedral, and had done work for York University.[179] Feilden was personally dismayed at the break with Denys Lasdun, which he regarded as a "major tragedy both for the University and for the cause of architecture". Fielden was "profoundly and visibly moved" but agreed to take over to "save something from the wreck" and carry on the Lasdun plan as far as possible to prevent it disintegrating into mediocrity.[180] He told his colleagues at Feilden and Mawson that "we must treat this campus as the most modern conservation area in the UK".[181] Frank Thistlethwaite insisted that the overall Lasdun plan and style be retained. Also, by chance, Sir Nikolaus Pevsner was visiting UEA at the time and urged David Luckhurst of Feilden and Mawson to the same effect. Bernard Feilden and Gordon Marshall wrote a "Guide Book for Project Architects" on style and materials to "keep the vocabulary". Accordingly the Lasdun concept would be preserved. Even the same building materials were to retain the appearance: concrete blocks (Denys Lasdun used Forticrete, David Luckhurst Lignacite) in situ concrete and pre-cast concrete units, even though some Feilden and Mawson architects wanted to use other styles and textures like glazed tiling, for example. Feilden and Mawson were also less keen on flat roofs, which had problems entailing high maintenance costs. Feilden himself, although he greatly admired Lasdun as an architect, would have built the Plain in brick if he had been starting from scratch, but recognised that inflation had made concrete and glass inevitable.[182] Feilden, however, had strong feelings of loyalty to Norwich and to an extent to Thistlethwaite because of his proven enthusiasm for architecture. Feilden would use his own firm but also other East Anglian architects. In practice David Luckhurst, who had designed the Village and the Food Research Institute, became responsible for completing the Plain under Bernard

Feilden, and he was an admirer of Lasdun's work and plan. Feilden would be answerable personally to the Vice-Chancellor and the Planning Committee while the University's Planning Officer would be under him – obviating a difficulty Lasdun had found in his early days. Significantly Feilden did not discuss fees, since "money was not a prime consideration for him in considering the job".

Feilden met the Council Committee on 4 December 1968 and both sides were clear that the Lasdun concept should be continued on the Plain; indeed Feilden spent a day with Lasdun discussing this.[183] They addressed the vital issue of concrete and Fielden thought that they should carry on in this medium in the central area, though they might diversify further out. The new architect was sensitive to the need for the centre area to retain the Lasdun idiom, even sometimes producing an exact copy but otherwise trying to avoid plagiarism and making Lasdun's work a cliché. He argued that unity of material – concrete – would give a consistency of style as (a telling comparison by Feilden) the use of limestone did for those parts of Norwich Cathedral designed by many different hands over many centuries. One interesting technicality emerged in Feilden's discussion. Utilisation of space was extremely low in university buildings, about 4-5 per cent, compared with 80 per cent in state schools. He and the UGC would be looking to tighten this up at UEA. Both sides satisfied, Bernard Feilden's appointment was announced publicly and the new architect emphasised his continuity with his predecessor: "Mr Lasdun has laid the foundations of what is possibly one of the finest universities in this country and we will follow the spirit of this scheme".[184]

Feilden presented his Development Plan in April 1970. It combined some remarkable proposals, chiefly that the University should grow from 2700 in 1970 to 5400 in 1977 and to 10,000 by 1982. These astonishing projections were not in response to any requests or targets posed by the UGC but were based on "informal indications of the likely need for student places in the 1970s and 1980s".[185] I remember attending Bernard Feilden's presentation and being both impressed with his enthusiasm but sceptical that the plans could ever be fulfilled in the constant atmosphere of financial constraint in which we then lived. Needless to say, none of this came about due to successive cuts in the 1980s. Feilden nevertheless made some interesting propositions, some of which did have some bearing on the future. He was clear that the river valley landscape should be kept open with marsh or a broad as a valley bottom feature. Very importantly, he insisted that, since they could not continue with the five Lasdun ziggurats curving down to the river, the foreground landscape between Norfolk and Suffolk Terraces and the river should not be built on at all, thus preserving the Harbour. New residences would, however, be needed since only 2.5 per cent of UEA students lived at home. Accordingly he proposed that new land should be added to the Plain. This included Earlham Park, the playing fields of Earlham School, the slope from Bluebell Road to the river and, further afield, land on the other side of Colney Lane and land on Watton Road. UEA actually suggested a deal whereby they would give up 103 acres of river valley (on which there was no intention to build) in return for thirty acres of Earlham Park between the Plain and the Hall. The City, however, was rightly adamant that it would not release Earlham Park.[186] Since the University did not grow to 10,000 the extra land proved unnecessary. A conjunction of two of Feilden's ideas of that time, however, ultimately bore fruit. He suggested a joint project with the City for an athletics track at Lakenham. This came about but on the spacious grounds of Earlham School, which he had urged the University to buy.

Two years later in 1972 Feilden presented a revised plan more modestly devised for 6000 rather than 10,000 students.[187] The limitations were imposed by the inability to get more land for expansion and the need to think in terms of land already owned by the University. Feilden raised several pointers for the future. He envisaged that the Village could be rebuilt for student residences. He also wanted more residences built in Norwich itself and residences which could pay their way by being good enough to be used by the public during vacations, not only for conferences but as holiday flats. A Broad could be excavated by gravel extraction and he wanted the academic buildings of the Wall to be more flexibly used between arts and sciences. He also faced up to the contentious problem of the car park.

It was now accepted that car parking would be needed for a half of the university population of 6000. Since the existing capacity was only 2500 he proposed "cheap car decks" and some parking on the other side of the river, but no parking to be tolerated in the Harbour area. The question was also raised of how far Centres needed separate buildings. The Computing and Music Centres already had them while CEAS and the Language Centre were part of the Teaching Wall. But future intentions – Education, Climate – would raise issues of the siting of small buildings around the Lasdun concept. Care would have to be taken that the strong central Lasdun design would not be compromised by smaller buildings in different styles scattered around it. This had been one of Lasdun's parting fears. These were sensible, modest proposals and almost all came about apart from the mysterious "car decks".

Under Bernard Feilden as consultant architect, the rest of the Plain was fleshed out in the 1970s. As far as possible, the Lasdun aesthetic was maintained as was the concrete fabric. However some buildings were cheaper or visually duller than Lasdun would have intended and some were splendid in their own right. Since it was no longer possible to continue the expensive ziggurats, a new residential block, Waveney Terrace, was built in a line parallel to the approach road from Bluebell Road to the Plain. It was built by the Norwich Partnership (of architects) to house 750 students. The interest of the block is financial rather than architectural. The finance of residences had drastically changed between the 1960s and 1970s. Before 1969 student residences in universities were built with government money channelled through the UGC.[188] In that year Lancaster University pioneered the scheme for building residences with loan finance repaid from rent income. The UGC, wanting to direct its limited funds away from accommodation to academic buildings, thoroughly approved this and the last lodgings project totally grant aided by the UGC was that at Durham in 1971-72. Thereafter the UGC would provide 25 per cent of the capital costs of residence projects and the remaining 75 per cent had to be raised on the open market by private loan finance – "loan financed accommodation" (LFA). UEA accordingly borrowed £682,000 for building Waveney Terrace in the early 1970s, about the same amount as Lancaster. The sum and interest on it had to be repaid from student rents; for Waveney about 45 per cent of the rent went for this purpose.

After the grandeur of the Lasdun schemes, Waveney Terrace was easy to criticise – "designed to low cost limits imposed by loan financed schemes, the block could hardly be barer. It has minimum maintenance, with no painted surfaces and minimal furniture . . . they are certainly not equal to the rest".[189] How could they be? But students enjoy living in Waveney and it was a most efficient and financially enterprising response to the new realism of the 1970s.

A refectory block was built along one side of the central square which formed a social focus for the Plain. Taking advantage of the steep slope of the Plain, the refectory was on three levels with a refectory and kitchen on the ground floor, a popular coffee bar at walkway level, while on the top floor there was then a good class waitress service restaurant open to all. At last it filled a social gap on the Plain and began to bind it as a pleasant place for living in the early seventies. This was further enhanced by a Sports Hall by Birkin Haward opened in 1971. A big functional building, it is very popular, with two large sports halls. The largest is used for examinations and has also since 1973 been used as a suitably dignified hall for Congregations. It is the largest internal space in the University and has removed any urgency for a long mooted Mackintosh Hall which Denys Lasdun had assumed would be a key part of his plan. This was a major change in the overall view of the Plain. Denys Lasdun had been encouraged to think of one big central services building. Bernard Feilden's great contribution was the creation of an open centre in the Square, with services around it: the University House, the street of shops, Chaplaincy and Refectory. This lively social area is as distinctive a part of UEA life as the teaching in the Wall and the residences in the Ziggurats.

Arguably the most successful new building of the early seventies was the whole administrative centre at the north east end of the site. It was designed by David Luckhurst working for Feilden and Mawson and built by William Sindall.[190] It comprises offices for 200 administrative staff, a splendid Council Chamber seating ninety-three, committee rooms and a suite of offices for the Vice-Chancellor's staff.[191] Various factors shaped this. Since Arts II was on one side of the walkway all the Registry had to be on the other side; hence to maximise the space, it curves round towards the Sports Centre and the curve itself strengthens the appearance of the entrance. A wild area of trees was carefully kept behind the curve. Also the Vice Chancellor insisted that his office should have a view of the Square. So the Registry had to be on one side and the Council House on the other. There is a direct internal connection between the Vice-Chancellor's Office and the Council Chamber through an internal staircase, enabling ease of access for the Vice-Chancellor, and also a discreet opportunity for elderly Chancellors to retire for a nap in the VCO between Congregations. Originally Luckhurst had intended a passage linking the entrance with the the Square, but since this would have passed directly underneath the VCO, presenting serious security problems, this was scrapped; hence the oddly weak junction between the Registry and the Council House. Luckhurst designed the carpet and also the long tables of the Council Chamber, which were made by Brook Marine of Lowestoft, boat-builders with hydraulic presses strong enough to mould the wood. Indeed local craftsmen were used as far as possible, for the flint knapping in the foyer, the finely crafted ceiling of the Chamber, the lead-faced doors of the Chamber and the steel security doors (presented by Feilden and Mawson) of the House itself.

The massing of the concrete shapes reflects Lasdun's work in achieving the same "cascading" from a boldly tall tower down through four stepped levels to a solid Council Chamber block. The concrete of the complex is relieved by interesting detail of windows and outlooks. It provides the Plain with a strong entrance which Lasdun admitted he had not had time to achieve. The tall tower naturally draws visitors into the University and it is a generally uplifting assertion, enhanced by the University flag flying proudly on its roof. This was the Vice-Chancellor's idea though Luckhurst would have preferred a much taller flagstaff where the present Founders' Green now stands.

This new complex enabled the administration to move from Earlham Hall to the Plain in 1975 and marked a real break with the past. Patricia Whitt, the Vice-Chancellor's secretary caught the mood on leaving Earlham Hall:

> I must say it feels very sad to be saying goodbye at 5.30 – very lonely really although surrounded by forty-one packing cases, bare walls and perfectly cleared desks . . .

I'm now looking across Earlham Park to that lovely tree and it, the view, looks golden and green in the dullish evening since the grass is so dry . . . looking forward to the new suite on the Plain which was beginning to look somewhat civilised.[192]

The transition also removed the unfortunate feature that "administration" had been spatially remote from the students and faculty in the Village or the Plain. All were now together on the campus and the integration must have contributed to the abatement of the tension that marked the period of the troubles. Finally the building of the Registry block signified that the most troublesome architectural problem of the sixties had been settled. No longer was there to be a huge building combining all administrative, social and catering functions. Now all these were to be separately disposed about the Plain . The administrative block at the east entrance, the Students' Union and the catering building on respectively the south and west sides of the Square. None are too large and they can preserve their appropriately distinctive tones – the Registry quiet and dignified to impress visitors; the Union bustling, noisy and scruffy to please the young. Above all, the University was very relieved that this last major development on the Plain had been successfully completed at a cost of £500,000 "just as the lid slams down on the country's university coffers".[193]

Opposite the Registry and forming the other side of the entrance was the Arts II building. This carried on Arts I in a straight line and marked the completion of the eastern end of the Teaching Wall. It was designed by Denys Lasdun and it broadly identical to Arts I, save in that the corridors were much wider and the offices correspondingly smaller. This has extended social and circulating space. It is well used, though the office space is too small to hold seminars, which creates knock-on problems in the provision of seminar rooms. The advent of IT equipment in offices has reduced space further. The reason for this was that the wide corridor was intended to be used for coat lockers to save the need for a locker room, while reducing the depth of the studies improved their natural lighting. Arts II avoided a major problem that became evident in Arts I, where blue asbestos had been used for insulation. With the discovery that this could cause cancer, this all had to be stripped out in 1976 at a cost of £30,000.[194]

One of the most interesting developments of the 1970s was the creation of the Broad from the River Yare. Denys Lasdun had intended to divert the bend of the river to bring it beneath the lowest crescent of residences, never built. It was always in Lasdun's mind that a water feature as well as landscape would offset the concrete. The Broad was something altogether more radical. It was estimated that it would have cost the University £25,000 in 1970 to have the Broad dug out, a prohibitive cost at the time. Frank Thistlethwaite was keen on having a marsh with reeds but George Chadwick, the Registrar, and Keith

Clayton preferred a lake. The origins of this idea were probably earlier than they were aware. Bridgid Rawnsley was working for Norfolk County Council on sites for mineral extraction in the mid sixties and identified the area by the Plain as one where gravel extraction would be acceptable to the Planning Department of the NCC. She also knew that if gravel were extracted then the workings would form lakes, themselves an attractive feature in planning terms. She was professionally acquainted with the Atlas gravel men, who ultimately undertook the work. She and her boss, John Palmer, fed this idea to DLP.[195] At UEA Keith Clayton, the Professor of Environmental Sciences, made auger borings into the gravel.[196] Then Bernard Feilden asked Atlas Aggregates to explore the possibility of a "no money" deal, whereby they would excavate the gravel free of charge leaving the University a landscaped sheet of water fed by the River Yare and flowing back into it.[197]

Work began in August 1973. The lake was to be not less than five acres but, if Atlas found enough gravel to be profitable, then they could go on to twenty acres. In practice they excavated eighteen acres, providing a lake some 800 yards long. They took 500,000 cubic yards of gravel, which was processed at their quarry at Colney nearby. Two islands were left to encourage waterfowl and bird life and the Broad is well stocked with fish. But apart from fishing no other sports are allowed. Sailing would be too disruptive and swimming is forbidden as too dangerous in the deceptively cold water. One student broke his back diving into the Broad when it was being constructed and there were two drownings in 1980 and 1981. On the completion of the project, in June 1978, Atlas presented a steel foot bridge to the University crossing the river and giving access between the Plain, Broad, river and Colney Lane. As well as being a visual amenity, the Broad is also used by BIO and ENV for ecological studies in a variety of habitats. Atlas won a Sand and Gravel Association (SAGA) award for their work.[198] Bernard Feilden well summed up the enterprise: "the University got a pleasing expanse of water for free with landscaping and an arched bridge added as a bonus. The public got an attractive riverside walk. Atlas got a satisfactory profit. Who can complain?"

The Broad had two other beneficial effects not initially predicted. First, it acted as a magnificent complement to the Sainsbury Centre not envisaged when work began. Indeed some assumed that it was part of Norman Foster's planning and that he was closely involved in the Broad, but it was a Feilden and Mawson project, though his SCVA was undoubtedly a beneficiary.[199] Secondly, the Broad relieved the University from pressure by the City to build between the existing Plain buildings and the river. Frank Thistlethwaite resolved to resist this at all costs and the Broad now effectively prevented any resort to this disastrous strategy.

One final aspect of the site which began to acquire a crucial and quite unpredictable significance was that of car parking. Denys Lasdun assumed that 25 per ent of the University population would be using cars and need parking, and that students would not be permitted to bring cars onto the site. Lasdun was briefed on that assumption and accordingly planned for what would have been sufficient parking places around the site on roads and the undercroft of residences. For example, his residence models show cars discreetly parked on the undercroft. But cars increased more than expected in the sixties, especially when students were allowed to bring them to University. By 1967 a proper car park was needed and this was planned to be at the entrance to the site, where it is now. But a number of interlocking factors then came into play crucial to the whole site development and out of all proportion in importance to the mere matter of parking vehicles. First, a separate car park was essential, since the City Council would refuse planning permission for the Arts II building until there were proper parking arrangements. The car park had become the prerequisite to any further building on the Plain.[200] The UGC refused, however, to provide capital sums for building car parks. This meant that the University would have to finance it out of its own funds, namely the Appeal. Yet the University Council rightly took the view that this would be an improper use of the Appeal, which had been subscribed for an endowment and residences. In any case to divert funds from the Plain buildings to the car park would baulk further development of the Plain. Here was a seemingly impossible squeeze. Without a car park the City Council would forbid any further development of the Plain. Yet to create one would drain funds from the Plain and stifle development in that way. Either way the further development of the Plain was to be jeopardised. A proposal was for the Appeal to provide the capital costs to be repaid over fifteen years from a charge on users, but this was never implemented. The car park was built, however, though simply as surfaced ground, not as a multi-storey as Lasdun envisaged or as Feilden's "car decks". Few staff who grumbled about car park charges had any idea how important this issue was to the whole building programme.

When Frank Thistlethwaite left office in 1980 the University of East Anglia had largely been built, the Plain with the Lasdun design and the Feilden and Mawson continuations of the Lasdun concept and plan, and Norman Foster's Sainsbury Centre which we discuss later. It is the boldest and most integrated campus design of any of the new universities of the sixties. Frank Thistlethwaite reflected, perhaps with some surprise, that "looking back over fifteen years it bears a remarkable, and to my mind satisfactory resemblance to the early ideas".[201] Through his choice of architects and support of their plans amid great difficulties it remains one of the chief legacies of the departing Vice-Chancellor and the most strongly designed of any of the new campuses of the sixties by one of the foremost architects of the day.

Table 6 Building Capital Costs (in £s)

31 July	Village	Boiler House or Site Works	CHEM	BIO	Library	Arts	University House	Residences	Sports
1963	201,274								
1964	411,026								
1966	1,141,492	87,953	125,052	25,507	1519	12,892	132	172,302	847
1966	1,428,892	395,830	397,431	280,192	17,965	138,244	155	511,726	25,597
1967	1,698,478	642,432	742,185	835,747	120,244	457,517	3206	1,068,923	32,537
1968	1,811,790	700,882	919,821	1,133,826	341,186	706,951	21,514	1,159,382	80,119
1969	1,834,779	738,183	969,269	1,193,027	503,203	811,273	21,514	1,210,973	125,275

31 July	MAP	Lecture Theatres	Computer Centre	Workshops	Car Parks	TV Centre	Restaurant	Fifers Lane 2 Blocks
1963								
1964								
1966								
1966								
1967	245	6066	76	4011	926			
1968	27,939	104,346	211,519	11737	21,988	200		
1969	28,922	203,904	300,263	13972	25,910	200	37	124,248

Table 7 Expenditure on Land, Buildings, Equipment (in £s)

	Purchase of land or buildings	New Constructions	Alterations	Furniture and Equipment	Scientific Equipment	Fees and Expenses	Total
1969	90,290	4,788,818	322,273	1,309,756	1,306,788	1,044,157	8,862,082
1970	90,290	5,466,912	327,457	1,416,590	1,310,710	1,287,760	10,210,803
1971	90,290	6,438,404	343,759	1,663,800	1,864,782	1,523,954	11,924,989
1972	90,290	7,860,967	357,604	1,857,844	1,979,302	1,650,288	13,796,295
1973	90,290	8,634,047	386,259	2,149,840	2,324,312	1,774,163	15,358,911
1974	90,290	9,151,184	492,157	2,348,141	2,710,272	1,874,348	16,666,392
1975	90,290	9,488,144	548,029	2,499,101	3,290,259	1,959,408	17,875,231
1976	90,290	9,860,528	643,213	2,587,290	3,549,611	2,290,752	19,021,684
1977	90,290	11,812,250	719,561	2,628,014	4,048,936	2,477,368	21,776,419
1978	90,290	12,906,533	831,676	3,012,083	4,323,378	2,650,493	23,814,453
1979	90,290	13,339,879	1,103,237	3,071,310	4,672,183	2,749,050	25,025,949
1980	90,290	13,748,856	1,358,623	3,227,536	5,229,662	2,841,157	26,496,124

Table 8   *The Building Programme, 1963-1980*

	Building	Architects	Main Contractors
1963-5	The Village	Fielden and Mawson	
1956-6	Boiler House	Denys Lasdun	A. Monk & Co
1966	Chemistry	Denys Lasdun	R.G. Carter
1967	Biology	Denys Lasdun	R.G. Carter
1967	Arts I	Denys Lasdun	R.G. Carter
1968	Computing Centre	Denys Lasdun	Ford & Carter
1968	Library I	Denys Lasdun	Costain Construction
1969	Lecture Theatres	Denys Lasdun	Costain Construction
1970	Arts II	Denys Lasdun	R.G. Carter
1970/1	Waveney Terrace	Norwich Partnership	Kerridge
1971	Sports Centre	Johns Slater & Howard	Bush Builders
1971	Restaurant	Feilden & Mawson	Bush Builders
1971	Chaplaincy	Feilden & Mawson	Bush Builders
1972	Waveney Terrace	Norwich Partnership	Bush Builders
1973	University House and Shops	John Slater & Howard	R.G.Carter
1973	Science Building	Feilden & Mawson	R.G. Carter
1973	Medical Centre	Feilden & Mawson	R.G. Carter
1973	Music Centre	Arup Associates	Bush Builders
1974	Library II	Denys Lasdun and Feilden & Mawson	Sindall
1975	Senate House	Feilden & Mawson	Sindall
1976	Porters Lodge	Feilden & Mawson	W.F. Pointer
1977	Maintenance Building	Edward Skipper	W.W.Gould
1978	Sainsbury Centre	Norman Foster	R.G. Carter
1979	Orwell Close	Anthony Faulkner	Bush Builders
1980	Wolfson Close	Anthony Faulkner	Sindall

6

A Time of Troubles

On campus the Maoist and Marxist, whose main business up to
now seemed to be internecine quarrel found a mass of activist
support . . . Hate and revolutionary zeal rages . . . a state of minor
terror reigned.[1]

Malcolm Bradbury, *The History Man* (1975)

If ever there was a university which does not deserve such things
it is East Anglia under your guidance.[2]

Sir Denys Page, 7 June 1971

At the 1966 Congregation the Vice-Chancellor urged his first graduates to
embark on "subversive activities". It could be regarded as part of the light
whimsy that is often a part of Congregation rhetoric. At its most serious it was
a hope that his "do different" graduates would use their trained minds to
question and change things in the outside world for the better. He could not
have predicted that within such a short time the University would endure a
grim period of "subversive" turmoil that lowered its public image to an
absolute nadir. He was also forced to wonder whether he himself was being
faced with real "subversive activities", part of a national and international
movement, sinister and destructive.

In the early years of UEA the student body, which was very small, was
generally orderly, happily busy and well regarded by the people of Norwich. It
was partly a consequence of the community spirit engendered by the Village.
There had been a naive letter to the press in February 1965 in which two
students accused the people of Norwich of being apathetic and "absolutely
dead" and assured them that the University would now give them a social
centre.[3] It aroused some resentment but otherwise 1965 passed peacefully.

Yet the winter of 1966-67 saw rumblings. There were student protests
against war toys in Norwich toyshops before Christmas. Internally there was
a boycott of dining halls because of the requirement of prepayment for meals.
This was renewed and the requirement cancelled in March. But in February
1967 Norwich experienced its first full-scale student demonstration. It was
over the government's intention to raise fees for foreign students at British

universities from £70 to £250. There was no strike or boycott of lectures but it took the form of reasoned speeches in the centre of Norwich by four totally respectable UEA students and faculty – future executives of Oxford University Press, the BBC, a future Master of a Cambridge college and the leader of the Conservatives at UEA. It could hardly be more proper and was praised by the police. But it aroused hostility in Norwich on the grounds that taxpayers did not pay for students to attend political meetings and foreigners should pay more in any case. The war toy and foreign fee demonstrations gave rise to a mild cartoon in the local press depicting a UEA scarf protesting – still affectionate but the thin edge of a wedge.

Internally there were troubling signs of slackening morale. There was pilfering of cutlery in the restaurant,[4] incidents of serious rowdyism and vandalism in residences,[5] and an excessively bawdy production of *Lysistrata* did the University no good in the eyes of the respectable.[6] But this was offset by the goodwill acquired by students for such public spirited activities as clearing the banks of the Wensum and the Yare, their large response to blood donor sessions, the VSU. The retiring President of the Students' Union, Philip Goodstein, ended his session quite satisfied with the good sense of students and the trust between them and the authorities.[7]

The start of the new academic year in 1967 marked a major change. The student numbers rose to 1724, more than doubling in two years. More importantly most of the University moved from the Village to the Plain, and the Lasdun buildings formed the focus of the University. As Malcolm Bradbury pointed out, it was a change from small scale in the Village, with its overtones of "Outward Bound, Oxbridge and Carnaby Street", to big University on the Plain.[8] This created a potentially dangerous spatial distancing between the mass of students on the Plain, the Vice-Chancellor and the Administration in Earlham Hall in the Park, and the Students' Union in the Village. Lost for ever was the moderating influence of living in the Village, its sense of small-scale community and softened environment.

Problems began to intensify. The Labour Club started a rather good political review *Can Opener* in February 1968 and began to organise protest meetings about Vietnam. These spread beyond Norwich to the nearby Lakenheath USAAF air base and Dow Chemicals in Kings Lynn, makers of napalm. This culminated in the major riot at the US Embassy in Grosvenor Square attended by UEA students.[9] This raised the whole consciousness of students about the Vietnam War.

Three serious areas of alienation began to emerge. Relations with the City deteriorated. Norwich landladies were refusing to let flats to noisy and dirty students. Students accordingly tried to pose as young "executives" to avoid the ban and the *Daily Telegraph* had some fun with this.[10] More seriously a survey by *Mandate* showed that two thirds of Norwich people had never visited UEA and barely a fifth had any idea of the size of the University. The student image was not helped by the *Rag Magazine* for 1968, a shoddy and smutty production and a sharp decline in tone from 1967.

Secondly, there was an alienation from the faculty. Staff-student seminars began to be held in May to discuss "the crucial breakdown between the JCR and the SCR", though the meetings themselves merely left the "feeling of a division between 'them' and 'us'".[11] To break down this division a group of students first picketed and then occupied the SCR to "integrate" with faculty. It was of little surprise that such action merely intensified rather than mollified this "alienation"; indeed it can have had no other intention. This was a significant new tactic.

On 13 May 1968 Princess Margaret made the first of two closely spaced royal visits to the University. The Princess was well regarded by the founders of UEA. Indeed Sir Roy Harrod had originally suggested her as Chancellor but, since she already held that office at Keele and fulfilled the office there "with great zest", it was thought inappropriate to ask her to divide her loyalties.[12] The students affected to see the visit less as an honour than as "unsought for, unwanted, uninteresting", a disruption of normal life and the presentation of a false illusion.[13] They could not have known that the Queen disapproved of her sister's visit also. If anything had gone seriously wrong it would have jeopardised her own visit shortly afterwards; even some minor trouble would focus unwarranted press attention. The Queen's judgement was right.

The Princess stayed for one and a half hours and saw the residences and the chemistry laboratories, and some French language teaching which interested her since her own French was good and she recognised some of the passages. All this was unremarkable but she also visited the Village on an unscheduled visit. Indeed the Chief Constable was alarmed as her car swept off there contrary to his plans. There she encountered a group of students – who could not have known of her surprise visit – who tried to make her the focus of an impromptu protest. The porter's official report described it so:

> A group of students numbering five moved close to the Royal Party and one of them, a male, endeavoured to ignite a paper carrier bag which was made in the guise of the Union Jack. In this attempt he was not successful but he immediately tore the paper bag in half and with a vocal ejaculation of either B . . . (?) or Bolshy threw the torn halves at the feet of the Royal Party.[14]

Another porter took the names of six students. What had been shouted was "Vietnam murderer" and one long-haired youth said he was just protesting about "society in general".[15] A series of chance photographs of the incident show the Princess and the Vice-Chancellor approaching a tall fuzzy-haired youth, a girl in a plastic raincoat and another in a mini-skirt. The Princess's smile turns blank with incomprehension, the Vice-Chancellor stares ahead glacially as they walk on, and Pro Vice-Chancellor Roy Campbell, following behind, turns to confront the trio. Princess Margaret made light of it; "Oh good! I've been protested against", she told the Vice-Chancellor.

The Union sought to distance itself from the discourtesy. The President, Richard Sandbrook, described the students concerned as recognised anarchists with no respect for the Union, University or anything.[16] *Mandate*, otherwise hostile to the visit, took the line that "protesters should never regard Royalty as a quick way to cheap press coverage".[17] At one level the incident was absurd or trivial but it was also profoundly important.

First, it sharply turned the City and region against the University, whose public esteem plummeted. The national and international press seized on the event. The President received fifty hostile letters and fifteen landladies at once refused to take any students. It was easy to get the impression that Royalty had run the gauntlet of crowds of students screaming obscenities and hurling flaming Union Jack flags. Secondly, it indicated to the anarchists that they had immense potential media power. It only needed a few individuals to do something odd or unusual in the presence of a camera and this would be given coverage out of all proportion to the event and the numbers involved. There was no need to win over large numbers of students; the press could effectively demonise the whole student body for the actions of a handful of the eccentric or disturbed. This was a powerful tactic used with increasing effectiveness in the coming months.

Thirdly, nobody was punished for the incident. This too was not lost on the anarchists. The University at that time had rules for dealing with drunks but not for outrages that brought it into disrepute. Accordingly the long-haired youth continued to play a part in subsequent disturbances and press photographs for the rest of the year, wilder in appearance and confident in his immunity. Fourthly, at the time of the Princess's visit, Essex University was in turmoil with a "free university", boycotts of lectures and bricks thrown through their Vice-Chancellor's windows. Up to this time UEA was thought of as respectable as Essex was radical and rowdy. Now the two universities of the east were thought of as equally despicable. Indeed the unfortunate vagueness of "East Anglia" became easily confused with Essex, the reputation of the one tarnishing the other. Fifthly, the Princess's visit, in *Mandate's* words "marked the start of civil war".[18] It began a sequence of troubles and the decline of UEA's public image and support, in keeping with the experiences of other universities at the same time.

The visit of Princess Margaret was followed by that of the Queen on 24 May 1968. The Queen is the Visitor of the University and as early as 1963 the Vice-

Chancellor was already thinking of a suitable time to receive Her Majesty.[19] It was appropriate to wait until there were buildings on the Plain and the chosen date enabled Her Majesty to combine the opening of the new Norfolk County Hall with an afternoon visit to UEA. In the previous month the Vice-Chancellor and Mrs Thistlethwaite had gone to Windsor to dine with the Queen and stay overnight as a pleasing introduction.

There was some fuss of students objecting to the spending of what they claimed was £200 on a water closet for the personal use of Her Majesty in Earlham Hall. In fact the entire cost of both royal visits was only £428, so the supposed costs of the closet were exaggerated for effect.[20] In between both royal visits the Vice-Chancellor was asked on television if he could guarantee that there would be no trouble for the Queen's visit.[21] He responded that, when there was so much trouble elsewhere, he could not guarantee anything but he relied on the fair play of the students and the leadership of the Union officers. The Palace privately asked him if he still wanted to go ahead and he unhestitatingly said yes.

The visit went quite well. The Queen walked past banners proclaiming "No to Anarchy, Yes to Monachy" and "UEA Welcomes the Queen." The "r" in "Monarchy" had been left out and inserted as an afterthought. Some photographs show it; some have it missing.[22] The Queen commented, "it is a pity that our side cannot spell as well as theirs". A Scottish Nationalist carried a Home Rule banner and thereby attracted enormous attention from the tabloids as a "protester". Richard Sandbrook, the President of the Students' Union, with typical grace, took tea (Earl Grey No. 3) with Her Majesty in defiance of instructions from the Union.

The adverse aspect of the visit was the holding of an alternative seminar on "Democracy in the University". About 200-300 students and staff attended this and about as many lined the route to greet the Queen. The seminar was held on the grass below the walkway on which the Queen was making her way between buildings. It was frankly intended as a gesture of dissent. The "seminar" discussed various aspects of student representation, the quality of teaching and so forth. These were perennial matters that needed discussing somewhere but not in public,[23] in the middle of a royal visit in the presence of the press while a sit-in at LSE was taking place at the same time.[24] The seminar was damaging. The press were looking for some action and a minor scuffle between "royalists" and "seminarians" provided a photo opportunity, though it was claimed that it "was staged entirely for the benefit of television."[25] Sandbrook personally deplored the "seminar" as "scandalous" and made strenuous efforts to stop it.

It further turned East Anglia against the University. The Norwich and Norfolk Ypres Association, who were shortly to attend a Buckingham Palace

Garden Party, decided to use the occasion to present a petition to the Queen asking her to "punish unruly students".[26] A handful of troublemakers insulting Princess Margaret could be dismissed as exceptional, but 200-300 deliberately ignoring the Queen was a much more substantial gesture. Moreover, some faculty played a significant part and this drew the flak of local hostility onto teachers as well as onto students. Nobody was punished, which emboldened some faculty for an ongoing tussle with the administration, as we shall see later. The people of Norwich took their revenge. The Rag which raised £3000 in 1967 and whose target for 1968 was £3500 raised only a paltry £400.[27]

Another minor revenge of the City was the banning of students and staff from Backs, a popular wine bar in the centre of town, on the grounds of their "ill manners, foul language, filthy habits and worn filthy dress". Sandbrook admitted that "the image of this University in the city of Norwich is at an all time low". Amazingly, he successfully negotiated with the managing director of the parent company to allow the University back.[28] But when the Union, passing beyond all reason, voted to take legal action against Backs and make the manager apologise, Sandbrook, whose term of office was drawing to a close, had no option but to resign as President.

There was a curious sideshow to these royal involvements. It was commonly believed that Princess Anne was intending to come to UEA as a student in 1968. The rationale was that she already had a schoolfriend from Benenden at UEA and it was near to Sandringham. The visit of Frank Thistlethwaite to Windsor, where he met Princess Anne earlier in the year, seemed to add weight to this. In fact the Vice-Chancellor and Princess Anne sat next to each other at the Windsor dinner and had a private conversation on this matter. She told him that she did not really want to go to university and he advised her to wait and possibly to go to a Commonwealth university when she felt ready.[29] Princess Margaret subsequently thanked the Vice-Chancellor for his helpful advice to her niece. The public, unaware of this, took the view that Princess Margaret and the Queen were really visiting UEA in 1968 with Princess Anne's future education in mind. The press took up the story widely with UEA being referred to as "the prestige University of East Anglia". Even the Barcelona press claimed that "la universidad East Anglia es una de la mejores de Inglaterra". Princess Anne's A level grades obviated her as a serious candidate, however, and UEA's increasing reputation for radical disruption removed it as an appropriate host.

The Summer of 1968 saw the eruption of Paris students in the événements.[30] The Nanterre campus, which had become a focus of student discontent in 1966, was closed. Daniel Cohn-Bendit marched to occupy the Sorbonne, which was then cleared by the police forcefully. This created an impression at UEA. Richard Owen, a student in EUR, spent some time with student leaders at the Sorbonne and stressed to UEA students their attempt to establish links with workers.[31] Susan Clarke, another EUR student, was given a Travelling Scholarship by the National Federation of Business and Professional Womens Clubs (hardly a revolutionary organisation) to visit France to study student unions.[32] There was an awareness of French events, acquired by most students from reading newspapers rather than any contact with Richard Owen or Susan Clarke, but in some minds it raised thoughts. Could adolescent rudeness to royalty escalate into a full-scale revolt with student unrest helping to unseat a government, as had succeeded in Belgium after unrest at the University of Leuven and as was being attempted against De Gaulle in Paris?

A valuable consequence of the troubles of the summer of 1968 was a reorganisation of the disciplinary structure. The structure was devised of a Discipline Committee for day to day misdemeanours, a Senate Discipline Committee for more serious matters, and an Appeals Committee to take appeals from the latter. Students had full representation on all committees and indeed a majority on the first of them. This was almost totally satisfactory and has broadly existed to this day, though the first-instance Disciplinary Committee has been replaced by a Disciplinary Officer. Also in 1968 the Vice-Chancellor remained Chairman of the Appeals Committee, a position from which he is now rightly distanced. The other major reform was the appointment of a full-time Dean of Students to take over from Marcus Dick, who had borne a crushing burden in addition to his academic duties. The new Dean was a remarkable man, John Coates. He was a Colonel with a DSO for wartime undercover exploits in Hungary and with Tito's partisans. He had followed this with a diplomatic career. He was a Finno-Ugrian linguist and had added a Cambridge doctorate to his many other accomplishments. "He is clearly quite a man" someone jotted on his papers.[33]

As well as these reforms the University obtained good publicity on the opening of the Library by Lord Franks, which seemed to reassert what the purpose of the University was as an academic institution. The Lasdun building attracted admiring attention and in a sincere gesture the Vice-President of the Students' Union joined the Ypres Association, which had been so critical of UEA, in laying a wreath at the Remembrance Day service in 1968. But this period of rapprochement was to be rudely interrupted.

On 2 December 1968 John Wells, the satirist, came to UEA to give a serious talk about Biafra. Since 1967 Biafra had been trying to declare its independence from Nigeria and the British Labour government was accused of abetting the genocide of the Biafran Ibos by the Hausas and Yorubas by its supply of arms to Lagos. Wells gave a useful and informative talk on this to the Socialist Society, attended by 150 students of all persuasions.[34] Wells, who had recently attacked the government on TV over Biafra, raised the issue as a British Vietnam for the Left to seize on as an object of guilt and moral recrimination.

In this context Roy Jenkins came to UEA two days after Wells's visit to make a televised programme with Robin Day on the future of democracy in Britain. It was to be the first of a new series called "University Forum", to find out what new ideas were fermenting in the universities. In hindsight it was a bizarre idea. Jenkins was Chancellor of the Exchequer yet he set aside the best part of a day's work to come to Norwich to talk to students. Who could have thought that students would have had enough to say to sustain one and a half hours' discussion or that this would merit nationwide attention? For Robin Day the project was one of mild desperation amid "unhappy years" in which he was being given less to do in *Panorama* and took up an "unsatisfactory assortment of now forgotten series".[35] The trip to Norwich was one of them. Jenkins, a miner's son with an aristocratic style, was not loved by the Left even before his defection to the Social Democrats. He arrived at Norwich Station smoking a cigar.

The television programme was a shambles. Students who had just seized on the Biafran issue attempted to take over the programme, and there was "jeering and counter jeering, catcalls, abuse and slow handclapping made almost continued bedlam".[36] Cards were held up purporting to show the number of Biafrans killed minute by minute. Leaflets were showered on the platform. Any attempt to discuss the future of democracy (which looked increasingly bleak on this showing) or to question Jenkins about the economy vanished, which infuriated the serious Left which genuinely wanted to press Jenkins over this issue. The pro-Biafrans were equally infuriated by Day's refusal to accept their issue for discussion.

Although Auberon Waugh was unusual in supporting the pro-Biafra action,[37] the overwhelming national reaction was appalled. Here at first hand were television images of rowdy, uncontrolled, mindless, tax-supported layabouts who tenanted the new universities. The public reputation of UEA plummeted along with other universities – a mass sit-in was taking place in Birmingham at the same time. Only two groups had cause to be satisfied. The technicians on the cameras were delighted with a most lively ninety minutes of television in what had hitherto been regarded as a docile university. They were also relieved that all their equipment had not been smashed, as it might have been at Essex. UEA was good for a "mini television riot".[38] More seriously, the revolutionary Left saw the passion aroused by the meeting as "a step towards building an effective opposition within this University".[39]

Early in the next year the London School of Economics was closed down by a further sit-in on 23 January. This led to threats of a proposed sit-in at

Earlham Hall in solidarity. If it had taken place it would have been the first sit-in at UEA, but the issue would have been so weakly second-hand that it would have been a tactical mistake. To inject some kind of fire into the event the President of the Students' Union demanded ludicrous assurances from the Vice-Chancellor "that similar political action will not be taken here" and that he would not erect steel gates all over UEA (steel gates were an issue at LSE) or victimise faculty. The Vice-Chancellor, who was away in Zambia and who had no intention of wasting money on steel gates, was asked to "clarify his position". It must be "the most important day in the University's life so far" claimed the sit-in leaflet with grandiose pomposity. On his return, the Vice-Chancellor replied coolly that he could not possibly respond to hypothetical situations which did not exist.[40] It was an absurd non-event but showed the reflective impact that troubles elsewhere could have. It also foreshadowed the threat of the sit-in strategy and moved Frank Thistlethwaite further in his increasing belief that he was faced with serious attempts at disruption.

Throughout 1969 there was an ongoing ripple of discontent and unrest about minor issues. There were attacks on the catering system and the running of the bookshop, and faculty and technicians were furious about proposals for car parking charges. Students protested about "sex spies" and porters checking up that members of the opposite sex were not in residence rooms after 11.30 p.m. – a rule abolished in June. There was a demonstration about the decision to grant an honorary degree to Sir Humphrey Gibbs, the former Governor of Rhodesia. To Liberals he was a plucky opponent of Ian Smith's UDI regime; to the Left merely a complaisant representative of the wealthy Rhodesian farming aristocracy. His connection with UEA was that his niece was Sir Edmund Bacon's wife, Gibbs and Bacon had been close friends at Cambridge.[41] The decision to hold the award of DCL to both Gibbs and Bacon in the City Hall merely transferred a demonstration to the centre of Norwich. The matter was controversial even in Senate, where a substantial minority voted against the Gibbs' doctorate.[42] In November UEA students held a large demonstration against the Vietnam War and an East Anglian Association for Peace in Vietnam was formed and sponsored by Second World War pacifist Benjamin Britten – UEA's Music Adviser. Some students tried to proselytise revolutionary ideas in local schools. Underlying all this was a constant ground bass of petty crime which was symptomatic of declining morale, a tide of nastiness on which fomenters of discontent could thrive.[43] The appointment of a psychiatric social worker to the Dean of Students office was a sign of the times.

In early 1970 some Edinburgh University students broke into their own university to find "political files" and some incriminating documents from Warwick were published. So UEA was again drawn into an issue not of its own making or particularly relevant to itself. The Vice-Chancellor made a statement, "I can state categorically that the University as a matter of policy does not compile information about the political affiliations or opinions of students".[44] Students had academic progress record cards kept by advisors and Schools, and there were files kept by the Medical and Appointments Officers[45] which were confidential as were those of the Dean of Students on welfare and disciplinary cases. That was all. Nevertheless the NUS Secretary compiled a lengthy report of matching tedium listing all kinds of inocuous files and procedures. He could not resist a note of paranoia: if there were political files, where were they? "In a warehouse in Norwich perhaps?" The Vice-Chancellor assured the President again that political opinions were no business of the University.[46] The files issue was important in some other universities but at UEA. In 1970 the matter was discussed in terms of disclaimers about non-existent, hypothetical circumstances of which UEA had no experience. Fantasies about "a warehouse in Norwich" as about "steel gates" sowed seeds of mistrust which were to blossom in 1971.

A much more serious issue that was to inflame 1970 was that of Barclays as the University's banker. Barclays was appointed UEA's bank by the Executive Committee on 18 July 1960 in dubious circumstances. When the matter was about to be discussed R. Q. Gurney, a local director of Barclays, simply said, "I propose Barclays". This was an improper use of influence and would not have been allowed in local government practice for example. Sir Edmund Bacon, who was a Director of Lloyds, felt scruples about putting forward his own bank and the Gurney proposal was not challenged. There was some historical sentimentality about the old Earlham-Gurney-Barclays link. Also it was true that many of the leading enterprises and institutions of Norwich banked with Barclays. Even so there should have been some proper tendering for best terms. The account of the new University was going to be one of the greatest prizes in the region and it should not have been so lightly bestowed at the behest of one with a vested interest.

For the first decade it did not matter. But in 1967 R. Q. Gurney expressed opposition to the sanctions against Rhodesia and was attacked by Shane Guy, the President of the UEA Liberal Society and a former Foreign Office official.[47] On the return of the students for the new academic year 1970-71, however, the Union urged all members to withhold the payment of bills until the University offered an alternative account and determined to follow such a policy itself.[48] The Vice-Chancellor then addressed the Students' Council on 12 October to make clear his position. He explained that he was deeply opposed to apartheid in South Africa, that he had devoted a lot of time to universities in Black Africa, notably Zambia and that he was Chairman of the East African Working Group of the Inter-University Council for Higher

Education Overseas. His credentials in this regard were impeccable. But he justified retaining the Barclay account on three grounds.[49]

First, he believed that the University needed to uphold its independence by not making decisions dictated by political considerations and he cited Clause 22 of the Charter as the justification for this. Second, choosing Barclays as the University bank was itself not a political act, it was merely the bank with local connections. It did not imply that the University endorsed all the bank's investment policies. In any case the decision had been taken before his appointment. Thirdly, although Barclays was involved in South Africa yet it also did a great deal of good in developing Black Africa. It was a good and courageous speech. It also informed students, who would not have known how significant a figure Frank Thistlethwaite was in helping the development of higher education in East Africa, though his invoking of Clause 22 was less convincing. It was to no avail. The Union decided to set up its own alternative account into which to pay bills. In 1970 the issue came to a head. Students were being urged to boycott Barclays Bank on various interlocking grounds. Barclays DCO was the biggest bank in South Africa and a mainstay of the apartheid economy. It was also active in Rhodesia, now run by Ian Smith's UDI regime. More specifically Barclays was financing the Cabora Bassa Dam in Mozambique. This dam, it was claimed, would supply power to South Africa, at a cost of displacing 24,000 black Mozambicans. R.Q. Gurney intervened again, denying that Cabora Bassa would benefit Rhodesia and urging Thistlethwaite to counter "false propaganda".[50] On 30 April 1970 the Students' Union resolved to ask the University to close its account with Barclays. Council considered this on 1 June and decided against it on the grounds that the University could not distinguish between the relative degrees with which different business organisations were involved in the South African economy. Moreover the University "must preserve its institutional neutrality in political matters".[51]

At this point the Vice-Chancellor's speech to the Students' Council was subject to an incisive critique by Dr David King.[52] Dr King was no ordinary protester. He was a South African himself and knew the issues at first hand. He was also one of the ablest men on the faculty to have passed through UEA, a future FRS, Professor of Chemistry at Cambridge and Master of Downing College, Cambridge and Chief Scientific Advisor to the Government. He convincingly pointed out that Clause 22 did not prevent UEA doing political things; it prevented the University imposing a religious, racial or political test on its *members*, not on its bank. Clause 22 forbade the University from exercising racial discrimination. It was untenable to cite it as a reason why the University should not punish its bank for supporting racial discrimination. On the contrary, if Clause 22 obliged the University to take a stand against racialism, it was more logical to suggest that it had a duty to take a stand against apartheid by disengaging from its bank than to suggest that the clause was a reason why it should not so disengage. The University also did many things that had political implications and could not help doing so. It had just told Mrs Thatcher that it opposed student loans rather than grants. BIO's research for the USAAF could also have been cited. King's argument was persuasive and sixty faculty supported the students' right to open an alternative account. The sixty included sixteen actual and future professors, including some soon to be most distinguished figures – King himself, Paul Kennedy (later Professor of History at Yale and UEA Hon. Litt.D.), C. D. Scott (later FBA), Martin and Patricia Hollis (the former a later FBA, Pro Vice-Chancellor and the latter a Life Peer).

The campaign against Barclays was an NUS one and not of course confined to Norwich. It worried the bank, which in 1970 spent £107,750 on student advertising, compared with Lloyds £63,750 and £26-28,000 by Nat West and the Midland.[53] Barclays claimed to have secured 48 per cent of freshmen accounts in 1969 so they had much to lose. Lord Cranbrook, the University's Treasurer, was worried too.[54] He thought that the Council was getting too used to appeasement. He despised the "woolly minded cliches" of the Countess of Albemarle in support of the alternative account and, in a veiled threat suggested that East Suffolk County Council would only continue to support the University if it stood firm against calls to change the bank account.[55] There was an impasse. 322 students were paying their bills into a trust fund, another 300 were delaying the payment of their bills.[56] The University was withholding £26,600 from the Students' Union – Manchester University was doing the same. Accordingly, on 16 November 1970 the Council agreed to open a separate account with a bank nominated by the Students' Union but not to terminate the Barclay account. The voting was seven laymen and nine academics, including the Vice-Chancellor, *for* the alternative account and six laymen and two academics *against*.[57] Thus there was an even balance of laymen for and against the alternative account; it was not a matter of academics outvoting laymen. The proposer of the motion in favour of the alternative account was Lady Albemarle, supported by the Vice-Chancellor and the Bishop of Norwich, Bert Hazell a former Labour MP for North Norfolk,and Arthur South a local businessman and a Labour councillor and a founder of the University.[58] Lady Albemarle was in favour of an alternative account but would have opposed a change of bank altogether. In the Vice-Chancellor's view the second account was justified since "the humane choice was to recognise this means whereby students could bear witness to their conscientious objections on this issue".[59] For Frank Thistlethwaite educated at a Quaker school these words about bearing witness and conscientious objection carried serious meaning and he welcomed Bishop Fleming's moral support. The money not paid into Barclays was kept with Lloyds and then transferred to the Midland as the alternative bank with less involvement with South Africa than the others.

This was too much for some. Lord Cranbrook, the Treasurer, resigned in protest. He was no supporter of apartheid, indeed he was one of only six Conservative peers who had voted in favour of sanctions on Rhodesia. Moreover his son-in-law was a coloured South African. But there were further cross-currents since his own father-in-law Sir Frederick Seebohm, was Chairman of Barclays DCO, the very bank being complained of. Lord Cranbrook resigned from the Council and his Treasurer's post since he believed that Council was abdicating authority under student pressure. Professor R. H. Campbell, the much respected Pro Vice-Chancellor, resigned all his University offices and maintained a dignified silence. Sir Roy Harrod resigned from the Court, as did eight local Conservative MPs led by Sir Harry Legge Bourke.[60] Some regarded this as little loss, since they rarely attended it anyway. The MPs were invited to lunch at UEA and Legge Bourke, after an impassioned letter to the Vice-Chancellor, urged Council to reconsider. At the lunch of MPs Roy Campbell did most of the talking. He told them that he personally considered that what the University had done was wrong but that the MPs were wrong to have reduced the age of majority without considering the implications for universities. Campbell's impression of Legge Bourke and the MPs was that they were out to make political capital from the incident. They went home unconciliated but did not create further trouble.[61] Timothy Colman then privately contacted many local businessmen in a damage limitation to prevent them turning against UEA. They had a narrow shave when Charles Pitt Steele of Norfolk County Council Education Committee tried to stop their £15,000 grant to UEA but without success.[62] Barclays also took this seriously. Sir Frederick Seebohm, and three Barclay directors, met with representatives of the NUS who convinced him that they were not merely a "rentacrowd" but were well-informed and genuinely concerned about the issues.[63] The *Eastern Daily Press* well expressed what many in Norwich must have thought. It considered the Council decision to allow an alternative account as wrong. It praised even-handedly the dignity of Roy Campbell, the humane attitudes of the Vice-Chancellor, the responsible conduct of the Students' Union and admitted the genuineness of the concern about South Africa. Yet "Danegeld has been paid and the Dane will be back".[64] There was also one more hidden effect in that from 1971 the University did not invest again in Barclays Bank as part of its portfolio. It was the sole exception to the University's practice of not interfering with the investment policies of its merchant bank, Lazards.[65]

Then there was the car park. We have seen something of the car park in considering the building of the Plain. The car park, however, had a greater significance as an episode in the politics of the University and became part of the story of the troubles. The only way to build the car park was with capital from the Appeal which had to be repaid from a charge on the users. These charges were first levied in 1967-68 but increasing opposition to them grew with ramifying consequences.[66] Due to the opposition the Council agreed not to levy charges in 1968-69 until the matter had been explored further, but a scale was drawn up for 1969-70, moderated according to salary ranging from £2 – £10 a year. Even the Vice-Chancellor paid £5 for his place at Earlham Hall. His Personal Assistant, in a note reminding him, added "the whole thing is a lot of humbug." It soon became more than that. Many people felt that, since other major employers in Norwich offered free parking as a fringe benefit, UEA was in effect imposing salary cuts on its employees through its car park charges. This was especially true since the University seemed to have so much space and was built at Earlham for precisely this reason. It was argued that this was a change in conditions of employment.[67] The AUT's national policy was that universities should not charge for car parks and UEA AUT would not comply with any charges.[68] The students also agreed to support the AUT and the ASTMS (Association of Scientific Technical and Managerial Staff).

The ASTMS also threatened a strike. This was most significant. Many faculty were dissatisfied with the AUT as too "professional" and "establishment", and not an effective fighting force. They were making common cause with technicians by joining the ASTMS, more militant, even working-class in constituency. The car park issue gave the ASTMS a splendid opportunity to gain members and show itself a high profile organisation prepared to take on management.

This resulted in a meeting on 19 December 1969 at the Department of Employment and Productivity.[69] The conciliators suggested that free car parking should be made available to all and when the free area was full then a paying area should be used. Accordingly the car park was divided with a free area distant from the Plain, by Bluebell Road, and a paying area near to the University buildings. This, however, did not satisfy. The AUT remained totally opposed to all charges,[70] and the ASTMS raised the stakes by demanding a public enquiry into the finances of UEA.[71] More seriously the School of Biological Sciences actually did have a one-day strike. They were at the most extreme western end of the site, furthest from the free car park in the east. They were used to parking on some adjacent land but now found that they were to be charged. On 26 January 1970 they struck for one day in protest. The Establishment Officer, J. M. Brewin, then wrote to all grades of staff in BIO asking them to affirm that they had not been on strike that day or they would suffer a day's deduction of pay.[72] This totally inflamed the situation. Professor Jack Kitching, a former Dean, complained to the Vice-Chancellor that it was the "pinnacle of discourtesy" that he (an FRS and an OBE) should be asked to affirm that he had been doing his duty. Professor J.R. Jones fairly pointed out that it was the University's job to note who was present before deducting salary, not to ask staff whether they were there or not.[73] The prestigious Professor Roy Markham, Director of the John Innes Institute, refused to visit the Plain and BIO under these parking conditions.[74] Others sent more abusive letters, one sending the Establishment Officer's letter to his solicitors – probably intended as a melodramatic gesture but shrewder than he thought, as we shall see. Yet again car park charges were abandoned by the Vice-Chancellor on 30 January 1970, as they had been in September and November 1969, to avert further strikes.[75]

This was not the end of the matter. Indeed in 1970 the car park dispute raised some very profound issues and moved from politics into political and legal theory not contemplated at UEA before. Professor R. H. Campbell asked a former colleague, Professor Donald Robertson, the Professor of Industrial Economics at Glasgow University, to comment on UEA's situation. He replied in a long thoughtful paper.[76] He took the view that "many of the duties of academics are deliberately underdescribed", so it was virtually impossible to relate duties to specific blocks of time and in any case they could be rearranged. So it was impossible to tell, certainly in the short term, whether a duty was being declined or rearranged, "the situation is bound to be somewhat ambiguous". It was also very doubtful whether it was legally permissable to require an individual to make a self-incriminating statement as Brewin had tried to do. Yet such an illegal statement would be the only way to verify a strike. Indeed the lecturer who had sent Brewin's letter to his solicitor had acted quite correctly. We cannot know what opinion he got back but it would probably have been to ignore the letter as invalid. Campbell was already getting similar advice. He told Robertson that,

> our Solicitors say that they do not think an individual can, in law, declare themselves to be on strike in the way academics might be asked to do. Given the point that nobody can in practice determine when another academic has gone on strike with complete certainty, you are faced with the incredible situation that an academic cannot go on strike at all.[77]

The basic point was that an individual cannot attribute a breach of contract to himself so "in practice a short strike by an academic cannot be proved with adequate certainty".[78] The point was reinforced by Professor Kitching, who had complained of the "pinnacle of discourtesy". He claimed that he had rearranged his classes "on academic grounds", so "it could not be established that a strike of Faculty had occurred". In any case – a crucial point – it is for a Dean to decide whether the academic duties of a School were being carried out, not the Registrar and still less an administrator like the Establishment Officer.[79] Here was the Gilbertian situation that Campbell and Robertson had foreseen. A whole School could cease work to create the pressure of a strike; yet, by rearranging its work, by refusing to affirm that it was on strike, and with the support of a Dean doing the same, no strike could be proved.

The argument was moved onto a higher plane by Gordon Tilsley (himself a lawyer) who saw it in almost philosophical terms. His view was that *employees* can strike and, in English conventions, although they lose pay their jobs are kept open for them and they return to them after the strike and relations resume. In his view, however, "the academic staff are so much part of the government of the University" they are "members of the Corporate Body". As such, for academics to strike against their own corporate body is to put themselves beyond the pale, since their status "and these privileges exact the duty of loyalty to the government of the University".[80] This was a harking back to the Cambridge common room and the "community of scholars". Yet by 1970 many faculty had come to regard themselves as employees having to defend themselves against management. The car park issue highlighted this and the Establishment Officer's letter brought home the point even to senior figures like Professors Kitching and Markham, who were pushed, to their surprise, into a dissident position.

Dissent on a larger scale was expressed by the rise of the ASTMS, one of the major consequences of the car park crisis. The ASTMS began to organise in early 1970. Roy Hay in February wrote of the need to recruit more widely and use the "perfect opportunity to capitalise on the extreme discontent at the ineffectiveness of Assembly and of the AUT".[81] They then asserted their position by asking for negotiating rights on the grounds that the AUT did not represent their interests.[82] The University already recognised the ASTMS for technicians but was uneasy about admitting it alongside the AUT for faculty. The ASTMS claimed membership among one in eight of academic staff at UEA by 1976.[83]

A committee established to consider this came to the view that the University could not undertake "discussions with ASTMS other than in conjunction with AUT which already operates in this field" and advised ASTMS to collaborate with AUT.[84] They did, however, concede that the University "would be prepared to accept representation by ASTMS on local matters only in respect of ASTMS faculty members". ASTMS continued to flourish, attracting radical faculty who often took the side of dissident students in the troubles.

The car parking issue, therefore became a very important theme in the troubles. It aroused the antagonism of both students and faculty which fed into the general malaise. It caused the first strike ever among faculty noted for their loyalty. It also raised more fundamental questions about whether faculty could strike, and most deeply of all, it rifted older notions of the community. Faculty who by striking denied their metaphysical status as part of the corporate body then found themselves threatened by management as employees. It also raised a clash of authority between the Registry and that of a Dean. The unrest also provided an opportunity for the ASTMS to organise, to challenge the AUT and claim recognition from the University as a more militant vehicle for faculty representation and protest.

It was not the Barclays or car parking issues, however, which plunged UEA into the depths of the troubles, it was the much more sinister issue of drugs. In January 1968 it was claimed that 600-1000 young people in Norwich had taken drugs and that there were thirty to fifty pushers in the city, but only a tenth of consumers were being treated by doctors for addiction.[85] Professor Roy Emerson acted as Chairman of the Norwich Action Group on Drugs, though UEA students were not seen as as problem. On the other hand, Roger Niven, the retiring President of the Students' Union, in a valedictory statement in the Summer of 1969, said that the Union should "get tough with vandalism, theft, public drug taking, drug pushing and hooliganism", which suggested that it was an issue by 1969.[86] I was the warden of a small hall of residence from 1965 to 1967 and, although I was concerned about some heavy drinking, there was no trace or suspicion of drug taking. In fact the first time that the Dean of Students heard of the presence of drugs at UEA was in January 1967.[87] The first UEA student prosecuted in Norwich for possession of cannabis was in January 1970.[88] Various drug-related matters began to trouble the Vice-Chancellor from 1969. The brother of a girl at UEA wrote privately to him early in 1969 expressing his concern about drugs and promiscuity at Fifers Lane.[89] Also in the summer of 1969 an expedition went to Morocco and one of the members established a drugs contact there. A packet of cannabis sent from Morocco was intercepted by the police, whose subsequent investigations revealed further drug possession in the expeditionary group.[90]

The most important case with the most profound repercussions, arose in 1970. An American student was found to be a user of cannabis, LSD and amphetamine. His rooms were raided by the Norwich Drug Squad in December 1970 resulting in a court appearance, a fine and suspended prison sentence in January 1971.[91] However the matter did not end there since he was then taken before the Senate Disciplinary Committee for a breach of General Regulations 10 (3).[92] Believing that he would only be severely reprimanded after the punishment he had already received in the magistrates' court, he admitted to his wider use of drugs. He was sent down from the University and the expulsion was upheld on appeal. This raised profound issues – that a student could be placed in double jeopardy and punished twice for the same offence both inside and outside the University; that more confessed evidence was taken account of at the second hearing than had been available at the first; and that the Dean of Students, who was concerned primarily with welfare and who was privy to all kinds of welfare information, was also the prosecutor in disciplinary cases able to use his background knowledge. A further emotive issue in this case was the fact that the student, if expelled, would be drafted to fight in Vietnam. Ironically his father was a senior officer in the US Army. Here was a heady brew of potential grievances.

The students took action. A petition of a thousand signatures was raised and there was a march to Earlham Hall. An Extraordinary Union General Meeting attended by 450 students was held on the night of 8 March 1971. This agreed that the student should be readmitted, that the Students' Union should have a veto over non-academic disciplinary cases, and that the Arts Building should be occupied.[93] 300 students did this when the meeting broke up at 8.45 p.m. The Union, although calling for the abolition of rule 10 (3), tried to stress that it was not a drugs issue but one about the unfairness of double jeopardy and student representation on the Disciplinary Committee. The NUS and nine other Student Unions sent messages of support.[94] The Vice-Chancellor refused to readmit the student or discuss the matter while the Arts Building was occupied and emergency arrangements were made for the relocation of teaching. The sitters-in described themselves "The Arts Block is filled with people who are talking together and looking happy and listening to good sounds . . . and besides the fun scene there are rooms for academic study if that is what you really want to do."[95]

The University clarified its position. It reminded students that the disciplinary procedures and committees had been agreed with the Union three years before. What many may not have known was that 10(3) "was promulgated partly at the request of the student representatives who were concerned to establish that drug taking was an offence and that the existing more general regulation did not make this sufficiently clear". The University must also have its own regulations to be able to proceed independently of the civil courts. The Code of Discipline was to be reviewed in the summer as a routine matter and not, it was stressed, in response to the sit-in.[96] The sit-in was called off on 17 March leaving behind £2013 worth of damage.[97]

Much emphasis over this case had been on constitutional quasi-legal matters, but it was not forgotten that drugs lay behind it. A rare attack on the sit-in was candid, "for many people it boils down to this, SOC SOC is protecting the heads from the people outside so they can smoke their pipe in peace".[98] There can be no doubt that there had been a great increase in drug use and a stepping up of measures to counteract it. Prosecutions for drug offences in Norfolk and Norwich nearly doubled from forty-seven in 1969 to eighty-nine by 1970.[99] The Mid Anglia Drugs Squad numbered twenty-seven officers and there was increasing police activity on campus.[100] The local MP, Dr Tom Stuttaford, made a strong attack on the University, demanding from the Home Secretary, Reginald Maudling, a police investigation into drug-taking at UEA.[101] He claimed that it was "rife" at the University and that UEA was "associated with the use and passage of drugs within the city of Norwich". The Senior Porter at Fifers Lane also thought that "a high percentage of students were on drugs". [102] Dr Stuttaford was especially knowledgeable in this area, being in charge of the City Dispensary dealing with addicts. In his view the University and city drug scenes did not intermingle. Dr Stuttaford knew the criminal who ran Norwich drugs but thought that UEA supply came from elsewhere; if the University had been in Norwich itself, drug provision would have been easier to control. He was concerned at the discovery of needles and syringes at Horsham which suggested hard drugs and not just cannabis hence his use of the word "rife".[103] But "rife" was disturbing as was his well-known comment that Norwich had lost "a second-rate golf course for what is rapidly becoming a third-rate university".

Some firm evidence to test Dr Stuttaford's assertion was provided by a working party on the use of drugs which reported on 1 March 1971.[104] This concluded that there was "widespread usage" of cannabis, with 200-500 occasional and forty to fifty heavy users. But there was little use of LSD, with about ten to twenty-five users, and there was no question of heroin or cocaine. The report concluded that "drug taking was not a major problem at UEA at present", though there had been a significant change in the last two years with more students coming to University already experienced in drug use in their own homes. In fact the Senate Disciplinary Committee had heard seven drugs cases between December 1968 and October 1971.[105] The working party could propose little save to reinforce that the University would not condone the use of cannabis, an illegal substance. But it suggested that the Medical and Counselling Services be built up to deal with student drug-users and that more information be made available.

The drugs issue caused anxiety to all universities not only on moral and medical grounds but because of the liabilities they incurred as host institutions.[106] Under the Dangerous Drugs Act 1965 every officer concerned in the management of premises where cannabis was smoked could be guilty of a criminal offence. Even for a tutor to report an incident would be self-incriminating. A case in Cambridge aroused concern among Vice-Chancellors, who were only assuaged by an assurance that prosecutions would not be made before consulting the Home Office.

The attitude of the Left to drugs was divided. Jack Straw, as President of the National Union of Students, campaigned against the use of cannabis – then as now.[107] One or two members of the International Socialists were cannabis users but the leadership was not and took the view that the more serious people were about politics the less they approved of drugs.[108] The Spartacus League by contrast much more commonly approved occasional cannabis smoking; indeed the leading supplier at UEA was a member of the SL. But there were dilemmas here. Cannabis smoking could be seen as part of some anti-orthodox life style along with pop music, dress and hair fashions "playing a part in breaking people away from middle class morality".[109] But there was an anti-capitalist suspicion of the drug-dealer as a businessman. There was also suspicion of "mind-expanding" LSD (made in the Chemistry laboratories) as dulling political fervour and seriousness. Cannabis smoking was undoubtedly common among the Spartacus League, like drinking, but LSD and heroin were regarded as dangerous and reactionary. There was only one heroin addict at UEA in those days, a Turkish postgraduate, nothing to do with political action and a pathetic warning to others.

While the 1971 sit-in was in progress it became merged with the issue of preliminary examinations. Those taking part in the sit-in regarded it as a betrayal to abandon the protest to take part in examinations. Underneath this was a genuine concern that preliminary examinations served no useful purpose.[110] The preliminary courses by contrast did fulfil many functions. The Vice-Chancellor regarded the first year as an important pause after A level in which a student could reorient himself. He was no lover of excessive testing and was disappointed that some Schools regarded the preliminary year as an opportunity to start specialist professional training as soon as possible. In SOC the preliminary course was important as a means of introducing students to a range of subjects not familiar to them from school, but there was no deep commitment to the need for an examination. There was a clear difference between Arts and Science Schools. The Arts Schools took a higher calibre of student and there was less need for an examination to detect those who might not be capable of proceeding to Honours. To mount full-scale examinations for all to find the occasional inadequate was a waste of time – especially since students were being continually tested by coursework. Science Schools by contrast took a poorer quality of entrant, some of whom really were unsuitable for Honours and who needed weeding out. The Science Schools, liked to use the preliminary course as an early part of the Honours course and appropriate for examination testing. Students were quick to sense these ambivalences, especially the doubtful value of preliminary examinations in the Arts Schools, and to make an issue out of them. Hence part of the sit-in advocated the peaceful boycott but not disruption of preliminary examinations.

Some students did try disruptions by banging on the roof of the Assembly Hall in the Village where some examinations were taking place. They were called off in consequence. Similar attempts to stop those in the Sports Centre on the Plain failed. This led to two students being heavily fined £35 by the Senate Disciplinary Committee and given suspended expulsion.[111] This in turn led to a further demonstration outside Earlham Hall and the handing in of a petition signed by 905 names against the punishment of the disrupters. It was the largest manifestation of discontent of those years.[112] It was also moderate, not condoning the disruption but protesting against the punishment. The petitioners included three future Deans and, to my knowledge, very many students of respectable and sensible reputation. The matter was taken up again in the next academic year by the President of the Students Union,[113] and it was followed by a powerfully argued document from the Deans of the Arts Schools rehearsing the now familiar arguments,[114] care in admissions admitted very few incapable of Honours, the preliminary examinations wasted too much time and interrupted the teaching, coursework made it unnecessary, it was too soon after A level. Accordingly the preliminary examinations were abolished in the Arts Schools from 1972 but retained for the Sciences. There was a sad footnote to these turbulent events. Between the sit-in, the preliminary examination disruption and the disciplinary hearing Marcus Dick, the former Dean of Students, died.[115] He had been walking with his wife and daughter when he collapsed with a heart attack on the beach at Cley. He had handed over his responsibilities as Dean and so missed the worst of the troubles, though they must have saddened him. He was only fifty but looked much older.

In May the turmoil intensified with the disclosure of "secret files" of letters between the Dean of Students office and the Residence Manager of Fifers Lane. These were about students suspected of drug use and cohabitation, and about liaison with the police on criminal matters.[116] To look at now they are hardly outrageous but part of the exchange of information about students, especially if they are engaged in criminal activity. But at that time of heightened tension they appeared sinister. In consequence a group of faculty signed a protest memorandum calling for a separation of the disciplinary and welfare systems, an enquiry into the methods by which the Dean of Students obtained information, and expressing the view that the Dean was "unsuitable" for his office. Twenty-six faculty signed the first two sections. On the first point they had some justification; it *was* necessary to separate discipline and welfare and was subsequently done. The second point about gathering information was not as interesting as they thought. The Dean of Students obviously received reports from Resident Tutors, porters and other staff, as one would expect. The fact that Dr Coates had been a distinguished figure in military intelligence and a behind the lines secret agent led to lurid suspicions of secret spy networks at UEA set up by a masterspy Dean. This was fed by the notorious "Strangelove Memorandum" about the need to protect the Medical Officer by attributing information passed on by him about drugs to others.[117] To those so inclined it suggested a cloak and dagger world of duplicitous relations between the Dean of Students' office, parents, the police and doctors with information being "extracted bit by bit" from one to test against another – all as an operation covered by a mysterious codename. It was easily forgotten that the memorandum had been disclosed as the result of a criminal break in during the sit-in. Clandestine to the last, the original "Strangelove Memorandum" was never returned to the University but still exists in a secret location.

The third point attacking Dr Coates as "unsuitable" was unwarranted and only nineteen signatories signed this.[118] Eleven were a group of the Left in the School of Economic and Social Studies. Another group of five were Biologists. A press conference on 6 May 1971 revealed the heightened passions.[119] Douglas Baker, the Assistant Dean, deplored "a handful of dedicated fanatics who believed that any methods no matter how low were justified if they furthered their extremist aims, have caused appalling damage to human relationships at the UEA in recent weeks". John Coates referred to the "froth, filth and scum" at the University. The Council meeting of 24 May deplored the "unprofessional conduct" of the nineteen, expressed its confidence in the DOS and offered help in any libel action he would wish to take.[120] They also decided to take legal advice to see if the conduct of the nineteen was "disgraceful" to the extent of meriting dismissal – a threat which the nineteen took very seriously. In this poker game there was actually no serious intention to sack the nineteen but several of the nineteen themselves were genuinely anxious. It was determined, however, to require an apology for the insult to Dr Coates. In this the University was advised by Dr Frazer Noble, the Vice-Chancellor of Leicester, who urged some strong gesture. After various meetings a settlement was reached by 23 June when the nineteen issued a statement that they "intended no slur on the character or sincerity" of the Dean or his Deputy. Dr Coates and Mr Baker accepted this and regarded the matter as closed.[121]

A major consequence of the troubles was a review of the whole structure of disciplinary matters. A commission of enquiry was set up by the Senate on 29 April 1971. It consisted of five faculty and five Student Council representatives under the Chairmanship of Raymond Frostick, a Norwich solicitor and Labour Councillor.[122] The fundamental issue was the need to reorder and possibly separate the functions of welfare and discipline. The commission quickly found that regulations were scattered through many documents and that "few people in the University have a clear idea of this overall structure". Also, before 1968 cases had been dealt with by the Vice-Chancellor or Dean of Students. Both these features of scattered codification and the personal involvement of high-level officials were indicative of a primitive structure inappropriate for an expanding institution. In the pre-Frostick system the DOS could summarily hear cases himself; above him, since November 1968, was the Joint Discipline Committee and the Senate and Senate Appeals Committees. In residences there were Residence Courts. Frostick grasped the main issue and recommended that "the Dean of Students should no longer have power to make regulations, powers of summary jurisdiction or prosecuting duties". They thought that Residence Courts should be retained, though they had heard few cases. The old prosecuting functions of the DOS should be devolved to two proctors with powers of summary jurisdiction, hearing and fining while prosecuting more serious cases before higher disciplinary committees. The Vice-Chancellor was to be entirely removed from the disciplinary system. They saw no role for a student veto over disciplinary decisions as impossible to arrive at without a public meeting of the Union, but they proposed two more students on the Senate Discipline Committee.

They had some useful recommendations on drugs. They argued that since the use of drugs was illegal the University had no need for a special regulation about them, any more than about assault or fraud. Accordingly it recommended the abolition of Regulation 10(3). But they retained the principle of double jeopardy. A student dealt with in the courts could be sent down to protect the interests of the University, just as professions protected themselves. Three student members wrote minority reports arguing for a student veto on disciplinary decisions or a system entirely run by the Students' Union. But overall the Frostick Report was welcomed as a lucid and totally sensible analysis of the way forward.

John Coates, in a thoughtful critique, still wanted the DOS to retain overall responsibility for both discipline and welfare. In his view the two could not be entirely separated, even if the DOS was no longer involved himself personally in disciplinary aspects.[123] This was a helpful modification to the commission's stance. In practice the DOS retained responsibility for discipline and for disciplinary policy, as Dr Coates wanted, but he devolved its jurisdiction to a Disciplinary Officer from whose activities he remained quite separate. It sounds metaphysical but has worked well since.

The second major issue heightened by the troubles was that of student participation in University government. In October 1968 the CVCP and NUS issued a joint statement on this. The NUS sought an "effective student presence". In welfare matters "it was quite appropriate"; also as regards the curriculum the faculty should have the final say but student views must "properly be taken into account", whereas in staff appointments and promotions both sides agreed that student participation was inappropriate.[124] These mild and sensible proposals were met with exaggerated national press coverage referring to "student *rule*" and "power to the students" in the inflamed atmosphere of the time. In the following month the NUS secured a similar joint statement with the LEAs, "the NUS seeks effective student pressure on the Governing Body and on all relevant committees".[125]

The system at UEA in those days gave students a limited role. There was a Joint Committee of Senate and the Students' Council and the Graduate Students Association to discuss matters of student affairs and make recommendations to the Senate. A Standing Student Welfare Committee was a joint committee of Council, Senate and Students. The Presidents of the Students' Union and the GSA attended Senate and Council only at the invitation of their chairmen. Students sat on all disciplinary committees – the Joint, Senate and Appeals. The Students' Council and GSA were requesting membership of the Senate and Council and this was being considered by the Senate.[126]

The Students' Union wanted four full members of Senate and Council. The University had allowed students onto these bodies for a trial period until the end of the academic year 1969 but could not accord them voting rights without changing the statutes. Roger Niven, the President of the Union, had argued that "we are not asking that we should control the University. We rather believe we are one of the main sectors of the University community and should be included in the government of the community by the community as such". This was excellently put, its reference to "community" well judged, and the *Eastern Daily Press* gave it its full support. 1969 was in any case a crucial year in that following the recommendations of the Latey Committee the voting age was lowered from twenty-one to eighteen and this increased student claims for voting representation in their own institutions. In the same year Jack Straw, then President-Elect of the NUS (and later Labour Shadow Secretary of State for Education), made a very able and widely received Granada Guildhall Lecture arguing that students should not have control of their universities but on the other hand consultation was insufficient. The irresistible demand was for representation.[127]

But still the students were not given voting rights. In October 1970 the Vice-Chancellor gave his annual interview to *Twice*, who raised the matter again.[128] He sidestepped the issue, by claiming that the students put their views "extremely well and forcefully", but gave no explanation of why there was still no voting. A year later Arthur South an influential member of the Council said he was firmly in favour of student voting rights and regarded it inevitable some time in the future.[129] The failure to grasp this issue of student voting, which looks in retrospect totally reasonable, caused resentment which underlay the troubles. But the atmosphere of mistrust engendered by the unrest probably increased resistance to the change. It was easily overlooked that, although there was no student voting rights on Senate and Council, UEA was very liberal in allowing student representation on a wide range of other committees, as we shall see. But in the eyes of dissidents this was no substitute for full representation on Senate and Council.

There was a final flurry of trouble when the Senate on 12 January 1972 rejected claims for student control of the disciplinary system or (failing that) veto over disciplinary decisions. This had been a claim of the minority of the Frostick Committee. Within a few days, on 7 February, students occupied the Arts Block for two days. After it had finished Senate met again and rejected a proposal to outlaw direct action and set up a committee to implement the Frostick Report. But most importantly they agreed to delete the contentious Regulation 10 (3) on drugs which had brought the troubles to such a head over the American student affair.

All these events at UEA did not take place in a vacuum, they were but part of a wider context of change and turmoil which they reflected and with which they sometimes interacted. In particular there was a slackening of traditional standards and a challenging of existing authorities in many areas of British life. The publication of *Private Eye* in 1961 and the starting of *That Was the Week that Was* in 1962 accustomed a generation to regard authority with an ironic and questioning eye. The spread of the contraceptive pill in the mid 1960s, the abolition of the death penalty in 1965, the Abortion Act of 1967 and the legalisation of homosexuality between consenting adults in the same year, the abolition of stage censorship in 1968 and the liberalisation of the divorce laws in 1969, all signalled a rapid shift away from traditional constraints on behaviour. Following the Divorce Reform Act of 1969, divorces sharply increased from around 50,000 a year in 1969 to 105,000 by 1973.[130] Over the time of troubles the likelihood of a student coming from a broken home doubled. How far this brought unhappiness and grievance to UEA in these years we can only speculate. The adulation of pop singers (with MBEs for the Beatles in 1965), the advent of the mini-skirt in 1964 ushered in an era of noise, hedonism and the claims of youth culture – sex and drugs and rock n' roll. At a more serious level the young were aware of other changes in their own lives. Between 1968 and 1972 numbers in comprehensive schools over-took those in grammar schools, which suggested a change in value systems, and the reduction of the age of majority to eighteen in 1969 gave the young political power.

Frank Thistlethwaite and several others saw this reduction in the age of majority as a central element in a new situation. The public at large was still expecting universities to discipline students as if they were at school. But at a stroke their status had been changed to that of independent, voting adults, less willing to accept an *in statu pupillari* status from a paternalistic *alma mater*. Britain as a whole was also in a curious psychological condition at this time: its population was quite the most satisfied with life of any European country and also the most optimistic about the future. Yet it was also by far the most dissatisfied about the state of its democracy. Here was a tension between happiness but political dissatisfaction and expectations of change that could feed unrest.[131] All these shifts were not lost on students. They knew they were coming into a world where rapid changes in values were normal and where old-established assumptions and power relationships could be overturned. They were also coming to a University opened in 1963 whose short life had been underlain by less than a decade of intense national change.

It was also a period of increasing unrest in universities internationally.[132] Troubles began at Berkeley, California, in 1964 and paralysed that campus for most of the decade. In 1965 the Free University of Berlin emerged as a centre of student protest, and in 1966 Nanterre became a focus of student disruption in Paris. 1967 saw the start of the compulsory draft for Vietnam, alienating many of student age in the USA from government policy. Wearing long hair and using drugs became a gesture of that alienation. It is an interesting fashion statement that during the troubles the Presidents of the UEA Students' Union from 1969 to 1972 all sported beards, and the last two very long hair and no tie for their official portraits. Long hair became the norm for Presidents until 1976.[133] In the same year there were the first significant British university troubles, with the revolt at the London School of Economics against the appointment of Dr Walter Adams as Principal on the grounds of his supposedly inadequate opposition to apartheid in Rhodesia.[134] Internationally matters escalated in 1968 as troubles at Leuven University led to the fall of the Belgian government. The *événements* in Paris in 1968 led to the closure of the Sorbonne and further disruption flamed at Columbia, Stanford, Rome and Prague as part of the "Prague Spring". Depths of nastiness were plumbed in the disruption of universities in China in the Cultural Revolution of these years and in the shooting of students at Kent State in the USA in May 1970.

Nothing in Norwich was ever of this degree of seriousness, but nonetheless the students had some objectively rational grounds for discontent. First, the promised increase of the student grant of £40 had been halved in 1969.

Accordingly, the cost of living had increased by 29 per cent since 1962 but the grant by only 12.5 per cent. Secondly, students no longer felt that their experience of a low and declining standard of living would be compensated by lucrative and fulfilling careers later on. It was clear by 1970 that there were more graduates than jobs and that degrees were no longer passports to attractive careers. This was especially so for arts graduates but also for biologists, in whom UEA had invested heavily.[135] The local press suggested, "it would be fatally easy to say that we have overdone it" and urged graduates to turn to skilled trades since the future would lie with "the graduate working with his hands".[136] In any case national unemployment levels had risen sharply in this period from 2.5 per cent in 1968 to 4 per cent by 1972. Graduates could easily feel that they had been betrayed by an expansion which had raised expectations that could not be met. If they had wanted to be craftsmen they would have left school at sixteen, not five impoverished and delayed years later. Some sense of this betrayal was conveyed in a letter written by a teacher visiting some ex-pupils who wrote to her friend the Dean of Students about the disappointment she found,

> They have, they say, been given to believe that all they had to do was to be good, take O levels and A levels to go to University . . . and that with a vast amount of specialised knowledge accumulated . . . they would have the choice of several very good jobs. Now they say Society has let them down – they are not enjoying University and they are terrified of what awaits them.[137]

It is one of the saddest document in the University Archives.

The strains of the rapid expansion, from 113 to 2603 in the sixties, were also evident by the end of the decade in a perceived fall in academic standards. The 1970 external examiners' reports were consistently the worst in the University's history. Even in the much vaunted biology the standard was "low in comparison with other universities". The examiner strongly advised against further expansion, unless a higher calibre of student could be admitted. In chemistry there was "low overall performance" which was "rather disappointing". The external examiner was so concerned about the "woefully weak tail" that he interviewed them all and found them not only ignorant of the subject but "having no interest at all in Chemistry". In physics "the decline in overall performance has not been arrested", and in mathematics the "overall performance was disappointing", with half the candidates obtaining only third class degrees or worse. In the arts, history contained a "stodgy and uninspiring lump" of students, and those in Russian were "most unsatisfactory" and "not fit to regard themselves graduates in Russian". The headlong twenty-three fold expansion of the sixties had clearly entailed some barrel-scraping of students not entirely fit for their studies. Under-performing students like this, bored with their work, compounded the low morale that underlay unrest.[138]

There were also things wrong with the University itself. The environment was at its absolutely least attractive. The "community" intimacies of the Village had been left behind. The concrete of the Lasdun buildings was as yet unsoftened by the creation of a total ambience. Demonstrations were enacted in a scenery of concrete blocks and still developing building sites. Keva Coombes, the President of the Union, told a visiting reporter, "the architecture has a subtle effect on people – it destroys their sense of community. Relations between staff and students are also cool".[139] Spatial dispositions were also unfortunate at that time. The Students' Union was still in the Village and ten minutes walk away from the Plain; "most people don't bother to come over during the day", said Coombes. The administration was separate from both, being still in Earlham Hall; "the Vice-Chancellor for instance is never seen about the campus", claimed Coombes exaggeratedly. These dislocations were an inevitable consequence of that stage of the University's development. But it was unfortunate that it coincided with the period of unrest.

There were also undoubtedly defects in the organisational set up at that time. The Nineteen and their more moderate supporters were quite wrong to insult the Dean of Students but they were right in their analysis that welfare and discipline should be separated, as they have been since. To have the same individual acting as the senior responsible person for welfare and also as the gatherer of information to prosecute wrongdoers (often the same kind of information relevant to welfare problems), also acting as the chairman (judge) of disciplinary proceedings, involved too many subtle conflicts of interest and grounds for suspicion. It was extraordinary that the University went through these years without a separate Disciplinary Officer as recommended by the Frostick Reports.

It was also a weakness that the students had no voting rights on Senate and Council. The national age of voting had been reduced from twenty-one to eighteen in 1969. Moreover students had won generous democratic concessions in 1970 in being able to vote in local political elections both at home and in Norwich and in the General Election either at home or in Norwich.[140] They were very conscious of these democratic rights, which were superior to those of Cambridge students. It heightened their feeling of exclusion from a say in the running of their own university. They had made progress. Students were admitted to School Boards in 1968-69 and then acquired voting rights there in the 1970-71 session. Other devices, such as joint staff-student committees in Schools, and student representatives electing convenors to call student meetings to discuss grievances, followed in 1969-70. Yet voting rights in Senate and Council eluded them.

The Vice-Chancellor was cautious over this because he had come to the view, as early as July 1968, that increased participation in the government of the University by students would merely lead to more and more demands until the students gained "student control of the universities", which he had to resist.[141] This was a crux of the matter. The Vice-Chancellor had changed his mind. He used not to think that disturbance was part of some wider plan of disruption by "organised subversive elements", but he came to think "I have been too innocent". The disturbance would not go away since the subversives "are out to break it" (the system of free universities). He was also particularly dismayed by some of his junior staff, "fanning the flames of their revolutionary anarchism". This was the cruel enigma. Would unrest be satisfied with reasonable reform or did there lie behind it a genuine revolutionary movement intent on nothing less than total control?

The unrest was spearheaded by a range of Left Wing Socialist groups. The most important were the International Socialists (the later Socialist Workers Party), who formed a branch in Norwich in 1969.[142] They did not normally meet at the University but in private homes and then at the Red Lion Pub in Bishopsgate. Their members were few, about eight faculty, less than ten students and about twenty townspeople. Their aims for society at large were certainly revolutionary, to replace the capitalist system by opposition to "all ruling class policies and organisations" and their replacement with "workers control over production and a Workers State".[143] But their aim within the University was not actually revolutionary but reformist. There was no belief that taking over the University would lead to a wider revolution; the aim was to democratise the University.

The social class of International Socialist faculty was rather comfortable middle class. The parental background of the seven International Socialist members of the nineteen was – "wealthy", "American money", "modest", publican, pharmacist, commercial traveller, a clergyman. At the University the IS was focused on faculty and rather middle class but they also aimed to recruit non-university working class supporters in Norwich. They were well organised with subscriptions, meetings and branches and also acted through the ASTMS trade union.

The other major body was the Spartacus League, part of the International Marxists Group.[144] This was the British Section of the Fourth International founded by Trotsky. The Spartacists appealed to committed Marxist intellectuals among students rather than faculty. Also, in contrast to the IS, most students in the Spartacus League, were working class. They did not seek student control over the University but they did want control of the disciplinary system and more say in course content. They wanted a socialist government which would reform the universities, but did not envisage UEA as a socialist university in a non-socialist country, nor did they believe that some kind of revolution at UEA would contribute to a national revolution. It is plain that both the IS and the Spartacus League were actually more modest in their aims and realistic about the limits of their power than it seemed at the time.

There were various other much less influential Left groups. The Revolutionary Students Socialist Federation was formed nationally in November 1968 and embarrassed the University by unsuccessfully trying to politicise local schoolchildren with pamphlets. They were Maoists and Trotskyists but had only a brief existence and fell apart in 1970 as the IS and SL became more significant. The East Anglian Libertarian Group were anarchists who may have been an element in the Roy Jenkins trouble but were otherwise insignificant. Both the IS and SL tended to despise anarchists. The Labour Party and the Communist Party were largely inactive among students, the latter not even in existence at UEA until 1971. The Socialist Labour League – strong on discipline and negligible in ideology – had virtually no appeal to students. Overarching all these was the Socialist Society, SOC SOC, which was not a political party but the forum for various Left students with its own publication *Can Opener*. SOC SOC was part of the Students' Union (as IS and SL were not) and so it was necessary that all Left sympathisers were part of it in order to qualify for Student Union money for organisational costs. There were about fifty members of SOC SOC and probably 250 students sufficiently sympathetic to the views of the far Left. This was the set-up of Left protest, dominated by the International Society and the Spartacus League, to a great extent due to the high abilities, and deep personal commitment of the organisers of both groups at this time.

A plethora of reasons of a broad nature were put forward to account for unrest. For the Spartacists it was a sense of betrayal. Universities justified themselves in terms of the disinterested pursuit of intellectual truth, cultural achievement and liberal values, and attracted students on those terms. Yet, when they arrived, they were disillusioned to find that their education was really intended to serve "the changing manpower needs of the capitalist world market".[145] Students who believed that they were joining a free community of scholars soon also found that it was controlled by a Council of large landowners, bankers, businessmen and accountants, some with some rather right-wing and Southern African sympathies. It fuelled old-style Marxist feelings of class conflict in some students. Another contrasting analysis saw unrest as the result of too much freedom.[146] Activists were characterised as children of middle-class, professional, liberal-minded parents who were reacting to the abrupt liberation from the strict control of school. This view appealed to some notable UEA personalities. Douglas Baker, the Assistant

Dean of Students, attributed part of the unrest problem to boredom created by excessive benevolence and liberalism and "the absence of a need for personal struggle".[147] A.E. Dyson, a UEA English lecturer who achieved national fame as the editor of *The Black Papers*, took a similar partly spiritual view that student unrest arose from "shapeless and irrational freedoms" creating "neurosis and unhappiness" for lack (in his view) of sufficient structure and discipline.[148] Roy Campbell also saw the problem that "so many of the protestors come from middle class homes where they have been pampered".[149] He too thought that this was exacerbated by the reduction in the age of majority. Accordingly the students both rejected the constraints of being *in statu pupillari* but at the same time wanted all the welfare privileges of being looked after. The Scottish tradition, which Campbell came from, did *not* lay stress on welfare as did the Oxbridge one that UEA inherited through Frank Thistlethwaite and Marcus Dick. Some people saw insufficient welfare as a problem, the lack of contact of staff and students out of working hours and the absence of students at weekends. The Dean of Students found the lack of staff-student mixing a major fault and rather unrealistically wanted more families of staff living in residences and faculty paying as much attention to joining in student functions as marking essays.[150] Psychologists began to take an interest in UEA and pinpointed the separate first year residences at Fifers Lane as the root of the problem. There the isolation of freshmen prevented their acculturation to the norms of their seniors.[151] Paradoxically the revolutionaries saw the dispersal of residences by years as a factor weakening their impact.

The conflicts were also underlain by a fundamental difference of view about the whole status of the student. As well as the change of student status from disenfranchised minor to a major with full national voting rights, they also began to think of themselves as consumers. In his influential Granada Lecture of 1969 Jack Straw emphasised the role of students as "consumers of education", and Roger Niven, one of the ablest Presidents of the UEA Students' Union in these years, took up this terminology. It was quite understandable that many members of Council, professors, businessmen and former military officers should think of students as pupils, employees and subordinates to be controlled and disciplined on the analogy of the school, firm or regiment. It would have required an effort of imagination for many in authority to regard themselves not as the bosses but rather the employees of the students who were cash-paying consumer customers, some of whom were dissatisfied with the service. The Barclays incident most clearly focused this issue. The "consumer" relationship of the student to the University is more evident in the late 1990s than it was in the late 1960s but that is when it began and for some there could be no meeting of minds over it.

An interesting insight into the perceptions of the Vice-Chancellor about the causes of unrest is given in a paper he gave to American University Presidents in 1969.[152] He identified the rapid growth of the universities and their raw newness, the fact that many students inevitably did not get to the universities of their first choice, the large working class element who were first generation students and who often brought trade union attitudes with them. He also thought that there was a lack of parental authority and too much permissiveness in the home that carried over to university, whose large scale, after school, left students feeling confused. He thought that many students lacked career motivation and merely drifted into university, and he understood the Left suspicions that their education was merely training them as "industrial fodder" or was too theoretical and arid to be "relevant". He had no illusions about the faculty; pressurised to publish, many took to careerism rather than a dedication to students and the institution, "committeeing but not committed" as he put it. There is no doubt that the Vice-Chancellor had given a good deal of perceptive thought to these matters and could be much more candid in a private meeting abroad than he could be publicly in Norwich.

How large was the disaffected student body? It certainly increased from the neglible to the substantial within a short time.

Date	Event	Number involved	Total UEA students
1968	Insult to Princess Margaret	5-7	1724
1968	Alternative seminar at visit of the Queen	200-300	1724
1968	Roy Jenkins speech	200	2123
1970	Barclay refusals	322 pay into Trust fund 300 hold bills, refuse pay	2603
1971	March sit-in	300 start-500 peak	2603
	Vote to continue sit-in	648	2603
1971	Vote for resignation of DOS	500-600	2603
1971	Petition against punishment of preliminary examination disrupters	905	2603

It is always said that unrest is the work of a small minority and not typical of the mass of students. Adherent members of the various Socialist groups referred to earlier were very few but by 1971 it is evident that a quarter and eventually a third of the student body were making positive gestures of hostility to and dissent from University policies. At this level unrest could not be dismissed as an untypical minority concern.

As well as students, there was also a group of junior staff whom the Vice-Chancellor regarded as "fanning the flames". This was true, though with small numbers. There was clearly a small group of radical protestors undeniably of the Left. Yet it would be wrong to think of even the hard core as disloyal drop outs. On the contrary, many were people of calibre, and people from whose aptitudes for administration in quieter times the University was later to benefit. Many were from one School, Economic and Social Studies. So the cliché of the radical sociologist protesting lecturer had some truth in UEA's case. Here were people whose studies and cast of mind was speculative, given to questioning society and politics, eager for change and with little stake in the status quo. It lent weight to those who regretted that there was no ballast of engineering, law and medical students at UEA – hard, fact-based disciplines of a vocational nature leading directly to serious lucrative careers.

Yet in spite of what trouble we had, it is remarkable that there was not more and that UEA was seen as a relatively pacific university. For example, considering adverse references to UEA and other sixties universities in national studies of university unrest, Norwich came off very lightly.

Adverse References

Source	UEA	Sussex	Lancaster	Essex	York	Kent	Warwick
Crouch 1970[153]	nil	2	nil	13	3	nil	2
Rooke 1971[154]	6	23	7	29	11	8	17
Gould 1977 [155]	nil	21	46	44	9	nil	16
Total	6	46	53	86	23	8	35

Essex was by far the most disruptive, and UEA always feared that because of Essex's vaguely "East Anglian" location something of its then riotous reputation would, by a confusion in the public mind, rub off on Norwich. UEA played no part in the investigations of the Parliamentary Select Committee on Student Relations. It was not visited (as Essex was, where the Committee was roughed up), no witnesses were called from UEA, and it was not even referred to. UEA was consistently regarded as no great cause for concern or comment – which would have surprised some Norfolk residents who thought of it as a hotbed of chaos. In spite of some "revolutionary" aims, violence played no part in the disturbances at UEA. Compared with the national and international scene UEA's record was a mild one. The Librarian visiting Heidelberg University found the place in turmoil, with strikes, fighting in the streets and three law suits pending. He comforted Thistlethwaite, "So our problems seem small in comparison".[156] It would also be misleading to give the impression that UEA was paralysed during the troubles or even during sit-ins. A student explained,

> classes continued surprisingly undisturbed in relocated sites outside the Arts Building. Serious students had no real difficulty in reaching their teachers for lessons or discussion. The science buildings have never been influenced anyway and the library remains the usual hive of constructive activity.[157]

In my own diaries of these days there is no reference to the sit-ins but to classes and meetings which were clearly attended by students; both worlds coexisted. In any case, we should remember that in events like this there is always a large mass whose motives range from the apathetic to the mildly curious. A semi-detached participant recalled,

> I remember the sit-in of 1971 although I can't remember why it happened. We attended student union meetings where people shouted and jumped up on tables . . . as in most revolutionary movements, the masses do not really know what is going on and if they follow it is through curiosity or chance rather than conviction.[158]

It is then relevant to ask not only why there was any trouble at UEA but why there was not a good deal more. Revolutionaries were interested in this angle in assessing their own limited success.[159] First, it could be argued that the dispersal of students into differently located residences isolated the different years from each other and "consequently there was no generalisation of personal experience". Secondly, UEA lacked large numbers of postgraduates who in other universities provided leadership in student movements. In 1969-70 there were 248 postgraduates out of 2358 students. Thirdly, some students felt that the system of seminars, and especially continuous assessment grades, acted as a form of control with many students unwilling to acquire reputations as troublemakers with non-radical teachers. Fourthly, the social complexion of students, "Home Counties, middle class and anti-militant", worked against revolutionary fervour.[160] The proportion of students from fee-paying schools and of upper middle-class backgrounds in the early intakes must be remembered. Fifthly, the generally conservative cast of mind of this very traditional rural area, the prosperity of Norwich and relative lack of disaffected unemployed youth removed much non-university local support for a revolutionary movement. Sixthly, the Council led by Bacon kept steady and did not overreact. Indeed Timothy Colman actually kept a note in the papers he took to Council, reminding himself not to overreact. The aristocratic elements on the Council were personally very tolerant of student aberrations. This would have surprised many on the far Left who regarded the aristocrats as their natural class enemies who would be troubled by such hostile disturbance. Nothing could be further from the truth. Sir Edmund Bacon was never shocked by student nonsense. He and his kind were used to getting into scrapes at their public schools and varsities and, to be frank, did not take academic work too seriously anyway. This paradoxically gave Bacon and hence the Council an "unrattled" strength.[161] They needed it in the face of various hysterical letters sent to the Vice-Chancellor in 1971, one urging him to hand over the University to the Head Porter, another to turn back to God or face national disaster!

Finally, and very importantly, UEA was already a very liberal university with a good deal of student representation on committees. Of twenty-three types of committee surveyed by the CVCP in 1971 UEA had student representatives on eighteen of them.[162] This compares with nineteen for Leeds, seventeen at Essex, sixteen at Durham and Kent, fifteen at Lancaster, thirteen at Bristol, ten at Liverpool and a surprising seven at Sussex, though Sussex allowed a large student representation on Senate. UEA responded also quite quickly to legitimate grievances as in the disciplinary reforms of 1968, the appointment of a full-time Dean of Students, the change in policy over Barclays, the Frostick Report and its implementation. UEA's genuinely democratic policy, even before students gained voting rights on Senate and Council, mitigated what would otherwise have been a legitimate source of grievance.

At one level the disturbances, national and local, had remarkably little effect. The universities did not spearhead a Marxist revolution; on the contrary, since 1970 Britain has experienced twenty-three years [to 2001] of Conservative governments for which, presumably, a large proportion of this "revolutionary" generation of students voted. Nor did it lead to the collapse of the universities under student control. Yet on the adverse side the disturbances harmed the universities and UEA in particular. They ended the honeymoon of the new universities and turned public opinion against the universities, students and faculty. It created a climate of opinion in which cuts of increasing severity could be made in government spending on higher education. The soaring costs of such expenditure were already causing concern before 1968 as current expenditure on the universities rose from 0.3 per cent of the GNP in 1961/2 to 0.49 per cent by 1966/7, when it stood at £198 million excluding maintenance grants. The unrest made it politically acceptable to allow the real value of the student grant to decline from an index number of 100 in 1962/3 to 82 by 1973/4.[163] The impact on UEA was immediate. Students applying in 1970 to go to university in 1971 fell nationally by 10 per cent and at UEA by 15.9 per cent.[164] Employment prospects collapsed. UEA students going into direct employment fell from 39 per cent in arts and 31 per cent in sciences in 1967 down to 17 per cent in arts in 1971 and 18 per cent in sciences in 1971. The University also lost some money as Yarmouth stopped its annual £4000 grant to the University.[165] Conversely Dr Lincoln Ralphs notified Bacon that the County Council would withdraw the grant of any student refusing to obey the rules of the University, but no case arose.[166] The troubles also left the Vice-Chancellor temporarily receptive to a possible change of career. When Noel Annan invited him to apply for the directorship of the British Museum in 1972, he admitted that "after twelve years starting this place I'm ripe for a change".[167] But he changed his mind the next year and remained at the helm throughout the seventies.

Yet, in spite of these adverse effects, paradoxically the troubles left some lasting benefits to UEA. They prompted thinking about the need to separate discipline and welfare and led to the creation of a properly organised structure of disciplinary committees without the inappropriate involvement of the Vice-Chancellor or Dean of Students. They also led to the allowing of student voting rights on University bodies and eventually on Senate and Council. The troubles over preliminary examinations were even salutary, not only in leading to their abolition but in prompting some more basic thinking about the purpose of examinations in a system already heavily monitored with coursework assessment. The Dean of Students' Office became more formalised with a virtually full-time Dean of Students and a new psychiatric service. Finally, the troubles established a tradition of manageable "political theatre" whereby protest – so long as no violence against the person was involved – was permitted and not punished. Personal violence, by contrast, was severely dealt with. It is only since 1987 that there have been any regulations against occupying buildings for example. Most important of all, these years saw an important shift from regarding students as minors in *statu pupillari* to enfranchised majors, consumers and cash-paying customers who have their rights and will have their say.

7

Administration and Finance

> Let us regard the University as a medium sized fast developing
> business concern with an annual turnover of £1 million a year.[1]
>
> Frank Thistlethwaite, October 1968

While the chief purposes of the University were scholarly research, teaching
and the care of students, behind the scenes it was held together by an efficient
administrative structure and nourished by flows of cash. For most of the
Thistlethwaite years this was managed by George Chadwick, the Registrar.
Frank Thistlethwaite made the analogy of a civil service department in which
the Vice-Chancellor was the Minister and the Registrar, the Permanent
Secretary responsible for academic, financial and buildings affairs. Harold
Mackintosh left the choice of Registrar largely to the Vice-Chancellor: "Well
Frank, you're the man who's going to have to work with him, it's up to you".[2]
George Chadwick had been the Deputy Registrar of King's College,
Newcastle since 1957. He had been educated at Liverpool University gaining
his B.Sc. in 1939 and subsequently served as a commissioned officer with the
Royal Corps of Signals and the Allied Control Commission in Austria. After
the war he became a schoolmaster at Liverpool College before entering
university administration.[3] Barry Stevenson was the next appointment as
Finance Officer, then Chadwick in turn appointed S.W.C. "Bill" Holland
CBE, a retired colonial administrator as his deputy. They were joined by Cory
Dixon, from Liverpool University, recommended by the UGC as Estates
Officer, but soon to be succeeded by Gordon Marshall in circumstances we
have already seen.

However efficient the main chain of administration, the Vice-Chancellor
was uneasy that there was a danger that everything could be filtered to him
only through the Registrar and he was concerned not to become too remote.
Accordingly he developed his own Vice-Chancellor's Office on the analogy of
a Minister's private office. This was to be his eyes and ears, his own personal
staff. The key figure throughout Frank Thistlethwaite's years – and those of
the two succeeding Vice-Chancellors – was Patricia Whitt, who joined UEA
in November 1962 from the BBC. Her work as secretary to the Vice-
Chancellor grew to that of a Personal Assistant, her official title from 1967,

recognising the realities of her position. Frank Thistlethwaite recalled that "she established a style in the dealings of my office, formal but accessible and friendly towards the outside world, this also permeated at many levels within the University contributing much to the sense of community which characterised the place".[4] Her outstanding contribution was rewarded with an MBE on her retirement in 1990. Others in the Vice-Chancellor's Office, the VCO, were Frank Albrighton, the Information Officer and a succession of able Administrative Assistants, John Wood, Alan Jones and Colin Latimer.

The University started off with the basic structure laid down by the Charter. The Council was a mixture of senior academics and distinguished laymen from the region; landowners, lawyers, businessmen and accountants, under the chairmanship of Sir Edmund Bacon. This brought an essential lay expertise to the running of the University, especially in financial matters, as was broadly common to all chartered universities. The Senate on the other hand is the academic body deciding academic policy. In the very early days there was very little paper work and few committee meetings, which gave surprising power to the Vice-Chancellor. Frank Thistlethwaite recalled, nostalgically, "one day I simply said to our little Senate : 'Let there be a Dean of Students and let Marcus Dick be he' and that was that".[5] He also decided on sixty-five as the retirement age without discussion. It was not to last and by the end of the decade there were twenty-four senate committees ranging from the Library to Higher Degrees, from American Exchange to the various Disciplinary Committees. There were also ten joint committees of Senate and Council dealing often with student matters, welfare, residences, sports, health, appointments and the like. Harold Perkin identified UEA as a new university which (like Essex and Warwick) had opted for a select Senate, about the same size as Council, to which not even all professors could expect to be elected. Such universities accordingly also had Assemblies for wider representation.[6] At UEA's Assembly all members of faculty (teaching staff), and other academic related staff were entitled to attend, to discuss matters being considered by the Senate and Council. Most important, however, to most people were the School Boards, emphasising the strength of the Board as the basic academic unit.

Boards had their different styles. Professor Norman Sheppard recalled being asked:

Why is it that the School of Chemical Sciences appears to operate with almost military efficiency whereas the School of Biological Sciences seems to lurch from crisis to crisis?" The differences showed in the conduct of the School Board meetings. The first Chemical Sciences Board meeting was dealt with so efficiently by Alan Katritzky – most of the topics having been previously aired or decided upon within the School – that it lasted for less than half an hour. I was in fact very annoyed because it seemed to me that the lack of discussion was discourteous to the senior Registry representative who was the Secretary to the Board. I soon found out however that this was much preferred to the other extreme at Biological Sciences (referred to in the Registry, I was told, as "The Commune") where the afternoon Board meeting commonly only completed discussion of half the agenda by 6 p.m.[7]

Two Deans of Biology complained to the Vice-Chancellor about the extent to which administration and committees diverted energies and time from teaching and research. Thomas Bennet Clark told the Vice-Chancellor, "I used to think that the University of London was a bit over-burdened by attendance at committees but here we seem to be nearly three times as bad",[8] while Jack Kitching (an FRS like Bennet Clark and like him deeply devoted to research) not only resented the diversion of time from scholarship to politics and even more the fact that this "brings out the worst in human nature".[9] EUR in the late 1960s was also a School given to long meetings and personally acrimonious debate. This was not just a matter of style, loss of control or personal relations. Behind it lay a profound problem of which the Vice-Chancellor was well aware, namely, how to reconcile the efficiency of "line management" authority with the collegiality of the "community of scholars" demanding a high degree of democratic representation and lengthy debate. In most Schools there were young radicals who declined to accept the professoriate as Germanic/Scottish type "bosses". They also saw not only the Boards but also the Assembly as a battle ground. Some not only wanted to replace the Vice-Chancellor as Chairman of the Assembly with an Assembly-elected person but also wanted Assembly to have the right to overrule Senate decisions. Both would have been contrary to the statutes and did not come about. It is worth noting that some of these "radicals" were not irresponsible troublemakers but serious politicians in local government. Some eventually moving from academic life at UEA to be elected to Parliament. So there were tensions of democracy and control and at the end of the decade it was decided to review the structure of administration and representation.

This took the form of the Frame of Government Committee (FOG) and, running parallel to it, in January to July 1969, a survey by an outside management consultant, Industrial Administration Ltd. The concerns of FOG resolved into four issues; the role of professors; the role of Assembly; whether there should be overarching bodies for the Arts and Sciences above the Boards; and, finally, the rights of students to representation in university government.

In the sixties some professors took a high, even extravagant, view of their position. This was actually quite contrary to the Vice-Chancellor's conception of their role. Frank Thistlethwaite has since, though not at the time, explained that he wanted to "relax the hold of the professoriate which the Academic Planning Board thought one of the less desirable features of the redbrick model" and that he was "positively hostile to an ex-officio, hierarchical professoriate".[10] He also firmly believed that Schools should elect their own Deans and that it was not necessary for a Dean to be a professor. John Tarrant in 1974 was the first non-professorial Dean. That he is, to date, the only one of the UEA faculty himself to have become a Vice-Chancellor suggests the rightness of this policy. On the contrary, some science professors (notably Katritzky and Glauert) felt that they needed to be given a special status which the UEA constitution and the Vice-Chancellor's own attitudes did not give them. In particular they felt that it was important that Deans should be appointed from professors by Council and not from the whole body of faculty by the Board of the respective School, "an unfortunate method".[11] Formally Deans are appointed by Council on the recommendation of the Senate on the recommendation of the School Board, but not necessarily from professors. Their argument was that in the sciences the large numbers of technical staff, expensive equipment and research projects required a high level of consistent leadership. They were fearful that there was a growing tendency for junior faculty to regard the School Board as "the ultimate authority for running a School". If so, their fears were justified; less so was the launch into autocratic arrogance, "such a system based on voting in which the views of the least and the most experienced count the same is completely unacceptable to us".

Behind this view and Thistlethwaite's positive hostility to it lay an old academic debate which had long preceded UEA. There were two traditions of university governance in Britain. That of Oxford and Cambridge had rested on the autonomy of the colleges and college fellows. In the nineteenth century they had been suspicious of the rise of their respective universities as central authorities and of the professoriate as university officials. Their suspicions were that increased university power would divert funds from the colleges and destroy their independence. The professors would also try to assert authority over fellows in departments, breaking down the college community of scholars in which fellows and professors were equal. A strong autocratic professoriate was also associated with the reception of Germanic ideas of university government. This in turn was linked with an emphasis on the importance of research, especially in the sciences and especially chemistry (Katritzky's subject) in which the German universities excelled. This tradition was replicated in England in the civic redbrick, in contradistinction to the ancient universities. Thus the Germanic, redbrick (and Scottish) tradition of a strong autocratic professoriate, with rigid hierarchies associated with the management of central university science laboratories devoted to research, clashed with the Oxbridge tradition. The latter emphasised college autonomy, equality between fellows living in a fairly democratic community of scholars, self-governing by election and suspicious of professorial authority from outside. The Vice-Chancellor was essentially a Cambridge college fellow and his instincts inclined to that tradition. His view of UEA governance was one "grounded on an assumption of sodality, of community. It was this which I wished to infuse into the government of UEA".[12] The Glauert-Katritzky memorandum raised all these deep issues again, though they probably did not appreciate how temperamentally opposed Frank Thistlethwaite was to their position. Running a large chemistry laboratory may require a considerable autocracy. Sir Christopher Ingold, who approved their memorandum, thought so. But the Vice-Chancellor was unwilling to run the whole university on that basis.

The issues of the Glauert-Katritzky memorandum were taken up by FOG.[13] Some professors made similar demands – a guaranteed minimum of professors on Senate, and all professors to be sent Senate papers whether Senators or not. They demanded a definition of the role of the professor to prevent Deans and Boards eroding what they saw as their leadership functions. The matter blew up into a vigorous debate over the Winter and Spring of 1970-71. It was argued, against the professors' submission, that professors had no formal distinction or definition in Charter, Statutes or Terms of Appointment and that there was no difference between them and other faculty in these terms.[14] Not all professors were heads of sectors nor did sector heads need to be professors. Martin Hollis put it well, that professors need have no special role in the managerial structure. Junior lecturers accepted administrative posts without needing, and probably for the very lack of, a formal chain of command, "in general the professor already holds the high cards and I can see no reason whatever to make them trumps!".[15] This exactly caught the mood of Senate which discussed the matter in February and March 1970. They did not accept that professors should have special responsibilities or powers or role. They did not need to be sector heads nor did sector heads need to be professors. This was very much in line with what McFarlane, Groves and Hollis (all arts men) had been arguing.

Alan Katritzky mounted a counter-attack trying to rally the science professors to demand "a reasonable degree of managerial authority and freedom from an excessive degree of administrative constraint".[16] A senior professor of Biology put in a bit of special pleading, claiming that he was in an "utterly unsatisfactory" situation that he had no part in planning the teaching of the biology courses which had been taken over by a Teaching Committee.[17] It is remarkable that this distinguished scientist, who was an FRS and OBE, did not feel he could use his personal authority to influence these matters. The scientists were getting very exercised over this and it was further stirred when the chemist David King proposed that professors could be removed from sector headship by a vote of the Board.[18] This was exactly the nightmare that Katritzky wanted to avoid. It is pleasingly ironic that when King shortly afterwards left UEA to take up the prestigious chair at Liverpool, he ran his department on traditionally redbrick – and Katritzky-influenced – authoritarian lines.

FOG and the Senate ignored the scientists counter-attack and continued to deny any special definition or role to professors. Lincoln Ralphs, observing this from outside, agreed with Senate. His own duties as Chief Education Officer of Norfolk had never been defined; the post was what he made it. He added wisely that "the more precisely a post is defined and its functions set out the less effective it becomes". Thistlethwaite replied in agreement.[19]

Another issue which taxed FOG, with equal futility, was the creation of Boards of Faculties. The idea was that since there were ten Boards by 1969, and inevitably going to be more, then rather than have each of these individually feeding into Senate it would be neater to have Boards of Faculties between them and the Senate. An Arts Board would cover EAS, EUR and FAM, one for Social Sciences would cover SOC, and DEV, one for Sciences BIO, CHE, ENV, MAP.[20] Such Boards would have appointed examiners and created regulations for courses and degrees. They would have created super-Dean posts for a few academics attracted to the massive administrative and committee work it would have entailed.

Although such a scheme had an aesthetic symmetry, it would have created an extra layer of administration, bureaucracy and paperwork. The Academic Planning Board had rejected the idea of an intermediate layer for this reason. The Registrar, however, continued working on plans and indeed produced six versions at different times. By June 1971 FOG decided to recommend to Senate the creation of Committees for Arts and Sciences to coordinate the School Boards under them.[21] The reasons advanced were that by 1976-77 there would be six Arts and Social Science Schools and seven Science Schools. More and bigger Schools would generate more work for Senate and there would "be a serious lack of coordination". What was needed was for Schools to "march in step and not get out of line" (why?).[22] It was a mixture of tidy-mindedness and optimistic vagueness but lacking a convincing argument. It did not convince Senate, which took the view that "since the present system worked well it was unnecessary to change it".[23] The matter was shunted drearily between Senate, the Development Committee and the Registrar into 1972, when Senate rejected it yet again in May. By then FOG had ceased to be and the Boards of Faculties never came into being.

A third area of concern was that of Assembly. A "Committee of Two" (Professor J. W. McFarlane and Dr D.A. King) had been set up by Senate to consider the role of Assembly.[24] They held a conservative view that Assembly should include faculty and administrators of administrative assistant rank and above, and that it should discuss matters of broad academic interest before they passed to Senate and Council. Some, however, wanted to go further. Professor Norman Sheppard proposed that Assembly should have the right to make Council and Senate "think again" about their decisions, as Congregation at Oxford and Regent House at Cambridge did.[25] This found support from other respected and conservative figures.[26] There was even a suggestion that Assembly should appoint the lay members of Council![27] Some of the more extreme views began to cause concern outside the University. Timothy Colman, the Chairman of the Finance Committee, told the Vice-Chancellor that a proposal that all financial matters should pass through Assembly before coming to Council "fills me with alarm".[28] The Vice-Chancellor took some advice on Norman Sheppard's point from Sir Frank Lee, who was on a committee looking at the role of Regent House, Cambridge. Lee told Thistlethwaite that giving more power to a body like Regent House – or the UEA Assembly – was "inimical to efficient administration" and that it was preferable to strengthen Council.[29]

In practice there was little to worry about – or hope for. Assembly was a fairly moribund body, rarely reaching attendances of a quarter of its members. In any case 52.4 per cent of those were content that "the powers of Assembly should remain as they are at present" and the Chairman agreed that "the majority of members ... do not accept the case for a dramatic shift in power".[30] The Committee of Two and FOG had caught the mood in leaving Assembly as it was, not giving it powers over Senate and Council.

The fourth major area considered by FOG was that of student representation in university government. The existing situation was that almost all of forty English universities and component colleges of the University of London allowed students to attend Council in some way, the most restrictive being York, where they were "occasionally invited". At only eleven were students full members with voting rights. UEA allowing four students on Council was generous, exceeded only by Aston (eight) and LSE (six), and equalled by only four others. As regards Senate, only Westfield allowed students voting rights, though ten universities allowed more students to attend than UEA did and thirteen fewer. So UEA's position as regards students attending Council and Senate was on the generous side of the normal.[31]

The Students' Council at UEA asked for four full student representatives on Senate and Council, two on the Appointments Board and Library Committees, and one on that arranging public lectures.[32] Roger Niven, the President, followed this up with a memorandum to FOG asking for four full voting members, on the grounds that "students as consumers wish to comment upon the goods they are being presented with ... we are not asking that we should control the University but they [the students] are one of the main sectors of the University community".[33] The Joint Committee of Senate and the Students' Council backed this, as did the AUT.[34] FOG accordingly had no difficulty in accepting this proposal, but "it is clear at this stage the student representation could not be formal members of the Senate and Council since full membership cannot be achieved without changes to the Statutes". In the interim, however, they thought it would be valuable for students to gain experience by participating for an experimental period and "the student representatives should be treated as far as practicable as full members".[35]

Later in the year, while the experiment was continuing, the President of the Students' Union was invited to extend his activities by attending meetings of the Finance, General Purposes and Planning Committees.[36] In 1970 School Boards were asked to report on student representation on their own Boards. "All Boards had expressed satisfaction with the arrangements for student participation at Board Meetings",[37] and most suggested that students should have full membership to vote and initiate motions.

FOG reported to Senate that arrangements for students on Senate and Council should continue for the academic year 1970-71 and that students be allowed full voting rights on Boards from Autumn 1970.[38] Student representatives should also be appointed to the General Purposes Committee, as well as the President attending Development, Finance and Planning Committees. Matters rolled on to their inevitable conclusion. The Deputy Registrar reminded FOG that the Privy Council was receiving several applications from universities to change their charters and statutes to admit students onto governing bodies.[39] The Privy Council had to be satisfied that student members would be genuinely elected representatives of the student body and would not participate in "reserved [confidential] business." FOG then immediately invited Senate and Council to apply to have the Charter and Statutes amended to admit four students each as fully voting members of Senate and Council. This was done in 1972 and FOG was at long last dissolved.

FOG was both more and less important than it seemed. It was concerned with three issues for which there was little support and which were of minor significance – more power to professors, Academic Boards, a greater role for Assembly – and one absolutely crucial one – political representation for students ultimately granted in 1976. Having the fourth discussed along with the other three avoided the University seeming to concede to student demands purely as a result of the troubles, as we have seen. It made sense to consider student rights in the context of a broader revision of university governance rather than as a one-off response to student pressure. Student representation was the only one of these four issues that came to anything and, as soon as it did, uncontentiously FOG ceased its work. Professor Katritzky, who was still sending in sheafs of documents about his rights and powers found that the game had finished.

Partly overlapping with FOG, the Council in December 1968 appointed Industrial Administration Ltd, a firm of management consultants, to conduct a survey of UEA's administrative structure. They began work in January 1969 and reported in June. In the early sixties the University was so small that everyone knew everybody else; in the first year of the University everybody was on Senate and on the School Boards. So there was initially no difficulty in communications or in integrating policy between the Senate, its Committees and Boards. The problem was that inevitably the increasing size of the University would change this.

The management consultants made a number of recommendations.[40] At the School level they suggested that Directors of Studies should be appointed to have "ultimate authority" for the interpretation and administration of policy in teaching and research. It was unclear what this was supposed to entail or what the relationship was to the Dean, especially since one part of the report referred to the Dean's role as "coordinator and guide" and to *their* "ultimate authority". They also dubiously suggested that dealing with Admissions could be dealt with by full-time administrators, which under-estimated the academic role in the selection and attraction of applicants.

The report also made several apposite suggestions. They appreciated that Boards were growing large and needed standing executive committees. Senate, they recommended, should be limited to fifty members who should individually sit for three rather than two years. They were rightly concerned that Senate was getting too involved in detailed administrative business. Far too many documents were also being passed to Senate and 60 per cent of the documentation related to only 10 per cent of the discussion. It wasted enormous amounts of administrative time in preparing these documents and reading them.

As regards other committees they thought that membership could be more strictly limited to eliminate purposeless participation ("committeeing without being committed" as the Vice-Chancellor put it) but that substitutes could be allowed. They recommended a Development and Planning Committee, reporting to Senate and Council, following the implementation of the building programme. They also sensibly suggested that the University needed a means of disseminating information. The *UEA Bulletin* used to do this in the early and mid sixties but by the end of the decade it had become merely a vehicle for articles and opinion rather than factual detail. Finally, in a section which attracted little attention, the consultants included a pregnant sentence on student representation. "The students would gain most from representation on select committees where they can influence the formulation of policy directly concerning themselves, and Senate and Council where they can register their votes on general university government". It was an early endorsement of students' claims for voting rights on Senate and Council.

The Frame of Government Committee received the report and made a favourably cool response.[41] They found the report "competent" and were pleased that "no major faults or deficiencies are revealed and in consequence the recommendations do not suggest that any radical changes should be made". They agreed that Senate could devolve work to other committees and concentrate itself on "policy and principle". They interpreted the consultants' call for Directors of Studies as meaning in effect sector heads for specific subjects within Schools, whether professors or not. Accordingly the Dean and sector heads could make up the steering or standing executive committees called for by the consultants. They were doubtful about the need for deputies or extending membership of Senate from two to three years.

Finally, FOG via the Senate reported tersely to Council on the reception of the consultants' report.[42] They had accepted the recommendation that Senate authority be delegated more, that the size of committees be restricted, and membership of Senate be limited to fifty, and that chairmen of committees be given executive authority especially for acting quickly in vacations. They refused the recommendation on the need to appoint deputies for people who could not attend committee meetings. Also they thought that the Appointments Board and Student Welfare Committees should still report to Senate and not to Council. They saw no need to amalgamate committees or change the term of office of Senate members or create Directors of Studies or Executive Committees. In practice sector heads running sectors and acting with their Deans had already come about *de facto* and needed no formal authorisation.

The Industrial Administration investigation was a useful exercise, even though nothing striking was revealed or needed to be done. Their most significant statement, on student voting rights in Senate and Council, fed into the favourable FOG view on this which resulted in change. The management consultants' private view, which they could hardly put in print, was that UEA was really run (and well run) by six people; all the rest, all the committees and administrative structures, probably did not matter very much one way or the other.[43] This view expressed off the record to one of the six was a realistic measure of the University, as probably of many large organisations.

Following FOG and its input from Industrial Administration Ltd, a joint

committee of Council and Senate was appointed in 1972 to review the constitution of the University. This presented its Final Report in November 1974.
The most important change was that of the Council which had hitherto
comprised seven members of local authorities of Norfolk and Suffolk, twelve
coopted lay members and thirteen members of Senate. The changes reduced
the Senate membership from thirteen to eight but added four members of
Assembly – reflecting the debate about the role of Assembly – two members
of non-teaching staff and four students. That there should be student representatives on the governing bodies of the University had been agreed by
Council in 1972 and was brought about from 1976-77. With this restructuring
the Council rebalanced its internal University members, including academic,
non-academic and student members, but with a lay majority being retained
as was required by the Privy Council.[44]

Senate too expanded its constituency. Each School's membership would
vary from two to four depending on the size of the School. But now a new
element was added with representation from the Library, research centres
and academic support services. The existing Assembly representation
continued and the five students who "attended" were increased to six with
full membership. The Boards remained the same and so most people would
have been unaware of the changes which were made by revisions of the
Charter and Statutes and came into effect on 20 December 1976. They
reflected "the increasing emphasis nationally on the involvement of all
employees in the running of the organisation for which they work".[45]

In the late 1970s the Vice-Chancellor had in mind a further change in the
organisation of top management. In the early 1960s he had chosen a unitary
arrangement by which the Registrar had responsibility for all the administration. The Vice-Chancellor came to think, however, that the workload of
administration had increased to such an extent that a division of function was
needed. The building of the Plain had massively increased the importance of
the Estates Office. Likewise the Establishment Officer's work had grown as
various categories of staff became unionised and engaged in collective
bargaining. The University now negotiated with its staff through two
committees, the Joint Committee for Faculty and Administrative Staff and
the Joint Committee for Non Teaching Staffs. In short the University was
becoming "an increasingly integrated and semi-industrial community". All
this imposed more strain on the role of Registrar. Frank Thistlethwaite
proposed that the old position of Registrar should be replaced by a dual
system by which the Registrar should look after Senate matters and a new
Bursar should deal with Council business – finance, estates, personnel and
industrial relations, those areas that had most increased in recent years. This
did not come about and George Chadwick, who had not been well in his last

two years, retired shortly afterwards (but we refer to this here as indicative of the connection between expansion and change and thinking about administrative reform).[46]

If some changes were the result of the expansion of the University and greater demands for representation, another arose from the need to cope with cuts in the 1970s. In the 1960s and first half of the 1970s the focal point of planning and resource application was the Development Committee of the Senate. This received the plans and estimates from Schools and other spending authorities, reported on them and sent them through Senate and the Finance Board to Council. This worked quite well in the context of the orderly quinquennial system of regular and predictable income whereby universities received substantial sums for their operation every five years from the University Grants Committee. With the collapse of the quinquennial grants in the mid 1970s the Development Committee became "unsuitable for taking hard and often speedy decisions in the context of retrenchment".[47] Since the Development Committee consisted of Deans and heads of spending units, they found it even more difficult to decide among themselves how to distribute the cuts they now had to bear rather than the expanding resources they were used to. Accordingly, in 1977 a Resources Committee was created as a joint sub-committee of the Development Committee and the Finance Board to allocate cuts, with a membership not so personally affected by their consequences. This was regarded by the Vice-Chancellor as a very effective body and meant that UEA pre-empted the recommendations of the later Jarratt Report by nearly ten years.

Before he left George Chadwick had, however, proposed a rationalisation of the Council committee structure such that Council business should be channelled through five Boards: Finance, Community Services, Staff, Forward Planning and Site Development. This came into being from August 1977.[48] George Chadwick retired in 1978 and was succeeded by Michael Paulson Ellis, a Cambridge classicist who had then trained as a chartered accountant, became a university administrator and who came to UEA from the University of Strathclyde.

Arguably the most important area of administration was that of the University's finances. Where did UEA's income come from and how was it spent? We can see the various components of the revenue account in Table 9.[49]

The first item was that of grants from Local Education Authorities in East Anglia. These were the earliest forms of income and in the first few years the largest. The sums and their donors are as shown in Table 10.

In the early sixties, as an earnest of the University's genuinely East Anglian base, both Norfolk and Suffolk counties and cities contributed substantially; indeed in the very first year Suffolk contributed slightly more (£38,001) than

14. Frank Thistlethwaite, the first Vice-Chancellor.

15. Appeal Garden Party, 1962: Viscount Cranbrook, Frank Thistlethwaite, Lord Mackintosh and Timothy Colman.

16. Gordon Tilsley, Timothy Colman and Sir Edmund Bacon, 1974, at the retirement of Sir Edmund as Chairman of the Appeal Committee.

17. Sir Lincoln Ralphs.

18. Sir Solly Zuckerman.

19. Lord Mackintosh.

20. Sir Charles Wilson.

21. The first executive, 1963.
Left to right (back) Alan Katritsky, Willi Guttsman, James McFarlane, Marcus Dick;
(front) Thomas Bennet Clark, Dick Ross, Frank Thistlethwaite, Ian Watt, George Chadwick.

22. The first Congregation, 1966.
Lord Franks conferring an honorary degree on Sir Charles Wilson.

23. Lord Franks, with his portrait and the artist Suzi Malin, 1984.

24. Owen Chadwick OM.

25. Sir Geoffrey Allen.

26. Three Vice-Chancellors and Miss Whitt.
Michael Thompson, Frank Thistlethwaite, Patricia Whitt, Derek Burke.

27. Lord Sainsbury, Norman Foster and Lady Sainsbury in the Crescent Wing,
September 1991.

28. Sir Michael Thompson.

29. Derek Burke.

30. Vincent Watts.

31. Dame Elizabeth Estève-Coll.

32. Michael Paulson Ellis.

Table 9   Revenue Account Income £

	LEA grants	Investments	UGC recurrent grants	Student Fees	Research grants	Total
1960-61	69,827	1295	-	-	-	71,122
1961-62	52,584	4383	-	-	-	56,967
1962-63	76,786	11,162	46	-	2230	83,366
1963-64	62,300	20,929	151,230	7879	17,509	240,870
1964-65	60,000	33,388	337,388	28,542	39,901	469,978
1965-66	60,000	41,874	552,970	60,742	113,760	795,899
1966-67	60,000	25,865	823,135	91,686	118,535	1,104,039
1967-68	60,000	20,425	1,145,467	135,583	196,849	1,458,150
1968-69	60,000	33,342	1,341,632	167,843	174,051	1,804,787
1969-70	60,000	49,856	1,599,906	191,705	148,831	2,070,080
1970-71	58,000	57,069	2,030,929	219,795	287,993	2,691,080
1971-72	55,000	58,911	2,474,578	229,682	326,900	3,195,513
1972-73	55,000	109,324	3,186,248	251,289	316,709	3,870,994
1973-74	39,000	261,700	3,864,859	268,726	354,756	4,635,727
1974-75	45,000	111,222	4,726,815	289,602	441,353	5,623,489
1975-76	30,500	117,782	5,748,558	537,557	760,601	7,234,440
1976-77	19,000	154,097	6,560,074	756,244	642,678	8,187,811
1977-78	17,500	156,183	5,936,315	1,957,015	680,348	8,810,013
1978-79	17,500	160,898	6,653,624	2,298,859	852,155	10,186,272
1979-80	17,500	237,987	8,747,483	2,738,272	1,358,353	13,208,896

Norfolk (£36,785). It was an act of public-spirited generosity from which they – unlike Norwich city – could expect to gain little. The Suffolk contribution diminished in 1975-76 and ceased thereafter. Lord Cranbrook was disappointed that Suffolk had not continued to support UEA more. Further afield Huntingdonshire and the Isle of Ely alternated in giving £2000. Gordon Tilsley saw clearly the need for this support both in practical and psychological terms. He told the Clerk of Norfolk County Council, F. P. Boyce, as early as the end of 1959, that the UGC was favourable to the Norwich movement and asked him to ensure that the Council would include an annual sum for the University in its estimates.[50] He was assured that £14,000 would be set aside.[51] Boyce too was sensitive to the public relations aspect, assuring his Chairman Sir Bartle Edwards that the UEA Promotion Committee would not need all this money but that it would be a psychological factor in dealing with the UGC and appealing to the public.[52] As other forms of income were introduced and increased so the LEA grants diminished in the 1970s and those from outside Norfolk and Norwich ceased altogether. But in the two or three years before the University actually opened these funds from regional LEAs gave UEA a solid start in comfortable circumstances.

Table 10   Recurrent Support from Local LEAs £

	Norfolk CC	East Suffolk CC	Norwich City C	Ipswich CBC	W Suffolk CC	Gt Yarmouth CBC	Huntingdonshire CC	Isle of Ely CC
1962-63	15,790	15,501	15,000	15,000	7500	5995	2000	-
1963-64	15,570	11,250	"	7500	5000	4000	-	2000
1964-65	15,500	11,050	"	"	"	"	2000	-
1965-66	"	"	"	"	"	"	-	2000
1966-67	"	"	"	"	"	"	2000	-
1967-68	"	"	"	"	"	"	"	-
1968-69	"	"	"	"	"	"	"	-
1969-70	"	"	"	"	"	2000	"	-
1970-71	"	"	"	"	"	-	1000	-
1971-72	"	"	"	"	"	-	"	-
1972-73	"	"	"	"	2500	-	-	-
1973-74	10,500	"	"	-	Now Suffolk CC	-	-	-
		Now Suffolk CC						
1974-75	5500	24,500	"	-	-	-	-	-
1975-76	5500	10,000	"	-	-	-	-	-
1976-77	"	-	13,500	-	-	-	-	-
1977-78	"	-	12,000	-	-	-	-	-
1978-79	"	-	12,000	-	-	-	-	-
1979-80	"	-	"	-	-	-	-	-

There was however, a reciprocal relationship of money flowing from the University to Norwich City Council. Even as the Village was being built in 1963, Keith Joseph at the Ministry of Housing and Local Government decided that the new universities should pay rates in full unless the local authority agreed to remit them. As with the older universities, the Treasury, through the UGC, would reimburse the universities, whose premises – like the new Village – were fixed on the same basis as commercial premises.[53]

The next major source was that of investments. In the first two years 1960-61 and 1961-2 the embryo university's finances were managed by John Barnard, the Borough Treasurer, and the first accounts were issued from the City Hall. There is no indication what he invested in but most charitable investments were then in gilts and local authorities while the instincts and traditions of his office would have been for the prudent conservation of funds. Appeal money was placed out short term with local authorities pending the building of residences. As the University and its finances were to grow and become more complicated they could not, however be left with a public-spirited local government officer to handle beside his main work. A merchant bank was required.

From 1962 the investments were handled by a merchant bank, Lazards. Some academic members of the Finance Committee expected that investment decisions would be taken by the Committee.[54] But they could hardly have the expertise and still less the time for this close day to day work. Accordingly, Basil Robarts, the General Manager of Norwich Union, offered to make enquiries about merchant banks and proposed Lazard Brothers & Co.[55] Local considerations were taken into account since one of the Lazards' directors, A. M. Marris, was on the main board of Barclays, had a residence in Norfolk and was known to Dick Gurney. Lazards were not, however, required to make a presentation of their record as fund manager or the comparative costs of their charges or state whether they would offer concessionary rates for educational institutions as some merchant banks did.[56] Nor were alternatives followed up. Buckmaster and Moore, who managed the investments of the Universities of Cambridge, Edinburgh and St Andrews and three major Cambridge colleges, offered their services to UEA but this was not pursued. There was a certain gentlemanly trust and local sentiment in the appointment of Lazards, as there had been about the appointment of Barclays.

In November 1962 Lazards laid out their strategy following a meeting with the Registrar. They agreed that £35,000 should be left in local authority mortgages to be managed by John Barnard, the City Treasurer. The University should build up a portfolio with half in equities and a half in fixed interest stocks, made up of a quarter gilt-edged stocks and a quarter in industrial

Table 11   Investments

	Capital	Short Term investment*	Equities	Fixed Interest	Property Unit Trusts	Income**
1960-61	69,200					1295
1961-62	151,894					4383
1962-63	277,439		95,979	181,460		11,162
1963-64	465,998		128,001	337,997		20,929
1964-65	471.349		131,602	339,747		33,388
1965-66	259,072		131,878	127,194		41,874
1966-67	202,716		142,392	60,344		25,865
1967-68	250,813		179,955	70,858		20,425
1968-69	213,832		127,420	86,412		33,342
1969-70	228,356		143,431	64,345	20,500	49,856
1970-71	366,620		243,844	94,796	27,980	57,069
1971-72	565,960	490,000	370,246	128,499	50,250	58,911
1972-73	574.080	1,175,100	262,761	182,399	68,650	109,324
1973-74	511,508	1,409,100	133,266	146,570	65,900	261,700
1974-75	718,931	1,258,100	292,818	297,481	88,725	111,222
1975-76	1,088,024	1,507,100	507,730	260,200	138,450	117,782
1976-77	1,535,577	2,229,100	537,883	542,529	157,250	165,097
1977-78	1,981,797	2,016,100	762,799	755,727	181,275	156,183
1978-79	2,361,686	1,773,317	882,200	832,700	260,350	160,898
1979-80	2,965,195	2,785,100	1,307,094	989,989	297,680	237,987

* held with local authorities, building societies, savings banks.
** income from investment in Trust, Consolidated and Special Funds

debentures and loan stocks. Lazards would deal at their discretion without prior reference to the University and charge 30 shillings per £1000 of market value on the last valuation of the calendar year.[57]

Reviewing these conditions, Barry Stevenson, who had just been appointed as the Finance Officer, considered that the 50 per cent in equities was too low and urged something more like 65 per cent. Robarts thought the fees normal but still thought the University should have pressed for lower charitable rates such as other merchant banks offered. The University accepted the terms but insisted on at least 60 per cent in equities. The initial advice of Lazards' E.W. Grazebrook on 50/50 balance was quaintly old-fashioned, disregarded the long bull market since 1950, and even more, disregarded the views of Lazards' own head of intelligence J. R. Cuthbertson. These were that "I think there is now quite a strong case for getting as fully invested in equities as trust deeds allow and for laying out new money steadily in the same direction … the case for equities seems irresistible".[58] C. A. Cooper, with whom UEA now dealt at Lazards, was of the same view. The invested fund increased from £192,000 in 1963 to over £566,000 by 1973, yielding usually around 5 per cent in the 1960s. As equities did well, so their proportion of the fund was as high as 77 per cent by 1969.[59]

The early 1970s posed problems for the financial management of the University as investors ran into the sharpest stock market crash since the war with inflation soaring from 5 per cent to 20 per cent. This called for radical changes in financial policy and is worth closer consideration. At the start of 1972 Timothy Colman, the Chairman of the Finance Committee, presciently thought that the bull market would last until September 1972 to be followed by a sharp fall.[60] He was absolutely right, Lazards agreed and hoped they would "see the cliff before the rest of the lemmings".[61] Not quite. Investors were already tumbling over the cliff in July when Lazards erroneously thought higher ground could be achieved.

The response to the stock market fall 1972-74 was, however, otherwise well judged as investments were redeployed (percentages of investment).

	1971	1972	1973	1974
Fixed interest securities	24.8	22.3	18.2	14.4
Equities	67.4	66.8	46.4	28.5
Property Unit Trusts	7.7	9.0	12.1	14.1
Cash	0.1	1.9	23.3	43.0

The shift from equities is evident. New alternatives were chosen in these years. First, this cash was invested in short-term investments at very high rates of interest (necessitated by the high inflation) offered by local authorities, building societies and savings banks.[62] Secondly, the University moved into property through property unit trusts to diversify its investment. These policy changes in the early 1970s under Timothy Colman's Chairmanship of the Finance Committee 1970-73 were an effective protection of the University against the worst fall in share values and rise in inflation since the war.

The financial advisers were rather caught out by the sharpness of the nadir of the crash of March 1974 (with the advent of Harold Wilson) and the rapidity of the recovery in the late summer of 1974 and through 1975. Lazards were still urging caution in buying shares in February 1975,[63] though these doubled in value between January and April in that year. By March UEA was clear that Lazards had been overcautious in missing the recovery by several months,[64] and Lazards themselves recognised "we had been too cautious in not investing sooner".[65] What this examination of the crucial years 1971-74 indicates, however, is the appropriate movement between types of investment to react to sharp stock market fluctuations and inflation. It also shows that there was an interplay between Lazards, the Finance Officer and the Chairman of the Finance Committee. It was not all left to the merchant bank and an experienced businessman like Timothy Colman could offer an expert opinion. After these crisis years the investment in equities resumed strongly, but a substantial amount still remained in fixed-interest gilts and high-yielding short-term investment. Fortunately the taste for property invest-ment continued to grow. This was appropriate as the property market soared, the average price of a house rising from £10,000 to £25,000 between 1973 and 1980, and real house price annual changes rose from minus 10 per cent in 1975 to plus 15 per cent by 1979. By and large the management of this crucial area of discretionary investment income was well judged in some of the most hazardous years since the war.

The largest element in the University's income was the University Grants Committee recurrent grants. These rose from £46 in 1962-63 to over £8,700,000 by 1979-80. The UGC acted as an intermediary between the universities and the government as their paymaster. Especially in the 1960s universities were keen to preserve concepts of academic freedom and univer-sity autonomy against direct government interference. On the other hand, Parliament and government had to safeguard the public interest of the taxpayer providing these funds. The UGC was the "buffer" between these interests and the conduit by which government money came to the universi-ties. Sir John Wolfenden, the Chairman of the UGC, described the system:

Universities are asked to submit to the UGC, once every five years, a detailed account of their expected income and their hoped-for expenditure for each year of the forthcoming quinquennium, distinguishing between capital spending and annual recurrent costs. Their income, for these purposes, includes income from endowments, investments, rents, students' fees, research contracts – everything except what they have in former years received from the UGC. Their expenditure includes the salaries of the academic and administrative staff, wages of laboratory technicians, books for the library, laboratory equipment, maintenance of build-ings and grounds. The income is "expected", because it is within narrow limits predictable: the expenditure is "hoped for" because it will not be realised without a massive contribution from UGC funds towards it. Students' fees, paid in part by local authorities and in part by parents, not by the UGC, cover less than one-tenth of what a student actually costs. (Halls of residence and other forms of university-managed student accommodation, once built, are required to be self-supporting and do not enter into the annual balance sheet.) Capital spending is, obviously, the cost of a new laboratory or library or residential hall. Plainly, the gap between expected income and hoped-for expenditure is enormous, especially in a period of expansion. That is the gap which the UGC is concerned with and that is the amount of money which is the meat of each university's submission.[66]

The UGC would assess the financial submissions of the universities critically and discuss them with Vice-Chancellors. It would then propose a total sum to the government, which the Treasury usually regarded as excessive, and would allocate to the UGC less than requested. The UGC in turn would distribute this to the universities. Recurrent annual income was on a quinquennial basis to allow for some forward planning – at least up to five years. Until 1974 the quinquennial grant was automatically supplemented for inflation. When it ceased to be so it was the first shock to university funding and a presage of cuts to come.[67] The recurrent allocation was made as a block grant. That is, the universities justified their demands in carefully itemised detail but the money they received was not tied to these items. The universities were trusted to spend the block of money they received for annual expenditure prudently at their own discretion with "virement" between salaries, books, maintenance and so forth. Capital expenditure was allocated by Parliament on an annual, not quinquennial basis. This was for buildings only, commissioned by the universities but subject to detailed cost scrutiny and approval by the UGC's architectural staff.

When UEA began, it dealt with a UGC still directly linked with the Treasury as it had been since its origins in 1919. But the creation of the new universities and the expansion of all, old and new, in response to Robbins, necessitated new relations. The costs and public expenditure soared and made the direct Treasury link inappropriate. The Treasury was not a spending department, indeed its duty was to demand cuts and savings in spending departments. The increase of universities and their increasing cost also made it anomolous that they were kept in a privileged position isolated from the rest of education. So in 1964 the UGC came under the Department of Education and Science along with its competitors in other levels of education. Another change consequent on this was the opening of the finances of UGC and individual universities to the scrutiny of the Comptroller and Auditor General and Public Accounts Committee, who reasonably wanted scrutiny of the £200 millions a year of public money spent on universities. This was the financial system under which UEA began its formative years.

In the first quinquennium UGC money expanded generously from £46 (before the University actually opened) to £823,135. There were some unusual features in UEA's relations with the UGC over this first quinquennium. First it appeared that any revenue derived from the endowments raised by the Appeal would simply be deducted from the UGC allocation. The Vice-Chancellor went to see the UGC and "said that he found it very difficult to see how any endowment money really helped the University since it was taken into account by the UGC in the quinquennial settlements". The Chairman agreed that the Vice-Chancellor was right.[68] After some pondering, however, the UGC agreed that UEA could use the endowment income as it wished on the pragmatic grounds that, if the UGC did not agree to this, it would all vanish in expenditure or capital purposes anyway.[69] The UGC was also accommodating about UEA's heavy initial costs. They calculated the costs per student in the initial build up of the first three "new" universities.[70] Thistlethwaite justified this on the grounds that he wanted a fast build up, and was including not only scientists in the first cohorts but postgraduate scientists. After economies of scale began to operate there would be a convergence of costs in all new universities to about £600. One UGC official thought that "East Anglia looks like being a bit expensive" but concurred.

	Sussex	York	East Anglia
Year 1	1620	?	1863
Year 2	760	600	900
Year 3	695	560	700
Year 4	633	535	600

There was an atmosphere of generosity, but not extravagance, about the University in those days. The fitting up of Earlham Lodge as the SCR, running headmasters' conferences to introduce the new university, enabling advisers to provide hospitality for advisees all created an attractive, welcoming image necessary for a new institution seeking to make a reputation. The relative youth of the faculty, however, kept salary costs moderate before "incremental drift" of an ageing faculty became a problem. Yet these halcyon days were not to last. In 1967 there was a national cut back on scientific equipment. Hitherto universities were given a capital grant to cover the cost of new equipment when each new building was opened. But new equipment in old buildings had to be paid for out of current accounts.[71] This old system favoured the new universities which were opening new buildings all the time as they expanded and had the costs of their equipment paid accordingly. The new system from August 1968 was that the annual equipment grant, whether for old or new buildings, should be an overall sum for each university. In practice a new university like UEA would have new buildings opening but no longer the automatically linked funds to equip them. UEA's scientific equipment grant continued to rise but at a drastically reduced rate 1968-70 before resuming in 1971. UEA, like all universities, was beginning to learn the problems of stop-go finance created by a failing economy.

The 1967-72 quinquennium was surrounded by much contradictory advice. The UGC letter of 20 December 1966 recognised that the universities were "sensitive to national needs and anxious to play their part in meeting them".[72] There was talk about the need for closer university-industry collaboration and the "crying need" for scientists and technologists. Yet the memorandum of guidance saw no need for new departments or an expansion of students in a whole range of vocational subjects – agriculture, Russian, biology, management, medicine, architecture – the first five of which were at various times part of UEA's aspirations in the sixties. By contrast they wanted a "large increase" in the Social Studies. Accordingly, in spite of the rhetoric of the December letter, the effect of the UGC allocation was to prevent UEA from becoming more vocational.

The quinquennial allocation for 1967-72 to UEA was £6,928,700, which was less than the £8,912,000 asked for. This was allocated

1967-68	1968-69	1969-70	1970-71	1971-72
£1,107,800	£1,251,500	£1,379,000	£1,522,800	£1,667,600

The rank order of the grants to new universities for 1971-72 showed UEA in a good light – Sussex £2,300,000, UEA £1,600,000, Warwick £1,400,000, York and Kent £1,300,000, Essex £1,100,000. The fact that the grant was less than expected meant, however, that the hopes to expand to 3600 students had to be cut back to 3000. Proposals for new Schools of Management and Technology and Molecular Technology and Engineering were abandoned and Law and Medicine receded into the future. It also left UEA with its bias towards the liberal arts – 67 per cent of students in arts and 33 per cent in sciences as opposed to the ratio of 56 : 44 it had hoped for. Although the increase in UGC grant increased from £11,000,000 to £16,000,000, this took no account of inflation.[73] The UGC grant per student fell slightly from £642 to £629 while inflation increased by 36 per cent 1967-72, exacerbating the effect of non-supplemention of UGC grants.

UEA also found the UGC, itself subject to Treasury pressure, increasingly niggardly in contrast to the early sixties. For example, in 1969 the UGC was refusing to finance a small footage of University House since it would be a profit-making bar. This was the first time that they had troubled about this kind of trivial detail. Frank Thistlethwaite complained in exasperation to another Vice-Chancellor that "we will soldier on but we find the micro climate of the UGC office has changed rapidly towards a new ice age".[74]

The 1972-77 quinquennium began badly with the universities having no clear figures for planning into the seventies. The responsibility for this lay not so much with the UGC as with the Secretary of State Margaret Thatcher (20 June 1970 to 3 March 1974). The fierce unpopularity of the universities following the student unrest meant that few were concerned about the headaches passed on to the Vice-Chancellors. A "provisional" grant was provided for 1972-73 pending the Secretary of State's announcement in December and the UGC's allocation in January 1973 – four months late. The provisional grant, only £170,000 greater than that for 1971-72, was grim enough. The *THES* surveyed some universities, including UEA, which replied that "the grant was such that the increase in the number of academic staff was severely restricted, with a consequential deterioration of the staff-student ratio".[75]

The UGC letter for the quinquennial allocation 1972-77 arrived in January 1973 and indicated that by 1976-77 UEA was to have 4568 full-time equivalent students, slightly fewer than the 4803 asked for. Crucially the recurrent grant was

1972-73	£3,019,000
1973-74	£3,320,000
1974-75	£3,570,000
1975-76	£3,894,000
1976-77	£4,232,000[76]

The 1972-77 quinquennium was wrecked by the raging inflation of these years. In the second half of 1973 the price of oil rose from five to fifteen dollars a barrel, then up to forty dollars by 1979. This forced inflation up to over 25 per cent a year after an annual average of 3.8 per cent in 1950-67 and 7.5 per cent in 1968-73. Keith Clayton thought the later years' allocations "very tough indeed". Clayton was concerned that there was going to be a 14 per cent fall in the allocation per student, also there would be a decline in the staff-student ratio from 1 : 10.3 to 1 : 11.5.[77] UEA was also to be hard hit by likely salary settlements in these very inflationary years. It was now exacerbated by "incremental drift", the annual progression of young staff up the incremental scales irrespective of pay settlements. Clayton also urged the necessity of savings in the early years of the quinquennium to cover the later ones. This was foresighted; indeed Clayton was surprised to find that many universities did not do calculations on the later years of the allocation but merely moved on from one year at a time.[78]

Adverse as this was it was exacerbated by the successor Labour government from March 1975, whose inability to control inflation began to wreck the finances of the quinquennial allocation and call into question the whole tradition of five year planning. Also, seeking a soft target, the government was denying the university teachers' pay claim. A UEA faculty lobby of the House of Commons on 6 May 1975 focused discontent with the whole financial situation. Professor J. R. Jones, a former Pro Vice-Chancellor and now Chairman of the UEA Association of University Teachers, noted that "the AUT was a modest body being turned into a militant one".[79]

A few days later the Vice-Chancellor gave serious warnings about the finances of UEA: "I accept that in a time of acute national economic difficulties we all have to tighten our belts, but in doing so I hope that we will not be so shortsighted as to damage irreparably the institutions that are the foundation of our higher education."[80] The Quinquennial Allocation system had broken down. The original allocations were so inadequate in the face of the mid seventies inflation that grants were now being made annually with revisions and top ups. This accounts for the disparity between the original UGC figures for 1972-77 cited earlier and the final UGC figures in the table of revenue. But even the new grant for 1975-76 of £5,700,000 (revised up from £3,800,000, itself raised to £4,900,000) was quite inadequate. This forced UEA into even more economies with a freeze on new appointments and replacements in May 1975, and cuts in hours of hourly paid staff. Since four fifths of UEA's expenditure was on wages and salaries, this was the only way forward. The Vice-Chancellor feared a shortfall of £400,000 by 1976.

The University staggered on to the end of the grim 1972-77 quinquennium, any possible planning in tatters. In March 1976 the UGC made the allocations for 1976-77. The Vice-Chancellor regarded his £5,900,000 as adequate and lifted the freeze on new appointments. But the respite was not to last. In September 1976 Sir Frederick Dainton of the UGC told universities to expect a 4 per cent real cut in resources for 1977-78. UEA reacted gravely with a renewed freeze on appointments, with twelve teaching posts left unfilled and a cut of 5.7 per cent on all staff and non-staff budgets. Most hurtfully UEA came to be talked of as a university which might be closed down, along with Stirling and Essex.[81] Dainton made it clear, however, that the UGC had never considered removing any university from its grant list. UEA estimated that its real cut would be about 2.5–3.0 per cent, which, with an extra 1 per cent for incremental drift made, say, 4 per cent, which was as bad as expected. The UGC grant actually declined absolutely in 1977-78 for the first time in the history of the University. The sharp rise in UGC grants in the final two years of Frank Thistlethwaite's Vice-Chancellorship was no sudden surge of generosity but an inevitable response to the second oil price shock, when oil prices rose to forty dollars a barrel and inflation rose to over 20 per cent. Finally, three points should be stressed. The UGC recurrent grants were quite the largest source of income for the University, about three quarters in 1970 and two thirds by 1980. This made it all the more dangerous that the measured quinquennial grants and planning that had shaped university finance since 1919, and still did in UEA's early days, broke down under the extraordinary inflation of 1974-75 and 1979-80. It destroyed the possibility of planning on anything more than an annual basis: grants were announced late, that for 1975-76 revised twice. But, thirdly, apart from 1977-78, the grants did actually increase. There was not yet the nightmare of coping with inflation with diminishing absolute sums. That was to come in the 1980s, as we shall see.

Finally, there were fees which were paid by the students' LEAs. The UGC and the CVCP consulted on the level at the start of each quinquennium to aim at making fee income about 11 per cent of total expenditure. The Robbins Committee recommended that this proportion should be raised to 20 per cent and the CVCP likewise proposed this to the government in December 1965. The government decided against this, although it required a substantial increase in overseas students fees.[82] At UEA fees were 9.8 per cent of total expenditure in 1967-78, but the raising of the proportion to 20 per cent became a long-term aim. This came about in 1977-78 and it remained 20-22 per cent for the remainder of the decade.

This revenue was then distributed as the expenditure of the University. The largest items were on Teaching and Research, Maintenance of Premises, Administration, and Student facilities in the following proportions.

| | Percentages of Expenditure | | | |
	Teaching and Research	Maintenance of premises	Administration	Student facilities and amenities
1966	67.5	12.9	13.1	4.7
1970	66.8	17.4	10.0	3.7
1975	66.6	16.4	8.2	4.0
1980	67.3	18.0	7.2	3.3

Teaching and research remained a remarkably constant 66-67 per cent and student amenities 3-4 per cent. The chief changes were the declining proportion spent on administration as it bore its share of the cuts and academics took on more administrative work. Also the maintenance of premises inevitably took a larger share as the buildings increased and the older ones deteriorated. The overall expenditure grew as shown in Table 12.

The expenditure rose as one would expect. Early surpluses were allowed to go into deficits to take the strain of the early years of expansion from 1963. The interesting feature is that from the start of the 1972 quinquennium the University systematically transferred surpluses to a quinquennial reserve to meet the inflationary demands of the end of the quinquennium. So the deficits of 1974/5, 1977/8 and 1978/9 were met with transfers from these reserves. Accordingly the "balance" at the end of the year was kept at a constant notional figure of £61,390. This skilful deployment of the quinquennial reserve was an important cushion in the fluctuating finances of the 1970s. The University was well served by its Finance Officers Barry Stevenson and Bob Newstead, and by a succession of lay Treasurers and Chairmen of the Finance Committee with a wide experience of business and accountancy: John Barnard (Borough Treasurer), Lord Cranbrook (farmer), W. Rowan Hare (Managing Director of Reckitt and Colman), Timothy Colman (farmer

Table 12   Growth of Overall Expenditure (£)

	Expenditure	Surplus	Deficit	Balance at end of year
1960-61	1925	69,197	-	
1961-62	12,724	39,953	-	14,004
1962-63	71,787	11,579	-	25,583
1963-64	246,071	-	5201	382
1964-65	477,889	-	7911	7529
1965-66	807,208	-	11,309	18,838
1966-67	1,020,811	83,228	-	59,390
1967-68	1,380,011	78,139	-	82,529
1968-69	1,796,902	7885	-	82,414
1969-70	2,175,791	-	75,192	7223
1970-71	2,680,733	10,347	-	17,570
1971-72	3,151,693	43,820	-	61,390
1972-73	3,602,287	268,707	-	61,390
1973-74	4,509,507	126,220	-	61,390
1974-75	5,791,293	-	167,804	61,390
1975-76	7,211,381	23,059	-	61,390
1976-77	7,899,354	288,457	-	-
1977-78	8,891,717	-	81,704	-
1978-79	10,335,479	-	149,207	-
1979-80	13,207,307	1589	-	-

and newspaper proprietor), Colonel Geoffrey Dicker (accountant). Yet it was always in the Vice-Chancellor's mind that, if anything went wrong with the University's finances, he alone was the accounting officer to Parliament and he might have to explain himself to a parliamentary committee. It happened to one of his fellow "new" university Vice-Chancellors but never to him or to UEA.

UEA was a well-administered and financed institution and this enabled it to withstand the strains imposed by organisational change and financial stringency in the sixties and seventies and to face the much more testing times of the eighties.

8

The Sainsbury Centre

I was too stunned the other evening to be able to convey the depth
of my appreciation for your very generous remarkable
intentions.[1]

Frank Thistlethwaite to Sir Robert Sainsbury, 8 June 1968

Frank Thistlethwaite always intended that UEA should have a School of Fine
Arts, which began in 1965,[2] and he also wanted an Arts Centre associated with
it. In this he was encouraged by a friend, Andrew Ritchie, a friendship whose
influence on UEA was to prove fruitful in two ways. He had first met Ritchie
in Cambridge when they were visiting a former colleague of Ritchie's wife,
Jane, who chanced to be a neighbour of the Thistlethwaites. It was a further
coincidence that Jane Ritchie proved to have been a friend of Mrs Jane
Thistlethwaite's sister. Ritchie was the head of British Art at the Museum of
Modern Art in New York before becoming Professor of Fine Art and Director
of the Gallery at Yale. The friendship of the Ritchies and Thistlethwaites grew
closer.

Ritchie encouraged Frank Thistlethwaite in his view of an Arts Centre. As
early as 1962 Thistlethwaite noted a useful conversation with Andrew Ritchie
in which the latter approved of the idea of a small gallery and library and
suggested that, since they could not realistically build a collection of paintings, they should concentrate on prints instead.[3] He further suggested that
they could get a good art historian from the Courtauld Institute or they might
find a Frenchman or Dutchman who would bring colour to the University.
Indeed Ritchie later suggested that UEA could make a feature of specialising
in Dutch painting, because of its geography and the affinity of the Norwich
School of Painting to the Low countries.[4]

Thistlethwaite envisaged that an Arts Centre for the new School of Arts
would cost between £300,000 and £500,000 and should comprise a theatre
for 500 people which could also be used for music and film. The upper floor
of the building should be an art exhibition gallery with ancillary rooms for
studios, rehearsal and dressing rooms.[5] The University had applied to the
Max Rayne Foundation in 1965 for finance but without success. They were
advised to reapply in 1967 but sights were being lowered. A Music Centre was

to be financed by the Nuffield Foundation, a large lecture theatre would be used for drama and it was proposed to use the Library Concourse or the brick-built section of the Library in the Village as an art gallery. They decided to settle for that and not to reapply to Rayne.[6] An approach to the Wolfson Foundation at about the same time was likewise unsuccessful.

It was in this time of lowered expectations that relations between Frank Thistlethwaite and Robert Sainsbury drew closer. Here again Andrew Ritchie had a role to play. He invited Frank and Jane Thistlethwaite to meet his circle of friends in the London art world, which included artists such as Henry Moore, dealers, collectors and benefactors. Among the last were Robert and Lisa Sainsbury.[7] Sainsbury was a grandson of J.J. Sainsbury, the founder of the grocery and supermarket firm. After Cambridge, Robert Sainsbury had qualified as a chartered accountant. He joined the company in 1930 and rose to be a Director in 1934, Joint General Manager in 1938, Deputy Chairman in 1956 and Chairman in 1967.[8] In the last year he was knighted for his services to the arts notably as Chairman of the Trustees of the Tate Gallery. When they made their gift to UEA in 1973 Sir Robert had retired from Sainsbury's but was joint President. Over the years Sainsbury and his wife Lisa had built up a major personal art collection. He recalled "starting over forty years ago, shortly after leaving Cambridge in 1927 I became a passionate acquirer of differing forms of art which excited me and which I could afford".[9]

Another link was Robert Sainsbury's daughter Annabel, who, quite independently, was considering coming to UEA to read mathematics and physics, which she did between 1966 and 1969. Annabel Sainsbury and her parents stayed with the Thistlethwaites at Wood Hall in 1965 as part of the looking round UEA. Robert Sainsbury then decided to start helping the University with donations with which to buy expensive art books that would otherwise have been beyond UEA's budget. He forwarded £1000 from the Sainsbury Charitable Fund in 1967 and £2500 in 1968. Those gifts were anonymous, to avoid embarrassing his daughter. The good use to which the University put these sums impressed Sainsbury with its seriousness about art. So too did the University's attempt to gather a collection of prints with £10,000 from the Council. The Sainsburys' admiration of the architecture of Denys Lasdun further focused their attention on UEA.

Accordingly, as Thistlethwaite recalled, the Sainsburys "were responsive to the idea of lending us pictures and pieces of sculpture for display in the University". The Thistlethwaites discussed this with the Sainsburys at various social meetings at the latters' London home in Smith Square.[10] It was at one of these meetings that Sainsbury suggested that he might leave their entire art collection to UEA. After a dinner on 30 May 1968, Thistlethwaite expressed his astonished gratitude in the extract at the head of this chapter. In July Sir

Robert Sainsbury referred to their "chat the other day" about leaving the collection to UEA. But he reasonably needed assurances about where it was to be housed.[11] Sainsbury suggested that if an arts centre were to be built then "he did not rule out the possibility that his estate might be in a position to contribute handsomely".

The matter remained in abeyance. The University could not afford to build an Arts Centre. Problems of student unrest with the occupation of buildings made it unthinkable for the Sainsburys to give their valuable collection for display in buildings where security could not be guaranteed. Thus the Vice-Chancellor "began to wonder whether we should ever be able to take advantage of the Sainsbury's good will". But in 1973 the situation clarified.[12] The Sainsburys saw their entire collection in a stunning, specially designed display in the new Kröller-Müller gallery outside Amsterdam. This raised their intentions from giving their collection to UEA to something even more astonishingly ambitious. It is worth recounting Frank Thistlethwaite's own words:

> Early in 1973 when Jane and I were taking sabbatical leave in California Patricia Whitt received a phone call from Sir Robert saying that he and Lady Sainsbury would like us to spend a night with them when we return to England because there was something they wished to discuss with us. And so we duly appeared at 5 Smith Square. Over dinner Bob and Lisa outlined their proposition to us. Recognising the intractability of our problem – our inability to fund, either from our own exiguous resources or from Government grant, the capital and recurrent income for such a project – they proposed to give their collection to the University of East Anglia outright together with the sum of £3,000,000 to cover the cost of a building and an endowment, the income of which would be used to continue to buy art objects to add to the collection. We were momentarily stunned. We knew the Sainsburys were wealthy but, in our somewhat academic naivety, we had never dreamed of such munificence, that Bob's unassuming modesty masked such a veritable Maecenas.

Why was this collection so important? In 1973 it was composed of about 400 paintings, drawings and sculptures. About a quarter was European work of the nineteenth and twentieth centuries, including pieces by Henry Moore, Francis Bacon and Giacometti – to all of whom Sainsbury had been an important early patron. His first significant acquisition had been in 1933 when he purchased Henry Moore's *Mother and Child* (1932) in green Hornton stone. Other modern artists represented were Degas, Seurat, Rouault, Modigliani and Picasso among others. In addition a major part of the collection comprised 169 pieces of so called primitive arts from Africa, Oceania and the Americas, including a bronze head of an Oba (King) from Benin, sculptures from Polynesia and Melanesia in the Pacific, and Eskimo, Indian and pre Columbian art from North and South America. There were

104 works of Egyptian, Sumerian and Greek sculpture through to Byzantine and Celtic items and a few of the twelfth century and later. There were also twenty-two pieces from Far Eastern civilisations, including a Khmer female torso from Cambodia, perhaps Sir Robert's favourite of the whole collection. It was symbolic that Sir Robert's first major purchase had been the *Mother and Child* in 1933, about the same time he bought a Chinese Tang pottery figure. In the next year 1934 he acquired in Paris an African wooden head from Gabon, his first piece of Primitive Sculpture. These initial objects purchased in 1933-34 signalled the three main directions – Modern, Primitive and Antiquities – the collection, and his taste, were to take.[13]

The unifying theme of such disparate material was that the objects should convey sensual pleasure. Sainsbury admitted to being "a hedonist in matters of art" and that "my personal reaction to any work of art is primarily sensual".[14] Sir Robert insisted that the collection was very much a joint enterprise with his wife Lisa. All the items reflected both their tastes, "it has been a joint collection, the result of a shared voyage discovering the cultures that appealed to us".[15] There was no doubt of the importance of the collection. Sir Norman Reid, Director of the Tate Gallery and an honorary graduate of UEA, said at the time that "the Sainsbury Collection is unique in Britain and celebrated throughout the world". The collection itself was priceless. Its insurance value was £3,500,000,[16] although all the items were irreplaceable, and its estimated value about £4,000,000 and £5,000,000.[17] What was equally remarkable was the other part of the gift, the £3,000,000 endowment from Sir Robert's son David Sainsbury. This was to build a gallery to house the collection and provide an endowment for the continued development of the collection. All in all Frank Thistlethwaite described it as "the most munificent private gift of its kind to a British university since the War".[18]

Why had Sir Robert chosen UEA for his munificence? Apart from his personal connections with Frank Thistlethwaite there were other considerations. He did not wish to give it to London, Oxford or Cambridge, already well stocked and endowed with the Courtauld, Ashmolean and Fitzwilliam Museums. Cambridge might have taken the collection but wanted to disperse it among its existing museums, which was unacceptable to Sir Robert. He thought that a new university would be more appropriate for a collection of modern art. He admired the work of Denys Lasdun and UEA's sculptural Lasdun buildings. A university that had commissioned such work would be likely to be sympathetic to his own taste. He had been "greatly impressed with the courses offered by the School of Fine Arts and Music and its potential as a prime magnet in this country for students in this particular discipline".[19] This would provide the context for his collection since he did not want to leave it as a simple museum. He wished it to be the centre of lively activity, of study and enjoyment by students. A strong School of Fine Arts, to which UEA was committed, would provide this. Beyond this Sainsbury wanted his collection to reach out to the mass of non-specialist students, "to give them the opportunity, when young, of learning the pleasures of visual experience, of looking at works of art from a sensual, not only an intellectual point of view".[20]

The lawyers got to work. Sir Robert himself had already drawn up the first document embodying his intentions in March 1973.[21] The collection of works of art was to be given to the University. The Gatsby Charitable Foundation established by David Sainsbury would provide a fund of £3,000,000 to build and endow an Arts Centre to house the collection. Not more than half of this £3,000,000 was to be spent on the building, the rest was to provide an endowment for a purchasing fund. This would be used to acquire works of art and art books, and to provide fellowships and pay for conservation. By works of art Sir Robert Sainsbury intended to include ethnographic artefacts, applied and decorative arts; he wished to exclude, for example, postage stamps or manuscript sheets of music. In case of dispute after Sir Robert's death, the Director of the Fitzwilliam Museum Cambridge would be the final arbitrator.

There were some problems to be resolved. The Sainsburys retained the right to possess the collection during their lifetime. Indeed part of it would still be in their home in Smith Square and rotate between there and the Sainsbury Centre. Full ownership would pass to the University after their death. The Inland Revenue accepted this and confirmed that it would exempt the collection from death duties.[22] The Sainsburys also claimed the right to continue buying for the collection those pieces which they deemed appropriate. More controversially they wanted to retain the right to sell items and to approve the investment policy of the endowment. This was rightly queried by the shrewdly vigilant Timothy Colman on the grounds that nobody could guarantee their capacities into extreme old age. These requirements were omitted from the final version of the deed of gift.[23]

There was also the problem of the UGC. Sainsbury's reasonable assumption was that the University would bear the cost of running the building. This depended on the UGC being willing to accept this as a reasonable charge on the block grant it gave to the University. The Vice-Chancellor sounded out Sir Kenneth Berrill, the Chairman of the UGC and an old Cambridge friend. He agreed that a sum would be included in the forthcoming grant to cover the recurrent costs of the Sainsbury Centre. The UGC grants were then block grants, that is to say each university received a global sum not broken down into specified items of expenditure. That internal allocation was up to UEA itself. Before the grant was made Sir Kenneth Berrill was succeeded by Sir Frederick Dainton,[24] who agreed with his predecessor's assurance. Sir Robert was as grateful to the UGC for their understanding as they were to him for his generosity.[25] This was important since Sir Robert saw his Centre not just as an old-fashioned museum. It was to be a vital part of the University, housing the School of Fine Arts with its teaching and research function, and playing a social role with the Senior Common Room, public restaurants and coffee shops. The UGC recognised this wide purpose and provided not only for its recurrent costs but £600,000 towards its capital costs – notionally the teaching and social areas.

The Sainsbury's £3,000,000 was transferred to the University in the form chiefly of British and American shares (Boots, ICI, Marks and Spencers, Coca Cola and Kodak, for example) and cash at the merchant bank Warburgs. The shares did not include those of the firm J. Sainsbury itself, since it had only just become a public company in June 1973. The various deeds were to be signed at a ceremony on 26 November 1973, which was a complex occasion much surrounded with mystery. To preserve confidentiality the Council had to meet first without knowing the purpose of the meeting. The Vice-Chancellor explained the nature of the gift and its background.[26] As he spoke the small silver Peruvian pre-conquest figurine of a llama stood on the table in front of him, a symbolic gift and foretaste of the riches to come. He pointed out that if UEA declined the offer it would go to another university and that they should and could not refuse it. He finished stirringly, "the name of Sainsbury will stand alongside those who have created the great centres of art in British universities from the seventeenth century to the present century: Ashmole at Oxford in 1677, Fitzwilliam at Cambridge in 1816, Courtauld at London in 1932 and now Sainsbury at East Anglia in 1973. I put the proposition to you".

The Council accepted the windfall with amazement. The lawyers, waiting in the wings, completed the signing of the legal documents and a press conference was held to announce the momentous event. The nation's press had been summoned but, like everyone else, they were kept in the dark about the significance of the occasion. This caught some of them out. The arts editor of the *Financial Times* could find no one to go to Norwich and accordingly missed the most important event linking finance, business and the arts in Britain since the 1930s.

Once the gift had been made and announced it was a matter of urgency to get on with building the Centre, lest its costs be overtaken by inflation. A building sub-committee of the Development Committee was set up to supervise the project. It consisted of Rowan Hare of the Council, Andrew Martindale, the Professor of Art History, and Gordon Marshall, the Estates Officer, who was to manage the building. In practice so personal was this project to Sir Robert that this subcommittee met in Sir Robert's dining room in Smith Square, rarely convened and most of the decisions were taken by Sir Robert Sainsbury and the Vice-Chancellor.[27] It was an unusual arrangement but understandable in the circumstances.

The starting point for the project was not the architect but the designer. The display of the collection at the Kröller Müller museum had been designed by Kho Liang Ie, an Indonesian Dutch designer working in Amsterdam. He was most famous as the designer of the interiors of Schiphol (and subsequently of Lagos) airport. Sir Robert Sainsbury was clear that Ie should design the new Sainsbury Centre for Visual Arts, the SCVA. Frank Thistlethwaite spent half a day with Ie and found that he was much more of a designer than an architect, but he already had a working relationship with the architect Norman Foster. The Vice-Chancellor told Sir Robert Sainsbury that Ie "knows Foster extremely well and no doubt he would discuss Foster with you."[28] Coincidentally Foster's name was included in the list of seventeen possible architects for the SCVA drawn up by Gordon Marshall the Estates Officer. The Vice Chancellor notified Bernard Feilden the Consultant Architect to the University, that they were considering Norman Foster.[29] He also asked the opinion of Sir Hugh Casson, since Ie "has already established a relationship with Norman Foster over an architectural project in the Netherlands".[30] Casson replied warmly, "I am also a great admirer of Norman Foster . . . a man of great energy, drive and enthusiasm" who had worked in Casson's office for a while.[31]

Foster had been on Gordon Marshall's short list and also on Robert Sainsbury's and he had worked with Kho Liang Ie.[321] Accordingly, he seemed ideal, in spite of his youth. He was then thirty-eight, a graduate of Manchester University's School of Architecture and of Yale. He had been working with Richard Rogers but had relatively little record. His early buildings were commercial, notably some port facilities for Fred Olsen, the Norwegian ship owner. But he had recently attracted a great deal of attention with his new building for Willis Faber in Ipswich. Gordon Marshall knew this and Sir Robert went to see it. It was, however, the Fred Olsen Centre (1968-70) which clinched Sir Robert's decision in favour of Norman Foster rather than the Willis Faber building (1970-75) as was frequently assumed. After talks with the Vice-Chancellor, the latter agreed to recommend Norman Foster as the architect and the Council formally appointed him on 25 April 1974. Sir Robert Sainsbury and Foster then made a short tour of Germany and Scandinavia visiting and discussing new buildings, getting a closer view of each other's tastes.[33]

Foster, Ie, Marshall and Sainsbury were already meeting in the latter's home and taking key decisions before this.[34] They decided to bring in Lanning Roper as landscape architect, roughly divided up the space by purposes and took the crucial initial decision to have no natural light for the art works. Gordon Marshall was concerned that the whole enterprise should not merely become Sir Robert working at home with the architect. It had to be meshed in with University government and Marshall insisted that he should be present at such meetings. Bernard Feilden had also to keep a positive role.[35] As well as Sir Robert's munificent generosity, there was also a large UEA input of land and labour and a considerable amount of public UGC money involved. This had not to be lost sight of. There was also some unease among local Norwich architects who had hoped for a competition in which local men could take part. Timothy Colman, addressing the Norfolk Association of Architects, emphasised the international status of the collection and hence the building that was to house it.[36]

Norman Foster and Kho Liang Ie had started off in a partnership specifically formed to create the SCVA. Sadly Ie shortly afterwards died of cancer and so all the interior design work was also taken over by Norman Foster Associates but was kept true to the spirit of Ie's aesthetic.[37] Foster had to meet many demands, several unrealistic and irreconcilable. The Sainsburys were insistent that the SCVA should be a living and working environment of bustling activity, both academic and social, thrown open to the public as well as the University. The art historians under Andrew Martindale were concerned that this concept would conflict with quiet scholarly study. They feared that academic activities and lecturers in their studies would become "peepshows" for visitors perambulating the building. They wanted spacious offices with an outlook onto the Broad.[38]

The art historians assumed that the UGC norms of 156 square feet for lecturers rooms could be raised to 170 square feet in the SCVA, allowing ample space for teaching and projecting slides in the study.[39] The Senior Common Room had high hopes of a variety of discrete rooms of different sizes and "access to a sunny lawn".[40] The SCR Committee at this time suggested to Norman Foster that they could use their own original fine furniture from Earlham Lodge in the new SCR. He was politely noncommittal. Clearly their chintzy Victoriana was to have no place in the high tech environment burgeoning in his mind any more than suites of cosy separate rooms.

There was the fundamental problem of the location of the SCVA. Various possibilities were raised. A site west of the biology garden was too remote. It could have been at the entrance to The Plain partly bridging the approach road. This would have given a spectacular entrance to the University but at enormous cost. If it were placed between Norfolk and Suffolk Terraces then most of it would have had to be underground, combining prohibitive expense with lack of visual impact. Sites near to the Music Centre or at the foot of the mound would have been too remote from access roads and parking. Hence the chosen site was adjacent to the end of Norfolk Terrace. This would have near access to roads and paths, it could be linked to the walkway and there was plenty of room to expand.[41]

As Norman Foster's long metal hangar-like concept became plain in drawings and plans by the summer of 1975, so the University's consultant architect, Bernard Feilden, became uneasy. He had "reservations from the aesthetic point of view", since Feilden and Foster had "two differing philosophies of architecture".[42] Feilden had specific objections. He had been appointed "to humanize the University as left to me by Lasdun", but he felt that Foster's building ran counter to this policy.[43] The County and City planning authorities might create planning difficulties because of the large scale of the building, which might be regarded as intrusive in the Yare Valley. "The layman will imagine that Norman's building is like the large agricultural buildings with its tubular shape."[44] Moreover, since most of the building was single storey, its volume of space was out of proportion to its floor surface, which would entail high energy and air conditioning costs. Such a length of metallic construction would need expansion joints which would leak, the cladding would streak and discolour. Feilden saw it as a high-cost short-life building with problems and an intrusive aesthetic. In brief, while Feilden was happy to remain consultant architect for the rest of the University, he wanted to withdraw from responsibility for the SCVA.[45] In practice the SCVA and Lasdun buildings juxtapose interestingly. While Norman Foster is reputed to dislike concrete,[46] Sir Denys regards the relation of the buildings as "a Rolls Royce next to a citadel". The motor car analogy was apt since Volvo used the SCVA in its advertising in 1990, to suggest high-tech futurism.

Another problem was soaring costs. Between the announcement of the gift in November 1973 and the opening of the building in April 1978 there was sharp inflation as prices virtually doubled, halving the value of the money part of the gift. Aware of this and the threat to the building, David Sainsbury added 286,464 Sainsbury shares (worth about £450-500,000) to the endowment fund for the SCVA. David's sister Annabel in the next year gave £120,000 towards the building as a result of which the costs of the walkway entrance, spiral staircase and part of the foyer are regarded as having been met by her generosity.

The costs of the enterprise were very worrying and constantly shifting. The original assumption of Sainsbury's £3,000,000 gift was that the building would cost £1,500,000. By July 1975 Gordon Marshall thought that the total cost of the building would be £3,244,000.[47] By November 1975, on the eve of building, it was reckoned as £3,295,000,[48] and by 30 June 1976 when the building was underway, at £3,515,000: more than the entire original gift, even absorbing the endowment element. By December 1977, when the building was nearly finished, the building cost £4,032,397, including over £3,000,000 from the Sainsburys and £632,000 from the UGC.[49] Sir Robert Sainsbury was resigned to paying for the insurance and conservation out of his own pocket, the endowment element having vanished. Sir Robert made it clear that he could no longer subsidise the School of Fine Arts, SCR or restaurant element, which was covered by the UGC. As the costs soared he observed "it looks as if there will be very little of my son's original £3,000,000 left to form an endowment fund".[50] The recurrent annual running costs were estimated at £126,700, but these would fall on the UGC rather than the Sainsburys.[51]

So much money was put into this project by the Sainsbury family between 1973 and 1976 that for clarity it is worth setting this out here:[52]

1. 570 works of art worth about £5,000,000 in 1976, possibly worth ten times as much in 2000.
2. The original endowment of £3,000,000 given by David Sainsbury 26 November 1973.
3. £93,171, the interest on £3,000,000 between the time it was set aside and the date of the gift.
4. 286,000 J. Sainsbury shares given by David Sainsbury on 10 November 1975, then valued at £1,500,000.
5. £50,000 to the cost of the building from the Robert and Lisa Sainsbury Charitable Fund April 1976.
6. £120,000 given by Annabel Sainsbury, now Mrs Peter Kanabus, August 1977.
7. £632,000 contributed by the UGC towards the costs of building.
8. £25,000 paid by Sir Robert Sainsbury towards the costs of the opening ceremony in April 1978.

This £4,395,171 just about covered the £4,200,000 costs of the building. Norman Foster, referring to objective quantity surveyors' calculations, regarded the gross costs of the building as very reasonable. The costs per square metre of the Burrell Gallery in Glasgow were £650, of the Museum of London £570, of the National Gallery extension £900, all of which were high compared with the £375 of the SCVA. Handscombes estimated that without furniture, fittings and fees the SCVA, "was a £2,800,000 project" and its metre cubic space costs "dramatically low".[53]

What did the University get for the money? A rectangle, 403 feet in length, 114 feet wide and 33 feet high, like a slender silver cigarette box or aircraft hangar. Structurally it is of steel with anodised aluminium cladding panels sealed with neoprene gaskets. The original aluminium cladding panels are no longer there since they began to be corroded by the layer of insulating phenolic foam. These were replaced in 1987 by new aluminium panels with inert rockwool insulation which have served well since.[54] There is a double-skin wall within which the services are housed. Inside there is a ground floor area of 46,013 square feet with two mezzanine floors of 9295 square feet. One of the mezzanines was originally used for the SCR, the other as a display and study area. The greater part of the ground floor is for the display of the Sainsbury collection in free-standing cabinets or on screens allowing a three-dimensional observation of the objects. There is also a separate gallery for special and visiting exhibitions. The internal walls are not intended to bear the weight of paintings as in most galleries. An interesting consequence of this was that when Lady Albemarle offered thirteen ancestral portraits to UEA in 1979 they had to be declined, since there was nowhere in the SCVA to hang them. The north west of the building is a restaurant, for University and public use, with stunning views through plate glass windows to grass and woodland. It was the Vice-Chancellor's idea to have the outside area illuminated so that people attending a dinner in the SCVA at night could enjoy the outlook through the glass to a sylvan theatrical stage set. Under snow the aspect is magical.

Between the restaurant, kitchen and the collection is the academic area of the former School of Fine Arts, now School of World Art Studies and Museology. This contains the studies of the faculty and the 90,000 slides and 180,000 photographs for teaching. At the south-east end of the building is the reception area, sales desk, a conservatory of hydroponic plants and the Gallery café. Visits were made to major galleries in England and Holland and it was concluded that it was essential for the SCVA to have shop and café facilities.[55] The reception area can be entered either at the ground level or from a link between the concrete walkway and an interior spiral staircase leading elegantly down from the wall to the ground. Underneath the whole length of the building is a basement for the storing and conservation of art works, entered by a large loading bay and ramp. This basement is remarkable. Buckminster Fuller, the famous American architect, visited the SCVA and asked how *heavy* the whole building was. Foster calculated that the above ground building weighed 1000 tons out of a total of 4000 tons. The basement was 8 per cent of the volume but 80 per cent of the weight and the basement cost two thirds of the whole.[56] Nonetheless, museum experts regard the basement storage space as rather too small in proportion. At the south-eastern end of the building is an area for visiting exhibitions and this south-eastern end is, like the north-western, terminated by a huge plate-glass window giving an aspect out onto the Broad.

A most remarkable interior feature of the SCVA is the regulation of light by louvred blinds which adjust automatically to exterior sunlight conditions. The first Director, Alan Borg (later Director of the Imperial War and Victoria and Albert Museums) described it:

The main south east window and the roof are covered by louvred blinds which are adjustable and automatic. A predetermined light level can therefore be maintained with the movement of the blinds controlled by light sensors . . . Natural light is combined with a highly sophisticated artificial lighting system designed by George Sexton . . . all the lights are in the roof space, where concord tracks allow an almost infinite variety of fittings and several point sources can be trained on an individual object.[57]

George Sexton's design of layout and lighting was crucial to the success of the building. It focused attention on the small objects and prevented their being overwhelmed by the open space of the huge interior.

The SCVA was described as "a remarkably elegant functional building, the equivalent of the early industrial revolution sheds, warehouses etc".[58] This was a perceptive observation. The Centre was in effect a great shed or envelope to house the collection and its attendant activities. The impressive use of the railway station shed, as in the Musée d'Orsay in Paris, lay a few years in the future, while Toni Garnier's magnificent nineteenth-century slaughterhouse in Lyons was already being used for artistic displays. The great shed, in contrast to the palatial suites of enclosed rooms of Victorian art galleries, is an exciting new form. The SCVA is sometimes described as a sophisticated aircraft hangar.[59] Indeed Norman Foster, a keen pilot, usually arrived at UEA by helicopter and the SCVA foreshadows his later design of Stansted Airport. The hangar analogy was reflected in a rumour current at the time. It was said that the Russians had detected the Centre by spy satellite. Its hangar design and its mysterious underground delivery ramp, whose entrance was masked by a wood, aroused their suspicions that it was a missile site. They asked to come and inspect it. If the story is a myth, it is certainly *ben trovato*. True but equally bizarre the almost flat roof needs regular cleaning for unforeseeable reasons. Rubbish collects there, not only leaves but stones and piles of old bones and fishing tackle dropped by seagulls flying overhead after feeding trips in the nearby Broad.[60]

The building is spectacular but easily overlooked is the way in which it is complemented by landscape gardening. This was by one of the most distin- guished practitioners, Lanning Roper.[61] Roper was the garden consultant for the National Trust and did much private work for clients including the Sainsburys. Undergrowth was cleared, major trees brought to prominence and flowers planted. But most remarkably the surrounding area was contoured (to half inch levels) to relate the building to the slope of the valley and the Broad. Yet again Cyril Loynes, the bulldozer driver who had worked for Denys Lasdun, used his skill. The perfect reflection of the light from the south-east windows of the SCVA in the Broad was the carefully calculated result of this work, an effect disturbed by the subsequent creation of the Crescent Wing under the slope.

The quality of the building has been recognised in many ways. It won the RIBA award in 1978 when Gordon Graham, the President of the RIBA, described it as "one of the three most outstanding buildings created this century".[62] In the same year it won the Finniston Award for Structural Steel Design. In 1979 it gathered a British Tourist Board Award and the R.S. Reynolds Award, the leading American accolade. Foster was the only architect in the twenty-two years of the Reynolds Prize to have won it twice, the first time for his Willis Faber building in 1976. In 1980 the SCVA was named Museum of the Year. The overall importance of the architecture at UEA following the acquisition of the SCVA was recognised internationally in 1979 when, in that year, the New York Museum of Modern Art held a very important exhibition on the best world architecture of the last two decades. Seven British university buildings were selected – three from Cambridge, two from Leicester and two from UEA, the Lasdun buildings and the SCVA.[63] In 1984 the SCVA was voted one of the world's top buildings in a poll of fifty-eight architects conducted by the *Illustrated London News*. Durham Cathedral, the winner, received five votes, the SCVA three – without the vote of Norman Foster who, as one of the judges, modestly did not vote for himself.[64] This was an astonishingly distinguished position architecturally for a new university to have achieved in a mere thirteen years.

Not everything was perfect. Most immediately the Fine Arts faculty felt that their personal accommodation was inadequate. Andrew Martindale tried to uphold the interests of his department and complained of the rooms, lack of light, ventilation or privacy. Also at 8 feet x 20 feet they were too small for teaching and smaller than those they were leaving. In all Martindale thought that his School's accommodation had "been very drastically compromised in the interests of an imaginative grandiose overall architectural concept".[65] Certainly to the outsider there does seem an incongruity between the lavish space of all the other parts of the building and the cramped quarters of the academics who work there. The problem was that these academic areas had to be financed by the UGC and, with the extraordinary inflation eroding the value of the £3,000,000 gift, Sir Robert Sainsbury was not able to cross-subsidise the teaching and administrative areas as he might have hoped. There were other problems. As a minor matter, Foster thought in retrospect that he could have designed the cladding panels to be less monotonous and a "richer mix".[66] The spiral staircase from the linking walkway proved too weak and had to be strengthened. But this should not detract from what is a splendid building, still genuinely exciting in the manner of a great railway station or airport.

The SCVA was formally opened in the first week of April 1978. There was a series of private views over three days during which a thousand guests came

to the Centre – artists, architects, collectors, scholars, journalists and representatives of universities and arts organisations and galleries. Uniquely, the
entire Sainsbury collection was on display at the same time. A private train
transported guests from Liverpool Street Station. Sir Robert was much
moved. He told Frank Thistlethwaite, "if before any of this started, someone
had told me that I would one day – as I did on Saturday evening – stand in a
building containing our collection and be completely happy in all respects, I
would have said it was not on – this semi miracle has in fact happened and I
really could not be myself more thrilled".[67] The University expressed its gratitude by according the degrees of Hon. Litt.D. to Sir Robert in 1977 and to
Lady Sainsbury in 1990.

There was some expression of dissent at the opening which raised legitimate issues. The Students Union objected to £10,000 being allocated by the
Council to the costs of the opening, £25,000 of which was borne personally by
Sir Robert. More seriously there was an apprehension that the running costs
of the building would fall on the University. They were of course supposed to
be covered by an unspecified part of the UGC block grant. But since this was
not itemised it could never be known either way. Some feared that "the
Centre is likely to run at a considerable loss which will further cripple university finances and lead to even larger cuts in existing staff facilities.[68] In practice the Vice-Chancellor was not anxious that the SCVA was a drain in his
day, as the block grant seemed to have met it, but the UGC accounting practices of those days made it impossible to prove – which gave a lever to critics.
More widely there did seem to be an incongruity between the increasing cuts
imposed on the University (and all universities) on the academic side and
UEA's owning and running a lavish building devoted to a multi-million
pound art collection.[69] There was no possible trade-off here. There was no
question of Sainsbury money being transferred to worthy pursuits like scientific research or student sport, nor of money being drained from the latter for
the Sainsburys' collection, which was a pure gain to the University. It would
have been unthinkable not to receive it and enjoy it. Sir Robert accepted the
protesting flysheet in good humour as he entered the building on his great
day.

The SCVA then embarked on its everyday life. Gordon Marshall, the
Estates Officer, became General Manager and Dr Alan Borg was appointed
Keeper. Borg was Assistant Keeper of Armouries at the Tower of London and
hence could claim to be moving from the oldest to the newest museum in the
country. He was a product of Oxford and the Courtauld Institute and had
taught at various universities including Princeton before taking up his post at
the Tower in 1970, moving to the SCVA in June 1978.[70] The Centre was run by
an SCVA Board set up on 1 August 1977 and responsible to the Council. There

were also the Trustees of the Sainsbury Purchasing Fund who would assume the purchasing powers on the death of Sir Robert Sainsbury. Both the Board and the Trustees were responsible to the Council of the University. Sir Robert sat on the Board but legally could not be a trustee of his own fund.[71]

There were teething troubles in public access to the gallery. Sir Robert had originally wanted a limit of only six groups of six people in the art collection at any one time. This was rather unrealistic since to have had a maximum of only thirty-six visitors in the building would have made the staffing, book-shop and catering quite uneconomic.[72] Sainsbury's original intention was that there should be no entrance fee, in which case entrance numbers would be immaterial. Sir Robert accepted the economic argument and agreed to a two hundred person limit in the exhibition area and an entrance fee of 25p.[73] Another contentious matter was the admission of children. Children over five were originally charged full price. Then, within a few days of the opening, children under twelve were denied entry altogether. This aroused much bad feeling locally and adverse press comment.[74] Accordingly in June this decision was reversed and children were allowed in at weekends. With these sensible adjustments, and stimulated by great media interest and publicity, 28,000 people came to the SCVA to see the Sainsbury Collection between April and August 1978.[75] Yet there remains the problem of reconciling the aims of wide public access but providing an experience of quiet contemplative enjoyment. This is so for all major museums and galleries and not special to the SCVA.

The SCVA was keen to create good relations with the City and region. To this end Frank Thistlethwaite asked Lady Zuckerman to form the Friends of the Sainsbury Centre and become its chairman.[76] The Friends were to "support encourage and assist the activities and development of the SCVA".[77] The fifty members already in the Corps of Guides would prove a useful basis. Daphne Powlett became the Secretary and Malcolm Freegard the Vice-Chairman. At their inaugural meeting on 2 February 1980 they recruited 150 friends, paying an annual membership fee of £4. For this they could attend special social events, though it was not intended that they would be involved in fund-raising; indeed they were not expected to interfere at all. Sir Norman Reid, the former Director of the Tate Gallery, in a witty speech at the inaugural meeting gave a gentle warning, "I have several times contemplated founding a group of Enemies [of the Tate] as the only effective means of keeping our Friends in order". Mercifully, this has not proved necessary at the SCVA. The SCVA also sought to appeal to a wider constituency by the use of social space in the Centre. A trial concert by the Aeolian Quartet in the conservatory on 9 March 1979 was a success and it was agreed to allow the use of the conservatory for concerts. But its use was tightly controlled by the

Vice-Chancellor and restricted to events connected with the fine arts under the aegis of the University.[78]

It was hoped that the prestige of the Sainsbury Collection would attract other gifts. In June 1978 Sir Colin and Lady Anderson gave their collection of Art Nouveau to the SCVA. Sir Colin was a director of various shipping companies, including P & O, and banks, including the Midland.[79] His passion was in the world of arts as Chairman of the Trustees of the Tate Gallery, a trustee of the National Gallery and Provost of the Royal College of Art. He had attended the opening of the SCVA only two months earlier and must have almost immediately decided to leave his own collection to UEA. This consisted of 120 pieces, including mainly French furniture by Gallé and Majorelle, glass and ceramics by Tiffany and Lalique, and most forms of Art Nouveau.[80] For those who appreciate the rather severe modernist forms of many of the Sainsbury pieces the subtly swirling lines of Art Nouveau are an interesting contrast. Art Nouveau was not the Sainsburys' taste but the long straight lines of the surrounding building offset both.

The Centre also attracted sculpture from Henry Moore, whose early patron Sir Robert Sainsbury had been. The building is surrounded by three pieces. Both east and west windows look out onto one while a third is placed on the north front. Two are part of the Sainsbury Collection and the third is on indefinite loan from the Tate. Moore came in person to the Centre in October 1978, along with Sir Robert and Norman Foster. Moore sited his sculptures by looking at full-size silhouettes in different locations from different angles. They came to be absorbed into the landscape over the years, though two were relocated when the Crescent Wing was built.

For Sir Robert Sainsbury the transfer of his collection to the SCVA was a major change though, after the initial show of the entire Collection, a part would always be retained at his home in Smith Square before recirculating back to Norwich.[81] He could not help remaining passionately involved with his objects and the SCVA which housed it. There were some matters over which Sainsbury was unhappy: he had wanted all visitors to the Collection to be in groups under the supervision of guides, which proved impracticable, and he took exception to an advertising poster, postcards and a catering brochure. He decided to withdraw from the management of the SCVA in which he had remained perhaps too close in ways which conflicted with the duties of the Keeper and General Manager. In 1979, however, there was a serious difference between Sainsbury and Gordon Marshall over air-conditioning. The original design of the SCVA had not incorporated air-conditioning, the volume of air space being so large, but the stifling heat of the summer of 1978 prompted reappraisal. Sir Robert generously offered to pay for air-conditioning but Gordon Marshall resisted it on the grounds that it was unnecessary and would add soaringly to the running costs which would fall on the University. Sir Robert's deep attachment to the building and his collection culminated in his proposal that Norman Foster should build a house on the campus near the Centre in which the Sainsburys could stay during their visits.[82] The security aspects of an elderly multi-millionaire living on campus in an unprotected house surrounded by priceless art treasures caused deep unease. The fears of kidnap, burglary, student occupation and strains on the University security system were but the most obvious problems, so Sir Robert was dissuaded from his plan. Some regret that the University did not take the opportunity of having a Norman Foster house on the site for use by distinguished visitors in the Sainsburys' absence. In spite of these difficulties the Sainsburys' generosity continued to enhance the work of the Centre. He established the Sainsbury Studentships financed by the Sainsbury Art Trust. These started in October 1979, worth £3000 a year each and the first named, privately endowed research studentships the University had received.[83]

As well as the Sainsbury financial contribution, the UGC met recurrent costs. In 1976 these had been estimated at £126,700 a year. This fell on the University and ultimately on the UGC and at their 1979 visitation the UGC suggested that the University should seek direct government support of the SCVA.[84] In 1978 Sir Arthur Drew's report on museums suggested that certain major museums like the Ashmolean and the Fitzwilliam should be supported with grants direct from the government, since they served the interests of the public beyond their university communities.[85] The SCVA surely fell into this category. The Secretary of State for Education (Shirley Williams when the report was published, Mark Carlisle from May 1979) had not decided what to do about the Drew Report, but it was a possible source of finance for the future. But up to 1980 the SCVA was still dependent on the block grant and the Vice-Chancellor had no unease that it was damaging to the rest of the University's finances.

The creation of the Sainsbury Centre was a splendid combined achievement. The extent of Sainsbury generosity was remarkable. Inflation and the passage of time has tended to dull awareness of this. But the £3,000,000 endowment provided by David Sainsbury would by 2000 be worth £20,000,000 and the value of the collection was valued at £40-50,000,000 in 1994 and much more now (2000). The objects have increased from about 600 in 1978 to over 1400. The money called forth creativity – the architectural skills of Norman Foster and Foster Associates, the structural engineering of Tony Hunt,[86] and the design imaginations of Kho Liang Ie and George Sexton and Lanning Roper the landscape designer. The University provided the land, the administrative skills of Gordon Marshall and Alan Borg, and the expertise of the academics of the School of Fine Arts under Andrew Martindale. The School became one of the top three art history departments in the country with a rare Grade 5 in the UGC research assessments. At the heart of the enterprise was the friendship of Sir Robert Sainsbury and Frank Thistlethwaite, a friendship that happily survived as Thistlethwaite was delighted to attend Lady Sainsbury's eightieth birthday celebrations in Kew Gardens in 1992. It was the combination of all these elements that made the SCVA a significant institution that added lustre to the Sainsbury name and transformed the public image of UEA.

The Street looking towards the Square
(*J. M. Kingsley-Lewis*)

9

The End of the Beginning

When I was recruited it was as a kind of academic impresario, charged with putting a new sort of show on the road. Now I find myself a sort of educational politician, holding prime office in a very unstable kind of political system.[1]

Frank Thistlethwaite, 26 August 1972

Following the period of troubles, the University embarked on an optimistic decade in the 1970s. The Vice-Chancellor led various moves to help stabilise the situation and present a positive image of the University. In December 1971 he played the Mozart double piano concerto with Philip Ledger and the University orchestra. He then took sabbatical leave for two terms in 1972-73 (including visits to Africa, France and the USA). On his return he made some positive speeches reviewing the first decade of the University, stressing that the plan "has worked very well" and foreseeing new Schools of Electronics, Computing and Law to meet demands for more relevance from the University.[2] He also reminded the Norwich community not only of the public services provided by the University but of the £1,800,000 (1970) rising to £3,000,000 (1973) annually with which it enriched the regional economy.[3] It was a point worth reiterating more at the time. Behind the scenes the Vice-Chancellor undertook a series of private dinners for local business and professional leaders enabling them to see the University and meet senior professors, keeping in touch with individuals and firms who gave to the Appeal in the early days. Timothy Colman, who helped to organise the guest lists, told Thistlethwaite that "this type of entertainment will be very benefi-cial to the University generally".[4] Scarcely less important, the Vice-Chancellor kept up good social relationships with a whole range of student politicians, sportsmen and actors invited to Wood Hall for drinks in the drawing room and croquet on the lawn.[5] Beneath the surface UEA was also particularly generous to its students. Its spending on student support services was among the highest of the "new" universities in the 1970s and far higher than the national average. It all helped to create a more optimistic mood in the University in the 1970s and easier relations with the student body.[6]

The 1970s began with some plans negotiated between the University, the CVCP and the UGC. The CVCP foresaw the need for 450,000 university places in Great Britain by 1981, a doubling of student numbers over the decade. On the other hand, they admitted that there would be difficulty in providing resources for higher education proportionate to this increase. Consequently this expansion would only be achieved by accepting reductions in the amount spent on each student in the 1970s. This in turn might be achieved by the substitution of grants by loans, part-time and correspondence courses, two year degrees, four term years and more students living at home. There might be savings arising from economies of scale but it was admitted that nothing was likely to yield sufficient savings as much as deteriorating staff student ratios.[7] It raised a number of issues that were to shape thinking in the 1970s.

UEA had already begun some planning under Peter Hill, the Professor of Economics. He noted that the number of eighteen year olds would rise sharply from 649,000 in 1974 to 798,000 by 1980. But of these there was likely to be a near doubling of those who gained three A levels, from 50,000 in 1972 to 90,000 by 1982. He foresaw that UEA would have to expand faster than the average, since it had potential capacity and surrounding space.[8] Most of this expansion was likely, however, to be in the arts and social studies because that is where the largest demand and the students with the best A levels were to be found. This was partly associated with the rapid increase of girls taking A levels in arts subjects. He saw no evidence of a swing back to science or any expectation of an ample supply of science students. Hill predicted a second major university expansion in the mid to late 1970s and concluded that "UEA should plan to expand as fast as it considers desirable . . . without worrying in the slightest whether or not the supply of qualified students is going to be available".[9]

On the basis of this, the Senate replied to the CVCP document drawing out its implications for UEA. They accepted that providing university education for all on the present basis would be too costly. But they "saw no merit in resisting expansion", since UEA could absorb 5000 students. Indeed they felt powerless to resist expansion but drew attention to the "dangerous implications of doubling numbers on the cheap". The most serious implication they well recognised was a deterioration of the staff student ratio which would have adverse effects on seminar size and small group teaching, research time, and contact with students.[10] UEA replied to the CVCP on these lines, "that UEA may expand very considerably" though pointing out the adverse effects, not least of which would be the fact that a large expansion of the output of graduates would create a "national slump in graduate employment"; but that was a governmental, not a UEA, concern.[11] The 1970s thus began with a mixture of moods. There was the excitement of challenge which the demands for further expansion presented. It was also gratifying that these continued demands seemed to validate the expansion of the 1960s which had called institutions like UEA into being. Yet such positive sentiments were modified by unease that expansion could be overdone and would carry costs in terms of the maintenance of standards.

Some detailed planning was already being done by the Academic Planning Working Party sitting from 1967-69 and looking forward into the seventies.[12] They floated ideas for a School of Medicine, suggesting that the West Norwich Hospital be rebuilt on land adjacent to the Plain (presaging, by thirty years, developments of the late 1990s). Professor Katritzky proposed a School of Molecular Technology, dealing with materials science. Schools of Management Technology and Law were likewise advanced – both of which eventually came about. Professor J.W. McFarlane arguing that most of the expansion would be on the arts side (for lack of scientists coming from sixth forms), suggested studies in comparative literature, later created, and an imaginative School of Liberal Science to draw arts students into scientific thinking, which never was.[13]

UEA was accordingly well prepared for the UGC letter which asked UEA to expand to 4650 students by 1976, with 500 more arts students than scientists.[14] The UGC admitted that nationally staff student ratios would deteriorate to 1 : 8.5 in the 1972-77 period but fairly pointed out that it had been 1 : 8.1 in 1957/9 (the same as 1969/70). Ratios had in fact been extraordinarily favourable at 1 : 7.6 in the 1963-66 period when the new universities were starting up. So the deterioration of the 1970s, much foreseen and feared, was only a slight deterioration from the 1950s, not such a headlong decline as the impression was sometimes given. The UGC envisaged a "large expansion" in Social Studies which suited UEA very well. Otherwise the UGC was cool about UEA's plans. It thought there was no need for business and management studies since there was a lack of university teachers in the subject. The demand for Russian, to which UEA had made a serious commitment, was small. In fact Russian was by far the easiest subject nationally in which to obtain university entrance in the late 1960s, suggesting an over ample supply of places to applicants.[15] Computing too would be held up by a shortage of high-level research workers in the field while law was a matter for future consideration with no immediate prospect. The UGC wanted UEA to expand with more of the same but the University's attempts at fresh curricular thinking were nugatory in the early seventies.

This was a pity in the light of future job prospects for students. The Appointments Officer, seeing little prospect of expanding careers in government, industry, commerce, the professions and arts subject teaching, urged the need for vocational schools of engineering, medicine, law, and business management – precisely the expensive areas which the UGC had closed off from expansion as far as UEA was concerned.[16] Professor Peter Hill took a totally sanguine view. UEA should expand as fast as possible in the 1970s "without worrying whether or not the supply of students will be forthcoming and without trying to match supply and demand – either the demand for university places or the demand for employers for student output".[17]

So the wish to expand continued. In 1976 the Vice-Chancellor foresaw that UEA would be a likely "choice for growth", since it had spare capacity and it needed to introduce more vocational and applied subjects to balance the curriculum – contrary to the intentions of the UGC in the early part of the decade.[18] This was prescient, since in the next year the UGC proposed a target of 4900 students by 1990-91, which was in line with UEA'S own strategic plan of 5000 by the end of the decade. This would entail a 30 per cent increase in UEA's numbers in four years, compared with a national anticipated increase of three per cent.[19] By 1978 the target had been raised again to 5000 by 1981-82, one of the highest increases of any university in the country.[20] As part of this expansion it was envisaged that accountancy, urban studies and psychology would be introduced. The freeze on new posts which had been introduced in the financial crisis of 1975 was to be lifted to make the expansion possible.[21]

These much-publicised developments heartened the University but caused some unease in the city. As early as 1973 Sir Edmund Bacon was expressing concern that an expanding UEA was going to exceed its planning permissions, and it was going to unbalance Norwich by having too many people employed by one industry (the University) and this risked a certain amount of anti-UEA feeling.[22] Questions were raised concerning where the extra 1500 students were to live. The city was clear that there were not enough lodgings, possibly only 500 extra, to cope with them. The University would have to build more residences itself and it was criticised for not having made plans for more residences or discussing the implications with the city. It was piquant that three of the City Councillors most critical of the situation were themselves connected with the University – Patricia Hollis, chair of the Housing Committee, Michael Ashley, a lecturer in SOC, and Valerie Guttsman, the wife of the Librarian.[23]

The expansion from 3367 students in 1975/6 to 4114 by 1980/1 did take place and the UGC visitation on 27-28 February 1979 congratulated the University on achieving this. But no further expansion was envisaged. The UGC tone was cautious. The University was urged that thinking of a School of Technology was " unwise" though some electronics might be done under the umbrella of physics. Nor should archaeology be contemplated. In an interesting hint the UGC thought that UEA's attitude to the staff student ratio was "rigid" and "inflexible", implying that more students could be taken in to be taught by fewer staff.[24] The UGC was right to be cautious since in May 1979 the Labour government was replaced by the Conservatives under Margaret Thatcher. In her analysis, excessive public spending was a key factor in Britain's poor economic performance. Severe cuts would have to be imposed, with higher education bearing its part. Memories of the troubles and the hostile reception of Keith Joseph on his speaking tours of universities did not endear the universities to the incoming government. Joseph had visited Norwich in November 1976 and had received a rough reception at UEA, having just come from a meeting with businessmen in the city at which he had already promised tax and public expenditure cuts.[25]

The promise was delivered in 1979, as the June budget of that year cut £30,000,000 from higher education. In October the UGC letter confirmed that there would be no increase in university funding in real terms "for a number of years" and foreign students would have to pay the full cost of their courses. The Expenditure White Paper in November 1979 cut educational expenditure for 1980-81 and specifically £12,000,000 from universities.[26] The UGC was clear that there would be fewer new places in universities in the coming years in sharp contrast to the expansion of the late 1970s.

Frank Thistlethwaite, reflecting some years later, saw underlying weaknesses which had left the universities vulnerable to cuts, culminating in the sharp policy change of 1979. In the mid 1960s responsibility for university finances and the UGC passed from the Treasury to the Secretary of State for Education and Science, "what had once been a sub-budget was now a large, eye-catching sum in the Parliamentary estimates" open to attack.[27] Secondly, the UGC, which had operated a system of quinquennial block grants, could not defend itself; the universities had no effective collective voice and believed too much in "cosy, confidential words to Ministers and Permanent Secretaries". Thirdly, the CVCP was ineffective. Frank Thistlethwaite himself had been part of a ginger group trying to vivify it but "we made very little headway". In sum, the universities "had no political clout".[28] The refusal to take seriously Shirley Williams' 1969 proposals for economy, and a seeming inability to curb student unrest, had alienated the universities from likely supportive constituencies. So over a three year period support for the universities was cut by 15 per cent and by 1983 two thousand academic staff were lost. It brought to an end the whole Robbins era.[29]

UEA responded by suspending its 1979-80 estimates. Far from continuing the expansion, the UGC in August 1979 advised a 6 per cent cut in student numbers.[30] A freeze on new appointments was reimposed as estimates for the deficit UEA might face ranged from £30,000 immediately to £781,000 by 1984.[31] The students held a one day strike in protest at the cuts and a brief occupation of the Registry, but with no expectation of influencing matters.[32]

Both the students and University were especially concerned about the new requirement that overseas students would have to pay full fees. Overseas students made up about 12 per cent of British university students at that time. The UGC now required all universities to cut back their overseas students to 93 per cent of their 1975/6 total. This would affect UEA, which was then embarking on growth with a small proportion of overseas students which would become even smaller. The arguments in favour of overseas students were familiar: they enhanced the academic and cultural life of the community; they created good will for Britain among future elites in emerging countries; and cemented connections with the Commonwealth to which we had moral obligations. Even if the subsidy to their fees had been £1500 a year, each student brought in £1740 in foreign currency.[33] The new policies would entail charging overseas students £3500 a year, three times the existing level. Frank Thistlethwaite felt the matter keenly since he had been personally involved with East African universities and the establishment of the University of Zambia. Taking a wider view, he reminded the House of Commons Foreign Affairs Committee that Britain had developed a close network of forty universities in twenty countries in Africa and South East Asia, initially starting universities and now helping them with graduate training.[34] All this would be jeopardised.

Amid the high politics of surges of growth and disappointing cutbacks that marked the 1970s, the University did not lose sight of the fact that its main purpose was an academic one. And here development and diversification remained impressive. The School of English and American Studies continued to flourish. New initiatives enriched the curriculum. The MA in creative writing began in 1971 and the first graduates in comparative literature were produced in the same year. After some delay both Film Studies and Drama began in 1976/7, the former under Charles Barr from the British Film Institute. Theatre Studies began with Julian Hilton and Tony Gash. Hilton combined a first class degree in English from Oxford with practical experience at Covent Garden, Munich Opera House and in German TV. He came from a theatrical family, Jack Hylton the band leader being his uncle while his father was Chairman of the Adelphi Theatre. Tony Gash similarly combined a first class degree with training at RADA. This combination of academic excellence with practical vocational experience was a healthy new strain much needed by UEA. A theatre was essential for such studies and, at a cost of £40,000, the Hall and stage area in the Village were reconstructed and properly fitted.[35] The editorship of the prestigious journal *Theatre Quarterly* also came to UEA.

The general vitality of the School was enhanced by two new scholars who came to the University in this decade. Paul Kennedy in 1970 and Harry Allen in 1971. Kennedy was one of the most distinguished historians ever to pass through UEA. His remarkable output of seven books and thirty-five articles in the 1970s was already establishing the international reputation that was to take him to the Dilworth Professorship at Yale. No narrow selfish careerist, he was a devout Roman Catholic and gave valuable time to private charitable work with the St Vincent de Paul Society. He even had a shadowy minor career as a racing journalist and tipster. His extremely energetic lifestyle was masked by a genuinely modest unassuming charm and UEA rightly honoured him with an Honorary Litt.D. in 1994. Harry Allen, by contrast, came to UEA at the end of his career, already distinguished as a pioneer of American studies and as a Second World War infantry officer with an MC. He held the Chair of American History at University College London and was Director of the Institute of United States Studies. While Professor of American History at UEA, he also served as Chairman of the British and European Associations for American Studies in the 1970s.[36] The energy of such scholars were but part of the ferment of EAS at this time with history, literature, drama, film and linguistics, both English and American. Indeed in Allen's deanship of 1973-76 some forty books were produced by EAS and then ten alone 1979-80. It was not surprising that, when all the other departments of English in Britain were asked in 1976 which they rated the best in their subject, 4.2 per cent cited UEA – the only university outside Oxford, Cambridge or London to be cited for English and the only UEA School to receive this national peer recognition.[37]

Closely linked with EAS in its historical aspects was the Centre of East Anglian Studies under the direction of Hassell Smith and Keith Clayton. This continued its policy of studying aspects of the city and region from different disciplinary viewpoints. Central to the decade was the Norwich Survey directed by Alan Carter, with the support of the City of Norwich and the Department of the Environment, which uncovered the archaeology and medieval manuscript sources of the early history of Norwich. Their discovery of 800 timber-framed buildings and fourteen tons of pottery gives some indication of the scale of the survey. Also on the historical side a transcription was made of the Bacon Manuscripts in the Norfolk and Norwich Record Office, resulting in the presentation to Sir Edmund Bacon of the published papers of Nathaniel Bacon of Stiffkey in 1979. A record was also made of all the surviving medieval stained glass in Norfolk and Suffolk, while a major bibliography of Norfolk history was compiled and published. The strength of CEAS was that it studied not only history but economic and geographical aspects. Morgan Sant ran an important project on the location and movement of industry in the region in conjunction with economists in SOC. There was also one on rural transport and accessibility and another on Norfolk tourism. Such studies brought CEAS into the sphere of regional policy analysis and consultancy. The CEAS advised the East Anglian Regional Planning Board and the Regional Strategy Team, while CEAS's Chairman Lord Walston (following Michael Riviere) was also Chairman of the East Anglian Economic Planning Council. [38] Under Keith Clayton, the director from 1973, historical and economic interests were joined by his own environmental geographic concerns. As the Norwich Survey finished so it was succeeded by a Department of Environment financed study of the East Anglian coast with voluntary "wave watchers" mapping the movement of sand and shingle and the "coastal budget" of erosion and accretion.

CEAS, however, had a fundamental problem concerning the finance of its projects. They depended on specific outside sponsors, governmental and charitable, but it was difficult to get funds for projects where the project leader was not already being paid a salary by his university. Yet CEAS had a shortage of staff on tenured university contracts who could make such applications. It was necessary for CEAS researchers also to be teachers on UEA salaries. This led to another problem, For example Paul Ashbee, a research archaeologist, taught courses on his subject. The UGC, while welcoming the work of CEAS, nonetheless hoped that "it would not be used as the thin end of a wedge to introduce an undergraduate course in archaeology".[39] In practice this was disregarded, as it had to be. There already were courses in archaeology and even UEA graduates getting jobs in archaeology on the strength of them in the 1970s. These were lively days for CEAS when it was genuinely multidisciplinary in character, with deans from arts and sciences and having a direct input not only into teaching but into the wider world of regional policy making.

The School of European Studies, work lay in the history, literature and languages of Germany, Russia, France, and distinctively, Scandinavia. Their problem for most of the early 1970s was a declining interest among schoolchildren in learning European languages, inappropriately coinciding with Britain's entry into Europe. It was also feared that the rather general title of the School did not indicate that language teaching was one of its major concerns. So the School restyled itself as the School of Modern Languages and European History in 1978-79. At a stroke this increased student applications after seven barren years. To emphasise the language aspect new courses were started in translating and interpreting. There were closer links with the Bell School of Languages in Norwich, with their tutors becoming honorary members of EUR. Although there was a diminishing interest in English students learning European languages, there was a reciprocal development in the contrary direction. Many students came from abroad to learn English –

Germans through DAAD (the German Academic Exchange) and French from the law department of Aix-en-Provence. For lack of hard-core language specialist students new options were created with minors in SOC, comparative literature combining English and European literatures (mostly in translation), and "joker" lecturers (as they were called) in sociology and classical history. The Comparative Literature initiative led to a large conference at UEA which founded the British Association for Comparative Literature, which "gained international recognition for UEA as a centre of comparative literary studies in Britain". Indeed it was the only undergraduate course in the country. Yet it raised questions of whether it was an appropriate study at first degree level, especially in an institution with difficulties in finding enough students with language skills in one foreign language let alone those needed for comparative work.

European history thrived and indeed claimed to have more research students than any university outside Oxford, Cambridge or London. The quality of EUR faculty was high, eight achieving chairs at other universities, including A.G. Cross and R.J. Evans at Cambridge. Especially noteworthy was Professor James McFarlane, who completed his great work on the Oxford edition of Ibsen and was awarded the Commander's Cross of the Royal Norwegian Order of St Olaf. However the decade ended on a low note as the UGC report on Russian Studies recommended that the excellent UEA Russian department be closed and dispersed. It was a problem for the future.

The School of Social Studies (renamed Economic and Social Studies from 1977-78) continued to flourish in the 1970s. It was a large School with 600 students and sixty faculty reflecting the generous staff student ratio of those days. It was also very disparate comprising economics, sociology, philosophy, economic history and development studies. The range of publications in the early 1970s reflected this, from mathematical logic to eighteenth-century roads, from Socratic irony to cattle in Kampala, from OECD accounts to the spread of spina bifida. This in itself might suggest a School becoming too large, diverse in interests and ripe for some splitting and reshaping. Indeed the hiving off of the development economists and sociologists into a new School of Development Studies in 1973 rationalised SOC's range somewhat.

There was a concern to introduce more mathematics into the culture of the School through the appointment of a social statistician and beginning a joint programme with MAP. It was significant that the Dean in the early 1970s was Professor Roy Emerson, a former engineer. SOC continued its concern to make its studies relevant to the outside world. In 1974-75 an interdisciplinary research project began on the location of non-manufacturing activities in manufacturing in the UK, sponsored by the Department of Industry and the EEC Commission. The sociologists too undertook major projects on the study of day centres for the elderly funded by the Department of Health and published in 1978, making UEA a major innovator in this field of socio-medical research. They also engaged in a study of the rehabilitation of ex-prisoners in employment. Such work carried through into the teaching of the MA in Social Work started in October 1976. But the proposed BA degree in Welfare Studies was abandoned in the cuts at the end of the decade. The economists too sought more relevance by the creation of a degree in Business Finance and Economics.

Curricular development took interesting directions in other areas. Politics was introduced in 1975, filling in the gap evident since Ross and Dick had persuaded Thistlethwaite to drop it from his original plans. The history degree was started in 1976 joining together history courses from different Schools. Increasingly students in SOC with little taste for economics or philosophy had begun to block together history courses in EAS and EUR. This new degree regularised this and in due course was to lead to the separate School of History.

One of the most interesting instances of the School reaching out was a summer course put on for students from the University of Riyadh in Saudi Arabia, a mixture of English language taught by the Bell School and British institutions taught by SOC to provide the context. But perhaps the most intriguing and poignant relic of these years is a large collection of Kalahari bushmen's artefacts collected in anthropological fieldwork by Margo Russell. It remains in a fine glass cabinet in Arts I and now looks as abandoned as the programme on social archaeology of which it was to have been a part but which the cuts of 1979 killed off.

As we have just seen, an early split from the over large School of Economic and Social Studies was the new School of Development Studies created in 1973. This had its origins in 1967 in the Overseas Development Group within SOC. It purpose was to study the economic, political and social problems of overseas, especially developing countries. It was also distinctive in that its faculty had to spend part of their time teaching at UEA and part working abroad on projects in the Third World – as it was then coming to be called. It ensured that studies and teaching back in Norwich were constantly nurtured by first-hand experience. Another distinctive feature was the turning of the ODG into a commercial limited company which won contracts from the Ministry of Overseas Development, the United Nations Food and Agriculture Organisation and individual countries. As a company it made profits from its contracts which it returned to the University to provide scholarships for overseas students. With a hundred students and eleven staff DEV provided one of the first large undergraduate programmes in such studies usually regarded as postgraduate. This work covered almost every developing country – regional planning in Tanzania, the impact of road building on income distribution in Nepal, sand control in Oman, advising on census taking in Ethiopia, agrarian reform in Peru.[40] They brought a multi-disciplinary and interdisciplinary approach of economists, agronomists, geologists and anthropologists to their researches and consultancy work.

The School also started an experimental farm in 1976 at Colney near the Plain. This was to develop cultivation techniques of farming relevant to developing countries. For example, they developed forms of harness for efficient oxen ploughing, using their own Guernsey cows; they devised cheap forms of wind power and reservoirs; and managed orchards and bee hives – all relevant for training Third World peasant farmers in small-scale production on programmes funded by UNFAO. They regularly displayed their activities at the Norfolk Show. DEV faculty had the air of men who led rugged lives in exotic places and stories abounded of their exploits. One drove across the Sahara in a jeep topped up with crates of Vichy water. Another redesigned the sacrificial enclosure at Mecca where annually a million beasts were slaughtered in thirty-six hours, with horrendous problems of blood and carcass disposal. Perhaps the most surreal experience was of an ODG member in Ghana who needed to get to the airport in circumstances of some urgency. As he stood by the road an ambassadorial motorcade of American cars approached, also on its way to the airport. The lead car stopped and an elegant lady opened the door and beckoned to him – "Get in, I'm Shirley Temple". So it was, Shirley Temple Black, her country's ambassador to Ghana. ODG men had to be prepared for anything.

In the 1970s music continued to flourish. In 1973 Philip Ledger left to become the Director of Music at King's College, Cambridge. His successor was Peter Aston of the University of York, a composer and editor of the music of George Jeffreys, an English seventeenth-century musician. The University Orchestra, University Choir and UEA Singers continued very active in performing in the region, at the Norwich and Norfolk Triennial Festival and at Aldeburgh. Perhaps the most distinctive development was that in electronic music recording. Tryggvi Tryggvason, an Icelandic engineer formerly from Decca, presided over "Boris", "Ethel", "Sally" and "Anton", a series of electronic sound generators, mixers and recorders.[41] The studio received an enormous stimulus in 1976 with the gift of a powerful computer from Willis, Faber and Dumas, the insurance brokers. This gift was the result of a personal contact between Mrs Maggie Smith (later MBE), the secretary of the School of Music, and Mr Ross Knight of the brokers. This could be used to control the electronic music synthesiser up to BBC standards. The existing synthesiser had a memory of 256 "events" but the new machine raised it to 800 per inch, with tapes over 2000 feet long.[42] By the end of the 1970s UEA had almost unrivalled electronic music facilities – the National Theatre used it, for example. It also had some of the most advanced recording facilities. They began recording in 1974-75 with "Songs and Dances of Fourteenth-Century Italy", not only the first UEA record but thought to be the first record produced by any British university music department.

Art history, still linked with music in the School of Fine Arts and Music, by the early 1970s was able to offer a complete coverage of teaching from the Roman Empire to contemporary times. An interesting innovation was taking students to Venice for the Spring term to study Venetian Renaissance Art, an extremely popular and enriching option. The department also acquired two resources. A vast slide and photographic library was being built up, ranging from sculpture in Provence, medieval panel painting in Norfolk, Isoken furniture and Dalmatian architecture, all originally photographed for the department as well as thousands of other pictures needed for teaching. Most importantly the department moved into the Sainsbury Centre in 1977-78 with its collection, itself a first-class teaching tool. It also enabled the range of teaching and research to be extended back to pre-Columbian and Tribal Art. National attention was focused on the department as it hosted the Annual Conference of the Association of Art Historians in 1979, showing off their glorious new location in the Sainsbury Centre. In 1973 Peter Lasko, who had brought the department into being, left to become the Director of the Courtauld Institute, which was itself, in spite of Frank Thistlethwaite's original intentions, something of an intellectual progenitor of the excellence of art history at UEA.

In the sciences the School of Biological Sciences was one of the oldest established Schools and it continued its existing strengths, ranging from broad ecology to the electronic microscopic study of molecules – from the Breckland meres and studies of inland waders and salt marshes to the DNA of grasshoppers and yeasts of strawberries and grapes. Yet the School seemed to be operating under certain strains. They were conscious that the demand for their students did not match the output. In 1971 they were saddened that only about a third of their graduates were taking up occupations relating to biology and wondered if their third year was too specifically related to research for those who did not need it. Throughout the early 1970s they became more aware of the difficulty of their graduates getting jobs relating to biology. The estimate that the stock of biologists needed by 1980 was only likely to be 58,000 admitted that there was bound to be a professional over-production. At the same time there was a steady fall in sixth formers taking biology in the 1970s. This may have reflected in a diminishing quality of students, for example twenty-eight out of the intake of 1976/7 failed their first year course. The School was caught in a declining demand both for its course and for its student output. It began to look as though this had not been such a good horse to back in the 1960s.

BIO's reaction was to join other science Schools in a course unit system devised to enable other students in the University to take BIO courses. They also established joint degrees in biophysics and ecology with MAP and ENV in 1980. Interestingly they did not respond by making the degree more general or less demanding, which might have been appropriate for students not even coping with the first year and not going into specialist biology careers. The University had set its face against ordinary degrees, which could have had a part to play here. But to diminish the level of teaching might have been seen as a downgrading of the School, which would have had adverse effects on its research reputation. This remained high with 760 publications being produced and £1,026,015 being received in research grant money. Especially valued locally, BIO also reached out to be of service to the community. It collaborated with the Norfolk and Norwich Hospital, and work on the cataracts, diabetes and foot disorders proved points of contact.

The School of Chemical Sciences too continued to drive hard at its research publishing 1129 articles and books in the decade and attracting £1,273,794 in research grants from outside. The School, however, had problems common to some other science Schools. There was a continued national decrease in the applications for university places in chemistry and this problem of admissions reduced the size of the School, whose output fell from sixty-nine in 1971 to fifty-eight by 1980. More important the School had to deal with a lower quality of student. For example, the proportion of firsts and 2/1s fell over the decade from 22 to 19 per cent while that of thirds and below rose from 40 to 49 per cent. To have nearly half the graduates gaining third class degrees and lower suggested a marked disparity between the very high international quality of the research of the School and what was possible in terms of the teaching. There was also a sharp contraction in employment opportunities for chemists in industry, consequently half the firsts and several of the Ph.Ds became school teachers. Much of the rhetoric of the sixties about the need of industry for scientists was beginning to ring hollow by the 1970s. In turn this must have influenced the decline in applications for science degrees. Chemistry's position was worsened by the severe financial constraints of the 1970s. It could not afford to replace or even promote faculty. Rather bizarrely one lecturer of international reputation moved straight to the prestigious ICI Brunner Chair at Liverpool and thence to the Chair at Cambridge without even being promoted to a senior lectureship at UEA.[43]

Since many graduates went into schoolteaching, the School responded appropriately. It continued to develop chemical education with its unique professorship in the subject. Professor Frank Halliwell had been appointed professor of chemical education in 1967 and on his retirement in 1971 he was succeeded by Professor Malcolm Frazer, who continued to develop the subject energetically. Aware that a specialised rigorous chemistry degree was not appropriate for many of their students, CHE set up a course on Chemistry and Society dealing with demography, the environment and food supply, linking science and social science interests. They sought to attract more students by mounting a new B.Sc. with a year in the USA at the University of Massachusetts. Finally, the School started advanced diplomas in organic chemistry (ADOC) and teaching and research in organic chemistry (ADTROC) to enable graduates in work in industry and teaching to update their knowledge. CHE was maintaining a high quantity and quality of research while also seeking to cater for the needs of its less academic and specialised students.

The problems of Biology and Chemistry were felt more acutely in the School of Mathematics and Physics. They recognised that there was a "national situation of retreat from the basic discipline of mathematics". [44] The subject was seen as too difficult and theoretical, applications were falling off and many applicants were not capable of the rigours of a full honours degree. This forced the School to consider ways of adjusting to adversity which were good for it and the University generally. This adjustment took three forms: embracing practical work of value to industry; reaching out to other Schools in the University; and accepting the need for work of less than honours degree standard for less able students.

Mathematics and physics were always likely to seem to the layman more rarefied than the applied sciences but some members of MAP made efforts to apply their work to industry at some points. Drs Matheson and Wright devised an automatic ellipsometer for detecting, for example, rust on railway lines. Norman Riley did work on the aerodynamics of slender wings for the Ministry of Defence and became a consultant to the Director of the Royal Aircraft Establishment at Farnborough. In adjacent but lighter vein, Professor Riley was also an authority on the aerodynamics of fast swing bowling. Nearer home the School became involved in research into deaf aids with the Norfolk and Norwich Hospital, which itself had a physics department. Probably of greatest significance for the future was the School's recognition of the increasing relevance of electronics. They started physics with electronics in 1974/5 partly to appeal to students who might be attracted by a more applied branch of the subject. With expertise built up in this area, they were able by 1979 to enter into an agreement with Midwich Computer Co. to mount short courses for them as part of an effort "to stimulate industrial involvement in the growth of electronics in the School". [45]

Within the University MAP made several initiatives to relate themselves to other parts of the University. In particular they offered mathematics and physics teaching to other Schools and started the Inter School Statistics group in 1975-76, of special value later to accountants. The curricular cooperation between Schools was facilitated by the implementation of a course unit system with a slotting system in 1973, the forerunner of the Common Course Structure. Professor Norman Cusack of MAP took a leading role in this and it enabled other scientists to "slot" MAP courses into their degrees.[46]

Within MAP itself the School had to address the problem of its poor application rate and the poor performance of many of its students when they arrived. They were constantly troubled by the numbers of students who failed or only obtained pass degrees. They admitted that many students seemed to hit an intellectual barrier of difficulty in their second year and that they would be better diverted to an ordinary degree at that stage. They started remedial classes at preliminary level in 1974-75 but were dismayed by 1976-77 that fewer than a half of the students succeeded in reaching the level of a second class degree. They announced the starting of an ordinary degree in 1978-79. By then the graduating class was only forty-one, the smallest for ten years.

MAP had tried to adjust but behind their immediate problems lay the fundamental question of whether the University should be continuing to support a School with perpetual problems of admissions, low student academic performance and high unit costs. The admissions problem was insoluble since it was part of a national trend. The poor performance of students suggests that a too rigorous degree was being presented to students, many of whom would have been better studying something more practical at technical college – as the enthusiasm for electronics suggested. There was no doubt, however, of the quality of the faculty. Peter Chadwick gained his FRS there in these years and several others departed for chairs elsewhere. Most notably UEA became a world leader in the study of photons, which gave information about the atomic and electronic structure of materials. From 1978 UEA pioneered the equipment for this technique "the only such apparatus in Britain".[47] But there was a cost to pay which other parts of the University had to bear. The forty-one graduates of 1977-78 had been taught by nine professors and readers. At the same time SOC was producing an output of over 150 with ten professors and readers and negligible overheads and gearing up for yet further expansion. It was then unthinkable for a "proper" university in the 1970s to jettison physics teaching but the question was already being raised which successive Vice-Chancellor's addressed, set aside and then only finally grasped with the closure of physics, in the late 1990s. Computing, based in the Computing Centre, but otherwise closely linked with mathematics and physics became a separate School in 1973 and grew progressively as physics declined.

By contrast the School of Environmental Sciences was perhaps the most confident of the science Schools. It produced its first graduates in 1970-71 with no tail, unlike CHE and MAP. The admissions position remained sound throughout the decade, with the highest A level scores of any School in the University. Moreover, in spite of cuts, it was able to grow from its first year's intake of fifty and a School size of 150 at the start of the decade to an intake of 120 and total size of 360 by the end. It as also the most financially successful School, attracting external research grants of £1,400,000 plus some additional foreign currencies.

One of the attractions of the School was the intrinsic interest, even excitement of the work. For example Mr Norman Croften-Sleight very generously took undergraduate field courses across the North Sea in his vessel *Opportune Star*. The School also had its own catamaran, Envirocat, which sank but was salvaged in 1975. The faculty were probably the most wide-ranging in their research cruising in the North East Atlantic, visiting scientific equipment on oil rigs, studying vegetation in the Samburu region of Kenya, and agriculture and rural transport in Bangladesh. Some work was strikingly of global import. Notable was that of Frederick Vine (who was elected to a chair in 1973 and FRS in 1974), whose work on ocean floor evolution and continental drift was of world repute. But also the School did a great deal of work of direct East Anglian value, including studies of pollution and mud in the North Sea. Of especially regional policy significance were Keith Clayton's studies on coastal erosion. He argued the controversial but compelling view that money spent on coastal defences was largely wasted; it was better to let some areas be eroded and be deposited elsewhere on the coastline. Expenditure should be used to compensate losing landowners rather than on futile attempts to hold back the sea. The School also controversially focused attention on the Norfolk Broads. Its work showed the connection between the depositing of sewage in the Broads, the spread of algae, the death of aquatic plants and birds, and the fear that an attractive amenity could end up as a series of stagnant pools. The University also found that most people living around the Broads did not know that their sewage ended up there and that they were prepared to spend more to prevent it. The School had important influences on policy about the coastline and Broads to the annoyance of some but the benefit of most.[48] These issues attracted the attention of the national press to ENV and to UEA generally. Whereas it was difficult for the public to understand the relevance of some of the other science Schools, ENV was always good for a story and had a flair for publicity to provide it. They were also, more than other science Schools, very conscious of policy issues and some of their research spread over into SOC and DEV areas of economics and sociology. Reflecting this, they also mounted an interdisciplinary course on

Energy, Materials and Society. ENV was one of the liveliest and most attractive centres of activity in the University.

A specialist area of ENV which rose to prominence in the 1970s was the Unit of Climatic Research established in 1971 on the initiative of Keith Clayton and with sponsorship from the Nuffield Foundation, Shell, BP and others.[49] Its first Director was Hubert Lamb who had been in charge of the Meteorological Office's research on climatic variation and was Chair of the United Nations World Meteorological Organisation. Their aim was to look at trends in world climate, using historical records and radio carbon dating of deposits, and they were already much concerned about the impact of pollution on climate.[50] Professor Lamb came to Norwich as "the ice man", attracting much attention for his prophecy of world cooling and a future ice age within 10,000 years. Within a few years in Norwich, in which the heat wave of 1975-76 had intervened, he had switched to warning of global warming with dire predictions of forest and crop belts being shifted, melting ice caps and drowned cities. A holocaust within a century was an even more exciting prospect than an ice age in ten millennia and it all helped to shape contemporary attitudes to global warming. It also drew much attention to UEA, as did two international conferences in 1973 and 1975 which he hosted in Norwich. Most importantly Lamb attracted financial sponsorship from seven leading insurance companies who were also making their own studies of climate patterns and calling on the research of the UEA Climate Unit with a view to minimising their insurance losses from storm and flood.[51] Lamb retired in 1978 but had made a considerable impact in his years at UEA, recognised by the conferring of an honorary Doctorate of Science in 1981.

As well as the Climatic Research Unit, the seventies saw some very useful innovations in the area of vocational social sciences in law, social work and education. At the start of the decade the University had indicated that it wanted a Law School as part of its concern to provide more vocational courses. UEA was allowed to start its Law School in 1977. The founding professor was David Bentley, formerly an assistant parliamentary counsel and teacher at LSE and tutor in jurisprudence at Christ Church, Oxford. The Norwich Law Society sold its library to the University without which teaching would not have been possible. Some controversy surrounded the creation of yet another law department. All universities desired one as a mark of professional prestige and UEA was pleased to have taken precedence over York, Essex and Lancaster. Although there was great student demand to study law, employment for law graduates was not increasing commensurately. Bentley, however, saw his new School not only as serving a professional purpose but as finding an interdisciplinary role with links with EUR and SOC through Common Market law and with ENV over environmental and planning law.

In one respect Law would be different from most UEA Schools in that it would not be interested in postgraduate research. Bentley took the view that the best lawyers were drawn to practise in the profession not to research and that what research the profession needed was best concentrated in the Centre for Socio-Legal Studies at Wolfson College Oxford. In any case research should not be undertaken by those who had not already been in professional practice.[52] It was a salutary view insisting on the primacy of undergraduate teaching. But within the year Professor Bentley resigned to return to government service and was replaced as professor and dean by Professor Gareth Miller, a solicitor, who has given leadership in the School and University ever since.

Another innovation was the creation of the two year master's degree in social work in October 1976. This would train social workers and probation officers. There was evident need for this, as only 37 per cent of local authority social workers were qualified at that time. These deficiencies in the profession were highlighted locally in the death of a baby in King's Lynn. Moreover, such training would naturally arise from the rather applied kind of sociology already developed by Professor Roy Emerson, with his medical interests, in SOC. The course was to be open to graduates of all subjects and was run by Dr Martin Davies, a former probation officer, civil servant and academic from the University of Manchester, soon to become editor of the prestigious *British Journal of Social Work*. UEA was one of only six universities providing such a course and was heavily subscribed.[53] There was some anxiety that the course would fall victim to the cuts. The *THES* even claimed that it had been abandoned after only two months, but reports of the demise were exaggerated.[54] The build up was slower, but doubled from October 1978. Firmly established, it drew part of its funding from Norfolk local authorities, which it in turn served through joint appointments with the South Norfolk Area Social Services Team and the Probation Office of Norwich Prison; "such arrangements offer the maximum benefits through interaction between teaching, practical application and research".[55]

Finally, there were exciting developments in the creation of a major School of Education. In 1972 a Centre for Applied Research in Education (CARE) was created to undertake research in curriculum and teaching, to help LEAs and schools as a consultant and to offer the University an advisory service on teaching methods and curriculum. They engaged in projects in small group teaching, teaching about race, computer-assisted learning and much else, drawing funds from the Ford, Nuffield and Gulbenkian Foundations and the Department for Education and Science. In 1973 they began teaching, but only at the postgraduate MA level.

The most important development in the area, however, was the merger with the local Teacher Training College at Keswick Hall. The college was one of the oldest in the country, having started as the Diocesan Training Institution in the cathedral close in 1840. After many vicissitudes and some changes of location the college came in 1948 to Keswick Hall, a fine Georgian house belonging to Quintin Gurney on the south-west outskirts of Norwich.[56] Quintin Gurney was already the Chairman of the College governors and a director of Barclays Bank. He had leased his property, Keswick Hall to the College on a ninety-nine year lease at a nominal rent. This was a very generous action of a genuinely Christian gentleman and the College was much in his debt. He was the father of Richard Quintin Gurney, an early supporter of the University as we have seen.

There had been increasing links between Keswick and UEA in the 1970s. In October 1975 the University validated a fourth year B.Ed. taught by Keswick for students with the BA. This was followed by a full four year B.Ed. and then, in 1978, by the part-time B.Ed. for serving teachers. It became evident that graduate work was the way forward for the College and the cessation of preparing for the Teacher's Certificate, the last intake for which entered in 1977.

While this was developing, there was new national thinking about the nature of teacher training. Many teacher training colleges were closing down in the 1970s. It was also government policy, following the James Report, that those remaining should have closer links with other institutions of higher education, the logic of which might ultimately be merger. This was the path for which Keswick was destined and some faculty were already upgrading their academic qualifications by studying for higher degrees at UEA.

The movement for the merger of Keswick and UEA was a fairly long one. Principal Canon John Gibbs had asked UEA about validating the B.Ed. as early as 1966, but the University's reasonable reaction was that it was then too busy establishing itself to take on extra external responsibilities. However in the early 1970s an urgency was brought to the situation. Lord Eric James's Committee in 1972, while warning of an over academic bias in teacher training, recognised that there would be cases "where such mergers are geographically possible the integration of Colleges of Education with other sectors is educationally appropriate".[57] As James was about to report Canon Gibbs presented his views to a joint meeting of Keswick and UEA, urging that the college and the university were just such a case which James might have had in mind.[58]

In 1972 Canon Gibbs, who became a bishop, was succeeded as Principal by William Etherington. He had come from St Martin's College, Lancaster, which was already very close to the university there and presented an example of what might happen in Norwich. He initially found UEA full of good will but unconcerned about concrete action. Then early in 1972 following "a splendid lunch . . . things were very different and there appeared to be genuine enthusiasm for exploring possibilities".[59] In 1973 matters began to crystallise. A White Paper in December 1972 considered the expansion of the non-university higher education sector and recognised that some colleges "wanted more complete integration with the university sector".[60] The subsequent DES circular proposed a reduction in teacher training places from 114,000 to 60-70,000 and urged colleges of education to integrate with universities.[61] For Etherington the position was plain and shaped by various considerations. There was little future for an independent specialised college of education. He could not diversify Keswick into technical subjects since the Norwich City College already covered that area, and in any case the Charity Commissioners to whom Keswick was answerable were also opposed to a merger with the City College. He needed to become part of a university to escape the financial control of the DES, which was now hostile to specialised teacher training and whose policy was to run down church teacher training colleges. His own experience at St Martin's, Lancaster, had been one of a teacher training college well linked with a local university, and his own ambitions were to raise the academic levels at Keswick – as had been done at St Martin's. The logic was inescapable. Keswick as it was might be threatened with closure; it needed to merge with UEA, and UEA would benefit from a new vocational School. I was involved with some validation and teaching at Keswick at the time, though knowing nothing of the background of these developments. I recall being asked by a Dean what I thought of closer links with Keswick and replying that anything that brought more vocational studies to the University was highly desirable. The mood was in the air.

Etherington pressed his views and sounded out those at UEA in late 1973. Keith Clayton foresaw a big arts expansion in which Keswick could play a part.[62] Frank Thistlethwaite was less sanguine and saw all kinds of difficulties, especially in absorbing a Church foundation; "no institutional association can be foreseen", was his view at that time.[63] In 1976, however, the Niblett Report recommended the merger of Keswick and UEA, and the DES supported this.[64] So from 1977 things moved swiftly. A joint committee under the chairmanship of Malcolm Frazer reported in October 1978 recommending the creation of a new School of Education and ironing out the details and especially that Lawrence Stenhouse's excellent educational research unit CARE should retain a separate existence within the new School.[65] Bill Etherington, the Principal, became the first Dean of the School. It was an immensely complicated merger involving the DES, the UGC, UEA, the College, the Church of England Education Board, the Charity Commission, the District Valuer and the Gurney family. It was to the credit of Malcolm Frazer, Bill Etherington, Dame Rosemary Murray the Chair of the Keswick Governors, and Bridget Watson, a tirelessly able UEA adminis- trator, that the merger was accomplished in the summer of 1981.

This raised an interesting point of principle for the University, which was willing to contemplate a split site with the Plain and Keswick Hall in a pleasant but remote location some three or four miles apart. It was envisaged that a School of Education would remain there and be joined by the School of Law. The lawyers were adamantly resistant to being isolated from the rest of the University in this way and it would have created considerable administra- tive and logistic problems. The problem was obviated by an unexpected intervention by the UGC. The UGC refused to accept the existing leasehold tenure of the property and insisted on purchase. Accordingly the College bought the Hall outright from James Gurney, the son of Quintin, for the very small sum of £30,000, the cost of a good family home but hardly of a Georgian mansion with grounds. James Gurney sold it with great generosity in the spirit of his family's munificence to UEA and, preceding that, to the church and education generally. Yet hardly had UEA bought the Hall from Keswick for the same small sum that had been paid to James Gurney than the UGC obliged the University to sell it commercially for a much larger sum as part of the 1981 cuts. James Gurney had reason to feel that he had been taken advantage of but the blame, if such there was, lay with the UGC and certainly not with the University. Timothy Colman was asked to explain the situation to James Gurney, yet another of the very private, delicate, high level services the Pro Chancellor was to render the University. However, the Gurney generosity was happily not lost since the proceeds of the sale were used to build the new EDU buildings on the Plain. UEA only agreed to the UGC demand for the sale on these terms and the UGC concurred. The other advantage was that LAW was then able to be located in Earlham Hall, which they much preferred to Keswick. The increasing activity of the Schools we have just been considering can be seen in the striking increase in research grants in this decade.

Table 13 Research Grants, 1970-1980

	BIO	CHEM	EAS	ENV	EUR	MAP	SOC	CEAS	CARE	COMP	DEV	TOTAL
1970-71	50,731	43,126	13,600 DM 500	88,689	1900	60,105	1117	4000				250,168
1971-72	9053	76,307 +17000$	-	20,664	-	25,103	16,366 125,000$	4970				152,443
1972-73	38,656	53,436	880 200$	52,445	-	6149	15,080 18,800$	7925	137,586			312,157
1973-74	8670	68,343	1100 2150 DM	143,000	3290	60,268	81,484	132,985	96,025	50,356	80,544	726,065
1974-75	32,718	56,830	5000 2240 DM	51,595	2575 16,000DM	32,899	4,797	21,142	47,739	18,970	84,837	359,102
1975-76	130,142	149,212	975 2000$	182,932	790 SKr 10,000 DKr 25,000	125,708	25,849	33,615	31,888	-	19,170	700,281
1976-77	127,043	163,031	3095	170,139	2950	40,847	55,784	39,020	9448	-	-	611,357
1977-78	135,402	162,969 8000$	1250 198,150$	151,438	10,300	-	12,637	63,586	42,896	-	24,753 490,000$	605,231
1978-79	300,898	355,545 160,000 BFr	14,354	149,027 132,850	4145	131,417	65,848	58,283	59,308	288,000$	51,500	1,190,375
1979-80	192,646	142,643	1875	294,719 72,500$ 11,700 SKr 2500 DKr 5000 NKr	6764 14,717$	142,375	90,185	61,656	113,760 42,399$	93,926	76,280 562,000$	1,216,829 and other currencies and uncosted assignments.

£ unless otherwise stated.
DM Deutsche Mark; BFr Belgian Francs; SKr Swedish Kronor; DKr Danish Kroner; NKr Norwegian Kroner.

These moves towards vocationalism in the balance of studies at UEA were essential at the time in the light of UEA's modest performance in the job market.

Table 14   *Future Occupations of UEA Graduates (percentages).*

	Research further academic study	Postgraduate teacher training	Other full-time training	Direct employment	(Industry)	Unemployed or unknown
			ARTS			
1968	8.7	19.1	8.7	25.7	7.1	33.3
1969	-	-	-	-	-	-
1970	9.2	12.7	6.6	29.9	7.1	39.1
1971	4.9	14.6	5.5	19.3	4.4	51.2
1972	7.6	16.5	5.7	17.7	2.8	45.9
1973	4.3	13.8	5.7	18.7	2.3	42.7
1974	5.5	12.8	5.1	20.3	4.7	41.9
1975	7.0	16.0	5.0	12.0	?	42.0
1976	7.0	17.7	6.4	20.1	1.5	32.0
1977	8.9	14.1	6.7	19.8	3.2	27.6
1978	5.6	13.0	7.4	20.4	2.8	32.6
1979	7.7	11.0	6.1	30.9	6.1	24.1
1980	5.6	12.3	11.1	29.0	5.6	28.9
			SCIENCES			
1968	17	10.8	1.5	48	30.2	20.9
1969	-	-	-	-	-	-
1970	15.9	13.0	2.5	30.7	16.3	34.4
1971	16.1	14.3	1.1	18.4	5.6	42.8
1972	14.0	22.3	5.2	20.0	5.6	34.0
1973	14.5	14.5	4.6	30.7	17.0	43.1
1974	15.1	10.1	4.1	28.9	11.5	32.1
1975	18.0	7.0	2.0	17.0	-	41.0
1976	19.0	10.1	3.9	29.6	11.5	24.3
1977	16.4	13.1	2.0	31.2	13.4	24.8
1978	19.0	9.5	1.9	37.7	15.8	17.1
1979	16.3	8.0	1.6	42.6	15.4	20.5
1980	19.6	8.7	2.1	38.0	15.4	22.2

In both arts and sciences, entering teacher training was the most popular occupation, with the possibilities of further research and postgraduate degrees being much more common in the sciences (15-20 per cent) than the arts (5-10 per cent). A higher and increasing proportion of arts graduates trained for another career after graduating. As we might expect, more scientists found jobs on graduating (20 per cent rising to 40 per cent) than arts (20 per cent rising to 30 per cent). But what concerned many was the low proportion going into industry. Single-figure percentages in arts and usually 10-15 per cent even in the sciences. What was disturbing was the very high proportions who were unemployed or unknown, though the very high levels of unemployment of the early 1970s had improved somewhat by the end of the decade. The severe unemployment nationally of 1971 and 1972 was the highest since the war and naturally reflected in graduate unemployment, 51 per cent for arts and 42 per cent for scientists in 1971. It was undoubtedly compounded by the suspicion of graduates and universities in general as an aftermath of the student unrest of the time. The "unemployed" and "unknowns" were classified together, however, and we cannot know how many of the "unknowns" were working at something and how many in the disaffected mood of the time were cocking a snook at the system by declining to respond to requests for information. Yet it was unfortunate that, even when the economy improved, UEA was shown to have the worst unemployment record of any British university for the 1975-79 period.[66] *The Financial Times* in 1974 published a league table of "useful" universities, with UEA and Essex at the bottom and with dark suggestions that they be closed down.[67]

The high levels of unemployment and lack of contribution to industry caused a good deal of concern both inside and outside the University. Deans' retreats in 1974-75 expressed anxiety about the quality and quantity of students and wondered whether the University should modify its curriculum to make it of more practical use. All were aware, however, that the UGC would block any moves to introduce technology, engineering and always had done. Pro Vice-Chancellor John Fletcher at the 1977 retreat presciently urged that it was "irresponsible to encourage students into academic careers when they should be thinking of industry and commerce instead".[68] Fletcher caught some of the very prevalent attitudes of the time. When Jim Prior was addressing a political meeting at UEA at the time of the 1974 General Election, he asked the students how many intended to take up industrial careers and only three hands were raised.[69] The "uselessness" of much of UEA, especially its emphasis on arts degrees – producing 300 more arts graduates than scientists by 1974 – their unemployment, the need to retrain and the mismatch with the needs of the economy came under strong local attack.[70] Attention was drawn in 1978 to a twenty-five-year-old EAS female graduate working on a roadside verge maintenance gang for Norfolk County Council under her gang leader, also a UEA graduate.[71] It raised questions about the appropriateness of spending public money in over-educating graduates who were to undertake jobs done in earlier decades by paupers as workhouse outdoor relief. Also, nationally, the social rate of return on university first degrees fell from 9 per cent in 1971 to 6 per cent by 1980 as the graduate output expanded.[72] Such sentiments fed into the public acceptance of severe cuts in higher education which began in the next year. Accordingly UEA's running an Insight course to encourage students to think of business careers was much welcomed.[73]

Students remained perhaps insufficiently aware of the problems that awaited them and got on with enjoying student life, which undoubtedly improved for them in the seventies. Facilities for them greatly increased, their representative power in the University was extended, and a better relationship between the University and the City was established after the troubles. In December 1976 elected student representatives became for the first time full speaking and voting members of the Council and Senate after some years as observers. This was a final resolution of one of the major demands of the troubled years. By this time the number of sabbatical officers had also increased from one, the President of the Students' Union, to four. The Vice-Chancellor's 1977-78 Report specifically noted what a pleasure the new style of student executive was to work with. With political power came more economic advantage as the Union in 1980 took financial control of the campus supermarket, the Fifers Lane bar and the shop in the Street.

Facilities for students were also greatly extended. Above all the new Sports Centre was opened on 22 February 1971 by Sir Stanley Rous, the Vice-President of the Football Association and a Suffolk man. Haydn Morris, the manager of the British Universities' rugby team and an English and British Lion international, was the first director. It provided large playing areas for badminton, basketball, squash courts, a twenty-eight foot climbing wall and practice halls for fencing and gymnastics.[74] It was available not only to the University but to the city and county. Within a year the Centre was attracting 1520 "performance attendances" a week in the Autumn and Spring Terms and 1210 in the summer. Squash was the most popular sport and two more courts were added in 1976.

1970 saw the start of Nexus, a television service with three cameras in a studio and two cameras in an outside broadcast unit for students to make their own programmes.[75] These were transmitted for two hours daily at lunchtime. It was an entrée into media careers for some, a stimulating recreation for most and it developed what would later be regarded as "communication skills". In retrospect we can also see it as an early stage of what was to develop as media studies, one of the most successful and fastest growing academic disciplines of the 1990s, both at UEA and elsewhere. Nexus also showed public spiritedness by inviting 200 pensioners to see Princess Anne's wedding to Captain Mark Philips projected on multiple TV screens as one big screen in University House.[76] Also on the entertainment side drama continued very prominent among the hundred or so clubs and societies run by the Union, with no less than thirteen productions in 1976-77. And by the end of the decade the Union was running fifty-four pop concerts a year.

It was also remarkable how altruistic much student activity remained, continuing traditions of the 1960s. The rags thrived and by 1977 had raised £17,000 since their inception in 1964, having overcome a period of public hostility during the troubles.[77] The seventies also saw some of their wittiest rag stunts. In 1975 there was the great coypu hoax. The coypu was a South American rodent introduced into East Anglia for fur farming. Many had escaped and were a menace, not least for undermining river banks. Students dressed in official white coats and purporting to hunt down the last coypus isolated several Norfolk villages closing traffic in or out. Norfolk villages, were once more targeted in 1977 with a bogus plan to rename all places with duplicate or confusing names, of which there were many. Old and New Buckenham for example were told that they both had to choose completely new and different names for postal purposes. It aroused ire but was a genuinely funny satire on the quaintness of Norfolk village nomenclature, still more on the local government and Post Office bureaucracy and its terminology. The value of rag was vividly seen in 1979 when it raised over £900 to buy a bionic arm for a little Norfolk girl. The record £4097 raised that year was distributed by the Lord Mayor, Mrs Valerie Guttsman, the wife of the University librarian.[78]

The Students' Union ran a Teenage Youth Club for fourteen to sixteen year olds and a Saturday Childrens' Club for eight to ten year olds. The attraction of these two for the youngsters was the use of the new Sports Hall. The Dean of Students' Office told the Vice-Chancellor that the clubs "consist mainly of very sensible young people trying to do a very worthwhile but difficult job in providing for young people they think of as being worse off than themselves".[79] Out in the county the students ran a Conservation Corps, with a hundred members helping a Norfolk farmer plant 200 maple trees along the Norwich-Stoke Holy Cross Road and helping wardens in Nature Reserves.

The largest and most prominent organisation was Student Community Action, which started in 1974. This was a wider grouping having at its core the original Voluntary Service Unit of the 1960s. About 350 students were involved in nineteen projects – over 10 per cent of the student body. Their activities were impressively wide ranging.[80] They visited the mentally handicapped children of Little Plumstead Hospital and built an adventure play-ground for them, the Eaton Hall School for emotionally disturbed children, the St Andrews and Hellesdon Hospitals for the mentally handicapped, the Wednesday Club for the similarly afflicted at Princes Street United Reform Church. This care for the mentally handicapped by young people themselves blessed with high intelligence is especially poignant. It was also especially valued by psychiatrists as part of therapy, "what we do is provide a little love" said a volunteer.

Others too were served, prisoners at Blundeston and Forncett Grange, the Meals on Wheels service, Shelter, Third World First, while the Blood Transfusion Unit was served to capacity through the generosity of students in the mid 1970s. All this and a multitude of activities from tea and chat, to painting and decorating and Christmas parties improved the image of the University and cemented relations of the University and the City. These activities were expressions of sheer virtue in their own right, the chief way in which the University was a force for good in its region.

The students engaged in such charitable activity were generally happy and self-confident. But there was also a minority of students with troubles of their own and during the seventies the University made urgent attempts to meet their needs. In 1970 there already was a psychiatric social worker and students consulted the ordinary doctors of the medical centre about psychological stress. But thereafter things developed partly influenced by the student unrest, which was in part manifestations of unhappiness. Nightline was established in 1971, a telephone contact whereby students feeling distress during the night could talk confidentially with others. Also in 1971 a second psychiatric social worker was appointed and thirteen more resident tutors. This restored the ratio of tutors to resident students to 1:58, what it had been in 1968 before it deteriorated during the troubles. In the next year a full-time Counselling Service under a Director of Student Counselling was established and Brian Thorne, the first full-time Student Counsellor at a senior level, started in 1973 with three part-time counsellors. Michael da Costa, a second full-time counsellor arrived in 1974, by which time a remarkable tenth of all students were consulting the service. It was a reminder to the University that, although it was educating intelligent adult minds, it was also dealing with emotionally developing adolescents, some of whom were finding life diffi-cult. The University's expertise in this area in the seventies was used to train counsellors elsewhere in the region. The Norfolk Association for Counselling was chaired by William Hallidie Smith of UEA and the Norwich Centre for Personal and Professional Development, opened in January 1980, acted as a training and consultancy unit for those in the caring professions, with UEA counsellors closely involved.

Student Affairs were generally presided over by the Student Amenities Policy Committee (the Amenities Policy Committee from 1974/5). Much of the day to day work was done, however, by the "Tuesday Club" under Dr C.C. "Kiff" Matheson, the future Dean of Students. This met weekly (and still does), acting as a lightning-conductor for all manner of problems. An enormous effort was put into improving student amenities in the 1970s. I (and my future wife) sat on the SAPC under the chairmanship of John Coates as Dean of Students. We were always impressed by the care and concern to improve things and meet reasonable student demands. This broad policy and care of detail by the Tuesday Club did much to remove discontents and improve the relations between the students and University. The good feeling by the end of Frank Thistlethwaites' period of office was a palpable contrast with the tensions of the beginning of the decade.

The Library continued to expand through a difficult decade with imagination and response to technical change. The stock rose from 182,718 items in 1970-71 to 414,112 by 1979-80, and issues over the same time from 133,868 to 274,979, while its annual grant increased from £122,711 to £324,860. Certain "real term" indicators deteriorated however. The staff student ratio moved up sharply from 1974/5. By this year the library had thirteen unfilled posts out of a complement of fifty-three when the financial freeze hit them, and the matter only slightly recovered by the end of the decade. The grant per student increased by 1.7 per cent. However the Brown index of book, periodical and binding costs rose by 2.9 per cent, exceeding the increase in grant and much exceeding the grant per head. One response was simply to cut opening hours and close at weekends in 1975-76. The Library sought to offset these resource problems by the reception of technology. A computerised system of issuing was introduced in 1971 by a team lead by Dr Christopher Aslin. In 1975 this Collectadata system was replaced by the Singer 10 system for the instant recording of issues and returns, more complex but satisfactory than the older system. UEA actually pioneered the use of the Singer 10 system and shrewdly got it cheap.

In spite of the constraints there were a number of other major advances.[81] A second stage of the Library was approved by the UGC in November 1970. The first two floors were handed over by Sindalls in July 1974, a little late, but with a lot of shifting and extra work, got ready for the new academic year in 1974. The Library also made some notable acquisitions. The Norwich Law Society transferred its own library from the Norwich City Library to UEA to support the new School of Law. Unpredictable good fortune saved the collection from destruction in the City Library fire of 1994. Also 1975/6 saw the final transfer of books from the Norfolk and Norwich Subscription Library. Agreements for this went back to 1967, since the Subscription Library could no longer afford to maintain its Victorian building and stock. The purchase of the collection saved and brought many delightful old biographical, travel and literary works to UEA. The Library is the heart of the University, set by Denys Lasdun as a donjon centrepoint of his academic city and, under Willi Guttsman and his staff, like much else in the University, it thrived amid difficulty in this decade.

The 1970s, and Frank Thistlethwaite's period of office, finished on a buoyant note according to various indicators. Students had increased from 2358 to 4114 over the decade. The quantity and quality of applicants to UEA rose sharply in the later years. The UEA applicants rose 1.7 per cent, considerably in excess of the national change of 1.3 per cent. Accordingly the ratio of UEA applicants to the national pool fell from 1:90 in 1976 to 1:63 by 1980.[82] The quality also rose as the proportion of UEA with three A levels increased from 63 per cent in 1976 to 70 per cent by 1980. The proportion of firsts and 2/1 degrees 1976-80 was also good at 29.5 per cent. The national average was 29.8 per cent.[83] Even the figures for UEA graduate unemployment improved from the middle to the end of the decade. The Vice-Chancellor was to leave the University in good heart.

In 1980 Frank Thistlethwaite was sixty-five and due to retire. As the year approached, so he received proper tributes of public recognition. He had been awarded an Honorary Doctorate of Humane Letters by the University of Colorado in 1972, elected to an Honorary Fellowship of his old college St John's, Cambridge, in 1974 and in 1979 was made a Commander of the Order of the British Empire. After his retirement the honorary degree of D.Sc. was conferred on him in 1994 by the University of Minnesota. Of notable interest and unusual for an academic, he was admitted as an honorary Fellow of the Royal Institute of British Architects. This was particularly appropriate for the Vice-Chancellor of a University which had commissioned such notable international figures as Sir Bernard Feilden, Sir Denys Lasdun and Sir Norman Foster before they had reached the apogee of their careers. It was a special pleasure for Frank Thistlethwaite himself, with his lifelong interest in architecture.

As part of the retirement proceedings the Vice-Chancellor was presented with a portrait of himself. This was done by Michael Noakes, who had painted portraits for St John's College, notably of Paul Dirac. Frank Thistlethwaite made enquiries of his old college about Noakes's work and was clearly satisfied. Very wisely Mr and Mrs Noakes were invited to stay at Wood Hall and were guests at dinner and luncheon parties in October 1979, so that they could get some idea of the Vice-Chancellor's personality and range of facial expressions prior to his formal sittings. Three took place between December 1979 and February 1980 and the portrait was ready for presentation by 30 June 1980. It is an excellent likeness, capturing the outgoing humanity and humour as well as the authority of the sitter. When displayed at the annual exhibition of the Royal Society of Portrait Painters one lady observer ignorant of the subject was heard to remark, "well he looks a nice old boy". It hangs now in pride of place in the foyer of the Council House and grows in depth with regular viewing.[84]

As 1980 unfolded the Vice-Chancellor's final months took on the form of a triumphal procession with farewell suppers given by Schools, dinners with Deans and the Wines Committee of the SCR, a farewell concert by the Aeolian Quartet, and the launching of a Rowing Club boat named *Frank Thistlethwaite*.[85] One of the most imaginative events was a summer evening cruise on the Bure river in the motor cruiser "Aquarius" belonging to Patricia and Martin Hollis. Its exclusive party consisted of former Harkness scholars at UEA who sailed from Horning to dinner at the Petersfield Hotel.

A fund was raised from members of the University and well wishers. 374 individuals and various corporate bodies and groups subscribed £3861. A modest amount was spent on commissioning a silver beaker for the Vice-Chancellor, made by Gerald Benney, the silversmith of the University mace. A brooch in the design of a spider's web was specially made for Jane Thistlethwaite by Robert Kramerson, a young American silversmith. But at the Thistlethwaites' insistence the cost of personal gifts was kept down so that the bulk of the fund could go to the Frank and Jane Thistlethwaite Fund.

The fund has an imaginative purpose. It is entirely at the disposal of the Vice-Chancellor of the day to be used for any purpose which the Vice-Chancellor considers would benefit the University, "the ideas would be the Vice-Chancellor's own".[86] Frank Thistlethwaite had sometimes felt baulked that any proposal of expenditure had to pass Senate and Council, and any such proposal that seemed non-essential always met objections that it was unaffordable in times of stringency. The Fund, by being independent of all University committees, would obviate this. Nobody could apply for it but the Vice-Chancellor would use it entirely at his own discretion. But only the interest, not the capital, was to be used and accordingly he proposed that the Fund lie fallow to accumulate for some years before the interest be tapped. By 1990 it had reached £9629 but had still not been used.[87] In due course it will become an increasingly valuable resource to embellish the University as the Vice-Chancellor hoped.

Frank Thistlethwaite took his formal farewell at the final Congregation of 4 July 1980, when Lord Franks conferred upon him the Honorary degree of Doctor of Civil Law.[88] At the same session honours were conferred on Sir Peter Pears and on Lord Zuckerman, who had played so large a part in the formation of UEA since the earliest days of the Academic Advisory

33. The first students arrive in the Village, October 1963.

34. The Alumni Reunion of 1996.
Frank Thistlethwaite and Dame Elizabeth Estève-Coll standing to the right, Nicholas Brooke seated on the left and Willi Guttsman on the right, Robert Ashton standing on the extreme left, Richard Snelling seated fourth from left.

35. A kitchen in Suffolk Terrace.

36. A bedroom in Suffolk Terrace.

37. A history seminar, 1965. The teacher is Richard Shannon, the second student from the right is the novelist Rose Tremain.

38. Work in a biology laboratory, 1965.

39. Richard Snelling addressing an early Student Union meeting in the Village Hall 1965.

40. The visit of the Queen, 24 May 1968.

41. Students leaving the arts block, after occupation, and marching to Earlham Hall, 17 March 1971.

42. A protest against administration.

43. Demonstrators in a snowstorm, on the visit of Robert Jackson, 21 November 1988.

44. The Students' Union during an election.

45. The Square.

46. The Square.

47. Rugby football at Fifer's Lane residences, January 1985.

Committee. To the consternation of the audience, Lord Franks normally so much in control on such occasions, having conferred degrees on Sir Peter and Lord Zuckerman then declared the proceedings closed, having seemingly forgotten the main business of the afternoon. The humour of the incident and his resumption had the beneficial effect of breaking what would have been considerable tension as the Vice-Chancellor took his position for the conferment. The Public Orator, Dr Randall Baker, praised the Vice-Chancellor for the alliance of tradition and innovation which had been the "hallmark of the distinctive contribution Frank Thistlethwaite has made to intellectual and academic life in this country", and he included Jane Thistlethwaite, "his chief Anglo-American interest who "reinforced the Thistlethwaite promotion of cultural life in the region".

Frank Thistlethwaite then replied, thanking various individuals and bodies who had helped to bring UEA into being, likening its progress to sailing a ship through changeable waters.[89] All went smoothly until he used as a peroration a passage from F.M. Cornford's *Microcosmographia Academica*. He addressed the students seemingly very directly and personally "try very hard to remember what it was like when you were young, there is no reason why your brains should ever get woolly, or anyone should wish you out of the way. Farewell". A touch of emotion came into his voice on the phrase "when you were young", creating an electric atmosphere of sympathy and empathy among young and old alike. The speech was followed by a long standing ovation from the congregation which included nine past and present Presidents of the Students' Union. Many of these were successful and busy men who had travelled specially for the occasion as a genuine mark of respect with which the Vice-Chancellor was held by the student body. After this Lord Franks declared the proceedings closed – for the second time – and the procession exited amid much tension relieving laughter.

After the Congregation a ceremony was held in the conservatory of the Sainsbury Centre at which Lord Franks presented the silver beaker and the brooch, as "a token of the high regard and deep affection" with which the Vice-Chancellor and his wife were held. Now, in lighter vein the Vice-Chancellor referred to the *Pirates of Penzance* lyric about the police force: "Yes, Yes, we go, Yes but you don't go", as one leavetaking ceremony followed another. "At last they really go", he concluded.

But not quite. For a day of joy ended in anguish. After a quiet unwinding dinner at the Maid's Head in Norwich Frank and Jane Thistlethwaite returned to Wood Hall and decided to christen his new beaker before retiring. As he recalled, "carrying it on a tray from the hall into the library I tripped over the step . . . breaking my fibia badly down towards the ankle. The result was a month in hospital and a summer recovering on crutches. Not part of this leavetaking".[90] Patricia Whitt told the Ritchies "all the shine has been taken off the gingerbread – it is such a cruel stroke of fate . . . he was terribly tired after so many extra engagements".[91] The Vice-Chancellor formally stayed in office until 26 September and then in October departed for his long deferred holiday in Crete, able to feel at long last that he really had left UEA.

There were many official expressions of regard on Frank Thistlethwaite's retirement, as we have seen. But in some ways the most potent are the very private or the unplannable. Here are two to finish with. In 1978 he received a letter from a former student, "the University has an overall quality of goodness, consideration and civilisation in the best senses of those words . . . I shall leave with a feeling of respect and gratitude to all involved". The Vice-Chancellor replied, "I do not think I have ever received a more touching letter from a UEA student than yours to me. I am immensely grateful to you for it . . . it is most heartening that UEA should mean so much to you".[92] So heartfelt on both sides, it is the finest pair of documents in the University Archive. The other tribute was the first Grand Reunion held in 1985, the tribute was not so much the holding of the reunion but the fact that 900 of the 2,000 graduates to that date returned to show an interest in their old university – a far higher proportion than any other of the new universities of the sixties achieved.[93] This too reflected something of the attitude of alumni to alma mater and to its creator.

On their retirement the Thistlethwaites moved to Cambridge and Frank resumed his academic career. He was awarded a Leverhulme Emeritus Fellowship in 1981 to work on the history of migration to the USA, and in 1986 became Visiting Professor of History at the University of Minnesota. This resulted in his book on Dorset Pilgrims, a study of west country men and women who emigrated to New England in the seventeenth century. This was followed by books dealing with the history of his family's cotton firm in Burnley and his own early life, his wartime years and career as a Cambridge don.[94] His happy retirement at Cambridge was enriched by being back in the Cambridge swim as an Honorary Fellow of St John's and Chairman of the Friends of the University Library. Yet it was immeasurably saddened by the death of Jane Thistlethwaite in 1992, a sadness shared at UEA, conscious of the contribution she too had made to its creation.

10

Making the Cuts

They were cutting the numbers of students, cutting the courses, cutting the secretaries, cutting the porters; they were cutting the playing fields, cutting the student accommodation, cutting the library, cutting the teaching buildings. They were also cutting the staff. There were those who suspected that the people in the university registry – who, as it happened, were not on the whole being cut – were undertaking the exercise with almost an excess of enthusiasm.[1]

Malcolm Bradbury, *Cuts* (1987)

The UGC is going to announce, probably some time in May, the distribution of the available funds to each university, based on an assessment of their research record and the viability of their departments. There are rumours that one or two universities will be closed down completely.[2]

David Lodge, *Nice Work* (1988)

Frank Thistlethwaite was succeeded as Vice-Chancellor in October 1980 by Michael Thompson. Thompson, then aged forty-nine, was the professor of Experimental Physics at Sussex University. He came with a distinguished career, a first class degree and D.Sc. from Liverpool University, work at Harwell Atomic Energy Research Establishment in the 1950s and 1960s with visiting posts at Chalk River in Canada, the Brookhaven National Laboratory on Long Island in USA, and the Australian National University in Canberra. He also had wide administrative experience not only at Sussex University but in NHS matters in the Brighton and Sussex region, and also as a consultant to various industries and the UKAEA and as director of the Alliance Building Society. Indeed one of his areas of expertise was in computers and the part they could play in building societies. The appointment of a physicist as Vice-Chancellor was in keeping with a trend of the time: in 1985 thirty-six out of the forty-five Vice-Chancellors were scientists.[3] He was a tall, lean, fit man fond of swimming and of sailing, joining the Royal Norfolk and Suffolk Yacht Club. He created a very favourable impression after his appointment. Sir Edmund Bacon told Frank Thistlethwaite, "I was very much impressed with your successor. It must be a great relief to believe that you are handing on all you have built up over the years to someone who looks as though he will be able to carry on your good work".[4]

Thompson came with certain views. He was keen to involve the public in the University in various ways and not merely through formal membership of Council and Court. He felt that "one of the failures of universities in the sixties was in convincing people at large that universities were doing anything worthwhile". The need to create public support for universities, and the awareness of how little there was of it when the cuts bit in the 1980s, became an urgent concern. "It is important to convince local people at least that there is something worthwhile going on on campus." At Sussex he had been closely involved with the Town and Gown Club, establishing contacts between the University and Brighton, and wanted to see what could be developed in Norwich. Above all he felt, and conveyed, a sense of optimism about his coming years which were to prove more difficult than he could have predicted.

Professor Thompson's arrival almost coincided with that of the Conservatives under Margaret Thatcher, who came into government in 1979 with the intention of reforming or cutting back the universities. Six reasons lay behind what seemed to be the necessity for this. First it was necessary to reduce public spending. Under Harold Wilson and James Callaghan it had usually been around 45 per cent of GDP, reaching 47 per cent in 1975. High levels of public spending were regarded as responsible for high inflation and interest rates. It also supported a large public sector which it was thought desirable to reduce in the interests of increasing private enterprise. Accordingly the Conservatives determined to diminish public spending and got it down to 38 per cent by 1988. Moreover, since public spending was never covered by taxation, the shortfall was met by public borrowing, the Public Sector Borrowing Requirement (PSBR). As a percentage of GDP this too was regarded as too high, being usually 8-10 per cent in the years 1974-76 and still 5-6 per cent in 1979-81. The Conservatives squeezed it down to 3 per cent and then 1 per cent in the early eighties, and then were actually able to repay public debt at the end of the decade 1987-90.[5] Cutting expenditure on the universities would contribute to this general drive to cut public expenditure and the PSBR as a whole.

Secondly, although the costs of the universities were a small part of total public spending, about 3 or 4 per cent, yet they were relatively high cost. Kenneth Baker's view was that "change was necessary because Britain was running a high cost education system with a relatively low level of output".[6] Even Robin Marris, who was hostile to Joseph's policies, showed that at £22,507, teaching and administrative costs per student in Britain were more than Belgium, France and Italy, and about the same as Germany. Britain had more university teachers in proportion to students than Canada, France, Italy, Japan, Switzerland and the USA but educated fewer first degree students per thousand population than any major power.[7] It was a system ripe for squeezing, either spending less or certainly forcing the existing system to educate more. It was also inequitable, since higher education in Britain absorbed four times the resources per student given to primary and secondary education, a disproportion greater than, any other advanced country.[8] Some rebalancing could be justified.

Thirdly, there was increasing scepticism that the expansion of higher education since the early 1960s had had any beneficial effects on the economy. Considering some key indicators, percentage growth per year:

	1960-73		1973-79	
Real earnings[1]	2.1		0.5	
Inflation[1]	4.8		14.7	
Unemployment	1.9		3.4	
	1960-64	1965	1969-73	1979
GDP[2]	3.1	2.5	3.0	3.0

1. Leslie Hannah in Paul Johnson, *Twentieth Century Britain* (London, 1994) p. 347.
2. B.W.E. Alford, *British Economic Performance 1945-1975* (Cambridge, 1998) p. 14.

Between the starting of the new universities and the advent of Margaret Thatcher, growth in real earnings had declined, inflation and unemployment risen and GDP remained notably unchanged. There was little evidence that the expansion of universities had had any beneficial effects on the economy and, since the costs of their expansion had contributed to high public spending, there seemed more gain than danger in cutting them.

Fourthly, there seemed even less reason to sustain the universities as student demand was likely to fall sharply. The numbers of eighteen year olds were due to fall from 941,000 in 1983 to 630,000 by 1994. The fall in the age group for social class groups I and II was, however, much less than for the population at large and they were the chief prospective entrants to universities. There was also a rising trend of women going to university and more mature students. Government statisticians calculated that, taking various factors into account, student numbers could fall from 565,000 in 1983/4 down to anything between 525,000 or 492,000 by 1996/7. Intelligent guesswork if no more, but some sort of fall was certainly expected. Nobody was predicting a rise over these years.[9] Sir Michael Thompson recalls that this was quite the most telling argument deployed by the civil service to justify cuts.

Fifthly, the universities could be accused of either not responding to demand for university places or of being institutions for which there was no rising demand. The surprising constancy of the age participation ratio at 13.8 in 1970/1 and 13.2 in 1981/2 could be interpreted in either way. But if there was no rising demand over the 1970s then it added strength to the argument that there would be even less by the mid 1990s in the demographic downturn.[10] Moreover, the universities had failed to increase their appeal more widely across the social classes. The age participation ratio of the "middle class" had risen from 19.5 in 1961 to 27 in 1977, while that of the "working class" had risen only slightly from 3.2 to 5 over the same period. The universities could be accused of conservatism and not facilitating social change as much as Robbins, and supporters of his Report, would have expected. It left them open to charges of needing some kind of radical reform. But that the middle classes still saw the universities as their special preserve was to later cause trouble for Sir Keith Joseph, the Secretary of State for Education, as we shall see.

Finally, there were deeper psychological factors behind the university cuts. Education was seen as a "secret garden" controlled not by dedicated professionals but by under employed, self-seeking, inefficient academics. Margaret Thatcher saw it as part of her radicalism to take on various "establishments" – doctors, lawyers, the Stock Exchange. Kenneth Baker recalled "the academic establishment at the universities was the first professional middle class group whose practices and interests was challenged by the Thatcher Government".[11] The government also sensed that the universities were vulnerable in public opinion due to their inability to curb student unrest. When Vice-Chancellors would visit Joseph to discuss finance he would easily divert them by berating them about student disturbances.[12] The middle classes still thought of a university education as desirable, but the status of "student" still carried opprobium. The image of the university teacher in the media at this time from *The History Man* to *The Edge of Darkness* and *Educating Rita* was dreadful – lazy, lecherous, corrupt and drunk. The universities would be easy targets as the 1981 cuts showed. Such were the considerations in the mind behind the furrowed brow and anguished mask Sir Keith Joseph presented in these years.

Joseph wanted the overall cut back in student numbers to be accompanied by a shift in the balance of studies, to reduce those studying the humanities and increase scientists, technologists or engineers of use to industry. There was a common belief that British universities produced far more humanities than science students and that this was damaging to the economy. Joseph's proposals accordingly gained support from this belief. In fact it was unfounded. In the 1970s British universities had a higher proportion of students studying science and technology (38.2 per cent) than Germany, Canada, USA or Japan and were only slightly exceeded in France. Britain had a smaller proportion studying humanities and social sciences (28.3 per cent) than any major country.[13] This was still so in the eighties, when 34 per cent of British graduations were in science and engineering compared with 21-22 per cent in Germany, Japan and the USA.[14] This was partly brought about by the upgrading of polytechnics to universities. The frequently complained of shortages of technologists for industry arose not so much from the balance of studies as the low overall output of British universities. They were now being asked to reduce this low output further and the policy of re-balancing was but a part of the wider problem. It was also likely to be thwarted by the fact that science and technology places remained unfilled in universities – 1100 in 1986.[15] UEA, however, really was heavily humanities biased. When Thompson arrived in 1980 UEA had only 32 two per cent of its students in the sciences, as opposed to 38.6 in the Humanities and 29.4 per cent in the social studies. Accordingly, in UEA's case the requirement to rebalance disciplines was apposite.

"Selectivity" came to be an important watchword and principle of these years. It came to operate on three levels. First, that there should be a selective preference for the sciences in whatever cuts were made. Secondly, that not all universities should suffer "equal misery" was favoured by the AUT, but "selectivity" by many Vice-Chancellors and especially the UGC. It gave a role to the latter to use their detailed knowledge of individual universities in making cuts. It also enabled them to preserve what was best in the system amid what was to be lost.[16] Finally, the concern for selectivity led to an increasing belief that, even within the sciences, resources should be concentrated in the best, large departments. This led to the Oxburgh Report on Earth Sciences in 1987 and the Edwards Report on Physics in 1988, shortly after Thompson's term. Each had respectively positive and adverse implications for UEA.

There was also a belief held by Joseph and the UGC that universities should rely less on public funding and seek more private funds. Joseph expressed this in measured terms that they should "inch towards" this position but that it was an "illusion" that there could be a "sudden transformation".[17] The UGC was more strident. Its Chairman, Sir Edward Parkes, warned Vice-Chancellors to seek private funds "on a massive scale" or go bankrupt.[18] UEA's balance of income for research at this time was 61.5 per cent from the public and 17.1 per cent from the private sector, with 21.1 per cent unknowable but probably predominantly public.[19] For UEA in an area so lacking in manufacturing industry there were limitations on the extent to which they could move from public to private finance. Such were the government policies which were to face the new incoming Vice-Chancellor.

Michael Thompson had scarcely been in office for a few days when he attended a meeting with the UGC. He reported that "on the national front it seemed likely that the financial situation would get worse and that higher education might be the target for a series of cuts", but that UEA had "no reason to be pessimistic." [20] He had more reason to be pessimistic than he thought. The UGC letter of 30 December 1980 notified universities that there would be a reduction of £30,000,000 for the fiscal year 1981/2, which would represent a fall of about 5 to 6 per cent. This was worse than earlier discussions had led Vice-Chancellors to expect and they were advised that "some reduction in the present level of activity will be inescapable".[21] The grant allocation letter would follow next Spring. UEA felt it had no need to await this with trepidation, as it had operated a moratorium on new posts for a year and tight budgetary and establishment control would continue.[22] In the meantime the University determined to maintain the unit of resource, that is the real income per student. This had actually fallen by 13 per cent since 1974 and it was not a nationally agreed policy to preserve it, so there was some wishful thinking in UEA's belief that it could sustain it. UEA anticipated that there would be a slight fall in home students offset by overseas full-time students, giving an overall total of about 4006.[23]

There were difficulties, however, in assuming that more overseas students could offset deficits at home. From 1980 overseas students had to pay full cost fees, unsubsidised by the British taxpayer. By 1981 a three year arts degree at a provincial university cost over £12,000. The home student was unaware of it, since fees were paid as part of the grant, but the overseas student had to find them out of his own pocket. The burden was increased by the inflation and strength of the pound of those years. Accordingly, in October 1980 UEA admissions of foreign students plummeted to a half of what they had been in 1979, and applications for 1981 were another 39 per cent down by January. The University was concerned that the loss of overseas students was reducing both the cosmopolitan character of the student body and its recurrent income. Moreover, countries which formerly regarded themselves as having links with the UK now felt "consternation and disillusion" at the new fee policy and were turning to universities in USA, Canada and Australia instead. There was also visa requirements, which particularly upset members of the "white" Commonwealth. Professor K. N. Bhaskar and Dr J. G. Harvey accordingly were sent in 1980 on a seventeen day trip to visit thirty-two institutions in Hong Kong, Singapore and Kuala Lumpur to sound out the market and its problems.[24] They made sensible proposals about producing publicity material, recognising the Hong Kong A level, keeping personal contacts and dealing with applications promptly. These could hardly be enough to counteract such problems, though great effort was put into the problem, with trips to Latin America and USA. Universities and the CVCP were ambivalent about the new "full cost" policies. There was outrage at the discrimination against non-EC countries but, on the other hand, the opportunity to earn money that came from independent (non UK government) sources was welcomed. UEA went after the money, hence the Bhaskar mission stressing business and law which were attractive to Asian students. Consequently, overseas students, having dipped from 325 in 1980/81 to 278 in 1981/82, recovered a bit to 292 by 1982/83, but there was not much expectation of recovering to 1980/81 levels.[25] One mitigating factor was the CVCP's Overseas Research Student scheme (ORS), which provided the difference between the home and overseas fees for research students. UEA had been quite successful in these. The imposition of full cost fees on overseas students was one of the first of the cuts.

In May 1981 the UGC notified Vice-Chancellors that the situation was even worse than they thought. The expected cuts would be 8.5 per cent for home students which, with a loss of income from overseas students, would amount to a total loss of "at least 11 per cent and possibly significantly more".[26] This was an aggregate figure and variations in allocations between universities would follow. But the UGC made it clear that research should be protected with the cuts fall on teaching; it was a stage in the tilting of priorities in university activity towards research at the expense of teaching. The University reckoned that it had surplus reserves of some £460,000 with which to absorb the expected cuts.[27] The Vice-Chancellor reassured the Court that there was no need for "alarm or despondency" since UEA "should be well placed to cope with the future".[28]

In July the two crucial UGC letters arrived.[29] The first was couched in general terms to all Vice-Chancellors. The loss of resources to the universities would be between 11 per cent (the UGC estimate) and 15 per cent (the CVCP estimate). Student numbers would fall by 5 per cent and the unit of resource by 10 per cent. Overall the UGC wanted a slightly greater than average cut in the arts, a "substantial reduction" in social studies, and a small increase in business studies, physical sciences and engineering and technology. This would change the balance of students among arts, science and medicine from 50 : 41: 9 in 1979/80 to 48 : 42: 10 for 1981/2.

The second letter was specifically about UEA. UEA's recurrent grant was to fall from £11,710,000 in 1981/82 to £10,950,000 for 1982/83 and £10,280,000 for 1983/84. Students were to fall from 4300 in 1980/1, to 3760 in 1979/80 and to 3640 by 1983/84 or 1984/85. More drastically, UEA was advised to discontinue linguistics and drama, phase out Russian and reduce social studies more than the arts. In the sciences they wanted a reduction in the physical sciences and biology. The Vice-Chancellor estimated that there would be a percentage decrease in income of 12 per cent between 1981/82 to 1983/84 and a reduction of 500 in student numbers. He saw "no insuperable financial problems" but was surprised at some of the UGC advice about departments.[30]

UEA had some initial grounds for optimism. Its cut was a little less than the average. Some observers thought that UEA had been very lucky in 1981, receiving the fifth lightest cut even though it had the fifth lowest A level entry levels.[31] The cuts imposed on Salford, Bradford and Aston at this time were over 30 per cent. Also UEA's reserves were larger than originally expected, £958,000 and there were seventy-six unfilled posts of all kinds, which gave flexibility. When the University took a considered view of the future, however, it was clear that the cuts would affect UEA in the next few years more than immediately. A surplus of £958,000 in 1980-81 would reduce to one of £155,000 by 1981-82, then move to a deficit of £1,000,000 by 1982-83 and £2,100,000 by 1983-84.[32] There was some flexible ambiguity about the timing of the cuts. The Universities wanted them spread over five years, Keith Joseph was insisting on three years, but the UGC told UEA that "it would not be seen as significant if the reduced totals were not achieved until 1984-85", which eased things somewhat. Nonetheless it was pointed out that the cuts would coincide not with a period of reduction in the number of eighteen year olds but an increase. Eighteen year olds reached a peak in 1982-83, but even the cohort of 1984-85 was larger than that of 1980-81: "over the period covered by the cutback in funds and student places the number of candidates applying to universities will increase". The cuts would fall not only on the universities but on – largely middle-class – parents and their children.

Following the initial document of September 1981 the Vice-Chancellor and Resources Committee worked on the University's detailed response to the cuts, resulting in a major report in March 1982 which merits particular attention. [33] The Review of Activities was initiated by the Vice-Chancellor. He had undertaken similar exercises at Harwell and at Sussex, and saw that this was necessary for UEA. He set out to find out the strengths and weaknesses of each School, getting each of them to draw up vital statistics and explain them to him in personal interviews. This was an unusual occasion when Lord Franks as Chancellor was appealed to for advice. As Chairman of many inquiries, Lord Franks advised the Vice-Chancellor to let all comers come and talk to him and then write up a report himself. Thompson saw that he had to design policies for flexibility and to identify growth points. He had not been satisfied with procedures at Sussex, where fair shares for all had led to equal immiseration irrespective of merit. He also saw the need to reorder the subjects at UEA into cost centres – for example art and music needed to be distinguished – as essential for financial planning. He rejected the staff student ratio as the basis for resource distribution since research expenditure, and the need for laboratory or studio teaching (as in physics or music) was so labour intensive. As selectivity had to be accepted so too the problem of the viability and even closure of some subjects (physics and Russian) also had to be faced. The Vice-Chancellor personally chaired the sessions running into hundreds of hours in 1980-81, on which the selective cuts of the Review were based.

The Review reminded members that the University faced a deficit of £2,100,000 by 1983-84, which represented 12.5 per cent of the projected expenditure of that year. Former cuts had usually been in the rate of expansion, but now it would be a real retraction. There was a real cut of 17 per cent in higher education and an expected 10 per cent deterioration in the unit of resource between 1979-80 and 1983-84. UEA's own cut was 12.5 per cent and student numbers were required to fall by 434 (10.7 per cent of UEA's 1981-82 target) to 3640 full-time home and EC students. This reduction was distributed as 379 (13 per cent) in the arts and 55 (5 per cent) in sciences. As a wholly hypothetical exercise, UEA estimated that seventy academic and eighty-one non-academic posts would be lost, hopefully by compensated voluntary redundancy. When the cuts had been made, the universities were given to believe that there would be level funding; there would be no further contractions as a matter of policy. But how were the immediate cuts to be addressed?

The University made it clear that it would broadly follow the UGC's advice but not down to the last detail, since "we know this University better than the UGC does". This was not a cavalier remark but the Vice-Chancellor's carefully considered view based on his lengthy and painstaking investigation into the strengths and weaknesses of Schools. They considered various ways of making the cuts. "Random vacancy", waiting to see who resigned, would most likely lead to the vanishing of sectors whose faculty could most easily find jobs elsewhere. "Excision of limb", or cutting out whole schools, was not feasible: there were no areas weak enough to need such amputation and it would entail massive compulsory redundancies. "Proportionate cuts" would make small units unviable and make the rebalancing required by the UGC impossible. Simply following UGC advice was not favoured either, since they proposed expanding areas where UEA was weak and cutting or abolishing some areas where it was strong. The only way forward was "selective choice", retaining almost everything yet operating selective differential cuts on all.

In digest form this is what the Resources Committee proposed. The percentage cuts emanated initially from the Vice-Chancellor following his review of activities with minor adjustments from the Resources Committee itself (Table 15).

The cuts would be facilitated by voluntary staff reductions of seventy academic and eighty non-academic posts, and eased by extra income generated from 298 overseas students. The Resources Committee declined to accept the UGC proposal to close drama and linguistics, but it did agree to cease Russian

Table 15   *Resources Committee Proposals*

School	Action	Cut	Expenditure 1983-4
Education	Merge CARE	16 per cent (£171,000)	£970,000
EAS	Retain linguistics and drama	16 per cent (£165,000)	£1,029,000
EUR	Discontinue Russian 1983.	16 per cent (£164,000)	£1,025,000
FAM		8.5 per cent (£38,000)	£403,000
CEAS	Cease September 1983	–	–
DEV		13 per cent (£63,000)	£488,000
LAW		7 per cent (£21,000)	£296,000
SOC	Absorb Social Work	18 per cent (£230,000)	£1,278,000
BIO		10.7 per cent (£118,000)	£1,100,000
CHEM		7.5 per cent (£71,000)	£952,000
Computing and Accountancy		Nil	£568,000
ENV		7.5 per cent (£65,000)	£853,000
MAP		6.6 per cent (£49,000)	£738,000
LIB		12.5 per cent (£63,000)	£956,000
AVC		17.9 per cent (£35,000)	£195,000
Computing Centre		7 per cent (£25,000)	£496,000
SCVA		12.5 per cent (£16,000)	£129,000
Safety		3.5 per cent (£2,000)	£57,000
Administration		12.5 per cent (£155,000)	£1,296,000
Maintenance	Staff	12.5 per cent (£211,000)	£3,330,000
	Heat, light, water	3.8 per cent (£30,000)	
Staff, student facilities and amenities – SSFA		15.5 per cent (£71,000)	£459,000
Students' Union		15 per cent (£33,000)	[SU declined to prepare a submission].
General Educ. Expenditure		27 per cent (£44,515)	£165,150
Other Expenditure		24 per cent (£23,000)	£55,840
Other Funds		13.2 per cent (£26,355)	£199,170
		Total Cuts £1,889,870	

as a full degree subject after 1983. It also proposed to close the CEAS but this met such protest in the region that it was retained, as we shall see. SOC was cut severely, as the UGC proposed, but little attention was paid to proposals to cut back ENV more than other sciences. The Review of March 1982 is one of the great documents of UEA's history – clear, judiciously argued, fairly balanced and arrived at after painstaking investigation chaired by the Vice-Chancellor. It inspired confidence that the crisis could be managed. The immediate task was to take UEA through the cuts to 1985 and this it did. In presenting the cuts to the public the Vice-Chancellor stressed their serious but non-catastrophic nature, but emphasised to the region that they would affect "the services the University could offer ... to the local community and East Anglia as a whole".[34]

The overall effect was to reduce student numbers, tilt the balance away from social sciences and humanities to science, and reduce costs per student.[35]

	Percentage of students in different areas			Costs per student by sector 1981/2=100
	1979-80	1981-82	1983-84	
Education	–	8.5	8.5	
Humanities	38.6	36.2	35.6	96.6
Social Sciences	29.4	24.8	23.5	97.2
Science	32.0	30.5	32.4	97.5
	100.0	100.0	100.0	
Student Numbers	3863.0	4124.0	3700.0	

Better news came in a further UGC letter in May about the University's recurrent grant for 1982-83 and revised provisional grant for 1983-84; this brought an improvement of £200,000 a year over what was expected in the July letter.[36] Also the savings through staff leaving was going quite well. It was estimated that 116 staff of all kinds had to leave by 1984 and already in 1982 it was certain that eighty-six would do so, seventeen by a premature retirement compensation scheme and voluntary severance and sixty-nine by natural wastage. Another thirty were still sought by 1984, but mostly in the non-academic and related areas where turnover was more fluid.[37] Nationally universities were losing staff rapidly. By November 1800 academics and administrators had taken voluntary redundancy over the last year,[38] and by the end of the year £41,000,000 had been paid out in redundancy money. It was already worrying that staff were leaving on a greater scale than the reduction in student numbers. Most of these were in the important areas of engineering, technology, computing and accountancy that Joseph wished to encourage.[39]

Shedding staff was the only effective way of making cuts, but UEA assured faculty that compulsory redundancy would be very unlikely and this gave considerable confidence at this time. Indeed the difficulties of compulsory redundancy were made clear by events elsewhere. When Brunel and Aston Universities leaked or revealed redundancy plans in September 1981, the AUT made it clear that any such attempts would be contested legally. By October several universities were frankly admitting that large numbers of academics would have to be shed. Even one so strong as Bristol envisaged losing 150.[40] By November the stakes were raised and rumour was now not only of individual redundancies but of whole universities having to close down. Mark Carlisle had stated that no university would be forced to do this but in September he had been replaced by Keith Joseph. The UGC now admitted that whole institutions could possibly close and three thousand academics would lose their jobs. The Vice-Chancellors thought that it was more likely to be 5250, or an eighth of the profession.[41] The first test case of a university trying to sack lecturers with tenure was at the London University Institute of Orthopaedics, but it was contested by the AUT and did not proceed.[42] The first case of a lecturer actually being made redundant was at Dundee, but she was reinstated by an Industrial Tribunal.[43] These London and Dundee cases indicated that responding to cuts by compulsory redundancy was very difficult and likely to fail. As regards UEA, Michael Thompson made it clear that compulsory redundancy would be an absolutely last resort and he had every expectation of getting through without it.[44]

The May 1983 report on the implementation of cuts was optimistic, good progress had been made and no compulsory redundancies would be necessary in 1983-84. Deficits for the future were estimated as 1983/84 £244,000, 1984/85 £124,000, 1985/6 £139,000. Confident of the future, the University proposed to make new allocations to the Library, to energy saving and to provision for about six or seven new research studentships.[45] Overall the expenditure of the University was to be £17,700,000 for 1983/84. Balances (surpluses of income over expenditure carried forward cumulatively) of £2,400,000 brought forward into 1983/84 would remain at £1,900,000 at the end of 1985/86. The staff would be reduced by a hundred and the student intake would be reduced, in spite of an unprecedented rise to 15,000 applicants for 1100 places. This reduction had to be made, since a few universities (not UEA) which had tried to avoid reducing students or even tried to increase them had had their UGC grant cut accordingly.

If the University left for the long vacation in 1983 in a reassured mood, worse was to come. The Conservatives were re-elected with an increased majority and following this, Nigel Lawson brought in a budget requiring further public spending cuts. The government must have seen that the cuts on universities in their first period of office had met with little public resistance: the middle-class parents whose offspring made up the bulk of university applicants either had not understood the implications of the cuts for themselves or approved of them. The increased majority of the returned government seemed to endorse their policies and call for more. So universities were to be cut by £23,500,000.[46]

The UEA had received assurance that student numbers for 1984/85 were likely to be the same as those for 1983/84,[47] but there was no assurance about level funding, although Edward Parkes reminded Keith Joseph that he had given "indications" about "more or less level funding". Parkes asked Joseph about his future intentions.[48] Joseph's long-delayed reply presaged further difficulties for the universities in the light of the Lawson budget.[49] He agreed that he had formerly hoped to retain level funding, but now (September 1983) "I cannot give any undertakings". Pressures on public spending were going to be severe, universities were going to have to be less dependent on public funds, and they should move to even more technological, scientific or engineering courses. Most ominously they should consider a reduction of 5-10 per cent in funds by the end of the decade, and a further 5 per cent in the five years beyond that, in an overall drive to reduce public spending as a proportion of GDP. Accusations of broken promises flew.[50] It was becoming evident that the cuts on universities were not merely those of 1981 but were to be ongoing and perpetual. Yet there was another twist. The universities had come to accept a situation of fewer students and less money. Then in September Keith Joseph asked UEA to take more students, especially in vocational and technological subjects, since he intended to squeeze public sector polytechnic and college higher education.[51] Universities should accept some of the burden shed by the polytechnics and colleges.[52] It was evident that some strategy was needed: was contraction or expansion of students wanted, in a condition of level or contracted funding? Sir Peter Swinnerton Dyer FRS, Sir Edward Parkes's successor at the UGC, started devising such a strategy for the 1990s. But his assumptions were depressing, asking the universities to contemplate a reduction in resources of up to 1 or 2 per cent in real terms in each of the next five years and 1 per cent a year for the next five years thereafter. He also asked ominously how universities would cope with a 15-20 per cent fall in student numbers between 1989/90 to 1994/95 and whether "a significant number of institutions" should be closed.[53] The UGC was thought to have a "hit list" of universities to close,[54] and some believed that only fifteen or sixteen universities would survive until the end of the century.[55]

These years were made all the more worrying for UEA in that the grant for 1984/85 was originally announced as £14,400,000, then £13,820,000 (which was an error), then not fully restored to £14,060,000. This could have resulted in either surpluses of £71,000, if the inflation rate were 4 per cent, but deficits of £67,000 if 5 per cent, which was quite unpredictable. The Finance Officer regarded the UGC letter "one of the most unhelpful ever received". In fact inflation rose gently from just under to just over 5 per cent between 1983 and 1985, making deficits inevitable.[56] UEA's response to the UGC request to contemplate 1 or 2 per cent cuts was forthright, even exasperated. Thompson told Swinnerton Dyer that his questions had started from the wrong viewpoint. They already assumed falling student demand for university places, which was questionable, that vocationalism must determine educational relevance; and that "vocational" had slipped into being equated with science. This overlooked the fact that many non-science subjects like accountancy, law, music and education were vocational at UEA and elsewhere. The UGC also assumed further cuts. In the Vice-Chancellor's view the debate should begin not with these assumptions but with the contribution higher education had to make – new technology, tackling unemployment, increased leisure, updating training.[57] UEA made it clear that research would certainly suffer from further cuts but they would increase part-time and mature students.

UEA calculated that a 1 per cent cut over six years to 1990 would amount to £1,080,000 and 2 per cent to £2,160,000. This compared with the £2,100,000 (12.5 per cent) cut sustained by UEA in 1981-84. Yet what had been done in 1981-84 was not repeatable in 1984-90 for two good reasons. UEA had prepared for the first cuts by an anticipatory freeze on new posts for two years; moreover, staff over fifty who wished to take retirement had already done so. The leeway existing before 1981 was no longer there after 1984.[58]

Planning had become very difficult, if not impossible. The stalwart Finance Officer, R. A. Newstead, made further calculations. He thought that reserves would be exhausted by 1986-87, leaving a shortfall of £628,000 by the end of that year; thereafter deficits could be anything between £416,000 or £1,008,000 for the next three years.[59] In fact the reserves fell from £1,600,000 in 1983 to £973,628 by 1986. This highlights UEA's great weakness: that its reserves were too small in relation to its annual turnover of around £20,000,000. This was in part due to UEA's relative youth, accentuated by the non-science bias that had been a feature Thompson inherited. Sir Michael was pleasantly surprised on going to Birmingham University to find there reserves of more than £80,000,000 to use flexibly.

If UEA, like all universities, was in a quandary by mid 1984, public opinion was becoming more aware and angry about the situation. There seemed to be no policy for higher education, just a concern to cut expenditure at all costs. The UGC was accused of having become "an agonised sub-mandarin" doing the bidding of its Department of Education master but beyond Parliament's questioning. The Vice-Chancellors likewise were criticised for being "curiously muted" and, unlike the doctors, unable to advocate their case, prefer-ring "tacit submission" to "judicious challenge".[60] The universities had been picked on not because they were conspicuously slack but because they were soft targets, since their funds were more easily regulated by Whitehall than areas of the education system receiving funds through local authorities. The loss of the quinquennial grant system, wrecked by inflation, had also been replaced by nothing but annual cash limits with consequent impossibilities of planning, and endless recalculation by individual universities of guessed at and constantly changing figures. Also insufficient thought was being given to the balance of scholarship, vocational training and research it, merely being assumed, fallaciously, that all institutions should do them equally.[61]

Public confidence was not reassured by the views of the Parliamentary Under Secretary of State dealing with universities, Peter Brooke. He had genuinely believed that the universities had experienced no cuts at all in 1980-81 and 1983-84, and that a 25 per cent increase in cash had resulted in "virtu-ally no change" in real terms. Then a session with Lord Flowers had convinced him that there really had been a cut of 8.75 per cent – itself containing an error and a confusion over calendar and academic years.[62] Brooke's position was a curious one – being part of a government calling for severe public spending cuts, having it believed that they were being carried out in universities, and yet himself purporting to believe that they were not. It also suggested an abyss of ambivalent policies which were based on figures nobody could trust. This impression was further intensified when the Royal Statistical Society demolished Department of Education assumptions that student demand would diminish by 20 per cent or 25 per cent over ten years and that 100,000 places were unnecessary. The Royal Statistical Society argued, on the contrary, that there would be a rising demand to the end of the century. The Department of Education accepted its error that its projections had been as much as 96,000 student places too low.[63] So were all these cuts really necessary after all? It was in this confused summer of 1984 that Lord Robbins died in May. He had been dismayed by the cuts of 1981, and furious with the UGC, and must have passed away saddened at such an undermining of the ideals of his Report of 1963.

Following the returns from universities, the UGC published its report in September 1984 on a Strategy for Higher Education at the same time as a parallel report for the National Advisory Body (for LEA colleges and poly-technics). They called for an increase of 14 per cent or 49,000 students in universities and polytechnics to 600,000 over the next three years and a sustaining of this position until 1990 at least.[64] As economic growth improved, so demand for graduates would increase and improvements in secondary education would likewise augment more teenagers qualified for university entry. This was in flat rejection of government assumptions of a fall in demand of student places of 30-70,000 students. To meet this they also called for government grants to universities to be held level to match inflation for at least six years. But extra funds should be made available for science and technology, essential research, updating adult skills, early retirement schemes for the old, and new blood posts for the young. They had no doubt that the 1981 cuts had done severe damage through the system, and that at least 11,000 young people had been denied a university education. This was a "forthright" document and welcomed by Lord Flowers, chair of the CVCP, as such. It seemed to suggest that the UGC and the CVCP, which had been criticised for being too accepting of government policy, were now, under Swinnerton Dyer and Flowers, to become much tougher in defending the universities. It was the first time that UGC advice to the government had been published. Keith Clayton of UEA, who had just left a period of office on the UGC, pointed out that this report was in line with the kind of advice UGC regularly gave to the government in private. He denied that the UGC had been supine but confessed "I am far from confident that published advice will quickly lead to an improved government response".[65]

While the Council was engaged with the cuts it received a broadside from one of its members, Ian Coutts. Mr Coutts was an accountant and a former Leader of Norfolk County Council, and a member of the Audit Commission. He had a reputation as a "man of the political right" and "Mr Cuts".[66] He served on the UEA Council as one of the representatives of Norfolk County Council. Then in 1984 he criticised UEA in *The Times* on 5 December 1984, followed by a speech in Norwich reported nationally in the *Daily Telegraph*.[67] Among other things he deplored that UEA had fifty-five porters, which he saw as equivalent to the police force of a town the size of King's Lynn, and that students were cosseted by having room cleaners. He called for the cutting of such non-academic staff to a quarter of its existing number. The University defended itself, pointing out that non-academic expenditure had been cut by 15 per cent,[68] that the comparison with King's Lynn was invalid, since Coutts left out of account all the non-police private security staff employed in that town, and that an irreducible level of security was necessary at UEA because of the open campus and its very valuable equipment. Coutts replied that his strictures applied not only to UEA but to universities generally. It is always salutary for institutions to receive constructive advice about economy but the suggestion to reduce non-academic staff to a quarter was hardly realistic or helpful. Also, having failed to convince his peers in Council, it was questionable practice to carry on the debate in the public press. Coutts's intervention should, however, be seen in the context of recent events which showed just how important the service staffs were.[69]

The inappropriateness of Coutts's complaints about the amount spent on security by the University was brought home by a few nasty events which showed the University vulnerable to criminal outsiders. Early in 1982 attention was drawn to sex attacks, with the Union reporting thirty incidents experienced in a survey of the three thousand women students at UEA. These ranged from exposure, indecent assault and a case of rape (not reported to the police). The problem was inevitably the totally open nature of the campus with woods and grassland around. "We don't want to turn this [campus] into a walled citadel", replied the University. Cost was also an element. However much was spent on lighting and security porters, only further expenditure could reduce this problem. For lack of those resources Campus Watch was set up to encourage students to be more vigilant of intruders.[70] The need for this was emphasised in April 1982 when the University was astonished to find a heroin dealer living in and trading from a campus room illegally sub-let by a student. This criminal was nothing to do with the University but it further brought home the University's vulnerability and the need for vigilance.[71] In August 1983 the University's land was invaded by a "Peace Convoy" of 150 people (forty of whom were arrested for drugs offences) in fifty vehicles who stayed for three weeks. The University gained an injunction to have the squatters removed and they became a matter for the Sheriff and the police, since it was a problem far beyond the capacities of UEA's security staff. Finally, and worst of all, in May 1984 a porter, Bill Wilson, was attacked by youths attempting to steal a bicycle and sustained serious head injuries from which he never fully recovered. It reminds us of the courage the security staff sometimes have to show in carrying out their duties in protecting all members of the University. The hunt for Mr Wilson's attacker was led by Detective Chief Superintendent Maurice Morson, head of Norfolk CID, who secured a conviction and jail sentence for the criminal. It was the University's good fortune that Mr Morson on retirement shortly afterwards became head of UEA's security staff in 1987. Mr Wilson never returned to work and the "Bill Wilson" Room in the Students Union commemorates his self-sacrificing action.

We have recalled these various distasteful episodes because they draw out certain wider features of UEA's life at this time. It is notable that these scandals did not reflect discreditably on UEA itself (as they might have done in the early 1970s). They were perpetrated by criminal outsiders. It also brought home to the people of Norwich that there was a price to be paid for maintaining open access for the public to its landscape and facilities. One consequence of these events was the introduction of Closed Circuit Television Cameras to UEA in 1984 by Maurice Morson, who had already pioneered its use in Norwich.[72] Finally, to return to the original point, they showed beyond doubt that Ian Coutts's suggestions about cutting security and bed making staff were inappropriate. They are front line defences against outside criminality on an open campus. The cuts in University finance in turn limited the University's capacity to strengthen or extend this defence.

Over the turn of the year 1984/85 the UGC and DES laid down key planning figures and assumptions for the next few years. In November 1984 the UGC embarked on yet another survey of universities, indicating that principles of selectivity would be introduced such that some universities could improve their financial position relative to others within constrained overall resources. The UGC calculated that students would decline from 565,000 in 1983/84 to 511,000 by 1999/2000.[73] In January 1985 Sir Keith Joseph reiterated his demand for more students in subjects of vocational relevance, notably science and engineering, wanted small departments rationalised and provided £4,000,000 for science laboratories.

In February 1985 the University was notified of its recurrent grant of £14,710,000,[74] which was the second highest of the new universities. Nonetheless UEA expected annual deficits of just over £500,000 and the exhaustion of its £1,300,000 reserves by 1986/7. The Resources Committee of UEA asked all spending authorities to prepare for a cut in resources of 3.5 per cent by the end of 1986/7 and leave posts unfilled.[75] The Vice-Chancellor did not pull his punches as he told the Court that UEA faced "a very sombre outlook indeed" and that prospects for the future were "worse than ever".[76]

In March 1985 the Jarratt Committee reported and this had implications for the cuts and their management.[77] The committee had been set up in April 1984 by the CVCP as a Steering Committee for Efficiency Studies in Universities under the Chairmanship of Sir Alex Jarratt, the Chairman of Reed International and Chancellor of Birmingham University. With him were three other industrialists (from Cadbury, Plessey and Ford), six academics, one university registrar and two civil servants. This well-balanced team brought forward well-considered proposals. They began by stressing that universities were "assets of immense national importance" and "serious consequences would follow if excellence ceased to be their objective, or if they were deprived of the ability to pursue it". The Committee was severely critical of the government. Its own funding horizons were too short, making forward planning by universities impossible because of the constant chopping and changing: "rapid changes in funding are not conducive to efficient use of resources". The UGC had come to be seen too much as a tool of the DES. It should make its views about the prospects and directions for higher education known publicly, have some overall planning framework and, if necessary, manage the system more – as when its advice on departmental closures was ignored in 1981. As regards the universities themselves, Jarratt made pertinent requirements. Councils should govern institutions with a Vice-Chancellor seen not only as an academic leader but as a chief executive. Each university should have a "rolling academic and institutional plan", and a planning and resources committee, to develop forward planning. As regards staff, their standards should be maintained by staff development, and annual appraisal and performance indicators such as research publications. Press reception was favourable though it was not appreciated that the capacity of universities to do their own planning was undermined by "the wilfully disconnected nature of the Government's approach to higher education".[78]

Jarratt did not have very profound implications for UEA because it already met many of its key requirements – a Council, Senate, executive Vice-Chancellor, a Resources Committee retitled "Planning and Resources" in the Jarratt terminology. The Deans were given more power as a Committee of Deans replacing the Development Committee to engaged in strategic planning. There were minor budgetary changes, and annual appraisal introduced for all from the Vice-Chancellor downwards. UEA was already well run, so press comment that Jarratt was going to lead to a "massive shake up" for universities and that dons would have to "put their house in order" did not much apply to UEA. But it was a step forward towards greater managerial control at the University.

The central engine of planning was the Planning and Resources Committee (PRC) which first met in 1986. It was partly a response to the Jarratt Report of 1985, which called for such as body in all universities. It was also a more appropriate body for deciding on cuts than the old Development Committee (from the 1960s) or the Resources Committee (from the 1970s). With the new PRC those two older committees ceased. The new PRC consisted of the most senior officers of the University (Chairman of Council, Treasurer, Vice-Chancellor and two Pro Vice-Chancellors) plus two members each from the Council and Senate. It was accordingly more distanced from Schools and Deans, who felt that they had lost some influence which they used to exercise through the Development Committee. Deans, however, still continued to meet informally with the Vice-Chancellor, as they had done since Frank Thistlethwaite's day. The new PRC was, however, firmly within the existing structure as a Joint Committee of Senate and Council, not as body imposing its authority from outside. Also, recommendations of the PRC were communicated to the Committee of Deans.

Following closely on Jarratt came the long awaited Green Paper in May 1985. This began by stressing the importance of the universities for meeting the need for qualified manpower. In three highly admonitory introductory paragraphs it stressed the need for universities to get closer to industry and commerce, serve its needs and encourage an entrepreneurial spirit in students as of prime importance. Universities could be of greatest use by training those with an enterprising attitude of mind in science, technology and mathematics, and indeed vocationalism was largely seen in these terms. Hence the need to balance subject studies more in this direction. Yet this should be seen against a background in which the eighteen- and nineteen-year-old population of Great Britain would fall by 33 per cent between 1984 and 1996. So far public expenditure on higher education had been £2700 million in 1980-81 and £3400 million in 1984/85, a reduction in real terms of 3.5 per cent.[79] No more money could be promised and some departments, even institutions might have to close.

The Green Paper aroused hostility both nationally and at UEA. Enoch Powell condemned it as "barbarism to attempt to evaluate the content of higher education in terms of economic performance". East Anglian MPs, like Robert Rhodes James of Cambridge, said he could not accept further contraction and resigned as the government's higher education liaison officer and Clement Freud of Ely called the Green Paper a move from the "unacceptable" to the "intolerable".[80] Even the *Daily Telegraph* slated it for its philistinism, false statistical assumptions and attempts to impose uniformity, and likened it to an attempt to keep a dying mule working carrying heavier loads with less and less food.[81]

At UEA the Vice-Chancellor was scathing and condemned the Green Paper as "depressing and disappointing ... the Government is once again thrusting a crisis on the universities", in precisely the way Jarratt had urged that it should not. There was no point in the government asking for more science and technology to meet the national need without the resources.[82] Professor Owen Chadwick, the new Chancellor, in appropriately historical and reflective mood, sadly contrasted the tone of the Green Paper and its wish to "direct higher education to be more serviceable to the industry and material prosperity of this country" with the Newmanite values he admired of universities as custodians of "a sense of beauty ... moral right ... a broader judgement of wisdom ... the civilised life ... culture". [83] Perhaps surprisingly, Margaret Thatcher took this kind of expression to heart and was saddened that Thatcherism in education had become equated to "a philistine subordination of scholarship to the immediate requirements of vocational training".[84]

In the aftermath of the Green Paper, Tony Newton, Under Secretary of State at the DHSS, made a visit to UEA and was "hustled away".[85] Sir Keith Joseph himself came to UEA at the end of the year to discuss the Green Paper with the Vice-Chancellor, Colonel Geoffrey Dicker, the chairman of Council, and Raymond Frostick. It was regarded by the Vice-Chancellor as "a useful and constructive exchange of views". Sir Keith found "everything was put firmly but courteously", but the President of the Students' Union, Ian McKenzie, found he was "listening but not hearing ... he did not get the message".[86] In fact the visit had elements of absurdity which were not revealed at the time. Sir Keith arrived by plane and had read the wrong briefing documents. In a confused state of mind and completely ill prepared, he thought he had come to *Essex* University. Spoiling for a fight with "subversives" he began by berating the Vice-Chancellor (the Director of a Building Society) for being a Communist! Such was the ridiculous side of the Minister responsible for education in these years.

It was not only the central funds of the University that were cut; the universities also experienced cuts through student grants, ESRC grants and VAT. The value of the maintenance grant in real terms fell on an index (1962/63 = 100) from 88 in 1980/81 to 81 in 1983/84 and 82 in 1984/85. Up to 1985/86 each student was entitled to a minimum award, regardless of income. The minimum award was worth £410 in 1983/84; by 1984/85 it had halved to £205 and by 1985/86 it had been abolished. Likewise up to 1984/85 students were reimbursed by their local authorities for travel between home and university. From 1984 this was abolished and replaced with a flat rate sum of £100, in effect limiting each of six journeys (two per term) to £16.[87] John Powley, the Norwich South Conservative MP, spoke against this in Parliament, pointing out the disadvantage to universities like UEA, but to no avail.[88] UEA students "sat in" at the Norwich Conservative Club to protest against grant cuts but to no more effect than John Powley's speech. It is hardly surprising that the political bias of UEA students was to the Left. In 1983, 38 per cent of students claimed to be Labour and 15 per cent Liberal or SDP, with only 20 per cent support for Conservatives.[89]

One particular specialised area of cut suffered by UEA in 1980s was the loss of ESRC grants. The Economic and Social Research Council (so renamed by Sir Keith Joseph) gave grants to students studying for postgraduate degrees. Far too few, however, were successfully completing their dissertations. Attention had first been drawn to the matter in 1981, when UEA was disclosed as the thirty-sixth worst university at completing ESRC Ph.D.s.[90] In 1985 the ESRC decided to impose sanctions by denying grants to poor performers for the next two years. These included UEA, which was then placed fifty-one out of sixty-four grant-receiving institutions with only one submission from fifteen students who had registered in 1979 and 1980. It was no comfort that University and King's Colleges of the University of London were even worse, or that the Arts schools at UEA were worse than the social sciences. At the end of 1985 five of the fourteen blacklisted institutions were reprieved by the ESRC, but not UEA, which remained one of the nine still excluded from grant.[91] Taking the long view only fifty-two students, registered in the academic years 1976-77 to 1981-82, had completed research degrees in Social Sciences at UEA by 1986, a mere 33 per cent. The arts percentage was 22 per cent and the sciences 73 per cent. Most of the non-science Ph.D.s at UEA simply gave up.

The University apologised and hoped to improve the situation, but there were deeper issues here. The truth was that anyone who embarked on a Humanities Ph.D. in these years was ill advised to do so and even more so to trouble completing it. Such a degree could only be of use in an academic career and these were precisely the years, 1981-86, when the average academic salary fell below the level of inflation while non-manual average earnings rose fifty percentage points above it.[92] In any case any aware postgraduate would have been conscious of the constant cuts, shedding of staff, threats of closures in the university sector he might have expected to enter. What is remarkable is not the low levels of completion but that anybody bothered to complete at all, and the naivety of the ESRC in expecting the situation to be otherwise in the state of higher education at that time. I recall the case of a young man at UEA undertaking a Ph.D. on German history who acquired a knowledge of German, the country and a German wife, and abandoned his studies and set himself up as an Anglo-German businessman. He counted as a UEA and ESRC academic "failure" but was precisely the kind of entrepreneurial success that Margaret Thatcher and Keith Joseph were rightly calling for. This example illustrates another issue raised at the time; that the ESRC should have recouped its lost expenditure from the withdrawing student, not penalised the institution and thereby putative future students who were blameless. With the sciences it was quite different. UEA was the fourth best university for science Ph.D. completions.[93] But here there were ample routine openings in chemical and electrical companies requiring large numbers of doctoral postgraduates. Also many UEA Ph.D.s derived from work at the John Innes Institute. UEA graduates were accordingly pretty acute in sizing up this arts-science labour market and acting rationally. But the University lost some money thereby.

In 1984 the Treasury also added to the burdens on universities by imposing a 15 per cent VAT on building, alterations and repairs, from which Universities were not exempt. Proposals to impose VAT on books would have crippled university library facilities but this was scotched by MPs. Also Sir Keith Joseph's proposal to charge a contribution to parents with tuition fees had to be scrapped in December 1984, after a back-bench revolt by the 1922 Committee. Ideas of student loans and a tax on graduates likewise came and went through Joseph's fertile mind. But perhaps what troubled him most was the issue of tenure. One of the barriers inhibiting the flexibility of universities in making cuts was the tenure of faculty. Short of total incompetence or moral turpitude it was impossible to dismiss a lecturer, and, since salaries were the most important element in university costs, they imposed a rigidity against the implementation of cuts. The rationale for tenure was that academics should have the freedom to pursue seemingly "useless" areas of inquiry or unpopular and unorthodox ideas without fear of loss of livelihood. The security of tenure was also seen as a compensation for the relatively low salaries of academics. But by the 1980s the academic "job for life" was seen as a peculiar privilege resistant to change. The government had incurred costs of £200,000,000 in compensation for those who took early retirement after the 1981 cuts and had no wish to repeat this. From early 1984 the government raised the idea of limiting tenure and Sir Peter Swinnerton Dyer of the UGC added his agreement. In December 1985 the DES notified universities that the government was intending to introduce legislation to enable universities to terminate the appointments of academic staff for reasons of redundancy or financial exigency. This would not apply retrospectively to existing faculty but would to any new staff appointed after the legislation or to staff already in permanent posts who accepted promotion. Rather oddly, a lecturer who by his hard work was promoted to a senior lectureship lost his tenure thereby. The law was not passed until 1986, and it gave only partial flexibility after then, but it was a direct response to the cuts and was yet another feature diminishing the attractiveness of university life.

Things got worse in May 1986 when the UGC made its allocation of the grant for 1986/7.[94] This was for the first time based on teaching and research criteria and selective judgements on research formula funding. UEA did badly. Whereas there was a cash increase of 3.1 per cent for English universities overall, and 1 per cent for Great Britain, UEA suffered a 0.5 per cent fall. It was one of nine English universities out of thirty-seven which were given cash – and by implication even greater real – cuts. Even worse, the UGC recognised that university costs as a whole had typically risen by 1.5 per cent more than general inflation, since wages and salaries, rates and book prices tended to rise more than inflation – the relative price effect. Accordingly the university system would face a squeeze on its costs rather more than 2 per cent a year due to this relative price effect. For UEA to receive a cash *cut* in these circumstances was all the more serious. Only Warwick and possibly Bath could have had any real gains from the May allocations. This was a new scenario: amid overall losses for the system as a whole there would be gainers and losers and this time UEA was among the losers. UEA's poor showing was not due to any lack of quality but due to its high costs per student, especially in academic areas. The UGC wanted this squeezed out. The Finance Officer calculated that it would entail a deficit of £1,186,000 by the end of the year even if posts were frozen saving about £200,000.[95] This 0.5 per cent reduction was bad enough but it could have been worse, since UEA was advised that it was being supported by a "safety net" and that this would be followed by further reductions of 3.7 per cent below the average in each of the years 1987-90. The Finance Officer calculated that these cumulative cuts would entail a deficit of £3,000,000 by 1989-90.[96]

The University saw that it was necessary to respond to the poor allocation of May with yet more planning – this resulted in "A Forward Look".[97] This was the product of the Planning and Resources Committee, a series of meetings with Schools chaired by Pro Vice-Chancellor Roy Church and John Tarrant, and voluminous performance indicator data gathered by Ron Walker and subsequently Alan Jones. The University reviewed its activities yet again in the light of a 15 per cent cut in resources and a 13 per cent deterioration in UEA's costs per student. It was accepted that most areas would have to suffer cuts, but there were four or five proposals of particular interest. The problem of physics inevitably re-emerged. It was far too expensive, and its faculty size was too small to be acceptable as one of the smallest physics departments in the country.[98] Yet it had no hope of attracting enough students to justify an increase in faculty and its links with other science schools were too slight. The review raised the possibility of closing it altogether. The other sciences would be given some protection or modest cuts.

Substantial cuts would have to be imposed on the Social Studies Schools. But one interesting idea was to create a new School of Economics and Business studies combining economics and accountancy, building on a successful inter-school degree in business finance. Perhaps regrettably, the School of Economic and Social Studies rejected this option. In the pure Arts Schools there would be cuts, but the most interesting proposal here was for all the historians to regroup in a School of History, since there already was a successful history degree taught collaboratively by them. The next decade was to see the closure of physics and the creation of the School of History in 1994, as the 1986 review had proposed. The difficult position of SOC in the 1990s suggests that an Economics and Business Studies School should have been given more attention.

But the main puzzle remained unresolved. UEA had been "punished" by the UGC in May not for its poor quality but for its high unit costs per student, although UEA's staff student ratios were in line with national averages.[99] UEA was spending too generously. It was already evident in 1984 that, in the range of subjects that UEA taught, it spent more per student than the national average. This was so of all subjects, with the exception of biological sciences and creative arts. UEA was especially generous in the fields of chemistry, accountancy, education and the social sciences. UEA also spent rather more than the national average on educational technology, the SCVA and SSFA and staff costs, and all matters benefiting students, their teaching and welfare. UEA was actually rather a good place to be as a student in the 1980s, though few would have known the underlying financial reasons.[100] But when comparative costs became a criterion in grant allocation in 1986 it was adverse for UEA. Michael Thompson was due to leave at the end of 1986 to become Vice-Chancellor of Birmingham, but Forward Look left behind many valuable ideas for his successor in facing up to further cuts which were clearly to be ongoing. How far were the cuts implemented in Thompson's years? Paradoxically, and contrary to so much of the rhetoric about cuts, students actually increased over his period of office from 4343 to 4742.

Student Numbers

	Full-Time		Part-Time		Total
	UG	Graduate	UG	Graduate	
1980-81	3634	480	66	163	4343
1981-82	3742	545	161	166	4614
1982-83	3653	566	190	217	4626
1983-84	3519	604	208	243	4574
1984-85	3494	646	199	260	4599
1985-86	3566	718	200	258	4742

There was a temporary dip between 1983-85 but an overall gain. A slight fall in undergraduates was, however, offset by a rise in graduate and part-time students. Faculty slightly contracted from 418 to 415. UEA more successfully carried out the government's intention of tilting the balance of studies away from arts to sciences. This was evidently so with faculty, but less so with students, where a slight fall in the proportion studying arts were more than offset by an increase in those in the social studies. However these were vocational studies in law and education.

	Student percentages			Faculty percentages		
	Science	Social Studies	Arts	Science	Social Studies	Arts
July 1980	35.4	30.2	34.3	37.4	30.3	32.2
July 1986	32.9	33.4	33.6	42.5	32.1	25.4

In spite of the slight rebalancing to vocational studies UEA still remained predominantly an arts and social studies university, though with the Arts Schools taking the largest proportion of students with the smallest proportion of teachers.

But the real extent of the cut was financial:

	Recurrent grant		Inflation
1981/2	£11,710,000		
		3.18%	28.5%
1986/7	£14,896,000		

A number of features became evident from this. Even accepting the need for cuts because of the need to cut public expenditure and to respond to a falling birth rate, one is impressed by the lack of smooth long-range planning. The cuts came in fits and starts, and universities were given the impression that matters would be stabilised after 1981, but that proved to be only the beginning. Of course the Conservatives could not know that they would be in office for eighteen years from 1979 to 1997, otherwise something more considered from the outset, clearly signalled and carefully implemented over some years might have been preferable. It was galling for universities to be accused of having no long-term plans when their paymasters clearly did not have any either. Accordingly, vast amounts of university time was spent making plans, and drawing up and revising budgets year after year; knowing that the goal posts were constantly changing and that any carefully worked out figures would be rendered meaningless by the next UGC letter. Policies came and went almost as afterthoughts – student loans, parents paying for tuition fees, VAT on books; all creating an atmosphere that the government was more concerned to intimidate the universities and their students than work out a coherent sustained plan. The refusal of a doctorate to Margaret Thatcher by Oxford University in 1985 added to these tensions. Yet some new developments were to be welcomed, in particular the move to basing each university's grants on performance indicators rather than simply numbers of students. These performance indictors included research quality, which recognised just how good some unfashionable or newly founded universities were and how the reputations of some older institutions rested on historical rather than contemporary virtues. Taking account of costs per student was fair, though this was to UEA's disadvantage. But it was all a proper spur to effort and efficiency. The work of academics certainly became less attractive in these years, with a quite sharp relative decline in salaries, the assault on tenure, the requirements of appraisal and now regular pressure to publish in conjunction with a deteriorating staff and student ratio and unit of resource. The proportion of academics who regretted their choice of profession rose from 19 per cent in 1976 to 31 per cent by 1989.[101] But UEA was able to hold to its promise not to impose compulsory redundancies. Perhaps most strikingly these years saw the very considerable increase of managerialism in the university sector as a whole. It arose inevitably from the incessant demands for information by the UGC, DES, CVCP and the consequent need for planning structures right through the University. Many academics had their time almost entirely diverted to committee work, budget calculations, and the writing of reports to an unprecedented extent. This made the University more reflective and aware of itself, its activities, priorities and costs, which was desirable and what the DES and UGC intended. But it seemed to make administration more intrusive, acquiring more authority over the academic side. This trend was to develop. Yet Michael Thompson was insistent that these years should not entirely be taken up with enduring cuts and responding defensively to the UGC. The University had to develop and innovate academically and to this we now turn.

11

Innovation without Growth

I think it is most important for the academic health of the
University that innovation should still occur. We have got to learn
the art of innovation without growth.[1]

Michael Thompson, October 1980

The University was determined not to expend all its energies in coping with
the cuts in these years. On the contrary, the early eighties was a period of
considerable innovation which showed a resilient spirit and sustained
morale. Admissions in the Thompson years were generally optimistic but
experienced the rise and fall of national trends. Applications had been
increasing steadily since 1976 and continued to do so into the early 1980s.[2]

	Applications to UEA	Change on previous year	Total applications to UCCA change on previous year
1980	11,983	+ 18.2	+ 1.8
1981	13,826	+ 15.4	− 0.6
1982	15,155	+ 9.6	+ 3.6

Applications to UEA in 1982 were double those of 1975 while the national
increase was that only of 34 per cent. The rise in applications was probably
due to two factors. The number of eighteen year olds was rising to a peak of
932,000 in 1983 before falling steadily by 34 per cent to 1995. Also the severe
unemployment of the early 1980s may have persuaded many school leavers to
seek a degree as a further insurance in the job market, or a university place as
a temporary refuge from the dole queue.

The healthy state of admissions enabled all universities to make the political
point that the universities were being cut precisely at a time when demand for
their services was never greater. UEA was rightly keen to publicise that there
were twelve or so applicants for every place at UEA.[3] Publicity and public relations became even more important. The prospectus was seen as the main tool
for improving the quality of applicants, with the Vice-Chancellor's Annual
Report as a major means of projecting a favourable image, regionally and

wider. The design with clear text and colour photographs was an innovation, emphasising UEA's distinctiveness and drawing attention to the strengths of Science Schools like ENV and Chemistry. For fullness of information and attractiveness of design, those of Sir Michael Thompson's years are some of the best of all UEA Annual Reports. Sir Michael attached great importance to this and attributes much credit to Joanna Motion, the Information Officer.

This became more so from 1983, the demographic peak of eighteen year olds. At UEA the "seven fat years" were over and a consistent decline set in, partly expected, but worryingly worse than the national average.

	Applications to UEA	Change on previous year	National trend	UEA fall	National trend
1983	14,511	−4.2%	+ 0.5per cent	1982-6	
1984	14,237	−1.9%	+ 0.7per cent		
1985	13,341	−6.3%	Not comparable	−15%	−0.4%
1986	13,021	−2.4%	Not comparable		

The University was particularly concerned about the admissions problems of the Science Schools not least because all universities were supposed to increase their proportion of students in science and technology at the expense of arts. To address this the University commissioned a research report which threw much light on attitudes to UEA in the 1980s.[4] UEA's overall image was "average" alongside UCL and Nottingham (which was flattering), below the "up and coming" category (like Warwick) but above the "poor quality" which included two other sixties universities. At about the same time *The Times* listed UEA as "rising in popularity" below the thirteen most popular.[5] The category of "average" was defined as "modern but not young, ordinary, OK, enjoyable time, acceptable degree, often little known". On the "map" of parameters of perceived quality of student life and academic reputation, UEA was seen as providing a good student life but being just on the negative side of academic reputation. It was inferior to York and Warwick but much better than Essex, Kent and Lancaster. UEA was also thought of as much more arts and social sciences based. The report pulled no punches, "UEA is likely to appeal to outgoing, friendly people who are looking for a pleasant place to go for three years but on the negative side it is unlikely to appeal to those who regard themselves as "high flying" academically and want to…end up with a good job and good prospects." Even those who liked the courses had reservations about "the rural location and concrete campus." The perception of UEA science departments by sixth formers was discriminating but modest.

ENV with 4.2 on a 5 point scale was seen as good. Biology, Chemistry, Computing and Mathematics rating 3.0–3.5 as average but Physics at 2.9 rather low in reputation. A curious psychological feature detected by the report was that students at UEA were very happy, even proud, to be there but felt that UEA was publicly underrated and were accordingly reticent about expressing their appreciation of the institution. "This reticence of current students can of course be highly damaging to UEA. It does nothing to reinforce the confidence of the outside world."

What was to be done? The consultants proposed that UEA market itself as a "new breed" university – exciting, modern, lively, relevant to the modern world, job-oriented, "the University for Today and the Future". It should stress its logo, use a slogan "UEA, the University of Today", change its name to UEA at Norwich, stress the hi-tech, "make more noise in popular media". This was all sensible and much came about but also behind the public relations, more substantive developments took place.

First there was the concern to attract overseas students with Professor Bhaskar's successful mission to South East Asia, though this was also motivated by a concern to mitigate a sharp fall due to grant changes, as we have seen. Another response to declining numbers of eighteen-year-old applicants was to take more mature students. The Admissions Report of 1984-85 noted increasing numbers of such applicants and observed that "as the number of eighteen-year-olds in the population falls steadily to 1995 mature candidates may become an important feature of the admissions scene".[6] In fact the proportion of mature students at UEA was steadily around 18 per cent, compared with a national average of 8.8 per cent.[7] This may have been stimulated by a mature UEA student, Jean Rennie, who achieved much publicity as the oldest student in Britain, having started in October 1981 at the age of seventy-four. Yet Mrs Mukerji (as she was known) illustrated the difficulties of such older students: she found the degree much harder than she had imagined, as her memory had deteriorated. She obtained a pass degree but claimed to have "loved every minute of the last three years".[8]

Jean Rennie was a full-time mature student but the University also saw opportunities in attracting part-time students. EAS introduced a part-time degree in history for mature students, admitting four students in October 1980 and another five in January 1981.[9] The twenty-seven who started the programme included a baker, a dentist, two doctors, seven teachers, including a music and a drama teacher, five housewives, a nurse, a toy manufacturer, a market gardener, a businessman, a clergyman, a telephonist, a local government clerk, a restaurant owner, an ex VAT inspector, a TV producer, and a school secretary, most in their forties and fifties. Their motives were well expressed in a report of 1983.

For some of the teachers, there is clearly a vocational element, as they are teaching at schools which have only recently become comprehensive. Other students consider that they "missed out" on formal education in their teens and still have a sense of loss. Yet others have professional qualifications but have hungered in more recent years for historical and liberal studies. Some have been devouring five or six historical biographies a week; others have taught themselves additional languages; several have slowly built up O levels and then A levels at evening class, and have now refused promotion, taken a drop in their income, switched to part-time work or taken on night shifts in order to do the part-time degree.[10]

Fifteen were women and twelve men. The successful entrants were but a proportion of the 130-150 enquirers a year, leading to about sixty applications. Some applicants had to be rejected as too old and others as insufficiently prepared, so to accommodate the latter a summer "bridge course" was devised. This degree yielded clear benefits to the University. It brought in a body of students "a joy to have around . . . committed, motivated, enthusiastic, forthcoming, adventurous". They brought a mature stability and example to the younger students and a wider experience of life which added to the tone of the University. This was evident in the seminar grades gained by the early intakes to 1983 – ten firsts, twenty-four 2/1s, twelve 2/2s – well above average of most undergraduates. Second, the success of EAS's pilot scheme prompted other Schools to follow suit. FAM began to offer part-time degrees and, as an extension of the EAS history degree, a history programme spanning both SOC and EAS was devised.

History and literature, accessible and with broad general interest, were particularly suitable for mature students. But the success of history as a part-time subject was also matched by the emergence of history as a specialist single-subject degree. The original thinking of the University was that history should be a component of interdisciplinary studies in many schools – relating to literature, economics, languages and so forth – but not studied by itself. Gradually keen student historians started combining history courses across different schools to create their own home-made history degrees. The downturn of admissions and the attractions of the part-time history degree urged the University to give greater prominence to the subject. From 1986 it was presented prominently in the UCCA handbook and a separate history brochure compiled. It was an important stepping-stone towards the creation of a separate School of History in 1994, as we shall see.

In the early 1980s the University also began to pay more attention to continuing education and the possibility of some kind of extramural activity.[11] Norfolk had a stimulating focus for this at Wensum Lodge and, although there was low level co-operation with the University, it was thought that there could be a great deal more if the University wished to increase its activity. In effect UEA was already involved in continuing education through taking mature students and part-time students in EAS, FAM and SOC, providing INSET in-service courses for teachers and various cultural activities for the general public. By 1986 it was evident that the University's activity in continuing education had expanded beyond the acceptance of part-time and mature students. There were chemistry postgraduate degrees for people in industry, the surprisingly large part-time MA in Education with ninety-four students taught from Norwich and forty-four doing the degree based on the Cambridge Institute of Education. A large number of short professional courses had also been created, nine by EDU for teachers ranging from autism to using calculators, seven in law from insolvency to data protection put on for the Law Society in conjunction with the Norfolk and Norwich Law Society. Social Work ran training schemes in Essex and Chemistry courses on spectroscopy for industrialists. UEA also deepened its connections with the region, validating Access courses at the Norfolk College of Arts and Technology (NORCAT) at King's Lynn and the Norwich City College. More directly there were joint courses with Norwich City College in languages and business, and one proposed on film and video with Suffolk College.[12] This did not yet lead to a full-blown School of Continuing Education. The reasons were clearly the existing strength of the University of Cambridge Extramural Board and the WEA in the still sparsely populated region. In any case, in this time of cuts everywhere else, it was hardly feasible to spend resources on starting a new School. Even so these years saw a remarkable concern to spread the University's activities more widely across the region, to create better links with the College sector and to be of more service to less orthodox students, part-time and mature. It also moved the UEA climate of opinion towards creating a Board of Continuing Education including an agreed transfer of extramural provision from Cambridge which came about in 1992.

Language was another area where admission difficulties prompted innovative response. EUR admissions had fallen drastically in the 1970s, possibly because it was not clear to applicants what "European Studies" was. EUR responded by offering degrees in double and single honours languages, making available a range of subsidiary language options and the introduction of an MA course in Teaching English as a foreign language (TEFL). The possibility of specialising more in languages gave a sharper vocational edge to the degree than the mix of history, literature and some language could provide. This emphasis on languages was reflected in the change of the name of the School to "Modern Languages and European History" in 1978. This in turn placed an additional demand for language teaching, especially French, and accordingly tutors whose chief expertise was in literature or history took on language teaching in addition, which they were competent to do.[13] A further development was a useful initiative for a degree combining languages taught at UEA and business studies at the Norwich City College. The College had much experience in higher education courses in business for the B/TEC and HND. This combination was to prove very attractive to employers.[14] This initiative was also interesting in that Dr John Lewis, the new Principal of the City College from 1983, had expressed an intention to work more closely with the University and start its own degree work though not in competition with UEA.[15]

One way in which the UGC expected UEA to respond to the cuts was by closing its Russian department. The establishment of Russian departments had become rather too fashionable in the sixties, when it was believed that the importance of the USSR meant that Russian would have to be the second language of significant numbers of educated people. There were plenty of teachers due to National Service courses in Russian creating a corpus of linguists. Noel Annan's advice to UEA's APB in the 1960s had also highlighted Russian. By the 1980s there was an excess of this provision and the UGC's Atkinson Report in 1980 recommended the contraction of Russian at nineteen universities and the phasing out of the subject at seven, including UEA, Lancaster and Sussex.[16] UEA, however, had an increase in new students in 1980, six new undergraduates and one postgraduate compared with two in the previous year. The new Vice-Chancellor and John Elsworth went to see the UGC to discuss the Report and thought afterwards that UEA "could solve its own problems".[17] Nothing very drastic happened to Russian but the six teachers of 1981/2 had shrunk to four by 1986/7. The same literature courses were offered (even one more by the later date) both in Russian and translation. It had been suggested that the UGC was embarrassed by the drastic proposals of the Atkinson Report. It was only partially followed at UEA; no sanctions followed but a little money was saved.

The University had rather more cause to be anxious about the employability of its graduates than its admissions.[18]

Destination of Graduates at 31 December (percentages)

	1979	1980	1981	1982	1983	1984	1985	1986
			ARTS AND SOCIAL STUDIES					
Unemployed or unknown	24.1	28.9	26.0	29.3	29.1	31.3	28.0	22.5
Permanent salaried post	30.4	29.0	29.1	34.2	34.7	31.9	37.6	36.5
				SCIENCES				
Unemployed or unknown	20.5	22.2	26.7	25.6	23.2	25.3	22.5	15.9
Permanent salaried post	42.6	38.0	32.9	37.3	42.3	40.1	43.9	46.4

The rising unemployment was predictable in the light of national trends. Teaching was the most common employment for arts graduates and manufacturing industry the most usual outlet for scientists, though the most striking increase was the sharp swing towards accountancy as a profession.[19] It was generally pleasing that more graduates went into permanent salaried posts than were unemployed or unknown, but the latter figures were rather high and rising. More worrying the *Financial Times* annually published a league table of the employability of graduates across all the universities. In 1980 UEA was thirty-fifth out of forty-four, in 1981 thirty-eighth, in 1982 thirty-ninth and by 1984 forty-second.[20] As the national unemployment situation deteriorated, so did UEA's position in relation to other universities. The legacy of its heavy emphasis on the arts and social studies and interdisciplinary liberal education still left it vulnerable in the harsh labour market of the 1980s, in spite of attempts to move to more vocationalism. UEA was severely criticised locally for its arts bias, for its neglect of work-related education, its belief in a general education "which supposedly equips one to tackle anything in life", and for continuing "to churn out large numbers of graduates with nebulous rather than specific relevance to the world of work".[21] UEA's modest employment record and especially its annually publicised low ranking in the FT league tables must have been a factor in the worse than average decline in admissions after 1983. It also contributed to the perception highlighted in the 1983 report that sixth formers thought of UEA more as a pleasant place to be than as a preparation for a good job. After Michael Thompson left, the University ceased publicising its employment figures to the Court and the public. They were the consequence of a legacy from the past and posed a challenge for the future.

The problem led to a scheme called Nudge to help the hundreds of unemployed graduates in Norfolk – presumably not all from UEA. It was run by Anita Boekee, who experienced unemployment after graduating in 1980. Her project, funded by the Manpower Services Commission, helped some 300-400 graduates in the early 1980s.[22] Another development to ameliorate the graduate employment situation was a course run by the Norwich City College Department of Management under Dr Bruce Potter from 1982. It was a ten-week course for twenty graduates, five of whom in the 1983 intake were from UEA.[23] The original idea was to prepare graduates for jobs, combining seminars and tutorials with Friday work experience with firms. By 1984 this had developed into the more ambitious Gateway Scheme. This now aimed to help the performance of small companies by seconding a graduate to assist in devising and implementing a growth project. These included matters like market and sale plans and the application of computer systems. It was a joint initiative of the City College, UEA, the Norwich and Norfolk Chamber of

Commerce and the YSC. It was now more considerable than the first scheme, combining five weeks training in small business strategy and management, followed by twenty-week secondment to business. The graduates were paid by the YSC and so were cost free to their employers. It enabled, for example, a UEA graduate with a – not very saleable – degree in development studies to convert to become a manager in publishing.[24]

UEA also looked to its own curriculum to make more graduates vocationally employable and to draw closer to industry. A potentially important new development was that for a Department of Electronics, as MAP had seen the need to become more vocational and practical in order to increase its attractiveness. They established a working party on electronics which recommended a full degree programme in the subject, which was accepted by the Senate in November 1980. Following this Anglia Television offered to endow a Chair of Electronics for five years on the understanding that the University would continue to fund it thereafter. There would be a degree combining electronics, physics, mathematics and computing, with short courses provided for Anglia TV engineers. The University foresaw no great difficulty with this, since half the units of the degree could be provided from those already taught in MAP with existing faculty. It could all start in October 1992. MAP's working party really wanted this to be the seed of a new School of Electronics, but the UGC would not allow it. UEA had been forbidden to start engineering from the 1960s, but it was a major error on the UGC's part still to be so discouraging of electronics as late as the 1980s. It was as if the UGC, so focused on implementing cuts in the 1980s, was losing sight of what positive developments were necessary for the national interest.[25]

The new professor in the Anglia TV chair was Douglas Lewin from Brunel University, where he was Professor of Digital Processors and head of the Department of Electrical Engineering.[26] He began optimistically stressing the ample job opportunities for his future students, the increasing use of computers in all walks of life, and the urgency of such developments to the national economy. But he soon ran into a fundamental problem. His course had originally been conceived as physics-based, to keep costs low and use existing, underutilised expertise. Yet he was developing it as an engineering programme requiring professional engineering staff and at least twenty of them, not five as he already had. He also stressed that his Department needed professional accreditation from the Institution of Electronic and Radio Engineers or the Institution of Electrical Engineers. Without expansion and more engineers as teachers he would not get accreditation, and without accreditation he could not attract students or substantial external funding. Nor would they be able to do much to meet the five to six thousand vacancies in electronic engineering posts identified by the National Electronics Council in 1983.[27] In any case electronics was too small a part of the Norwich economy to provide a base for such studies at UEA. The problem was insoluble. There was no question of UEA, while coping with the cuts, acceding to his demands and expanding what would have been a very high-cost department contrary to UGC advice. As it was electronics was already quite the most expensive subject in the University, at a cost of £5576 per student in 1984/5.[28] Lewin resigned in 1986, accepting a post at Sheffield, sadly dying shortly thereafter of cancer. But while a full programme could not be attempted, it had at least established electronics in the University and a laboratory still bears Lewin's name in commemoration. But behind this lay the culpability not of UEA but of the UGC and government policy in not developing electronics in the 1980s.

Another appointment which brought the University closer to industry was that of a professorship of environment risk, the first in the country. This was financed by the Wolfson Foundation for the first five years and the first occupant was Dr Lewis Roberts, CBE, FRS, a director of the AERE Harwell, where he had been a colleague of the Vice-Chancellor. He was to focus on such matters as disposal of toxic and radioactive wastes and pollution by fertilisers and acid rain.[29]

The University saw the need to establish even closer links with industry and in these years it took two distinctive forms, the creation of a Science Park and the appointment of an Industrial Liaison Officer. A recent government report in 1983 had called for closer research links between higher education and industry, seeing Science Parks as a way of doing this.[30] Plans for a Science Park had originally initiated with the Norwich Chamber of Commerce and the City and County Councils in 1982, with the University expressing a distant interest.[31] By early 1983 the UEA Village had become the proposed site to develop "new small businesses mainly in the high technology field".[32] This was warmly welcomed by the local MPs including John MacGregor, who had first-hand knowledge of large American Science Parks linked with universities. MacGregor's ministerial colleague, Lord Young, was also especially keen on such parks. He pointed out that in 1982 there were only two of them in Britain, but by 1985 there were twenty-one. Yet only Bradford and Warwick Universities had parks approaching the size of that of Cambridge, the notable pioneer.[33] UEA wanted to be part of this rapidly developing trend, so £70,000 was allocated by the University from its Capital Fund for the Science Park.[34] Planning permission required restrictions on the size of units and especially prevented the resulting complex being sold off to a private developer as an unacceptable industrial estate in Earlham.[35] Two high-tech companies, Synergy Computer Systems and Oasis Electronics, started in the Village in 1984 while there were still some University-occupied academic buildings there. The Park did not develop as well as was hoped but it was a useful initiative typical of the enterprise culture of the 1980s. As well as the money for the Science Park, £50,000 was allocated for "pump priming projects which would promote links between the University and industry and which would bring benefits to the University",[36] and a Director of Industrial Liaison was appointed. But it proved difficult to develop industrial links and to make a University like UEA more industrially minded given the characteristics of the region.

A further symbolic reaching out to industry in the region was the recognition of the British Sugar Corporation Laboratories in Colney Lane as an Affiliated Institute of the University with twelve research staff. There had been joint projects of BSCL and CHE and BIO. It put the BSCL on the same footing as the John Innes Institute and the FRI – "the more contacts of this kind which the University has the better".[37]

This was very consciously part of Michael Thompson's strategy. At the John Innes Institute Professor (later Sir) David Hopwood had made vital discoveries in the development of genetically modified crops. David Sainsbury was personally interested in this and was minded to give a substantial sum (eventually £15,000,000) through his Gatsby Trust for a laboratory to advance these researches. It was this that enabled Michael Thompson to persuade the Agricultural Research Council that its Plant Breeding laboratory should be in Norwich, not in Cambridge. The Sainsbury money and Thompson's intervention were the key. These matters developed from 1987 after Michael Thompson had left, as we shall see in the next chapter, but his initiative had been crucial in what was to follow. This was to become the Norwich Research Park in Colney Lane, which was quite different from the abortive Science Park in the Village in Earlham.

Science was also stimulated by new faculty. As the government was concerned to reduce university faculty overall and encourage older members to take early retirement, so it saw an advantage in replacing some of them with younger "new blood" scholars. £100 million was to be made available over three years for bringing "new blood" into the universities mainly in natural science and technology and for boosting information technology.[38] The build up of new blood posts and UEA's share of them was as follows:

	National	UEA	
1983	242	3	Plus 1 IT
1984	349	6	
1985	200	4	
		13	

Of these two were CHE, four MAP, two BIO, two ENV, one FAM, one EDU and one CEAS.[39]

The posts were satisfactorily filled, though it was difficult for universities to recruit lecturers in IT, where university salaries were half those offered in industry. A third of the 116 "new blood" posts in IT remained unfilled.[40] What might have been a good idea in the national interest was rendered nugatory by the broader concerns to cut the universities at all costs. But UEA gained some benefits. Information Technology also had an impact on UEA in the early eighties with the significant computerisation of the University. The existing ICL 2904 administrative computing equipment had been installed in 1975 and by 1983 was out of date. The manufacturers no longer made it or provided spare parts and they declined to service it. It was updated in various ways. For example, two magnetic tape decks were installed for the processing of salaries, a requirement of the national banking system. The existing 28k word and 130 mbyte disc store capacity of 1977 had been augmented by a further 68k and 280 mbytes between 1980-83.[41] A new computer was needed not least because from 1985 UCCA would be introducing new online admissions procedures, enabling the University, and then Schools, to communicate their decisions instantaneously and directly to UCCA. The University selected the Hewlett Packard Series 3000 as the best replacement and this was planned to deal with admissions and student records from 1984 and payroll and financial accounting from 1985. The cost of the new system was £175,000, though paradoxically with savings of some £32,000 a year over the old ICL system. This reflected the rapid advances in computer technology, and its cheapening and increased reliability.

At the same time the University Computing department was thriving. Robin Forrest became Professor of Computing Studies in 1980. Research grants of £120,000, including £40,000 from IBM, had been attracted by the UEA team, who worked on computer design and graphics to solve problems in industry – jet engines, car bodies, machine tools and even the *Star Wars* film special effects.[42] But the cuts had even hit this unit. They had many more schemes than they could develop and, as Forrest noted, "the real shortage is manpower. We have plenty of students waiting to come in, but not the places".

There was much talk about IT in Norwich at this time, partly because John Garrett, the MP for Norwich South, was the Opposition spokesman on industry with special responsibility for high technology. He was keen on stressing the potential of Norwich as a key centre where IT could develop with the Stationery Office, insurance companies and UEA.[43] Later in 1982 a major IT exhibition was held sat the Hotel Norwich with both Norwich MPs, David Ennals and John Garrett, stressing its importance.[44] When Professor Forrest had been at Cambridge in the 1960s he had helped to found a group from whom some seventy computer related firms had sprung up in the area, and it was hoped that UEA as a centre of IT in Norwich would likewise generate industrial activity, partly through the Science Park.

It was not only in service to industry, science and IT that UEA drew closer to the community but also through artistic initiatives of wider public appeal. In 1984 the East Anglian Film Archive was donated to the University by David Cleveland, the assistant director of the AVC. Cleveland had founded it in 1976 and over the years had collected 600 films relating to the region from 1902. An immensely valuable resource, historic films from the archive are used in lecture/showings and gain a wider audience through their frequent use on television.[45] In music the much loved subscription concerts at UEA had to cease, a victim of the cuts. W. Rowan Hare, a long-standing friend of the University stepped into the breach and endowed a series of concerts in memory of his late wife. The first Dorothea Hare Young Musicians concert was consequently held in January 1983.[46] In drama the Village Theatre in the old Assembly Hall was given a major facelift by the Kenny Trust (the gift of two UEA graduates of the Sainsbury family, Annabel Sainsbury and her husband Peter Kanabus. Kenny was the name of their adopted child) and renamed the Kenny Theatre. It opened in March 1984 as a technically equipped theatre with an audience capacity of 320 in a raked auditorium. It was to be used for student drama and new companies such as the Minotaur Theatre Company – UEA drama students in their spare time capacity. But it was also available for local drama and dance groups outside the University, a further service to the community.[47] Finally, the Norwich Survey, which had been at work for ten years and was threatened with closure due to the cutting of the City Council grant, was reprieved. The Council, the UEA and DES resumed as financial backers of the archaeological and building survey work of the Survey.[48]

That The Centre of East Anglian Studies might be closed as a contribution to cuts aroused a great deal of local protest. Indeed scarcely any aspect of the cuts so brought home to people of the region that the cuts fell not only on "the University" but on them, since CEAS was a key link between UEA and the region.[49] It raised an important issue of how far the University could subsidise the region when the criteria on which it is judged for funding paid no attention to such activity. CEAS was retained as a separate entity but had to rely more for its finance on its supporters outside the University. It also changed its focus at the suggestion of Professor Roy Church. When it began it was intended to cover all aspects of the region – historical, archaeological, environmental and economic. In its reprieved form it was to concentrate on local and regional history and archaeology, for which there was a large popular following. Far from attenuating, in this new focused form the Centre expanded. It acquired a "new blood" Lectureship in Regional History from the UGC in 1984, while the University itself funded a research studentship and the Royal Norfolk Agricultural Association also sponsored a studentship to study county agriculture in the twentieth century. The Centre also published the latest volume in the Stiffkey papers of Nathaniel Bacon. The presentation of a copy to Lord Townshend by Mr Timothy Colman, the Pro Chancellor and President of the Norfolk Records Society, in March 1984, was a happy celebration not only of the Bacon project but of the survival of CEAS in its new form.[50]

In spite of the cuts the academic work of the University continued successfully. It would be otiose to survey this comprehensively again but some new features caught the attention. The SCVA had its triumphs and changes. Dr Alan Borg, the Director, had formerly been Master of Blades at the Tower of London and he was able to secure the unique privilege of an exhibition of Tower Armoury treasures – the first time that any Tower exhibits had been allowed out to any other museum. It was also unique as Norwich Union's first venture into arts sponsorship. Over 10,000 people booked to see the magnificent exhibition even before it opened. The SCVA also began to attract gifts, a sculpture from Dame Alix Meynell and a collection of nineteenth-century watercolours and drawings of Norfolk churches from Mrs Veronica Berry. In 1983 Alan Borg left to become the Director of the Imperial War Museum, and later of the Victoria and Albert Museum. He was succeeded by Graham Beal from the Walker Arts Centre in Minneapolis.[51]

The library continued to grow from 414,092 volumes in 1980 to 583,368 by 1986 and annual expenditure from £321,000 in 1980 to £470,000 by 1986. One noteworthy achievement was the appointment of Mrs Jean Steward as the new National President of the Association of Assistant Librarians, surprisingly the first University Librarian to achieve this honour.[52] IT too was being further adopted in the library. The newly acquired Keswick Library needed computer-based cataloguing and Senate resolved that there should be application of computer automation to all library cataloguing. In the meantime the production of an up-datable catalogue on microfiche using the Birmingham Libraries Catalogue Mechanisation Project (BLCMP), was introduced from 1983 as a step towards eventual online interrogation of a computerised catalogue.[53] But most important was the retirement of the Librarian Willi Guttsman, who right from the beginning had led the Library from its sparsely filled shelves in Earlham Hall in 1962 to the Lasdun buildings of 1968 and 1974 with a book stock of over 500,000 volumes. His successor was David Baker from the University of Hull. He had a first class degree in music from Cambridge, was a FRCO (at the age of seventeen one of the youngest) and became organist of Wymondham Abbey. Perhaps not unconnected with this, he also brought an expertise in IT to bring the Library into a new high technology world.

There were some areas where UEA work had considerable implications for policy regionally, nationally and internationally. Keith Clayton continued to press his argument that schemes to prevent coastal erosion were a costly waste of resources and, in spite of the acceptance of a £820,000 scheme of defensive work at Sidestrand, his views that "the sea will always win in the end" were increasingly influential in Whitehall.[54] In another area of influence Professor Timothy O'Riordan, one of the leading authorities on the Broads, became Chairman of the Broads Authority Strategy Committee in 1980. It brought UEA science in defence of the Broads against other interests – marsh drainers, speed boat users, nitrate and phosphate effluent pumpers.[55] The School of Environmental Sciences also made the largest ever survey of Norfolk's landscape and 100,000 plant and wildlife habitats.[56] The climatologists continued to disturb. They were suggesting that not only were earth temperatures rising but that this was linked to increasing air pollution. Their work was part of the US Department of Energy's multi-million dollar research programme and an important root of present policies to reduce pollution to diminish the greenhouse effect and the consequent disaster of global warming.[57] They also advised Oxfam about fluctuating flood and drought weather conditions.[58] Likewise the School of Development Studies advised, and were critical of, Bob Geldof, following the £50,000,000 raised by Live Aid for Third World famine, impressing on him the importance of the kind of small-scale, low-cost projects (like their new oxen pump) that were their expertise.[59] We could refer further to work on cataracts using non-animal tissue, the monitoring of the Sizewell B nuclear power station inquiry and much else. But the point is made that UEA's research in these difficult years not only remained highly active but much of it became highly policy-oriented. Those who sought to denigrate the universities as ivory towered "groves of Academia" were well wide of the mark as far as UEA was concerned.

The overall emphasis on research, developing under Thistlethwaite in the 1970s increased even more sharply in Thompson's years. Graduates increased:

	Graduate numbers (excluding PGCE)	PCGE	All graduates as percentage of total students	Percentage excluding PGCE
1979-80	556		13.4	
1980-81	561		13.2	
1981-82	628		14.3	
1982-83	550	124	16.2	13.2
1983-84	606	120	17.8	14.8
1984-85	665	111	18.7	16.0
1985-86	738	109	19.8	17.3

The Research Committee in 1983 had a policy to achieve a graduate population equivalent to 14 per cent of total student numbers, and this was achieved. For example, as is evident in the above table, it was the policy to change the School of Education's activities from undergraduate initial teacher training to the postgraduate certificate. At the same time the research of Lawrence Stenhouse, who died in 1982, and Jean Rudduck and Barry Macdonald in the already existing Centre for Applied Research in Education was encouraged. When the Research Assessment Exercises began in 1986, research in chemistry, mathematics, computing and history was shown to be better than average, that in physics, electrical engineering and accountancy below average, and the rest average. This began to matter as one of the criteria for the UGC assessment of the recurrent grant.[60] Even more impressively external research grants massively rose:

Table 16   External Research Grants
(£ unless otherwise stated)

	1980-81		1985-86
BIO	263,226		689,201 + 71,000 Belg.fr.
CHEM	150,067		901,082
COMP	8000	SYS	940,272
DEV	104,440	DEV + ODG	109,259
SOC	77,244 + 212,400 DM		308,718
EAS	1650 + $1,40		5429
ENV	254,000 + $155,000		852,914 + $159,025
FAM	1472	AHM	700
MAP	84,951		209,165 + 6900
			+ BF 65,800
			+ BR 300,000
EUR	5912		8350
CEAS	69,106		100,617
CARE	21,632		14,406
	1,041,700		4,140,113
	[+ 212,400 DM]		[+ $ 165,925]
	[+ $156,400]		[+ 136,800 BF]
			[+ 300,000 BR]

This nearly fourfold increase in research grant income at a time when the price level rose by 1.4 over the same period represented a real cultural change in favour of research with some major Schools, with ENV and CHE emerging as big winners and spenders.

The 1980s, with its financial cuts, could not be a period of lavish building such as Denys Lasdun had enjoyed in the 1960s and Norman Foster in the 1970s. But UEA was determined not to stagnate under the cuts, either architecturally or academically. The University, however, did need a new building to replace the loss of Keswick Hall as the home of its new School of Education. The new Education Building was designed by Rick Mather on the recommendation of Norman Foster. It was an innovative use of capital resources, since the sale of Keswick Hall and land at Colney enabled this new building. Mather was then best known for remodelling the interior of old terraced houses in London and the design of restaurants. I recall a presentation he made of his work. There moved before our eyes photographs of plush eating places in Hong Kong, London and elsewhere, cocktail bars with curvaceous counters and secluded lighting and much expensive glass and steel. We were enchanted but wondered what this had to do with a financially hard-pressed university in the austere 1980s. Mather had also never designed a freestanding building of any size before. £500,000 was available, however, from the government as a consequence of UEA's relinquishing Keswick Hall. Mather "created a horse-shoe building, open to the south west, angled at 45 degrees to Lasdun's teaching wall, chiefly because he wanted to create a protected south-west facing courtyard".[61] The building had many interesting and beneficial features. Mather had no obligation (as had Feilden and Mawson) to continue the Lasdun idiom either in style or texture. There was some unease in the City Council's planning development subcommittee that the design was so dissimilar to the existing buildings around. But the University insisted that the development plan had to be flexible and the Lasdun style "was not for all time". Foster and Mather were proposing a radical change in style with the tile cladding. There was some comment about the cylinder of the Climatic Unit building being a "gasometer" but Mrs Pauline Corker well summed up "it will provide a visual break which will be extremely acceptable, I like it". And the plan was approved.[62]

Although his location was dominated by the back of the Teaching Wall, the Education Building formed a distinctive contrast. Eschewing the concrete of the surrounding buildings, it has clean, white-panelled, glazed blockwork cladding over a reinforced concrete frame which weathers well. Unlike Lasdun's very regular horizontal bands of concrete and glass, Mather delighted in irregularity of fenestration which adds to the interest of the exterior. Also, while Mather's exteriors seemed like boxes and cylinders, his interiors were more complex than those of the Lasdun buildings. The pathways through the area pleasingly thread through grassy areas and pools, in and out of buildings, unlike the straight lines of the Lasdun walkways. One sees Mather's instinct for interesting curves and the relevance of those elliptical cocktail bars. Also very importantly, the new building filled in part of the back spaces of the Teaching Wall. The backs of some of Lasdun's buildings – the residences and Teaching Wall – could be as unattractive as the fronts were splendid. The area had also become a clutter of overflow parking. The building also embodies much of Gordon Marshall's insistence on low maintenance – no paint, or paint on plaster, window frames coated with stove enamel, floors covered with carpets which were a third cheaper to clean than hard floors. The relation of Marshall and Mather was regarded as a "monument to successful patronage".[63] The new School of Education Building was opened in October 1984 by Lady Enid Ralphs CBE, the widow of Sir Lincoln Ralphs, distinguished in her own right as Chairman of the Magistrates' Association and a former lecturer at Keswick College.[64] The Education Building was joined by new premises for the Climatic Research Unit in 1983-84, also by Mather. In nice contrast to the School of Education, this was a cylinder but of the same white cladded exterior. The money (£275,000) for this was generously provided by the Wolfson Foundation, which shortly after also contributed to another wing to the Education Building for the use of SYS. The whole complex, built by R.G. Carter of Drayton, forms a delightful contrast to the adjacent concrete cliff of the back of the Teaching Wall. It is intriguing that Rick Mather has recently been chosen to bring some stylistic variety to the concrete of London's South Bank and it is thought that his experience of doing this at UEA influenced this choice.[65]

One issue which might have affected the building environment of the Plain was a proposal in 1981 to sell off the playing fields of Earlham School for £250,000. This was a time when Michael Heseltine was insisting on the sale of council houses and Norwich was engaged in a dispute with him over this. The proposal came from Judith Walpole, the Chair of the Education Committee of Norfolk County Council, who envisaged a housing estate cheek by jowl with the University. She also suggested that the children of Earlham School, having lost their playing fields, could use those of UEA instead.[66] This was strongly opposed by the University and the City Council and the ill-judged scheme was abandoned.[67] It left the environs of UEA unencroached by inappropriate buildings and, more importantly, left them free as valuable site for splendid sporting facilities, a running track and then a swimming pool for the use of UEA, City and County jointly, much later in the year 2000.

The new buildings at UEA presented an optimistic view of the fabric, yet one way of responding to the cuts was to defer maintenance on the existing fabric. In sum, over six years it was estimated to save £1,475,000 by this deferment. They ranged from £2000 for expansion joints in the Sports Centre to £200,000 saved by not cleaning and painting the Sainsbury Centre. In between, decaying concrete, window frames, flat roof repair and boiler tubing and much else had to remain neglected.[68]

The University also offset part of the losses of the cuts by the sale of land at Colney to BUPA for £100,000 for the building of a private hospital.[69] There was protest from some opposed on principle to private medicine, but it brought a useful addition to the capital needed for new building. As low quality farmland the University had valued the DEV farm at £821 an acre in 1981, but they were able to sell it to BUPA as commercial building land for £14,285 an acre.[70] DEV did not lose since they moved to a new site south of Watton Road, where the Rural Technology Field Laboratory was established. But most tellingly the building of a hospital on the western boundary of the Plain in the 1980s, followed by the Norfolk and Norwich Hospital in Colney Lane in the 1990s, strengthened UEA's claims to move into medical education some years later.

The cuts also forced UEA to think of its property in commercial terms. The residences provided two thousand beds and made UEA the biggest hotel in Norwich. To capitalise on this the University devised and advertised Norfolk Heritage Study Tours as a package holiday from £150 to £200 a week from 1981.[71] The University was fortunate in having Roger Lloyd as its conference organiser. He came with commercial experience at Colman's and J. Walter Thompson, and built up UEA's conference business in the 1970s and was Chairman of the Norwich Tourist Association.[72] UEA accordingly benefited from being part of Norwich's general thrust in tourism management.

Morale at the University was raised by three splendid events. In 1984 Lord Franks retired as Chancellor, shortly before his eightieth birthday, having served for nineteen years. This was marked by the commissioning of a portrait by Suzi Malin.[73] It depicts an aloof, mandarin side to Franks's personality, rather than the courteous charm more frequently seen at UEA, but it is a very finely drawn portrait and now hangs in the Council Chamber.

Franks's successor was the Rev. Professor Owen Chadwick, the ecclesiastical historian. His career of remarkable distinction began early as he combined a first class degree with gaining three rugby blues. He became Regius Professor of Modern History at Cambridge, Master of Selwyn College, Vice-Chancellor of Cambridge, President of the British Academy, KBE and a member of the Order of Merit. He also had long links with UEA. He was one of those academics with homes in north Norfolk who served on the promotion committee to establish a University in Norwich and was already an honorary Litt.D. of UEA. By curious chance, as a sideline to his major work on the Victorian Church, he had written *Victorian Miniature*, a study of a clergyman who lived in Wood Hall which, a century later was to become the residence of UEA Vice-Chancellors. He was a keen walker and sailor when in Norfolk, and still very fit and spry. He had a manner of walking as if absorbed in thought but, like an old rugby three-quarter, ready to move swiftly in some unexpected direction.[74] He could also be extremely witty. In his inauguration speech he reviewed the tragic ends of several University Chancellors who had been executed. "The Office has risks", he observed dryly in his slow, reflective voice with perfect timing. I have rarely seen a Congregation so swayed by the skilful use of appropriate humour. The new Chancellor also involved himself in areas of University life beyond his duties. He attended a Christian group and also an away day of historians, where his recollections of Nazi Germany gripped the meeting. The University could hardly have been more fortunate in its new Chancellor as a successor to Lord Franks.

Secondly, attention was favourably focused on the University when it became the host to the British Association for the Advancement of Science in September 1984. The organising committee was chaired by Timothy Colman with Professor Malcolm Frazer, the Dean of Chemistry and a Vice-President of the Association playing a leading part. This is a major annual event which had previously been held in Norwich in 1868, 1935 and 1961. Now, for the first time, UEA could provide a venue.[75] About three thousand people attended for a week of wide-ranging sessions. These inevitably included East Anglian and UEA interests – climate, political and social change in Norfolk, nature conservation, the Halvergate Marshes. These were rather ENV/SOC/BIO interests rather than MAP/CHE, but rightly in keeping with the emphasis on conveying the social aspects of science to a wider public which is the BA's purpose. It was a grand occasion, an honour for the University, and also consistent with Michael Thompson's stated aim of explaining university activities to the outside world.

Thirdly, UEA formed a former Students' Association and held a splendid reunion. It had become evident during the cuts that the universities lacked support in public opinion. When the Vice-Chancellor attended the House of Commons in 1982 about the cuts only two MPs met him, David Ennals and John Garrett of Norwich; the other ten MPs on the Court did not trouble to do so.[76] The universities even seemed to lack friends among their own graduates. To rectify this Kent and Lancaster Universities started graduate associations in 1983 and Sussex reformed an existing one. UEA had had a UEA Society, organised by graduates and mostly based in London, but this had declined by the early 1980s. This was possibly due to the tragic death of Alastair Gordon in the Moorgate underground crash in 1975. A chemistry graduate he had been a stalwart of the society. What was needed was a revived Association, efficiently administered and funded from the University and nationwide in scope. The benefits to both sides were clear. The ex-students could get continuing career advice, social events and reunions, and use of UEA facilities. The University could secure some influence in the outside world, receive feedback about careers and the relevance of the curriculum, and some members might contribute to the University financially. But the University was insistent that the new Association was about "friend raising" rather than "fund-raising" and "fund-raising is the expression of a relationship not the basis of a relationship".[77] There were 19,000 former students at this time. The Association was duly formed in 1985 and a successful reunion held in September of that year.[78] Twenty-two years after the admission of the first students, it was a necessary milestone in the creation of a mature university.

How was UEA shaping up as a good performing university in these years? If we look at the class of degrees, they certainly improved. The percentage of firsts and 2/1s gained by students increased markedly in almost all Schools while thirds declined.[79]

	1sts and 2/1s		3rds	
	1980	1985	1980	1985
BIO	35.0	59.2	20.6	13.2
CHEM	19.3	50.0	38.6	19.4
Computing and Accountancy	21.2	48.6	36.4	15.3
DEV	26.2	38.2	7.1	7.3
SOC	29.4	36.9	13.9	7.8
EAS	33.4	51.3	7.0	3.1
ENV	48.9	45.5	6.7	12.1
FAM	43.1	36.2	6.9	7.3
LAW	17.0	23.5	29.8	14.0
MAP	23.6	14.6	36.4	27.4
EUR	37.7	47.1	2.9	3.1
Average	30.4	41.0	18.7	11.8

The exceptions to improvement and change were ENV and FAM, which already had unusually high levels of good degrees; and, at the other end of the spectrum, MAP, which was continuing to have difficulties in attracting quality students. The reason for the improvement may well relate to the very high levels of unemployment, usually in the range of 10-12 per cent, and reaching three million by 1982, some of the highest of the post-war years. This concentrated the minds of the students on the need for a good degree to get a job. Good as this improvement was, UEA's performance was slightly lower than the national average.[80] In 1983 and 1984 the national average of firsts and 2/1s in subjects studied at UEA was 41.3 per cent compared with UEA's own performance of 35.25 per cent. The excellent ENV most exceeded the national average. The problematic MAP with its lack of good students was a notable underperformer. But the overall sharply improving academic standard is one of the chief features of these years.

In response to the cuts, the University went on to the offensive by forcefully reminding Norwich and the region of what it contributed.[81] A lot of research brought economic benefits to the region and specifically to agriculture. There was the work of BIO on crop pest (cereal aphid) outbreaks, diseases in oilseed rape and peas, the ecology of weeds and the behaviour of cows, rabbits and turkeys; DEV's work on organic farming and soil structure; and CRU's on rainfall and climate trends. There was also research on social welfare problems, problem drinkers, primary health care, and care of the elderly in collaboration with the Norwich General Practice Training Programme and the Norfolk Area Health Authority. ENV and BIO contributed much research to local environmental matters, the Norfolk Broads and their problems, the salt marshes of the Norfolk coast and the Breckland heaths, while Great Witchingham Wildlife Park benefited from studies in animal behaviour. Culturally UEA had much to offer in local history through CEAS, archaeology, music, drama and the film archive, which needs no reiteration. In public life some 110 members of UEA faculty served on public bodies – political, advisory, charitable and the rest.

Then the University moved on to the tough argument about cash. This paragraph was so concise and hard hitting that it is worth quoting in full:

> The annual wages bill of the University is £11.75 million gross (but excluding contributions to National Insurance and superannuation), leaving about £8 million to be spent by University employees in the region. The University employs 1857 people (full- and part-time), most of whom live in the locality. In addition there are some 4000 students in residence each spending annually at least £2000 in the area or collectively some £8,000,000. Studies elsewhere of the economic benefits of a new university suggest that for every £1 spent by university employees and students another £0.20 of income is generated through stimulation of local services. This would suggest that the existence of UEA has raised regional income by approximately £19,000,000: this in turn has probably led to the formation of about 1000-1200 additional jobs in the surrounding area.

This was a time when universities were too often under attack and forced on the defensive, while many in Norwich still have regarded UEA as a resort of useless, long haired layabouts. It was salutary for Norwich to be reminded that UEA was a powerful economic dynamo and nucleus of expertise in its midst, something to cherish out of self-interest in times of high unemployment, if not for more high-minded motives.

In December 1985 Michael Thompson announced his intention to resign on 31 December 1986 to become Vice-Chancellor of the University of Birmingham.[82] He had not sought the Birmingham post but his positive stewardship of UEA in difficult circumstances had caught the attention of the authorities there. He and his wife Sybil were presented with a fine cabinet at the leave taking and he left for Birmingham, where his career was rewarded with a knighthood in 1991.

12

The Next Step Forward

The UEA has come to maturity and Norfolk and Norwich is very
much richer for it being here.[1]

Gillian Shepherd, 3 July 1995

The new Vice-Chancellor was Derek Burke.[2] Then aged fifty-seven, he was
born in Sutton Coldfield, the son of a managing director of a group of engineering companies who had left school at fourteen. Burke himself studied at
Birmingham University, gaining his B.Sc. and then Ph.D. in chemistry.
Research at Yale followed and then at the National Institute for Medical
Research on the anti-viral and anti-cancer drug interferon. He was appointed
a Lecturer in Biological Chemistry at the University of Aberdeen in 1960 and
then as the founding Professor of Biological Sciences at Warwick University in
1969 at the age of thirty-nine. His career changed again when invited to join a
new biotechnology company, Allelix, in Toronto as Scientific Director and
Vice-President. This was Canada's largest biotechnology company, with a staff
of 150 and a budget of 16,000,000 dollars. After four years the Vice-
Chancellor's post at UEA drew him back to Britain where three of his children
remained. As he reflected, "I like the country, and I owe it a great deal". He
brought to UEA many valuable qualities. He was a first-rate biochemist,
particularly relevant at UEA with its adjacent John Innes and Food Research
Institutes. He brought considerable administrative abilities and business experience. The rolling strategic five year plan, the monitoring of expenditure, and
negotiating between firms and universities were all familiar parts of his work
at Allelix. He had little patience with the anti-business attitudes he had
encountered in some quarters at Warwick University in the early 1970s. As well
as being a scientist, manager, businessman, he was also a committed Christian
interested in ethical issues and, on his return to Britain, served on various
national church committees. In appearance he was tall with a slight stoop and
a broad, open face. His personal interests included opera, listening to music
and walking his samoyed dog. He was a family man with three daughters and a
son. His wife, Mary, was an American with a doctorate in English Literature
whom he had met at Yale and who was to be an essential well known and much
liked support in the work he was now to undertake at UEA.

In January 1987 he found a university rightly proud of its achievements, and with happy students and staff, but anxious over its finances, since it was due to lose something like 17 per cent of its income over three years. There were different views as to how to tackle the financial problems; one group maintaining that the modest reserves should be used up to meet the immediate deficits, another wanting to close down some science Schools as too expensive. But the new Vice-Chancellor had the advantage of a continuity of transition. Between his appointment in the Summer of 1986 and his taking office in January 1987, he attended meetings with Michael Thompson and the two Pro Vice-Chancellors. Accordingly, he was familiar with the proposals of "Forward Look" and agreed with them.

As the new Vice-Chancellor he felt the need for a clear statement of what the University was about, a mission statement followed by an agreed strategic plan. Universities were in any case being urged by HEFCE to produce mission statements.[3] The new agreed mission statement declared that,

> UEA Norwich is a premier research and teaching university. We are dedicated to the advancement of learning and the increase of knowledge both to satisfy the aspirations of individuals and to contribute to economic, social and cultural progress at regional, national and international levels.

This was to be achieved by sustaining academic excellence, developing UEA's national and international role in teaching and research, strengthening the regional role in contributing to the life of East Anglia, preserving the interaction of research and scholarship, and providing a rewarding experience for students, a supportive environment for staff and allocating resources accordingly.

As well as the overall mission statement there was a strategic plan, a new venture for the University. Burke inherited "A Forward Look" from Thompson's last month in office in 1986. After extensive discussion in the University, Burke wrote the first draft of a strategic plan which was then discussed by Schools, Assembly and Senate before final adoption. This set a pattern, reviewing proposed student numbers, finances and detailed recommendations for cuts across Schools. Thereafter various planning documents resulted in "Growth and Change, 1990-95: a Strategic Plan" in January 1990, setting out aims, objectives and strategies – curricular, administrative and so forth. It set out several aims, to increase student numbers by 20-25 per cent, establish a common course structure, increase interaction with the Colney Lane Institutes, collaborate with other East Anglian institutions, develop the site, make the use of IT a routine activity, and affirm research and teaching excellence. All these aims were achieved.[4]

From 1993 the horizon was changed, looking towards the end of the century. A document called "The Strategic Plan: UEA 2000" was published annually from 1993 with the mission statement, with a checklist of progress in aims. We shall see some of the achievements later in the chapter. But some general points are worth making about the process. The University had probably never felt itself so formally managed. The new Planning and Resources Committee inherited from Michael Thompson's last year 1986 remained the chief planning body. In spite of its carefully devised constitutional position, it did arouse some resentment from some Deans and Senate who felt rather downgraded, dealing with decisions following debates held elsewhere. Senate could and did overrule the PRC, but usually on matters like the Library and student services. It had to be recognised, however, that, following Jarratt and a decade of managing cuts, some body had to be responsible for making realistic disinterested, if unwelcome proposals within a more managed system. Also, as we shall see, there were many new initiatives and careful planning was needed to keep these moving forward with proper priorities. The Vice-Chairman of the PRC was Dr John Tarrant, himself part of a noteworthy constitutional change. In 1989 he was uniquely appointed Deputy Vice-Chancellor, dealing mainly with estates and financial matters. He bore much of the burden of these busy years and was rewarded with the Vice-Chancellorship of Huddersfield University in 1995.

Burke's years, like those of his predecessors were bedevilled by problems of finance. Between 1988 and 1993 public funding per student in English universities and colleges was reduced by 26 per cent in real terms and the Exchequer Recurrent Grant fell from 54 per cent of higher education income in 1989/90 to 44 per cent by 1994/5.[5] As he entered office, UEA's grant was to be increased by 0.7 per cent from £14,968,000 to £15,073,000 for the period 1987-89 but, with inflation, this would represent a real cut estimated at 4.5 per cent, the fourth worst cut of any university. It would have been worse but for a "safety net" and overall UEA expected a shortfall of £4,300,000. This was disappointing since Sussex, Warwick and York all made substantial real gains. Immediate student anger was expressed in "Stop the Cuts" sit-ins in the Registry and elsewhere. Surprisingly it was not then a disciplinary offence to occupy University buildings but this was rectified in June 1987.[6] Disciplinary action was taken against two students since a porter and receptionist had been bruised in a melée in the Registry foyer. The "Stop the Cuts" gestures were patently futile, and fortunately they did not mark the beginning of a long period of unrest as in 1968-72. The firmness with which the new Vice-Chancellor dealt with the matter was beneficial to his standing.

The University had applied for a £4,000,000 grant for "streamlining", which meant enabling eighty-five staff to retire to make the cuts, but only half of this was secured,[7] which meant spending reserves which it was feared could be depleted in three years. UEA was not, of course, alone in this. It was estimated that all universities would be in deficit to the extent of £200,000,000 by 1989/90.[8] The cuts were made in 1988 but, as the specific figures for 1988-89 and 1989-90 were published in successive years, it appeared that year after year UEA was being signalled out for particular displeasure. In 1988-89 it was as the second most severely cut university, exceeded only by the Manchester Business School. The *Daily Telegraph* cuttingly described UEA as one of a handful of universities on a "downward escalator" to presumably imminent bankruptcy and extinction.[9] Burke resented this expression and pointed out that "we have lost courses, lost subjects, lost people and we have been damaged", but the University had shed two hundred staff, become leaner and was "refocused into areas of strength".[10]

A first sign of recovery was the splendid achievement of UEA in raising over £5,000,000 from outside sources for research in the first six months of 1989-90. This placed UEA in the top twenty universities in Britain for research income. This was vital since the UFC annual grants to individual universities were partly based on income they could raise in this way. Accordingly, in the declaration of the 1990-91 figures, UEA's grant was raised from £14,586,000 to £14,715,000, now one of thirty-four universities with raised grants and no longer among the sixteen suffering cuts – now ironically including Kent, Lancaster, Warwick and York. This was very important for UEA, since it indicated for the first time in the Burke years that there was no inevitable "downward escalator" to which UEA was condemned. Things could improve by effort and action. UEA also had a nice positive balance of income and expenditure in 1988-89 which placed it among the thirty-five solidly solvent universities and well clear of the eighteen in deficit (including the prestigious Cambridge, Edinburgh, Bristol and Manchester).

If 1990 suggested better times for UEA, yet this year saw an interesting experiment which ended in confusion for all universities and which needs some explanation. In April 1987, Kenneth Baker's White Paper proposed to replace the UGC with a Universities Funding Council (UFC), while polytechnics were to be freed from local authorities and placed under a Polytechnics and Colleges Funding Council (PCFC) with a strong business membership. Both would "contract" with their client institutions, and grants would be based on these contracts and their performance. This was expected to create two leagues of universities, the elite doing research, the rest largely confined to teaching and training; or, some condemned to close. This approach was regarded as especially appropriate for expensive sciences, where resources were best concentrated in ten to fifteen universities and not wasted among small poor departments. Indeed a pilot study of earth sciences for the UGC had classified departments in this way, with UEA coming out as one of the

leading research elite. But the wider implications were that ten British universities could lose their chemistry and physics departments and become liberal
arts colleges. UEA was not regarded as likely to be one of the ten, but physics
would certainly have been vulnerable. These plans for the two leagues
(researching or teaching) were abandoned in 1988 after heavy opposition in
the House of Lords.

The contracting idea remained. This idea was that the funding body would
contract with a university to produce, say, fifteen philosophers or a hundred
engineers for a "guide price". Universities would then compete among themselves, and with polytechnics, to produce so many graduates of a certain
discipline at the lowest price. It would drive down costs as institutions
undercut each other below the guide price. The government could influence
the type of graduate produced and encourage a shift to producing (high guide
price) scientists and technologists rather than (low price) humanists. The
prices ranged from £8500 per student for clinical medicine down to £2200 for
law and politics. Also, since the contracts would be for four years, it would
reintroduce some stability back into university funding. The dangers to
university autonomy and of government dictation were plain but it was an
interesting attempt to bring the competitive disciplines of the market to academic change.[11] It rather assumed that Cambridge as a producer of engineers
or LSE of economists would be shunned by the funding councils if they were
underbid by a cheaper contract offered by, say, "Coketown" Poly. Derek
Burke was scathing, "the guide prices will fall and there will be an inevitable
fall in the unit of resource. This is a deliberate policy".[12] The "guide prices"
were already too low and the implication was that they would have to be
topped up by private fees.

Chaos then ensued as the universities, predictably, agreed to stick to guide
prices, refused to compete and undercut each other, and put in bids at the
maximum guide price. Only 7 per cent of bids were below the guide price.
The UFC in turn threw out all the bogus bids.[13] Burke was disappointed that
the UFC had rejected his bids and thereby wrecked a four-year plan based on
them.[14] It was a return to "hand to mouth" annual budgeting, and it was also
"a grotesque insult to the universities" as the CVCP put it.[15] Burke's predecessor, Michael Thompson, now at Birmingham, was also outspoken against
it. Many were pleased that the Vice-Chancellors had stood up to the government and wrecked the system.

Following the failure of the bidding system, universities were locked into a
system whereby they were forced to expand. From 1990-91 the balance of
public funding was shifted from cash-limited recurrent grants to tuition fees
to encourage universities to recruit more students. This was therefore an
important element in the growth of UEA in these years from four thousand to

seven thousand students. Then from 1991-92 the single tuition fee was replaced by three band levels, rewarding laboratory and workshop (science and technology) over classroom (arts) courses, to encourage a shift to the sciences. From the same year annual assumptions were made about improved efficiency; overall efficiency gains of 1.5 per cent had to be made, rising to 2 per cent in 1994-95. There was no standing still under this system; a university either had to expand or contract into insignificance. It was seen as a major national success for higher education in which UEA participated fully.[16]

By 1992 the UFC based its grants on a combination of money partly for teaching, itself based on numbers of students, and partly for research. Under this system UEA's grants rose steadily from £16,100,000 in 1990/1 to £20,400,000 by 1993/4. These years 1990-93 were optimistic ones for UEA after the difficult initial years. Yet a new squeeze hit the universities with a 14 per cent cut in teaching funds, which threatened to wipe out £2,000,000 from UEA's income in a further drive to reduce government spending. UEA was forced to cut its intake by 150,[17] and student numbers were capped, preventing the University from offsetting the impact of cuts by higher undergraduate recruitment. Six universities – though not UEA – were plunged into serious financial difficulties.[18]

In 1995 HEFCE gave UEA a 1.9 per cent increase in grant, in effect a real 3.25 per cent cut, exacerbated by a further cap of student numbers. This was about average for England's established universities and actually fourth out of the seven universities of the sixties. The 1995 allocation was the most complicated so far. Each university's grant was based on its research performance and student numbers. The research allocation (R) was dominated by the quality related (CR) component, taking account of the research quality of a university as measured by the result of the 1992 Research Assessment Exercise of individual subjects. Teaching allocations (T) were based on recruitment in the previous year, provided that the cap on home/European award holders – the Maximum Aggregate Student Number (MASN) – was not exceeded, and on each university's average level of funding per student. The MASN cap was to regulate student awards and hence local authority expenditure on grants. Both the R and T elements were subject to an efficiency gain of 1.5 per cent per annum. The T element had been so subject for the previous two years, the R element now for the first time.[19]

The *Financial Times* with customary lucidity, noted that public funding per student had fallen in real terms from an index number of 100 in 1989/90 to 73 by 1995/6.

> The squeeze on student funding seems likely to worsen. Under grant allocations to higher education in England for the 1995/6 academic year, funding for teaching and research will rise by 2.1 per cent to £3.2 billion. Taking into account the

expected 2.3 per cent increase in student numbers and assuming annual inflation of about 3 per cent this could mean a real decline over the previous year of some 3.4 per cent per student in this type of funding.

One Vice-Chancellor described it as an experiment to see how much more could be squeezed out of universities, "it could be an experiment to test to destruction".[20]

These were national problems of which UEA was only a part. Burke could take satisfaction that UEA's finances had improved as follows:[21]

	Income £ million	Of which UGC, UFC, HEFCE, £ million	Research Income £ million	Expenditure £ million	General Funds Reserves £ million
1987-88	27.8	16.2	3.1	28.1	
1988-99	29.0	17.2	4.4	29.0	
		Now UFC			
1989-90	38.1	19.0	6.3	37.3	7.4
1990-91	42.1	16.1	8.4	41.5	7.4
1991-92	45.8	16.7	8.7	45.4	6.3
		Now HEFCE			
1992-93	52.9	19.1	9.7	51.1	7.4
1993-94	57.3	20.5	9.8	56.0	8.0
1994-95	62.3	25.8	11.5	61.1	

Overall income had risen strongly and, as regards state funding, UEA's position was respectably middling. The key element had been the increasing research income from outside sources, important in its own right and, through the formulae on which the overall state grant was calculated, a factor driving up overall income. It was no longer one of the most cut universities and on a "downward escalator".

Burke inherited proposals for cuts which could have threatened or closed various departments but which had been rejected by Senate just before he arrived. The School of Education, highly peer rated (eighth best for research and ninth for teaching),[22] sustained a 30 per cent cut in resources, largely because the merger with Keswick had made them hugely overresourced, with too many teachers for the number of student places. But they revived. The CEAS, which had staved off fears of closure in recent years, flourished under Hassell Smith and Richard Wilson. It launched a £200,000 appeal at Wood Hall in 1987 to provide an endowment to cushion it from the University's finances.[23] Music too seemed under threat from cuts in 1987 but this aroused a packed public protest meeting at Norwich City Hall.[24] Music was saved and raised £123,000 by public appeal, specifically to endow scholarships to maintain expert tuition for voice and instruments.

The most threatened and most strongly defended School was, however, Development Studies, "DEV". UEA was the only university in Britain which offered development studies at all levels. The threat to close its undergraduate teaching programme and cut staff from twenty-seven to fifteen led to questions in Parliament,[25] and personal interventions from Edward Heath and Dame Judith Hart, the latter of whom described DEV as the "Jewel in the Crown" of UEA. It was a time of acute awareness of Third World poverty (the Ethiopian famine, the Brandt Commission, Bob Geldof's Live Aid concert). In fact DEV had been the only School refusing to accept its cut and the threat to close its undergraduate degree, if it did not do so, was a means of calling its bluff. In any case, there were problems over its undergraduate applications and their quality. DEV accepted its cut, survived, and went on to become very successful under the new system.

More contentious was the reprieve of Physics, the only science department under threat of closure. It had many problems. It was too small to be viable. The UGC regarded the minimum viable size for such a department as twenty full time staff and two hundred students. UEA had only fifty-one students and the entire faculty of MAP in 1986-87 was only twenty-seven, about half physicists. The staff student ratio for physics was 1 : 5.3, about half the national average for the subject and vastly below the staff student ratio for other UEA Schools, most of which were 1 : 10-14. Other Science Schools attracted over £1,000,000 a year in outside research funds but Physics only drew in £250,000, while Physics research output per head was much below BIO, CHE, and ENV.[26] Since the early 1980s it had been, in the words of one Pro Vice-Chancellor, "a financial haemorrhage on a massive and crippling scale", an ungrasped nettle. The UGC report revealed UEA's position starkly. Its Physics Department was the fifth smallest in the UK, but the fifth most expensive. It had the seventh most generous staff/student ratio and the lowest research income of all.[27]

Yet physics was a core science discipline and many argued that no first class British university could continue without it. Physics too was an important component of the interaction with the Research Institutes, especially IFR. So strenuous efforts were made to save the subject. A number of staff took early retirement, a new professor was appointed who gave more vigorous leadership, the degree course was redesigned and renamed "Interdisciplinary Physics" and, for a while, all went well. More students and some excellent new staff were recruited, the grant income improved; an Advisory Board under the Chairmanship of Sir Sam Edwards FRS gave invaluable advice and physics was retained. But it remained a high cost problem and the strains of saving money and bearing an increasing student load were absorbed by the Humanities Schools.

A key feature of Burke's years, 1987-95 was the considerable expansion of student numbers from four thousand to seven thousand, driven partly by funding policies as we have seen. Burke had regarded UEA as too small when he arrived, restrained by the constant cuts of the eighties. The original strategic plan had been to increase from four thousand to five thousand five hundred by 1994/5; but, having already achieved that target by 1992, UEA aimed for 8000 plus 1800 part-timers by the year 2000.[28] This rate of growth would keep UEA in line with the expansion of higher education in the UK as a whole. It caught national attention as "one of the most ambitious expansion plans of any university".[29] Nearer home it aroused unease in Norwich that this expansion would create a housing crisis in Norwich. Some in the City Council resented it as another episode of UEA's ignoring the implications of its actions for the city.[30] It was to be a powerful motive behind the building expansion and provision of more residences.

National policy did not always help such expansion. The government, having called for the provision of higher education for a third of eighteen-year-olds – to which UEA was responding – then decided that this was unaffordable. So UEA had to cut its projected first year intake for 1994 by 8 per cent and keep to a total student body of 5050 (in practice exceeded).[31] In spite of these constraints the overall expansion of the Burke years was impressive and drove many other changes.

Student and Academic Staff Numbers

	U/G	P/G	Total students	Academic staff
1986-87	3693	1095	4788	526
1987-88	3757	1133	4890	544
1988-89	3724	1084	4808	535
1989-90	3882	1200	5082	547
1990-91	3873	1369	5242	597
1991-92	4174	1453	5627	629
1992-93	4700	1592	6292	632
1993-94	5268	1772	7040	641
1994-95	5434	2063	7497	604

If the University was to expand its student numbers, and to diversify its studies, then more buildings were needed. Rick Mather, who had designed the buildings for the School of Education, the School of Information Systems and the Climatic Research Unit, was asked by the University to produce a Development Plan for the future development of the site.[32] He identified certain key areas and their possible use, some realised and some still potential. He proposed first of all a new road to come sweeping into the Plain from the west, with an entrance in Colney Lane and providing a link between UEA and the A47 Southern bypass. As regards the site itself, he was insistent on maintaining the Lasdun principles – keeping building to the Central area, preserving the Parkland and maintaining viewpoints to the road as the Plain's central visual feature. Within the central area he envisaged Site A (an area of greenhouses and a biological garden) as possible residences which could be developed immediately. Site B, the area on the southern side of the road, he thought of as academic buildings. This is where the Elizabeth Fry and Constable Terrace buildings were to be located. Site C was by the hard play and mound areas at the Bluebell Road end of the site. He saw this as a site for residences: what became Nelson Court. He also proposed building on the grass area between Waveney Terrace and the University Drive approach from Bluebell Road (Site D). He was dismayed at the bleak mess of the bus turn-around by the Students' Union, Site E, and proposed clearing away the clutter of cars and recyling bins and then building a theatre there to liven it up. Finally, he saw the vast car park, Site F, as the potential site for a major public building like a concert hall – as Denys Lasdun had. Mather discussed his plans with Sir Denys Lasdun and also with Bernard Feilden and Norman Foster.[33] Sir Denys was especially supportive, although Mather was distinctively changing the "language". Mather thought the high-level walkways no longer possible and he saw his patterns rather more in terms of ground-level main streets and courtyards. Enthused by his own ideas, Mather then asked the University if he could design some of these buildings himself. Sites B, C and E were developed as he had envisaged.

In 1989, following Mather's plan, it was announced that the University was to embark upon a new building plan to prepare UEA for the twenty-first century. Two blocks of residences for a total of 1100 students, an Occupational and Physiotherapy Building and a Drama Studio were planned. They were to cost £20,000,000 from the University's capital reserves, outside grants and, most innovatively, outside loans raised through a Business Expansion Scheme organised by Hodgson Martin. Investors bought shares at a discount and, with tax relief and after five years received £1.50 per £1 share tax free. The residences built with this money, Nelson Court and Constable Terrace, were owned by Hodgson Martin until early 1996 when they were bought back by the University and the debt discharged. It was a tax efficient, low-cost way of raising capital.[34] Nelson Court and Constable Terrace were also partly financed by the sale of the original Village site in Wilberforce Road in 1989, the proceeds of which also were used for the Studio Theatre and hockey pitches.

Constable Terrace facing south towards the Sainsbury Centre accommodates about 600 students in a long gently curving terrace of three and four storeys, with a very elegant roof cornice with lighting underneath the rim, defining the roofline shape, providing light in a dark area and an evocation of the cocktail bars he had shown the University before building CRU. The finish is fine with ash veneer woodwork, plastered white walls and carpeting. There is also a "wonderful external concrete spiral staircase, the core of which is covered in a sea-green mosaic and with railings which are striations of black steel rod". [35] Equally important the building was so energy efficient that recycled heat from the inhabitants kept the building warm with super insulation and double-glazing. Stale air from shower rooms and kitchens is recycled to living rooms and kitchens.[36] This elegant terrace was opened in 1993 and gained a RIBA regional award in 1995, one of twenty-three won by UEA since it started.[37]

Rick Mather also designed Nelson Court for another 600 students at a cost of £6,000,000. Nelson Court and Constable Terrace have the same interior design. They are in effect series of terraced houses, a ten bedroom house behind a front door. They both have en suite facilities fabricated off site and dropped in with a crane.[38] This was an important change from the principle of staircase and corridor which had shaped the Thistlethwaite-Lasdun thinking of the 1960s. In practice the new residences were more like the terraced houses in the city which students were used to renting. The en suite facilities and high degree of finish was intended to appeal to students, now in the 1990s enjoying a higher standard of living at home than they would have done in the 1960s. The market was well targeted since a questionnaire had found that many students were prepared to pay more for better residences. The increasingly important conference trade also demanded better than normal student rooms. The students themselves now had a wide range of choice from the perfectly acceptable to the rather good.

In 1989, after the University had persuaded the Health Authority that it would provide courses, it was also decided to build a new £3,900,000 school for occupational therapists and physiotherapists. There was a shortage of therapists in the region and the new training centre would go some way to redress this. UEA gave the land free while the costs of construction were to be met by the Department of Health and the East Anglian Regional Health Authority, the latter to be the owner of the four storey building.[39] It was designed by John Miller and Partners to contain teaching areas, workshops and a gymnasium, and was opened for the new School of Occupational Therapy and Physiotherapy in 1993. Most excitingly, the building was formally opened by the Queen on 25 May 1994 and named the Queen's Building. On her tour of the building the Queen expressed her keen interest in ligaments, her grandson Peter Philips having damaged his knee in a rugby accident.[40] It was a pleasant visit, less overwhelmingly special than that of 1968 but more relaxed and with no fears of any trouble from the new generation of students. A further occasion for pride was the winning of a regional RIBA award for the Queen's Building, which was then one of five runners-up for the RIBA Building of the Year (won by the Eurostar terminal at Waterloo).[41]

John Miller and Partners also designed the £4,200,000 Elizabeth Fry Building, built by Willmott Dixon and opened in January 1995. It provided teaching facilities, lecture theatres and seminar rooms, chiefly for the School of Health and Social Work, but is widely used. The building is technically of considerable interest. Its three storeys and 30,000 square feet is heated by the equivalent of two domestic size boilers. Peter Yorke noted that "the heat efficiency of the building is phenomenal. Air is passed through hollows in the floor to warm the building's structure which acts as a night storage heater in winter while in summer the building is cooled by night time ventilation". Yorke and the architects had been to Stockholm to look at public buildings similarly heated and ventilated. Triple- glazed and seven times more airtight than the standard building, it was the first building of its size in Britain to be so serviced,[42] and "the latest example of the UEA's commitment to architecturally, environmentally friendly buildings".[43] In September 1995 it too won a regional award of the RIBA. The Vice-Chancellor noted that the new buildings, Constable Terrace, the Queen's Building and Elizabeth Fry, had altered spatial relations on the Plain: "they're changing the way the University works, as the centre of gravity has shifted away from the top end of the Teaching Wall towards the new buildings. And they've drawn the Sainsbury Centre into the University rather than it being a bolt on".[44]

As part of the building expansion, the University acquired a new theatre. Since the early days of the University drama had been staged in the hall in the Village. In 1984 this was reshaped and re-equipped as the 320 seat Kenny Theatre, financed by the Kenny Trust. In 1987 this was lost when it was decided to sell off the Village, then increasingly dilapidated and isolated from the Plain. Part of the money from the sale of the Village could be used to build a new theatre on the Plain. This was done and the new purpose-built Studio Theatre was opened by Harold Pinter in January 1994. It is designed by Rick Mather and seats up to 200 with very flexible arrangements of seating and performing space. Although enjoyed by many for entertainment, it is very much a teaching resource for drama students being trained in acting, directing and the technical aspects of theatrical presentation. Its opening was a happy event with several existing and future theatrical honorary graduates of UEA – Pinter himself, Timothy West, Prunella Scales and Ian Emmerson, the Director of the Maddermarket Theatre, performing or attending.[45]

Also on the artistic side the Sainsbury Centre acquired a major 20,000 square foot extension. The £8,000,000 cost was met by David Sainsbury's Gatsby Trust. Norman Foster was once again the architect and decided to build it underground, following on from the eastern end of the SCVA to avoid interrupting the line of the main building. It is beneath a large grass area which is level with the end of the building. The area between the greensward and the resumed slope of grass down to the Broad is filled with a striking fan-shaped façade of glass, hence its name "The Crescent Wing". It provides natural light for an exciting curving interior corridor which leads into the extension and looks out to the Broad. Lit from within, it provides another reflection in the Broad. It was built by Woolf Construction and its special technical interest was the need to keep moisture out of this under-ground structure which is embedded in soil through which water is constantly seeping. Coffey Brothers, Irish specialist contractors in water-containing structures, devised the complicated unseen proofing and drainage system.[46] The extension provides a splendid suite of offices, a very well-equipped exhibition area, and space for storage and the display of stored items. It also houses advanced conservation laboratories for the SCVA's own use and for teaching, and the Sainsbury Research Unit (1988) under Dr Steven Hooper, an authority on Oceanic art and already well known to the Sainsburys from his work at the British Museum.

UEA also extended its sporting facilities in these years. In 1989 a fine running track was built by the Norfolk Athletics Trust in the grounds of Earlham High School. In 1993 its management was taken over by UEA, to be part of a major sports venue with a new hockey centre to be shared between the University and athletes from Norwich and Norfolk. UEA invested £500,000 in this with the Sports Council and Norfolk County Council each contributing £100,000. They were opened in June 1993 by the hockey interna-tional Lucy Youngs from Aylsham. It created the East Anglian Regional Hockey Centre, second only as a national centre to that at Milton Keynes.[47] The hockey centre, like the track, was a great success, more than 71,000 people using the Centre in its first year.[48] Although primarily intended for hockey, the floodlit artificial turf pitches could also be used for football training and five-a-side matches. This was all leading to the vision for a £5,500,000 super stadium for the year 2000 with a twenty-five metre swimming pool. It would make Norwich and UEA the sporting centre of Norfolk with facilities capable of staging international events. Lottery money was applied for and £100,000 raised locally. The final raising of the money and building occupied the time of Burke's successors and the final complex opened in 2000 for the millennium.

The Village site in Wilberforce Road underwent major changes in these years. In 1987 it was decided to sell off the Village site, which had outgrown its purpose as the nursery of new Schools and was now very dilapidated.[49] It was sold to property developers in 1989 for £4,000,000 at the height of the property boom. Four years later the University bought part of the site back for £750,000, "a pretty good piece of business" as the University observed.[50] UEA now needed the space to build student residences to replace Fifers Lane. Accommodation costing £11,000,000, and also financed by a BES scheme, was built by Team Services for 713 students. It now meant that UEA could provide University residences for 3000 students, some three fifths of undergraduates.

The building of new residences on the Village site in Wilberforce Road was necessitated by the closure in 1994 of those in Fifers Lane which had been occupied since 1965. The 591 bedrooms at Horsham had become hopelessly uneconomic, losing £100,000 in the last year of operation, while refurbishment including essential fire precautions, would have cost over £3,000,000. The Fifers Lane site was leased from the City and County Councils until 2006 and the Council was as unwilling to forego the rent as was the University to refurbish for so short a period. Within a month vandals were breaking in, smashing windows and fittings, drug taking and fire raising. Even worse the continued rent and upkeep was costing the University £130,000 a year and it could hardly spend more on security for buildings unused and yielding no income. It aroused resentment from some who wanted to use the buildings to house the homeless, while students paying higher rents at Earlham began to regret the loss of the low £26 rents at Horsham. The University hoped to dispose of the property to an interested third party but redevelopment would entail the demolition of the existing buildings and, in any case, it was generally appreciated that it was the City, not the University, which owned the site. The dilemmas remained insoluble, Horsham remained a millstone and a dereliction but it was a sad end to a period of UEA's history which many students regard with affection.[51] UEA was eventually released from its lease in November 1998.

We cannot leave this without considering two aspects of site development, one away from the Plain and the other abortive. The first was the location of a new hospital for Norwich. Although it was not part of UEA, it had implications for it and the University intervened in the deliberations. The site preferred by Norwich District Health Authority and the Regional Health Authority was Hellesdon. But the hospital consultants wanted a site in Colney and in 1987 Derek Burke put the Colney case to the Regional Health Authority, thus being among those who convinced it to change its mind in favour of it in spite of local Colney opposition. In 1990 a nine hundred bed

£104,000,000 hospital was approved by the Health Secretary, Kenneth Clarke. A major new hospital on the western edge of the University near to the new BUPA hospital and the life science and health Schools made logistic sense and strengthened UEA's ambitions for a Medical School. But the decisive influence was that of the consultants rather than UEA. Finally, there was one major idea for developing the site which did not materialise. The Norfolk Record Office was located in Norwich City Library, which had been destroyed by fire in 1994. The Library was to be rebuilt on its Bethel Street site, but it was proposed to relocate the Records Office in a £10,000,000 centre at UEA. This would have created a major History Centre at UEA combining the UEA Library, the UEA and County Archives, the CEAS and the East Anglian Film Archive, a splendid partnership of University and region.[52] It did not come about. There was some feeling that UEA was too distant from Norwich, that there was insufficient space for the extra building around the Library and that it would clutter the Lasdun design. The key factor, however, was that lottery money was not forthcoming and the plan was shelved, but it was a bold vision backed by the Vice-Chancellor. Both hospital and Records Office projects were in keeping with the aim of drawing the University, City and County closer.

In research and teaching UEA remained lively and innovative in these years. A key element in this on the science side was the creation of a major Research Park of remarkable power and prestige which came together alongside UEA. Burke on his arrival had stressed that "we are committed to this inter-reaction with local industry".[53] In 1990 the University won approval to develop a Science Research Park in the Yare Valley off Colney Lane, overcoming the objections of conservationists, notably the Yare Valley Society.[54] New developments from 1987 were to add to the complex. In that year David Sainsbury's Gatsby Charitable Foundation gave £15,000,000 over ten years to create the Sainsbury Laboratory at the John Innes Institute. This was to develop genetically modified disease-resistant plants to remove the need for chemical protection. In the same year the Ministry of Agriculture and Fisheries announced that it would create a new £5,000,000 central food laboratory complex at Colney Lane, replacing two smaller existing offices in Norwich and one in London. The site was further augmented by the Cambridge Laboratory opened in 1990.[55] This was part of the former Plant Breeding Institute Laboratory in Cambridge. Following privatisation, part was taken by Unilever and the research side came to Norwich.[56] This now large complex of buildings was formally opened as the Norwich Research Park in November 1993 by John MacGregor the MP for South Norfolk, who described it as, "probably the greatest concentration of facilities concerned with crops and food research anywhere in the world".[57] By then it comprised the Ministry of Agriculture's Food Science Laboratory, British Sugar's technical centre, the John Innes Centre (including the Sainsbury and Cambridge laboratories) and the Norwich Laboratory of the AFRC Institute of Food Research. To these would shortly be added the Nitrogen Fixation Laboratory, which moved from the University of Sussex. The John Innes Institute had now become so large, with 625 scientists, three leading laboratories and a budget of £13,700,000, that it was renamed the John Innes Centre, with Derek Burke continuing as the Chairman of Council.

The Norwich Research Park (NRP) was a major international centre of excellence in biotechnology and perfectly positioned adjacent to the life sciences buildings of UEA. Burke reflected that "the links with the Norwich Research Park are a priceless asset for UEA. UEA benefits from the teaching skills of scientists at NRP, some holding professorships at UEA, a hundred scientists working in NRP were taking research degrees at UEA.[58] What had developed was a major international research park, but not a science or business park of local firms such as the business park enthusiasts of the 1980s may have hoped for.[59] The Norwich Research Park is an altogether grander concept. In its narrowest definition it is a piece of land on which the major research laboratories around Colney Lane are located. More widely, it includes the new hospital (the Norfolk and Norwich University Hospital) and the Chemistry and Biology Schools of UEA. Most ambitiously, some see the NRP as a broad concept comprising the whole of UEA, the research laboratories and the hospital. It is a powerful vision far beyond the idea of a business park of local firms adjacent to a university.

The connection with the University was further cemented by Derek Burke's personal position. In 1988 he was appointed Chairman of the Advisory Committee on Novel Foods and Processes. This new body replaced an earlier advisory committee, since new expertise was required in biotechnology and genetic engineering because, as Edwina Currie observed, "many novel food projects will involve the use of genetic engineering".[60] Burke brought his experience of this from Canada, "we have learnt how to modify organisms by changing their genetic make up and it is now beginning to be possible to use this in food production".[61] There were further links in that Professors Peter Richmond and David Southgate of the Food Research Institute were also members of the committee. The first approval for a genetically engineered food was given by Burke's ACNP in 1990 to a form of yeast designed to make bread rise faster. Through the Vice-Chancellor, the FRI and the Sainsbury Laboratory, the network of scientists around UEA played an important part in the innovation and regulation of the new technology.[62] In various ways, collaboration with institutions in the Research Park enriched UEA's own scientific work. For example UEA's interdisciplinary tradition, notably in biochemistry, was evident in its work in colloid science. This dealt with materials such as paste, emulsions and food, with expertise spread over the Schools of Chemistry, Physics and Biology and the Institute of Food Research. A colloid group was formed in 1987 and a Biocolloid Centre based at UEA and the IFRN and with links with the Norfolk and Norwich Hospital.[63] Also Norwich was in the forefront of the study of pathogens and plants. BIO and the John Innes Institute provide a concentration of expertise in molecular plant pathology which is unique in the UK.[64]

Physics, having been reprieved, thrived remarkably in spite of its small size. Eschewing expensive "big" physics, the new approach stressed the interdisciplinary potential of the subject. An interdisciplinary physics degree began in 1988 using optional units from physics, electronic engineering, chemical, biological and environmental sciences. A leading part of this new focused research, under Professor Paul Coleman, was the use of positron beams to study the surface properties of metals. As part of this, Coleman developed a positron microscope which could map tiny defects in surfaces, of considerable importance for the electronics industry. The School also had links with the Research Park, due to its reputation in semi-conductors under Professor John Davies. Davies noted "that reputation got us the equipment that allowed us to carry out the interdisciplinary work : that is how interdisciplinary work often develops".[65]

UEA became a major centre of metallobiology. This examines the role of metals in biological processes, for example calcium in bone formation, and sodium and potassium in nerve transmission, while the importance of trace metals such as iron and zinc to the body are well known. UEA's specialism was the study of metalloproteins by spectroscopic and kinetic methods and the University was designated by SERC as its UK Centre for Research on Metalloproteins. This work is led by Professor A.J. Thomson (CHE), who became an FRS in 1993 for his work, and Professor Colin Greenwood (BIO), reflecting the interdisciplinary nature of the work. There is close collaboration with the IFRN, for example, on the intake and storage of iron by animals. It is a prime example of interdisciplinarity between UEA Schools and the IFRN in the Research Park and of relating academic research to practical advances in agriculture and medicine.[66]

The School of Environmental Sciences continued as one of the premier centres of science at UEA. By the mid 1990s ENV was concerned with a remarkably wide range of research studies, the recreational value of woodland (using Thetford Forest), the climate and chemical composition of the Weddell Sea in Antarctica, ocean circulation in the North Atlantic and the effect of melting Polar ice, the extraction of sustainable resources in the Brazilian rain forest, and fishing in Vietnam. The School also acquired an interesting resource in the Weybourne Atmospheric Observatory, a former Second World War gunnery blockhouse and cow byre. This, linked with other observatories worldwide, monitors the quality of air over Norfolk and found it remarkably polluted. ENV also continued with its long-standing occupations – global warming (1993 was the sixth hottest year on record and nine of the thirteen warmest years, since the 1850s, were in the 1980s and 1990s), the controversy over the need for, or irrelevance of, sea defences, and the ecology of the Broads embodied in the Broads Plan of 1987. ENV had gained over £20,000,000 in research grants between 1990-1995, a grade 5 research rating in 1992 and, showing the links between teaching and research, and "excellent" rating in the Teaching Quality Assessment in 1994.[67]

It was environmental concerns that attracted the largest research grant ever to come to UEA, £2,000,000 from the ESRC in 1991 to finance a new Centre for Social and Economic Research on the Global Environment (CSERGE) based jointly on UEA and University College London. The purpose of the Centre is to examine areas such as climate change and global warming, biodiversity loss, the adaptation of institutions to environmental change, the problem of the ozone hole and the study of environmental risk – all established UEA fortes.[68]

As well as these major developments, UEA research and teaching can be seen to relate to biomedical research, industrial and literary matters. At a time when the siting of the new hospital was being debated, UEA became noted for some areas of biomedical research. Dr Ian Gibson of the School of Biological Sciences researched into gene therapy, how healthy genes could be made to take over from defective ones to treat cancers and other diseases. Norfolk's "Big C" Appeal had provided over £300,000 for cancer research at UEA and in 1993 they received a further £100,000 to work on leukaemia. Dr John Leslie, consultant haematologist at the Norfolk and Norwich Hospital, regarded UEA's genetic-based research as "the best hope of finding an effective treatment" for the disease.[69] In the course of this the UEA researchers discovered a molecule responsible for spreading tumours from one part of the body to another; consequently, a further £120,000 grant was received in 1994 from the Association for International Cancer Research.[70] Much attention was drawn to BIO's research in this year 1994 with the opening of the Francesca Gunn laboratory. Francesca had been the infant daughter of the Norwich City goal keeper Bryan Gunn who had died of leukaemia. £100,000 of the appeal raised in her memory was generously given to UEA to dedicate a laboratory to her, opened by her parents in 1994.[71] As well as leukaemia the laboratory works on breast, kidney, colon and testicular cancers. They received a further £24,000 from the Bryan Gunn Fund in 1995. In 1997 Ian Gibson became a Member of Parliament, where he continues his forceful concern for cancer and medical research.

Also of major importance was George Duncan's work on cataracts. What was distinctive was his refusal to experiment on live animals which would have had to be blinded. Instead he used lenses initially taken from cattle and pigs killed in slaughterhouses, and then entirely human lenses removed in operations and kept in the East Anglia Eye Bank at the West Norwich Hospital. Cells from these were grown in the laboratory with a view to eventually growing whole lenses in tissue culture. This was in keeping with the "Big C" policy of not supporting research involving animals. The UEA work was supported by a major pharmaceutical company and anti-vivisection groups, Animal Aid and the Humane Research Trust, who gave their largest ever grant of £250,000 to make UEA a "world leader in the use of human tissue technology".[72] In 1991 a Biomedical Research Centre was created at UEA to promote collaboration between UEA, its affiliated institutes and local hospitals. This provided an umbrella for the work in cataract and cancer cell research, and provision was made for doctors from the Norfolk and Norwich Hospital to carry out research in UEA laboratories.[73]

As well as the medical science arising from BIO, the University moved strongly towards health education in the early 1990s. In 1990 a Centre for Health Policy research was created to combine the interests in this area of social work, sociology, law and then physiotherapy and nursing.[74] Then in 1991 the Vice-Chancellor outlined his plans for honours degree courses in occupational and physiotherapy to the College of Occupational Therapists Conference in Norwich.[75] Tribute should be paid to Eileen Bumphrey, the regional occupational therapist. It was her personal crusade to get better training for occupational therapists in East Anglia. Two things were then distinctive about her thinking. She wanted this training in a university and also combined with physiotherapy. It was unusual for both types of therapists to train together. UEA became a pioneer of such training creating a new professional area, interdisciplinary in form and winning contracts from the Health Service rather than HEFCE. Accordingly, the new School of Health and Social Work was established in 1993 comprising occupational therapy, physiotherapy and social work while the Queen's Building was opened in 1994 as we have seen. This was joined by the Health Policy and Practice Unit established under Professor Shirley Pearce (a native of Norfolk) in January 1994. This engaged in clinical psychology training and researched into such matters as eating disorders, learning difficulties and Alzheimer's disease. They work closely with GPs and the training of junior hospital doctors.[76] Finally, in 1995, UEA started a new School of Nursing and Midwifery. This was the former Norfolk College of Nursing and Midwifery, with bases in hospitals in Norwich and King's Lynn. UEA already validated their awards. It brought 450 full-time and 1000 part-time students, and ninety staff to UEA.[77]

This close engagement of UEA with health education was a remarkably rapid and intense change between 1990 and 1995. With the building of the new hospital nearby it positioned UEA as a credible location for the future School of Medicine.

UEA also served local industry in remarkably diverse ways. Bernard Matthews, the Norfolk turkey farmer, and the University collaborated on a £200,000 project to introduce computer control on production lines to meet the demands of hygiene standards. The project was led by Professor Rodney Coates, head of electronic systems engineering at UEA who valued such practical work for developing degree courses.[78] Electronics also figured in MAP's work for British Telecommunications in the development of speech recognition machines. Language teachers also reached out to Norwich businesses. The chemical firm of May and Baker in Sweetbriar Road had been taken over by the French firm Rhône Poulenc, which necessitated managers learning French. UEA devised a ten-week course with emphasis on language speaking, which was taken by about a dozen senior managers.[79] Likewise twelve members of the solicitors Mills and Reeve attended courses in French and German to prepare for European legal work.[80] In an unusually specialised area, Dr John Turner devised a genetically engineered strain of willow resistant to "watermark" disease. The work was financed partly by cricket bat manufacturers who feared the ruination of their industry, since the best willow for bats *Salix Alba Caerula*, was the most vulnerable.[81] Most cricket bat willows were grown in East Anglia; indeed it had been intended to use willows on the Plain for this purpose (Chapter 4). UEA also started a two-year MBA in 1992 with financial support from the Norfolk and Waveney Training and Enterprise Council and nineteen students (selected from forty-five) including a pub manager and the general manager of Jarrolds office equipment. Under Tony Brown, the Director of Management Education, it was a successful service to local managers and entrepreneurs.[82] Following this a new School of Management was set up in September 1995, comprising the accountancy sector from the School of Information Systems, the research staff in SYS working on computers in Teaching Initiative and the Director and Deputy Director of Management Education. The Dean of the new School was Professor Keith Fletcher from Strathclyde Business School. The new School took over responsibility for the MBA and MA in human resource strategy programmes, and the undergraduate degrees in accounting and business management.[83]

In the literary arts the Arthur Miller Centre was opened in May 1989 to honour the distinguished American dramatist and his connection with UEA. The opening was celebrated with a high level seminar, a gala performance at the Theatre Royal and a dinner for 300 at the Sainsbury Centre.[84] UEA also had a major department of Scandinavian studies. James McFarlane and Janet Garton started the Norvik Press to publish critical books on and translations of Scandinavian literature.[85] Garton's contribution to Scandinavian studies was subsequently honoured with an MBE and a Cambridge Litt.D., unique for UEA at the time. In the early 1990s the Fine Arts section of the old FAM were retitled World Art and Museology (WAM), reflecting the global range of both art and artefacts studied in the SCVA. Professor John Onions had actually suggested changing the name of the SCVA itself, but Sir Robert Sainsbury, declining this, proposed the change in title of the School instead.

An important new development was the creation of the School of History in 1994. The degree in history had existed since 1981, taught by historians in the various Schools of EAS, EUR and SOC. It cut across the first Vice-Chancellor's interdisciplinary early planning of the University. Various factors lay behind this. There had been a certain tension between historians and letterists, linguists and social scientists in their own Schools in competition for resources. Interdisciplinarity, especially in times of successive cuts, had led to conflict rather than cooperation. History as a subject was given insufficient prominence in University publications, where it appeared in subsections of other subjects, confusing or deterring potential applicants. Most significantly the continued success of the history degree, in spite of the difficulties of organising and advertising it, suggested that there would be enough student support to sustain a separate School. Also the University, aware of recruiting difficulties in some Science Schools realised that it needed a School that was likely to be successful as regards admissions. The pressures of the Research Assessment and history's likely excellent performance in this, if properly categorised and grouped, was a further convincing consideration. Almost all the historians were eager to join the new School. A Centre for Historical Studies had been created in 1993, but this still perpetuated difficulties of operating across different Schools. Before the creation of the Centre sixteen historians expressed a willingness to go ahead as a School but thirteen were unwilling (mostly American and art historians); yet after the creation of the Centre there was unanimous support for establishing a School. The American historians in EAS preferred to keep their literary links, though their American history units continued to be part of the History degree. Art historians in WAM of course remained in WAM as expected. Under Professors Roy Church and Colin Davis, the patient creation of the School of History was one of the most striking examples of leadership and cooperation at this time.[86] But it also illustrates one of the difficulties of making change within the institution of those days. The Vice-Chancellor and both Pro Vice-Chancellors were opposed to this innovation in spite of the compelling arguments for it. It was more usual then to contemplate adding on new Schools from outside than an internal reconfiguration of the original Schools.

One of the major achievements of the Burke years was in establishing closer links with the region and especially Suffolk. In his first year in office, the Vice-Chancellor attended a meeting in Ipswich to meet businessmen and farmers and "the crucial importance of Suffolk in its [UEA's] affairs was underlined by him".[87] As an early earnest of this, he had appointed a short course development officer, with contacts with 250 firms throughout the region, through which they anticipated improving their service to the region.

A key strategy was to establish closer links with the colleges. In July 1991 Burke wrote to the Principals of all the Colleges of Higher and Further Education in Norfolk and Suffolk proposing to form a Regional Federation "to identify common issues, share problems and provide mutual help wherever possible".[88] He had received positive responses from all nine colleges and held two constructive meetings. Accordingly, the Regional Federation was launched in November 1991.[89] College students would be able to come to UEA, the colleges' own degrees could be validated by UEA, and joint courses could be offered by both. It would lead to "a major realignment [giving] the region a better coordinated, more flexible and improved quality of educational opportunity".[90] It was no coincidence that UEA took a stand at the Suffolk Show for the first time in June 1991.

In the next year Suffolk College in Ipswich became the first associate college of UEA. In April 1993 the Suffolk Colleges became independent of Suffolk County Council and established closer relations with the University.[91] Suffolk College, with 30,000 students, was the largest, offering twelve degree courses, four at Master's level, as well as its predominant further education work. It established links with UEA in electronic education, easy transition from its BTEC diploma to UEA's electronics degree having been arranged.[92] Lowestoft College, with 1400 full-time and 10,000 part-time students, had inevitably close links with the sea, fishing and with maritime, oil and safety matters. Lowestoft had connections both with UEA and the Anglia Polytechnic. Finally, Otley College, with 4500 students, was one of the most interesting, specialising in agricultural, horticultural and animal husbandry and rural management issues broadly. This suggested potentially close links with UEA and its ENV and BIO expertise.[93] In 1993 they started a B.Sc. in environmental conservation and ecology validated by UEA. Indeed Professor Keith Clayton of ENV for some years after his retirement was employed by UEA to keep up personal contact with the Suffolk Colleges, notably Otley. These developments were so successful that by 1993 there were proposals to make Suffolk College into a University of Suffolk. This was not an outlandish expectation, since Suffolk College already had 30-40 per cent of its students in higher education (the HEFCE requirement was

55 per cent) and Suffolk had no university at all in the county. On 1 August 1996 Suffolk College became a University College of UEA, a title it later had to cease using in the light of government decisions.

UEA made further contacts with Suffolk and East Anglia, generally through its Extramural, then Continuing Education Departments. In 1991 UEA created the Centre for Continuing Education, which took over the running of extra-mural studies in Norfolk and East Suffolk from Cambridge University, which had hitherto run all extra-mural education in East Anglia. Christopher Barringer, who had been Cambridge's resident tutor, then became UEA's first Director of Extramural Studies. At that time in 1991, a thousand students took sixty-seven courses run by UEA; by 1995 when Barringer retired, over three thousand were attending more than a hundred courses in twenty locations from King's Lynn and Cromer to Ipswich and Aldeburgh.[94] The most popular subjects were local history, archaeology and landscape, ecology, ornithology, botany and climate. It all cemented good academic relations between UEA and Suffolk.

The colleges were not only important in their own right but also acted as feeders of undergraduates to UEA. They ran Access courses which students could take as alternatives to A level. Suffolk College provided Access courses as did Norcat at King's Lynn, while Lowestoft not only did so in its base town but at Blyth House, Saxmundham.[95] UEA aimed to increase its intake of students from the region from 15 per cent to 20 per cent from ten colleges in Norfolk and Suffolk.[96]

Relations with the region were complicated by the creation of Anglia Polytechnic University in 1991. It was the result of the merger of the Essex Institute of Higher Education in Colchester and the College of Arts and Technology in Cambridge in 1989. This was designated as a Polytechnic in May 1991 and then as a University in November the same year. In a decision fiercely opposed by UEA, the Privy Council agreed this title as Anglia Polytechnic University.[97] To have "The University of East Anglia" and what was increasingly known as "Anglia University" in the same region was a source of confusion to outsiders and of irritation to both universities. Now they are increasingly emphasising APU as their title, which makes for clearer recognition. There were further confusions in that APU had four campuses, four associate colleges and two franchise colleges scattered across four counties.[98] Colleges in Norwich, Great Yarmouth and King's Lynn were linked with APU rather than UEA, whereas most of the Suffolk colleges are linked with UEA. It was also easy for sixth formers at higher education fairs to get the impression that UEA was a Norwich out-campus of the main Anglia University somewhere to the south.

It was paradoxical that while UEA was establishing stronger links in

Suffolk there were not similar relationships with the Norwich City College. In Burke's early years relations seemed promising as Access courses began at the College in September 1987, which were acceptable for UEA entrance and welcomed by Professor Burke as "new and exciting".[99] In 1992, however, Norwich City College not only celebrated its centenary but became an associate college of Anglia Polytechnic University, whose degrees it then taught. Professor Burke thinks that UEA and the Norwich City College were just too physically close. "You'll eat us for tea", was the comment of Dr Jack Lewis, the Principal of the City College, and Burke thinks that they were probably right. The College became independent of the County Council in 1993 and Dr Lewis retired in the same year but leaving his successor Caroline Neville with the College already linked to APU – and not UEA – for six degree courses. The arrangement is not immutable and overall the initiatives in reaching out to colleges in the region and especially in Suffolk were one of the achievements of the Burke years.

The extended relationships with regional colleges raised questions of UEA's identity and name. It prompted renewed calls to retitle UEA as the University of Norwich. Some of the most successful universities of the sixties were nominally linked to cities – Warwick, York, Lancaster – even if they were not actually in those cities. The arguments against change, however, were that UEA had recently adopted a strong logo style and nomenclature. The UEA (since 1966) and UEA, Norwich (since 1985) had become UEA, Norwich, University of East Anglia since 1990 with heavy bars above and below the logo since 1991. The University could not forget that "Where is the University of East Anglia?" had once been asked as a question on the quiz show "Brain of Britain", so unclear to the public was its corporate identity and location. To change the title again would risk it being thought of as a 1990 university rather than a more established one of the 1960s. "UEA" was by now a strong brand name, well known in higher education. Also to become "The University of Norwich" would have run counter to the strenuous efforts of the 1990s to make UEA more relevant to the region as a whole.

A major change, more controversial than the rest, was the attempt to create a modular common course structure with a reshaping of the academic year into two long, fifteen-week semesters. This was to replace the traditional arrangement of three ten-week terms with end-of-year examinations in the Summer term. The arguments in favour of the system were compelling. Students would study three units per semester over four honours semesters (years two and three). Each unit would be worth twenty credits, thus a degree would be gained with 240 credits. This would yield several advantages. Schemes could be drawn up of a range of choices which had to be taken in one's home School, allowing further credits of free choice to be taken in another School. Credit standardisation ensured that the workload for a unit was the same in different Schools. Not only would it facilitate movement between Schools within the University but it was anticipated that it would lead to flexibility of students moving between universities. More widely, this new modular credit system would enable foreign, European and American students to come to UEA and take units of compatible credits which they could fit into their degrees back home. Semesterisation followed from this, since most other university systems operated with two semesters a year rather than the traditional three terms. A fifteen-week semester allowed enough time to learn a quantity of work and to examine it within the semester, as a ten-week term did not. It was a key factor in the new system that there should be "portability" of credits, that each learned portion of work should be tested at the end of the semester so that a grade could be determined and, if necessary, carried away to another School, university or country. It was a further extension of the continuous assessment with which UEA had long been familiar. The final clinching argument was that many other universities were making the change and that UEA had better follow suit, or even be in the vanguard. UEA went over to the modularised semesterised Common Course Structure in September 1993, just before a committee chaired by Lord Flowers at the end of the year recommended that other institutions should follow the pioneering lead of Stirling and several Polytechnics.[100]

Although the CCS seemed so justifiable in its planning stage, when it began to operate from 1993 difficulties began to emerge which undermined support for it. The twice-yearly examinations created problems of timing. There were insufficient days for revision in the second semester. External examiners complained of the lack of time for the examinations, marking and refereeing, and their lack of control over the first semester. The teaching of the second semester was fragmented by the Easter Vacation. Some arts subjects found the system unhelpful for the long-term development of understanding, seeing connections between themes over different units over a year or more.[101] It did not lead to a flow of students between British universities. Only a third of universities had credit transfer schemes;[102] and, although twenty nine universities ran two-semester systems, there were twenty different patterns to the academic year and no attempt to coordinate them.[103] Nor did it increase the flow of students between Schools in the University. To protect their budgets Schools often set up their own versions of units available in other Schools. As the official report on CCS observed, "CCS ought in theory to prevent such duplication of effort, but finance is the overriding factor".[104] CCS helps the reception of foreign students but, since they are unwilling to return to the University to take examinations, they tend to do special coursework variants of units.

Dissatisfaction with the CCS modular system led to a strong movement in favour of a return to terms and end-of-year examinations. From the year 2000 there will be two terms of twelve weeks and a summer term of six weeks for substantial examinations at the end of the year. CCS, modularity and semesters were a bold imaginative plan supported by many convincing arguments. But operationally there were too many problems, some of which threatened standards. No other issue caused so much trouble and controversy in these years.

Of more lasting beneficial effects on teaching were developments in Information Technology (IT) in these years. This was especially so in the Library. 1986/7 saw the completion of the latest phase of the computerisation of circulation procedures using an ICL System 25 mini-computer. By 1987 the Library had automated circulation control, book ordering and accounting and periodicals listing. In 1987 the UGC awarded the Library £32,000 to enable it to mount the machine-readable catalogue on the University's computer network. Anyone on campus can now look up any item on the catalogue using a computer.[105] Beyond that, the Library acquired the software for Cambridge University's Online Public Access Catalogue (OPAC) which was to be the basis of a UEA system designed as a joint project between the Library and the Computing Centre. In conjunction with this, the Library's card catalogue was converted to machine readable form. In the early 1990s access to other academic library catalogues increased. With the cooperation of libraries and computing centres, it became possible for UEA to provide access to the Institute for Scientific Information's citation indexes, and BIDS (the Bath ISI Database Service) provides the most powerful bibliographical tools available.[106] Individual academics also found their lives transformed by E-mail in these years. Personal computers were put in all offices so that "it is now commonplace for users on the UEA data network to contact routinely colleagues elsewhere". The Join Academic Network (JANET) was completed, interconnecting all the universities in the United Kingdom and, through EARN, internationally.[107]

In other ways the University was concerned to raise standards in teaching. Biennial reviews of all units began in 1988, surveying their quality content and reception.[108] This was followed by the starting of the annual personal appraisal of all staff in 1989,[109] discussing their teaching, research and administrative contributions. Staff Training and Development began in 1988 under Ruth Goodall and about this time, the regular distribution of questionnaires to students giving feedback on the teaching of units. In 1994 a complex appeals procedure was devised and also arrangements for students to complain about the "professional unsuitability" of staff.[110] All these procedures brought teaching under greater control. They were in keeping with managerial practices in commerce and industry outside the universities. To an extent they were a response to the public demand for accountability, but above all they were a fair recognition of students as cash-paying customers now making financial sacrifices and deserving a fair return. In practice the quality of teaching at UEA was good, as we shall see in the next chapter.

The late 1980s also saw a shift in the attitudes of students towards something more worldly and less radical. In 1987 Karin Smyth, the Students' Union President, noted that her role was less "swashbuckling radical and political" than it used to be. "There's been a shift to the Right in perceptions" and more cooperation with the University authorities.[111] A Gallup Poll of students nationally at this time also discovered a Thatcherite upper middle class in the making.[112] Three quarters of them regarded themselves as hard working, 94 per cent as happy or very happy (the "very happy" far exceeding the general population). Industry was the first choice of career, with setting up one's own business and the City or financial services also high, as they were in rank order of most respected professions. After ten years of Thatcherism teaching was by far the least respected job. Among self-perceptions "ambitious", "responsible", "self-reliant" and "realist" ranked very high, whereas very few admitted to be a "rebel" or "radical". Fifteen per cent already owned a portfolio of shares. The *Daily Telegraph* was delighted to characterise students as "happy New Realists" preparing for "the real world". This was a national survey but UEA fitted the pattern well. Jo Abra, the SU Welfare Officer, suggested that "in the sixties the main aim of going to university was to experience life, but now people want to get a good degree to get a good job", while her interviewer reflected that "in many ways campus life [at UEA] was becoming an extension of yuppie Thatcherite Britain".[113] The ever-perceptive Malcolm Bradbury caught the mood and wrote a television drama *Anything More Would be Greedy* (Anglia TV 1989) about high-flyers carving out careers in the business and political world of Thatcherite Britain. "I began to notice this new breed appearing in my classes" at UEA, he said.[114]

The new mood was also reflected in a revised Students' Union constitution.[115] Its preamble noted the change in Union and student activity from political activism to social and commercial activity :

> We have reluctantly had to accept that the days of "mass student activism" have gone. Involvement in the Union has moved away from political decision making and towards the social side of student life. Although we are attracting more people than ever to our discos, gigs, shops, bars, clubs and societies, we have recently found it more and more difficult to encourage people to stand for elected posts and to attend General Meetings.

The revisions sought to address the lack of involvement. Affiliation to the National Union of Students was no longer to be automatic but was reviewed every three years. The minimum number of General Meetings was cut from three to one per term, since they were seldom well attended. If important issues arose they could be decided by policy ballots in which more were expected to participate, while four new sabbatical officers were created to deal with executive matters. Most students preferred to be involved with the Union through its social and commercial activities.

Student media thrived. "Livewire", the student radio station won the Guardian/NUS award for the best student radio station in 1993, having scooped the BBC on the outbreak of the Gulf War and Mrs Thatcher's resignation.[116] Shortly afterwards, it gained a licence to broadcast to the city on FM and not merely to UEA. Not to be outdone, UEA's student newspaper *Concrete* and its magazine *Bucket of Tongues* both won *Guardian* awards in 1995.

The Union also became involved in the Waterfront in King Street in Norwich. This was an old warehouse on the River Yare, ideal for pop music events. UEA had always been good at mounting social events in the LCR but the Waterfront was a useful extra facility. In 1985 the Norwich City Council agreed to finance it. This proved insufficient and UEA became engaged in 1989, giving a £90,000 grant towards the then estimated costs of £773,000. After further loans and grants from others, the building opened in 1990. It was relevant to the University as a social venue for rock concerts attended by students and, at one time, it was thought that it would replace the Kenny Theatre. The project tottered on with further grants from various bodies (not UEA) until it fell into liquidation with debts of £360,000 in January 1993. In December of that year the UEA Students Union took over its running rent free, taking a loan of £70,000 to refurbish the premises. It may have been thought a foolhardy commitment but the Union had more than a decade of successful business experience and an annual commercial turnover of £4,000,000.[117] Moreover attendance was enthusiastic and it served a valuable social purpose for students.

The disc jockey John Peel, an honorary graduate of the University, lent the moral support of his attendance at the reopening in December. The local press also praised the students for taking on the challenge and making a profit by 1994.[118] The City Council had confidence in the SU as managers of its property and continued to provide further grants. It remained under UEASU management a vibrant centre in addition to the LCR for local bands, sixth form parties, gay and lesbian nights, some university drama and all round rave ups which added to the attractiveness of student life at UEA.

Generally content as students were, they were affected by a fundamental way in which they were financed. From 1962 students who gained a place in an institution of higher education were awarded means tested grants and tuition fees were paid. The increase in students from 4 per cent to 30 per cent of eighteen-year-olds and the move from elite to mass higher education was placing an intolerable burden on public finances. To tackle this schemes were devised to reduce the rights of students to public money and replace it with loans. The minimum maintenance grant was abolished in 1985. In 1986 entitlement to supplementary and unemployment benefits in the Christmas and Easter Vacations was removed along with housing benefit for students in halls of residence. The question of student grants prompted a legal ruling in which UEA actually played a central part. This was a Court of Appeal decision that, although students were not eligible for social security benefits during vacations, they were eligible if they were intercalating, that is interrupting a degree and not receiving grant money or a loan and not allowed on campus.[119] In 1990 students were made ineligible to claim unemployment benefit, income support, housing benefit and, most importantly, the grant level was frozen at the 1990 level while student loans with no interest payment were introduced to offset the declining value of the grant.[120] The loans were to be provided by the government-owned Student Loans Company and were to be repaid by the graduate within five years of graduation, unless they were earning less than 85 per cent of the average wage. In 1994 the grant, frozen since 1990, was cut by 10 per cent as the first step to a 30 per cent reduction between 1994/5 – 1996/7, compensated by more loans.

There were arguments on both sides. The government argued that grants for all could not be maintained in an age of mass higher education. Loans would make possible the projected expansion and indeed facilitate the entry to university of students from lower social classes. It could also be argued that, even with 30 per cent attending university, it still left 70 per cent who did not and it was not self-evident why the poor should pay taxes to provide higher education for the minority who were likely to earn higher incomes as a result. Better the students pay for themselves, regarding it as an investment which they would recoup in higher earnings in later life. If they regarded a degree as an investment paid for by themselves, students would be likely to work hard, also be demanding on their tutors and choose studies leading to useful and remunerative careers which would make the curriculum sensitive to the market. Robert Jackson, the Minister charged with these reforms, came to UEA on 21 November 1988 to rehearse these arguments before a mass meeting of students. He was greeted with black balloons and a sceptical, prickly but orderly audience.[121] The Vice-Chancellor remained publicly opposed to loans, as did the Students' Union, on the grounds that it would deter the poorer working class, unused to incurring debt, from going to university.[122] It would entail poverty during student life and debt in the early years of working and hold back expansion.

How did this work out, nationally and at UEA? The students claimed that they were plunged into unbearable debt. In 1994 a "debtometer" set up by the Union on campus recorded £160,000 of debt.[123] Yet shortly afterwards Barclays revealed that the East Anglia debt at £1732 per head was considerably below the national average of £2233 in 1995.[124] In any case, only about half of students applied for loans suggesting that the rest were not troubled by the new system.[125] In 1993/4 47 per cent of students nationally took out a SLC loan; at UEA the proportion was 48.4 per cent.[126] Also, rather contrary to impressions of outrage, a survey of 1993 found only 17 per cent of students "worried" or "concerned" about loans and 23 per cent positively pleased with the new system.[127]

There is, however, no doubt that some UEA students fell into a lifestyle of poverty. The UEA Medical Officer, Dr P. Coathup, noted that a few students "ate so badly and lived in such poor conditions, they smelled of poverty, and a have-and have-not gap was developing between them and those supported by well-off parents".[128] Various students interviewed referred to large debts of about £5000, "you are constantly worrying about it", and the difficulties of finding part-time work to reduce debt. "I have spoken to students who have not eaten for three days."[129] The mundane diary of a third year girl student in 1995 exemplified this in revealing a lifestyle of baked beans, bread, tinned tuna, pizza and chips. A cause for concern for Mum.[130] The safety net was the Vice-Chancellor's Fund operated by the Dean of Students Office, there was a sharp rise in disbursements of this 1994/5 "indicative of the increasing level of student hardship".[131]

With poverty went increased student stress. The numbers of students attending the Counselling Service rose from 408 in 1987/8 to 495 by 1994/5, some 6.4 per cent of the undergraduate body. Taking into account the increase in student numbers, this was actually a slight decline in the proportion of students consulting the Counselling Service. The Director found, however, that their work was growing because numbers of counselling sessions and sessions per client increased more sharply. The Director of Counselling identified several causes behind this: "dire financial circumstances and anxiety about money"; an increasing anxiety to perform well academically for fear of unemployment in a tighter job market; and the "increasingly competitive and materialist ethos which is permeating the whole of society". Government policies and cutbacks increased stress for some students and others found the new CCS system with twice yearly examinations created "intolerable stress". Of course we must remember that those who felt acute distress were only a minority of students and many brought depressions and family problems with them. Nor was this unique to UEA but part of a national trend found by counsellors.[132] But it was an underlying trend of these years. It was also the case with staff. A report of 1995 found that 83 per cent felt that stress was adversely affecting their health, with 40 per cent feeling the effects of overwork.[133] These findings and Brian Thorne's particular interest in training prompted the creation of the Centre for Counselling Studies in 1992 to train more counsellors, and in 1996 the University (as opposed to the Students') Counselling Service was created. Brian Thorne, the Director, found strong support and interest from the Vice-Chancellor deriving from their common Christian belief.

Those not generally so troubled by these problems were mature students and the University was eager to serve the region by admitting them. Access courses prepared older students for university entrance as the alternative to A Levels or Open University foundation courses. Access programmes were provided by Norwich City College, Lowestoft and Great Yarmouth, and there were others out in the county at Watton and Thetford feeding students to UEA or Norfolk College in King's Lynn (NORCAT), itself teaching degrees validated by UEA. By 1997 45 per cent of UEA students, were mature students which was a higher proportion than any of the "new" sixties universities.[134] Two merit special mention and stand for all. Toni Woodrow, a former personnel officer at Danepak and former Open University student, gained a literature and history degree at the age of seventy-two.[135] Most remarkable was John Knight, who graduated in 1995 at the age of seventy-eight, probably UEA's oldest ever student. He was already an OBE, a senior partner in a major law firm, freeman of St Edmundsbury, with forty years of service as a local government councillor. He too graduated in history.[136] "It beats coffee mornings and bingo", said Mrs Woodrow.

These years were marked by pleasing events, often symbols of recognition and good for morale. Owen Chadwick retired as Chancellor and was succeeded by Sir Geoffrey Allen FRS. Sir Geoffrey, then aged sixty-six was a former Chairman of the Science and Engineering Council and Professor of Chemical Technology at Imperial College, London. He had close links with industry through his study of polymers and as former head of research and member of the Board of Directors of Unilever, while abroad he was executive adviser to the President of Kobe Steel in Japan. He was installed at a ceremony in St Andrews Hall on 6 July 1994.[137] He has proved to be a remarkably "hands-on" Chancellor, in contrast to the style of Lord Franks, and this is greatly appreciated by successive Vice-Chancellors. The Robert and Lisa Sainsbury Art Trustees made a donation of £4,500,000 to mark the golden wedding of the donors in 1987. Half went to the endowment fund of the SCVA and half to the Sainsbury Unit for the Arts of Africa, Oceania and the Americas. The University was further heartened by a remarkably generous bequest of £700,000 left by Lord Zuckerman, who died in 1993, "in recognition of the benefits I have received from my association with the University".[138] In 1990 Mrs Irene Platt bequeathed £250,000 to create the Platt Centre for "the study and teaching of modern foreign languages at the University" in memory of her father James Platt a noted linguist.[139] Finally, most eye-catching, a Class 86 locomotive running between Norwich and London was named "UEA Norwich, The University of East Anglia" and was unveiled by John MacGregor, the South Norfolk MP and then Transport Secretary on 5 July 1993.[140]

Perhaps most important and uplifting was the University's celebration of its own Jubilee 1963-88, styled "Twenty-Five Years of Excellence". On the initiative of the Vice-Chancellor, and, following proposals from Christopher Smith's working party, a whole range of exciting events took place. There was a Class of '63 dinner, concerts, an exhibition on the history of the University, Sir Denys Lasdun gave a lecture on his buildings, loyal greetings and gracious reply were exchanged with Her Majesty the Queen, Arthur Miller visited in connection with the opening of the Arthur Miller Centre and a gala performance of his work, there was an Open Day, a civic service and a special graduation in the Theatre Royal.[141] Prince Charles visited the University in November, arousing remarkable enthusiasm on the part of the students. Security went to pot as the Prince mingled with hundreds of students along the walkways. One told him frankly that he did not approve of monarchy, to which the Prince, with equal frankness, replied that he was sorry to hear it. After a visit to the CRU the Prince departed by helicopter. Never has Lasdun's grass "Harbour" been seen to better theatrical effect, hundreds of students accompanying the Prince walking down between Norfolk and Suffolk Terraces, the helicopter lifting off amid general cheering, its lights flanked by room lights from the Terraces. Shortly afterwards, Princess Diana visited UEA in 1990. All these events drew creditable attention to the University and boosted morale.

In Burke's later years *The Times* started publishing league tables of universities, which threw light on UEA's strengths and weaknesses at the time.[141] UEA's overall position was modest and declining slightly from thirty-seventh out of ninety-six in 1993 to thirty-ninth in 1994 to forty-fourth in 1995. UEA had certain evident strengths. It admitted students with good entry grades, its Library spending was good and consistent. Students' accommodation was very attractive and its research record activity and proportion of postgraduates were high up the league tables. The teaching record was also good. By 1995 three departments had been assessed as excellent – Environmental Sciences, Law, Social Work, one of thirty-eight universities with three or more excellent departments.[143] So far the picture depicted was of a university very attractive to students. Indeed in 1991 UEA was the eleventh most popular university in terms of applications per place[144] while the drop out rate at 12.2 per cent was low.[145]

Yet UEA was pulled down by three things. First the employment record of graduates was problematic and, although improving, was in the lower third of all universities. The unknown or unemployed among UEA graduates were usually 16-18 per cent, though rising to 20 per cent in 1991. Usually only about a third went directly into employment. Burke already identified this as a weakness: "the percentage of our new graduates who go directly into permanent employment is less than the UK average and this is sometimes the subject of adverse comment".[146] This was an old recurrent problem, as we have seen in earlier chapters, these early *Times* league tables were open to criticism, however, since they did not weight universities for subject mix. High initial unemployment was a feature of the big Arts Schools but much less so for the Science and vocational Schools. It was a continued reflection of the Humanities, non-vocational bias of UEA's spread of activities going back to the early days. A survey of 1990 showed that the best employment opportunities lay in engineering, business-related subjects and computing, towards which UEA was moving, and the worst in life sciences, social sciences, languages and arts to which UEA had been committed in its early days.[147] Measuring the employment of graduates in the same year as graduation was, however, not entirely fair. In two surveys studying what had happened to UEA graduates three years after graduation it was found that:

Output of	In full time employment	Studying	Unemployed
1993 as at 1996	77 per cent	16 per cent	3 per cent
1995 as at 1998	75 per cent	8 per cent	1 per cent

Very few were unemployed after a short time, the vast majority were in full-time employment and proper graduate level jobs.[148]

The second feature was the modest ranking of UEA students gaining firsts. This was consistently below national levels. UEA's proportion of firsts in these years 1985-1994 was around 4 per cent rising to 8 per cent whereas the national averages were around 7 per cent rising to 9 per cent.[149] One factor behind this may have been the coursework continuous assessment where it was much more difficult to keep scoring first class grades consistently than in examinations. This was especially so in the Humanities. The proportion of firsts was higher in the Sciences, Chemistry, Mathematics and Environmental Sciences for example. This was another way in which the earlier legacy of subject mix was still influencing UEA in the late eighties and early nineties. Moreover, most students were happy to aim for (and employers accept) good

2/1s and probably calculated that it was not worth the extra effort gaining a first. This could only be an advantage in academic jobs whose attraction was not remotely commensurate with the additional striving.

It is also possible to look at this more closely in terms of subjects. *The Times* began ranking the top twenty universities by subject area. In 1993 UEA was in the top twenty for humanities (10), social sciences (19), languages (14).[150] In 1994 it was so placed in the social sciences (13), visual and performing arts (15), biological sciences (11), physical and mathematical sciences (20), humanities (19).[151] In 1995 UEA was in the top twenty for environmental science (1), chemistry (15), law (17), economics (20).[152] By 1996 there was a leap forward and UEA appeared in the top twenty for chemistry, computing, development studies, history, law, and music and was the best in the country for environmental science and social work. Of the ten UEA subjects included in the surveys, eight were in the top twenty enabling the University to claim that it was "firmly among the top twenty of Britain's 104 Universities".[153]

There was no doubt of UEA's research strength and of the improvement in it in these years. This was now knowable from the regular Research Assessment Exercises (RAE). In 1989 UEA had an average score of 3.15 (out of 5) and ranked seventeenth out of all universities, with history, art, and social work top rated (5) and internationally outstanding. By 1992 UEA was pleased with its improved performance, its average score rising to 3.47, though its rank order fell to 27, and it had been overtaken by all the other sixties universities except Kent. It was pleasing, however, that three departments were internationally outstanding – environmental sciences, art history and social work – and eleven were rated either four or five. Improvement was also evident in that, whereas in 1989 85 per cent of staff were working in units recognised as nationally or internationally outstanding, this had risen to 96 per cent by 1992.[154] Four subjects were rated at 5 and 10 at 4. Things improved further in the RAE of 1996. The average score rose yet again from 3.47 to 3.69 and the top five rated departments rose to eight, while twelve departments all improved their ratings.[155] UEA's research performance in these years was good and continued to improve. The value of UEA's research grants and contracts rose from £3,700,000 in 1987/8 to £12,600,000 by 1994/5, and its research expenditure rose from £2,800,000 to £9,400,000 over the same period.[156] Burke rightly regarded it "an outstanding achievement for a university just thirty years old".[157]

Derek Burke retired in September 1995. In personality he usually showed a cheerful nature, energetic and optimistic. Yet he was also capable of robust temper and, some thought, of a certain impetuosity. He believed in the importance of leadership and good management. Privately he held Christian beliefs and this could reflect in his concern for the distressed. It was also much appreciated when from 1989 he began a series of receptions for staff of twenty-five years service at which they were presented with a copy of the watercolour of UEA painted by Jeremy Barlow. Mrs Mary Burke was widely liked for her presence about the University and as the hostess of their entertaining at Wood Hall. Her opening of Wood Hall to, for example, the Womens' Coffee Club was valued as continuing the style of Jane Thistlethwaite as a gracious and welcoming Vice-Chancellor's lady.

Derek Burke himself had been honoured by being appointed a Deputy Lieutenant of Norfolk in 1992, awarded the CBE in 1994 and, received an Honorary Doctorate of Science and Emeritus Professorship of the University. He retired to Cambridge and Walberswick and continued his work as Chairman of the ACNFP, dealing with now contentious genetically modified food issues and as adviser to the Parliamentary Science and Technology Committee. His period of office had been one of considerable advance in many fields as he handed on his achievements and problems to his successor.

13

The Pursuit of Excellence

Our mission is to sustain and develop international standards of
academic excellence in all our Schools of Studies.[1]

UEA Mission Statement, 2000

The last five years have been unusually marked by the periods of office of two
Vice-Chancellors, Dame Elizabeth Estève-Coll and Vincent Watts. They are
best considered together because the period as a whole was so short and
Dame Elizabeth's tenure was prematurely terminated by illness. In any case
many of the intentions which Dame Elizabeth had hoped to carry out were
taken up by her successor and the initiatives and achievements of the one
merged with those of the other.

Derek Burke was succeeded by Dame Elizabeth Estève Coll in 1995. She
came with quite the most remarkable background of any of UEA's Vice-
Chancellors.[2] Born in Ripon and educated at Darlington High School, she
studied variously in Oxford, France and Trinity College Dublin but withdrew
at the age of nineteen to marry an officer in the Spanish merchant navy, José
Estève-Coll. She then lived at sea with her husband between 1959 and 1967
voyaging through Europe, the Arctic, South America and the Far East. On her
journeys she read extensively and, on leaving the sea, she studied as a mature
student for a first class degree in the History of Art at Birkbeck College
London. Thereafter she rose rapidly as an information officer and librarian at
Kingston Polytechnic before becoming Librarian of the University of Surrey
and then Keeper of the National Art Library at the Victoria and Albert
Museum, of which she became Director in 1988. Her period of office at the V &
A was marked by energy and change, creating a new Department of Research,
doubling visitors from 850,000 to 1,700,000, and raising sponsorship for eight
new galleries. The ironic Saatchi and Saatchi slogan "an ace caff with quite a
nice museum attached" attracted both attention and attendances. Here was
entrepreneurial flair, high administrative ability and a career soundly rooted
in higher education that would suit UEA. Raymond Frostick the Chairman of
Council praised "her strong leadership qualities, her ability to articulate a
vision for a complex organisation and her experience of representing a
national institution both in the UK and internationally at the highest level,

make her ideally suited to lead UEA in the years ahead." He might have added her deep Anglo-Catholic religious belief. It is significant that four of her eight Desert Island Discs were devotional music.

Dame Elizabeth was headhunted by Saxton Bampfylde International, the first time that UEA had recruited in this way. This was in itself significant. Half the shortlisted held jobs outside the university world. Saxton Bampfylde looked for people with industrial or other management and presentational skills with the ability to market and direct complex organisations. The use of Saxton Bampfylde and the appointments of both Dame Elizabeth and Vincent Watts from outside higher education were important but successful breaks in trend.[3]

Dame Elizabeth's initial reaction on arriving at UEA was a favourable one, but she found certain tasks in front of her. She was impressed with the commitment of staff to teaching and research, but she thought UEA lacked a cohesive external image and that the University did not blow its trumpet enough. This had been brought home to her when she told a friend that she was going to UEA; the response was "Oh, that's the place at Colchester isn't it?" She also wanted to look at managerial and organisational arrangements, which "clearly creaked a bit", and to involve UEA more in local training in industry and commerce. Finally, she thought that UEA was doing too many things across too wide a spectrum, which needed prioritising.[4] Dame Elizabeth was cruelly denied the opportunity to carry through these aims, since, scarcely a year after her arrival, she was diagnosed as having multiple sclerosis and on 2 December 1996 she announced her decision to retire in September 1997. As Pro Vice-Chancellor R.A.Y Jones well expressed it, her departure was "a total tragedy for the University and for her personally".[5] The sense of loss was genuine. People working closely with her tell of her charisma, her ability to give people she encountered her total attention and to leave them feeling enhanced and also arouse affectionate loyalty in associates. With the exception of Frank Thistlethwaite's final Congregation, I have never experienced the University's collective good will towards a Vice-Chancellor so strongly as at Dame Elizabeth's first Assembly. Dame Elizabeth retired to the South of France but happily returns to Norwich regularly, where her expertises in library and fine arts concerns are still put to valuable use. The first on the committee overseeing the creation of the new Millennium Library in Norwich and the second as she acts as the liaison between the University and Sir Robert and Lady Sainsbury.

She handed over to Vincent Watts as the new Vice-Chancellor, who was then aged fifty-seven. Like his predecessor, he was recruited with the assistance of Saxton Bampfylde, though with the University still in full control of the process. After a Cambridge education in economics and biochemistry, and a double first in natural sciences, he qualified as a chartered accountant with Arthur Andersen, rising to a partnership in Arthur Andersen Consulting.[6] He was an accountant, management consultant and authority on operational research and IT. He was closer, however, to higher education than this might suggest. He was deeply involved in the education side of the Institute of Chartered Accountants and, as head of recruitment for Arthur Andersen, knew a great deal about universities (as well as having a professor for a wife). He worked on several government projects and reviews of government departments for which he was awarded an OBE in 1998. A short, wiry man and extremely fit, he was a championship squash player and completed the London Marathon in 1994 at the age of fifty-four . He could still show his physical prowess by taking part in the annual charity abseil down the Teaching Wall. He was married, with two children. His wife, Professor Rachel Prosser, was a remarkable woman in her own right as Professor of Psychiatry at the UCL Medical School who became well known for her studies of post traumatic stress and the treatment of sufferers following the King's Cross Underground fire in 1987 and the Lockerbie disaster. She was tragically killed in a fall at Wood Hall in July 1998 when the new Vice-Chancellor had been in office for barely a year.

Vincent Watts brought a new management style. He holds from time to time an "Open House" in which he explains his plans, and the progress of the University, to large, well-attended meetings of all comers. In his first he made some interesting observations on the culture of UEA as he found it in his early days.[7] He found the University over-deferential compared with his earlier job, which carried the risk that staff were reluctant to refuse what they were asked to do and took on more than they could undertake efficiently. Decision making was still cumbersome – as Dame Elizabeth and Derek Burke had found before him – and he felt that Senate needed streamlining. He also followed Dame Elizabeth in believing that there was too much diversity, which needed rationalising. He liked the multidisciplinarity but found that the financial system worked against it. He emphasised the need to select twenty young people who would participate in the leadership of the University of ten years' time whose views would lead the way forward. As well as his Open House meetings, Watts also started regular surgeries whereby individuals could discuss matters concerning them. It all added to more open communications within the University and good morale.

Following the University's Strategic Plan, the Executive Group started a wide ranging review of the University's organisation and structure, called "Agenda for Change".[8] They felt the need to "revitalise the University's power to act as a united organisation". A central feature of this was the need to reduce the number of academic units and release academic time in administering them, minimise committees, concentrate support expertise to secure economies of scale and give more emphasis to skills development in teaching. "Agenda for Change" led to the report "Making the Difference".[9] This document set objectives to be achieved to sustain UEA as a world-class institution into the next century. As we have seen, there had been some slippage of UEA'S position in the – flawed – *Times* league tables, though in Dame Elizabeth's years UEA's position had risen sharply from forty-fourth to twenty-sixth. "Making the Difference" called for a progressive improvement in UEA's teaching and research, improving staff morale and motivation, increasing income streams from external sources. It also proposed the need for more coherent and focused strategies, minimising nugatory commitment of resources – suggesting a new look at physics. Organisationally the report also envisaged a three-tier managerial structure lead by an executive team, with groupings of Schools by cognate interests, such as humanities and social science, science, professional, each headed by a Pro Vice-Chancellor, all to be supported by a core of central services. Finally the need for an enhanced and more widely established image was identified – as it had been by Dame Elizabeth.

The "Making a Difference" Report in turn lead to a further major document "Creating our Future".[10] Five working groups of twenty-nine mostly younger members of staff considered the shape of UEA as it was to be in the year 2008. They were mapping the University they expected to inherit. The groups insisted that UEA had to be an internationally competitive research university with an international catchment of students. Only by being a research-led University could it sustain a virtuous circle of increasing research income, which would in turn increase HEFCE income, attract more postgraduates and hence more income, and more undergraduates attracted by research-led teaching. All departments were expected to be 5 or 5 star in their research ratings with 4 as the acceptable minimum. Teaching would itself be influenced by this in that it should relate to the research interests of teachers; indeed it was uneconomical for teachers to be teaching too many units to too small numbers in areas not related to their research. Amazingly UEA taught 300 degree programmes and 287 units with fewer than ten students per unit. This was now regarded as a diversity of choice to the extent of profligacy. Tutors were urged to "teach less" but deliver "better learning", reduce units and leave more responsibility to students for their own learning. The usual suggestions were made of the need to focus activities and also to project a more positive image of the University. It was for example not generally known that in the Research Assessment of 1996 UEA ranked eighth in the sciences for the whole of Britain, behind seven major civic universities.

In the meantime the new Vice-Chancellor planned a radical restructuring of UEA's academic organisation from 1998. An Executive Group replaced the Pro Vice-Chancellors meeting and Schools were grouped into the cognate groups, as we have seen, while the Senior Management Team brought together Deans, chairs of major committees and other senior officers. It was thereby hoped to reduce bureaucracy and improve information flow.[11] Pro Vice-Chancellors were increased to six from 1998. This delegation became the more necessary as the Vice-Chancellor became the Chairman of the East of England Development Agency in 1999, which took up two days a week. This was a strong system for sharing and delegating power and responsibility, but further plans met with opposition. It was proposed not merely to have cognate groups but to merge groupings of Schools into four super faculties. But this was not favoured. There was unease about the power to be wielded by "superdeans". Financially strong Schools could find themselves weakened by being linked with deficit ones. In some Schools it seemed to work. BIO and ENV supported CHE financially because of their valuable interdisciplinary links, but the formalising of the broader structure did not commend itself outside the sciences and it did not proceed further.

The finances of the University remained sound:[12]

						(£000)
	Income				Expenditure	Surplus (Deficit)
	Funding Council Grants	Tuition Fees	Research grants	Total		
1996-95	25,897	18,164	11,508	67,750	66,872	878
1996-97	25,881	18,068	11,762	67,644	69,079	(1444)
1997-98	26,982	19,632	12,180	72,999	72,011	88
1998-99	27,330	20,086	13,234	75,342	74,233	1109
1999-2000	28,120	21,634	15,706	82,758	78,861	3897

The continued squeeze arose from the "efficiency gains" required of the universities, in 1996-97 3 per cent, in 1997-98 3 per cent, and in 1998-99 2 per cent with the assumption of 2.75 per cent annual inflation. As Vincent Watts explained, "We're planning the next five years, but we are having to do it in the terms of a 10 per cent reduction in income. Effectively the government is saying that we will be teaching the same number of students with 10 per cent less people, 10 per cent less books, 10 per cent less everything. And it is called an efficiency saving".[13] In his view the cuts over the last ten years may have been efficiency savings but no longer.

Student numbers continued to increase and staff numbers to fall and the staff/student ratio to deteriorate.[14]

		Students					
	UG	PG taught	PG research	Total	Academic staff	Ratio	Total staff
1995-96	7324	1392	735	9451	490	19.2	2075
1996-97	7529	1401	795	9725	491	19.8	2089
1997-98	7726	2085	847	10,658	451	23.6	2050
1998-99	9040	2467	1279	12,786	482	26.5	2051
1999-2000	9680	2187	959	12,826	488	26.3	2133

The University, in face of this, contemplated "top up" fees, following the Russell Group and consultation with the 94 Group, of which UEA was a part. UEA, along with many other universities, reserved the right to charge "supplementary fees" in the 1998 prospectus.[15]

Both Dame Elizabeth Estève-Coll and Vincent Watts made adjustments and innovations in the academic structure. One matter which had to be grasped was the Common Course Structure and the layout of the academic year. We have seen in the previous chapter the difficulties of the new system and the discontent, not least among external examiners, it aroused. This was conveyed to Dame Elizabeth and yet another process of consultation and deliberation ensued. After much discussion of variants, two terms of twelve weeks each followed by a summer term of six weeks for examining was agreed upon, to come into effect in the year 2000-2001. It would allow good spans of unbroken time for teaching a unit, give six weeks for revision, examining and assessment, and allow the examining of Autumn units at the end of the year. The good features of the old CCS could be retained, a Common Course university-wide catalogue of units, free choice across Schools, the credit system with everything assessed. It will give more space for teaching, avoid teaching and examining at the same time and give proper time for substantial annual examinations.[16]

Both Dame Elizabeth and Vincent Watts had to grasp the problem of physics. It had been reprieved in Derek Burke's years and developed its research creditably, as we have seen, raising its research rating from two to three in 1992 and to four by 1996. But its problems remained. Its intake of students had declined from thirty a year in the early 1990s to eighteen by the later part of the decade. Its staff student ratio of 1 : 5 and its annual deficits of £300,000 a year were insupportable.[17] The PRC in January 1997 proposed ceasing to take undergraduates but to continue research and service teaching in conjunction with the School of Chemistry. By 1998, however, "it was now clear that despite enormous effort the School would be unable to achieve the level of grant and research income that would secure its future".[18] It could not be supported without damage to UEA's other activities. Later in the year it was agreed that that the School of Physics should be closed from 1 August

1999 and that staff could be transferred to the University of Bath, which had a 4 RAE rating (like UEA) and was planning to expand.[19] It was a sad but inevitable end. Physics had never developed the prominence of chemistry, biology and environmental sciences, it was probably too expensive and had less opportunity to match the needs of the region. Its demise sent a message that no subject was indispensable within a university whose curriculum was constantly changing.

Another major change in the original "map of learning" was the break up of the School of European Studies. The School had £135,000 worth of debts and some of its research performance was low. Opinion was also sharply divided as to its shape and future. With the creation of the School of History most of its historians had moved to the new School, taking their RAE strength with them. This left the teachers of literature and the linguists and some others of broad social and artistic interests. Some believed that the way forward was through the development of media studies, applications for which had rocketed nationally from 1473 in 1986 to 32,862 by 1995.[20] Conversely it was argued that there was a diminishing demand for European literature on the part of sixth formers, with applications for EUR literature degrees falling from 315 in 1984 to 220 by 1990.[21] Eight lecturers in French either died, retired or moved away and were not replaced. Instead a lecturer was appointed to teach English television drama, no languages required. The original Thistlethwaite concept of integrated history and literary studies all infused with rigorous foreign language learning had disintegrated. The School was accordingly broken up in the only way that seemed possible. Five literary scholars (some very distinguished) transferred to EAS to form a large School of Literature, three with contemporary European interests usefully moved to the School of Economic and Social Studies and the remaining, largely language teachers formed a new School of Language, Linguistics and Translation Studies – LLT. This also contains the Centre for English Language and British Studies (CEB), the James Platt Centre and the Centre for Modern Nordic Studies and its successful Norvik Press. There was a tragic dimension to this since, amid the turmoil of the break up, the Dean of the School, Professor Roger Pipe Fowler died of a heart attack at the end-of-year party at his home. His funeral at the village church in Lingwood was packed to overflowing, a genuinely moving event, a tribute to Pipe Fowler and in a more shadowy way to the old values of EUR now departed.

As old areas changed so new ones developed. The University moved strongly into Japanese studies. Both the Chancellor, who was an adviser to Kobe Steel, and Dame Elizabeth had keen interests in Japan as had Sir Robert and Lisa Sainsbury. The Sainsburys proposed selling one of their pictures, Modigliani's *Portrait of Barakowski*, in Japan hoping to raise £8,000,000 to finance a Centre for Japanese Studies at UEA. Due to a downturn in the Japanese economy, it raised only £4,000,000 but the Centre went ahead, financed at £6,000,000, as the Sainsbury Institute for the Study of Japanese Art and Culture (SISJAC). It began, like UEA itself, in the Cathedral Close under Nicole Rousmaniere, a Japanese expert from WAM. A distinctive feature of SISJAC was its association with the University of London School of Oriental and African Studies. This provided access to its library in London and allowed a senior scholar in Japanese art, Dr Timon Screech, to devote half his time to SISJAC as a Senior Associate. In turn SISJAC funds a lecturer's post, the Sainsbury Lectureship, at SOAS.[22]

The middle of these five years saw the publication of the Dearing Report in 1997, the most important on higher education since that of Lord Robbins in 1963.[23] UEA contributed to the Report in that Dame Elizabeth Estève-Coll sat on the working group on the structure and governance of higher education. Also the University made its own submission. This emphasised that university funding was inadequate, and that this was being paid for in a deteriorating quality of student life and a substantial relative decline in the reward to providers of university education. It was quite unrealistic to expect every institution to raise standards in face of declining resources. If the government was unwilling to provide the necessary funds the beneficiaries – the students and the private sector – had to contribute if standards were to be maintained. UEA also called for a more selective distribution of funds to protect the 5 and 5 star rated subject departments, wherever they were, rather than create a superleague of universities containing pockets of mediocrity. This was sound advice and influenced some of the findings of the committee.

The Dearing Committee made important proposals which were to have implications for UEA as well as the higher education sector generally. They called for a resumption of the growth of student numbers to a participation ratio rising from a third up to 45 per cent. Within this he hoped to increase the intake from semi-skilled and unskilled manual workers' children. But in the context of students having doubled in the previous twenty years, but with public funding having been cut by 45 per cent in real terms, it was evident that government could not adequately finance an expansion of this nature. Dearing accordingly proposed that more of the cost could be passed to students as beneficiaries. They were to pay an annual tuition fee which would cover 25 per cent of the costs of tuition to be repaid through an "income contingent mechanism" with graduates repaying from earnings over several years. This was fair, since the personal rate of return on doing a degree was of the order of 11-13 per cent. David Blunkett accepted the principle of tilting the burden of cost more to the consumer but preferred in detail to abolish grants outright in favour of more loans, and to relate the student's contribution to tuition fees to their parental income rather than its being a flat rate. Dearing made several other proposals which will begin to affect UEA. The report suggested reducing the size of university councils and, following a governance review UEA has done this from September 2000. He proposed an Institute for Learning and Teaching in Higher Education to raise the quality and status of teaching in universities. All new staff will have to gain the associateship before passing probation. He thought that TQA had been valuable but, since almost all departments were satisfactory and better, he saw no need to continue it in the long term. Instead he considered that standards would be better regulated by a tough external examiner system. Externals would come from a pool of selected high-calibre academics released from their own universities and working a sixty day year on their external examining duties. Teaching was also to be more informed by communication and information technology work, "embedded" rather than "bolt on". There is a feeling through the Dearing Report that universities had put too much emphasis on research at the expense of teaching and that this should be redressed as a step towards giving the job of university lecturer a professional status it lacked. Since university lecturers were now to be seven year trained people (first degree plus Ph.D. plus associateship of the ILTHE), he questioned whether salary levels were really appropriate to attract such entrants to British universities claiming to be "world class in higher education". Accordingly, he urged that the proposed 6.5 per cent reduction in expenditure per student, which was to be imposed on universities 1998/9-1999/2000, be moderated to a 1 per cent per year as a more reasonable "efficiency gain". He also called for a three year rolling programme of finance to replace the annual uncertainties which had overtaken the old quinquennial arrangements. Many features of Dearing quickly appeared at UEA or were there already. There was increasing emphasis on IT, on staff training for teaching, for the incorporation of skills and work experience into courses. The TQA and external examiner system remain but may well change in the coming years.

In fact the quality of teaching at UEA was something on which the University could pride itself. An internal survey made at the same time as the Dearing Report found that 91 per cent of students had experienced inspiring teaching, which had stimulated their motivation (43 per cent) "to a significant extent".[24] Between 60 and 70 per cent found the seminars, lectures and practicals helpful, and 86 per cent found that they maintained their enthusiasm by experience of good teaching. As regards the future, 61-88 per cent of students in physiotherapy, law, accountancy, computing, history and chemistry were happy that the courses equipped them with the skills and qualities for employment. Perhaps most significantly 88 per cent of students felt that they had gained in self-confidence as a result of their teaching – especially women studying English literature. There was no room for complacency but there was a lot of good here which the report found "consistent with UEA's institutional commitment and the general ethos that values high quality teaching".

This high quality of teaching is now objectively measurable through the Quality Assessments.[25] In 1994 and 1995 Law, Social Work, Development Studies, and Environmental Sciences were assessed as "excellent" and History, Chemistry, Music and English as "satisfactory". In 1995 the classification changed and between then and 1997 all subjects presented – Sociology, Modern Languages, Electronic Engineering, Communications and Media, Dance Drama and Cinematics were " approved". Now subjects are assessed out of a maximum score of twenty-four. American Studies have scored twenty-four, OPT and the School of Health Policy and Film Studies twenty-three, History of Art, Biology twenty-two and Drama twenty-one. By 1996 only York, Warwick and LSE had more departments rated excellent or twenty two-twenty four points with the same or fewer departments assessed.[26] As well as this, the Quality Assurance Agency visited UEA in November 1997 to test that its procedures for quality assurance were satisfactory. They were "satisfied that the University was in general exercising proper stewardship of the educational experience that it provides and of the maintenance of the quality of that provision" and it was "properly discharging its responsibilities for the maintenance of the standards of its awards".[27]

In a University where teaching is to be research-led the RAE scores were also important. In 1996 the results were most creditable, with Environmental Sciences and Scandinavian Studies rated 5 star and Biological Sciences, Film Studies, Education and Professional Development, History, Pure Mathematics and Social Work receiving grade 5. Subject areas rated 4 and over rose from 14 to 16 – over 70 per cent of staff.[28] Eleven subject areas had raised their RAE rating between 1992 and 1996. Never content with past achievement it is now the aim to raise the proportion of staff in 5 and 5 star departments to 60 per cent for the RAE of 2001. It is notable that Environmental Sciences and Social Work have the extraordinary distinction of combining 5 and 5 star RAE scores with the highest teaching assessment ratings. Combining RAE and TQA ratings *The Times* listed UEA in the top twenty universities for History, Geography, Music, Social Work, Law, Computing, Chemistry and Environmental Sciences – eight out of the fourteen subjects surveyed.[29] In wider terms 87 percent of students at UEA completed their degrees, compared with a UK average of 77 per cent, and only 9 per cent of UEA students dropped out, compared with 16 per cent nationally.[30] The Vice-Chancellor rightly observed "these results are a huge tribute to the quality of standards and care that students can expect at this

University". These ratings are not merely matters of institutional pride since they relate to funding. Accordingly this translated into a 3.6 per cent increase in grant in the year 2000 allocations, the sixteenth best out of seventy-six universities and the second best of the "sixties" universities.[31] It was a good position to have reached after forty years.

Teaching not only has to be good, but there is an increasing awareness that it should prepare students for employment. Accordingly a new unit "Learning through Earning" was devised to start in 1999.[32] A series of seminars would encourage students to think about employment skills and during the summer vacation they take work experience, paid or voluntary. This was to encourage the teamworking and communication skills and develop the sense of initiative and drive necessary for employability.[33] Norwich Union is a keen participant in the scheme, which is partly financed by the Department for Education and Employment. The project also built on the success of the Skills Development Partnership run by Kay Sanderson, whereby small and medium-sized companies offer work experience to students mentored by a manager from a larger company. Individual Schools, like History, also offer Personal and Academic Development units encouraging students to think about future employment and their employability.

One of the most important of these new skills was IT, whose use continued to spread rapidly.[34] By the end of the decade 86 per cent of UEA staff used computers in their jobs and 91 per cent of the academics also used home computers for UEA work. This was mostly for word processing and E-mail, though about a third of faculty also used IT in teaching and just over a half used the Internet to provide and find information. As regards the students, more had become familiar with IT at school before coming to university and a half already owned their own computers before arriving. Once arrived they found IT training as part of their courses; essays were required to be word processed and there is twenty-four hour availability of computers in a specially accessed floor of the Library. By the end of the decade IT use was virtually total among students – 94 per cent used E-mail, 92 per cent library catalogues, 90 per cent word processing and 88 per cent the web. A nation wide student survey placed UEA in the top five universities for its computing facilities.[35] Intriguingly, the first and only novel specifically about UEA had communicating by IT as one of its themes – " Addicted to E-mail he tells me ... I simply shrug. He's just like the rest of us" – The villain communicated only with his P.C.[36] But, villains apart, the spread of IT made things easier, faster and ensured that students had a vital transferable skill for the world of work as graduates.

Research continued strongly and even so short a span as five years throws up highlights. Biochemistry continued to flourish and was enhanced by the

£3,000,000 Molecular Structure Centre and the Wolfson Fermentation Laboratory, both opened by Lord and Lady Wolfson in 1996. The Centre was unique in the UK, searching for new antibiotics and new chemicals for use in medicine and industry and in the role of metals such as iron in biology. This brought together researchers from UEA and the Norwich Research Park. The research needed a constant supply of bacteria and this was grown in the Wolfson Fermentation Laboratory. Also of particular interest in East Anglia, with its high level of nitrates in the water, is the study of the role of bacteria in the nitrogen cycle.[37] Biology and Chemistry also joined forces in developing the £900,000 Centre for Metalloprotein Spectroscopy strengthening, UEA's forte in metallobiology as we have seen. The School of Biological Studies also remained a centre of strength as Professor Gill Murphy received over £1,000,000 from the Medical Research Council for work on cell biology, especially relating to her specialism of arthritis.[38] The cancer and cataract work also continued.

UEA's increasing expertise in health education and the biochemical sciences related to medicine culminated in the award of a Medical School to the University in 2000.[39] Announced on 16 July 2000, it was the result of an initiative by the East Anglia Joint Venture Medical Programme of which UEA is a partner along with regional NHS Trusts and others. The new Medical School will bring 150 jobs and over 500 students to the University, with a first intake of 110 entrants from autumn 2002, to be housed in a new building near the existing Schools of Health Policy and Practice and the School of Occupational Therapy and Physiotherapy. They will take a five year course leading to the medical degree Bachelor of Medicine and Bachelor of Surgery (MB/BS) awarded by UEA. The new School will benefit immensely from its proximity to the new Norfolk and Norwich Hospital in Colney, the existing Health Schools at UEA (already with three thousand students), and UEA's Wellcome Unit for the History of Medicine. The Medical School is one of the most important developments in recent years and a further symbol of a mature university.

The School of Environmental Sciences is also the focus of especially exciting developments. A new Institute for Connective Environmental Research (ICER) will be built which will comprise existing and new centres. The former are CSERGE, the Centre for Environmental Risk, the Climatic Research Unit. These were joined in summer 1999 by the Jackson Environment Institute, which moved from University College London to UEA. This augmented UEA's research resources with another £5,000,000, "reinforcing the largest and most advanced combined environmental research programme in the UK".[40] To these will be added new Centres. Most notably UEA has been chosen as the location of the new national climate change research centre, the Tyndall Centre, in which UEA was preferred over Cambridge and Oxford and Imperial and University Colleges London. Also new will be SYNERGY the successor of the Great Yarmouth Recommissioning Partnership dealing with oil and gas in the North Sea. Finally the Fuji Corporation of Japan will send researchers and support Visiting Professorships and Fellowships from business around the world. ENV has recently gained over £20,000,000 of grants, which reinforce its position as the premier department in Britain and arguably in Europe. By 2017 it is envisaged that "there will exist a comprehensive scheme for the management of the global economy" and UEA "will be acknowledged as making the greatest contribution, relative to resource, of any single institute".[41]

In the Social Sciences "DEV" continues its wide international range of activity from the study of poverty and social decline in Central Asia and AIDS in India through to biological matters such as soil erosion and biodiversity.[42] It continues its farm, originally at Colney, but now on the slope down to the Yare adjoining the Plain. Its poor eroded soil (formerly used for strawberries and barley) is not untypical of Third World agriculture. The School of Social Work remains a jewel in the crown at UEA, with its regular 5 and 5 star in the RAEs of 1989, 1992 and 1996 combined with its "excellent" for teaching. Notable within it has been the work of Professor June Thoburn, a former senior child care officer in Norwich and expert on child care. She set up the Family Support Network in 1994, composed of researchers, practitioners and users who can access a central databank for research findings. In the following year, they launched the Centre for Research on the Child and Family for multidisciplinary research. The core work of the School is training social workers and, until 1995, probation officers. It offers a spectrum of degrees tailored to the needs of practitioners – the MA in international child welfare from 1996, the degree in psychosocial studies from 1997 and the doctorate in social work from 1998. They spread beyond the problems of families and children in the UK to deal with wider international issues such as child trafficking, street children and child labour drawing students and making studies internationally from Uganda, the West Indies and Romania among others. Under Professors Peter Wedge, Martin Davies, David Howe and June Thoburn, SWK has grown since 1975 to be the pre-eminent School of Social Work in Britain in the 1990s.[43]

The School of History also found part of its research agenda transformed as in 1998 it became home to a £1,140,000 Wellcome Trust History of Medicine Unit, one of only five such in the country. It arose from Professor Roy Church's membership of the ESRC Committee and his meeting senior administrators of the Wellcome History of Medicine panel there. The overture to submit a bid thus came to Roy Church privately and personally. The unit's role was to promote scholarly research and increase public awareness of the history of medicine. The unit was transferred from the University of Cambridge and built upon the existing strengths in modern and medieval medical history developed by Steven Cherry and Carole Rawcliffe and would make for greater collaboration with the Schools of Health, BIO, DEV and Environmental Sciences in a multidisciplinary History of Medicine Unit which would be unique.[44] In the following year 1999 the Wellcome connection was further strengthened when Professor Roy Church was commissioned to write the history of Burroughs Wellcome, 1880-1939, enhancing the School of History's international reputation for economic and business history.[45]

What is evident from these selected highlights is the importance of inter-disciplinarity. The overlapping interests of chemistry and biology in biochemistry and of both with environmental sciences is plain. But also with the social sciences DEV's work straddles biological, environmental biodiver-sity, health care matters through to social work researches in Central Asia. Conversely Social Work has interests in Africa and other foreign countries and in the developmental aspects of the position of children. In a less obvi-ously likely combination we have seen the relation of historical studies with the biochemical and health concerns of the Wellcome Trust. This is in keeping with the original Thistlethwaite ethos of the University, while the present Vice-Chancellor has also stressed that strong Schools will tend to have an interdisciplinary outlook and that those that become too insular will be vulnerable.[46]

The development of the estate of the University has been a mixture of disappointment and advance. It was not to be expected that the last five years would see the kind of building expansion of the Burke years. The plans to surround two sides of the Library with a major archive centre which as we have seen, failed in 1997 on the denial of heritage lottery money, although it was recognised that Norfolk had one of the most important county archives in Britain. By happy contrast the East Anglian Sports Park did win its lottery bid in June 1997. UEA itself is contributing £1,900,000 towards the costs and it is a genuine partnership of University and region. It now comprises the region's largest Sports Hall with squash courts, climbing wall and fitness centre alongside the athletics track and hockey pitches. Especially notable is an Olympic-size swimming pool sponsored by Bernard Matthews, the Norfolk poultry millionaire, as the Bernard Matthew's Olympic Pool. It provides UEA with one of the best sporting complexes of any university in Britain.[47] The total cost is £17,500,000, £14,600,000 of which has come from the lottery, the fourth largest lottery sports fund grant. The new Sports Centre leaves the problem of what to do with the existing Sports Hall.[48] The Students' Union hoped to make it into a giant gig centre for events too big for the Waterfront or the LCR. Other proposals are for a meeting point for business and the University and the future will decide, but it is pleasingly unusual for the University to have to take decisions over surplus resources.

In 1996 the University acquired a new Director of Estates and Building, Richard Goodall, a valuation surveyor and former head of property of Cambridgeshire County Council. He was joined in the same year by Mel Pascoe, a former power station engineer, as Energy Manager.[49] They might originally have seen their tasks as maintaining the existing stock of buildings, now mostly over thirty years old and increasing energy saving. Goodall, however, soon found himself overseeing schemes for yet further expansion. The University has plans for a three storey addition to the Biology buildings, a new building by the existing CRU structure for ENV costing £50,000,000. There will also be new accommodation for nursing under a Private Finance Initiative scheme, either on the Plain or by the Hospital. More building is also envisaged by the greenhouses for undergraduate health education, and there is a major internal reorganisation of the science buildings in the Wall resulting from the departure of physics. £700,000 will be spent on improving the LCR and improvement has already been made in 1999 to the shops in the Street.[50] The fabric of the estate will be no more static than any other part of the University in the immediate years to come.

The University continues to reach out to local business. As traditional sources of funding from the government have been squeezed, so all universities have had to turn outwards to their local business communities offering expertise in training, research and consultancy. At UEA this is facilitated by the Business Development Director, Tony Brown. UEA has established useful linkages.[51] It has a fruitful partnership with Virgin Direct, Norwich's fastest growing business, in helping employees to develop new ideas – "Virgin Ideas". Norwich Union also draws naturally to UEA and they use "data mining" techniques developed by the School of Information Systems for retrieving and analysing nuggets of data from vast databases. Thirdly, there is a substantial collaborative project between UEA's School of Biological Sciences and Nuclear Electric for the restoration of the landscape and ecosystems around the site of the Sizewell B reactor. Fourthly, Amoco, one of UK's largest oil producers, has turned to UEA's Centre for Environmental Risk to assess the impact of dealing with the piles at the base of offshore oil and gas structures. Finally, the HELIX initiative (Higher Education Links and Industrial Expertise) has won £500,000 from HFCE's Higher Education Reach Out to Business and the Community (HEROBC) to enable the Business Development Team to build further links with firms to create a one stop shop for business enquiries for I and CIT, energy and risk management and finance.[52]

Yet while serving local needs UEA is also a significant international university. By 1995/6 it received 1100 international students from ninety countries.[53] The chief sources were Japan, Cyprus and Malaysia.[54] Accordingly, UEA celebrated Japan Day in 1996 and received a visit from the Japanese ambassador Hiroaki Fujii and Madame Fujii. Likewise Dame Elizabeth and Sir Geoffrey Allen, who both had keen Japanese interests, visited Japan and other South East Asian countries together.[55] UEA alumni branches are found in Japan, Malaysia, Taiwan, Hong Kong, South Korea and Singapore in South East Asia, and Nepal and Sri Lanka in the subcontinent and in South Africa. UEA is also making exploratory visits to China, to Yunnan University in the south west, to Sechuan Province and the City University of Hong Kong, with a view to exchanging students and research. As well as students coming to UEA for normal degree courses, UEA has mounted courses for specific groups. Egyptian medical workers come to the prestigious School of Health for ten-week courses funded by the Egyptian government. This teaches nurses to undertake procedures and treatments usually reserved for doctors in Egypt but done by nurses in England.[56] Similarly, the Wellcome Foundation has funded students from Brazil, Kenya, Ruanda and Nepal to study wildlife conservation in the MSc in Applied Ecology.[57] Conversely UEA provides teaching abroad, CARE setting up a distance learning teacher training college course in Namibia.[58] In Ethiopia CRU's Declan Conway, an authority on the climate of the Nile, teaches courses on climatology as a contribution to that country's drought problem.[59] Ethiopians have also visited UEA to study the working of our Library. A lot of UEA's research has an international dimension, notably in the case of ENV, whose projects range from the Brazilian rain forest to the Arctic, from the Antarctic to the Vietnam coast. So strong is UEA's reputation in the Far East that it has prompted the extraordinary generous gift from David Wong, a Hong Kong businessman, who has financed a £25,000 annual fellowship in creative writing.[60]

In 2002 Vincent Watts leaves his Vice-Chancellorship to become full-time Chairman of the East of England Development Agency. He will be succeeded in 2002 by Professor David Eastwood, the Chief Executive of the Arts and Humanities Research Board. Many themes raised here will come to fruition or be resolved in the near future under the new Vice-Chancellor. But we leave the University at the end of the century and the end of its first forty years in good heart, immensely active over a wide range, and moving strongly ahead on the tracks of its clear strategic planning. Let us now turn to make some final reflections on the story and achievement as a whole.

14

Achievement

It really was a Crusade.[1]

Sir Timothy Colman, 26 August 1999

Over the relatively short span of UEA's history British universities have expanded from twenty-four in 1961 with 200,000 students to ninety-six universities with over 1,500,000 students by the end of the 1990s. Costs have risen from £198,000,000 in 1966/7 to seven billion pounds by the late 1990s. In 1961/2 public expenditure on higher education stood at 0.30 per cent of GDP and 1.15 per cent by 1994/5.[2] The proportion of the population going to university has risen from 4 per cent to over 30 per cent while the CBI calls for a further advance to 40 per cent and the government assumes 50 per cent by 2010.[3] In this UEA has played its part, growing from its original 113 students in 1963/4 to 12,000 by the end of the millennium. Generous as this expansion has seemed, it is still far short of the "mass" higher education found, for example in California, where some 80 per cent of students go to university.[4]

What is also remarkable is that expansion has taken place with comparatively little change in the assumptions that underlay the pre-Robbins selective system. There is still the belief that education should be largely supported by the state, that high standards should be maintained and a uniformity of standards secured by a reliance on good A level grades for entrance and on external examiners to link standards across universities. The three year degree is held to, chiefly in single subjects, and universities pride themselves on low drop out rates. Yet many of these assumptions, evident still at UEA, are handed on from a time when the university sector was a tenth of the size it is now. Martin Trow regards all these criteria as being inevitably strained by going beyond 15 per cent of age group entry to universities.[5]

Throughout UEA's history all universities have been buffeted by contradictory demands and accusations mirroring the above paradox. On the one hand, there are incessant demands for more expansion; on the other, there are claims that elite standards should be retained. Expansionists point out that, in spite of Britain's own expansion, it has consistently lagged behind other countries in the proportion taking higher education. It was so at the time of the Robbins Report and in most surveys of the 1970s and 1980s,[6] and was still so in the 1990s. In 1991 Britain's 28 per cent of eighteen-year-olds in tertiary education was less than eleven other European countries (and USA, Canada, New Zealand and Japan), "Britain still sends fewer young people to university than any of its major industrial competitors",[7] and it was still so in 1992/3.[8] Our expansion was only part of a movement common to all industrialised countries and hardly kept pace with most. The counter-argument was that the English system of higher education by being more selective was more cost effective in that almost all who entered universities graduated successfully. This was in contrast to European systems, which were much more open of access but exercised selectivity by failing less adequate students in examinations in the course of the degree. England placed an emphasis on selective efficiency, other systems on wider educational opportunity. Universities could accordingly be accused of dragging their feet to impede expansion, preferring the ease of teaching the well-qualified academic young to facing the challenge of a new type of student. The issue revived fiercely in 2000 with attacks by Gordon Brown and others on the "elitism" of English universities.

On the other hand, the fact that universities participated in the expansion at all led to counter-accusations of colluding in a fall in standards and the abandoning of supposedly elite qualities of the 1950s or even 1930s. Sir Maurice Dean, the Permanent Under Secretary of State at the Ministry of Education, in 1964 called the new universities of the sixties "Universities of Noddyland",[9] while Lord Boothby (Rector of St Andrews University) dismissed them as "mushroom" universities. It would have surprised critics of that time that within thirty years most of the new universities, including UEA, were quite regularly in the top third of *The Times* annual rankings, and Warwick was a member of the elite Russell Group. Three of the top eight universities for science in the RAE of 1996 were "new" universities of the sixties (UEA, Warwick and York).

The expansion has raised questions of whether standards could be maintained. Alan Smithers has noted, "we are pushing people with lower qualifications into the same system and then castigating universities where large numbers fail".[10] Yet this has not been a problem at UEA, where only 9 per cent of students drop out compared with a national average of 16 per cent.[11] This may be due to quite conscientious systems of monitoring student progress. Also with the modular system it becomes difficult to fail everything. Resits are allowed and, even in the case of failing to complete a full degree, then a pass degree, diploma or certificate may be gained with lesser quantities or work and achievement. This is a quite appropriate adjustment to mass higher education where there are many nuanced stages between the stark alternatives of successful honours graduation or failure as in the early 1960s.

In spite of its own expansion along with that of the university system as a whole, UEA is confident that it has maintained standards. In my experience the quality of the solid 2/1s and 2/2s remains remarkably consistent and the best firsts are probably even better than in the past. This consistency over time, when the proportion entering higher education has risen from 4 to 30 per cent, is puzzling, but four factors may lie behind it. First, UEA itself has not shifted from taking the top 4 per cent to the lower end of the top 30 per cent. In the 1960s it was probably taking the lower end of the top 5 per cent of ability, and in the 1990s probably students within, say, the top eight per cent.[12] Less attractive universities would be admitting down to the 30 per cent level. Secondly, UEA, like all universities, has been tapping ability neglected at school, especially that of mature students, more than capable of university education but unrecognised by the secondary modern and comprehensive schools of their youth. Four excellent firsts in the School of History in 1999 were mature women of this type. Thirdly, the University is careful at monitoring standards through Unit Assessment Committees as well as Boards of Examiners. Proportions of firsts and 2/1s remain at a very steady 60 per cent. Extraordinary variations can be corrected, as in the case of one School in 1994. Standards in any case are linked across universities by external examiners and now by the Quality Assurance Agency, with its benchmark standards. We have seen in the previous chapter UEA's excellent performance in these reviews and the Quality Audit's satisfaction with the University's procedures. Fourthly, students are almost certainly working harder than they did. The Director of Counselling has found increasingly in the 1990s that anxiety about work and perfectionism is a cause of stress and distress. This in turn is prompted by student awareness of the increased competition in the graduate labour market, itself a consequence of expansion. Finally, the quality of teaching has probably improved with Staff Development and Training since 1988 and appraisal of units by students, managers, biennial and quinquennial reviews. All these factors have helped to preserve and monitor standards in the face of increasing numbers.

There has also been a concern to preserve the ideal of the community. We have seen something the rhetoric and reality of this in the sixties in Chapter 4. This used to be expressed through an active Senior Common Room. It was a focus of recreational life when at Earlham Lodge in the Village. With development of the Plain it moved to a first floor suite in University House. In the 1970s splendid wine tastings and suppers took place there during the winter and at Earlham Hall and on its lawn during the summer. This was a high point of morale and good fellowship under the SCR chairmanship of R.A.Y. Jones. It was then given excellent facilities in the SCVA but it lost thereby a centrality of location and of purpose. The social focus shifted to Top Floor above the central refectory block; open to all grades of staff. Senior Common

Room gradually ceased to exist. Community became less spoken about and in some universities its passing was regretted and in some even welcomed. But Dame Elizabeth spoke of it at her first Assembly and Vincent Watts is insistent on it, stressing that "as a campus university we have a strong sense of community".[13] Creating our Future likewise stressed the need to treat students "as part of a community". But rhetoric is made real by, for example, the Vice-Chancellor's regular Open Days and the innovation of opening the Court to all comers. The "community of scholars" was perhaps a sentimental but real psychological force necessary to forging the enterprise in its early days and it is good to see this being recognised anew.

The University needs this solidarity as it has become subject to increasing intervention by the state, not least by Conservative governments which claimed to be "rolling back" the influence of the state. We have seen this with the demands of the UGC, UFC and HEFCE for ceaseless financial information, especially with the collapse of the quinquennial planning system and the successive cuts. To these have been added the Research Assessment Exercises from 1986 and the periodic Teaching Quality Assessment and Academic Audit. All this can be justified in terms of accountability for public money, but the accountability seems to increase as the money diminishes. Vice-Chancellor Derek Burke was moved to a certain exasperation: "The Government is increasingly more intrusive, demanding multiple levels of audit, repeated financial projections, poorly performed reviews of teaching, attempts to control our decision making more closely, surely by now we have proved more than adequately that we run a tight ship".[14]

This in turn has altered the internal culture of the University. As outside bodies impose on the University, so the central power within the University has had to increase its own control over constituent parts of the University. It was evident in recurrent demands for accountable data from Schools. More power has also passed to the Planning and Resources Committee, away from Senate (though PRC is a Committee of Senate and Council) and even from Deans. The Senate of 24 January 1996 lasted a mere forty minutes, though transacting the important business of absorbing CEAS into the School of History. A commentator queried "Should we congratulate ourselves on the thoroughness of the work undertaken elsewhere in the committee system which brought items to Senate so well argued and thought through that speechless assent was the only appropriate response?"; or should they be concerned " that Senate's democratic function had been neutered"?[15] Successive Vice-Chancellors have complained of the difficulties of decision-making and the need to streamline it. Accordingly, a more centralised managerial style has been necessary to enable the Registry to respond efficiently to the demands placed upon it by government and to manage change swiftly.[16] The senior management has proliferated from two Pro Vice-Chancellors, in the mid 1980s, to three including a Deputy Vice-Chancellor and now to six. But it can be argued that UEA is now a business and there are very many things to do. The former Registrar, Michael Paulson Ellis, was certain that UEA had became more managerial during his time as Registrar between 1978-1999 and significantly changed the job title on his passport from "University Administrator" to "University Manager".[17]

The curricular shape of UEA has been continually readdressed. Its origins reflected attitudes of the time – a belief in liberal education, in general mind training rather than a preparation for a first job. These were the attitudes of the first two Vice-Chancellors and it was reinforced by the UGC of the early sixties under Sir Keith Murray, who advised UEA, and other new universities, not to get involved with their local Victorian technical colleges and to keep their activities distinctly non-technical. This was also the clear view of Sir Charles Wilson and the APB. No engineering was to be allowed at UEA and there was no question of undertaking very expensive studies in agriculture, veterinary science or medicine. Nor at a lower level could UEA contemplate, for example, building, nursing or catering, more appropriate for technical colleges. It has been suggested that UEA could have disregarded the UGC in the sixties and gone ahead with some engineering, as Sussex, Warwick and Essex did. But it might have been risky to cross the UGC in those formative years, though UEA did disregard the UGC over law and archaeology in the 1970s and electronics in the 1980s. Sheldon Rothblatt suggests that high costs are "one strong reason why a liberal education ... is difficult to achieve under conditions of mass access".[18] In the UEA case this was not so since traditional liberal education was the inexpensive way to obtain rapid growth in the sixties. But it did leave UEA with an inheritance of an arts-humanities orientation with 45 per cent of faculty in the mid sixties teaching some form of literature or history. Strenuous efforts have been made over the years to include more vocational subjects relating to careers – education, law, accountancy, management, nursing, physio and occupational therapy, electronics, computing and social work – all of which can virtually guarantee first job employment and which give a good balance to UEA's range of provision.

Interdisciplinarity has always been a hallmark of UEA's approach to the curriculum. This was strongly argued by Frank Thistlethwaite at his appointment interview, accorded with the views of the APB and was carried through into the early planning, as we have seen. Chemistry was unusual in insisting on being a single-subject School in those days. Since then matters have shifted in different directions. In some cases there has been a move to specialist Schools. The creation of a School of History has forced EAS to become in effect chiefly a School of Literature, leaving EUR as a School of

Languages. Social Work split off from Economic and Social Studies to attain specialist excellence through independence. The Schools and Departments of Law, Drama and Education are also focused on their disciplines. The hopes for "new maps of learning", especially in some arts subjects, have not been entirely sustained. Perhaps more surprising is the jettisoning of subjects such as physics and French as demand from sixth formers diminished, and Russian as part of a national rationalisation. Conversely, UEA has responded to sixth form enthusiasm for media studies by strongly developing drama and film studies. Indeed some of the most successful careers followed by UEA graduates have been in the media, as we shall see – though paradoxically before such studies began. Yet if there has been a move away from interdisciplinarity in some areas of the humanities it seems to have grown in the sciences. We have seen this with Biology and Chemistry and Environmental Sciences. Chemistry nowadays has arguably more that interdisciplinary role that Thistlethwaite intended than it did in the early years of the University. The keen interdisciplinarity in the sciences owes something to the John Innes Centre and the activities of the NRP, where all these disciplines interrelate in matters to do with food and plants. The enthusiasm and expertise of the Vice-Chancellor Derek Burke as a leading biochemist undoubtedly contributed to this, while the prestige and size of the School of Environmental Sciences, a catholic user of all kinds of science in interconnected ways, was also a force. UEA has proved itself highly fluid and responsive to change in its curricular planning as specialisms emerge, subjects coalesce and fashions change.

In recent years the University has also become increasingly concerned that what students study should make them employable. This is reflected not only in the move to more vocationalism but in the teaching of "enabling skills" or "transferable skills" as they came to be called. They were justified on the grounds that "these were skills which were directly applicable beyond the University and it was suggested that an increased awareness on the part of students that they were acquiring such skills through the learning process would help lessen anxiety about the perceived non-relevance of non vocational courses".[19] So concerned was the Senate that it set up a group to consider it, including the Chairman of Nabisco. This rightly emphasised abilities in reading, writing, and verbal communication which were expected to develop through preparing essays and seminar participation. Particularly important were numeracy, "the capacity to see the meaning of numbers and the relations between them" and computer literacy, both "fundamental to basic management techniques". The scientists needed to be more literate and verbal and the arts students more numerate, all with a capacity for Information Technology. The Dearing Report was very keen that all universities should undertake such skill development and it led to Learning through

Earning and similar schemes and the rapid permeation of IT in the University in the 1990s. It was all part of an increasing recognition that the purpose of the University is not only liberal mind training, research and scholarship but preparing graduates for the world of work. It is one of the major attitudinal changes between the 1960s and 1990s.

UEA has undoubtedly been a good place for students. UEA spent generously, even very generously, on students in the 1970s and this was an element in the cuts imposed in the 1980s. UEA was also more democratic than most in allowing student representation on University bodies in the 1960s. Both these factors mitigated the severity of unrest in the Troubles and eased recovery from them. In the consultants report on Image in 1985 it was emphasised that UEA was well regarded by students as a good place to be. Its high degree of residential accommodation, now extraordinarily good sports facilities, a Union highly entrepreneurial in providing entertainments, some of the best buildings of any university since 1960 in one of the grandest valley landscapes, and a safe, lively and beautiful historic city, all contributed to an attractive lifestyle for students. 89 per cent of the graduates of 1996 said that they would recommend to friends the course they had done. 96 per cent would recommend UEA as a whole and 90 per cent thought that UEA had lived up to their expectations.[20]

In two ways, however, the University has not been able to serve the student body as would have been hoped in the 1960s. One expectation of the expansion of higher education, held by Robbins and others was that it would draw in more talent from the working classes. UEA has contributed to this but not very markedly. It always has been a rather middle-class, but not upper middle-class, university. In 1999 it took 82 per cent of its intake from state schools, which is the national average. Yet only 17 per cent came from the manual, semi-skilled or unskilled occupations, which was much less than the national average for university students of 26 per cent. All the 1960s universities took a lower than average working class intake and UEA (along with Warwick and York) was the least working class of all.[21] There is no bias involved on UEA's part but it probably reflects the fact that much of UEA's intake comes from the south east of England (45 per cent in 1993 and 1996) and not so much from the traditional "working-class" areas of the north west, north east and midlands (8.6 per cent in 1993 and 10 per cent in 1996).

Students have also had to suffer the decline in the unit of resource, the difference between expanding numbers of students and constrained finance. Between 1985/6 and 1993/4 expenditure per student in real terms on equipment fell from £426 to £259 and on books from £70 to £46.[22] University grants are subject to "efficiency gains", that is universities are expected to make up losses by greater efficiency in, for example, the use of IT, having fewer staff and larger classes. Yet efficiency gains can easily translate into quality losses. Fewer books are bought: by 1995 UEA was acquiring material at only 40 per cent of the 1970 level though it cost twice as much per student.[23] Small group seminar teaching on which UEA used to pride itself cannot be sustained as groups increase in size from eight or twelve to twenty or more. This is inevitable and common to all universities in response to declining resources per student.

UEA has been fortunate in the quality of its Vice-Chancellors. It is notable that several Vice-Chancellors had business backgrounds either through their family or their own careers. Frank Thistlethwaite's family owned and managed cotton mills. Michael Thompson's father was a former Indian army officer turned agricultural merchant, while Derek Burke's father owned engineering factories in the midlands. Some had business experience in their own early careers – Michael Thompson as a Director (then Vice-Chairman) of the Alliance and Leicester Building Society, Derek Burke as a Director of Allelix, Vincent Watts as a partner of Arthur Andersen. Some even continued their business interests while Vice-Chancellor, Thompson with the Alliance and Watts as the Chairman of the East of England Development Agency. Others have had major administrative experience in the public service, Frank Thistlethwaite in the wartime civil service in America and London, Dame Elizabeth Estève-Coll as Director of the Victoria and Albert Museum. This has brought great benefits to UEA, since running a university demands increasingly the skills and experience of management and business. It is also notable that both Michael Thompson and Vincent Watts have been experts in IT to industrial consultancy level. It is also interesting that all the wives of the male Vice-Chancellors have been academics in schools or universities.

Leadership and quality has been evident not only at the very top but in scholarship and administration. Something of this can be seen in distinctions awarded to faculty and administrators for their work at UEA. Professors Sir David Hopwood, Sir Angus Wilson and Sir Malcolm Bradbury have been knighted and Professor Andrew Motion appointed Poet Laureate. Professors Keith Clayton and Kerry Turner both of ENV are CBE's and Professor Roy Emerson and Roy Campbell, both of SOC, OBE's as are Malcolm Crowder formerly of the Estates Office and Michael Paulson Ellis the former Registrar. MBE's have been awarded to Patricia Whitt the personal assistant to three Vice-Chancellors and to Maggie Smith the secretary of the Music department and to Janet Garton the distinguished Scandinavianist. It is remarkable that the UEA course in Creative Writing, the pre-eminent one in the UK, has been led by two literary knights and the Poet Laureate.

A number of outstanding faculty have passed on to distinction elsewhere. Anthony Cross, Richard Evans and David King to the chairs of Russian,

History and Chemistry at Cambridge, Malcolm Bowie to the chair of French at Oxford, Paul Kennedy to the Dilworth Chair of History at Yale, and Alan Katritzky to that of chemistry at Florida. In the arts Sir Philip Ledger became Principal of the Royal Scottish Academy of Music while Peter Lasko CBE became Director of the Courtauld Institute, to be followed by Eric Fernie also from UEA. It is a pleasing irony that whereas Frank Thistlethwaite's original intention was that the UEA School of Fine Arts should not be like the Courtauld yet the School's destiny was to provide two successive Directors of the Institute. In an adjacent area Alan Borg progressed from the Directorship of the SCVA to the Imperial War Museum and the Victoria and Albert Museum where he succeeded Dame Elizabeth Estève-Coll. The greatest distinction has been life peerage to the historian and Labour local government politician Patricia Hollis as Baroness Hollis of Heigham, Parliamentary Under Secretary of State in the Department of Social Security.

UEA's contribution to the region has been invaluable and we have seen many instances of it. By the late 1990s 46 per cent of UEA's students came from Norfolk and Suffolk, and half from within a hundred mile radius. Conversely about a quarter of new UEA graduates of 1995 and 1996 are employed in the region. UEA as an employer and purchaser of services makes an expenditure of £66,000,000 in the region and, with the Norwich Research Park, it is the third largest employer in the region spending some £95,000,000. The University provides recreational services to the region with 250,000 visitors annually to the Sports Centre, 35,000 to the SCVA and 120,000 to Students' Union concerts and the Waterfront. Sharon Choa, following on the work of Peter Aston, has enhanced the very high quality of the University orchestra and choir, which gives great pleasure, for example in a recent performance of Britten's *War Requiem*. UEA gives special financial support to music because of its regional role. The University has had many research projects relevant to the region which need no full reiteration here. In the 1990s one may note funding from the regional NHS for eleven research projects in ENV and HEA. The Economics Research Centre undertakes economic and social surveys for regional organisations and the Centre for Environmental Risk Management has contracts with Norwich Union. BIO benefits from Bryan Gunn's leukaemia fund and the Big C (Norfolk and Suffolk's cancer charity) amounting to over £400,000. HIS has a significant reputation for local and regional history through the work of CEAS, while SYS has important schemes with Norwich Union and other local firms. We need not reiterate UEA's involvement with research and policy on the Broads and coastal erosion and the NRP as a focus of research for the food sciences. UEA is also significant in the training of local labour. Norwich City Council benefits from the University's provision of IT training and the Norfolk

County Council in food and biotechnology. There are many short courses in languages, management and much else and, as it becomes more vocational, the University produces a steady ouput of nurses, therapists, social workers, schoolteachers, IT specialists and managers, many of whom will serve the region. We have seen the striking endeavours of the University in creating links with the colleges in Norfolk and Suffolk and helping the development of Suffolk College and the creation of the Regional Federation in 1991. The establishment of the Government Office of the Eastern Region (GOER) has created a higher education forum which will facilitate further cooperation.[24] Finally UEA has contributed to local politics with Patricia Hollis, Peter Mercer, Alec Fisher, Michael Ashley, Brian Heading and Christopher Smith becoming councillors and George Turner and Ian Gibson Members of Parliament. Beyond that the participation of members of the University in local drama, music, literary, environmental and charitable activity is incalculable. UEA has always been determined to be not only a University of international and national standing but a force for good and usefulness in its city and region. As the traditional economy of Norwich changes, and the University and NRP grow in scale and wealth, so there is an increasing mutuality of interest between UEA and the City, the success of the University becoming even more vital to that of the city which gave it birth.

UEA's contribution to national life through its students is already paying rich dividends. We may analyse the careers being followed by alumni since the 1960s (Table 17).[25]

It is evident that students in the vocational and science schools tend to follow professions relating to their studies. Yet even students from Schools whose studies seem much less evidently to lead to careers do enter professions, even if not directly related. This was so with students from EAS, DEV and EUR. What is most striking of all is that only small proportions go into what one would regard as lower than graduate work – waiters, van drivers, buskers and the like; only in DEV was this significant. The public easily gets the impression that students are scruffy, long-haired, tax-absorbing layabouts. But in reality they are prosperous and serious professionals in the making. The benefits to society measured by the social rate of return on the costs of their education are an impressive 11 per cent per annum, a very good investment. And UEA has been making its contribution to this through successive generations of graduates. As UEA graduates have benefited themselves and society it is also pleasing to record that they have not forgotten the University. The Alumni Society has given £150,000 to UEA since 1990.

Most university students benefit themselves and society fairly anonymously. But some UEA graduates have achieved recognised distinction and celebrity. Judith Appleton, formerly of DEV, was awarded an MBE in 1985 for

Table 17   Occupations of UEA Alumni, 1966-2000

School	Following a profession taken related to the degree taken.		Following a profession unrelated to the degree.		In non-graduate work.	
	No	Per cent	No	Per cent	No	Per cent
SYS	66	97	2	2.9	0	0
MAP	62	84.9	7	9.5	4	5.5
LAW	28	82.3	6	17.6	0	0
CHEM	60	80	14	18.6	1	1.3
EDU	62	78.4	17	21.5	0	0
SOC	142	73.1	39	20.1	13	6.7
BIO	70	72.9	24	25	2	2.0
AHM	34	60.7	20	35.7	2	3.5
ENV	43	47.7	42	46.6	5	5.5
DEV	32	44.4	32	69.4	8	11.1
EAS	70	42.4	80	48.4	15	9
EUR	66	41.5	79	49.6	14	8.8
Total	735	63.3	362	31.2	64	5.5

her work for Save the Children in Ethiopia, the first honour to a UEA graduate. The novelist Kazuo Ishiguro is an OBE as is Richard Sandbrook, a former President of the Students' Union and Executive Director of the International Institute of Environment and Development. Ian McEwan, the novelist was awarded a CBE, in the Millennium honours of 2000. This was, pleasingly, the same honours list in which Malcolm Bradbury, a founder of the Creative Writing course which McEwan had taken as its first and (then) only student, was knighted. Other graduates have achieved academic distinction in their fields. Professor Sir Paul Nurse FRS is the Royal Society Napier Professor at Oxford and Director of Laboratory Research of the Imperial Cancer Research Fund and a Nobel Laureate. Christopher Wrigley was a dynamic President of the Historical Association and is Professor of History at Nottingham University.

UEA graduates have been remarkably successful in the media. As well as McEwan and Ishiguro, Rose Tremain is one of our leading novelists, Booker shortlist and Whitbread prizewinner, whose *Restoration* became an Oscar-nominated film. Jonathan Powell, the distinguished television drama producer (*Bleak House* and *Tinker, Tailor, Soldier, Spy*) became Controller of BBC 1 and then of Carlton Television. Michael Jackson was Controller of BBC 2 while Jenny Abramsky was Controller of Radio 5 and, subsequently head of BBC Radio. In front of the camera Selena Scott and Penny Tranter, the Meteorological Office TV weather presenter, are nationally, and Helen McDermott and Carol Bundock regionally, very well known. In less public profile areas Karen Jones, Managing Director of the Pelican restaurant group, which owns Café Rouge, is an outstanding example of a UEA entrepreneur while Jeni Mundy has carried the UEA sailing tradition to the highest level as a member of the all women crew in the Whitbread Round the World Yacht Race of 1990. Also in sport, Andy Ripley was an England and British Lions rugby international. UEA has been proud to recognise its own by conferring honorary doctorates on Nurse, McEwan, Ishiguro, Wrigley and King.

What of the future? This could go in any of several not mutually exclusive directions. First, under the present system of state control, accountability will continue to increase absorbing more time from the substantive activities of teaching and research. Noel Annan deplored that in 1994 a third of dons' time was being spent on administration compared with a fifth on research.[26] Some influential voices are concerned about this trend of universities receiving less money from the state while being subject to progressively more control.[27] The dependency of leading universities on state funds has halved but their regulatory burden doubled in the last twenty years. UEA received 72 per cent of its income from the UGC in 1964 but only 41 per cent from the HEFCE in 1994. As the proportion of income diminishes and regulatory control increases some strong universities are going to become "difficult" – as Oxford and Cambridge are over QAA "benchmarks" of standards.

Secondly, at the other pole is complete independence. This would be a university receiving no regular government money, except for special contracts, but with the freedom to determine its own level of fees charged to students and salaries to staff. This is the basis of the excellence of the best American universities.[28] This would call the bluff of various interested parties. The public demands first class higher education while being unwilling to pay higher taxes to pay for it. Higher education ranks low in priority compared with the health service and schools. Total freedom to charge fees would bring home to parent and students the real costs of education. It would also set up a genuine market, each university judging its position in the market by setting charges at a level to attract enough students who know what to expect, ranging from expensive excellence to inexpensive adequacy – or inadequacy which would lead to closure. Independence would remove the humbug that all universities are supposed to be excellent in everything, and the even greater humbug that an expensive state bureaucracy can enforce it so. The market broadly ranks hotels, restaurants and public schools and it could do so for universities. It would force students to make calculations: high fees and a high rate of return on investment in, for instance, law and medicine; low for for example for teaching. Independence would also make large industrial corporations face the real costs of training their professional labour and tilt more of the costs of higher education to them and away from the taxpayer. These free market arguments are not as outlandish as one may suppose. Nicholas Barr, influential on Lord Dearing's Committee, has advocated them.[29] Even more influentially Robert Jackson, the former Minister for Higher Education, advocated the possibility of independence and the matter was actually debated in Cabinet, but rejected on the grounds that it would lead to the closure of several universities. But it is an agenda in the wings (though also rejected by Dearing) and would be a release from the underfunded, overadministered situation universities are now in. UEA would survive, in a more focused form, but certainly not all its departments.

Thirdly, it can be questioned whether there will be in the future any need for a University at all, as a physical entity. The use of IT, television, E-mail and the internet may remove the need for thousands of young people to reside together in concrete structures attending lectures and tutorials in person. More teaching could be done by videoed lectures, the internet and texts on screen replace paper books from the library. UEA is excellent for IT – indeed the former Librarian is now Director of Information Services and an expert on IT. Mature students laboriously travelling in to UEA from north Norfolk and Suffolk villages may become an anachronism. There are limits to it, however, since a university is also a place of social interaction and personal communication. Indeed one very senior official of UEA told me half jokingly that "we are partly in the sex and entertainment business". This is truer than he thought. In the 1990s about a third of ex SOC, BIO and EAS women of the 1960s were married to UEA fellow graduates,[30] and 81 per cent of students in 1999 claimed (extravagantly) to be carrying on sexual relations with each other.[31] Electronics is no substitute. Electronic media will advance but the Plain is unlikely to be replaced by "virtual reality".

Finally, UEA may become a genuine University of East Anglia. R.A.Y. Jones, a long serving and experienced Pro Vice-Chancellor has speculated interestingly, "I envisage a truly East Anglian University, a federal institution with campuses in Norwich, Ipswich and Colchester".[32] The higher education institutions of the East Anglian bulge, which is a distinctive region, could become a large federal university, analogous to the Victoria University (Manchester, Liverpool and Leeds) before 1900. This would constitute a "big" university with over 30,000 students. Vincent Watts would like to see one big 40,000 student university in East Anglia (including, say, Norfolk, Suffolk, Essex and Cambridgeshire), similar in scale and power to an American state university and with the resources to be world-class in many areas. Successive Vice-Chancellors at UEA have felt that UEA was too small.

The birth rate, after falling from the mid 1960s to the end of the 1970s, then rising through the 1980s, is predicated to fall steadily through the first third of the twenty-first century. If this is so, the achievement of scale at UEA, or anywhere else in the east, may best be brought about by such an arrangement especially in so sparsely populated a region. An Association of Universities of the Eastern Region was created in 2000 with Professor David Bridges of UEA as Executive Director. If devolution goes further to the creation of a governmental region in the east and there are pressures for students to attend local universities then this is all the more likely.

Some see a conflict of purpose between the University regarding an important part of its function in serving the local region and its quest to become as world-ranking international research institution. The Creating our Future Group report, *UEA a World Class Future,* posed two alternatives, as "regionally focused university" or an "internationally competitive research" one and decisively rejected the former in favour of the latter. Yet inevitably there was some ambivalence since, although the regional focus was rejected, UEA was urged to be "significantly involved in regional activities" and regional funding opportunities "must be exploited to the full". In practice UEA will seek world-class excellence where it can without being so imprudent as to neglect its regional role which is considerable. Some of UEA's existing strengths encompass both the international and the regional. ENV has a world-class reputation in matters ranging from the Antarctic to Brazil yet it also serves the region through its studies of the Broads and coastal erosion. HIS not only studies national and international history but especially through CEAS has made major contributions to local and regional history. The work of the JIC and its connections with BIO and CHEM is of international significance but thereby benefits East Anglian agriculture. And there are many more. But there is a dissonance of emphasis between the COF Report and the Regional Strategy Task Group Report on UEA and the region. Perhaps UEA is doing too much. Vice-Chancellors Dame Elizabeth Estève-Coll and Vincent Watts have felt that UEA is trying to do too many things for its size. Part of this problem arises from the lack of industry in the region and of big universities nearby – unlike Yorkshire or the East Midlands for example. It forces UEA to take on a wide range of objectives which creates difficulties. All these matters, the balance of international and regional role and the focus of activity are for the future to resolve.

An institution derives its strength by pursuing energetically the activities of the present and planning for the future, as UEA does. Yet from time to time it is also salutary to look back as we have been doing. It arouses many desirable sentiments: gratitude for the work of all those academics and laymen who created and developed the University; pride in a great deal of achievement academic, architectural and in the intellectual and social formation of students; a sense of corporate identity, and commonality of interest in what some still like to think of as a "community of scholars".

The last word should go to one of UEA's greatest lay friends, Sir Timothy Colman, who retired as a member of the University Council in 1985 though continuing to serve as Pro Chancellor. He finally retired as Pro Chancellor in the year 2000 after nearly forty years of public service to UEA. Towards the end of our talk at Bixley Manor he said that he regarded the foundation of the University of East Anglia as the most important thing to have happened in Norwich in the second half of the twentieth century. When I expressed mild surprise at this high view he became most serious and reflective, as if looking back over the decades and wishing to impress his point on me, "Yes," he said, "it really was a Crusade."

Notes

Notes to Acknowledgements

1 *Annual Report of the Vice-Chancellor*, 1977-78 p. 12.
2 Professor J.R. Jones, file, The History of the University.
3 Letter, Professor J.R. Jones to Professor Andrew Martindale, 30 September 1980.
4 AVC tape 307.

Notes to Chapter 1: A University for Norwich, 1918-1960

1 Memorandum, "University College", 1947, Gordon Tilsley Papers, (GTP).
2 Susannah Wade Martins, *A History of Norfolk* (Chichester, 1984), Elsie McCutcheon, *Norwich through the Ages* (Bury St Edmunds, 1989), B. Green and R. Young, *Norwich the Growth of a City* (1981), and Frank Meeres, *A History of Norwich* (Chichester, 1998), are good on this background.
3 Percy Lubbock, *Earlham* (London, 1922), pp. 197-98.
4 R. H. Mottram, *East Anglia: England's Eastern Province* (London, 1933), p. 85.
5 Ibid., p. 2.
6 James Stuart, *Reminiscences* (London, 1912), chapter 9, on Norwich.
7 Alan Metters, *The Tech, 1891-1991* (Norwich, 1991). Prospectuses of the City of Norwich Technical Institute, 1901-1902, and thereafter. Norwich City College Archives.
8 Michael Sanderson, "The Civic Universities and the Industrial Spirit", *Historical Research* 144 (1988).
9 Frank Thistlethwaite, "The University of East Anglia", in M. G. Ross, ed., *New Universities in the Modern World* (London, 1966). Professor Thistlethwaite tells me that 1910 was a misprint.
10 *The Times*, 23 April and 29 July 1913.
11 "Proposed University College in Norwich", n.d. but 1946. Lincoln Ralphs Papers (LRP). "University College", a background paper to the 1946 movement, in GTP. There is no trace of the Norwich application in the UGC papers for 1919. PRO, UGC2/1. For the context Christine Helen Skinn, *Paying the Piper: The Development of the University Grants Committee, 1919-1946* (London, 1986).
12 Joyce Gurney-Read, *Trades and Industries of Norwich* (Norwich, 1988), pp. 7-10. I am grateful to Dr Christine Clark for this reference.
13 *EDP*, 26 September 1963.
14 It is suggested (in "University College" 1947) that the money raised was passed to the Memorial Chapel at the Cathedral. There is no evidence for this. NRO, DCN/106/1 Minute Book of the War Memorial Chapel Committee, 1919-32.
15 *EDP*, 18 January 1939 in Norwich City College Newscuttings Books.
16 *EDP*, 17 March 1939.

17 *Norwich Labour Monthly*, March 1939.

18 NRO, N/TC 35/5/9, Higher Education Sub Committee Minutes, 1937-40, p. 380, 21 April 1939. I owe this reference to Dr Alan Metters. The College had regular dealings with London University about College courses validated by the University.

19 *Higher Technological Education: Report of a Special Committee* (Lord Percy), HMSO, 1945.

20 1945 XIV *Scientific Manpower* (Sir Alan Barlow), Cmnd. 6824.

21 *EDP*, 29 March 1946. This was just before the Barlow Report.

22 Michael Shattock, *Making a University: Celebration of Warwick's First Twenty-Five Years* (Warwick, 1991).

23 *EDP*, 15 August 1946.

24 J.W. Beeson and W.O. Bell, "Proposal for University College in Norwich", 6 December 1946 (GTP). Lady Ralphs told me that her husband, Dr Lincoln Ralphs, was chiefly responsible for this document.

25 *Sunday Times*, 20 October 1946.

26 Memorandum, Lincoln Ralphs to W.O. Bell, 29 April 1947 (LRP).

27 Memorandum, "University College", n.d. 1947. Possibly a document presented to the UGC at the 14 May 1947 meeting.

28 The Norwich deputation consisted of Alderman F. C. Jex, Alderman Sam Peel, Percy Jewson, the Directors of Education for Norfolk and East Suffolk, and the Town Clerk of Norwich.

29 PRO, UGC 2/27 paper 7, October 1946, "Observations of the UGC on Matters arising from the Barlow Report".

30 Ibid., paper 3 January 1946.

31 Proposed University College for Norwich. Interview with the Chairman of the UGC, 14 May 1947, in GTP and UGC 7/212.

32 PRO, UGC 7/212, "Proposed Institution of Norwich University College", paper, September 1955.

33 PRO, UGC 7/212, copy of Paton's question and letter, H.A. de Montmorency to E. Hale, 1 August 1946.

34 PRO, UGC 7/212, various letters between Sir Will Spens and Sir Walter Moberly, 20 June, 14 November, 27 November, 29 November 1947, and the final letter, Spens to Bernard Storey, 12 March 1948.

35 Notes by the Town Clerk on an interview with representatives of the University College Hull, 10 October 1947, GTP.

36 Letter, Bernard Storey to W.O. Bell, 15 October 1947, about a meeting 22 October.

37 Gordon Tilsley, "Personal Reminiscence" (PR).

38 Sir Arthur South, interviewed 20 April 1995.

39 *Fifteen to Eighteen: Report of the Central Advisory Council for Education* (Sir Geoffrey Crowther), 1959, pp. 226-27.

40 *The Flow into Employment of Scientists, Engineers and Technologists* (Sir Michael Swann), Cmnd 3760, 1968, p. 45.

41 *The Age Group Bulge and its Possible Effects on University Policy*, Home Universities Conference, 1955.

42 *Higher Education* (Lord Robbins), Cmnd. 2154 (1963), p. 260.

43 *AUT Report on Policy for University Expansion*, May 1954, p. 9.

44 UGC, *University Development, 1952-1957*, Cmnd. 534, September 1958.

45 *Workers Educational Association, Norfolk Federation: Some Problems of a New University. Report of a Study Group*, July 1959.

46 W.G.V. Balchin, "Universities in Great Britain: A Geographical Conspectus", n.d. but 1959, typescript.

47 Typescript memorandum FBI to the UGC, "University Expansion and the New Universities", December 1959.

48 *EDP*, 18 October 1978. Obituary of Sir Lincoln Ralphs and conversations with Lady Ralphs.

49 *EDP*, 17 April 1958.

50 Sir Arthur South, 20 April 1995.

51 Mrs Valerie Guttsman, 12 June 1995.

52 *EDP*, 18 April 1958.

53 *EDP*, 21 April 1958.

54 *EDP*, 4, 10, 11 June 1958.

55 *EDP*, 5 June 1958, and letter to Lincoln Ralphs 4 June 1958.

56 Letter, Sam Peel to Sir Arthur South, 7 June 1958, LRP.

57 Lecture given at UEA by Sir Lincoln Ralphs, 22 January 1974. Text in LRP.

58 *EEN*, 27 April 1978.

59 Letter, T. C. Eaton to Lincoln Ralphs, 4 June 1958, (LRP), and to *EDP*, 5 June 1958. The address presenting T. C. Eaton for the honorary degree of M.A. at the Congregation, 4 July 1995, provides background but was unaware of his role in the 1958 movement.

60 *EDP*, 11 June 1958.

61 *EDP*, 12 June 1958.

62 *EDP*, 30 June 1958.

63 *The Times*, 30 June 1958.

64 *EEN*, 30 April 1970.

65 "University for Norwich", 8 July 1958. An account of the Purdy lunch, LRP. Sir Arthur had no recollection of this lunch or record in his papers. This account was in Ralphs' papers.

66 Note by the Town Clerk on the proposed University College at Brighton, 8 July 1958. Sir Arthur South's Papers (ASP).

67 Letter, Andrew Ryrie to Bernard Storey, 9 July 1958, GTP.

68 Memorandum on the meeting of Andrew Ryrie with Sir Keith Murray at UGC, 16 July 1958. Sir Keith Murray's own memorandum, 16 July 1958, PRO, UGC 7/212.

69 *EDP*, 10, 11 July 1958.

70 Letter, Raymond Fox to Lincoln Ralphs, 2 July 1958. LRP and Letter, Lincoln Ralphs to F.B. Boyce, 25 October 1958.

71 Address at UEA, 22 January 1974, LRP.

72 Letter, R. Q. Gurney to Lincoln Ralphs 11 September 1958, LRP. Richard Quintin Gurney b. 1914 was the son of Quintin Edward Gurney, 1883-1968, both landowners and bankers in the city and county. *Burkes Landed Gentry*, 18th edn, i, pp. 344-45.

73 Letter, Lincoln Ralphs to R. Q. Gurney 15 September 1958, LRP.

74 Letter, Andrew Ryrie to Lincoln Ralphs September 1958, LRP.

75 University for Norwich. Notes of a meeting 8 October 1958. (Copies in ASP, GTP).

76 *EDP*, 29 April 1958.

77 Tilsley, PR p. 13.

78 Letter, Gordon Tilsley to Arthur South 23 October 1958 and brief, "Proposed University in Norwich", ASP.

79 Gordon Tilsley PR pp. 18-19. Arthur South mistakenly thought that this meeting was an immediate consequence of the Purdy's lunch in April (*EEN*, 30 April 1970) but it followed the October meeting. Since Sir Arthur chaired both this is understandable.

Tilsley was unsure whether Ryrie was present at the meeting. South was sure that he was.

80   Gordon Tilsley, PR, pp. 20, 25.

81   Lord Mackintosh of Halifax, *By Faith and Work* (London, 1966), ed. A. A. Thomson.

82   Letter, Gordon Tilsley to Lincoln Ralphs 30 October 1958, LRP and letters between Lincoln Ralphs and Lady Fermoy 21, 30 December 1958, LRP.

83   Letter, Bernard Storey to Arthur South 25 November 1958, ASP.

84   Letter, F. B. Boyce to Lincoln Ralphs 4 November 1958, LRP.

85   Letter, D. E. Howell Jones to Lincoln Ralphs 17 June 1958 urging Ralphs to "jog Mr Gooch's elbow", LRP

86   Letters between F. P. Boyce and Lincoln Ralphs, 23, 25 October 1958, LRP.

87   Letters, Lincoln Ralphs to F. B. Boyce, 7 November 1958, Boyce to Ralphs 11 November 1958, and Ralphs to Tilsley 23 January 1959.

88   Letter, Lincoln Ralphs to Gordon Tilsley, 16 June 1959.

89   Gordon Tilsley, "The Prospects for the Establishment of a University of Norwich", 28 January 1959.

90   Proposed University of Norwich. First meeting of the Promotion Committee, 2 February 1959.

91   Tilsley, PR p. 24.

92   Steering Sub-Committee, 10 February 1959.

93   Letters, Denis Buxton to Gordon Tilsley, 5 January 1959 and to Lincoln Ralphs, 6 January 1959. Letter, Buxton to Sir Keith Murray 23 November 1958, PRO, UGC 7/212.

94   Notes of discussions at the office of the University Grants Committee, 20 February 1959, and UGC Memorandum, 23 February 1959. Possible University in Norwich, PRO, UGC 7/212.

95   Letter, Henry Maddick to Lincoln Ralphs 27 January 1959 and letters between them 31 December 1958, 2, 7, January 1959 LRP, and Tilsley PR, p. 30.

96   1 old penny = 0.41 new pence.

97   Letters, Ryrie to Tilsley and South, 12 March 1959.

98   Report of the Steering Committee, 11 March 1959.

99   Letter, R. V. Nash (Clerk of North Walsham Urban District Council) to Ralphs and Tilsley, 11 February 1959, LRP.

100 Report to the Education General Purposes Committee, 1 May 1959. Proposed University of Norwich.

101 Annual contributions made by Local Education Authorities, n.d. 1959/60, GTP

102 Letter, Gordon Tilsley to Sir Cecil Syers, the Secretary of the UGC, 11 May 1959.

103 Report of Education Committee to the Council with respect to the proposed University of Norwich, 27 May 1959, and comment of the Treasurer A. J. Barnard.

104 Submission to the UGC, November 1959, p. 8 and Tilsley, PR, p. 30.

105 Letter, Boyce to Ralphs, 23 December 1959.

106 Letters between Ralphs and Thomson, 15, 16 June 1959, LRP. Thomson told Ralphs that Herbert Butterfield, Master of Peterhouse and Regius Professor of Modern History was also "*very* favourably disposed" to a University in Norwich.

107 Tilsley, PR, pp. 51-53.

108 Letter, Tilsley to Lord Mackintosh , 23 October 1959.

109 Letter, Ryrie to Tilsley to July 1959, ASP, suggesting that "these people could now be formed into a Committee with Keith Murray's approval".

110 Summary of matters dealt with in a talk by Mr W. G. Stone, 6 July 1959.

111 Report by the Town Clerk . . . relating to the establishment of a Charitable Trust 4 February 1960. Andrew Ryrie seems to have suggested a trust as early as September 1958.

112 Letter, Murray to Hale, 17 June 1958, PRO, UGC 7/212.

113 Memorandum, Sir Keith Murray, 16 July 1958, PRO, UGC 7/212.

114 PRO, UGC, 1/7 Minute, 16 July 1959. UGC 2/57, University Expansion post 1963. Memorandum, November 1959. UGC 2/60, "New University Institutions", March 1960, for this change of policy.

115 Executive Committee, 4 August 1959.

116 Tilsley, PR, p. 47. Unfortunately a file of letters discussing the name is no longer in Gordon Tilsley's papers.

117 *Nautical Magazine*, February 1972, is a splendid example, describing the Head Porter of UEA remonstrating with his students at *Essex!* Senate Minute, 16 June 1971, debated changing the name for this reason.

118 Sir John Wolfenden, *Turning Points* (London, 1976), p. 153.

119 Letter, Lord Cranbrook to Lord Mackintosh, n.d. November 1960.

120 Notes of a visit to Nottingham University, 10-11 November 1959, GTP.

121 Submission to the University Grants Committee for the Establishment of a University of East Anglia, Norwich, November 1959.

122 Interview with the Sub-Committee of the UGC, 16 December 1959.

123 Typescript of Lord Mackintosh's speech to UGC, 15 December 1959.

124 Gordon Tilsley, note on the availability of lodgings, 31 December 1959 and letter, Tilsley to Sir Cecil Syers 22 January 1960.

125 Mackintosh, *By Faith and Work*, p. 252.

126 Letter, UGC to Gordon Tilsley, 19 April 1960. Mackintosh had actually been told earlier in a letter of 8 April for which he thanked Murray "with great joy", 12 April 1960, PRO, UGC 7/212.

127 Gordon Tilsley, "Founder's Green in the Memory", in David Baker and Christopher Smith, *Studies for Elizabeth Fudakowska* (Norwich, 1994) p. 15.

128 Letter, Gordon Tilsley to Lord Mackintosh, 20 April 1960.

129 Letter, Lord Mancroft to Lord Mackintosh, 22 April 1960. PRO, UGC 1/8, minute, 16 June 1960, agreed to drop the term "University College" for Norwich and Brighton.

130 Tilsley, PR, p. 66.

131 Press Release. Announcement of the Rt Hon. Viscount Mackintosh of Halifax, 20 April 1960. He was punctilious in using the term "University College".

Notes to Chapter 2: Laying the Foundations

1 Petition of the Promotion Committee of the University of East Anglia to the Queen's Most Excellent Majesty, 9 May 1963.

2 Letters, Sir Roy Harrod to Gordon Tilsley, 17 December 1959, 23 April 1960. Letter, Tilsley to the AAC, 27 April 1960.

3 Letter, W. J. H. Sprott to Gordon Tilsley 14 August 1960.

4 Letter, Bishop Launcelot Fleming to Gordon Tilsley, 3 September 1960.

5 Letter, Charles Wilson to Sir Solly Zuckerman, 23 November 1960. Papers of Sir Solly Zuckerman (SZP).

6　*EDP*, 1 December 1960.

7　Letter, Gordon Tilsley to Lord Mackintosh, 7 December 1960.

8　APB, notes of discussion with Professor Waddington, 4 January 1961, Professor Jack Dainty of UEA, who knew Waddington in Edinburgh, says that "Wadd's" style there was quite informal and not at all autocratic.

9　APB, notes on discussion with Dr J. F. Lockwood, 12 January 1961.

10　Waddington's age even began to concern Zuckerman. In Zuckerman's APB papers there is an interesting scrap n.d. but 1960 where Zuckerman ringed around Waddington's age fifty-five and began to doodle fancifully with the figures as if reflecting on them.

11　Letter, Sir Roy Harrod to Lord Mackintosh 18 January 1961.

12　Notes of a preliminary meeting of representatives of the Executive Committee to meet the APB.

13　Verbatim notes taken by Gordon Tilsley.

14　Sir Arthur South told me this, 20 April 1995.

15　Reminiscence of R.Q. Gurney to Frank Thistlethwaite, n.d. but late 1970s. Gurney's repeated misspelling of Sir Solly Zuckerman's name (which was a famous one) may be careless ignorance or possibly was a lingering resentment.

16　Verbatim notes taken by Gordon Tilsley. Also letter, Wallace Morfey to Frank Thistlethwaite, 3 December 1986, recalled the meeting.

17　Letter, Sir Solly Zuckerman to E. T. Williams, 30 January 1961.

18　Letter, Sir Solly Zuckerman to Charles Wilson and other members of the APB, 30 January 1961.

19　Letter, Launcelot Fleming to Gordon Tilsley, 3 February 1961.

20　Executive Committee, 31 January 1961.

21　APB, 9 February 1961.

22　Letter, Sir Keith Murray to Mackintosh, 6 February 1961.

23　Air letter, Mackintosh to Gordon Tilsley, 3 March 1961.

24　APB, 27 February 1961.

25　Letter, Charles Wilson to Gordon Tilsley, 2 May 1961.

26　*EDP*, 3 May 1961.

27　Letter, Gordon Tilsley to Frank Thistlethwaite, 21 August 1989, recounting this. I have not seen Murray's letter, which must be subsequent to that of 6 February 1961.

28　Letter, Lincoln Ralphs to Percy Lord, Chief Education Officer of Lancashire, 12 February 1962, LRP.

29　PRO, UGC 9/2/2. Letter, E.T. Williams to Sir Keith Murray, 24 May 1961.

30　Letter, Lincoln Ralphs to Percy Lord, 12 February 1962.

31　Letter, C. H. Waddington to Charles Wilson, 29 May 1961.

32　Letter, Charles Wilson to Lord Mackintosh, 30 May 1961.

33　Letter, C. H. Waddington to Lord Mackintosh, 4 June 1961, and Memorandum, "Reasons against my Going to Norwich".

34　Sir Charles Wilson, interviewed 5 June 1995, and Frank Thistlethwaite, tape 2.

35　Gordon Tilsley, notes on interviews, 27 July 1961, GTP. Also transcript of E. T. Williams notes in FTP.

36　Gordon Tilsley, "Founder's Green in the Memory", p. 16.

37　Letter, Gordon Tilsley to Lord Mackintosh, 29 July 1961. Frank Thistlethwaite was aged forty-six on his appointment.

38　Frank Thistlethwaite, curriculum vitae in FTP. *EEN*, 25 August 1961. Frank

Thistlethwaite, *A Lancashire Family Inheritance* (Cambridge, 1996), *Our War 1938-45* (Cambridge, 1997) and *Cambridge Years* (Cambridge, 1999) for his earlier pre-UEA career.

39 Frank Thistlethwaite, *Origins, A Personal Reminiscence of UEA's Foundation* (Cambridge, 2000), pp. 2-4, "How I was Appointed Vice-Chancellor".

40 Letter, Eric James to Frank Thistlethwaite, 27 July 1961, and Frank Thistlethwaite draft reply n.d. and James to Thistlethwaite, 12 September 1961. Personal correspondence, 1948-61.

41 File, "Jane Hosford Thistlethwaite" FTP, cabinet 1.

42 Letter, Lord Mackintosh to Frank Thistlethwaite, n.d. 1961. Terms of appointment and File "VC Personal Requirements", FT cabinet 1.

43 Thistlethwaite, *Origins*, pp. 50-51. Owen Chadwick, *Victorian Miniature* (London, 1960) is an account of a clergyman, William Wayte Andrew, who lived in Wood Hall between 1841 and 1887. The author was a future Chancellor of UEA.

44 Letter, Frank Thistlethwaite to Lincoln Ralphs, 22 August 1961, LRP.

45 Letter, Bernard Waley Cohen to Thistlethwaite, 22 September 1961. He meant "ante".

46 Letter, W.G. Munnings to Lincoln Ralphs, 11 July 1958.

47 Letter, Rev. C. G. Deeks to Lincoln Ralphs, 9 December 1958.

48 Letter, P. Reeves to Lincoln Ralphs, 16 January 1959.

49 Letter, Lincoln Ralphs to the editor, *EDP*, 20 January 1959.

50 Steering Committee, 30 July 1959.

51 Gordon Tilsley, note for file, 13 August 1959.

52 Finance Committee, 25, 30 November 1959.

53 List of principal industrial concerns, 15 December 1959.

54 Letter, Sir James Duff to Mary Duff, 28 September 1959, GTP.

55 Letter, Lincoln Ralphs to Lord Mackintosh, 10 February 1960, LPP.

56 Gordon Tilsley, "Use of Professional Services for Launching Appeals", 3 February 1960.

57 Memorandum by Dr M. A. Hooker on the work of John F. Rich & Co. Ltd, 26 April 1960.

58 Note of business at Raveningham Hall, 29 July 1960. Note of a meeting at the Dorchester Hotel, London, 3 November 1960.

59 *The Times*, 23 November 1960.

60 Letter, W. G. Stone (of Brighton) to Gordon Tilsley, 5 May 1960.

61 *UEA Bulletin*, December 1973, "Timothy James Alan Colman".

62 Appeal Committee, 6 November 1961.

63 Appeal Committee, 3 January 1962.

64 Letter, Landrum R. Bolling, President of Earlham College, 23 January 1960, LRP.

65 Appeal Committee, 18 December 1961.

66 Letter, Gordon Tilsley to T.J.A. Colman, 27 January 1962.

67 Letter, Herbert Dickerson to Michael Bulman, 12 February 1962.

68 Letter, T. J. A. Colman to Michael Bulman, 21 February 1962.

69 B. A. Holderness, *British Agriculture since 1945* (Manchester, 1985), pp. 49, 96-97, 104-18, 167.

70 Letter, T. J. A. Colman to Viscount Althorp, 4 January 1962.

71 Appeal Committee, 2 April 1962.

72 *EDP*, 28 April 1958.
73 Appeal Committee, 14 November 1961.
74 Appeal Committee, 9 March 1962.
75 Appeal Committee, 18 December 1961.
76 Appeal Committee, 15 January 1962.
77 Report of Osborne Peacock, 17 January 1962. They were also the advertising agents for John Mackintosh and Sons Ltd.
78 Appeal Committee, 5 February 1962.
79 *East Anglian Daily Times*, 27 March 1962.
80 Appeal Committee, 2 April 1962.
81 *Ipswich Evening Star*, 2 May 1962.
82 Appeal Committee, 18 December 1961.
83 Appeal Committee, 30 April 1962.
84 Letter, J. W. Beeson, Director of Education for Norwich, to Headmasters in Norwich, 23 March 1962.
85 *EDP*, 16 March 1962.
86 Letter, Timothy Colman to Lord Mackintosh, 22 March 1962.
87 *EDP*, 17 May 1962.
88 Lord Mackintosh's speeches at the press conference at Norwich City Hall and the evening reception at Norwich Castle, 17 May 1962. Lord Mackintosh's papers in the possession of Lady Mackintosh of Halifax. Photocopies in University Archives.
89 *University of East Anglia: The Background Story* and *What Kind of University for East Anglia?* The second takes account of the appointment of Denys Lasdun as architect.
90 Letter, Frank Thistlethwaite to Lord Mackintosh, 23 January 1962 recounting an interview with Murray.
91 Group Captain Montgomery, interviewed 2 March 1995. Letter, Montgomery to Timothy Colman, 9 January 1995.
92 *EDP*, 28 April 1995, Sir Arthur South interviewed by Colin Chinnery.
93 Lord Mackintosh's annotated typescripts of speeches, 4 November 1960, 1 March 1962, 9 March 1962, 1 May 1962, 17 May 1962, 26 April 1963, 18 April 1964, 12 November 1964, by courtesy of Lady Mackintosh of Halifax.
94 Lord Mackintosh, *By Faith and Work*, p. 256. The challenge was made at the City Hall Press Conference, 17 May 1962.
95 Particulars of donations promised up to 12 June 1962.
96 Appeal Committee, 7 June 1962.
97 Group Captain Montgomery remembered visiting Lord Althorp ("very clued up") on North-West Norfolk appeal matters and meeting Lady Diana as a toddler at this time, as does Frank Thistlethwaite. Lady Fermoy was Lady Diana's grandmother.
98 *East Anglian Daily Times* and *EEN*, 30 October 1962.
99 Second Subscription List, 30 October 1962.
100 *EDP*, 1 January 1963. G.B. Wilson, "Recollections of the First Lord Mackintosh", 1990. G.B. Wilson worked for Rowntree Mackintosh in Norwich for twenty-five years.
101 Mackintosh, *By Faith and Work* p. 260.
102 Mackintosh, *By Faith and Work* p. 267.
103 *Ipswich Daily Star*, 29 October 1962.
104 Third Subscription list, 10 May 1963.
105 Fifth Subscription list, 18 July 1963.
106 Michael Shattock, *Making a University* (Warwick, 1991).

107 Executive Committee, 15 July 1963. Over £1,000,000, out of £1,300,000, had been raised in East Anglia.

108 *East Anglian Daily Times,* 3 October 1963.

109 *EEN,* 30 November 1970.

110 *EDP,* 17 November 1973.

111 *UEA:The Silver Years,* UEA video, 1988.

112 *EEN,* 5 July 1980.

113 *Annual Reports of the Vice-Chancellor,* 1962-63 and 1963-64, has lists of these donations. Also file on "The UEA Collection of Plate" in FTP papers.

114 Council Minutes, 10 October 1966. The last reference to the Appeal in the University accounts lists it as £1,140,915 on 31 July 1969, which is clearly a misprint for £1,400,000 plus.

115 Minutes of a meeting of the Academic Sub-Committee, 8 August 1959.

116 Letter, Russell Taylor to the Registrar of MIT, 6 December 1958, and to Arthur South, 4 December 1958 ASP.

117 Note of a discussion with Mr J. F. Warren, 19 August 1959, GTP.

118 Note of a discussion with Mr F. Rayns, 20 August 1959, GTP.

119 Note of a discussion with Mr Ricketts, Secretary of RIBA, 25 August 1959.

120 Papers of Sir John Cockcroft, Churchill College Cambridge Archive Centre. 17/1 Memorandum to the Committee on Higher Education, 3 July 1961 (Robbins), and Evidence, 13 October, 17 November 1961.

121 Academic Advisory Committee, 6 June 1960.

122 Academic Advisory Committee, Statement of Representations, 11 September 1961.

123 Dr Corran was a distinguished food scientist who (among other things) created the modern Robinsons Barley water drinks for Colman's. He kept in close touch with Alan Katritzky and the Chemistry Department of UEA.

124 Letter, Rev. S. Myers to Lincoln Ralphs, 7 December 1960, enclosing resolutions concerning a Department of Theology. Letter, Bishop Fleming to Ralphs, 27 February 1960, and Notes on a Department of Divinity, 11 October 1960, by Launcelot Fleming. In LRP.

125 APB, 27 July 1960. Mysteriously the UGC started nominating an APB for Norwich over a month before notifying anybody in Norwich that consent for the new university had been given. UGC , 1/8 3 March 1960.

126 APB, Noel Annan, General Character of Norwich University, August 1960.

127 APB, Noel Annan, Proposed Scheme for Arts Studies at the University of East Anglia, 22 November 1960.

128 Letter, Sir Maurice Bowra to Frank Thistlethwaite, 12 September 1961. Interestingly Annan's plan of a sociology degree would have been eight sociology plus five other subjects.

129 Memorandum, 20 September 1960.

130 APB, 27/8 September 1960.

131 APB, A Department of Education for the University of East Anglia, 19 September 1960.

132 APB, 27/8 September 1960.

133 APB, 25 October 1960.

134 APB, 22 November 1960.

135 So thought Gordon Tilsley, who travelled back with him on the train from London to Norwich. Lady Ralphs said that Sir Lincoln was never crestfallen by temporary setbacks. His resilience in seeing the movement through to this stage was proof of this.

136 Michael Sanderson, "French, Languages and the Early Planning of UEA", in C. N. Smith, *Essays for Janine Dakyns and Michael Parkinson* (Norwich, 1996).

137 APB, 22 November 1960.

138 APB, Sir Christopher Ingold, "First Thoughts on a Plan for a Faculty of Science", 12 September 1960.

139 Sir Solly Zuckerman, *Monkeys, Men and Missiles: An Autobiography 1946-88* (London, 1988), pp. 124-27.

140 Letter, Sir Solly Zuckerman to Sir Christopher Ingold, 24 September 1960, SZP.

141 Sir Solly Zuckerman, "Environmental Sciences", 25 October 1960.

142 Recommendations of the Conference on the Need for Expansion in Marine Sciences. Royal Society, 11 November 1960.

143 Zuckerman, *Monkeys, Men and Missiles*, pp. 451-52.

144 Letter, Ralphs to S. W. Wooldridge, 29 October 1962, LRP.

145 Letters between Lincoln Ralphs and Dr Alice Garnett, 24, 25 January 1961, and 29 June 1965, LRP.

146 Letter, E.M. Yates to Lincoln Ralphs, 3 August 1965, LRP.

147 APB, 27/8 September 1960.

148 Lord Annan, "British Higher Education 1960-80: A Personal Retrospect", *Minerva* Vol.20 No.1 (Spring/Summer 1982).

149 APB, Zuckerman, "The Teaching of Biology", 25 October 1960.

150 APB, 25 October 1960.

151 APB, Noel Annan, "The Teaching of Biology", October 1960.

152 Letter, Sir Solly Zuckerman to Sir Christopher Ingold, 20 December 1961, SZP.

153 Note of a meeting between Frank Thistlethwaite and Thomas Bennet Clark at the Athenaeum Club, 20 December 1961.

154 Wolfenden, *Turning Points*, p. 158. Allocation of Quinquennial Grant, 1967-72. Memorandum of General Guidance Sections, 21-23 November 1967.

155 APB, 27/8 September 1960.

156 APB, Skeleton of Degree Courses in Humanities and Social Sciences, 20 September 1961.

157 Noel Annan, "Higher Education" in Bernard Crick, ed., *Essays on Reform, 1967: A Centenary Tribute* (Oxford, 1967), p. 32.

158 *The Years of Crisis*, Report of the Labour Party's Study Group on Higher Education (1962) (Lord Taylor). *The Structure of Higher Education*, Fabian Tract, 334 (1961).

159 Frank Thistlethwaite, Notes for a speech to the Executive Committee, n.d. but 1961.

160 APB, Report to the UGC, October 1961.

161 Letter, Sir Keith Murray to Lord Mackintosh, 24 October 1961.

162 Executive Committee, 16 January 1961.

163 Confidential Report of a visit by Sir Roy Harrod to University College of North Staffordshire, 12/13 March 1960.

164 Confidential Note by Sir George Barnes to Sir Roy Harrod, 20 June 1960.

165 APB, 12 December 1960 on constitutional discussions.

166 APB, 20 September 1961.

167 APB, Report to UGC September/October 1961.

168 Letter, Murray to Lord Mackintosh, 24 October 1961.

169 Frank Thistlethwaite, The Structure of Academic Government, n.d. but early 1962.

170 Petition of the Promotion Committee of the University of East Anglia, 9 May 1963.

171 Thistlethwaite, *Origins*, pp. 67-68.

172 Charter of the University of East Anglia. Text, 27 November 1963.
173 Thistlethwaite, *Origins*, p. 77.
174 *EDP*, 27 February 1964.
175 Thistlethwaite, *Origins*, pp. 78-79.
176 *EDP*, 9 April 1964.
177 *Suffolk Mercury*, 28 February 1964.
178 *EDP*, 27 February 1965.
179 *EEN*, 29 February 1964.
180 *Norfolk News*, 9 October 1964.
181 Typescript Reports of the Norwich Junior Chamber of Commerce, 1962/63-1964/65, kindly made available by Mr R.C. Frostick, conversation with Mr Frostick, 17 February 2000.
182 Letter, Bruce Henderson-Gray to Lord Mackintosh, 21 December 1959.
183 "Universities, Genuine Urban or Fake Suburban?", *Architects' Journal*, 19 May 1960.
184 *Higher Education*, p. 163.
185 Academic Advisory Sub-Committee, 8 August 1960.
186 There is a good first-hand account of this in Tilsley, PR, pp. 80-87.
187 Memorandum, "Proposed Norwich University", 1 August 1958, ASP.
188 Letter, Andrew Ryrie to Gordon Tilsley, 12 March 1959.
189 Letter, Gordon Tilsley to Arthur South, 22 April 1959.
190 Letter, H. C. Rowley to Alderman H. Frazer, 29 December 1958, ASP.
191 *EDP*, 8 and 19 August 1959.
192 Local Enquiry into an Outline Application . . . to Use 165 Acres of Land at Earlham for the Erection of the University of East Anglia, n.d. but late 1960, GTP.
193 Academic Advisory Sub-Committee, 8 August 1960.
194 Tilsley, PR, pp. 41-44, on the choice of Earlham.
195 Letter, Gordon Tilsley to Lord Mackintosh, 13 April 1960.
196 Letter, S. G. G. Wilkinson (for Minister of Housing and Local Government) to Gordon Tilsley, 16 May 1961.
197 R. G. Jobling, "The Location and Siting of a New university", *Universities Quarterly*, Spring 1970. Ray Jobling was a former lecturer at UEA.
198 Percy Lubbock, *Earlham* (London, 1922; 1963 edn), pp. 12-13. Alan Carter, "Earlham: the Hall in the Park", *Ziggurat*, 2, June 1986. Geoffrey Goreham, "Earlham Hall" *EEN*, 8 October 1983.
199 Thistlethwaite, *Founding*, p. 11.
200 FT, Cabinet 3. "Lord Mackintosh's Party", 11 December 1964.
201 Zuckerman, *Monkeys, Men and Missiles*, pp. 451-52.
202 Council Minute, 6 November 1967.

Notes to Chapter 3: What and How to Teach

1 Letter, Frank Thistlethwaite to Ian Watt, 26 October 1961.
2 Letter, Sir Keith Murray to Frank Thistlethwaite, 28 September 1963.
3 Frank Thistlethwaite, *Origins: A Personal Reminiscence of UEA's Foundation* (2000), p. 59.
4 Ian Watt, "The Idea of an English School: English at Norwich" *Critical Survey*, Autumn 1962. Watt and Thistlethwaite had been successively undergraduate friends,

then pupil and teacher, then Fellows at St John's College, Cambridge, in the 1930s and 1940s. Frank Thistlethwaite, *Cambridge Years* (Cambridge, 1999), p. 4.

5 Ian Watt, "The Seminar", *Universities Quarterly*, 18, September 1964.

6 *Report of the Committee on University Teaching Methods* (Sir Edward Hale), UGC, HMSO (1964), pp. 74-76.

7 "Teaching Methods", *UEA Bulletin*, 22 November 1965.

8 FT, interviewed by James McFarlane, audio tape 3, comments by McFarlane.

9 "Teaching Methods", UEA Bulletin, 22 November 1965.

10 Malcolm Bradbury, *The History Man* (London, 1975), pp. 127-28.

11 Roy Emerson, An Investigation of Student Opinions on Coursework Arrangements, Senate Minute, 19 June 1968.

12 R.B. Woodings, "The Seminar is the Message", *UEA Bulletin*, February 1969.

13 Senate Minute, 23 November 1966; Council Minute, 6 November 1967; Senate Minute, 10 May 1972.

14 Report of the Working Party on Staff Student Ratios, Senate Minute, 10 March 1971.

15 Thistlethwaite, *Origins*, p. 60.

16 Andor Gomme, "Publicity or Promise: The New Universities", *Delta*, 34, Autumn 1964.

17 Hale, *Report on University Teaching Methods*, p. 92.

18 Emerson, Investigation of Student Opinions on Coursework Arrangements, Senate Minute, 19 June 1968.

19 FT, tape 1.

20 FT, in Ross p. 57 .

21 FT, tape 3.

22 Minutes of the Deans in Arts Committee, 1962-63, 31 October, 20 November 1962. This committee met at FT's home in Cambridge.

23 Stuart Maclure, "The University of East Anglia", *The Listener*, 11 November 1965. Maclure was the editor of the *Times Educational Supplement*.

24 Roger Fowler, "Confessions of a Disappointed Idealist", *UEA Bulletin*, October 1968.

25 FT, tape 3 and in Ross p. 60.

26 Albert Sloman, *A University in the Making* (London, 1964).

27 Working Party on Proposals for Curricula and Examinations in Sixth Forms, Senate Minute, 10 May 1970.

28 Letter, S.W.C. Holland to D. E. Bennett (SCUE), 7 March 1972, in Senate Minute, 10 May 1972.

29 Senate Minute, 1 February 1967, the case of Thomas Forster.

30 Michael Sanderson, "The School of English Studies", *UEA Bulletin*, 29 May 1967.

31 Christopher Wrigley, MS Memoirs, pp. 23-38.

32 Senate Minute, 22 June 1966.

33 Thistlethwaite, *Origins*, p. 97.

34 Senate Minute, 26 October 1966.

35 FT, tape 6.

36 A. Hassell Smith, "The Centre of East Anglian Studies", *UEA Bulletin*, February 1969.

37 *EDP*, 9 June 1971.

38 *UEA Early Years*, AVC, tape 176.

39 Angus Wilson, *The Old Men at the Zoo* (1961), *Late Call* (1964), *No Laughing Matter* (1967).

40 Angus Wilson interviewed by Michael Sanderson, *UEA Bulletin*, 29 May 1967.

Margaret Drabble, *Angus Wilson: A Biography* (London, 1995).

41 "Creative Writing Twenty-Five Years Years On", Malcolm Bradbury interviewed by Kate Bull, *Ziggurat*, 17, Autumn/Winter 1995. Ian McEwan, "Cocker at the Theatre", *The Incredible Magazine*, 28 May 1971. A sharply moralistic attack on pornography in the theatre is an early example of his UEA work.

42 Michael Beloff, *The Plateglass Universities*, pp. 107-8.

43 *Annual Report of the Vice-Chancellor*, 1967-68, p. 40.

44 Thistlethwaite, *Origins* pp. 37-39.

45 Michael Sanderson, "French, Language and the Early Planning of UEA, 1960-66", in C. N. Smith ed., *Essays for Michael Parkinson and Janine Dakyns* (Norwich, 1995). There is a sympathetic portrait of Parkinson, Dakyns and their EUR work in W.G. Sebald *The Rings of Saturn* (London, 1998), pp. 6-9.

46 *Annual Report of the Vice-Chancellor*, 1963-64, p. 11.

47 *Annual Report of the Vice-Chancellor*, 1967-68, p. 48.

48 Anon., "UEA Goes to Russia", *UEA Bulletin*, 21 November 1966, for an account of such a tour.

49 FT, tape 2.

50 Thistlethwaite, *Origins*, pp. 41-43.

51 Memorandum, FT to Roy Emerson, 3 February 1975.

52 *East Anglian Daily Times*, 9 July 1965. R. Scase, "The Suffolk Sociology Project", *UEA Bulletin*, 7 March 1966.

53 *EDP*, 8 July 1969.

54 *EEN*, 11 August 1970.

55 Thistlethwaite, *Origins*, pp. 89-92.

56 Senate Minute, 9 March 1966.

57 Mike Faber, "The Overseas Development Group", *UEA Bulletin*, June 1970.

58 Letter, Frank Thistlethwaite to Derek Burke, 12 February 1990.

59 Letter, Frank Thistlethwaite to Benjamin Britten, 5 November 1963, BBP. I am indebted to Miss Rosamund Strode for her transcriptions from the Benjamin Britten Papers in the Britten Pears Library.

60 Humphrey Carpenter, *Benjamin Britten: A Biography* (London, 1992).

61 Letter, Imogen Holst to Frank Thistlethwaite, 29 May 1964 and reply by FT, 2 June 1964.

62 Memorandum by Philip Ledger, 20 October 1965. Holst's letter was of course sent to Ledger, 14 June 1965.

63 Letter, Frank Thistlethwaite to Benjamin Britten, 21 January 1965.

64 Letter, Benjamin Britten to Frank Thistlethwaite, 6 April 1965, BPP.

65 Peter Aston, in *Broadview*, February 1998.

66 Reference by Benjamin Britten, 14 January 1965.

67 Letter, Benjamin Britten to Frank Thistlethwaite, 6 April 1965, BPP.

68 Tom Roast and Peter Aston, "Music", in Ian Atherton and others, *Norwich Cathedral* (London, 1996).

69 Thistlethwaite, *Origins*, p.86.

70 *EDP*, 1 April 1967.

71 *EDP*, 3 June 1967.

72 Interview with Rosamund Strode, 14 May 1995. Miss Strode accompanied him.

73 Programmes of *Saul* and *War Requiem* kindly provided by Miss P. O. Whitt. I attended both.

74 Letter, Frank Thistlethwaite to Brian Young of the Nuffield Foundation, 5 November 1968. Senate Minute, 11 December 1968.

75 Letter, Philip Ledger to Rosamund Strode, 28 February 1994.

76 Memorandum on Beetham Arthur Leeman Batchelor provided by Rosamund Strode.

77 Arthur Harrison, "The Hesse Students", *Aldeburgh Festival*, 1963.

78 Rosamund Strode, "Founding a Music School at UEA: The Aldeburgh Involvement", 21 May 1994. Tape recording of a talk to the UEA Friends of Music.

79 Thistlethwaite, *Origins*, p. 84

80 Senate Minute, 3 November 1971. A. R. Martindale memorandum on the study term in Venice.

81 Thomas Bennet Clark, "Breaking Down Barriers", *Times Educational Supplement*, 21 September 1962.

82 *The Royal Society Report of the Ad Hoc Biological Research Committee*, November 1961.

83 Letters, T. Bennet Clark to Sir Solly Zuckerman, 29 March, 2 April 1962.

84 Letter, Sir Solly Zuckerman to FT, 3 June 1962.

85 Letter, Bennet Clark to Sir Solly Zuckerman, 8 June 1962.

86 *Sunday Times*, 7 November 1965.

87 T. A. Bennet Clark, "The Future Role of Biology", *Progress*, 3, (1965); Michael Sanderson, "Research in the School of Biological Sciences", *UEA Bulletin*, 24 April 1967.

88 *EDP*, 13 August 1969.

89 *EDP*, 28 June 1965.

90 Memorandum, T. Bennet Clark to FT, 14 June 1967, and sent by Thistlethwaite to Sir Solly Zuckerman.

91 AVC, tape 176.

92 *Report of the Agricultural Research Council for 1961-2*, p. 5.

93 *Committee on the Management and Control of Research and Development* (Zuckerman), HMSO, 1961.

94 Letter, E. G. Cox of ARC to FT, 20 June 1962.

95 Food Research Institute, Interview with Dr Curtis, 1980, AVC tape 71.

96 Michael Sanderson, "The John Innes Institute", *UEA Bulletin*, 3 October 1966.

97 "John Innes Institute", Finance and General Purposes Committee Minute, 24 June 1963.

98 Letter, Frank Thistlethwaite to Solly Zuckerman, 15 February 1966.

99 Senate Minutes, 23 June, 29 September 1965.

100 Paolo Palladino, "Science, Technology and the Economy: Plant Breeding in Great Britain, 1920-1970", *Economic History Review*, 49 (1996).

101 *EDP*, 5 May 1967; *EEN*, 17 August 1967.

102 Senate Minute, 19 May 1965, "The Fisheries Laboratory Lowestoft".

103 FT, tape 1.

104 *EDP*, 9 November 1961.

105 *East Anglian Daily Times*, 30 January 1962.

106 *Thetford and Watton Times*, 18 October 1963, reporting the Dereham Branch of the NFU.

107 *East Anglian Farming World*, 16 January 1964.

108 FT, tape 3.

109 Thistlethwaite, *Origins*, p. 94.

110 J. B. Hutchinson, "Proposals for a Faculty of Field Sciences", 20 January 1962. Hutchinson was Drapers Professor of Agriculture at Cambridge.

111 Letter, Frank Thistlethwaite to Sir Solly Zuckerman, 5 July 1965, SZP.

112 Letter, Frank Thistlethwaite to Sir Solly Zuckerman, 21 March 1987, SZP.

113 *Mandate*, 4 November 1968. "Environmental Sciences", *UEA Bulletin*, March 1968.

114 Thistlethwaite, *Origins*, p. 33. Norman Sheppard, "Recollections of the Formative Years of the School of Chemical Sciences of the University of East Anglia", typescript.

115 Alan Katritzky, "Highlights from Fifty Years of Heterocyclic Chemistry", *Journal of Heterocyclic Chemistry*, 31 (1994), cites this letter and Katritzky's view of Bennet Clark.

116 Suggestions for a School of Chemistry at Norwich, May 1962. Letter, Alan Katritzky to Frank Thistlethwaite, 23 May 1962.

117 Letter, Alan Katritzky to Frank Thistlethwaite, 8 June 1962.

118 Sir John Cockcroft Diaries, 1962, entries for June. Archives of Churchill College, Cambridge.

119 Letter, Sir John Cockcroft to Sir Solly Zuckerman, 13 October 1962.

120 Letter, Sir Christopher Ingold to Frank Thistlethwaite, 21 June 1962.

121 Letter, Frank Thistlethwaite to Sir Solly Zuckerman, 30 July 1962.

122 Letter, Sir Solly Zuckerman to Frank Thistlethwaite, 18 August 1962.

123 Letters, Alan Katritzky to Sir Robert Robinson, 2 August 1962, and Robinson to Katritzky, 7 August 1962.

124 Letter, Alan Katritzky to Frank Thistlethwaite, 16 August 1962.

125 Letter, Alan Katritzky to Sir Robert Robinson, 24 September 1962.

126 Letter, Sir Robert Robinson to Alan Katritzky, 4 October 1962.

127 Draft letter, Alan Katritzky to Frank Thistlethwaite, n.d. but September 1962.

128 Letter, Frank Thistlethwaite to Alan Katritzky, 18 October 1962.

129 FT, tape 1.

130 Interview with Sir Charles Wilson, 5 June 1995.

131 Interview with Alan Katritzky, 7 July 1995.

132 *Chemical and Engineering News*, 30 November 1964.

133 Introduction to the School of Chemical Sciences, Senate Minute, 22 June 1966.

134 Senate Minute, 23 November 1966.

135 Senate Minute, 5 November 1969, Report of the Working Party on Post Graduate Education, table 6.

136 *Annual Report of the Vice-Chancellor*, 1964-65, p. 34.

137 *Annual Report of the Vice-Chancellor*, 1966-67, p. 48.

138 Senate Minute, 28 September 1966.

139 Senate Minute, 29 November 1967.

140 Senate Minute, 7 February 1968.

141 PRO, ED 129/79, Letter, Frank Thistlethwaite to Royal Commission on Medical Education, 2 March 1966 and in Senate Minute, 9 March 1966. Senate Minute, 2 February 1966, a UEA Working Party on Medical Education met on 15 December 1965. Thistlethwaite had conveyed to UGC its "interest in establishing a School of Medicine."

142 *Royal Commission on Medical Education*, 1965-68, Cmnd 3569.

143 Council Minute, 18 December 1967, Proposal for a Medical School.

144 Joint meetings of University Faculty and local doctors, May to December 1969.
145 Report of the Working Party on a School of Molecular Sciences, Senate Minute, 1 February 1967.
146 Report of the Working Party on Psychological Sciences, Senate Minute, 12 May 1971.
147 *Annual Report of the Vice-Chancellor*, 1987-88, p. 6.
148 *British Business Schools, a Report by the Rt Hon. Lord Franks* (British Institute of Management, 1963).
149 Letter, Burke Trend to Sir Solly Zuckerman, 25 September 1964, asking Zuckerman to advise Professor Ross on this, SZP.
150 Senate Minute, 13 March 1968.
151 Thistlethwaite, *Origins*, pp. 29-31. FT, tape 1. Interview with Willi Guttsman, 12 June 1995. Obituary in *The Times*, 28 February 1998. On Elizabeth Fudakowska see Willi Guttsman, "Elizabeth Fudakowska: An Appreciation" in David Baker and Christopher Smith, *Essays for Elizabeth Fudakowska* (Norwich, 1994).
152 Joan Blunt, in *EDP*, 6 November 1964.
153 *Cambridge Daily News*, 4 December 1963. *Daily Telegraph*, 8 February 1964.
154 Report of the UGC Committee on Libraries, June 1967.
155 *EDP*, 26 May 1964, Press Release, "Holkham Books", Council Minute, 29 June 1964.
156 W. G. Guttsman, "Learned Libraries in Germany", *The Times*, 26 March 1965.
157 *EDP*, 23, 26 October 1968.
158 Report of the Librarian, 1970-71, Senate Minute, 3 November 1971.
159 Patricia Hollis, *Jennie Lee* (Oxford, 1997), p. 301.
160 *EEN*, 21 October 1963.
161 *Guardian*, 11 June 1965.
162 Asa Briggs, *The History of Broadcasting in the United Kingdom*, v, *Competition, 1955-1974* (Oxford, 1995), pp. 53, 476-77.
163 Council Minute, 11 October 1965.
164 PRO, UGC/7/925, "University of the Air, Miss Jennie Lee's Working Party".
165 Report of the Working Party on Television in the University March 1966, Council Minute, 6 June 1966.
166 *EEN*, 17 January 1967.
167 The Audio Visual Centre, Senate Minute, 6 November 1968.
168 *EEN*, 12 January 1970.
169 AVC Report, Senate Minute, 10 June 1970.
170 Malcolm Freegard, "The Audio Visual Centre", *UEA Bulletin*, June 1971.

Notes to Chapter 4: A Community of Scholars

1 The Bishop of Norwich, Launcelot Fleming, "Sermon at the Service of Thanksgiving . . . the Life and Work of the University of East Anglia", *Norwich Churchman*, January 1964.
2 *Annual Report of the Vice-Chancellor*, 1961-62, p. 7.
3 Gordon Tilsley, interviewed 27 January 1995.
4 CEAS, audio visual tape 295. BBC material.
5 *EEN*, 21 December 1963.
6 *The Times*, 15 October 1963.
7 Michael Sanderson, *The Missing Stratum: Technical School Education in England, 1900-1960* (London, 1994).

8 Noel Annan, *The Dons* (London, 1999), p. 159. The comment was by Sir Maurice Bowra.

9 Interview with Sir Charles Wilson, who recalled this, 5 June 1995.

10 *EDP*, 6 May 1963.

11 *EDP*, 7 October 1965.

12 *East Anglian Daily Times*, 24 May 1963.

13 *EEN*, October 1963.

14 *Daily Telegraph*, 29 November 1963.

15 Memorandum, Frank Mattison to Frank Thistlethwaite, 1 February 1965.

16 Frank Mattison, "Who Wants to Come to a New University?", *UEA Bulletin*, 17 January 1966.

17 Malcolm Cross and R. G. Jobling, "The English New Universities: A Preliminary Enquiry", *Universities Quarterly*, Spring 1969, p. 177.

18 Mattison, "Who Wants to Come to a New University?".

19 Cross and Jobling, "The English New Universities".

20 Harold Perkin, *New Universities in the United Kingdom* (OECD, 1969), p. 107.

21 Mattison, "Who Wants to Come to a New University?".

22 Mattison, "Who Wants to Come to a New University?".

23 *EDP*, 10 May 1967.

24 Frank Thistlethwaite in a speech at University of Skopje, April 1974.

25 UGC statistics, Senate Minute, 25 October 1967.

26 Senate Minute, 13 January 1971, 14 June 1972.

27 Senate Minute, 16 June 1971.

28 A Tape, University Stories, 1960-71, CEAS.

29 "Origins of Staff and Students", FTP, cabinet 3.

30 *Mandate*, 28 November 1967.

31 Sir Ivor Jennings, "Cambridge Graduates in the University of East Anglia and Elsewhere", *Cambridge Review*, 31 October 1964.

32 Letter, Sir George Barnes to Sir Roy Harrod, n.d. but May 1960.

33 File, "Responses of First Faculty" to a questionnaire from the author.

34 Notes for a speech to the Executive Committee, n.d. but 1961.

35 *The Times*, 25 January 1963.

36 *Mandate*, 34 and 35, May 1969.

37 Frank Thistlethwaite, *Origins: A Personal Reminiscence of UEA's Foundation* (2000), p. 13.

38 Letter, FT to Faculty, 23 October 1963, Personal Correspondence, cabinet 2.

39 Thistlethwaite, *Origins*, p. 13.

40 File, Jane Thistlethwaite. The UEA Women's Club.

41 *The Times*, 8 August 1963.

42 *EDP*, 25 June 1963.

43 *EDP*, 25 June 1963 and interview with Daphne Powlett.

44 Senate Minute, 30 September 1964.

45 Daphne Powlett, on CEAS, video 295.

46 Anthony Sampson, *Anatomy of Britain* (London, 1962), p. 236.

47 *Observer*, 3 May 1964.

48 Annan, *The Dons*, p. 151. Bowra and Dick were part of the social circle of Anne Fleming, wife of Ian Fleming, creator of "James Bond".

49 Thistlethwaite, *Origins*, p. 24.

50 Lincoln Ralphs, "The University and the Churches", LRP script for speech or article, n.d. but about 1960.

51 Christopher Wrigley, "Religion in the University", *UEA Bulletin*, 24 April 1967.

52 Michael Sanderson, "The Chaplains and University Religion", *UEA Bulletin*, 20 February 1967. These were estimates by the chaplains of their adherents. It is intriguing that thirty years later belief in God was actually greater among UEA students (60 per cent) but that in life after death (20 per cent) and the divinity of Christ (17 per cent) much less. *Concrete*, 18 October 1995.

53 FTP, tape 5. Donald Lindsay, *Friends for Life: A Portrait of Launcelot Fleming* (Seaford, 1981).

54 "Proposed Chaplaincy Centre", Council Minute, 8 November 1965, Senate Minute, 9 March 1966.

55 Letter, R. H.Campbell to Frank Thistlethwaite, 2 November 1966, in Senate Minute, 23 November 1966.

56 Senate Minute, 12 January 1967.

57 Senate Minute, 19 June 1968.

58 Senate Minute, 13 May 1970.

59 Frank Thistlethwaite, speech at the opening of the Chaplaincy Centre, 22 January 1972, in FTP, Personal Correspondence.

60 Letter, Rev. Francis Jones (the Presbyterian Chaplain) to Frank Thistlethwaite, 20 March 1969. Senate Minute, 28 May 1969.

61 Frank Thistlethwaite, "Of Doing Different" *Ziggurat*, No 4, May 1987; Adrian Smith, "Written Reminiscences", 7 September 1995; Richard and Margaret Snelling on BBC1, "Look East" 24 November 1999.

62 *Sunday Telegraph*, 25 October 1964.

63 *EEN*, 19 December 1968.

64 *EDP*, 13 November 1969.

65 *EEN*, 19 December 1968.

66 *EEN*, 22 December 1972.

67 *UEA Bulletin*, 7 March 1966, on the South African Student Scheme.

68 Cedric Lamb in *Decanter*, Summer 1966.

69 *Concrete*, 15 May 1996.

70 Council Minute, 18 December 1967.

71 *EEN*, 7 March 1964.

72 Leslie Halliwell, *Filmgoer's Companion* (London, 1990), p. 315.

73 FTP, "The UEA Debating Union, 1963-75". MS Memoirs of Christopher Wrigley.

74 *EDP*, 14, 15 May 1964.

75 *EEN*, 31 May 1965, *Norfolk News*, 25 June 1965.

76 Rosemary Todd, "The Visit to Rouen", *UEA Bulletin*, 7 March 1966.

77 *Chips*, 3 March 1967.

78 *EEN*, 1 August 1973.

79 *Square One*, 2 May 1967.

80 Christopher Wrigley, MS Memoirs, p. 88.

81 Eric Nicholls "Have You Found Your Ideal?", *Skop*, December 1964. *Skop* was the first UEA magazine, a rare, possibly unique, copy is in the papers of D. L. Marsh. Eric Nicholls later became a personnel manager with the Bradford and Bingley Building Society.

82 *EEN*, 15 February 1963.

83 *Daily Express*, 1 July 1972.
84 Appointments Officer's Report, 1965/6; Senate Minute, 1 February 1967; D. C. Ward, "Occupations of UEA Graduates", *UEA Bulletin*, 21 November 1966.
85 Senate Minute, 7 February 1968.
86 "Relations between Industry and UEA", Senate Minute, 29 May 1968.
87 Bertie Leigh, "Graduates and Careers", *Square One*, May 1968.
88 *EDP*, 1 May 1968.
89 Senate Minute, 10 February 1971.
90 Nigel Hawkes, "Our Concept of a Graduate Job is Changing", *New Academic*, 13 May 1971.
91 Appointments Board Report, 1970-71; Senate Minute, 8 March 1971.
92 *The Times*, 31 March 1971.
93 Working Party on Post Graduate Education in the University, Senate Minute, 5 November 1969. The Appointments Board did not publish statistics on postgraduate employment in the Vice-Chancellor's Reports.
94 Letter, Sir Edmund Bacon to Lord Franks, 9 January 1965.
95 Alex Danchev, *Oliver Franks: Founding Father* (Oxford, 1993); "Lord Franks of Headington", *UEA Bulletin*, 5, May 1966, an account of an interview of the author with Lord Franks in 1966.
96 *UEA Bulletin*, 5, May 1966, "The Installation of the Chancellor".
97 Frank Thistlethwaite *Origins*, p. 80
98 Senate Minute, 23 November 1966, Official and Academic Dress Regulations.
99 *Sunday Times*, 24 April 1966.
100 *EDP*, 25 April 1966.
101 Hugo Vickers, *Cecil Beaton* (London, 1985), p. 459.
102 Kenneth Clark, *Civilisation: A Personal View* (London, 1969), p. 346.
103 Letter, Frank Thistlethwaite to Lord Clark, 29 May 1969.

Notes to Chapter 5: Building the Environment

I am especially grateful to Mr Peter McKinley of Denys Lasdun and Partners who helped me with some of the wording of this chapter, especially on technical architectural matters.
1 Letter, Frank Thistlethwaite to Ian Watt, 26 October 1961.
2 Letter, Sir Isaiah Berlin to Frank Thistlethwaite, 3 March 1967.
3 Sir James Mountford, *Keele: An Historical Critique* (London, 1972), p. 225.
4 Frank Thistlethwaite, CV Appendix II Notes on Architectural Interests.
5 Steering Committee Minute, 18 January 1960.
6 Executive Committee Minute, 26 June 1961.
7 Letter, Leslie Martin to Gordon Tilsley, 27 July 1961.
8 Executive Committee Minute, 9 October 1961.
9 Frank Thistlethwaite, *Origins*, p. 56.
10 Report of the Committee on the Appointment of the University Architect, 15 November 1963.
11 *EEN*, 10 March 1962.
12 William J.R. Curtis, *Denys Lasdun: Architecture, City, Landscape* (London, 1994); "Denys Louis Lasdun" in *UEA Bulletin*, February 1965; Brian Connell interview in

The Times, 24 March 1975; Denys Lasdun Exhibition, Royal Academy of Arts, 6 February to 16 March 1997.

13 Interview with Sir Denys Lasdun and Peter McKinley, 7 October 1999.

14 Denys Lasdun, "An Architect's Approach to Architecture", *Journal of the Royal Institute of British Architects* 72 (1965), pp. 184, 195.

15 Denys Lasdun, *A Language and a Theme: The Architecture of Denys Lasdun and Partners* (RIBA Publications, 1976), "Denys Lasdun, the Evolution of a Style", *Architectural Review*, 145 (1969).

16 Lasdun, "An Architect's Approach to Architecture", p. 185.

17 Architect's Terms of Appointment and Letter, Lord Mackintosh to Denys Lasdun, 5 March 1962.

18 *EDP*, 10 March 1962.

19 Interview with Sir Denys Lasdun and Peter McKinley, 7 October 1999.

20 Brief in UEA Development Plan Report (a DLP document) 1969, Special Collections. These documents have been transferred to the UEA Archives.

21 Thistlethwaite, *Origins*, p. 56. Frank Thistlethwaite attributes the concept to himself but it was more accurately Denys Lasdun's.

22 Denys Lasdun, "The Architecture of the Urban Landscape", in Denys Lasdun, ed., *Architecture in an Age of Scepticism* (London, 1984), p. 139.

23 *EDP*, 1 February 1989.

24 Frank Thistlethwaite's comments on the brief in *Origins*, p. 56.

25 Executive Committee, 9 October 1961.

26 PRO, UGC/2/91 Paper, 14/63.

27 Interview with Mr D.J.F. Luckhurst, 4 August 1999, and *EDP*, 26 September 1963, for an account of the building. Another local firm of architects had actually been asked to design the Village, but as they were unable to make progress the work was transferred to Feilden and Mawson.

28 *Construction and Labour News*, 3 October 1963.

29 Early sketch plan of the Village n.d., FTP, cabinet 3.

30 Professor John Tarrant, the Public Orator, on presenting David Mawson for an Honorary MA, 4 July 1995.

31 *EDP*, 28 March 1963.

32 Letter, Sir Roy Harrod to Gordon Tilsley, 15 June 1960.

33 Letter, Sir Edmund Bacon to Frank Thistlethwaite, 25 September 1963.

34 PRO, UGC 2/110 Paper 196/64, 19 November 1964. The UGC agreed to provide a grant for the rent and refurbishment.

35 Tony Birks, *Building the New Universities* (Newton Abbot, 1972), p. 32.

36 *EDP*, 2 October 1969.

37 "UEA, Denys Lasdun and Partners", a talk by Alexander Redhouse and Peter McKinley, 15 February 1966.

38 Lasdun, "An Architect's Approach to Architecture", p. 196.

39 Denys Lasdun, "A Sense of Place and Time", *Listener*, 17 February 1966.

40 The UEA Development Plan (a DLP document), 1963.

41 *The Builder*, 3 May 1963.

42 Professor R.H. Campbell recalled this of that day.

43 *EEN*, 25 April 1963.

44 Development Plan Report 1969, Greater University, p. 35.

45 PRO, UGC 7/440, notes of a meeting 10 May 1963, Sir Keith Murray, the Vice-

Chancellor, Denys Lasdun and others.

46 PRO, UGC 7/440, Memorandum by Alexander Parnis, 20 February 1963. Parnis was Assistant Secretary to the UGC.

47 Executive Committee, 7 October 1963.

48 Denys Lasdun's speech to the Executive Committee, 30 September 1963. In fact Sir Keith Murray had made this clear to Lord Mackintosh but not to the Vice-Chancellor until January 1962. PRO, UGC 7/440, Memorandum by Sir Keith Murray, 19 January 1962.

49 PRO, UGC 7/440, Memoranda by A.E.L. Parnis, 20 February 1963, 26 April 1963, 6 May 1963, and E.R. Coplestone, 29 April 1963, and Sir Keith Murray's comments at the Meeting 10 May 1963 and Letter to the Vice-Chancellor, 1 May 1963. Coplestone was Under Secretary of the UGC then Secretary from 1964.

50 Report of the Committee on the Appointment of the Architect, 15 November 1963.

51 Letters, A.E.L. Parnis of the UGC to Gordon Marshall (the University's Estates Officer), 4 March 1964 and Marshall's reply, 19 March 1964.

52 Letter, Lincoln Ralphs to Frank Thistlethwaite, 1 November 1963.

53 Executive Committee, 30 September 1963.

54 Denys Lasdun's Statement to Council, 29 July 1966.

55 R.P. Dober, *The New Campus in Britain* (New York, 1965), p. 41.

56 Draft Building Programme, 1 November 1963.

57 *EDP*, 13 August 1965.

58 P.L. Young (of Anglian Building Products), "Pre-Cast Concrete: An Appeal to the Cheque Book", *East Anglian Daily Times*, 12 November 1968.

59 Executive Committee, 28 May 1962.

60 Personal information from Professor Norman Riley.

61 *Concrete: The Journal of the Concrete Society*, December 1968.

62 *Architectural Design*, May 1969, 7/6, "The University of East Anglia", for a full account of the design and building, *East Anglian Daily Times*, 12 November 1968.

63 Development Plan Report, 1969, pp. 52-53.

64 Curtis, *Denys Lasdun*, pp. 35-36.

65 Letter, Bernard Feilden to Frank Thistlethwaite, September 1989 in Correspondence with Participants.

66 The Boiler House Complex, June 1964, in Special Collections and File, Boiler House Complex in FTP.

67 Frank Thistlethwaite, tape 5.

68 A friend of the author's wife coming to a Russian course at UEA heard this and recounted the story to her.

69 Graham Martin, *From Vision to Reality: The Making of the University of Kent* (Canterbury, 1990), pp. 93, 98-99.

70 Curtis, *Denys Lasdun*, p. 22.

71 Willi Guttsman, Some Basic Ideas about the Library, August 1962.

72 Letter, Gordon Marshall to N. Wolf of the UGC, 5 February 1964.

73 Notes on Lasdun's draft plan, n.d. but 1963.

74 Interview with Willi Guttsman, 12 June 1995.

75 The Library Building, September 1964. Box in Special Collections.

76 Letter, Sir John Cockcroft to Frank Thistlethwaite, 1 August 1966.

77 Birks, *op.cit.* p. 40.

78 Letter, Willi Guttsman to the Vice-Chancellor, 17 November 1968.

79 Interview with Mr Michael Everitt of Feilden and Mawson, 5 August 1999. Various correspondence, George Chadwick, Denys Lasdun, Bernard Feilden, Gordon Marshall, 24 February 1971, 31 March 1971, 6 April 1971, in private papers of Michael Everitt.

80 Lecture Rooms Development Plan by Ian Watt, 3 July 1963, and Lecture Theatre Building, July 1966, Special Collection, Senate Minute, 27 September 1967.

81 Letter, A.E.L. Parnis to Cory Dixon, 9 August 1963.

82 Chemical Sciences, May 1964, Special Collections.

83 Letter, Davis, Belfield and Everest to Denys Lasdun, 27 November 1964.

84 Letter, C.R. Ross to Lord Mackintosh, 10 December 1964.

85 Ian Watt, Memorandum on the Arts Building, March 1963.

86 Arts Building, July 1964 and February 1967, in Special Collections.

87 Letter, N. Wolf to Gordon Marshall, 10 March 1964.

88 School of Biological Sciences, July 1964, in Special Collections.

89 Letters between Denys Lasdun and Frank Thistlethwaite, 30 September, 28 October, 1 November 1966.

90 Mathematics and Physics Building, 10 August 1966, Special Collections.

91 Interview with Marshall Hopkins, 8 July 1999; "Non System Building at UEA, UEA Science Building" in *Era: Journal of the Eastern Region of the Royal Institute of British Architects*, January/February 1974.

92 The Computing Centre, August 1967, Special Collections.

93 Letter, Sir Roy Harrod to Gordon Tilsley, 15 June 1960.

94 APB, 12 December 1960.

95 APB, 20 September 1961.

96 Frank Thistlethwaite, Student Residence as a factor in the Development Plan, APB, 10 January 1962.

97 Student Residence Paper II, 15 February 1962. The UGC *Report of the Sub-Committee on Halls of Residence* (W.R. Niblett) HMSO, 1957, p. 12, had also called for planners to consider "combining small groups of rooms into units . . . study bedrooms cluster round a small common room".

98 Interview with Professor R.H. Campbell, 6 June 1995, recalling Denys Lasdun.

99 Residential Accommodation, April 1964, Special Collections.

100 Memorandum, Cory Dixon, 14 August 1963.

101 Letter, Cory Dixon to Denys Lasdun, just before 26 August 1963.

102 Memorandum, Frank Thistlethwaite, 26 August 1963.

103 Thistlethwaite, *Origins*, p. 63.

104 Memorandum, G.H. Marshall, 4 February 1964.

105 Letter, N.D. Wolf (of the UGC) to Gordon Marshall, 26 August 1964.

106 APB, 1 February 1962.

107 Letters, Timothy Colman to the Vice-Chancellor, 26 November 1963, and to Lord Mackintosh, 25 September 1964.

108 Tony Birks, *op.cit.* p. 81.

109 Denys Lasdun, Statement, 29 July 1966.

110 Jonathan Mardle in *EDP*, 5 October 1966.

111 Letter, Philip Goodstein to Lincoln Ralphs, 28 February 1967. (LRP). Dr Ralphs was the Chairman of the Residences Building Sub-Committee.

112 Letters, Lincoln Ralphs to R.T. Skipper, 3 August to 9 September 1967.

113 Letter, Pamela Freer (Chairman of the Residents Committee) to Lincoln Ralphs, 12 December 1966.

114 Christopher Wrigley, MS Memoirs.

115 Richard Fawcett interview with Denys Lasdun, *Square One*, 2 May 1967.

116 Letter, Pamela Freer to Lincoln Ralphs, 12 December 1966.

117 *Times Higher Education Supplement*, 3 October 1975.

118 Letter, Frank Thistlethwaite to Cory Dixon, 21 May 1963.

119 Letter, A.E.L. Parnis to Cory Dixon , 8 August 1963.

120 Letter, Frank Thistlethwaite to Denys Lasdun, 6 November 1964.

121 Memorandum, Marcus Dick, 4 May 1965.

122 University House, Special Collections.

123 Senate Minute, 27 September 1967.

124 Letter, Timothy Colman to Frank Thistlethwaite, n.d. but February 1969.

125 Tony Birks, p. 83.

126 *East Anglian Daily Times*, 23 October 1965.

127 *Norfolk News*, 5 November 1965.

128 Frank Thistlethwaite, tape 5.

129 PRO, UGC 2/122 Paper 18/66, "UEA Great Hall".

130 R.H. Campbell, Notes of a meeting with the Vice-Chancellor, 21 February 1968. R.H.S. Crossman vetoed Norwich's expenditure on the project, which lapsed.

131 R.H. Campbell, Notes of a meeting with the Vice-Chancellor, 21 February 1968.

132 Senate Minute, 8 May 1972.

133 Letter, Denys Lasdun, to the Vice-Chancellor, 31 January 1968.

134 Denys Lasdun, Report on the Landscape and Playing Fields, November 1965.

135 Letter, Joan, Lady Evershed to Frank Thistlethwaite, 17 December 1966.

136 Letter, Brenda Colvin to Frank Thistlethwaite, 9 August 1968.

137 Interview with R.H. Campbell, 6 June 1995.

138 Brenda Colvin, Landscape Report, December 1967.

139 Access Road Correspondence, 1963-64.

140 Development Plan, 1963.

141 Letter, Gordon Marshall to Peter McKinley of DLP, 6 January 1965.

142 *EDP*, 25 March 1965.

143 Letter, Frank Thistlethwaite to Denys Lasdun, 27 May 1963.

144 *Guardian*, 5 December 1967.

145 *THES*, 3 October 1975.

146 *Spectator*, 7 August 1976.

147 Harold Perkin, *Innovation in Higher Education: New Universities in the United Kingdom*, OECD (1969), p. 95.

148 Tony Birks, p. 82.

149 MUF Architecture video tapes of UEA for the Lasdun Exhibition at the Royal Academy 1998 and interview with Malcolm Bradbury. Also Denys Lasdun's commentary on the National Theatre at the Exhibition. Sir Malcolm greatly admired the Lasdun concept and building designs, as he made clear to Sir Denys when they met sometime afterwards.

150 Letter, Vice-Chancellor to Denys Lasdun, 13 May 1964.

151 C.R. Ross, Memorandum to Deans, 15 May 1964.

152 Site Development Committee, 18 May 1964.

153 Letter, Denys Lasdun to Frank Thistlethwaite, 19 May 1964.

154 Letter, C.R. Ross to Denys Lasdun, 20 May 1964.

155 Letter, Denys Lasdun to C.R. Ross, 25 May 1964.

156 C.R. Ross, briefing to Deans, 29 May 1964.
157 Notes of a Meeting with the UGC, August 1964.
158 Notes on telephone conversation, Frank Thistlethwaite and Denys Lasdun, 14 July 1967, RHCP.
159 Notes of a meeting with the UGC, 19 January morning, 1968, RHCP.
160 Notes of a meeting with DLP, 19 January afternoon, 1968, RHCP.
161 Notes of a meeting with Denys Lasdun, Alexander Redhouse and Peter McKinley, 19 June 1968.
162 Letter, Timothy Colman to R.H. Campbell, 9 August 1968, RHCP.
163 Committee on the Relationship with the Architect, 7 October 1968; Letter, Frank Thistlethwaite to Denys Lasdun, 16 October 1968.
164 Committee on the Relationship with the Architect, 29 October 1968.
165 Committee on the Relationship with the Architect, 13 November 1968.
166 Memorandum, Peter Lasko, 13 November 1968.
167 Letter, Sir Edmund Bacon to Denys Lasdun, 21 November 1968.
168 *EEN*, 17 December 1968; *Daily Telegraph*, 18 December 1968.
169 Committee on the Relationship with the Architect, 29 October 1968.
170 Noel Annan, "Higher Education", in *Essays on Reform*, ed., Bernard Crick (Oxford, 1967), p. 29.
171 Letter, Jack Butterworth to Frank Thistlethwaite, 7 November 1966, which became a memorandum to the UGC, 23 January 1967.
172 Committee on the Relationship, 29 October 1968. UGC assumptions were that a building had to last for thirty years but Lasdun could hardly accept this limitation and Thistlethwaite thinks that he was right not to do so.
173 Ad hoc committee to agree terms, 21 October 1967.
174 Charles McKean, *Architectural Guide to Cambridge and East Anglia since 1920*, ERA Publications, RIBA Eastern Region (Edinburgh, 1982), p. 67.
175 UEA Development Plan: Recommendations for their Application for the Future, June 1969.
176 Tony Birks, p.74.
177 Denys Lasdun, Statement, 27 July 1966.
178 Council Minutes, 18 November 1968.
179 Bernard Feilden, see Senate Minute, 11 January 1989.
180 Notes for Frank Thistlethwaite on the meeting with Bernard Feilden, 23 November 1968 and Memorandum, Thistlethwaite to the Pro Chancellor, 25 November 1968 on this meeting.
181 Michael Everitt interviewed 5 August 1999.
182 Sir Bernard Feilden interviewed by Stefan Muthesius, 28 September 1995.
183 Committee on Relations with the Architect, 4 December 1968.
184 *EDP*, 17 January 1969.
185 Bernard Feilden, Development Plan, April 1970.
186 *EDP*, 3 September 1971.
187 Bernard Feilden Development Plan, 7 March 1972; *EDP*, 26 April 1972.
188 *THES*, 27 October 1972.
189 Tony Birks, p. 83.
190 Interview with Mr D.J.F. Luckhurst, 4 August 1999.
191 *Building Design*, 10 October 1975.
192 Letter, Patricia Whitt to Frank Thistlethwaite, 5 September 1975.

193 *EDP*, 2 October 1975.

194 *EEN*, 12 November 1976.

195 Interview with Mrs Bridgid Everitt (née Rawnsley), 5 August 1999. Miss Rawnsley shortly afterwards married Michael Everitt of Feilden and Mawson, who worked on the UEA Library.

196 Frank Thistlethwaite, tape 5, attributes much of the ideas to Keith Clayton.

197 Bernard Feilden, the University of East Anglia, the Broad, September 1989. Rosamund Reich (of Feilden and Mawson), "The Broad at UEA", *Landscape Design*, February 1980.

198 *EEN*, 22 April 1979.

199 *Architectural Review*, 164.

200 R.H. Campbell, "Summary of the Parking Provision", 20 February 1970, RHCP.

201 *Annual Report of the Vice-Chancellor*, 1975-76, p. 10.

202 Rick Mather Architects, *Development Plan for the University of East Anglia*, 14 June 1989, p. 55.

Notes to Chapter 6: A Time of Troubles

1 Malcolm Bradbury, *The History Man* (London, 1975), pp. 48-49.

2 Letter, Sir Denys Page to Frank Thistlethwaite, 7 June 1971.

3 *EEN*, 2 February 1965.

4 *EDP*, 14 February 1967.

5 *Chips*, 17 March 1967; *EEN*, 24 May 1967.

6 *EEN*, 6 June 1967.

7 Philip Goodstein, "Presidential Retrospect", *UEA Bulletin*, 29 May 1967.

8 Malcolm Bradbury, "The University of East Anglia" *Guardian*, 9 October 1967. His fictional view of the effects of increasing scale are in *The History Man*, pp. 64-65.

9 *Chips*, 26 March 1968, for a good account of the Grosvenor Square riot.

10 *Daily Telegraph*, 18 October 1967.

11 *Chips*, 31 May 1968. *Chips* printed its title in Cyrillic presumably to assert its solidarity with the revolutionary USSR.

12 Letter, Sir Roy Harrod to the Earl of Stradbroke, 30 April 1960, GTP.

13 *Mandate*, 21 May 1968.

14 Visit of HRH Princess Margaret, Porters' Reports, 13 May 1968, FTP.

15 *EEN*, 14 May 1968.

16 *EEN*, 14 May 1968.

17 *Mandate*, 21 May 1968.

18 *Mandate*, 7 October 1968.

19 Letter, Frank Thistlethwaite to Sir Edmund Bacon, 1 October 1963. Visit of HM The Queen.

20 Memorandum, Registrar to Frank Thistlethwaite. Cost of Royal Visits, "the Finance Officer thinks the amount is a fair one".

21 CEAS/296, videotape from Anglia TV.

22 *The Times*, 25 May 1968; *EDP*, 25 May 1968

23 *The Times*, 24 May 1968.

24 *Chips*, 27 May 1968.

25 CEAS/296, videotape records the visit and snatches of the "seminar".

26 Bertie Leigh, "A Tale of Two Universities", *Daily Telegraph*, 29 May 1968.

27 *EDP*, 2 June 1968.

28 *EDP*, 12 June 1968.

29 Interview Frank Thistlethwaite; and letter, Frank Thistlethwaite to Jill Thistlethwaite (his daughter), Easter weekend 1968, describing the Windsor visit.

30 Harriet Crawley, *A Degree of Defiance: Students in England and Europe Now* (London, 1969). Miss Crawley was there at the time.

31 *EEN*, 3 June 1968.

32 Senate Minute, 24 May 1967.

33 File, Dean of Students' Working Party, FTP.

34 *Chips*, 6 December 1968 gives a good account.

35 Sir Robin Day, *Grand Inquisitor* (London, 1989), pp. 152-53.

36 *Daily Telegraph*, 5 December 1968.

37 Auberon Waugh, "In Defence of Students", *Spectator*, 7 February 1969.

38 Jonathan Raban, "The Art of Disaster", *New Society*, 12 December 1968. Raban, later well known as a writer, was then a lecturer at UEA and present at the meeting.

39 "The Reason for the Jenkins Comedy", *Chips*, 6 December 1968.

40 Letters, Roger Niven to Frank Thistlethwaite and reply, 4 and 21 February 1969. File, Student Unrest.

41 Donald Lindsay, *Sir Edmund Bacon: a Norfolk Life* (Maldon, 1988), pp. 99-100. He had flown to Rhodesia to stay with and give moral support to his friend during the stressful time of the declaration of a republic in 1969. Obituary of Sir Edmund Bacon, *The Times*, 2 October 1982.

42 Senate Minute, 11 December 1968. Envelope on the voting on Sir Humphrey Gibbs's doctorate.

43 *Chips*, 21 February 1969.

44 Frank Thistlethwaite Statement, 23 February 1970, in file "Student Files, 1969/70".

45 D. Gowans, "A Report on the Individual Data System ... in the University", 9 March 1970.

46 Letter, Frank Thistlethwaite to Philip Garrahan, 6 March 1970.

47 *EDP*, 4 May 1967. Mr Guy later had a distinguished career in university administration as Secretary of Goldsmith's College, University of London.

48 Letter, Keva Coombes to Frank Thistlethwaite, 6 October 1970.

49 Frank Thistlethwaite Speech to the Students' Council, 12 October 1970.

50 File, Barclays Bank, letter, R. Q. Gurney to Frank Thistlethwaite n.d. but early 1970.

51 Frank Thistlethwaite's reply to the Resolution of the Students' Union of 30 April 1970 concerning Barclays Bank, 3 June 1970.

52 *Twice*, October 1970.

53 *The Times*, 31 October 1970.

54 Letter, Lord Cranbrook to Sir Edmund Bacon, 4 November 1970.

55 Letter, Sir Edmund Bacon to Vice-Chancellor, 11 November 1970.

56 *The Times*, 19 November 1970; *Twice*, November 1970.

57 Handwritten note in file on Barclays Bank.

58 *EDP*, 20 November 1970.

59 Typed note, 24 November 1970, in file on Barclays Bank.

60 Anglia TV interview with Sir Harry Legge Bourke, CEAS, videotape 296.

61 Interview with R. H. Campbell, 6 June 1995.

62 *EEN*, 25 November 1970; *EDP*, 21 December 1970.

63 *Twice*, January 1971.

64 *EDP*, 30 November 1970.

65 Memorandum, Frank Albrighton to Frank Thistlethwaite, 6 February 1976.

66 RHCP; summary of Car Parking Position, private memorandum, 20 February 1970.

67 Car Parking: A Financial Problem or a Moral Issue?, n.d. circa 4 September 1969, Car Parking file, FTP.

68 Memorandum, Prof. J. R. Jones (UEA, AUT) to Registrar, 4 September 1969.

69 Notes of a meeting at the Department of Employment, 19 December 1969.

70 Memorandum, David King to Frank Thistlethwaite, 23 January 1970.

71 Memorandum, C. S. Middleton to Frank Thistlethwaite, 27 January 1970.

72 Letter, J. M. Brewin to BIO, 30 January 1970.

73 Memorandum, J. R. Jones to J. M. Brewin, 13 February 1970.

74 Letter, Roy Markham to Registrar, 4 February 1970.

75 *EDP*, 31 January 1970.

76 D. J. Robertson, "Strikes in a University in Britain", March 1970, RHCP.

77 Letter, R. H. Campbell to D. J. Robertson, 9 March 1970, RHCP.

78 Letter, R. H. Campbell to D. J. Robertson, 23 March 1970, RHCP.

79 Memorandum, J. R. Kitching to Registrar, 1 May 1970.

80 Letter, Gordon Tilsley to Registrar, 29 April 1970.

81 Memorandum by Roy Hay, 23 February 1970, in file "ASTMS Recognition" in, RHCP.

82 Memorandum, Roy Hay and Michael Miller to Establishment Officer, 10 May 1970, RHCP.

83 Peter Wilby in *Times Higher Education Supplement*, 12 March 1976.

84 Report of the Working Party on Negotiating and Consultative Machinery, n.d. but after 1 June 1970, RHCP.

85 *EDP*, 13 January 1968, Dr Tom Stuttaford.

86 *EDP*, 3 July 1969.

87 Letter, R. H. Campbell to the author, 10 June 1995.

88 *EEN*, 2 January 1970.

89 Letters, R.N.S. Shawyer to Frank Thistlethwaite, 1 January, 10 April 1969.

90 Memorandum, Dean of Students to Frank Thistlethwaite, 29, 30 October 1969.

91 Envelope of documents on the case of an American student and drugs.

92 This regulation stated: "The University will suspend or preclude from further study or take such other disciplinary action as it may see fit against any student found in possession of a drug or drugs the possession of which, unless prescribed for that student by a registered medical practitioner, would render that student liable to prosecution."

93 Minutes of the Extraordinary Union General Meeting, 8 March 1971.

94 Student Union Newsletter, 9 March 1971.

95 Sit-in Newsheet, 11 March 1971.

96 UEA Newsletter, 15 March 1971.

97 Senate Minute, 24 April 1971.

98 "Black Bun goes to the Sit-In", 9 March 1971. "Heads" here will mean "dopeheads" or "smackheads" i.e. drug users.

99 *EEN*, 20 April 1971.

100 "Pigs off Campus", March 1971, and *Norwich Dope News*, April 1971 (produced at UEA).

101 *EEN*, 18 May 1971.
102 Frederick C. Wigby, *A Shilling, a Shuttleknife and a Piece of String* (Wymondham, 1984), p. 121.
103 Interview, Dr Tom Stuttaford, 29 April 1995.
104 Report of the Working Party on the Use of Drugs, 1 March 1971.
105 Report on the Code of Discipline (Frostick Report), October 1971, p. 8.
106 Dangerous Drugs Act 1965, Eliz. II c. 15; PRO, UGC 7/807 "The Taking of Dangerous Drugs by Students".
107 Jack Straw, "Desert Island Discs" BBC Radio 4, 12 July 1998.
108 "Analysis of UEA Events", March 1971.
109 "The Dream is Over", Spring 1971.
110 *The Boycott of Prelims*, leaflet, 12 March 1971.
111 *EEN*, 23 April 1971.
112 Petition, 22 April 1971.
113 Memorandum, Alec Gordon to Frank Thistlethwaite, 12 November 1971.
114 Preliminary Assessment; Proposals of the Arts Deans to Senate, 1 December 1971.
115 *EEN*, 19 April 1971.
116 *Twice*, 3 May 1971, reprints some.
117 Dean of Students to Deputy Dean, 20 February 1970, designated "Strangelove" by the DOS. "Strangelove" was the DOS code name for drugs matters, "Cupid" for sexual irregularities. *Dr Strangelove* was a film of 1963.
118 Memoranda, J. Gubbay and others on Welfare and Discipline, 7 May 1971 and another n.d. but a few days later, GCP.
119 *EEN*, 6 May 1971; *The Times*, 7 May 1971.
120 Letter, G. A. Chadwick (the Registrar) to Gerald Crompton (and others), 25 May 1971, GCP.
121 Newsletter, 23 June 1971, prints the documents.
122 Report of the Commission of Inquiry into the Code of Discipline and the General Regulations (Raymond Frostick), October 1971.
123 John Coates, "Where the Report Goes Wrong", *Kett*, November 1971.
124 Joint Statement of the CVCP and NUS, October 1968.
125 Joint Statement of LEAs and the NUS, November 1968.
126 Letter, Frank Thistlethwaite to CVCP, 9 December 1968.
127 Jack Straw, "Student Participation in Higher Education", in *Universities: The Boundaries of Change* (London, 1970).
128 *Twice*, October 1970.
129 *Twice*, November 1971.
130 *Independent*, 28 April 1995.
131 Arthur Marwick, *The Sixties* (Oxford, 1998), p. 759 citing a survey of 1973.
132 *Report of the Select Committee on Education and Science*, Session 1968-69, *Student Relations*, i; *Report 1969*, on this wider unrest.
133 Official photographs of Presidents of the Students' Union 1964-80.
134 Harry Kidd, *The Trouble at LSE* (Oxford, 1969).
135 *The Times*, 15 May 1970.
136 *EDP*, 15 May 1970.
137 Letter, to Dr John Coates, 6 November 1971.
138 Eve Warren, "The Disillusionment of an Aspiring Scholar", *Square One*, May 1968.
139 *Sunday Telegraph*, 16 May 1971.

140 *EDP*, 10 February 1970.

141 Frank Thistlethwaite, paper on Student Unrest and Discipline, 5 July 1968. A paper given to the CVCP at Cambridge.

142 Interview, Gerald Crompton, 30 May 1995.

143 "What We Stand For", *International Socialists*, June 1971.

144 Interview, John Ceybird, 28 December 1994.

145 John Ceybird, "The Capitalist University", *Student Union Handbook*, 1971/2. Also Stephen Wilson, "The Vice-Chancellor's University", *Kett*, May/June 1972, from a more libertarian non-Marxist view point. Dr Wilson was not associated with the Left.

146 Tom Burns (Edinburgh University), typescript, "The Revolt of the Privileged", July 1968. This was significant at UEA since it was sent by the Librarian to Frank Thistlethwaite and by him to all Deans.

147 Douglas Baker, "Boredom on the Pampered Campus", *Daily Telegraph*, 9 October 1971.

148 A. E. Dyson, "The Sleep of Reason", in C. B. Cox and A. E. Dyson, *The Black Papers*; (London, 1971); and A. E. Dyson, "The Structures We Need", in Rhodes Boyson, *Education: Threatened Standards* (Enfield, 1972).

149 R. H. Campbell, "Address to the Magistrates of Norwich on Student Discipline and Welfare", October 1970, RHCP.

150 Paper on "Student Welfare", by Dr M. Balls and others, 12 June 1970; and Memorandum by John Coates, 22 June 1970.

151 Letter, Roy Emerson to Frank Thistlethwaite, 28 July 1971, passing on the views of Dr. David Castell, a chief clinical psychologist. He might also have added a sad lack of rapport between the Senior Porter at Fifers Lane and the (terminally ill) Marcus Dick. Frederick C. Wigby *op.cit*, pp. 118-36.

152 Frank Thistlethwaite, "Student Relations in the Seventies", address to the meeting of American Presidents at Williamsburg,Virginia, 14-18 April 1969.

153 Colin Crouch, *The Student Revolt* (London, 1970).

154 M. A. Rooke, *Anarchy and Apathy: Student Unrest, 1968-70* (London, 1971).

155 Julius Gould, *The Attack on Higher Education, Marxist and Radical Penetration*, Institute for the Study of Conflict, September 1977.

156 Letter, Willi Guttsman to Frank Thistlethwaite, 3 June 1972.

157 J. N. Sivall in *EEN*, 17 March 1971.

158 Memoirs of Mary Vallanjon (1969-72), 15 October 1995.

159 Spartacus League, analysis of UEA events, March 1971.

160 Bertie Leigh, *Daily Telegraph*, 29 May 1968.

161 Interview with R. H. Campbell, 6 June 1995.

162 CVCP, *Student Membership of University Committees and Sub Committees*, May 1971.

163 Gareth Williams, "Higher Education Deflated", *New Society*, 21 November 1974. C.C. Matheson, "A Review of Financial Support for Students", 17 February 1986, Senate Minute, 26 February 1986.

164 *EEN*, 5 May 1972.

165 *EEN*, 12 March 1971.

166 Letter, Lincoln Ralphs to Sir Edmund Bacon, 28 April 1971, LRP.

167 Letter, Frank Thistlethwaite to Noel Annan, 21 December 1972.

Notes to Chapter 7: Administration and Finance

1　Frank Thistlethwaite, *UEA Bulletin*, October 1968, p. 13.
2　Frank Thistlethwaite, *Origins*, p. 9.
3　*EDP*, 4 January 1962.
4　Frank Thistlethwaite, *Origins*, p. 65. FTP, tape 4.
5　Frank Thistlethwaite, *Doing Different in a Cold Climate*, the St John's College Lecture, 25 October 1988, p. 4.
6　Harold Perkin, "The Government of the New Universities", in *New Universities in the United Kingdom* (OECD, 1969).
7　Norman Sheppard, Recollections.
8　Letter, Thomas Bennet Clark to Frank Thistlethwaite, 14 June 1967.
9　Letter, J. A. Kitching to Frank Thistlethwaite, 6 May 1971. Temperamentally Professor Kitching would have liked to have exercised more authoritarian control than he was capable of exerting. His public school background, private wealth and very conservative views distanced him from many colleagues, which added to the difficulties of the BIO Board, hence his comments here and subsequently.
10　Frank Thistlethwaite, *Origins*, p. 67.
11　M.B. Glauert and A.R. Katritzky, Responsibilities and Authority within Schools, 30 July 1968, SZP.
12　Frank Thistlethwaite, *Origins*, p. 69; Frank Thistlethwaite, *Cambridge Years, 1945-1961* (Cambridge, 1999), pp. 129-35.
13　Professorial submission to FOG, n.d. but *c.* 7 May 1969.
14　J. McFarlane and R.G. Groves, The Role of the Professor, 30 December 1970.
15　Letter, Martin Hollis to Frank Thistlethwaite, 5 December 1970.
16　McFarlane and Groves, The Role of the Professor, 23 April 1971.
17　Letter, J. A. Kitching to Frank Thistlethwaite, 6 May 1971.
18　Council Minute, 21 June 1971.
19　Letters, Lincoln Ralphs to Frank Thistlethwaite, 7, 11 June 1971, LRP.
20　George Chadwick, Paper on the Framework of Government, 4 June 1969.
21　FOG Committee for Arts and Sciences, Senate Minute, 3 November 1971.
22　FOG Committee for Arts and Sciences, Senate Minute, 3 November 1971.
23　John Wood to the Development Committee, 22 November 1971.
24　Report by the Committee of Two on the Government of the University, 15 January 1969 (mis-printed as 1968).
25　Memorandum, Professor N. Sheppard to FOG, n.d. but May 1970, and Recollections, "University Governance".
26　Eg. A. J. Boulton, "Assembly Again", and R. K. Harris, "Assembly and Democracy", both in *UEA Bulletin*, March 1973.
27　J. Biggart, "Bureaucracy or Community?", *UEA Bulletin*, March 1973.
28　Letter, Timothy Colman to Frank Thistlethwaite, 13 March 1970.
29　Letter, Sir Frank Lee to Frank Thistlethwaite, 28 May 1970.
30　R. K. Harris *op. cit.*
31　CVCP, Student Participation in University Government, October 1971.
32　Senate Minute, 6 November 1968.
33　Memorandum on Student Participation in University Government, December 1968.
34　AUT, Policy Statement on Student Participation, 6 January 1969.
35　FOG Minutes, January 1969.

36 FOG Minutes, 13 November 1969.

37 FOG Minutes, 28 May 1970.

38 Senate Minute, 10 June 1970.

39 Memorandum, S. W. Holland to FOG, 24 January 1972.

40 Industrial Administration Ltd, University of East Anglia, Survey of Senate and its Committtees, June 1969.

41 FOG Minute, 17 September 1969, and Senate Minute, 5 November 1969.

42 FOG Minute, 19 January 1970, and Senate Minute, 4 February 1970.

43 Private information from one of "the six", not the Vice-Chancellor.

44 *Annual Report of the Vice-Chancellor*, 1974-75, pp. 8-10.

45 *Annual Report of the Vice Chancellor*, 1976-77, p. 12.

46 Frank Thistlethwaite, "A Proposal for Administrative Reform", 5 May 1976.

47 Jarratt Report Working Group, Senate Minute, 25 June 1986.

48 *Annual Report of the Vice-Chancellor*, 1976-77, pp. 12-13.

49 From the Honorary Treasurer's Annual Reports and Accounts, 1960/1–1979/80.

50 Letter, Gordon Tilsley to F.P. Boyce, 17 December 1959, LRP.

51 Letter, F.P. Boyce to Tilsley, 18 December 1959, LRP.

52 Letter, F.P. Boyce to Sir Bartle Edwards, 20 December 1959, LRP.

53 *The Times*, 13 February 1963, *EEN*, 18 February 1965.

54 Sir Timothy Colman, interviewed 26 August 1999.

55 Letter, Basil Robarts to Lord Mackintosh, 17 July 1962. This and subsequent letters were in a surviving Investment Policy file retrieved from the Finance Office. Frank Thistlethwaite also knew of Lazards through Sir Robert Sainsbury.

56 Letter, Basil Robarts to George Chadwick, 2 August 1962.

57 Letter, E. W. Grazebrook to George Chadwick, 28 November 1962.

58 J. R. Cuthbertson, Head of the Intelligence Department, Lazard Bros, "Equities and Gilts in the Crystal Ball", March 1963 in Investment Policy file.

59 Letter, C. A. Cooper to R. A. Newstead, 18 September 1970, enclosing the figures up to 1970. Other figures from the Investment Policy File and Valuations of Securities by Lazard's. The distributed amount is from the file on the Consolidated Fund. This was set up on the advice of Professor C.R. Ross, former Bursar of Hertford College, Oxford, for items of expenditure like prizes.

60 Letter R. A. Newstead to C. A. Cooper, 17 January 1972, reporting Timothy Colman's views.

61 Letter, C. A. Cooper to R. A. Newstead, 24 January 1972.

62 Letter, G. P. Dawnay to R. A. Newstead, 12 February 1974.

63 Letter, Guy Dawnay to R. A. Newstead, 28 February 1975.

64 Letter, R. A. Newstead to Geoffrey Dicker, Chairman of the Finance Committee, 5 and 7 March 1975.

65 Notes of a meeting, 29 April 1975.

66 Sir John Wolfenden, *Turning Points* (London, 1976), p. 148.

67 John Carswell, *Government and the Universities in Britain, 1960-1980* (Cambridge, 1985), pp. 145-46.

68 PRO, UGC/7/27 Quinquennial Estimate, East Anglia, Memorandum E.R. Coplestone, 1 March 1963.

69 PRO, UGC/7/27 Memorandum, E.R. Coplestone, 13 March 1963.

70 PRO, UGC/7/27 Memorandum, W.H. Fisher, 11 March 1963.

71 *New Scientist*, 13 July 1967.

72 Letter, Sir John Wolfenden to Frank Thistlethwaite, 20 December 1966.
73 Frank Thistlethwaite in *THES*, 1 November 1968.
74 Letter, Frank Thistlethwaite to Charles Carter, the Vice-Chancellor of Lancaster University, 2 and 16 December 1969.
75 *THES*, 21 July 1972.
76 The Quinquennial Allocation, 1972-77 commentary by Professor Keith Clayton, 20 January 1973. Professor Clayton was acting Vice-Chancellor while Frank Thistlethwaite was on leave.
77 Keith Clayton on the Quinquennial Allocation, *UEA Newsletter*, 2 March 1973.
78 Letter, Keith Clayton to Frank Thistlethwaite, 21 January 1973.
79 *EDP*, 7 May 1975.
80 *EDP*, 10 May 1975.
81 Letter, W. A. Cramond, the Vice-Chancellor of Stirling University to the Editor of the *Daily Record* which had repeated this canard, 17 December 1976. Copy sent to Frank Thistlethwaite.
82 CVCP, Memorandum to the Secretary of State, 24 February 1967.

Notes to Chapter 8: The Sainsbury Centre

1 Letter, Frank Thistlethwaite to Sir Robert Sainsbury, 8 June 1968. The papers on the SCVA are in FTP, cabinet 2.
2 Frank Thistlethwaite, "The Sainsbury Connection", typescript in FTP, cabinet 1. See also Frank Thistlethwaite, *Origins*, pp. 105-14.
3 File, Jane and Andrew Ritchie, note by Frank Thistlethwaite, 2 August 1962.
4 Note by Frank Thistlethwaite, 27 July 1964.
5 "A Memorandum on the Arts Centre Project", 3 August 1965.
6 Memoranda, 9, 11 November 1968.
7 "The Sainsbury Connection", p. 2.
8 James Boswell, *The Story of Sainsburys* (London, 1969); Sir Robert Sainsbury, obituary in *The Times*, 4 April 2000.
9 Robert Sainsbury, cited by Frank Thistlethwaite in speech to Council, 26 November 1973.
10 File, Robert Sainsbury, 1965-68, letters, 21 March 1967, 8 April 1968.
11 Letter, Robert Sainsbury to Frank Thistlethwaite, 24 July 1968 and Memorandum by Frank Thistlethwaite, September 1968.
12 "The Sainsbury Connection", p. 4.
13 Steven Hooper, *The Robert and Lisa Sainsbury Collection* (Yale U.P., 1997) 3 volumes, including "A History of the Collection", pp. xxvii-lxxvii in Volume 1.
14 Sainsbury, "A Personal Choice", 20 November 1975.
15 Ibid.
16 Memorandum, the Finance Officer to Frank Thistlethwaite, 2 October 1979.
17 *Economist*, 8 April 1978.
18 "The Sainsbury Connection", p. 4.
19 Speech of Frank Thistlethwaite to Council, 26 November 1973.
20 Sir Robert Sainsbury, "A Personal Choice".
21 Proposed gifts by Sir Robert and Lady Sainsbury and their son David to the University of ——, 26 March 1973. The name of the university was left blank pending acceptance of the gift by the UEA Council.

22 Letter, Inland Revenue to Sir Robert Sainsbury's solicitors, 20 August 1973.

23 Memorandum, Timothy Colman, 9 November 1973.

24 Letter, Sir Frederick Dainton to Sir Robert Sainsbury, 16 November 1973.

25 Letter, Sir Robert Sainsbury to Sir Fredrick Dainton, 18 March 1975.

26 Frank Thistlethwaite, speech to Council 26 November 1973.

27 "The Sainsbury Connection", p. 5.

28 Letter, Frank Thistlethwaite to Sir Robert Sainsbury, 11 December 1973.

29 Letter, Frank Thistlethwaite to Bernard Feilden, 8 February 1974.

30 Letter, Frank Thistlethwaite to Sir Hugh Casson, 8 February 1974.

31 Letter, Sir Hugh Casson to Frank Thistlethwaite, 11 February 1974.

32 Frank Thistlethwaite, interview tape 6, 4 September 1980.

33 "The Sainsbury Connection", p. 6; Council Minutes, 25 April 1974; and letters, Frank Thistlethwaite to Norman Foster and Ko Liang Ie, 2 May 1974.

34 Notes of a meeting, 4 April 1974.

35 Memorandum, Gordon Marshall to Frank Thistlethwaite, 8 April 1974.

36 *EDP*, 1 May 1974.

37 SCVA, Building Committee, 14 January 1975.

38 Memorandum, Andrew Martindale to Frank Thistlethwaite, 17 March 1975.

39 Architects brief, Art History Sector, October 1974.

40 Draft brief for the Senior Common Room, 21 March 1975.

41 SCVA Building Committee, 8 October 1974, analysis of possible sites.

42 Frank Thistlethwaite, Statement to Council, 2 June 1975.

43 Letter, Bernard Feilden to Frank Thistlethwaite, 16 May 1975.

44 Letter, Bernard Feilden to Frank Thistlethwaite, 19 May 1975.

45 Letter, Sir Robert Sainsbury to Frank Thistlethwaite, 9 July 1975 *EDP*, 14 November 1975.

46 Norman Foster interviewed on "Omnibus", BBC1 24 March 1981.

47 Memorandum, Gordon Marshall, 21 July 1975.

48 SCVA Building Committee, 11 November 1975.

49 Letter, Sir Robert Sainsbury to Frank Thistlethwaite, 5 December 1977.

50 Letter, Sir Robert Sainsbury to Andrew Martindale, 31 August 1976.

51 Letter, Frank Thistlethwaite to Sir Frederick Dainton of the UGC, 19 November 1976.

52 Frank Thistlethwaite, memorandum to Council, 30 November 1977.

53 Letter, Norman Foster to Gordon Marshall, 22 March 1978.

54 *Architect's Journal*, 14 October 1987.

55 SCVA, Commercial Activities, a report by Roger Lloyd and Frank Albrighton, December 1977.

56 Norman Foster, "IQRC, Extracts from a Project Diary", in Denys Lasdun, *Architecture in an Age of Scepticism* (London, 1984).

57 Alan Borg, "The Sainsbury Centre for Visual Arts", *Museum Journal*, 78 (1979).

58 "The Gift", AVC 212, Anglia TV programme. Reg Butler, the sculptor, made this point. The film brings out George Sexton's contribution well.

59 Report, Butler Miller Associates, 8 August 1977.

60 *EEN*, 7 May 1982.

61 Jane Brown, *Lanning Roper and his Gardens* (London, 1987), pp. 148-52, obituary, *The Times*, 24 March 1983.

62 *THES*, 18 August 1978.

63 *Building Design*, 9 March 1979.

64 *EEN*, 29 May 1984.

65 Memoranda, Andrew Martindale to Frank Thistlethwaite, 27 July, 5 August 1976.
66 *Building Design*, 29 December 1978.
67 Letter, Sir Robert Sainsbury to Frank Thistlethwaite, 10 April 1978.
68 Flysheet, Sainsbury Centre picket, Joint Shop Stewards and Students Union Committee April 1978.
69 Memorandum, Gordon Marshall, 8 March 1978, "The Centre is not popular in the University." On the other hand, the success of the Sainsbury's financing of the SCVA must have been a factor in their creation of the Sainsbury Laboratory, SISJAC and the Kenny fund support for sports facilities.
70 *EDP*, 15 June 1978.
71 Memorandum, Sir Robert Sainsbury, 22 March 1977.
72 Memorandum, Gordon Marshall, 8 March 1978.
73 Letter, Sir Robert Sainsbury, 30 March 1978.
74 *EEN*, 11 April 1978; *EDP*, 14, 20 April 1978.
75 *EDP*, 16 October 1978.
76 Letter, Frank Thistlethwaite to Lady Zuckerman, 24 January 1979.
77 Newsletter of the Friends of the SCVA, March 1980.
78 SCVA, Use of the Conservatory, 1978-80.
79 *The Times*, 17 October 1980.
80 *EEN*, 6 June 1978. It was given a splendid complete display in the SCVA in April 2000.
81 *EDP*, 25 October 1978.
82 Letter, Sir Robert Sainsbury to Frank Thistlethwaite, 6 November 1979.
83 Memorandum, Alan Jones, 7 November 1978 and enclosed documents.
84 Memorandum, Alan Jones to Frank Thistlethwaite, 25 June 1979.
85 *Framework for a System of Museums* (Sir Arthur Drew), Report of a Working Party of the Standing Committee on Museums and Galleries, November 1978.
86 *The Times*, 23 January 1991.

Notes to Chaper 9: The End of the Beginning

1 Frank Thistlethwaite, "The Position and Role of the Vice-Chancellor", Address at a Conference at Exeter University 26 August 1972.
2 *EEN*, 15 May 1973.
3 NRO, ACC Eaton, 15 September 1977; "The Value of the University to the Economy of the Norwich Sub-Region", 22 April 1970. *EDP*, 17 November 1973.
4 Letter, Timothy Colman to Frank Thistlethwaite, 15 July 1975, File on Vice-Chancellor's Dinners.
5 File on Student Parties. One of these parties ended outrageously (or hilariously) as a croquet match dissolved into a brawl in the shrubbery after the Vice-Chancellor had left.
6 Senate Minute, 30 September 1981, "Expenditure and Cost per Student 1979-80", Lancaster £110, UEA £87, Essex £83, Kent £76, Sussex £71, Warwick £69, national average £66, York £44.
7 CVCP, University Development in the 1970s, 5 November 1969.
8 Development in the 1970s, Senate Minutes, 3 December 1969.
9 Academic Planning Working Party, the Demand for University Places in the 1970s, 14 January 1969.

10 Comments of the Senate on University Development in the 1970s, 3 December 1969.

11 Reply to the Committee of Vice-Chancellors on University Expansion, Senate Minutes, 3 December 1969.

12 Academic Planning Working Party file, 14 March 1967 to 28 November 1969.

13 J.W. McFarlane, "The Shape of UEA in the 1970s: One Man's Speculations", 11 February 1969, Academic Working Party file.

14 Letter, Sir Kenneth Berrill of UGC to Vice-Chancellor, 20 May 1970.

15 T.P. Hill, "Chances of Obtaining a University Place by Subject". Papers of the Academic Planning Working Party. 93.6 per cent of applicants in Russian gained places in 1966 and 86 per cent in 1967.

16 D.C. Ward, "The Flow of UEA Graduates into Employment", APWP paper, February 1969.

17 T.P. Hill, "The Demand for University Places in the 1970s", APWP paper, 14 January 1969.

18 *EEN*, 12 March 1976.

19 *EDP*, 2 December 1977.

20 *EDP*, 13 May 1978.

21 *EEN*, 14 October 1978, 11 May 1979.

22 Letter, Sir Edmund Bacon to Frank Thistlethwaite, 4 April 1973 and letters, Keith Clayton (who had just dined with Sir Edmund) to Frank Thistlethwaite, 20 March and 3 April 1973.

23 *EDP*, 18 May 1978.

24 Visit of the University Grants Committee 27/8 February 1979.

25 *EDP*, 13 November 1976.

26 *THES*, 16 November 1979, "'Briefing".

27 Frank Thistlethwaite, *Doing Different in a Cold Climate*, St John's College Lecture, 25 October 1988, p. 10.

28 Thistlethwaite, *Doing Different in a Cold Climate*, p. 11.

29 Lord Annan, "British Higher Education", *Minerva*, 1982, p. 19.

30 *EDP*, 22 August 1979.

31 *EDP*, 10 November 1979.

32 *EDP*, 8 and 23 November 1979.

33 *EEN*, 9 June 1979, giving text of letter, Frank Thistlethwaite to Mark Carlisle, Secretary of State for Education.

34 House of Commons Foreign Affairs Committee Session, 1979-80. Overseas Development Sub-Committee, Minutes of Evidence, 26 February 1980. Frank Thistlethwaite's evidence, question 305.

35 *EEN*, 29 November 1979.

36 *The Times*, 20 July 1988, obituary of Professor Harry Allen.

37 A.H. Halsey, *The Decline of Donnish Dominion* (Oxford, 1990), p. 83.

38 This and subsequent paragraphs are based on the *Annual Reports of the Vice-Chancellor*, unless otherwise indicated.

39 Visit of the UGC, 28 February 1979.

40 *Annual Reports of the Vice-Chancellor, EDP*, 28 February 1976, 18 February 1977.

41 *EDP*, 29 December 1975.

42 *EDP*, 2 April 1976.

43 Letters, Professors Sydney Kettle and Norman Sheppard to Frank Thistlethwaite, 16 December 1975 and 9 February 1976.

44 *Annual Report of the Vice-Chancellor 1976-77*, p. 89.

45 *Annual Report of the Vice-Chancellor* 1979-80, p. 95.

46 *THES*, 2 February 1973.

47 *Annual Report of the Vice-Chancellor*, 1978-79, p. 17.

48 *Evening Standard*, 21 September 1976; *EEN*, 19 March 1977; *Observer*, 19 June 1977.

49 Senate Minute, 10 February 1971.

50 *EDP*, 26 November 1971.

51 *EEN*, 24 March 1975, U.H. Morth, "Climatological Research", *New Scientist*, 30 November 1978.

52 David Bentley, interviewed in *THES*, 17 June 1977.

53 *EEN*, 24 January 1976; *THES*, 27 February 1976.

54 *THES*, 26 November 1976.

55 *Annual Report of the Vice-Chancellor*, 1978-79, p. 54.

56 Jack Bull, *The Story of Keswick Hall, 1839-1981*, n.d.

57 *Teacher Training and Education* (the James Report), DES, HMSO (1972) para. 5.37., p. 62.

58 Canon John Gibbs, "Notes of a Meeting at Earlham Hall", 16 March 1971, W.E. Etherington Papers. I am grateful to Mr Etherington for making these private papers about Keswick Hall available to me and for valuable conversations.

59 Letter, W.E. Etherington to Hugh Pollard, 26 April 1972. Pollard was the Principal of St Martin's College, Lancaster.

60 *Education: A Framework for Expansion*, Cmnd 5174, December 1972.

61 Circular 7/73, 26 March 1973.

62 W.E. Etherington, "Notes of a Meeting with Professor Keith Clayton", 14 November 1973.

63 W.E. Etherington, "Notes of a Meeting with the Vice-Chancellor UEA", 12 December 1973.

64 Principal's Report to the Governing Body on the Future of the College, 18 January 1977.

65 Final Report of the Joint Committee, October 1978. Malcolm Frazer was the Professor of Chemical Education and Chairman of the UEA Committee dealing with Keswick. He later became the Director and Chief Executive of the Council for National Academic Awards.

66 Anthony Sampson, *Anatomy of Britain* (London, 1982), pp. 138-39, citing *Financial Times*, 9 July 1981.

67 *EEN*, 8 February 1974.

68 File on Deans' Retreats, 1974-80.

69 Rosemary Bohr (née Spencer), letter of memoirs, 17 October 1996.

70 *EDP*, 9 October 1975, "Proceeding in Blinkers"; *EEN*, "Degrees of Usefulness" 12 July 1977.

71 *EDP*, 7 February 1978.

72 *The Development of Higher Education into the 1990s*, p. 58.

73 *EDP*, 20 April 1979.

74 *EDP*, 23 February 1971.

75 Malcolm Freegard, "A Mirror of University Life on TV", *THES*, 15 April 1977.

76 *EEN*, 9 November 1973.

77 *EEN*, 16 June 1977.

78 *EEN*, 7 March 1979.

79 Letter, Dean of Students to Frank Thistlethwaite, 30 April 1974.

80 *EEN*, 7 February 1975; *EEN*, 20 May 1975; *EDP*, 1 March 1976.

81 *EDP*, 11 April 1974.

82 Senate Minute, 1 December 1982, Admissions Review.

83 *Observer*, 20 January 1985.

84 File, Portrait by Mr Michael Noakes. Mr Noakes has become a portraitist of H.M. the Queen since the UEA commission.

85 Frank Thistlethwaite, Diary on Leavetaking, 1980.

86 Letter, Frank Thistlethwaite to Michael Thompson, 5 March 1983.

87 Letter, Derek Burke to Frank Thistlethwaite, 31 January 1990.

88 *EDP*, 5 July 1980; *EEN* 5 July 1980.

89 Speech of the Vice-Chancellor (4 July 1980) in the VC Speeches Box and audio tape of the 1980 Congregation. The written text has the words "to be young" but the record of the actual speech has "when you were young". Possibly this deviation from the text to make the words more personal and direct heightened the emotion.

90 Frank Thistlethwaite, Diary of Leavetaking 1980.

91 Letter, Patricia Whitt to Mrs Andrew Ritchie, n.d. but July 1980.

92 Letter, undisclosed correspondent to Frank Thistlethwaite, 12 June 1978 and reply, Thistlethwaite to correspondent, 14 June 1978. In this case, since the letter was expressing private sentiments, I am not printing the name of the writer.

93 "2000 Graduates Later" 1985, audio-visual tape 307; Vice-Chancellor Michael Thompson addressing the Students' Union.

94 These books recalling his earlier life were *A Lancashire Family Inheritance* (1996); *Our War* (1997); *Cambridge Years* (1999).

Notes to Chapter 10: Making the Cuts

1 Malcolm Bradbury, *Cuts* (1987), p. 40.

2 David Lodge, *Nice Work* (1988), p. 307.

3 *Observer*, 29 September 1985.

4 Letter, Sir Edmund Bacon to Frank Thistlethwaite, 10 October 1979.

5 *Financial Times*, 1 December 1995.

6 Kenneth Baker, *The Turbulent Years* (London, 1993), p. 233.

7 Robin Marris in *The Times*, 5 February 1982, citing 1978 figures.

8 *National Commission on Education*, 1995, p. 44.

9 *The Development of Higher Education into the 1990s*, (Cmd 9524, HMSO, 1985), pp. 11-13.

10 Gareth Williams and Tessa Blackstone, *Response to Adversity*, SRHE (London, 1983), pp. 16, 17.

11 Baker, *The Turbulent Years*, p. 233.

12 Morrison Halcrow, *Keith Joseph: A Single Mind* (London, 1989), p. 184.

13 Asher Tropp, citing *Education Trends in the 1970s*, OECD 1984; *Guardian*, 20 December 1985.

14 Robin Marris in *The Times*, 28 June 1985.

15 *Daily Telegraph*, 21 April 1986.

16 P.G. Moore, "University Financing, 1979-1986", *Higher Education Quarterly*, 41, January 1987.

17 Sir Keith Joseph in Parliament, 26 October 1984; *The Times*, 27 October 1984.

Exchequer revenue from Government as a percentage of the income of UK universities fell from 63 per cent in 1980 to 55 per cent by 1988. *Independent*, 4 November 1989.

18 *Daily Telegraph*, 1 October 1983.

19 UEA Accounts, 1984/1985. The average of both years 1984 and 1985 is research councils 38.5 per cent, government departments 16.1 per cent, local authorities 4.0 per cent, public corporations 2.0 per cent, industry and commerce 8.9 per cent, charities 8.2 per cent, overseas organisations 12.3 per cent, "other" 8.8 per cent.

20 Senate Minute, 29 October 1980.

21 Letter, Edward Parkes to Michael Thompson, 30 December 1980.

22 Senate Minute, 4 February 1981.

23 Unit of Resource, Senate Minute, 4 February 1981.

24 Far East Trip, Report by Professor K. N. Bhaskar and Dr J.G. Harvey; Senate Minute, 20 May 1981.

25 Overseas Student Recruitment, Senate Minute, 9 February 1983.

26 Letter, Edward Parkes to Michael Thompson, 15 May 1981.

27 Senate Minute, 20 May 1981.

28 *Annual Report of the Vice-Chancellor*, 1979-80; *EDP*, 16 May 1981.

29 Letters, Edward Parkes to Michael Thompson, 1 July 1981.

30 UEA Newsletter, 3 July 1981.

31 Geoffrey Walford, *Restructuring Universities: Politics and Power in the Management of Change* (London, 1987), p. 81, figure 4.1.

32 University Development, 1981-85, Senate Minute, 30 September 1981.

33 Resources Committee, Review of Activities Report, March 1982.

34 *EDP*, 12 March 1982.

35 Resources Committee Strategy for Higher Education, Senate Minute, 29 February 1984.

36 Letter, Edward Parkes to Michael Thompson, 20 May 1982.

37 Senate Minute, 1 December 1982.

38 *The Times*, 23 November 1982.

39 *Daily Telegraph*, 23 December 1982.

40 *The Times*, 7 October 1981.

41 *Daily Telegraph*, 5 November 1981.

42 *The Times*, 30 December 1981.

43 *Daily Telegraph*, 30 January 1982.

44 *EEN*, 7 November 1981.

45 Plan for implementation 1983-4, Senate Minute, 15 June 1983.

46 *Daily Telegraph*, 27 July 1983.

47 Edward Parkes to Michael Thompson, 26 July 1983.

48 Letter, Edward Parkes to Sir Keith Joseph, 26 July 1983.

49 Letter, Sir Keith Joseph to Sir Edward Parkes, 1 September 1983.

50 *The Times*, 12 September 1983.

51 Letter, Sir Keith Joseph to Michael Thompson, 29 September 1983.

52 *The Times*, 30 September 1983.

53 Letter, Sir Peter Swinnerton Dyer to Michael Thompson, 1 November 1983.

54 *The Guardian*, 8 November 1983.

55 *Daily Telegraph*, 9 November 1983.

56 Finance Officer's memorandum, 4 October 1983, Senate Minute, 9 November 1983.

57 Letter, Michael Thompson to UGC, reported in Newsletter, 30 March 1984.
58 Resources Committee Strategy for Higher Education, Senate Minute, 29 February 1984.
59 Plan for Implementation, 1984-85, Finance Office, May 1984, Senate Minute, 20 June 1984.
60 *Guardian*, 8 February 1984.
61 *The Times*, 12 March 1984.
62 *Guardian*, 8, 14 March 1984.
63 *Daily Telegraph*, 13 July 1984.
64 *A Strategy for Higher Education into the 1990s*, University Grants Committee, HMSO (1984).
65 Keith Clayton in *Guardian*, 17 September 1984.
66 *EDP*, 23 January 1985.
67 *Daily Telegraph*, 6 December 1984.
68 *The Times*, 8 December 1984.
69 *Daily Telegraph*, 6 December 1984; *EDP*, 11, 12, 13, 14, 15, 18, 19, 20 December 1984; *EEN*, 14 December 1984; *EDP*, 22, 23 January 1985, for the Coutts issue. Ian Coutts returned to UEA in the 1990s as a respected and successful mature student in history.
70 *EDP*, 22 January 1982; *EEN*, 27 February 1984.
71 *EEN*, 21 April 1982; *EDP*, 22 April 1982.
72 *Concrete*, 6 March 1996.
73 Letter, UGC to Michael Thompson, 19 November 1984.
74 Letter, UGC to Michael Thompson, 7 February 1985.
75 University Planning, Senate Minute, 27 February 1985; *EDP*, 5 March 1985.
76 *EDP*, 11 May 1985.
77 Report of the Steering Committee for Efficiency Studies: Universities (Jarratt) CVCP 1985; Senate Minute, 6 November 1985.
78 *The Times*, 2 April 1985.
79 *The Development of Higher Education into the 1990s* (Cmd 9524) HMSO 1985.
80 *The Times*, 22 May 1985.
81 *Daily Telegraph*, 28 May 1985.
82 *EDP*, 22 May 1985.
83 Owen Chadwick, *The Ups and Downs of Universities*, Keswick Hall Lecture, 1986, pp. 2, 4, 5.
84 Margaret Thatcher, *The Downing Street Years* (London, 1993), p. 599.
85 *EDP*, 8 June 1985.
86 *EDP*, 17 December 1985.
87 C.C. Matheson, A Review of Financial Support for Students, 17 February 1986, Senate Minute, 26 February 1986.
88 *EEN*, 21 July 1984.
89 *EDP*, 6 June 1983.
90 *The Times*, 15 January 1981.
91 *The Times*, 19 December 1985.
92 AUT, *UK Universities: Bursting at the Seams* (1993), p. 6.
93 *The Times*, 14 January 1981. The Chairman of the Science and Engineering Research Council at the time was Sir Geoffrey Allen, a future Chancellor of UEA.
94 Letter, UGC to Michael Thompson, 20 May 1986. This was co-incidentally Keith Joseph's last day in office before handing over to Kenneth Baker.

95 Finance Officer's Assessment of the 1986-87 grant, Senate Minute, 28 May 1986.
96 The UGC Safety Net, Finance Officer, 9 December 1986; Senate Minute, 17 December 1986.
97 Plans to 1990, A Forward Look; Senate Minute, 17 December 1986.
98 Review of Activities, Senate Minute, 17 March 1982.
90 Forward Look Report, Summary of Comments, Senate Minute, 17 December 1986.
100 Comparative Cost Units, 1984-85. Senate Minute, 25 June 1986. Nationally the average unit cost per student fell by 5 per cent in real terms between 1980/1 to 1986/7, *Higher Education: Meeting the Challenge*, Cmnd 114 HMSO (1987), p. 15.
101 A. H. Halsey, *The Decline of Donnish Dominion*, p. 289.

Notes to Chapter 11: Innovation without Growth

1   Michael Thompson, *EDP*, 2 October 1980.
2   Senate Minute, 1 December 1982.
3   *EEN*, 12 December 1981; *EDP*, 7 September 1983.
4   Teachers' and Pupils' Attitudes to and Images of Science at the University of East Anglia, November 1985, Senate Minute, 11 December 1985.
5   *The Times*, 3 September 1984.
6   Admissions Committee Annual Report, 1984-85.
7   Working Party on Continuing Education, Senate Minute, 9 November 1983.
8   Jean Rennie, *Cap and Apron to Cap and Gown* (Fakenham, 1985); *EDP*, *Daily Telegraph*, 3 July 1984.
9   Senate Minute, 26 November 1980.
10 "The Part-Time BA in History", Senate Minute, 9 March 1983.
11 Working Party on Continuing Education, Senate Minute, 9 November 1983.
12 Continuing Education, Senate Minute, 26 February 1986.
13 Report of the Working Party on Language Teaching 1981, Senate Minute, 17 June 1981.
14 Joint Programme in Modern Languages and Business Studies, Senate Minute, 15 May 1985.
15 *EDP*, 1 July 1983.
16 *THES*, 26 September 1980; *Report on Russian and Russian Studies in British Universities* (Prof. R.J.C. Atkinson), UGC, December 1979.
17 Senate Minute, 26 November 1980.
18 Senate Minute, 14 March 1987, gives employment data 1977-86.
19 *Annual Report of the Vice-Chancellor*, 1985/6, p. 61.
20 *Financial Times*, 21 January 1982, 26 January 1984, 14 November 1985.
21 Dennis Chaplin in *EDP*, 26, 27 September 1985.
22 *EEN*, 19 March 1982.
23 *EEN*, 12 November 1983.
24 *EDP*, 11 December 1984.
25 Working Party on Electronics, Senate Minute, 20 May 1981.
26 *EDP*, 12 November 1981.
27 Electronic Systems Engineering: An Investment for the Future, Senate Minute, 20 June 1984.
28 Comparative Unit Costs: Finance Office paper, Senate Minute, 25 June 1986.

29 *EDP*, 28 March 1985; *THES*, 22 March 1985.
30 *Improving Research Links between Higher Education and Industry*, HMSO, June 1983. UEA gave evidence to the Advisory Council for Applied Research and Development, whose report this was.
31 *EDP*, 30 April 1982.
32 *EDP*, 22 February 1983.
33 *Guardian*, 7 December 1985.
34 Senate Minute, 9 November 1983.
35 *EDP*, 25 May 1985.
36 Senate Minute, 23 May 1984.
37 Senate Minute, 1 December 1982.
38 Senate Minute, 9 February 1983.
39 Senate Minute, 15 May 1985.
40 *The Times*, 19 March, 20 November 1984.
41 "New Administration Computer", Senate Minute, 14 December 1983.
42 *EEN*, 13 May 1982.
43 *EDP*, 3 March 1982.
44 *EEN*, 15 October 1982.
45 *EDP*, 28 July 1983. Senate Minute, 9 November 1983.
46 *EEN*, 20 May 1982, 14 January 1983.
47 *EDP*, 8 March 1984.
48 *EDP*, 10 September 1982.
49 *EEN*, 26, 27 March 1982 typical of a spate of articles and letters in March and April 1983 in support of CEAS.
50 *EDP*, 27 March 1984.
51 *EDP*, 12 April 1983.
52 *EDP*, 26 June 1984.
53 Senate Minute, 17 July 1981.
54 *EDP*, 4 January 1985, 13 April 1985.
55 *EEN*, 8 November 1980; *EDP*, 3 March, 16 September 1982.
56 *EDP*, 14 June 1985.
57 *EDP*, 10 May 1985, 2 March 1984.
58 *EDP*, 13 October 1983.
59 *EDP*, 7 November 1985.
60 Senate Minute, 25 June 1986.
61 Stefan Muthesius, *Concrete and Open Skies*.
62 *EDP*, 4 February 1983; *EEN*, 2 September 1983.
63 *Architect's Journal*, 5 March 1986; Belinda Ward "A Lesson in Patronage"; and David Wild, "Appraisal".
64 AVC tape 568; *EDP*, 23 October 1984.
65 *Financial Times*, 21 August 1999. The Business, *Financial Times* weekend magazine, 19 February 2000, "Zen and the Art of Buildings".
66 *EDP*, 3 December 1981.
67 *EEN*, 5 January 1982.
68 Deferred Maintenance, Senate Minute, 15 May 1985.
69 *EEN*, 3 October 1981; *EDP*, 16 February 1982.
70 The School of Development Studies Farm, appendix I, Valuation, Senate Minute, 20 April 1981.

71 *EEN*, 19 February 1981; *Daily Telegraph*, 2 June 1982.
72 *EEN*, 16 January 1985.
73 *EDP*, 5 December 1984.
74 Owen Chadwick, Senate Minute, 18 March 1985; *EDP*, 11 May, 26 June, 5 July 1985.
75 *EDP*, 20 March, 5 September 1984.
76 *EDP*, 5 February 1982.
77 UEA Association, Senate Minute, 29 February 1984.
78 *EDP*, 23 September 1985.
79 First Degrees Committee, Senate Minute, 22 June 1985.
80 Senate Minute, 26 February 1986.
81 "The Economic Contribution of UEA to the Region", Senate Minute, 3 March 1982; *EDP* 16 October 1982.
82 Senate Minute, 11 December 1985.

Notes to Chapter 12: The Next Step Forward

1 Gillian Shephard, Secretary of State for Education and MP for South-West Norfolk; *EEN*, 3 July 1995.
2 Derek C. Burke, Curriculum Vitae, Senate Minute, 31 July 1986; *EDP*, 18 April 1987; *EEN*, 30 January 1987; *THES*, 29 September 1995.
3 *Ziggurat*, 16, Spring/Summer 1995, "Eight Years in the Hot Seat".
4 *Ziggurat*, 8, February 1990, "Growth and Change".
5 *The Financial Health of Higher Education Institutions in England*, National Audit Office, Report by the Comptroller and Auditor General. HC Session, 1994-95, 13, 2 December 1994, pp. 1, 13.
6 Senate Minute, 17 June 1987, made it an offence to "occupy any premises".
7 *EDP*, 16 May 1987.
8 *Independent*, 13 October 1987.
9 *Daily Telegraph*, 15 February 1989.
10 *EDP*, 16 February 1989.
11 *Independent*, 21 May 1987.
12 *Independent*, 1 March 1990.
13 *Guardian*, 26 October 1990.
14 *Guardian*, 6 November 1990.
15 *EDP*, 26 October 1990.
16 *Financial Health of Higher Education Institutions*, appendix 2, "Funding Changes".
17 *EDP*, 21 June 1994.
18 *Guardian*, 2 December 1994.
19 *THES*, 3 March 1995. Seminar by Alan Jones on university finances 1992 and information from Alan Jones.
20 *Financial Times*, 20 March 1995.
21 Annual Accounts of UEA for the period.
22 *THES*, 23 January 1987.
23 *EDP*, 23 May 1987.
24 *EDP*, 3 February 1987.
25 *Hansard*, 21 January 1987.
26 Research Committee Report, Senate Minute, 16 January 1991.

27 PRO, UGC/6/70, UGC, *The Future of University Physics* (Sir Sam Edwards), 1988.
28 Strategic Plan, February 1995.
29 *Daily Telegraph*, 6 November 1995.
30 *Daily Telegraph*, 17 November 1989.
31 *Financial Times*, 22 February 1994; *EEN*, 2 September 1994.
32 Rick Mather Architects, *Development Plan for the University of East Anglia*, 14 June 1989.
33 *Building Design*, 9 November 1990.
34 *EDP*, 2 February 1991.
35 Peter Dormer in *Independent*, 8 December 1993.
36 *Architect's Journal*, 7 November 1990.
37 *EDP*, 1 May 1995.
38 *Ziggurat*, 13 Autumn 1993, "New Residences".
39 *EDP*, 29 June 1989..
40 *EDP*, 26 May 1994.
41 *The Times*, 2 December 1994.
42 *The Advertiser*, 13 October 1995.
43 Peter Yorke *EEN*, 28 September 1995.
44 *Annual Report of the Vice-Chancellor*, 1993-94 p. 16.
45 *EDP*, 27 January 1994; *Ziggurat* 14, Spring/Summer 1994.
46 *Construction Weekly*, 7 March 1990.
47 *EDP*, 9 June 1993.
48 *EEN*, 28 November 1994.
49 *EDP*, 5 December 1987.
50 *EDP*, 9 March 1993.
51 *EEN*, 30 August 1994; *EDP*, 2 September 1994; *EEN*, 28 July 1995; *EDP*, 1 December 1995; UEA press briefing 30 November 1995.
52 *EDP*, 28 May 1995.
53 *EDP*, 4 May 1987.
54 *EEN*, 4 October 1990.
55 Senate Minute, 16 June 1990. Recognition of the Cambridge Laboratory as an Affiliated Institute of the University.
56 *Annual Report of the Vice-Chancellor*, 1990-91, p. 16, and information from Dr Peter Snape, 14 December 1999.
57 *EDP*, 13 November 1993.
58 "Science in the Park", *Ziggurat*, 15, Autumn/Winter 1994.
59 Segal Quince Wickstead, *Universities, Enterprise and Local Economic Development*, MSC, (HMSO, 1988).
60 *EDP*, 6 October 1988.
61 Ibid.
62 *New Scientist*, 3 November 1990.
63 *Annual Report of the Vice-Chancellor*, 1986-87.
64 *Annual Report of the Vice-Chancellor*, 1986-87.
65 *Annual Report of the Vice-Chancellor*, 1988-89; *Ziggurat*, 17, Autumn/Winter 1995.
66 *Annual Report of the Vice-Chancellor*, 1988-89 and 1992-93.
67 *School of Environmental Sciences Annual Report*, 1995.
68 *Ziggurat*, 10, Summer 1992.
69 *EDP*, 17 August 1993; *Ziggurat*, 13 Autumn 1993.

70 *EDP*, 11 March 1994.

71 *EDP*, 16 September 1994.

72 *EDP*, 3 February 1995.

73 *Annual Report of the Vice-Chancellor*, 1991-92.

74 *Annual Report of the Vice-Chancellor*, 1990-91.

75 *Therapy*, 25 April 1991, "The Profession of Occupational Therapy"; Senate Minute, 14 November 1990.

76 *Annual Report of the Vice-Chancellor*, 1993-94, pp. 6-7.

77 *Annual Report of the Vice-Chancellor*, 1994-95, pp. 6-7.

78 *EDP*, 10 June 1987.

79 *EEN*, 26 May 1991.

80 *EEN*, 29 August 1989.

81 *Sunday Times*, 11 June 1989.

82 *EDP*, 12 April 1995; Senate Minute, 15 January 1992, Management Education Steering Group.

83 *Ziggurat* 17, Autumn/Winter 1995.

84 *Annual Report of the Vice-Chancellor*, 1988-89; *EDP*, 12 May 1989; *The Times*, 16 May 1989.

85 *EEN*, 1 May 1987.

86 Professor R. A. Church, "A Strategy for History at UEA", Senate Minute, 24 October 1990. Working Group on the Future of History, Report, 9 June 1993, and Senate Minute, 15 June 1994, are key documents. There is a good account by Roy Church in *UEA History News*, October 1996.

87 *East Anglian Daily Times*, 8 December 1987.

88 Letter, Derek Burke to various Principals, 19 July 1991, Senate Minute, 13 November 1991.

89 Derek Burke Speech to Court, 15 May 1992.

90 *EDP*, 3 August 1991.

91 *East Anglian Daily Times*, 31 March 1993.

92 *EDP*, 19 May 1988.

93 Validation Committee, Otley College, 5 June 1990.

94 UEA Press Release, 31 August 1995.

95 *East Anglian Daily Times*, 27 June 1995.

96 *Independent*, 20 May 1993.

97 Senate Minutes, 13 November 1991, 4 March 1992, 17 June 1992. "Eastern Counties University", "University of Eastern England" (UEE) were other proposals.

98 *THES*, 10 May 1991.

99 *EEN*, 13 March 1987.

100 Working Party on a Common Course Structure. Senate Minutes, 13 June 1990, 6 March 1991, 13 November 1991, 15 January 1992, 4 March 1992. For the justification and planning of the system, *Ziggurat*, 13, Autumn 1993.

101 History in Universities Defence Group (HUDG), Survey of History Departments: A Report (1994), pp. 6-7. *Daily Telegraph*, 3 August 1995, for an attack by several major departments of history on modules and "pick and mix" degrees.

102 HUDG, p. 6.

103 *Independent*, 7 December 1995; Senate Minute, 25 January 1995.

104 Andrew Marfleet and Saville Kushner, *The Common Course Structure at UEA*, November 1995, p. 35.

105 *Annual Report of the Vice-Chancellor*, 1986-87.
106 *Annual Report of the Vice-Chancellor*, 1991-92.
107 *Annual Report of the Vice-Chancellor*, 1986-87.
108 Senate Minute, 8 June 1988.
109 Senate Minute, 9 November 1988.
110 Senate Minute, 15 June 1994.
111 *EEN*, 26 January 1987.
112 Gallup Poll in *The Times* and *Daily Telegraph*, 10 October 1988.
113 *EDP*, 27 October 1988.
114 *EEN*, 24 July 1989.
115 The New Union Constitution, 26 November 1990; Senate Minute, 16 January 1991.
116 *EEN*, 25 October 1993.
117 *EDP*, 21 February 1993.
118 *EEN*, 13 February 1995.
119 *EDP*, 21 February 1995.
120 *Guardian*, 16 November 1994.
121 *EEN*, 22 November 1988.
122 *Ziggurat*, 14, Spring/Summer 1994.
123 *EEN*, 8 November 1994.
124 *EEN*, 1 February 1995.
125 *Sunday Telegraph*, 3 November 1994, suggested 44 per cent. *EEN*, 1 February 1995, cited the SLC as suggesting "a half".
126 *Ziggurat*, 17, Autumn/Winter 1995.
127 *Daily Telegraph*, 26 August 1993.
128 *EADT*, 23 October 1995.
129 *EEN*, 21 September 1994.
130 *EDP*, 6 October 1995.
131 *Ziggurat*, 17, Autumn/Winter 1995.
132 Reports of the Director of the Student Counselling Service (Brian Thorne), 1987/8 – 1994/5. An Assessment of the Student Counselling Service, n.d. 1993/4.
133 Report of the Group for Staff Support and Fellowship, 1995.
134 *Creating our Future*, appendix 2. Citing HEFCE profiles of Higher Education Institutes, 1997.
135 *EEN*, 21 June 1988.
136 *East Anglian Daily Times*, 12 July 1995.
137 Sir Geoffrey Allen, Curriculum Vitae, Senate Minutes, 14 December 1983, 7 February 1994. *EDP*, 11 May, 7 July 1994. *University of East Anglia: The Installation of Professor Sir Geoffrey Allen*, 6 July 1994.
138 *EEN*, 17 September 1993.
139 Senate Minute, 13 June 1990; *Ziggurat*, 11, Autumn 1992.
140 *EDP*, 6 July 1993.
141 Report from the Vice-Chancellor on UEA 25, Senate Minute, 15 November 1989.
142 *The Times*, 14 May 1993, 27 May 1994, 19 May 1995.
143 *Daily Telegraph*, 23 August 1995.
144 *Sunday Times*, 27 January 1991.
145 *Observer*, 21 October 1994.
146 Planning for the 1990s, Senate Minute, 1 March 1989.
147 *An Overview of the Demand for Graduates*, HMSO, March 1990, p. 54.

148 Janet Anderson, *From UEA to Employment*, UEA 1997; *From UEA to Employment*, ii, UEA 1999.
149 Senate Minutes, 16 November 1994, 15 January 1995.
150 *The Times*, 12 May 1993.
151 *The Times*, 26 May 1994.
152 *The Times*, 19 May 1995.
153 *The Times*, 15 May 1996, and press release, 15 May 1996.
154 *Ziggurat*, 12, Spring/Summer 1993.
155 In the HEFCE grants for 1995-96, UEA was a respectable twenty-fifth with £8,100,000, *Independent*, 3 March 1995.
156 Senate Minute, 24 January 1996.
157 *Annual Report of the Vice-Chancellor*, 1992-93.

Notes to Chapter 13: The Pursuit of Excellence

1 UEA Strategic Plan, UEA 2000 Mission Statement.
2 *Broadview Bulletin*, 13 December 1994. UEA Press release, 13 December 1994. Most broadsheet newspapers published profiles, 14-19 December 1994. Desert Island Discs interview by Sue Lawley 20 October 1991 (made available by the BBC to the National Sound Archive, British Library) is most illuminating.
3 *Financial Times*, 14 December 1994.
4 *EDP*, Interview with Colin Chinery, 2 October 1995; *Broadview*, 8 February 1996; Dame Elizabeth's speech at Assembly, 6 March 1996.
5 *Concrete*, 22 January 1997.
6 Vincent Watts, Curriculum Vitae, Senate Minute, 7 July 1977.
7 Author's notes on the Vice-Chancellor's Open House, 28 November 1997.
8 Agenda for Change, a briefing note, 6 February 1998.
9 Making the Difference, 29 April 1998. Senate Minute, 14 June 1998.
10 Creating a Future: UEA, a World Class Future, September 1998
11 David Baker in *Broadview*, 18 October 1996.
12 *Annual Reports of the Vice-Chancellor and Accounts*.
13 Vice-Chancellor in *Concrete*, 3 February 1999.
14 *Annual Reports of the Vice-Chancellor and Accounts*.
15 "Top Up Fees", Senate Minute, 22 January 1997.
16 Green Paper, The Structure of the Academic Year, 22 January 1997. Senate Minute, 24 June 1998.
17 Planning and Resources Committee Physics Review Group. Senate Minute, 22 January 1997.
18 Senate Minute, 11 March 1998.
19 Senate Minute, 26 June 1998.
20 *Independent on Sunday*, 26 June 1995
21 European Media Studies with Honours Language Programme. Senate Minute, 12 June 1991.
22 *Broadview*, February 1999.
23 *National Committee of Inquiry into Higher Education: Higher Education in a Learning Society* (Sir Ron Dearing), HMSO July 1977.
24 Jon Gubbay and Lynn Preston, *The Student Learning Experience: Report of a Survey of UEA Students*, UEA May 1997.

25 PRO, UGC/22 Quality Assessment Reports.
26 *Daily Telegraph*, 21 August 1996.
27 *Broadview*, June 1998.
28 Research Assessment Exercise Results, 1996; Senate Minute, 22 January 1997; *Ziggurat*, Spring/Summer 1997.
29 *The Times*, 15 May 1996.
30 *Broadview*, December 1998.
31 *THES*, 3 March 2000.
32 *Broadview*, February, December 1998; *Concrete*, 11 November 1998.
33 *Staff IT Skills and Use 1999 Survey Report* (Janet Anderson), June 1999; *Student IT Use; 1998 Survey Report* (Janet Anderson), 1998.
34 Senate Minute, 24 June 1998, referring to a survey by Redmole.
35 Jon Buscall, *College.com* (London, 1999), p. 195.
36 *Ziggurat*, Spring/Summer 1997; *Broadview*, 16 October 1996.
37 *Broadview*, September 1999.
38 *Broadview*, May 1999.
39 UEA Press Release, 16 June 2000.
40 Presentation of Professor Trevor Davies (Dean of ENV) to UEA Court, 12 May 2000.
41 *Concrete*, 19 January 2000.
42 *Ziggurat*, Spring/Summer 1997.
43 *Ziggurat*, Spring/Summer 1995; *Broadview*, 1 August 1996; *Ziggurat*, Summer 1998.
44 *Broadview*, October 1997
45 *Broadview*, October 1999.
46 Vice-Chancellor's Open House, 9 November 1999.
47 Sport University. Welcome to Sport at UEA, n.d. 1998.
48 *Concrete*, 17 February 1999
49 *Broadview*, 8 February, 20 June 1996.
50 *Concrete*, 12 May 1999.
51 *Ziggurat*, Summer 1998.
52 *Broadview*, December 1999.
53 *Annual Report of the Vice-Chancellor*, 1995/6.
54 Senate Minute, 12 June 1996.
55 *Annual Report of the Vice-Chancellor*, 1996/7.
56 *Ziggurat*, Summer 1998.
57 *Annual Report of the Vice-Chancellor*, 1996/7.
58 *Annual Report of the Vice-Chancellor*, 1996/7.
59 *Ziggurat*, Spring/Summer 1997.
60 *Annual Report of the Vice-Chancellor*, 1996/7.

Notes to Chapter 14: Achievement

1 Sir Timothy Colman interviewed, 26 August 1999.
2 Figures from the *Dearing Report*, pp. 18, 20, 44.
3 The Chancellor of the Exechequer's budget speech, 21 March 2000.
4 Martin Trow, "Reflections on the Transition from Mass to Universal Higher Education", *Daedalus* 99, no. 1, Winter 1970.
5 Martin Trow, "The Robbins Trap: British Attitudes and the Limits of Expansion", *Higher Education Quarterly*, 43, Winter 1989.

6 Michael Sanderson, *Educational Opportunity and Social Change* (London, 1987), pp. 132-33, for these surveys.

7 *Independent,* 9 December 1993.

8 *Guardian,* 23 August 1995.

9 John Carswell, *Government and the Universities in Britain, 1960-80* (Cambridge, 1985), p. 62.

10 *The Times,* 3 December 1999.

11 Ibid.

12 In *The Times* League tables of 1998 (15 May 1998), UEA's entry standards ranked twenty-fourth out of ninety-six universities along with two others. If the best university was taking the top 1 per cent and the ninety-sixth the top thirtieth per cent of ability then UEA's position (24-26 out of 96) suggests that it was recruiting in the 7.5-8 per cent range of ability, not greatly different from the 1960s.

13 *Annual Report of the Vice-Chancellor,* 1996-97.

14 *Annual Report of the Vice-Chancellor,* 1992-93.

15 *Broadview,* 8 February 1996.

16 *The Changing Roles of University Leaders and Managers,* DES, 1991, is perceptive on the dichotomy of the "community of scholars" and "managerial" styles.

17 Michael Paulson Ellis, "A Registrar Remembers", Seminar at UEA 9 June 1999.

18 Sheldon Rothblatt, "The Limbs of Osiris: Liberal Education in the English-Speaking World", in Sheldon Rothblatt and Bjorn Wittrock, *The European and American University since 1880* (Cambridge, 1993), p. 69.

19 *Annual Report of the Vice-Chancellor,* 1986-87; "Transferable Skills", Report to the Committee of Deans; Transferable Skills, 9 May 1988, Senate Minute, 8 June 1988.

20 Janet Anderson, *From UEA to Employment*, ii, UEA, 1999.

21 *The Times,* 3 December 1999.

22 *Efficiency Gains or Quality Losses?,* AUT 1994.

23 The Future of the Library, a Green Paper presented to Senate, 15 November 1995.

24 Report of the Regional Strategy Task Group October 1997; Senate Minute, 12 November 1997.

25 Alumni Occupations, a sample of 1161 calculated from the first eighty pages of the printout provided by Mrs Hayley Garrard. The entries are anonymised.

26 Noel Annan, *The Dons* (London 1999) p. 294.

27 *The Times,* 2 December 1987; William Rees Mogg, "Cash is not Academic".

28 Charles Clotfelter, *Buying the Best: Cost Escalation in Higher Education* (Princeton, 1996).

29 John Ashworth, "Turning the Tables", BBC Radio 4, 23 February 1997.

30 Michael Sanderson, "Women at UEA in the 1960s", p. 189.

31 *Concrete,* 2 February 2000 "Sex Survey".

32 R.A.Y. Jones, in *Broadview,* September 1997.

Bibliography

Papers in UEA Archives

The most important are four filing cabinets of the papers of Professor Frank Thistlethwaite, the founding Vice Chancellor, 1961–80.

There are also the papers or photographed copies of the papers of:

Dr Simon Eden Green (student matters).
W.E. Etherington (the merger with Keswick College).
Finance Office, files on early investment policy.
Lord Mackintosh of Halifax (speeches in support of UEA).
D.L. Marsh (student matters).
Norwich Junior Chamber of Commerce, 1963–65 (support for UEA).
Sir Lincoln Ralphs (correspondence and papers on founding and early years of UEA).
Jeremy Schonfield (student matters).
Sir Arthur South (correspondence and papers on the founding of UEA).
Gordon Tilsley (committees and correspondence on the founding of UEA).
Lord Zuckerman (SZ/UEA/1–7).

Briefs and Plans for Denys Lasdun's design of the Plain.
Newscuttings Books of the University

Papers Relating to UEA in Private Hands

R.H. Campbell (Pro Vice Chancellor).
Gerald Crompton.
Michael Everitt (architect, Feilden and Mawson).
Michael Sanderson (UEA Diaries, 1971–2000).

Unpublished Typescript Memoirs of UEA

Rosemary Bohr (née Spencer).
John Cockings.
A. Hassell Smith.
Adrian Smith.
Professor Norman Sheppard,"Recollections of the Formative Years of the School of Chemical Sciences".
Professor Norman Sheppard, "University Governance".
Frank Thistlethwaite, "Origins" (subsequently printed).

Frank Thistlethwaite,"The Founding of the University of East Anglia".
Gordon Tilsley, "Personal Reminiscences".
Mary Vallanjon.
G.B. Wilson.
David and Jill Wright.
Professor Christopher Wrigley.

Sample printout of alumnae occupations, 1963–2000 (provided by Mrs Hayley Garrard).

UEA Official Publications

Senate Minutes
Council Minutes
Calendars
Prospectuses
Annual Reports of the Vice Chancellor
Annual Accounts
UEA Bulletin
UEA Newsletter
Broadview
Ziggurat

Student Publications

Chips
Can Opener
Concrete
Decanter
Incredible Magazine
Kett
Mandate
Phoenix
SKOP
Square One
Twice

Papers in Other Locations

Papers of the University Grants Committee in the Public Records Office, Kew

UGC Minutes, 1959–69, UGC, 1/7–17.
UGC Papers, 2/1 (1919); 2/27 (1946); 2/28 (1947); 2/57 (1959) University Expansion; 2/60 (1960) New University Institutions; 2/91 (1963) University Village; 2/ 110 (1964) Horsham St Faith; 2/122 (1966) UEA Great Hall.

UGC/7/27, Quinquennial Estimates, University of East Anglia, 1962–67.
UGC/7/212, Proposed Institution of Norwich University College.
UGC/7/440, Expansion of Universities post 1963, University of East Anglia.
UGC/7/807, Taking of Dangerous Drugs by Students.
UGC/7/925, University of the Air.
UGC/22, Quality Assessment Reports, UEA, 1994–97.
UGC 7/1306, Enquiry into Student Progress, 1968.
UGC/9/2/2, Subcommittee on New Universities.

Churchill College Cambridge, Archive Centre

Papers of Sir John Cockcroft, 17/1.
Memorandum to the Committee on Higher Education (Lord Robbins), 3 July 1961.
Evidence 13 October, 17 November 1961.
Personal Diary, 1962.

Norwich City College Archives

Prospectuses of the City of Norwich Technical Institute, 1901–39.
Newscuttings Books.

Norfolk County Record Office

N/TC 35/5/9, Minutes of the Education (Sub) Higher Education Committee, 12 January 1937 to 5 March 1940.
ACC, Eaton, 15 September 1977, Papers of T.C. Eaton on UEA.

Miss Rosamund Strode

Transcripts of correspondence between Benjamin Britten and UEA.

Personal Interviews

Lord Annan, 26/9/1996. Sir Malcolm Bradbury, 21/2/2000. Professor Derek Burke, 6/3/2000. Professor R.H. Campbell, 6/6/1995. John Ceybird, 28/12/1994. Professor Keith Clayton, 22/11/1999. John Cockings, 16/5/1996. Sir Timothy Colman, 26/8/1999. Gerald and Rosemary Crompton, 30/5/1995. Professor Jack Dainty, 18/4/2000. T.C. Eaton, 12/8/1996. Professor Roy Emerson, 31/7/1996. Michael and Bridgid Everitt, 5/8/1999. Sir Bernard Feilden, interviewed by Stefan Muthesius, 28/9/1995. Lord Franks of Headington, *c.* May 1966. Raymond Frostick, 17/2/2000. Willi and Valerie Guttsman, 12/6/1995. Marshall Hopkins, 8/7/1999. Professor Alan Katritzky, 23/6/1995. Sir Denys Lasdun, 7/10/1999. David Luckhurst, 4/8/1999. C.C. "Kiff" Matheson, 3/4/2000. Peter McKinley, 7/10/1999. Group Captain G.R. Montgomery, 2/3/1995. Professor Donald Osborne, 16/8/1996. Daphne Powlett, 19/4/1995. Lady Enid Ralphs, 1/3/1995. Judith Crabtree, 3/7/1998. W.Rowan Hare, 5/9/1996/ Barbara and Professor Geoffrey Searle, 14/7/1998. Professor Norman Sheppard, 17/7/1998. Sir

Arthur South, 20/4/1995. Rosamund Strode, 14/5/1995. Dr Tom Stuttaford, 29/4/1995 (by telephone). Professor John Tarrant, 27/3/2000. Frank Thistlethwaite, 9/12/1994, 1/7/1996, 20/8/1999, 10/11/1999. Sir Michael Thompson, 10/1/2000. Professor Andrew Thomson, 11/5/2000. Professor Brian Thorne, 21/1/2000. Gordon Tilsley, 27 January 1995. Vincent Watts, 18/4/2000. Patricia Whitt, 24/11/1999, 31/1/2000. Sir Charles Wilson, 5/6/1995. Sir Angus Wilson, *c.* May 1967.

Audio-Visual, Verbal and Recorded Material Relating to UEA

Audio-Visual Centre Tapes

71	Food Research Institute.
117, 173–75	Frank Thistlethwaite interviewed by James McFarlane.
176	Glimpses of Early Years.
209	University Stories.
212, 235	SCVA.
260	Roy Emerson.
280	The Education Building.
294,295,296,307	2000 Graduates Later.
568.	Audio Tape of the 1980 Congregation

UEA :The Silver Years   1988 (video)

Film in East Anglian Film Archive

Jos Haentjens, Universities in Britain, *The University of East Anglia,* 1973. UEA Norwich,1983–84.

Other Materials

Frank Thistlethwaite, interviewed by Professor James McFarlane, six audio tapes.
Michael Paulson Ellis, "A Registrar Remembers", UEA Seminar, 9 June 1999.
Denys Lasdun, Exhibition at the Royal Academy of Arts, 6 February-16 March 1997, and the original tapes on UEA made for the Exhibition by MUF.
Desert Island Discs, Radio 4 interviews by Sue Lawley:
  Dame Elizabeth Estève-Coll (made available by the BBC Sound Archives to the British Library).
  Rose Tremain, 12/10/1997.
  Jack Straw, 12/7/1998.
  Ian McEwan, 16/1/2000.

University of East Anglia: Special Reports

Industrial Administration Ltd, "The University of East Anglia, Survey of Senate and its Committees", June 1969.
Report of the Working Party on the Use of Drugs. March 1971.

Report of the Commission of Enquiry into the General Regulations and the Code of Discipline (Raymond Frostick),October 1971.

Butler Miller Associates, Report on the Sainsbury Centre for Visual Arts, 8 August 1977.

Resources Committee Review of Activities, March 1982.

Report of the Working Party on the Jarratt Report (Raymond Frostick),1986.

Rick Mather Architects, Development Plan for the University of East Anglia, 14 June 1989.

CVCP, Academic Audit Unit, Report of an Academic Audit of the University of East Anglia, April 1991.

Marfleet, Andrew and Kushner, Saville, "The Common Course Structure at UEA", November 1995.

"From UEA to Employment: A Survey of 1993 Graduates" (Janet Anderson),March 1997.

"The Student Learning Experience: Report of a Survey of UEA Students" (Jon Gubbay and Lynn Preston), May 1997.

Report of the Regional Strategy Task Group (David Bridges), October 1997.

"Student IT Use: A Survey Report" (Janet Anderson), 1998.

"Staff IT Skills and Use: A Survey Report" (Janet Anderson), 1999.

"From UEA to Employment: A Survey of 1996 Graduates", vol 2 (Janet Anderson), 1999.

Government Reports

Higher Technological Education, Report of a Special Committee (Lord Percy), HMSO (1945).

XIV Scientific Manpower (Sir Alan Barlow), Cmnd 6824 (1945-46).

UGC Report of the Sub Committee on Halls of Residence (W.R. Niblett) (1957).

UGC University Development, 1952–57, Cmnd 534 (1958).

Fifteen to Eighteen: Report of the Central Advisory Council for Education (Sir Geoffrey Crowther) (1959).

Report of the Agricultural Research Council (1961–62).

Report of the Committee on the Management and Control of Research and Development (Sir Solly Zuckerman) (1961).

Higher Education (Lord Robbins), Cmnd 2154 (1963).

Report of the Committee on University Teaching Methods (Sir Edward Hale), UGC (1964).

Report of the Royal Commission on Medical Education, 1965–68, Cmnd 3569 (1968).

Report of the UGC Committee on Libraries (1967).

The Flow into Employment of Scientists, Engineers and Technologists (Sir Michael Swann), Cmnd 3760 (1968).

Report of the Select Committee on Education and Science, Session 1968–69. Student Relations, vol i, Report (1969).

Education: A Framework for Expansion, Cmnd 5174 (1972).

Teacher Training and Education (Lord James) (1972).

Framework for a System of Museums (Sir Arthur Drew). Report of a Working Party of the Standing Committee on Museums and Galleries (1978).

Report on Russian and Russian Studies in British Universities (Professor R.J.C. Atkinson) (1979).

House of Commons Foreign Affairs Committee, Session 1979–80/ Overseas Development Sub Committee (1980).

Report of a Joint Working Party on the Support of University Scientific Research, Cmnd 8567 (1982).

Improving Links between Higher Education and Industry, Advisory Council for Applied Research and Development (ACARD) (1983).

A Strategy for Higher Education into the 1990s. UGC (1984).

The Development of Higher Education into the 1990s, Cmnd 9524 (1985).

Higher Education, Meeting the Challenge, Cmnd 114 (1987).

Strengthening the Earth Sciences (E.R. Oxburgh), UGC (1987).

Universities, Enterprise and Local Economic Development (Segal, Quince, Wickstead for the Manpower Services Commission) (1988).

The Future of University Physics (Sir Sam Edwards), UGC (1988).

Committee of Public Accounts, First Report. Financial Problems at Universities. HC Session, 1989–90 (1990).

An Overview of the Demand for Graduates (M.Rigg, P. Elias, M. White, S. Johnson) Department of Education and Science (1990).

Education and Training for the Twenty-First Century, Department of Education and Science, Cmnd 1536 (1991).

Higher Education, a New Framework, Cmnd 1541 (1991).

The Financial Health of Higher Education Institutions in England, National Audit Office, Report by the Comptroller and Auditor General. HC Session, 1994–95, no. 13 (1994).

Higher Education in the Learning Society. National Committee of Inquiry into Higher Education (Sir Ron Dearing) (1997). Main Report, Summary Report, Reports 2, 3, 7.

Reports of Other Bodies (CVCP, AUT etc)

AUT Report on Policy for University Expansion (May 1954).

"The Age Group Bulge and its Possible Effects on University Policy". Home Universities Conference (1955).

Balchin, W.G.V., "Universities in Great Britain: A Geographical Conspectus", typescript (n.d. but 1959).

Workers Educational Association, Norfolk Federation, "Some Problems of a New University: Report of a Study Group" (July 1959).

"University Expansion and the New Universities", Federation of British Industries, typescript (December 1959).

"The Structure of Higher Education", Fabian Tract, 334 (1961).

Royal Society, Report of the Ad Hoc Biological Research Committee (November 1961).

"The Years of Crisis", Report of the Labour Party's Study Group on Higher Education (Lord Taylor) (1962).

British Business Schools: A Report by the Rt Hon. Lord Franks. British Institute of Management (1963)

Professional Pay in Universities, AUT (1966)

University Development in the 1970s, CVCP (November 1969).

Student Membership of University Committees and Subcommittees, CVCP (May 1971).

Report of the Steering Committee for Efficiency Studies : Universities (Sir Alec Jarratt), CVCP (1985).

The Changing Roles of University Leaders and Managers, University of Surrey for the DES (1991).

"UK Universities: Bursting at the Seams", AUT (1993).

Report of the National Commission on Education (Sir Claus Moser et al.) (1995).

Books and Articles

(Place of book publication London unless otherwise specified)

Aldcroft, D.H., *Education, Training and Economic Performance, 1944-1990* (Manchester, 1992).

Alford, B.W.E., *British Economic Performance, 1945-1975* (Cambridge, 1988).

Annan, Lord Noel, "British Higher Education, 1960–80: A Personal Retrospect", *Minerva*, 20 (Spring/Summer 1982), pp. 1–24.

Annan, Lord Noel, "Higher Education" in Crick, Bernard, ed., *Essays on Reform, 1967: A Centenary Tribute* (Oxford, 1967), pp. 24–43.

Annan, Lord Noel, *The Dons* (1999).

Atherton, Ian, Fernie, Eric, Harper Bill, Christopher and Hassell Smith, A., *Norwich: Cathedral, Church, City and Diocese* (1996).

Baker, David and Smith, Christopher, ed., *Essays for E.F.[Elizabeth Fudakowska]* (Norwich, 1994).

Baker, Kenneth, *The Turbulent Years* (1993).

Beloff, Michael, *Plateglass Universities* (1968).

Birks, Tony, *Building the New Universities* (Newton Abbot, 1972).

Blackstone, Tessa, "Access to Higher Education in Britain", in Phillipson, Nicholas, ed., *Universities, Society and the Future* (Edinburgh, 1983), pp. 248–59.

Booth, Clive, "Central Government and Higher Education Planning, 1965–1986", *Higher Education Quarterly*, 41 (1987), pp. 57–72.

Borg, Alan, "The Sainsbury Centre for Visual Arts", *Museums Journal*, 78 (March 1979), pp. 167–69.

Boswell, James, *The Story of Sainsburys* (1969).

Bradbury, Sir Malcolm, *Cuts* (1987).

Bradbury, Sir Malcolm, *The History Man* (1975).

Briggs, Lord Asa, *The History of Broadcasting in the United Kingdom*, v, *1955-1974* (Oxford, 1995).

Brown, Jane, *Lanning Roper and his Gardens* (1987).

Bull, Jack, *The Story of Keswick Hall, 1839-1981* (n.d.).

Buscall, Jon, *College.com* (1999).

Carpenter, Humphrey, *Benjamin Britten: A Biography* (1992).

Carswell, John, *Government and the Universities in Britain, 1960-1980* (Cambridge, 1985).

Carter, Sir Charles, *Higher Education for the Future* (Oxford, 1980).

Chadwick, Owen, *The Ups and Downs of Universities* (Keswick Hall Lecture, 1986).

Chadwick, Owen, *Victorian Miniature* (1960).

Clark, (Lord) Kenneth, *Civilisation: A Personal View* (1969).

Crawley, Harriet, *A Degree of Defiance: Students in England and Europe Now* (1969).

Cross, Malcolm and Jobling, Ray, "The English New Universities: A Preliminary Enquiry", *Universities Quarterly* (Spring 1969).

Crouch, Colin, *The Student Revolt* (1970).

Curtis, William J.R., *Denys Lasdun: Architecture, City, Landscape* (1994).

Daiches, David, *The Idea of a New University: An Experiment in Sussex* (1964).

Danchev, Alex, *Oliver Franks: Founding Father* (Oxford, 1993).

Day, Sir Robin, *Grand Inquisitor* (1989).

"Denys Lasdun: The Evolution of a Style", *Architectural Review*, 145 (May 1969), pp. 345–48.

Dober, Richard P., *The New Campus in Britain* (New York, 1965).

Drabble, Margaret, *Angus Wilson: A Biography* (1995).

Dyson, A.E., "The Sleep of Reason", in Cox, C.B. and Dyson A.E., *The Black Papers* (1971), pp. 84–86.

Dyson, A.E., "The Structures We Need", in Boyson, Rhodes, *Education, Threatened Standards* (Enfield, 1972), pp. 126–33.

Earwaker, Julian, and Becker, Kathleen, *Literary Norfolk* (Ipswich, 1998).

Fawcett, Richard, "Today's Mud...", *Square One* (2 May 1967), pp. 31–34.

Foster, Norman, "IQRC: Extracts from a Project Diary", in Lasdun, Denys, *Architecture in an Age of Scepticism* (1984), pp. 112–33.

Gould, Julius, *The Attack on Higher Education, Marxist and Radical Penetration* (Institute for the Study of Conflict, 1977).

Gomme, Andor, "Publicity or Promise: The New Universities", *Delta*, 34 (Autumn 1964), pp. 2–19.

Green, Barbara and Young, Rachel, *Norwich: The Growth of a City* (1981).

Halcrow, Morrison, *Keith Joseph: A Single Mind* (1989).

Halsey, A.H., *The Decline of Donnish Dominion* (Oxford, 1990).

Harrop, Sylvia, *Decade of Change: The University of Liverpool, 1981-1991* (Liverpool, 1994).

Heyck, T.W., "The Idea of a University in Britain, 1870–1970", *History of European Ideas*, 8 (1987), pp. 205–19.

Holderness, B.A., *British Agriculture since 1945* (Manchester, 1985).

Hollis, Patricia, *Jennie Lee: A Life* (Oxford, 1997).

Jenkins, Peter, *Mrs Thatcher's Revolution* (1987).

Jenkins, Simon, *Accountable to None: The Tory Nationalisation of Britain* (1995).

Jennings, Sir Ivor, "Cambridge Graduates in the University of East Anglia and Elsewhere", *Cambridge Review* (31 October 1964), pp. 70–71.

Jobling, R.G., "The Location and Siting of a New University", *Universities Quarterly* (Spring 1970), pp. 123–36.

Johnson, Paul, *Twentieth-Century Britain* (1994).

Katritzky, Alan, "Highlights from Fifty Years of Heterocyclic Chemistry", *Journal of Heterocyclic Chemistry*, 31 (1994), pp. 569–602.

Kidd, Harry, *The Trouble at LSE* (Oxford, 1969).

Kogan, Maurice, and Kogan, David, *The Attack on Higher Education* (1983).

Lasdun, Sir Denys, *A Language and A Theme: The Architecture of Denys Lasdun and Partners* (RIBA Publications, 1976).

Lasdun, Sir Denys, "An Architect's Approach to Architecture", *Journal of the Royal Institute of British Architects*, 72 (April 1965), pp. 184–95.

Lasdun, Sir Denys, ed., *Architecture in an Age of Scepticism* (London, 1984).

Lasdun, Sir Denys, "A Sense of Time and Place", *Listener* (17 February 1966), pp. 229–31.

Lasdun, Sir Denys, "The Architecture of the Urban Landscape", in Lasdun, Denys, ed., *Architecture in an Age of Scepticism* (1984), pp. 134–59.

Lawlor, John, *The New University* (1968).

Lindsay, Donald, *Friends for Life: A Portrait of Launcelot Fleming* (Seaford, 1981).

Lindsay, Donald, *Sir Edmund Bacon: A Norfolk Life* (Maldon, 1988).

Lodge, David, *Nice Work* (1988).

Lubbock, Percy, *Earlham* (London, 1922; repr. 1963).

Mackintosh of Halifax , Viscount, edited by Thomson, A.A., *By Faith and Work* (1966).

McClintock, M.E. *The University of Lancaster: A History of the First Ten Years, 1964-1974* (Lancaster, 1974).

McCutcheon, Elsie, *Norwich through the Ages* (Bury St Edmunds, 1989).

McKean, Charles, *Architectural Guide to Cambridge and East Anglia since 1920* (ERA Publications, RIBA Eastern Region, Edinburgh, 1982).

Maclure, Stuart, "The University of East Anglia", *Listener* (11 November 1965), pp. 747–48, 750.

Martin, Graham, *From Vision to Reality: The Making of the University of Kent* (Canterbury, 1990).

Marwick, Arthur, *The Sixties* (Oxford, 1998).

Meeres, Frank, *A History of Norwich* (Chichester, 1998).

Metters, Alan, *The Tech, 1891-1991* (Norwich, 1991).

Moore, Peter G., "University Financing, 1979–86", *Higher Education Quarterly*, 41 (1 January 1987), pp. 25–42.

Mottram, R.H., *East Anglia: England's Eastern Province* (1933).

Mountford, Sir James, *Keele: An Historic Critique* (1972).

Muthesius, Stefan, *Concrete and Open Skies* (2001).

"Non-System Building at UEA: The UEA Science Building", *ERA: Journal of the Eastern Region of the Royal Institute of British Architects*, 36 (January/February 1974), pp. 11–17.

Palladino, Paolo, "Science, Technology and the Economy: Plant Breeding in Great Britain, 1920–1970", *Economic History Review*, 49 (February 1996), pp. 116–36.

Perkin, Harold, *Innovation in Higher Education: New Universities in the United Kingdom* (OECD, 1969).

Raban, Jonathan, "The Art of Disaster", *New Society*, 12 (December 1968), p. 871.

Rees, Harry, *A University is Born* (1989).

Reeves, Marjorie, *The Crisis in Higher Education* (1988).

Reich, Rosamund, "The Broad at UEA", *Landscape Design* (February 1980), pp. 11–17.

Rennie, Jean, *Cap and Apron to Cap and Gown* (Fakenham, 1985).

Robbins, Lord, *Higher Education Revisited* (1980).

Robbins, Lord, *The University in the Modern World* (1966).

Rooke, M.A., *Anarchy and Apathy, Student Unrest, 1968-70* (1971).

Ross, Murray, *New Universities in the Modern World* (1966).

Rothblatt, Sheldon and Wittrock, Bjorn, *The European and American University since 1800* (Cambridge, 1993).

Sampson, Anthony, *The Anatomy of Britain* (1962, 1965, 1971, 1982, 1992).

Sanderson, Michael, "'...And Will Girls be Admitted?' Women at the University of East Anglia in the 1960s", in Sutherland, Gillian ed., *The Transformation of an Elite? Women and Higher Education since 1900*, Papers at the University of Cambridge, September 1998, pp. 183–98.

Sanderson, Michael, *Educational Opportunity and Social Change* (1987).

Sanderson, Michael, "French, Languages and the Early Planning of UEA", in Smith, C.N., ed., *Essays for Janine Dakyns and Michael Parkinson* (Norwich, 1996), pp. 385–90.

Sanderson, Michael, "The Civic Universities and the Industrial Spirit", *Historical Research*, (February 1988), pp. 90–104.

Sanderson, Michael, *The Universities and British Industry, 1850-1970* (1972).

Scott, Peter, "Higher Education", in Morris, Max and Griggs, Clive, ed., *Education: The Wasted Years? 1973-1986* (1988), pp. 127–44.

Scott, Peter, "Higher Education", in Kavanagh, D., and Seldon, A., *The Thatcher Effect* (Oxford, 1989), pp. 198–212.

Scott, Peter, *The Crisis of the University* (1984).

Sebald, W.G., *The Rings of Saturn* (1998).

Shattock, Michael, *Making a University: A Celebration of Warwick's First Twenty-Five Years* (Warwick, 1991).

Shattock, Michael, *The UGC and the Management of British Universities* (Buckingham, 1994).

Shinn, Christine Helen, *Paying the Piper: The Development of the University Grants Committee, 1919-1946* (1986).

Simon, Brian, *Education and the Social Order, 1940-1990* (1991).

Sloman, Albert E., *A University in the Making* (1964).

Stephens, Michael D. ed., *Universities, Education and the National Economy* (1989).

Straw, Jack, "Student Participation in Higher Education", *Universities: The Boundaries of Change* (1970), pp. 7–27.

Stewart, W.A.C., *Higher Education in Post-War Britain* (1989).

Stuart, James, *Reminiscences* (1912).

Thatcher, Margaret, *The Downing Street Years* (1993).

"The University of East Anglia", *Architectural Design* (May 1969), pp. 245–69.

Thistlethwaite, Frank, *A Lancashire Family Inheritance* (Cambridge, 1996).

Thistlethwaite, Frank, *Cambridge Years* (Cambridge, 1999).

Thistlethwaite, Frank, *Doing Different in a Cold Climate* (St John's College Lecture, 1988).

Thistlethwaite, Frank, *Origins: A Personal Reminiscence of UEA's Foundation* (Cambridge, 2000).

Thistlethwaite, Frank, *Our War, 1938-45* (Cambridge, 1997).

Thistlethwaite, Frank, "The University of East Anglia", in Ross, M.G. ed., *New Universities in the Modern World* (1966), pp. 53–68.

Tilsley, Gordon, "Founders Green in the Memory", in Baker, David and Smith, Christopher, ed., *Studies for EF* [Elizabeth Fudakowska] (Norwich, 1994), pp. 13–17.

Trow, Martin, "Reflections on the Transition from Mass to Universal Higher Education", *Daedalus*, 99 (Winter 1970), pp. 1–42.

Trow, Martin, "The Robbins Trap: British Attitudes and the Limits of Expansion", *Higher Education Quarterly*, 43 (Winter 1989), pp. 55–75.

"Universities: Genuine Urban or Fake Suburban?", *Architects' Journal* (19 May 1960), pp. 744–46.

Vickers, Hugo, *Cecil Beaton* (1985).

Wade Martins, Susannah, *A History of Norfolk* (Chichester, 1984).

Walford, Geoffrey, *Restructuring Universities: Politics and Power in the Management of Change* (1987).

Ward, Belinda, "A Lesson in Patronage", *Architects' Journal*, 183 (5 March 1986), pp. 34–35.

Warnock, Mary, *Universities: Knowing Our Minds* (1989).

Watt, Ian, "The Seminar", *Universities Quarterly*, 18 (September 1964), pp. 369–89.

Watt, Ian, "English at Norwich", in "The Idea of An English School: Symposium on the New Universities", *Critical Survey* (Autumn, 1962), pp. 42–46.

Waugh, Auberon, "In Defence of Students", *Spectator* (7 February 1969), pp. 163–64.

Wesker, Arnold, *Roots: A Play* (1959).

Wigby, Frederick C., *A Shilling, a Shuttleknife and a Piece of String* (Wymondham, 1984).

Williams, Gareth, "Higher Education Deflated", *New Society*, 30 (21 November 1974), pp. 471–73.

Williams, Gareth, and Blackstone, Tessa, *Response to Adversity* (1983).

Wolfenden, Sir John, *Turning Points* (1976).

Zuckerman, Solly, *Monkeys, Men and Missiles: An Autobiography, 1946-88* (1988).

Index